THE CITY SHAPED

Urban Patterns and Meanings Through History

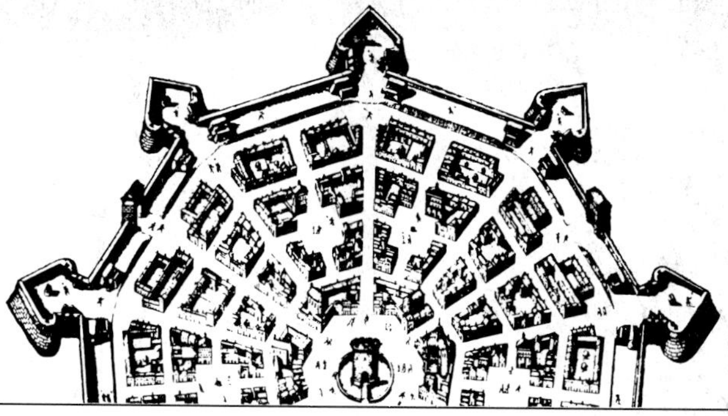

SPIRO KOSTOF

THE CITY SHAPED

Urban Patterns and Meanings Through History

Original drawings by Richard Tobias

A BULFINCH PRESS BOOK
LITTLE, BROWN AND COMPANY
BOSTON · TORONTO · LONDON

For
Vasiliki Pringu,
Leandros, and Rita
who were always there to come home to

Frontispiece 1 *The center of Siena (Italy). The Campo—the fan-shaped open space upper right—developed at the meeting point of three separate communities: the bishop's town around the cathedral (lower left), and two settlements to the east and north, reached by the two streets at the top of the photograph forming a Y, a junction that was carefully designed (see pp. 61–62, 70–71). Photo Compagnia Generale Ripreseaeree, Parma, Italy*

First North American Edition

Library of Congress Cataloging-in-Publication Data

Kostof, Spiro.
The city shaped / Spiro Kostof.
p. cm.
Includes bibliographical references and index.
ISBN 0-8212-1867-0
1. Cities and towns—History. 2. Cities and towns—Growth.
I. Title.
HT111.K63 1991
307.76—dc20 91-52813

Bulfinch Press is an imprint and trademark of Little, Brown and Company (Inc.)
Published simultaneously in Canada by Little, Brown & Company (Canada) Limited

PRINTED IN HONG KONG

CONTENTS

3 · THE CITY AS DIAGRAM *159*

4 · THE GRAND MANNER *209*

5 · THE URBAN SKYLINE *279*

ACKNOWLEDGMENTS

My two indispensable collaborators have been Richard Tobias, whose many drawings buttress and further the argument, and my long-time assistant Greg Castillo who organized the research, oversaw the heroic enterprise of illustrating the text, and was the daily liaison with the publisher. The credit for much that is good about the content and look of this volume belongs to the two of them, while the failings rest squarely, as they must, with the author. A generous grant from the Graham Foundation for Advanced Studies in the Fine Arts has aided in the preparation of the drawings. The Design Arts program of the National Endowment for the Arts also contributed in this effort.

The immodest range of the subject forced me often to seek the advice of experts. Many friends and colleagues came to the rescue, and I regret that I cannot name them all. As a token list, let me acknowledge the following: Nezar AlSayyad, Mirka Benes, Gene Brucker, Dora Crouch, Diane Ghirardo, Paul Groth, Diane Favro, David Friedman, Brenda Preyer, Jean-Pierre Protzen, and Marc Treib. The Walker Art Center consented to my re-use of some of the material on the American skyline which was originally delivered there in the Center's American Icons series and published subsequently in *Design Quarterly*. In the procurement of visual material, I must thank David Phillips of the Chicago Architectural Photo Co., Myron and Gail Lee, and at the University of California, Berkeley, Peter Bosselman of the Environmental Simulation Laboratory, Maryly Snow, and Dan Johnston. Elizabeth Byrne, Head of the College of Environmental Design Library at Berkeley, has given us invaluable assistance. Johan van der Zande helped us with some German texts, and produced the index – no mean task for a free-ranging book of this kind. To all of them, and the many others not mentioned, my heartfelt thanks. Finally, I would like to thank the staff of Thames and Hudson for their encouragement and meticulous care at all stages of the book's production.

S.K.

2 The city observed: Wenceslas Square, Prague, in 1835, engraving by Vincenc Morstadt. Originally a cleared strip of land at the city edge where the town's horse market was held, by the 19th century Wenceslas Square had emerged as Prague's most elegant promenade. The square has continued as the stage of the city's fortunes to this day: it was where Soviet tanks rumbled in to suppress the "Prague Spring" of 1968, and where crowds of protesters initiated the "Velvet Revolution" of 1989.

INTRODUCTION

THE CITY AS ARTIFACT

PRELIMINARIES

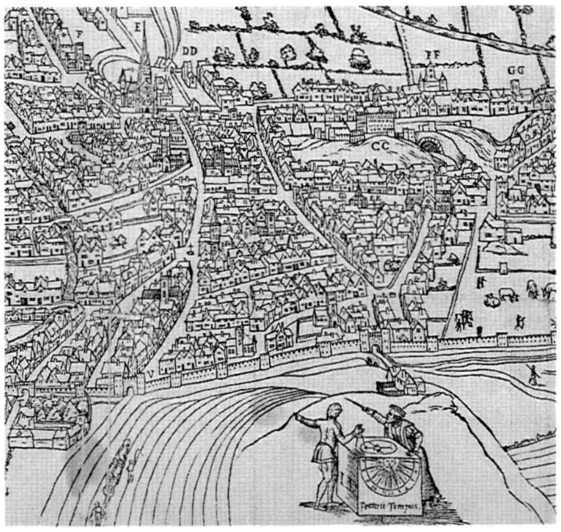

3 The city imaged: a detail of William Cunningham's woodcut map of Norwich, from The Cosmographical Glasse *(1559). Cunningham's map includes a self-portrait of the surveyor poised above his plane-table. The bird's-eye view, which accurately depicts the town's walled edge, curving streets, and densely built blocks, is the earliest surviving printed map of any English town.*

THIS book is an architectural historian's attempt to make accessible, to architects, urban designers, and the general public, the universal experience of making cities. It is about urban form and urban process. More specifically, it is a discussion of some patterns and elements of urban form *seen in a historical perspective.*

The emphasis is critical. There is a vast modern literature about urban form—how to make it and how to "read" it. From Camillo Sitte's *The Art of Building Cities* (*Der Städte-Bau nach seinen künstlerischen Grundsätzen*) of 1889 and all those other *Stadtbaukunst* books since then by the likes of Joseph Stübben, Albert E. Brinckmann and Werner Hegemann, down to the present generation of Gordon Cullen, Kevin Lynch, Rob Krier, and Michael Trieb, the professional eye of the designer has scrutinized urban configurations, and drawn prescriptive lessons from such scrutiny.

Urban design is of course an art, and like all design it does have to consider, or at least pay lip service to, human behavior. So this literature is full of references to the social implications of urban form. Is the gridiron plan tedious and disorienting? Do certain kinds of public places engender social interaction or discourage it? That sort of thing. These matters, since I am not myself a member of the designing confraternity, are on the whole extraneous to my inquiry, at least in so far as they are considered in the abstract, independently of specific historical context.

What concerns me has to do with how and why cities took the shape they did. Which is to say that I am not engaged with form in the abstract, or with form studied for its behavioral possibilities, but with form as a receptacle of meaning. And architectural meaning is ultimately always lodged in history, in cultural contexts.

Now the history of urban form can be used as a design quarry: it has routinely so been used. There is certainly nothing wrong with architects and planners being inspired by the old townscapes of Europe, say, or the medinas of North Africa. That is, in fact, the professionals' special gift—catching the distinctive quality of a street or a public space, being touched by it, wanting to incorporate that quality into their own designs. They do not need a historian for that. Where this mining of the past becomes objectionable is when the designer ascribes certain rationales to the forms he or she admires, rationales which are either innocent of history or else casually misrepresent it.

I remember that when I was asked to take part in an urban design seminar in Siena
1 several years ago, the common perception of this much admired city-form was that it developed spontaneously, filling and solidifying the shapes of its natural site. The landscape of medieval Siena was seen as testimony against those forceful designs imposed by planners and politicians in defiance of the dictates of topography and the comfortable rhythms of the townsfolk. Even people who ought to have known better reinforced this impressionistic reading of the great Tuscan hilltown. Lewis Mumford, for example, singled her out as proof of "the esthetic and engineering superiority of an organic plan."[1]

But I was not at all surprised to discover, as I looked into the historical circumstances of Siena's origin and growth, that she was coerced to take that shape, that her city-form was one of the most highly regimented designs of medieval urbanism (see below, pp. 70–71).[2] I was not surprised, because over the years I have witnessed numerous instances of false "reading" of past architecture, and have become settled in my mind that form, in itself, is very lamely informative of intention. We "read" form correctly only to the extent that we are familiar with the precise cultural conditions that generated it. Rather than presume, in other words, as practically everybody in the architectural world wants to presume, that buildings and city-forms are a transparent medium of cultural expression, I am convinced that the relationship only works the other way around. The more we know about cultures, about the structure of society in various periods of history in different parts of the world, the better we are able to read their built environment.[3]

There is no quick, easy way to appropriate the past. Walking in an old town center, sketching it and thinking about it, is instructive in a direct way. It is the first and indispensable step. But it will not tell us what really happened until we turn to the archives, the history books, the old maps—until we assemble all the evidence, some of it often contradictory, that will help explain how a particular downtown got the look it now has. That kind of evidence is what this book leans on to conduct its analysis of urban form.

To the form-seeker, for example, a grid is a grid is a grid. At best, it is a visual theme upon which to play variations: he might be concerned with issues like using a true checkerboard design versus syncopated block rhythms, with cross-axial or

Variations on the grid:

4 Florentine new town, 14th century.

5 Ideal city plan by Scamozzi, from his L'idea della architettura universale *(1615).*

6 New Orleans, a French colonial settlement, in 1760.

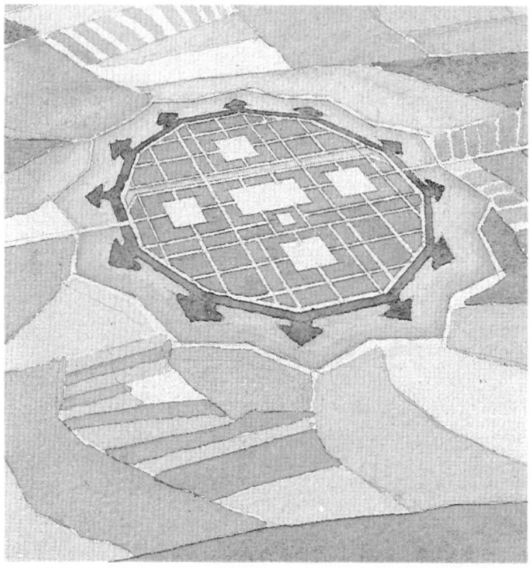

7 The state as citymaker. Rome's transformation under Fascist rule answered both the economic and ideological needs of the new regime. A public works program that exalted manual labor was launched in the mid-Twenties to alleviate unemployment. Labor-intensive demolitions like these at the Markets of Trajan (2nd century AD) stripped monumental ruins of their crust of picturesque tenement housing. The juxtaposition of these ancient fragments with modern traffic arteries (see p. 231) fulfilled a symbolic program equating imperial grandezza *with Fascist rule.*

other types of emphasis, with the placement of open spaces within the discipline of the grid, with the width and hierarchy of streets. To us here, on the other hand, how, and with what intentions, the Romans in Britain, the *bastidors* ("builders") of medieval Wales and Gascony, the Spanish in Mexico, or the Illinois Central Railroad Company in the prairies of the Midwest employed this very same device of settlement will be the principal substance of a review of orthogonal planning. We will have to come to grips with the fact that the grid has accommodated a startling variety of social structures—territorial aristocracy in Greek Sicily; the agrarian republicanism of Thomas Jefferson; the cosmic vision of Joseph Smith for the setting of the Second Coming in Mormon settlements like Nauvoo, Illinois, and Salt Lake City, Utah—and of course good old speculative greed.

For us, then, city form is neutral until it is impressed with specific cultural intent. So there is no point in noticing the formal similarities between L'Enfant's plan for Washington and the absolutist diagrams of Versailles or Karlsruhe, no point in discovering identical sinuous streets in medieval Nördlingen and Olmsted's Riverside, unless we can elaborate on the nature of the content that was to be housed within each, and the social premises of the designers.

Urban form and urban process, I said at the beginning. The second half of this program, urban process, may also not be self-explanatory. I use the phrase here in two senses.

One of them has to do with the people and forces and institutions that bring about urban form. Who designs cities? what procedures do they go through? what are the empowering agencies and laws? Content of this nature we will bring in as we need it, to explain elements of urban form, but we will not devote separate sections to it.

This is because the legal and economic history that affects city-making is an enormous (and, I might add, rather neglected) subject. It involves ownership of urban land and the land market; the exercise of eminent domain or compulsory purchase, that is, the power of government to take over private property for public use; the institution of the legally binding master plan, the *piano regolatore* of the Italians; building codes and other regulatory measures; instruments of funding urban change, like property taxes and bond issues; and the administrative structure of cities. That in itself is more than enough for an independent book.

As for designers of cities, this too is a huge assignment, and also not a very pressing one for the kind of inquiry we are undertaking here. As far as I know there is no general urban history written exclusively from this vantage, though of course there is some considerable literature in that direction. We know a lot about the big names: Hippodamus of Miletus; the designer of Renaissance Ferrara, Biagio Rossetti; Baron Haussmann of Paris; Daniel Burnham of Chicago; Le Corbusier. We know much less about names like Eric Dahlberg, Nicodemus Tessin the Younger, or Nicolas de Clerville, for example, busy designing cities in the 17th and early 18th centuries, and hundreds of others like them from the rest of history. We are well informed about Arnolfo di Cambio as an architect, but know little of his work as city-planner, even though it was his effort to draw up the plans of new towns like San Giovanni and Castelfranco, according to Vasari, that moved Florence to award him honorary citizenship.

Even this roster, properly reviewed, would account only for those makers of cities who can be called designers in the narrow sense. But cities are given shape by all sorts of people, by military engineers, for example, by ships' gunners (like those who laid out the early British port cities of India), and by administrators and state officials, from the *oikists* (leaders of colonizing expeditions) who gave us the great Greek towns of Sicily and the medieval lords of England and France and Spain who planted

8 The speculator as citymaker. Modern Los Angeles (California) is the product of a series of real estate booms which began in the late 19th century. In this 1920s photograph, developers survey open fields about to be transformed into marketable building lots serviced by a gridded network of streets and boulevards.

hundreds of new towns or *bastides* within their territories, down to modern planning commissioners like Robert Moses of New York and Edmund Bacon of Philadelphia. Cities are initiated by religious orders like the Cistercians in Gascony
113 and the Teutonic Order in eastern Europe, the Franciscan missions in Spanish Mexico and the *aldeias* of the Jesuits in Amazonia and central Brazil; by reformers and paternalistic industrialists; and by that legion of surveyors that laid out colonial towns in every age, and inscribed standard plans along railroad lines across much of the North American continent in the 19th century. A survey of this extraordinary crowd, their writings and the tools of their trade, would make a first-rate story. It would include the likes of Sir Henry le Waleys, town-planning advisor to Edward I of England in the late 13th century; Francesco Laparelli (1521–70) who designed
104 Valletta in Malta; James Oglethorpe who conceived Savannah, Georgia, in 1733, and Judge Augustus B. Woodward who devised the striking Baroque plan for
216 Detroit in 1805; Per Brahe (1602–80) the famous head of the Generalship of Finland, responsible for at least a dozen towns, Helsinki among them; Jan Pieterszoon Coen, who founded Batavia, now Jakarta, capital of the Dutch East Indies, in 1619; the Dutch engineer Franz de Voland, who drew the plans for Odessa and many other new cities in southern Russia during the reign of Catherine the Great in the later 18th century; and hundreds of others.

There are two reasons, beyond the obvious restraint of length, why this chronicle would not be germane to our story, except perhaps intermittently.

Pl.3 First of all, attention to "designers" tends to favor new cities like Palmanova or
192 Canberra, and ideal cities that were never built. I am interested, rather, in *real* cities—their creation and subsequent behavior. I focus on the theory of urban design, or on abstract urban schemes that are there to prove a point or propose a utopia, only when there is a tangible relation to the practices of actual town-making.

More importantly, many cities come about without benefit of designers, or once designed, set about instantly to adapt themselves to the rituals of everyday life and the vagaries of history. Who designed Athens or Calcutta? How many people beyond the immediate entourage and time of its founder, the caliph al-Mansur,
9 experienced the famous round city of Baghdad? "It hardly ever lived in the perfect shape conceived for it," Oleg Grabar writes; "even during the lifetime of al-Mansour suburbs were added, the carefully drawn internal divisions broke
10 down, and the Round City became only a part of the enormous urban complex of Baghdad."[4]

9, 10 Baghdad (Iraq): the geometric 8th-century ground plan, organized around the caliph's palace, was a casualty of the city's success. By the 9th century the sprawling growth of a thriving community had obliterated the original autocratic diagram.

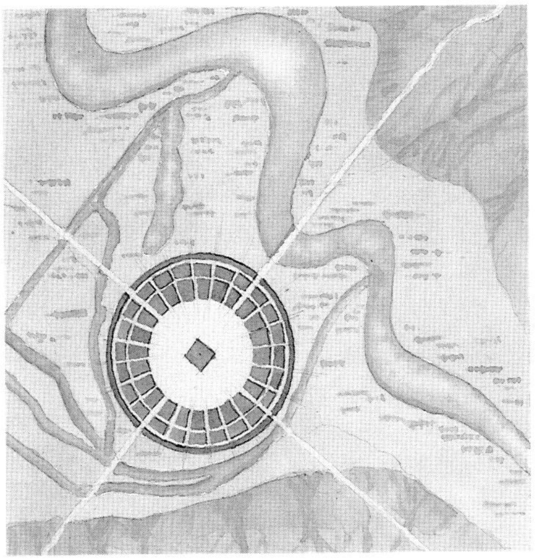

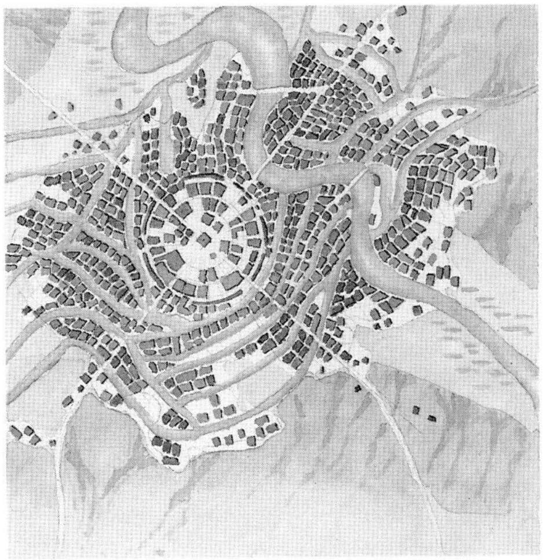

11, 12 The Campus Martius was Imperial Rome's monumental core. Only the Pantheon, recognizable by its round stepped dome (top), survived intact into the Renaissance. A millennium of stone scavenging and piecemeal reconstruction had disintegrated the Baths of Nero, the Odeon, and the huge Stadium of Domitian—its elongated imprint still legible in the Piazza Navona (bottom).

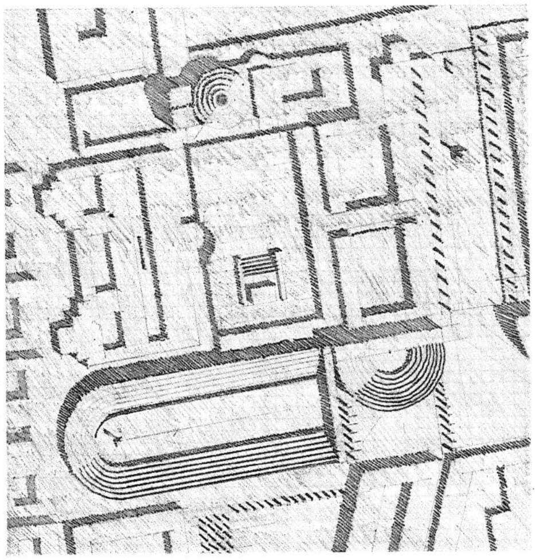

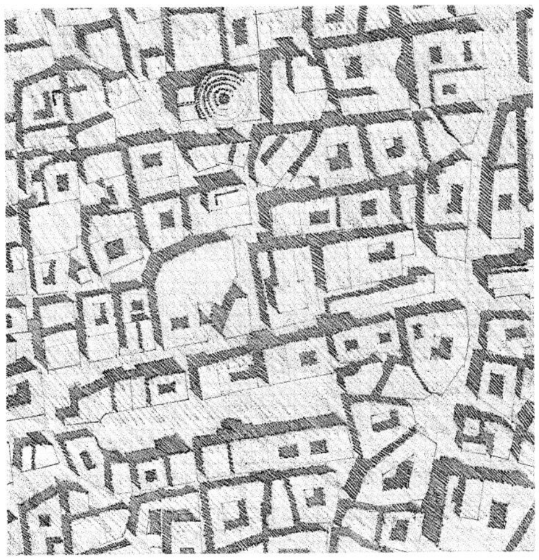

The second sense in which I use "urban process," on the other hand, is very much central to the purposes of this book. This refers, precisely, to physical change through time. The tendency all too often is to see urban form as a finite thing, a closed thing, a complicated object. I want to stress what we know instead to be the case—that a city, however perfect its initial shape, is never complete, never at rest. Thousands of witting and unwitting acts every day alter its lines in ways that are perceptible only over a certain stretch of time. City walls are pulled down and filled in; once rational grids are slowly obscured; a slashing diagonal is run through close-grained residential neighborhoods; railroad tracks usurp cemeteries and waterfronts; wars, fires, and freeway connectors annihilate city cores.

Let me give one dramatic instance, with the particulars of which I am rather intimately familiar. Consider these two pendant urban images. There is imperial Rome, a city of one million or more at its height, dominated by a stone construct of public buildings and porticoes, especially in the flatland of the Campus Martius *11*
within the crook of the Tiber; its predominant housing form, the multi-story apartment block or *insula*, crowds interstitial spaces between the public zones and the slopes of the famous hills. And there is medieval Rome, down to 50,000 or less at its nadir, crammed in the Tiber bend and across the river in Trastevere, detached two-story family houses obliterating almost completely the grand formal order of *12*

the imperial Campus Martius. How did it happen? How were the theaters and temples and amphitheaters and forums consumed? where did the 40,000 apartment buildings of ancient Rome go? how did we get this maze of sinuous streets and alleys out of the magisterial orthogonal arrangements of the imperial city? That is urban process at its most ostensible.

We are recorders of a physicality, then, akin to that of a flowing river or a changing sky. So we will be mindful of urban process, in this sense of the phrase, both as an ongoing concern in discussing each one of our themes, and as an overarching subject of conclusion.

AFFILIATES OF METHOD

Turning now to structure, it should be clear from the table of contents that this is not a conventional survey of urbanism through the ages, in the mode of A. E. J. Morris's

13 The city as a reflection of its governing power: Würzburg (Germany), the seat of the house of Schönborn, was transformed under their patronage into the extravagant Baroque composition shown in this broadside of 1723 by their architect Balthasar Neumann. The theatrical border, with its dynastic crest and commemorative disks including depictions of the new palace and chapel, reinforces the association of the city with its ruling family.

History of Urban Form (1974; 1979) or even Lewis Mumford's *The City in History* (1961). It assumes a basic acquaintance with the main lines of Western and non-Western urbanism as a sequential narrative, and chooses to focus, rather, on a number of formal themes treated freely—the discussion moving through historical time and geography as necessary.

There are other ways to structure a historical review of urban form, of course, and they have all been tried. Cities have been sorted out by country (it is enough to remember E. A. Gutkind's great work, *International History of City Development*, 1964ff.), by epoch, by geographic location. Wolfgang Braunfels's *Urban Design in Western Europe* (1976; English edition 1988) begins with the premise that cities designed themselves "as reflections of forms of government and ideals of order." His categories include cathedral cities, city-states, sea powers (Venice, Lübeck, Amsterdam), imperial cities, ideal cities, seats of a princely court (Turin, Munich, Dresden, St. Petersburg), and capital cities. The problems are obvious. In terms of its own premises, this organization suffers from the fact that cities are almost never singleminded. They may start out with a prime specialty, but they soon will acquire other uses. More serious, from our point of view, is that it is difficult to determine elements of urban design that would give commonality to each of these categories. What we are left with is a common political orientation (or a common economic structure if we opt for categories like harbor towns, market towns, agricultural centers, industrial towns) without a concomitant homogeneity of urban landscape.

Kevin Lynch, in his last book, *Good City Form* (1981), which is the best marriage I know of between a thoughtful inquiry into the history of urban form and a resultant theory of urban design, set up an organizing scheme that rewards scrutiny. His three categories, called "normative models," have less to do with political or economic order than they do with the prime motivation of the city, or its self-perception.[5]

The *cosmic* model, or holy city, takes the plan to be an interpretation of the universe and of the gods. It also encompasses Renaissance and Baroque ideal plans laid out as an articulated expression of power. Characteristic design features of this model are the monumental axis, the enclosure and its protected gates, dominant landmarks, the reliance on the regular grid, and spatial organization by hierarchy.

The *practical* model, or the city as machine, is "factual, functional, 'cool'," not in the least magical. It is the concept that motivates colonial towns and company towns, the speculative grid towns of the United States, Le Corbusier's Radiant City, and more recently still, the inventions of the British Archigram group and the arcologies of the Italian Paolo Soleri. A city, according to this model, "is made up of small, autonomous, undifferentiated parts, linked up into a great machine which in contrast has clearly differentiated functions and motions."

The *organic* model, or the biological city, sees the city as a living thing rather than a machine. It has a definite boundary and an optimum size, a cohesive, indivisible

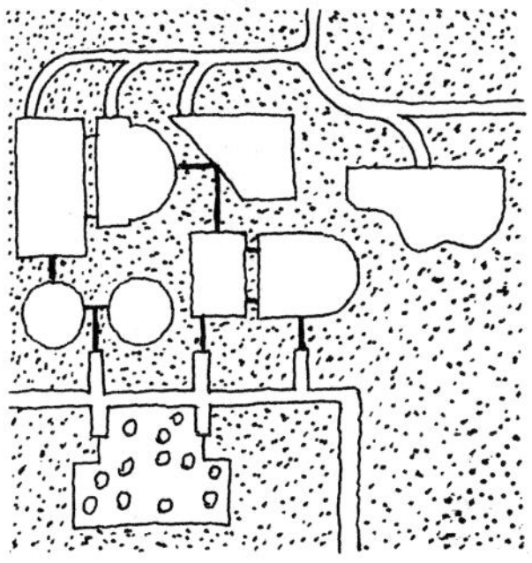

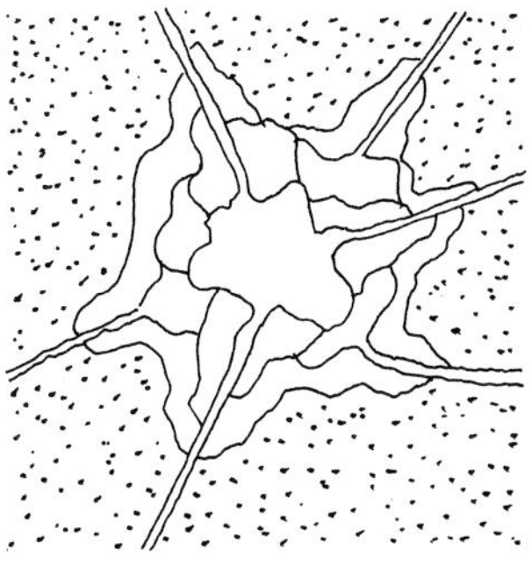

14 The cosmic city: a spatial diagram of social hierarchy.

15 The practical city: a functional construct of interrelated parts.

16 The organic city: an indivisible, living organism.

internal structure, and a rhythmic behavior that seeks, in the face of inevitable change, to maintain a balanced state. The creators of this model were the likes of Frederick Law Olmsted, Ebenezer Howard, Patrick Geddes and Lewis Mumford. Only this last model, limited as it seems to be to non-geometric urban patterns of the past and to the self-conscious "organisms" of garden cities, American "Greenbelt towns" and picturesque suburbs, possesses a more or less homologous morphology.

What is useful in this categorization—to which Lynch ultimately takes exception—is that it gives us some basic metaphors for the city, and these in turn supply both the language of discourse and the rationale for physical interventions. If the city is a machine that must function efficiently, it is subject to obsolescence, and needs constant tuning and updating. What is done to the city-form will be thought of as mechanical adjustments, to make the city work or run properly. If the city is an organism, and we speak of cells and arteries, it can become pathological, and interventions to correct the diseased form will be in the nature of surgery. Finally in the first model, the cosmic city, we are encouraged to discount all practical, technological, economic or sanitary explanations for the placement and layout of cities. That is what Joseph Rykwert did some years ago in a provocative book called *The Idea of a Town* (1976) *Pl.7* in which he set out to prove that ancient towns were, above all, symbolic patterns, conceived in mythical and ritual terms, and that seeking any rational or pragmatic logic for them was futile.

It bears repeating that the primary interest of this book is to elucidate the physical traits of the urban landscape without *a priori* theories of urban behavior. Persuaded by history that the same urban form does not perforce express identical, or even similar, human content, and conversely, that the same political, social or economic order will not yield an invariable design matrix, I choose to start, throughout, with the thing itself and work towards its meaning. How does the non-geometric city plan come about? what is the nature, and what are the permutations, of the ubiquitous grid? historically, in what ways has the city defined its limits? within the city, what divisions were implied or built? These are some of the topics of the chapters that follow, and of a companion volume, *The City Assembled*—these, and two prime components of the urban armature, namely, streets, and those spaces which, by common consent and legal restraint, were kept free of development and set aside for public use.

INTRODUCTION

Cities are amalgams of buildings and people. They are inhabited settings from which daily rituals—the mundane and the extraordinary, the random and the staged—derive their validity. In the urban artifact and its mutations are condensed continuities of time and place. The city is the ultimate memorial of our struggles and glories: it is where the pride of the past is set on display.

Sometimes cities are laid out by fiat, as perfect shapes and for premeditated ends. They may aim to reflect a cosmic rule or an ideal society, be cast as a machine of war, or have no higher purpose than to generate profit for the founder. A myth of propitiousness and high destiny may come to surround the act of founding. Or this act may be nothing more than a routinized and repetitive event. But whether born under divine guidance or the speculative urge, the pattern will dry up, and even die, unless the people forge within it a special, self-sustaining life that can survive adversity and the turns of fortune.

Pl.1 Benares (Varanasi, India), the approach to the Panchganga Ghat during the Kartik festival.

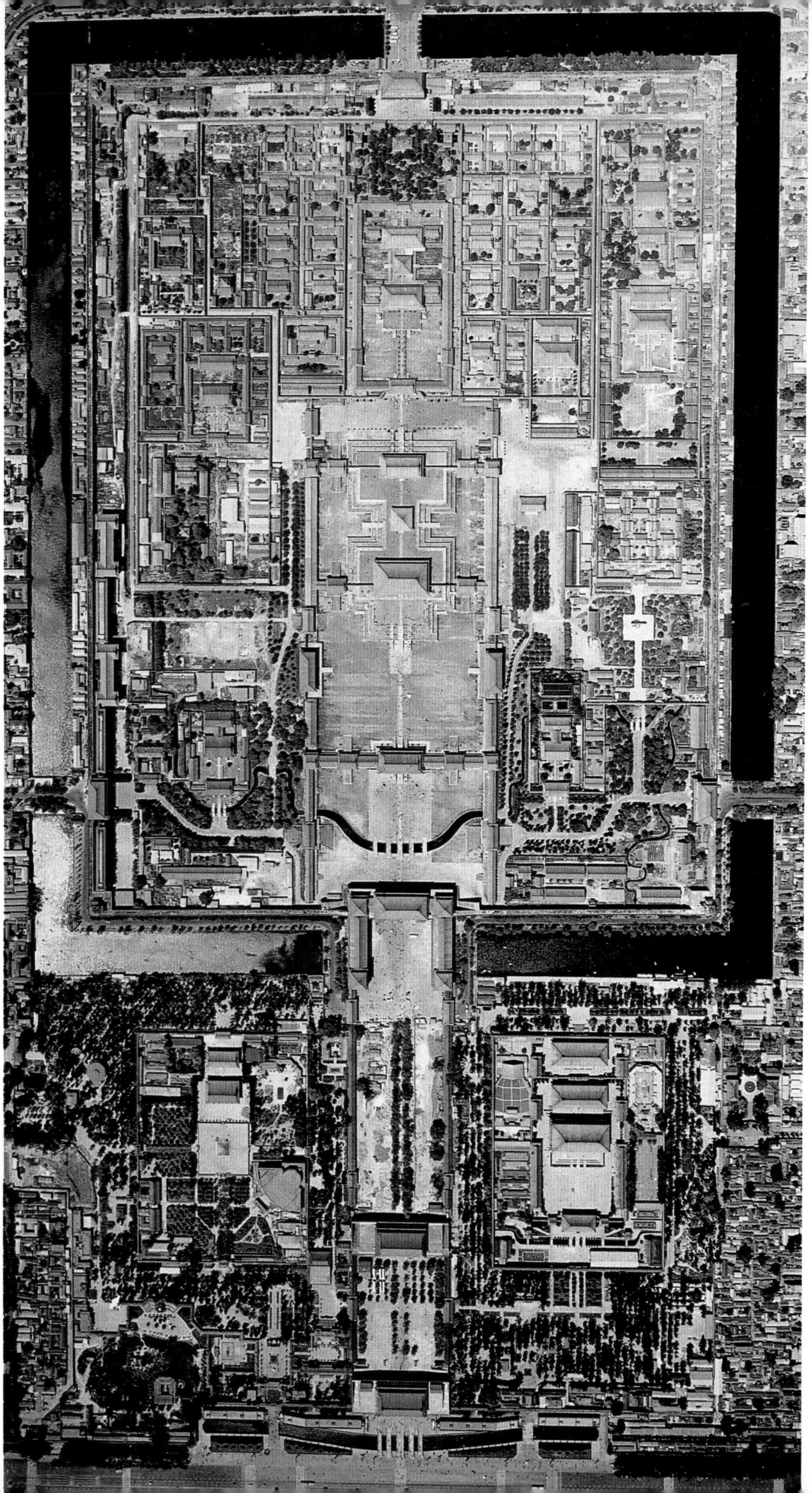

The city as diagram

Pl.2 left *An imperial diagram: the Forbidden City in Beijing (China), core of the concentric rectangles that organized the Ming capital as rebuilt from 1421. The palace compound, approached through gates (bottom), is islanded by a moat.*

Pl.3 above *A sunburst for warfare in the Veneto: Palmanova (Italy), created in 1593–1623. The Venetian commander and troops occupied the center, while barracks for foreign mercenaries ringed the city inside the original fortifications, pierced by three gates.*

Pl.4 Vienna, bird's-eye view by G. Veith, 1873. The dense medieval city clusters around the spire of St. Stephen's Cathedral in the background. Until 1857 it was tightly enclosed by a spacious ring of fortifications. Outside, suburbs, palaces, and churches—notably the very tall St. Charles's (left, by Fischer von Erlach, begun 1716)—had spread into the countryside. The demolition of the fortifications provided the opportunity for a composition in the Grand Manner, the new Ringstrasse, defined by planting and lined with monumental public and residential buildings in a variety of architectural styles. Moving forward in the left-hand quadrant, the twin-spired Votivkirche is followed by the neo-Gothic Rathaus, neo-Renaissance twin Museums, and Opera House (beyond the dome of St. Charles's).

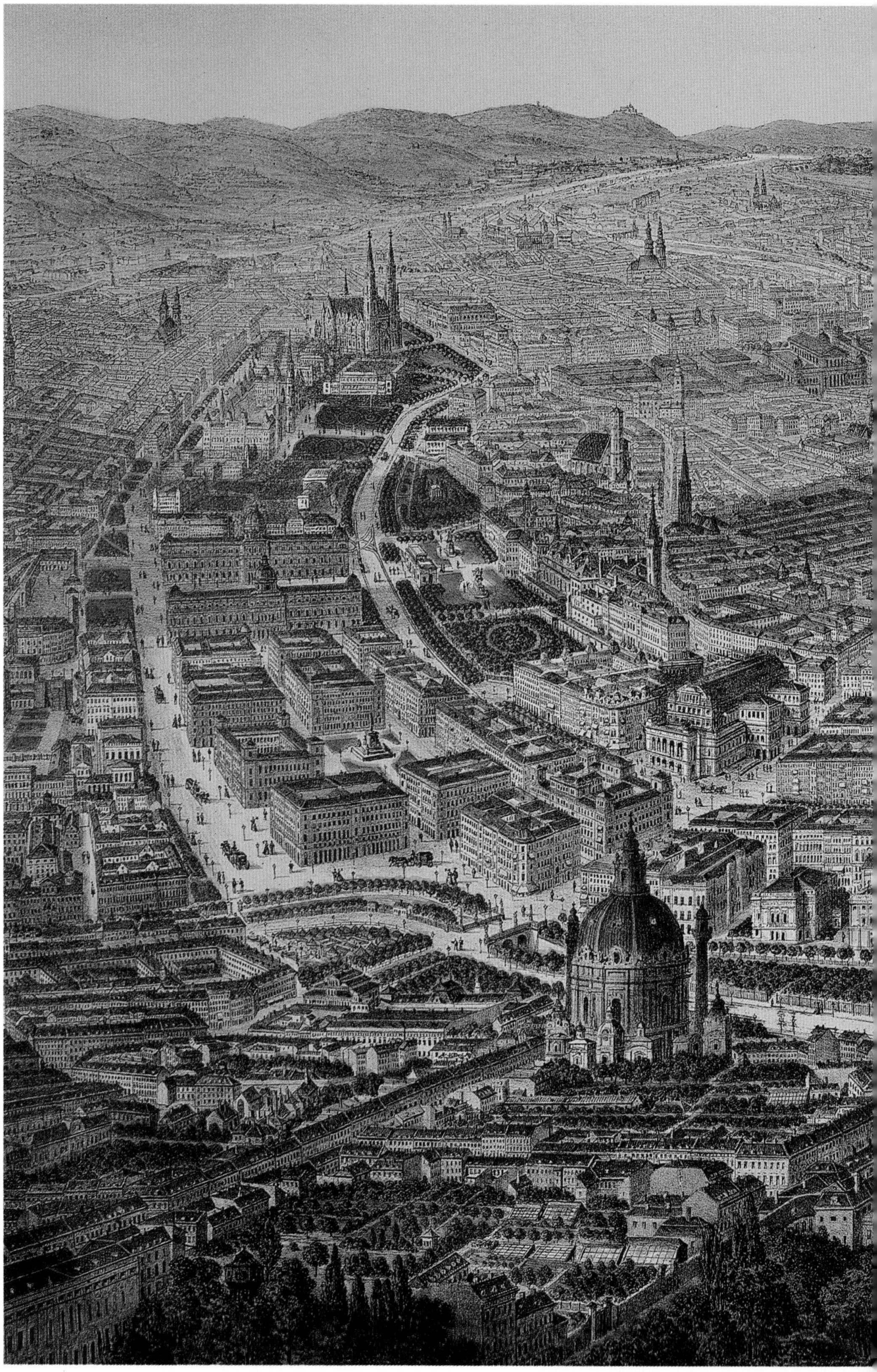

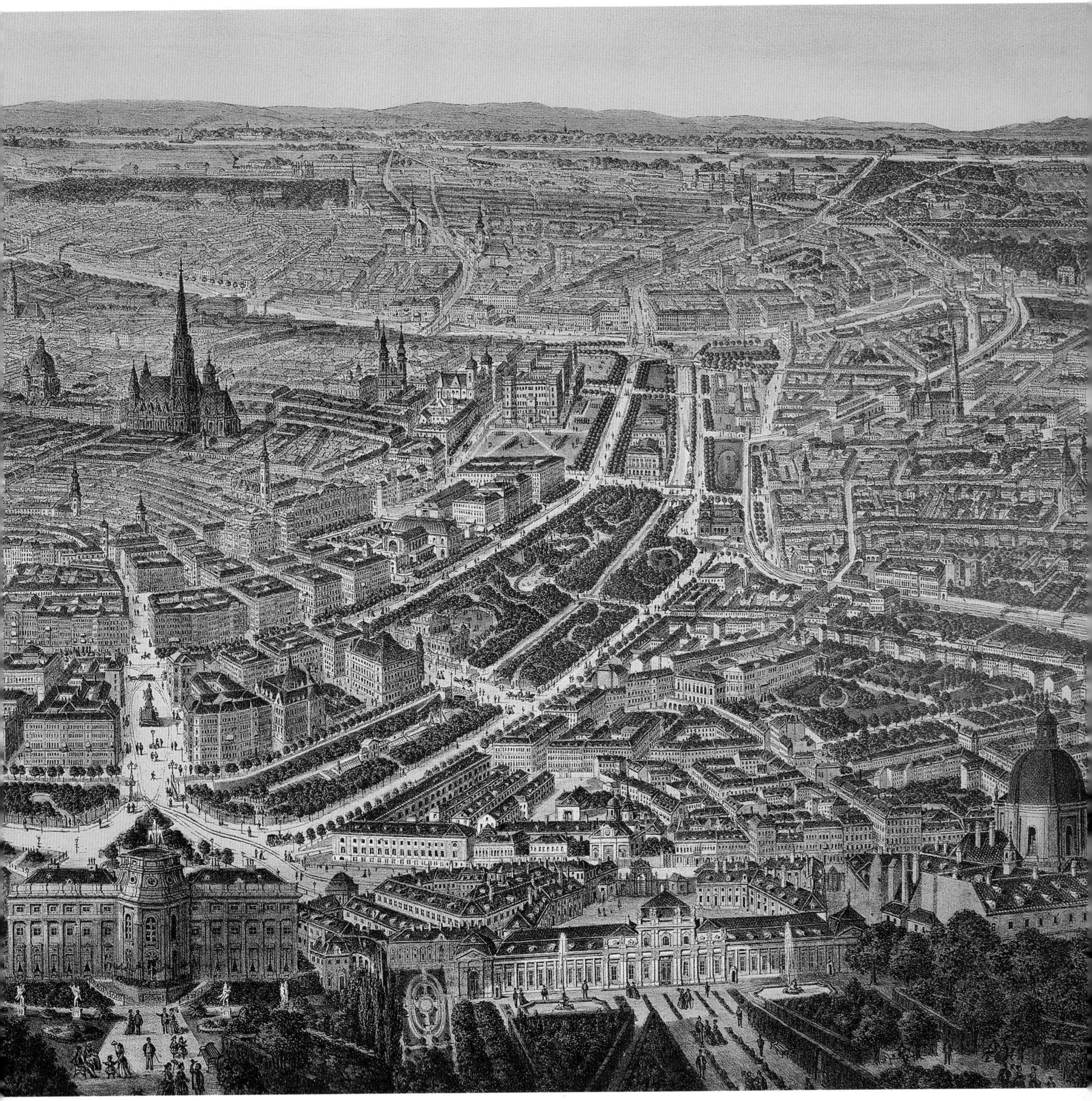

Commemorative city portraits

Pl.5 right *A somewhat schematic profile view of Naples (Italy) serves as backdrop to the triumphal return of the Aragonese fleet in 1464. The city is shown poised on a curve between sea and rising hills, its mark impressed on the sea by its famous lighthouse, on the hills by the monastery of S. Martino.*

Pl.6 below *This painting of Saragossa (Spain) in 1646 by J. B. del Mazo and Velázquez is, on the other hand, both specific and personal: it records the view from Prince Baltasar Carlos's room in S. Lázaro, looking out across the Ebro. To the left of the 15th-century Puente de Piedra is the cathedral of La Seo, with its curious Moorish dome; to the right, the city's other cathedral, of the Pilar (since rebuilt). Baltasar Carlos died in his room here, and the picture was completed for his father, Philip IV. The royal procession can just be seen on the far bank of the river in the center.*

Pl.7 left *Some urbanists have argued that ancient towns were shaped by symbolism rather than pragmatic logic. The mythical foundation of the Aztec capital Tenochtitlán (later Mexico City) in the mid-14th century is depicted in a page from the* Codex Mendoza. *At the intersection of four streams (recalling the four-part division of the city that remained well into the post-Conquest era), the location of the future capital is revealed through a sacred portent: an eagle perched on a cactus (*nochtli*) growing on a rock (*tetl*). "Cactus-on-rock" (*Tenoch*) is the name of the Aztec leader shown to the left of the eagle, as well as that of his new city.*

Pl.8 above *A diagram for the future: the interior landscape of a space colony, as projected by NASA.*

Bluntly put, my approach has a lot more to do with social history and urban geography than it does with the traditional fare of architectural historians. There are problems with both of these scholarly cultures. The social historian who tackles the city is often frustratingly vague about the physical frame of things. "For anyone interested in the landscape of a town it can be infuriating to pick up a book purporting to be a definitive history and find it goes into intricate details about borough organization in the thirteenth century and notable mayors in the eighteenth century, but tells little about its physical appearance at any date and does not even provide a plan."

This is a quotation from Michael Aston and James Bond, *The Landscape of Towns* (1976), a work which, confined only to England though it is and presented as a straightforward chronological survey, recalls rather directly my intent in the present volume and its companion. If there is one complaint to be lodged, it is that their book is too physical: there is not enough attention paid to the underlying explanations of urban form. And yet physical patterns always encapsulate an extra-physical reality. As one geographer put it, "Few social values and actions are so abstract that they fail to be reflected in material forms."[6]

My difficulties with urban geographers have to do with aims and means. Much of their effort goes to generating theory, which brings with it an insistence on measurement, statistical samples, and reductive diagrams. A practical side of these preoccupations is the definition of type independent of particular historical circumstance — a habit that parallels, with very different motives of course, the cavalier formal reductionism of the designer writing about urban form. But as one of their own, Harold Carter, observes, "if geographers reduce to abstract generalization the rich variety of urban places from Timbukto to Tottenham, from Samarkand to San Francisco, from Narberth to Nabeul, then theirs is an odd craft."[7]

Of their two principal jurisdictions, "the spatial characteristics of the city, and the characteristics of the city in space" (to use Carter's words again),[8] the second holds little fascination for me. The reader will find nothing here about favorite topics of the urban geographer like "the process of urbanization," "the growth of the city system" (or the distribution pattern of towns and the flow of goods and people within that pattern), and "the ranking of towns." A key monument of these concerns, central place theory, will barely be mentioned.

We are more in tune when urban geography turns to urban form proper and the interior structure of cities. Even here the vast literature is only very selectively apropos. Urban land-use and systems of land-rent, the location of industry in the city, the rural-urban fringe, the central business district—these are less appealing to me as theoretical matters of urban behavior than when they bear directly on the shape of particular cities. By the same token, the geographer's overwhelming economic bias in the discussion of urban form is at odds with an approach like mine that is fundamentally cultural, its steady emphasis on politics, social structure, and ritual.

Most apposite, as a tool, is the geographer's analysis of the "town plan"—a technique honed and publicized principally by M. R. G. Conzen.[9] What historians and practitioners of architecture loosely call urban fabric is comprised, for the Conzen school, of three interlocking elements. First, there is *the town plan* itself, which consists of the street system; the plot pattern, that is to say, land parcels or lots; and the building arrangement within this pattern. All this is taken at the ground level. This town plan the younger Conzen—M. P. Conzen—describes as "the cadaster or matrix of land divisions functionally differentiated by legally protected ownership." Then comes *the land use pattern*, which shows specialized uses of

17–19 The basic components of a town plan are identified by urban geographer M. R. G. Conzen as the town plan or street pattern (left)*, the land use pattern* (center)*, and the building fabric defining the city in three dimensions* (right)*.*

ground and space. Finally, there is *the building fabric*, which is the actual three-dimensional mark of physical structures on the land ownership parcel.

The difference is crucial. When architectural historians or architects engage in urban history, they habitually emphasize the street system alone. Edmund Bacon's *Design of Cities* is a well-known example. But urban process, in our sense of the phrase, is in large measure the story of urban development within the pre-existing frame or "ground plan." It manifests itself through changes in plot configuration, and the size and scale of the solid structures that occupy it. On this head at least, urban geography has much to teach us.

This so called morphogenetic approach, which puts all emphasis on the urban landscape itself, is judged as too restrictive by many geographers; they are usually the same ones who dismiss out-of-hand the *artistic* approach, their term for the strict formalism of the designer and the architectural historian. What is missing from the Conzen school, according to them, is a sense of economic forces, having to do with land values, the building industry and the like, which affect the physical growth and shape of the city. Building cycles, or varying amounts of constructional activity over time, are associated by these geographers, J. W. R. Whitehand perhaps foremost among them, with the familiar dogma of economic cycles. These peaks and sags in building activity affect new development at the fringe, as well as revisions in the urban core. Without denying the validity of this economic emphasis, or its contribution to an eventual theory of urban form, I must pronounce it, too, marginal within my limited charter.

PERIODS AND CATEGORIES

The thematic structure of my discourse, and its culturally inclusive range, limit reliance on traditional periodization. The term "medieval," conventionally finite for the West, is only of relative use when applied to China; "Renaissance" is of no use at all. Again, style periods methodically developed by art historians in the last one hundred years remain of limited relevance to urban form. There is as yet no credible effort to distinguish a Romanesque or a Gothic or a Rococo city, for example, except as a chronological convenience; but we are ready to recognize a Baroque urban esthetic (see "The Grand Manner," below), and at least one
140 historian, Kurt W. Forster, has interpreted the plan of Sabbioneta, the Gonzaga town of the 1550s, as a Mannerist grid.[10]

A more sweeping and simpler distinction, especially one that has the merit of being universally valid, would serve better in studies of my kind that undertake broad overviews. Fernand Braudel's roughly chronological divisions, inspired in part by Max Weber, are perhaps too tailormade for his own particular brand of history to be applicable beyond his system. They are restricted, at any rate, to the West. Type A, the open city, he identifies mostly with Greece and Rome. Here the town, whether walled or not, is "open to the surrounding countryside and on terms of equality with it." The medieval town is the classic case of Type B, the closed city: it is self-sufficient, exclusivist, and distrusts country folk and newcomers alike in its zealously guarded monopoly of industry and craft. Type C comprises the subjugated towns of early modern times, from the Renaissance onward, disciplined and sternly controlled by a powerful prince or state.[11]

For my purposes, I prefer an equally drastic but more ecumenical differentiation. The *pre-industrial city*, first postulated in a 1960 book of that name by Gideon *20*
Sjoberg, retains its usefulness despite serious objections to some of its premises. The definition, as it applies to our own concerns, specifies small size (very rarely over 100,000 people); lack of land use specialization; and little social and physical mobility. The social structure is primarily of two classes—an elite and a lower clas; the status of an intermediate stratum of merchants has been consistently overrated, according to Sjoberg. The center is taken up by government and religion and the residences of the elite. Occupational groupings are everywhere the rule.

The pre-industrial city, common to all civilizations of the old world for several millennia, still holds on here and there. But it has been overwhelmingly replaced by something else during the last several hundred years. Each of the themes I will take up in the succeeding chapters will have to consider the radical changes brought about by the appearance, in the relatively recent past, of the *industrial city*. If the *21*
critical date here is the 18th century, this can be pushed back to 1500 and even earlier, in so far as the industrial city may be said to have been prefigured by capitalism. The urban landscape was fundamentally transformed when urban land came to be seen as a source of income, when ownership was divorced from use, and property became primarily a means to produce rent. It was this "land-rent gradient" that, in the words of J. E. Vance, Jr., "ended the idea of the ordered city and economically encouraged *the segregation of uses*."[12]

The third category to distinguish, however brief its history to date, is *the socialist* *22*
city. Its cycle is not yet closed, but the basic features are already fully manifest. The central operative principle here is the abolition of capitalist ownership of land and property. This ban is actually by no means absolute in socialist countries. In Poland, for example, three-fourths of all farmland is still peasant-owned; in Yugoslavia this percentage is even higher. By and large, property is not expropriated "if it does not greatly exceed the acceptable per capita living-space norms and is used solely for shelter; thus private property persists in the housing sector in town and country."[13] But this selective leniency does not alter the fact that central planning determines the status, growth, and shape of the socialist city. It is the government which decides the size and look of the public spaces, the amount of housing, the size of the living units, patterns of transportation and questions of zoning. Rent and profit have nothing to do with these decisions. This at least has been the case until the recent populist revolution in eastern Europe, which may well succeed in privatizing property and installing a market economy along the model of the industrialised West.

As it has crystallized since the Second World War, the form of the socialist city shows these distinctive characteristics. In the center, the old business district has

20 The spatial characteristics of the European pre-industrial city are shown in this mid-17th-century view of Strasbourg (then Germany, now France) by Jan Jansson: a strongly defined city edge, and a dense, compact core accented by monumental public structures.

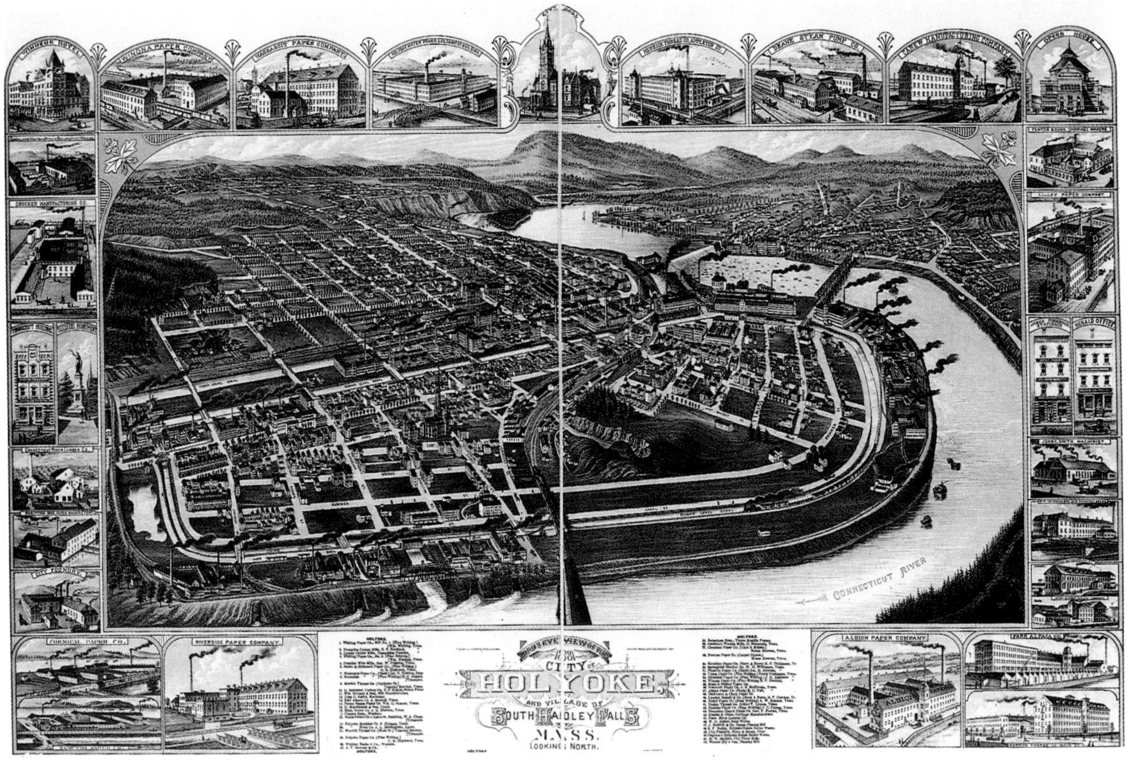

21 The industrial townscape is enshrined in A. F. Poole's 1881 lithograph of Holyoke (Massachusetts), a New England factory town. Manufacturing enterprises, hotels, and other monuments to private capital are celebrated in vignettes surrounding the bird's-eye view. The grid of subdivided lots, more densely occupied toward the town center, is a graphic reminder of a land-rent gradient and the profit motive for citybuilding.

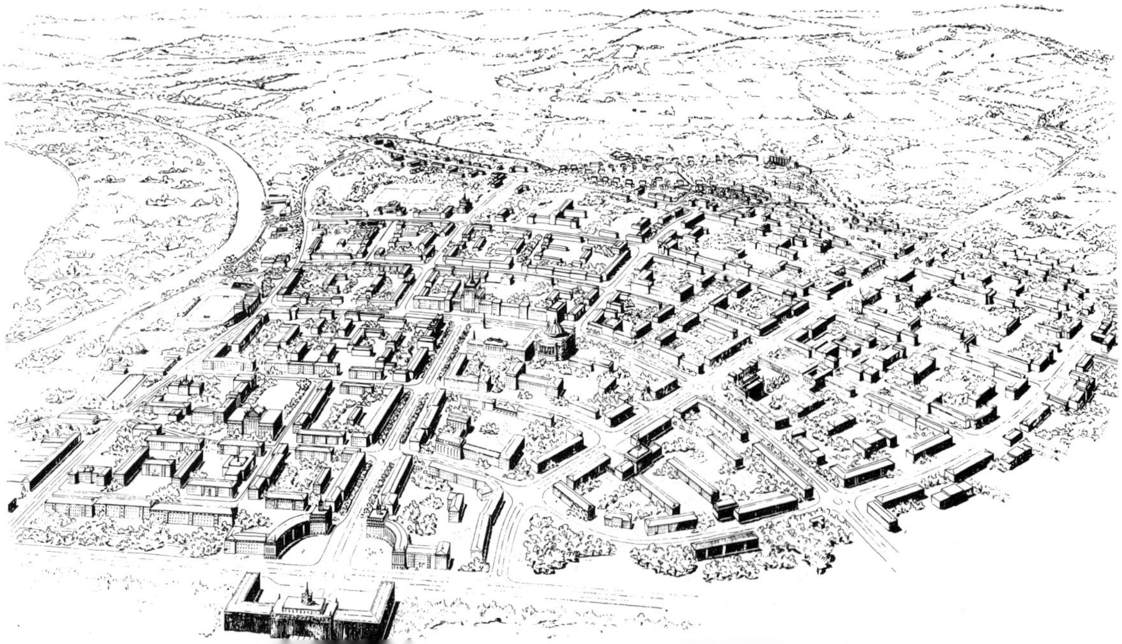

22 The socialist city of Stalinstadt (Eisenhütten-stadt) was heralded as East Germany's first planned new town and was designed in conformity with Soviet prototypes. The uniform density of settlement from edge to core and the large open spaces in the heart of town are made possible through centralized development authority and the rejection of differential land values. (From Deutsche Architektur, *1952*)

been replaced by a monumental administrative/governmental core. Sofia and East Berlin come to mind. A vast public space of a ceremonial nature occupies much of this central area where the thick of things had been. There is, in addition, a Park of Culture and Rest for the recreation of the working people, with promenades, tea rooms, picnic areas, and the obligatory socialist monuments. The housing consists of more or less equivalent neighborhood units, each focused on an industrial plant. This residential zone extends right from the inner city to the periphery in relatively high and even densities of population, in contrast to the increasingly low fringe densities of the capitalist-industrial city. Since the reliance on public transportation is much greater than in the West, urban growth follows officially determined transport routes. There are no squatter settlements. Again in total contrast with the Western, especially the North American, city, the retailing of consumer goods and banking take up an exceedingly small area in the urban landscape. The prominent presence is an architecture of public welfare goods and services.

THE CITY IN HISTORY

What is a city? how and when did cities begin?

The questions are posed because they would be expected in a book on the history of urban form. They are posed with the plea that we do not quibble about them. Definitions of the city, theories about its origins, and dogma about its behavior have consumed us. We have reached the point where the subject cannot be discussed at all without refuting or revising what others said. What follows is by way of clearing the air.

URBAN CYCLES

These days almost nobody believes in the diffusion theory any more—that is, that the city originated in Mesopotamia in the 4th millennium BC, and spread from there to the Indus Valley and China, and westward to Greece. With that premise, we only had to worry about one place and its cities in accounting for the birth of the urban form.

For one thing, it is now agreed, characteristics of some Neolithic settlements in Western Asia—Jericho, ᶜAin Ghazal, Çatal Hüyük, and Khirokitia are examples— 23
qualify them as towns; and that was about two or three thousand years *before* Mesopotamia. Jericho was girdled by a tremendous stone wall. ᶜAin Ghazal, also in Jordan, was three times the size of Jericho, with a population of 2,500–3,000 over thirty acres (12 ha.). The site yielded lifelike human statuary, luxury goods, and

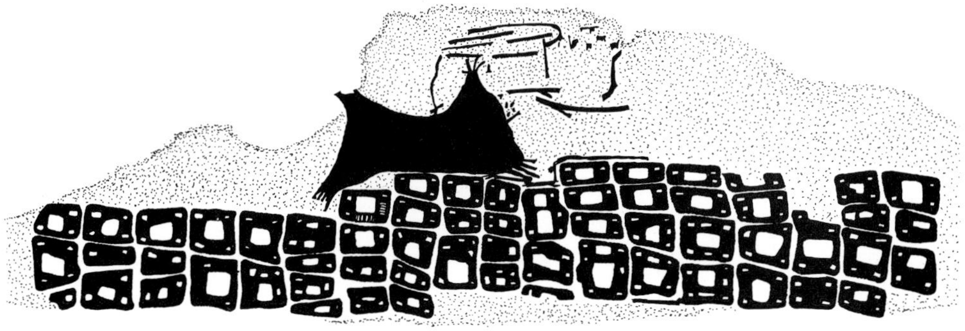

23 A wall-painting reconstructed from a shrine at Çatal Hüyük (Turkey) may be the oldest extant graphic representation of a town plan. The closely spaced rows of houses beneath a figure thought to represent an erupting volcano suggest the pattern of dwellings in this Neolithic settlement founded around 6500 BC.

small geometrical objects which may have been accounting tokens related to an
23 equitable allocation of resources.[14] Çatal Hüyük, in the Konya Plain, with perhaps 10,000 souls, disposed of a valued commodity, obsidian, the black volcanic glass that was the best material of the time for cutting tools; so it had the wherewithal for foreign trade. It had also public shrines and shops. Khirokitia in Cyprus had a street, the first I know of, and the unwalled settlement stretched along its length in a pattern of growth that was potentially open-ended.

There is a hiatus of at least fifteen hundred years between the demise of these proto-urban settlements and the rise of the first true cities in the mudplains between the Tigris and Euphrates some time around 3500 BC. In the Nile Valley urbanization came a little later, perhaps by 3000 BC. Then, a millennium or so after that, we have the cities of the Indus Valley, Harappa and Mohenjo Daro, which materialize rather suddenly and are abandoned as suddenly several centuries later. Between the death of these Indus Valley cities and the reappearance of urban life in India and Pakistan under the aegis of the Aryan invaders comes another time-gap of about one thousand years. In China the settings of the first cities were the western flood plains of the Yellow River and the lower Wei River valley: the earliest city was said to be Yin at Anyang, but earlier Shang capitals like Zhengzhou one hundred miles (160 km.) away have since been excavated. City genesis in South-East Asia—Burma, Malaysia, Indochina—is documented in the early centuries of the first millennium AD. In the New World, the Maya cities of Yucatan and Guatemala come first; Tikal and Uaxactun are among the oldest. In Peru, towns before the Chimú kingdom are obscure, but by the year AD 1000 Chanchan, with its characteristic walled citadel–compounds, had started its career as Chimú capital. In Africa, proponents of native, pre-European urbanization can point to Yoruba cities like Ibadan, Ogbomosho, Iwo, Ife and Lagos.

Two points need to be made in relation to this brief survey of urban beginnings.

First, we must stress the unevenness of urban development over space and time. At the very least, we have to conclude that the so-called urban revolution flared independently in several places on earth at different times, exactly as we now know to be the case with the Neolithic revolution. And this periodicity of city-making is a fact of history also for the West. In the Greek world, the Dorian invasion of about 1100 BC which brought down the brilliant civilization of Mycenae interrupted city life on the mainland and the Aegean islands for several hundred years. The long decline of urbanism after the "fall" of the Roman Empire is irrefutable, even if it has been perhaps overstated. The resurgence of new towns in the later Middle Ages had definite limits. Only after 1200 did the plantation of new towns extend beyond the Elbe and the Saale into eastern Europe and the Baltic shores.

At the same time, urban systems have an inbuilt stability, so that they can do without constant replenishment. Let us recall that in France, for example, the framework of the urban system which still holds today is the product of two periods of town foundation—the Gallo-Roman and the medieval. Out of 44 capitals of *civitates* in the Gallo-Roman period, that is, tribal territories identified for administrative purposes, 26 became *chef-lieux* of modern *départements* after the French Revolution when the framework of provincial rule that had prevailed under the *ancien régime* was restructured. From the mid-14th century on, little was added to this urban system, no more than a score of new towns between 1500 and 1800, and these were occasioned mostly by political ambition (e.g. the Duc de Sully's Henrichemont north of Bourges from 1608, the Duc de Nevers' Charleville near
146 Reims, also from 1608, Cardinal Richelieu's homonymous town from 1635, and of
238 course Versailles), by defense (e.g. Longwy and Neuf-Brisach, both designed by

Vauban), and by colonial ambition (the five ports of Le Havre, Brest, Rochefort, Lorient, and Sète).

In England, we find Roman towns, Saxon towns, and some 400 or 500 post-Conquest towns of the 12th and early 13th centuries, with long intervals of inactivity in between. And again almost nothing between the last of the medieval new towns, Queensborough and Bewdley, and the end of the 17th century, when here too, as in France, some new port towns were initiated, namely, Falmouth (1660), Whitehaven, Port Glasgow, and Devonport.

Second, if town-making, and urban life, are not a steady state of existence but surge and lapse in irregular cycles across the continents, alternate orders of human settlement should be given due attention. It is possible that we have made altogether too much of the city. Take the case of China. Most scholars now agree that in taking possession of their vast territories, the Chinese did not regard the city as the prime unit of settlement. What was important in penetrating and holding unsettled tracts was the expansion into them of systematic agriculture, centered in peasant villages. Once the land was tamed, one or more of these villages would be built up as centers of imperial authority.[15] The contrast is evident with Greece, Rome, or the opening up of eastern Europe by the Germans, say, where new towns were considered mandatory in the process of colonization.

URBAN ORIGINS

24 The origins of cities: markets. European fairs, like this one outside Arnhem (The Netherlands), provided a marketplace freed from many of the duties and franchises that encumbered long-distance trade. The biggest trade fairs took on the appearance of temporary cities, as shown in this detail of an engraving by Romeyn de Hooch (1645–1708).

The various schools of urban origins are familiar, and they often involve us in chicken-and-egg circumvolutions. Did this-and-such create the necessity for cities, or did an urban presence bring about this-and-such?

So it is with the concept of a surplus, i.e. that cities started when there was a shift away from a simple, self-satisfying village economy. Surplus production beyond the immediate needs of the community made possible the emancipation of some people from the toils of the land, and this created the opportunity for specialized tasks and the groups associated with them, namely, scribes, craftsmen, priests, and warriors. Surplus production presumes irrigation, and efficient irrigation systems presume a complex bureaucracy, and that means cities. So goes the argument.

But first of all, there really is no solid evidence that the rise of political authority in Mesopotamia, the putative birthplace of the city, was based on the administrative requirements of a major canal system. Secondly, surplus is a relative term. It has to presume a shift in priorities, the redirection of goods and services from one use to another, and not only and always an increase in production. In other words, changes in social institutions might be just as likely to precipitate changes in technology and complex notions about subsistence and surplus rather than the other way around.

The same holds for the city as a protected marketplace. In a thesis popularized by Jane Jacobs's *The Economy of Cities* (1969), cities are presumed to have developed as nodal markets; agricultural intensification then followed to feed the city. The trouble here is that a market was not always necessary in early towns, because long-distance trade was regulated by treaties and carried out by official traders. There is the instance of the Assyrian *karum*, for example, trading colonies of Assyrian merchants who settled just outside already flourishing towns in neighboring states like those of Anatolia. Trade by treaty was also practiced in pre-Columbian Meso-America, in pre-colonial West Africa, and probably in Shang China.[16] The self-regulating market, it turns out, may have been the exception and not the rule. What is more, local markets, even when they existed, did not always develop into cities, and neither, by the way, did fairs, those quintessential centers of long-distance trade, 24 common belief to the contrary notwithstanding. In fact, this is also true of the Middle Ages. As far as we can tell, no medieval fair ever gave birth to a city. Even Troyes existed before its famous fair.

Much the same problem arises with military and religious theories: the town as an agent of defense and domination, and the town as a holy place. To be sure, concentration of settlements for purposes of defense may have generated cities (why did they not start earlier, one wonders, since defense must have been a problem in pre-urban times too?). Then again, the reverse may be true, that once you have a concentration of people, you might need sophisticated defense. And shrines do not
25 always produce cities, though there is no doubting the great importance of cults and of a priestly hierarchy in the matrix of early cities everywhere, as Paul Wheatley and others have long argued.[17] This emphasis on the ceremonial cult center, I might add, is very much to be applauded as a necessary antidote against the excessive importance attached to trade by historians of the Western city.

All this is conveniently summarized in Harold Carter's recent book, *An Introduction to Urban Historical Geography* (1983), which concludes by quoting Wheatley:

> It is doubtful if a single, autonomous, causative factor will ever be identified in the nexus of social, economic and political transformations which resulted in the emergence of urban forms . . . whatever structural changes in social organization were induced by commerce, warfare or technology, they needed to be validated by some instrument of authority if they were to achieve institutionalized permanence.

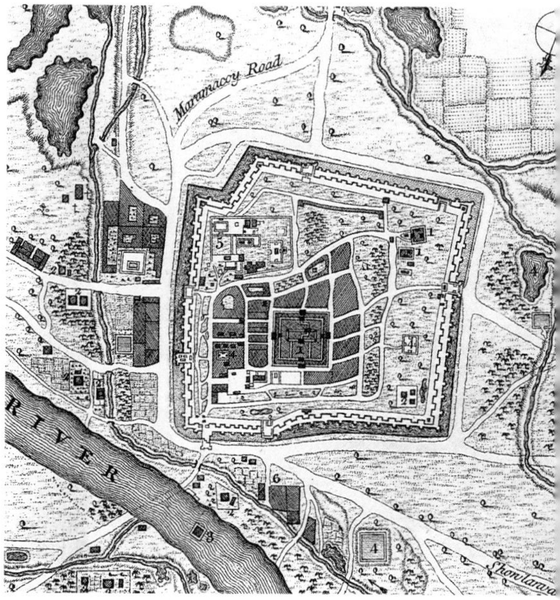

25 *The origins of cities: ceremonial centers. Madurai (South India) is depicted in this 18th-century plan as a concentric pattern of walls, open spaces and city blocks organized around the sacred kernel of its temple precinct, with its own square wall pierced by four towered gates or* gopuras.

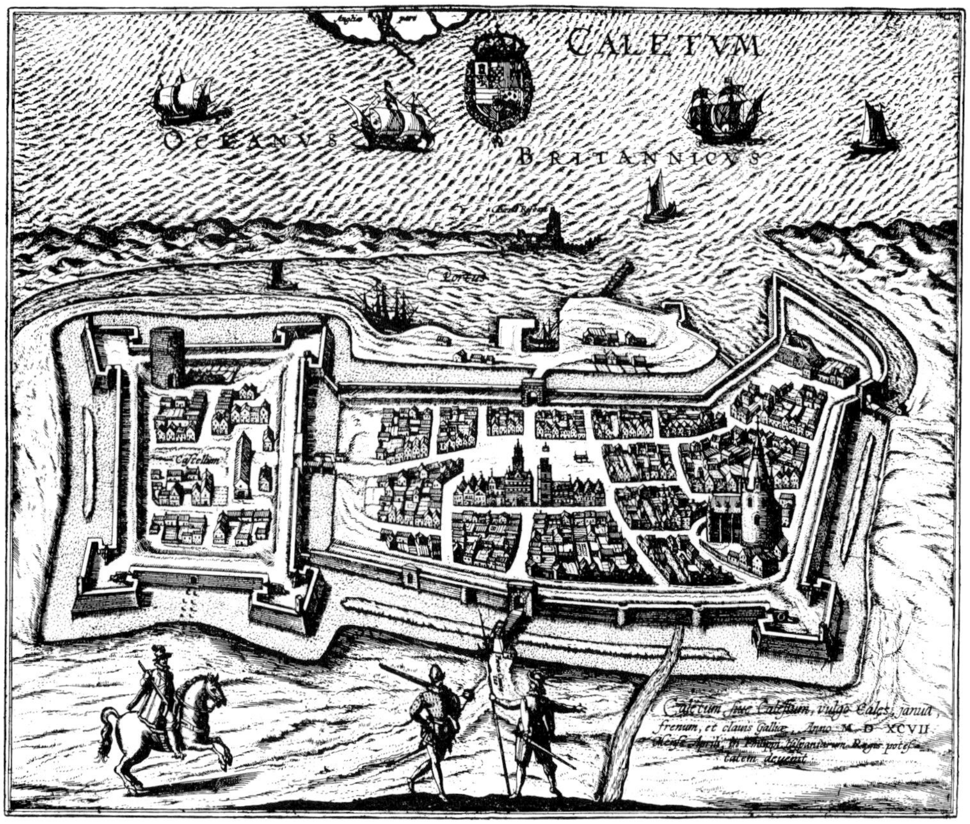

26 left *The origins of cities: military strongholds. The French coastal city of Calais was occupied by Edward III of England in 1346 to establish a firm grip upon the territory gained through military exploits. In the two centuries of rule by the British* goddons, *the city was transformed into an administrative fortress. The English foothold was recaptured by the French in 1558, despite a last desperate remodeling of its bastions in conformance with the state-of-the-art Italian prototypes, as shown in this late 16th-century engraving from Braun and Hogenberg's* Civitates Orbis Terrarum.

This instrument of authority, rather than any particular form of activity, was the
generating force for many towns. Sjoberg equated authority with social power. To
him the pre-industrial city was "a mechanism by which a society's rulers can
consolidate and maintain their power." The spread of cities into non-urbanized
areas had to do with "the consolidation or extension of a political apparatus, be the
result a kingdom or an empire."[18] Military conquest and political stability, more so *26*
than trade, create the need for cities. A conquering force requires administrative and
military centers in order to control newly won lands. Ibn Khaldun, the great Muslim
historian, made much the same point in the 15th century. "Dynasties and royal
authority are absolutely necessary for the building of cities and the planning of
towns," he wrote.[19] The catch, again, is who came first. You can argue, and some
have, that early dynasties needed an urban base as their mainspring. In the end, it
comes down to a seemingly unavoidable primary distinction between cities imposed
by an established political authority, and those which, in Wheatley's words, came
into being "as a result of the spontaneous readjustment of social, political and
economic relationships within the context of a folk society."[20] The latter process is
internal to a specific region, while urban imposition is the extension of urban
patterns from one region to another.

To take Japan as an example: the first cities developed, south of the Tohoku,
between the 4th and 6th centuries AD. The generating nucleus is said to have been
palace–capitals of chiefdoms that brought together a number of tribes, in the period
known as the Tumulus culture, in the Yamato region of south Japan. The fortified
palace that either incorporated or was surrounded by the personal administrative *29,*
staff of the ruler drew about itself an unplanned accretion of artisans, craftsmen and *30*
military retainers, and out of this social readjustment internal to the Yamato region
an urban form was born. Then, in the 7th century, capitals conceived as unitary
wholes and fully planned as orthogonal compositions make a sudden appearance,
beginning with Fujiwara occupied in 694, and Heijokyo (Nara) in the center of the *139*
Yamato plain some fifteen years later. The model in this instance was external, namely, the orthogonal planning of Chinese cities like Chang'an. It is uncertain whether *174*
the model was imported directly and adopted along with the Chinese government
structure, or whether it reached Japan through the intermediary of the Korean
kingdom of Silla with its Chinese-style capital on the site of present-day Kyongju. In
either case, it was an alien formula brought in and applied by a strong centralized
authority to a territory that had nothing to do with its creation.

If urban causality proves a tricky subject, we must also try not to make too much of the precise location, or the general geomorphic conditions, in which cities chose to manifest themselves. Cities, even those attributed to spontaneous processes inherent to a region, are never entirely processual events: at some level, city-making always entails an act of will on the part of a leader or a collectivity. To explain cities as the result of purely "natural" causes—accidents of geography or regional inevitabilities—is to indulge in a species of physical determinism incompatible with human affairs. There are, after all, many river crossings, convergences of land routes, and defensible outcrops which did not spawn towns. As Aston and Bond say, "Towns are built by and for people. Their regional and local sitings are the result of decisions taken by people and not of some inevitable physical control." And besides it is good to remember that, "Whatever the initial reasons for a town's foundation on a particular site, once established it generates its own infrastructure, transport network and so on."[21]

Shall we agree, then, not to fret too much about the single common empowering factor responsible for the origin of cities? None of the generative impulses mentioned above is unimportant. A positive ecological base; a site favorable to trade; an advanced technology that would include large-scale irrigation works, metallurgy, animal husbandry and the like; a complex social organization; a strong political structure—these are all relevant to the genesis of cities. The point is that some factors were probably interdependent in the emergence of some cities, and different ones among them may have motivated different cities: or, to put it more clearly, towns may have been spawned for specific reasons that have to do with the purposes they were intended to serve.

Urban form is generated through a variety of settlement processes.

27, 28 left *Through synoecism, several independent villages are consolidated into a single community.*

29, 30 center *Service precincts grow up near palace, temple, or fortress compounds, attracted by their concentration of wealth.*

31, 32 right *In the case of the Precolumbian city of Teotihuacán (Mexico), the administrative powers invested in the religious complex were sufficient to substitute a formal orthogonality for the pattern of villages that originally occupied the site.*

EARLY CITY FORM

Early cities came in many shapes. We must be willing to set aside, before we enter our main discourse, the seductive picture of cities growing organically out of village life, like mature trees out of green saplings. Whatever the incidence of such progressive development, let us not mistake non-geometric city form for the inevitable end result of the slow proliferous change of a simpler settlement form. There are many cases where the coming together of a number of prior settlements, speaking morphogenetically, produced towns of arbitrary irregularities. We mentioned the first Japanese towns, given life by the chieftain's palace. These, or for that matter the first Mesopotamian towns, probably owed their shape as much to some erratic social agglomeration around an institutional core as they did to natural adjustments or "biological" rhythms.

Secondly, there were from the start plenty of towns that did not in the least look natural or organic. Some, like El Lahun, were dormitory communities for workers, not full-fledged towns in reality. But they showed, for all that, the knowledge in Old Kingdom Egypt to design totally ordered environments, with streets, seriated housing units, and a residential hierarchy that is anything but random. And in cities like Mohenjo Daro we have a schematic orthogonal planning applied to the entire urban fabric; the blocks were of roughly equal size, and a rational distinction was made between main streets and the alleys that separated the houses.

No, whatever the actual practices of urbanization may have been, ancient traditions insisted that making cities was an intentional act, approved and implemented at the highest level. The gods made cities and took charge of them. The kings made cities, in order to set up microcosms of their rule. The city was a marvellous, inspired creation. An Egyptian document of the 7th century BC says that Ptah "had formed the gods, he had made cities, he had founded nomes. He had put the gods in their shrines." An earlier poem hails Amun and his creation, Thebes, "the pattern of every city." And so it continued through the centuries. As far as people's beliefs were concerned, cities were made, they did not happen.

This is not at all surprising, since in many ancient cultures, the city on earth was supposed to represent a celestial model which it was extremely important to reproduce accurately. Ritual proprieties like orientation to the four points of the compass, symmetrically arranged gates, and dimensions of round, magical numbers, had to be observed. Which in turn meant an artificial layout, often of some geometric purity. The gods knew such things and told the kings. If you could start from scratch, you could have the whole town properly conform to the prescribed ritual instructions. One's reign could then start auspiciously. History is filled with instances of new towns that augur new eras: Amarna for Akhenaten; Khorsabad for Sargon II; Baghdad for al-Mansur; Dadu for Khubilai Khan; Versailles for Louis XIV. A treasured advantage of these new starts was that the ruler could design an ideal population for his city, and coerce it to live in premeditated relationships.

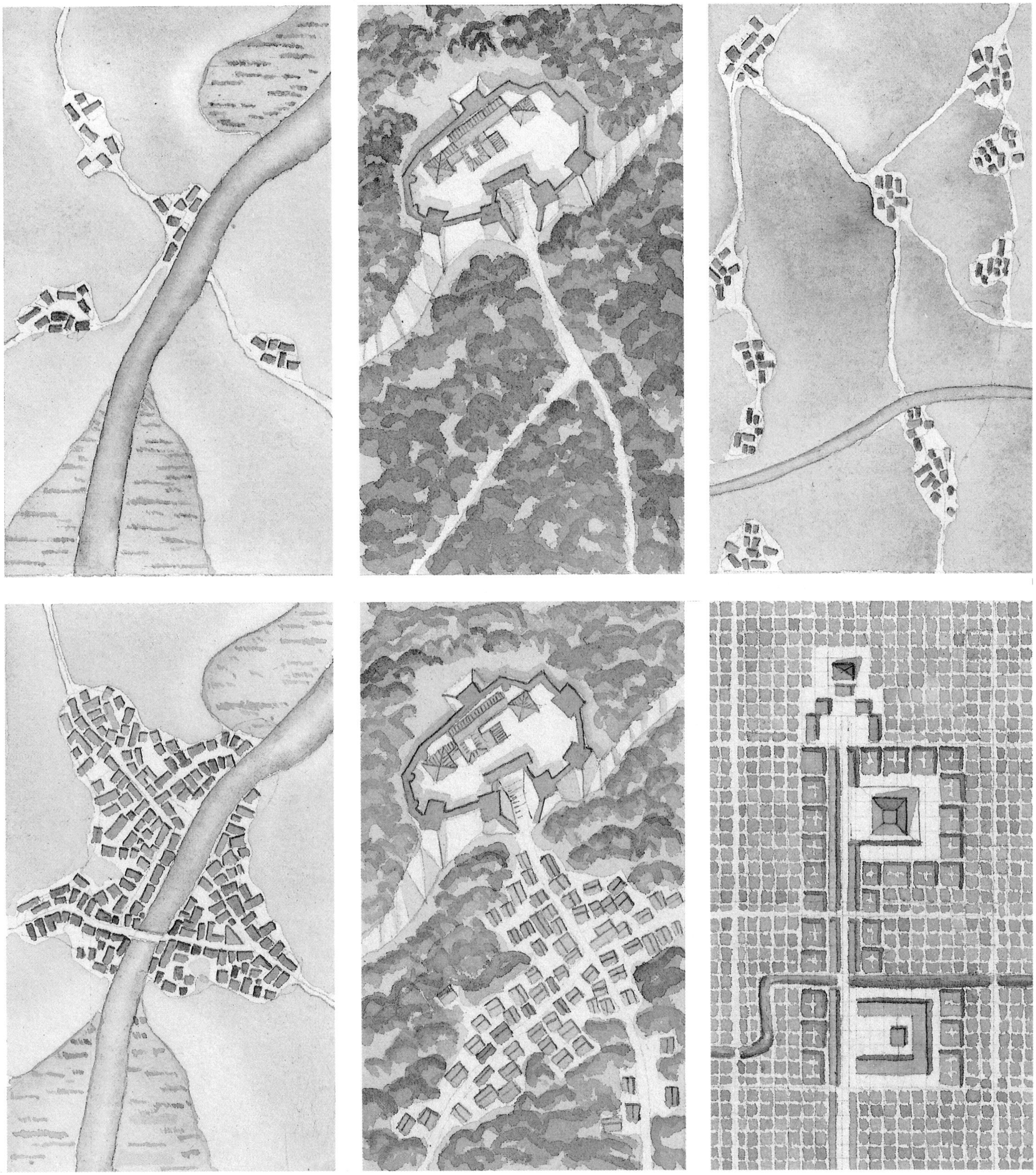

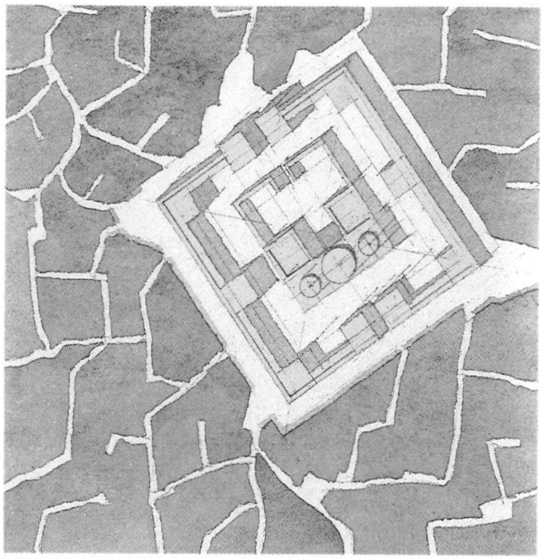

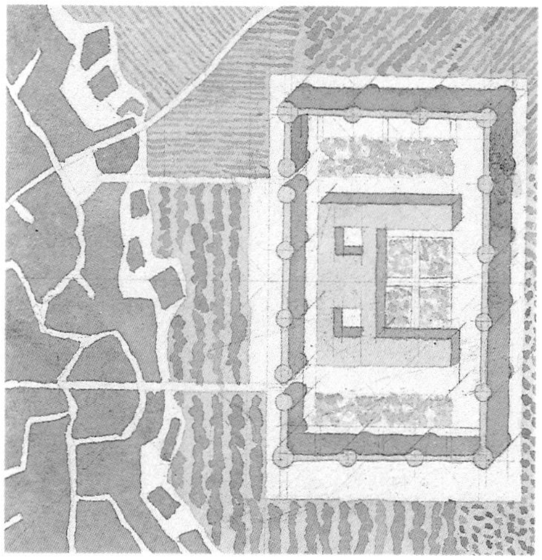

33, 34 Planted within the urban core or appended to the city edge, monumental temple and palace precincts provide a striking contrast to their urban setting in scale and geometric order.

If you had to work with something less perfect, a prior city you inherited, you could do two things. You could see to it that the central ceremonial complex
33, reflected the divine prototype—which is why temple–palace groups of otherwise
34 irregular towns are often planned in a formal manner that would stand in significant contrast to the rest of the urban fabric, both in scale and in its calculated order. Or you could add new quarters to the old town, ennobled with your very own dynastic monumentality and endowed with an exclusive population. This is the story of Assur and Babylon, of Cairo and Samarra, of Ercole d'Este's addition to Ferrara and
253 those of the Electors of Brandenburg to Berlin. The shape of many cities in history represents a serial growth of planned increments grafted to an original core, and one of the most revealing aspects of the urban landscape has to do with the ways in which these additions are meshed with, or purposely discriminated from, the older fabric.

Alongside the tradition of the divine–princely origin of cities, there seems to have been from very early on a counter-tradition that said humans, common people, urbanized on their own initiative, and the gods were not pleased about it. In the Old Testament it is easy to detect strong anti-urban sentiments. God created a garden, a paradise of Nature, an Eden, but "Cain went out from the presence of the Lord and dwelt in the land of Nod on the East of Eden . . . and he built a city." And later on again, journeying eastward, the offspring of Noah found a plain in the land of Shinar; "and they said, 'Go to, let us build us a city and a tower, whose top may reach unto heaven; and let us make us a name, lest we be scattered abroad upon the face of the whole earth.'" And the Lord promptly put an end to these blasphemous proceedings.

Are we to read into this the resistance of agrarian cultures, where God is everywhere, or localized in brooks and mountaintops, to the challenge of cities and the domestication, if you will, of the godhead? Or should we also see here the beginnings of populism, of bypassing central authority—the creation of cities by the will of the people, without benefit of kingship or priesthood; or the wresting of cities from such authority?

In the world of the Greeks, that notion will find its apogee in the concept of the *polis* where the community as a whole *is* the city. In the words of Nicias to the Athenian soldiers on the beach at Syracuse: "You are yourselves the town, wherever you choose to settle . . . it is men that make the city, not the walls and ships without them" (Thucydides vii.63). *Polis* gives us "political." Man, Aristotle wrote, is a "political" creature, one suited by nature to live in a city.

And how do we know this type of city? There will be in it no monumental settings except for the gods, no stone houses, no fancy streets. And there will be in it places where the citizens can come together to make decisions affecting their common fate and the way they want to live. And the city will be the measure of one's morality. Good people live in cities; they belong to a particular city that gives them their identity and self-worth. People who transgress morality are banished from their city. "No city hath he," Sophocles writes, "who dares to dwell with dishonor."

After the Hellenistic/Roman epoch when the city as a work of art, or *urbs*, prevailed over *civitas*, the city as a righteous assembly of people, we find again an assertion of community. This is what sustains some of the Roman towns despite their sorry state, their shrinkage, their bankruptcy, brought about by the disintegration of the empire. "Not the stones but the people," as Isidore of Seville put it in the 7th century in describing *civitas*. And when several centuries later the people regain control of their cities from their feudal overlords, once again there is a collective presence, a moral imperative, a parity of citizens in charge of their destiny and their city-form. Throughout the later Middle Ages, the struggle of the burghers to stand up to castle and cathedral, to lord and bishop, will dramatically inform the making of the urban landscape.

WHAT IS A CITY?

To conclude these introductory remarks, I think we can agree on some simple premises about cities, regardless of their origin, their birthplace, their form, their makers. Two sensible definitions, both from 1938, would allow us a good starting point. For L. Wirth, a city is "a relatively large, dense, and permanent settlement of socially heterogenous individuals."[22] For Mumford, a city is a "point of maximum concentration for the power and culture of a community."[23] Here is my gloss on these fundamental premises.

A. Cities are places where a certain energized crowding of people takes place. This has nothing to do with absolute size or with absolute numbers: it has to do with settlement density. The vast majority of towns in the pre-industrial world were small: a population of 2,000 or less was not uncommon, and one of 10,000 would be noteworthy. Of the almost 3,000 towns in the Holy Roman Empire only about 12 to 15 (Cologne and Lübeck among them) had over 10,000 inhabitants.

A few statistics will serve as future points of reference. There were only a handful of genuine metropolises in antiquity, among them imperial Rome in the 2nd century AD and Chang'an in the 8th. In the Middle Ages this prodigious size is matched by Constantinople, Cordoba and Palermo, the last two of which may have been in the 500,000 range in the 13th–14th centuries. Baghdad may have had as many as 1,000,000 inhabitants before it was destroyed by the Mongols in 1258. Again, we have Chinese parallels for such phenomenal concentrations—Nanjing in the 15th century, and, in the late imperial era, Beijing, Suzhou and Canton. Beijing remained the world's largest city until 1800, with a population of 2,000,000–3,000,000, when it was overtaken by London. Its only close rivals in the 17th century were Istanbul, Agra, and Delhi. Behind every enormous city of this sort, at least in the pre-industrial era, there lies a vast, centralized state. Without its ruler, the city is bound to wither or collapse.

B. Cities come in clusters. A town never exists unaccompanied by other towns. It is therefore inevitably locked in an urban system, an urban hierarchy. Even the lowliest of townlets has its dependent villages. As Braudel puts it, "The town only exists as a town in relation to a form of life lower than its own . . . It has to dominate an empire, however tiny, in order to exist."[24] In China, the urban hierarchy was expressed by suffixes added to the names of towns, like *fu* for a town of the first order, *chu* for one lower down, and *hieu* for one lower still. Similarly, there was a clearly defined urban hierarchy in Ottoman Anatolia of the 16th century headed by Istanbul, and descending through a number of regional centers of about 20,000 to 40,000 inhabitants each to two sets of lower-order towns of under 10,000 and under 5,000.

C. Cities are places that have some physical circumscription, whether material or symbolic, to separate those who belong in the urban order from those who do not. "Une ville sans mur n'est pas une ville" (a city without walls is not a city), J.-F. Sobry wrote in his *De l'architecture* of 1776. Even without any physical circumscription, there is a legal perimeter within which restrictions and privileges apply.

D. Cities are places where there is a specialized differentiation of work—where people are priests or craftsmen or soldiers—and where wealth is not equally distributed among the citizens. These distinctions create social hierarchies: the rich are more powerful than the poor; the priest is more important than the artisan. Social heterogeneity is also axiomatic. The urban population contains different ethnic groups, races, religions. Even in ethnically homogeneous cities, as the original Yoruba cities were intended to be, there might be slaves or transient traders.

E. Cities are places favored by a source of income—trade, intensive agriculture and the possibility of surplus food, a physical resource like a metal or a spring (Bath), a geomorphic resource like a natural harbor, or a human resource like a king.

F. Cities are places that must rely on written records. It is through writing that they will tally their goods, put down the laws that will govern the community, and establish title to property—which is extremely important, because in the final analysis a city rests on a construct of ownership.

G. Cities are places that are intimately engaged with their countryside, that have a territory that feeds them and which they protect and provide services for. The separation of town and country, as we shall see repeatedly in this book, is thoroughly injudicious. Roman towns do not exist apart from the centuriated land roundabout; great Italian communes like Florence and Siena could not exist without their *contado*; and the same is true of New England towns and their fields and commons. *Polis*, *civitas*, commune, township—all these are terms that apply to an urban settlement *and* its region.[25]

Often the city-form is locked into rural systems of land division. The Romans commonly correlated the main north-south and east-west coordinates of the centuriation—the division of rural land into squares that were supposed to be the theoretical equivalent of one hundred small holdings—with the cross-axes of the

35–43 Characteristics of cities:

A *Energized crowding*

B *Urban clusters*

C *Physical circumscription*

D *Differentiation of uses*

E *Urban resources*

F *Written records*

G *City and countryside*

H *Monumental framework*

I *Buildings and people*

A

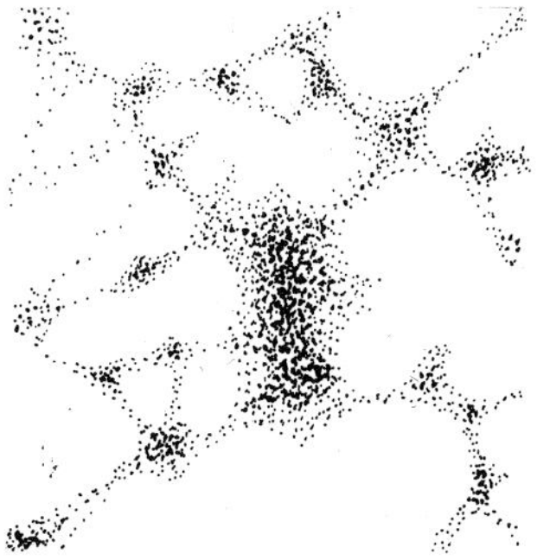
B

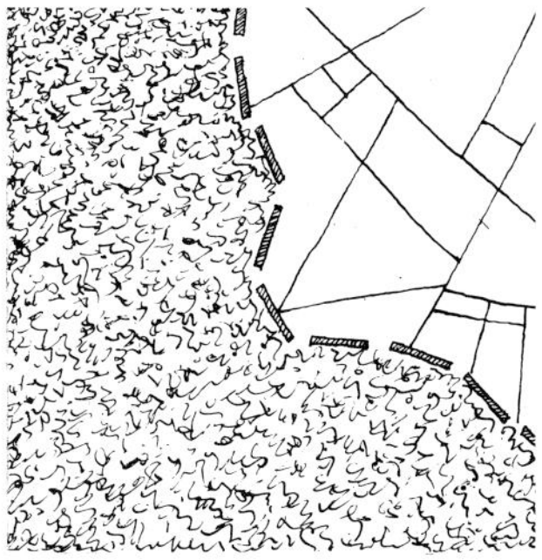
C

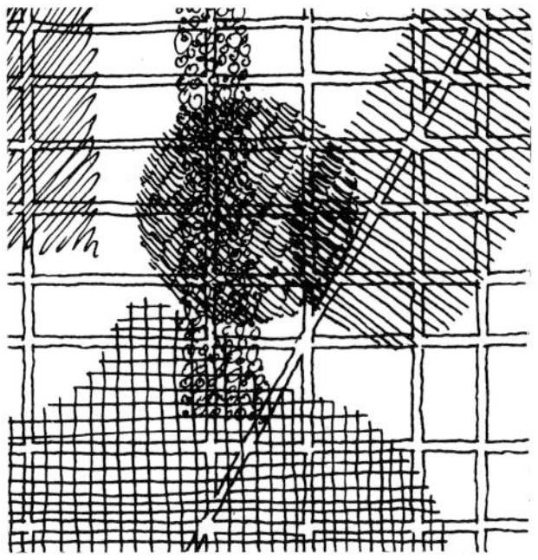
D

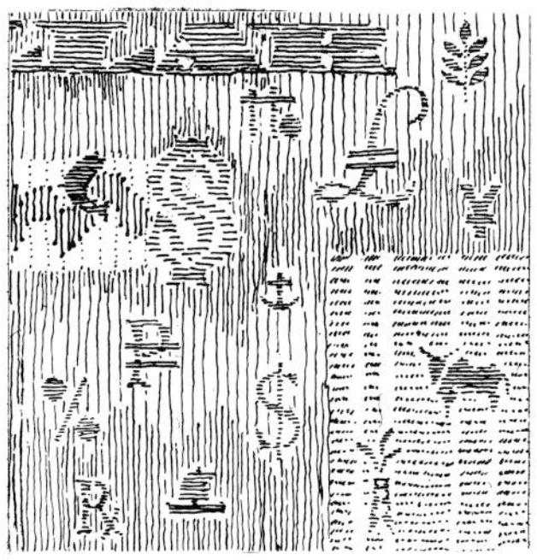
E

F

G

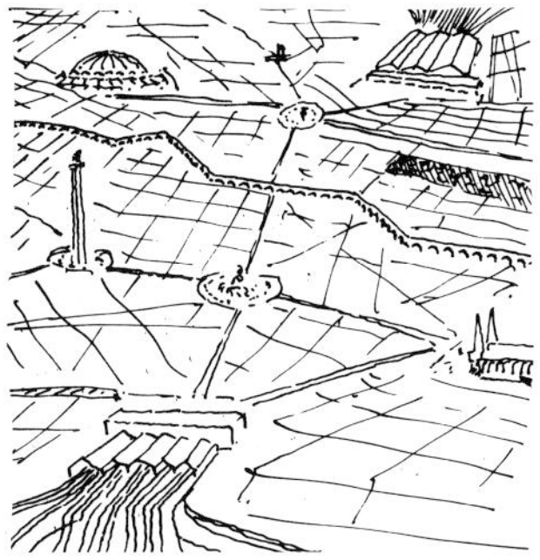
H

I

city. The National Survey that regulated two-thirds of the United States territory determined the placement and size of many towns (see "The Grid," below). It is, furthermore, of great interest to us that pre-existing rural property bounds will often influence subsequent urban lines, and determine the shape of urban development.

The question of which came first, town or country, is not simple. The first towns in the Middle East or China controlled and organized an already functioning countryside. In the opening of the American West, the towns preceded the farms and made their operations possible. By the same token, the strains of a deeply felt disagreement about the relative superiority of town and country can be heard throughout history. Two examples, as distant as I can make them. In China, the Confucian view that the proper function of the elite was to govern, that government presumed cities, and that the purpose of government was to civilize the countryside, clashes with the ultimately Taoist and Buddhist ideal of rural existence. Thomas Jefferson's agrarian republicanism had no use for cities in the structure of the young nation. Cities were "sores on the body politic."

H. Cities are places distinguished by some kind of monumental definition, that is, where the fabric is more than a blanket of residences. This means a set of public buildings that give the city scale, and the citizenry landmarks of a common identity. Technological monuments are also important: Rome had its aqueducts; Tikal, a large manmade reservoir; Anuradhapura in Sri Lanka, a hydraulic system of monumental proportions. In the public realm early cities under central authority chose to emphasize the palace and the temple. In the people's city, the princely palace disappears, or is translated into a palace of the people, and the temple is "secularized"—that is the case of the Greek *polis*, and that too is the case of the European commune in the Middle Ages with its *palazzo pubblico* or *Rathaus* and its "civic" cathedral.

I. Finally, cities are places made up of buildings and people. I agree with Kevin Lynch: "City forms, their actual function, and the ideas and values that people attach to them make up a single phenomenon."[26] Hundreds of new towns in every age of history were still-born, or died young. The majority of the grids laid out by railroad companies along their lines in the 19th century never fleshed out into real towns. Conversely, we can discount scholarly claims for the fully established and
173 long-lived Mayan sites or for places like Angkor Thom and Nakhon Pathom that they were not real cities because they had no resident population. These spectacular ceremonial settings and the priests and the builders and the artisans and the people selling them things belonged together. We will be well served, in reading this book, to recognize that there have been cityless societies, and times when cities were vestigial marks in a predominantly rural landscape. Let us recognize, too, that the urban and pastoral ways of life were at times contending social systems; and further, that the history of human settlement must be predicated on a rural-urban continuum, and that the city as a self-contained unit of analysis must be seen as conditional enterprise. For all that, the city is one of the most remarkable, one of the most enduring of human artifacts and human institutions. Its fascination is inevitable: its study is both duty and homage.

Ours is certainly not a story restricted to the past. At this very moment cities are being born *ab ovo*, either through the legal instrument of incorporation, or through parthenogenesis. Since 1950 more than 30 new towns were created in England. In France, along two preferential axes following the Seine Valley, several new towns for 300,000 to 500,000 each are in the process of building—St.-Quentin-en-Yvelines, Evry, Marne-la-Vallée. Others have been started outside the Paris region. In the Soviet Union we have many hundreds of recent new towns, closely associated with the spread of industrialization. In the United States, the "new communities" program introduced in the Sixties has had its own considerable offspring.

It is a long haul, from Jericho to Marne-la-Valleé. My ambition to encompass all of urban history through this thematic approach rests on a paradox. Cities in their physical aspect are stubbornly long-lived. As Vance put it,

> The most enduring feature of the city is its physical build, which remains with remarkable persistence, gaining increments that are responsive to the most recent economic demand and reflective of the latest stylistic vogue, but conserving evidence of past urban culture for present and future generations.

At the same time

> urban society changes more than any other human grouping, economic innovation comes usually most rapidly and boldly in cities, immigration aims first

44 Budapest's Marx Square—formerly Berlin Square—manifests a century of shifting urban culture in its streets and buildings. On the right, a remnant of the city's fin-de-siècle splendor is coaxed into the socialist era with a crowning red star. Across the street a glass-skinned commercial building and a multi-level thoroughfare interject a fragment of late modern townscape.

> at the urban core forcing upon cities the critical role of acculturating refugees from many countrysides, and the winds of intellectual advance blow strong in cities . . .[27]

The challenge in this book and its companion volume will be to seize upon and reconcile this vital contest between socio-economic change and the persistence of the artifact.

1 · "ORGANIC" PATTERNS

PLANNED CITIES AND UNPLANNED

THERE are two kinds of cities, the most persistent, and crudest, analysis of urban form would have us accept. It is not hard to tell them apart.

The first kind is the planned or designed or "created" city—Pierre
Lavedan's *ville créée*. It is set down at one moment, its pattern determined once and 47
for all by some overseeing authority. Until the 19th century this pattern invariably
registered as an orderly, geometric diagram. At its purest it would be a grid, or else a 147
centrally planned scheme like a circle or a polygon with radial streets issuing from 159
the center; but often the geometry is more complex, marrying the two pure formulas
in modulated and refracted combinations.

The other kind is the *ville spontanée*—the spontaneous city, also called "grown," 46
"chance-grown," "generated" (as against "imposed"), or, to underline one of the evident determinants of its pattern, "geomorphic." It is presumed to develop without benefit of designers, subject to no master plan but the passage of time, the lay of the land, and the daily life of the citizens. The resultant form is irregular, non-geometric, "organic," with an incidence of crooked and curved streets and randomly defined open spaces. To stress process over time in the making of such city-forms, one speaks of "unplanned evolution" or "instinctive growth."

Here is how one urban historian, F. Castagnoli, makes the distinction.

> The irregular city is the result of development left entirely to individuals who actually live on the land. If a governing body divides the land and disposes of it before it is handed over to the users, a uniformly patterned city will emerge.[1]

The issue, from this perspective, is order and its corollary, control. And so, depending on our view of things, we will either favor the planned city over the unplanned for its formal discipline, or else deplore its rigidity. Again, we might fault the random ways of the unplanned city—or find praise for its celebration of an eventful topography, the responsive and flexible evolution of its form, and its native ease with the rhythms of communal living.

For a number of reasons, this neat dichotomy, intended to simplify our appreciation of urban form, turns out to be more a hindrance than an aid.

45 Vézelay (France). A gracefully curved street traces a processional path to a Benedictine abbey with a church famous as the resting place of the remains of Mary Magdalen. The town's remarkable growth, fueled almost entirely by this religious distinction, ended abruptly at the end of the 13th century when Mary Magdalen's relics were discovered at St.-Maximin in Provence and Vézelay was deserted by its pious visitors.

46, 47 The irregular geometries of the ville spontanée *versus the ordered framework of the* ville créée.

At the outset, it is worth emphasizing that the regularity of the planned city is conditional. Streets that read as straight and uniform on the city plan may be compromised by the capricious behavior of the bordering masses.

48, The unpredictability is of two kinds. How the buildings relate to the street line
49 and where they stand on their lots have a good deal to do with the perception of geometric order. William Penn knew as much when he laid out the famous checkerboard of Philadelphia. His directives for its occupation reveal solicitude about holding to a common street line and about the spacing of buildings along the streets. "Let the houses built be in a line, or upon a line, as much as may be," he wrote. "Let every house be placed, if the person pleases, in the middle of its plat, as to the breadth way of it." In the 18th century, Baroque city-makers everywhere urged, or legislated when they could, that street-defining buildings be brought to the edge of
252 their lots in a straight line, and further, that they be given identical façades.[2]

The provision for a uniform appearance was intended to forestall the second kind of building activity that can dilute the effect of formal planning. Even when buildings are marshalled like troops along the lines of an urban grid, the degree of animation in their mass and, more essentially, variable height can result in picturesque formations believed to be congenital to the unplanned city. Manhat-
102 tan's inflexible grid dissipates above ground into compilations that can range from the miscellaneous to the fantastic.

If the experience of the planned city-form is conditional, the irregularity of the "unplanned" city is also a matter of degree. The curve is frequent but not canonical. What reads as an unordered arrangement is often a matter of straight street segments crossing at random angles, and linear elements broken with frequent angular bends. This is what Richard Pillsbury calls "the irregular pattern" in his classification of early Pennsylvania towns; a good example is Oxford in Chester County.[3] When these linear elements are steady enough to read as a distorted or
50 scrambled grid—this is the case of Naarden in Holland and Villeréal in France, both intentionally planted towns—we have license to play up the rule or the deviation.

This blurring of the basic duality of urban form, of the planned and the unplanned, has also a peculiarly modern twist. Since the early 19th century, a strand of planning that first emerges in romantic suburbs, and graduates into a full-blown alternative to the dominant practices of Western urbanism, has given us non-geometric layouts artfully designed to avoid the rigidity of geometric abstraction.

With their preference for curvilinear street systems, the broken line, accented spacing and spirited profiles, these layouts rephrase the tenets of "organic" cities in a selfconscious, emulative mood. We might allow ourselves to speak, therefore, of a "planned organicism" or, less awkwardly, "planned picturesque," and reserve its discussion to the final sections of this chapter.

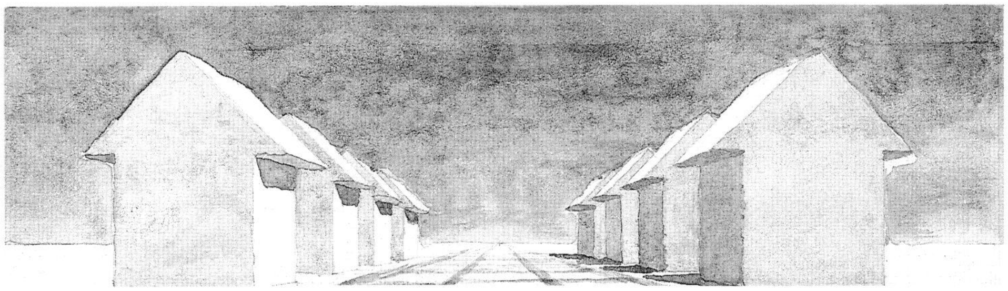

48, 49 The geometric regularity of a straight street can be reinforced by laws prescribing uniform setbacks, or diluted by variation in building location.

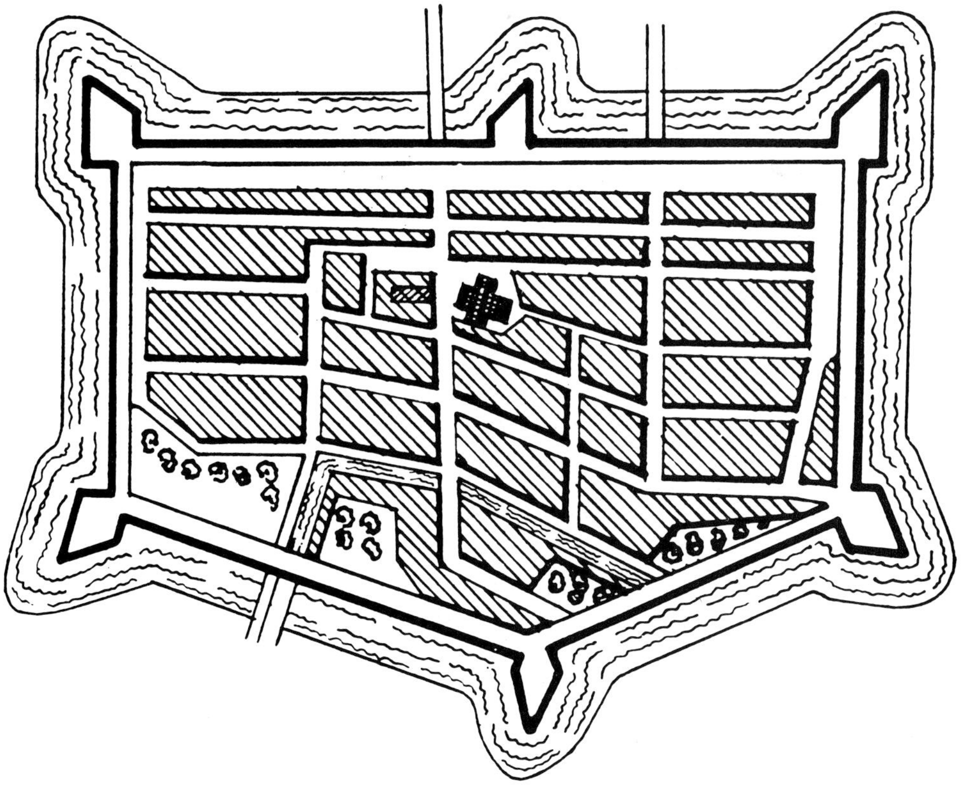

50 Naarden (The Netherlands) in 1632. The skewed street grid dates from its re-establishment as a nieuwestad *(new town) in 1350 under the order of Willem V, after a previous settlement was destroyed by fire. Its strategic position on the Zuider Zee led to Naarden's development as a fortified outpost in the early 17th century. (After Boxhoorn)*

51 Boston (Massachusetts) in 1877. An amalgam of irregular and rectilinear development is visible in John Bachmann's expansive town portrait. The meandering street network of the historic core around the domed State House (center) recalls the shape of the land and its country roads, the city's earliest formgivers. In the right background is the gridded development of the South End, a district built on landfill in the mid-19th century.

COEXISTENCE AND TRANSCRIPTION

If we were to scan several hundred city plans at random across the range of history, we would discover a more fundamental reason to question the usefulness of urban dichotomies based on geometry. We would find that the two primary versions of urban arrangement, the planned and the "organic," often exist side by side, as does
51 tidy Back Bay next to old Boston. In Europe, new additions to the dense medieval
253 cores of historic towns were always regular. Modern colonial powers overwhelmed
the native tangle of North African medinas and the ancient towns of India and Indochina with grand geometric designs, quickened by single-minded diagonals and accented by formal squares.

The point to be made is this. However instructive the contrast between medieval Ferrara and its Herculean Addition, or between Old and New Delhi, we are obliged to remember that Ferrara and Delhi are urban entities which cannot, historically and physically, be treated as permanently dichotomous. When the two components are not quite as discrete as in these two examples, or when there is more than one

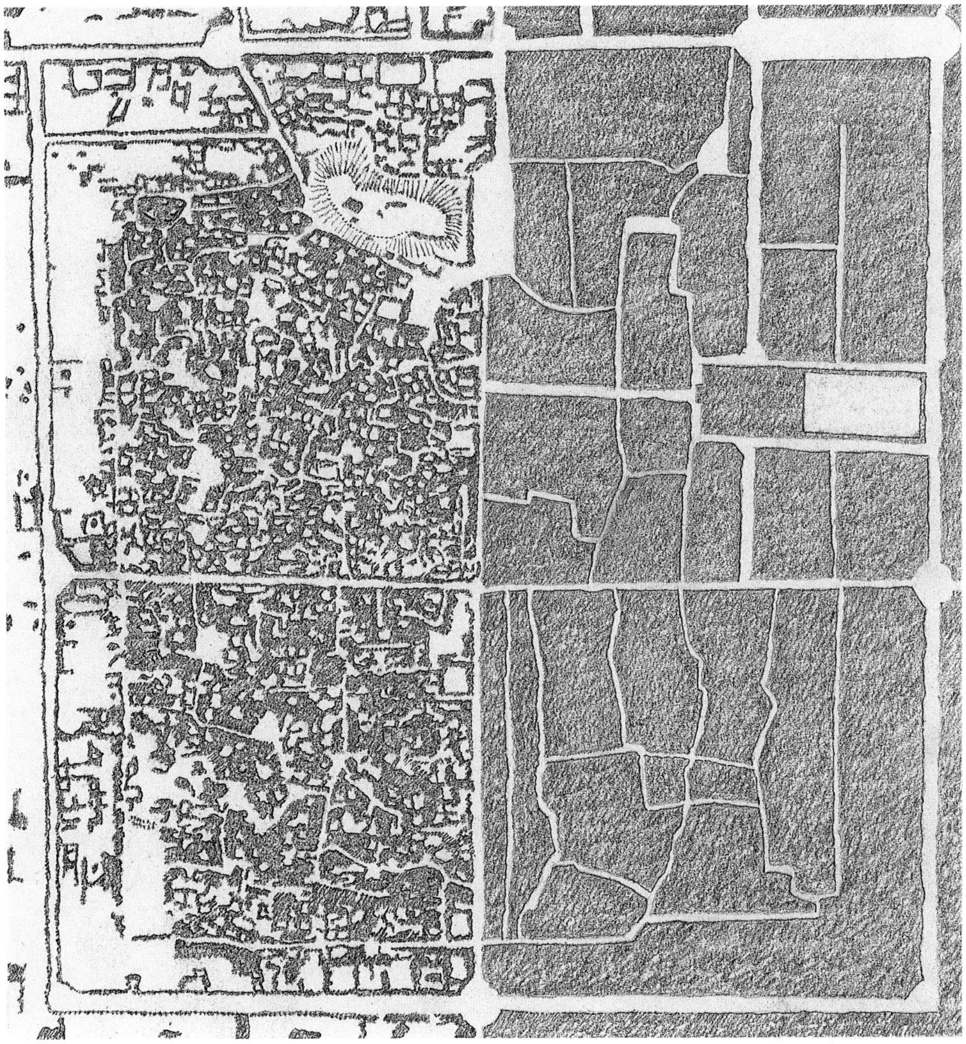

52 Herat (Afghanistan). This split plan shows the coexistence of a variety of urban geometries at differing street hierarchies. The city's supergrid, right, organizes a secondary street network within large quadrants. When Herat's maze of courts and blind alleys is added to the plan, left, this overall organization all but disappears. (After von Niedermeyer)

planned increment, the need to interpret the city as an intricate mesh, as the sum of its parts and the ledger of its history, is especially pressing.

Most historic towns, and virtually all those of metropolitan size, are puzzles of premeditated and spontaneous segments, variously interlocked or juxtaposed. The "organic" old core is itself likely to be a composite of several units; surrounding it will be an array of more or less orderly new quarters; along the city edge, and in unoccupied internal pockets, extemporaneous squatter settlements of recent years could effectively confound what legible consistency the urban form might have assumed in the course of its life. Cities, Wolfgang Braunfels appositely reminds us, "are the result of a self-renewing power of design."[4] It is questionable gain to divorce regular from irregular in this continuous effort of adjustment.

We can go beyond. The two kinds of urban form do not always stand in a contiguous relationship. They metamorphose. The reworking of prior geometries over time leaves urban palimpsests where a once regular grid plan is feebly ensconced within a maze of cul-de-sacs and narrow winding streets.

Look at the plan of old Herat, the westernmost large city of Afghanistan. A pair of 52
relatively straight market streets intersecting at right angles divide the city form into

square quadrants; these are bounded externally by roads that run parallel to the city walls, which themselves inscribe a near-perfect square. Within each one of the quarters a lively jumble of street elements prevails. Or so it might seem at first glance. In reality, a network of secondary streets can be detected without difficulty, starting at the four arms of the cross-axis and the peripheral roads, and crossing the quarters roughly north–south and east–west. The map of Herat drawn by a German officer, Oskar von Niedermeyer, in 1916/17 exaggerates this regularity by leaving out the short blind alleys that push out from the tracery of the rough grid. The probability suggests itself that Herat began as a regularly gridded city whose lines were frayed with use. A Hellenistic origin is not precluded, and it has also been proposed that Herat was laid out according to the strict prescriptions of the Indian architectural manual, the *Manasara* (see p. 104).[5]

In a more familiar, Western, context, the career of the once formally planned
164 Roman town (e.g., Caerleon in Britain, Aosta in Italy, Barcelona in Spain) in the aftermath of the Empire, we can reconstruct some of the steps in the process of deregulation. The background for the urban retrenchment and readjustment in post-Roman Europe is well known—depopulation, reduced circumstances, and a social revolution that consigned towns built for a pagan culture of multiple cults to the monotheistic religions of Christianity and, later on in some regions of the Empire, of Islam. There was no place in the new social structure for theaters, amphitheaters, temples, or (in the Christian case) baths. The civic institutions of the Classical city were also defunct, and as one consequence of this, the defense of public space was weak or non-existent. So the disintegration of the rationally ordered and publicly administered Roman *urbs* got under way. What happened can be described under three main headings.

53– First, there is *the freeing of movement from geometric order*. The grid is inflexible
55 in terms of human movement. We are not inclined to make right-angle turns as we go about from place to place unless we are forced to do so. With the impairment of municipal controls in the post-Roman city, natural movement soon carved short-cuts through the large rigid blocks of the grid. Tracks skirting or crossing the ruins of those public buildings for which there was no longer any use also crystallized into new streets.

At the same time, the circulation pattern relating to the central market, which sometimes coincided with the old Roman forum, was rationalized to suit the new urban conditions. In the closed economy of the Middle Ages, the town market was a precious asset; its privileges were stringently managed. Towns kept small. Market tolls levied against nonresident users were the town's main income, a fact which led townspeople to oppose open-ended immigration and growth. Within the town, the artisans' and shopkeepers' livelihood depended on their nearness to the market-place. The area around the market was the most prized; and after that, the streets leading to the town gates. The most advantageous layout from the shopkeeper's and artisan's point of view was the wheel—several streets radiating from the market out toward the city gates. But the Roman grid was impressed by a pronounced cross-axis, with the forum at or near the center. The sensible thing to do, then, was to push through the blocks at the points of least resistance.

Second, *the reorganization of the blocks*. In Roman times the residential
57 structure was of houses of single unrelated families, three or four to a block, and, in the more crowded cities, multi-story apartment buildings or *insulae*. In Islamic
56 towns, on the other hand, a very different residential structure prevailed. The population grouped itself into neighborhoods according to kinship, tribe, or ethnicity. The through-streets in this case constituted the dividing lines among these

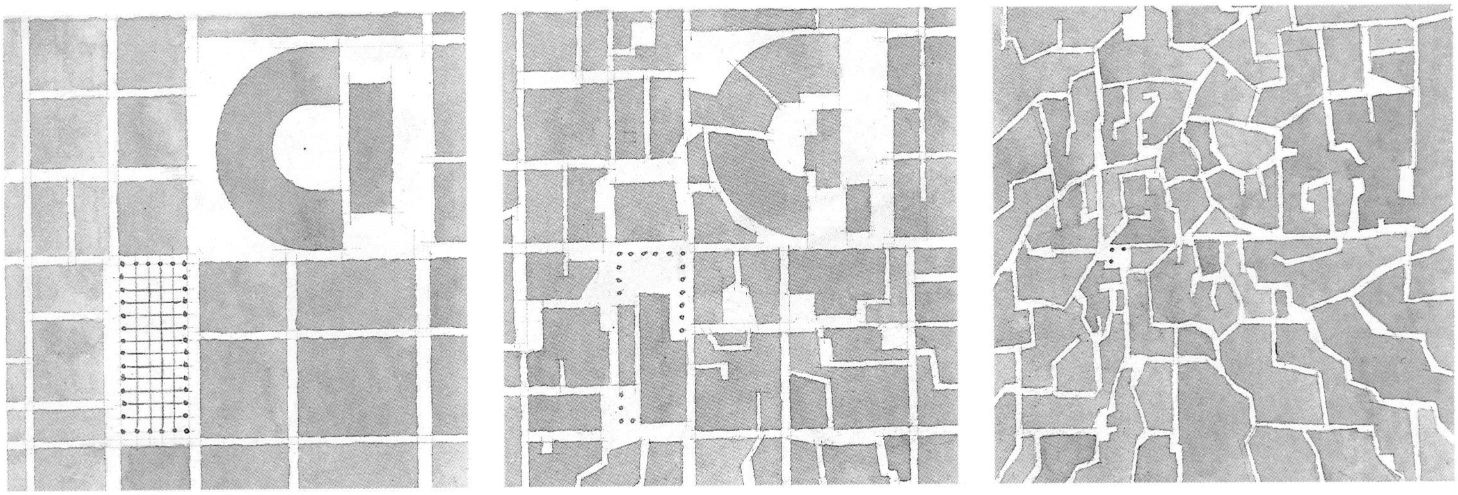

53–55 *The gradual transformation of a gridded Roman colony into an Islamic city.* Left: *The solidly framed Roman grid is punctuated by an open-air market and an amphitheater.* Center: *The city's new Islamic population appropriates these public monuments for private use, and mid-block pathways begin to violate the orthogonal street pattern.* Right: *The transformed city is one with a minimum of open public space. Straight passages along the winding system of narrow lanes offer the merest suggestion of the original layout.*

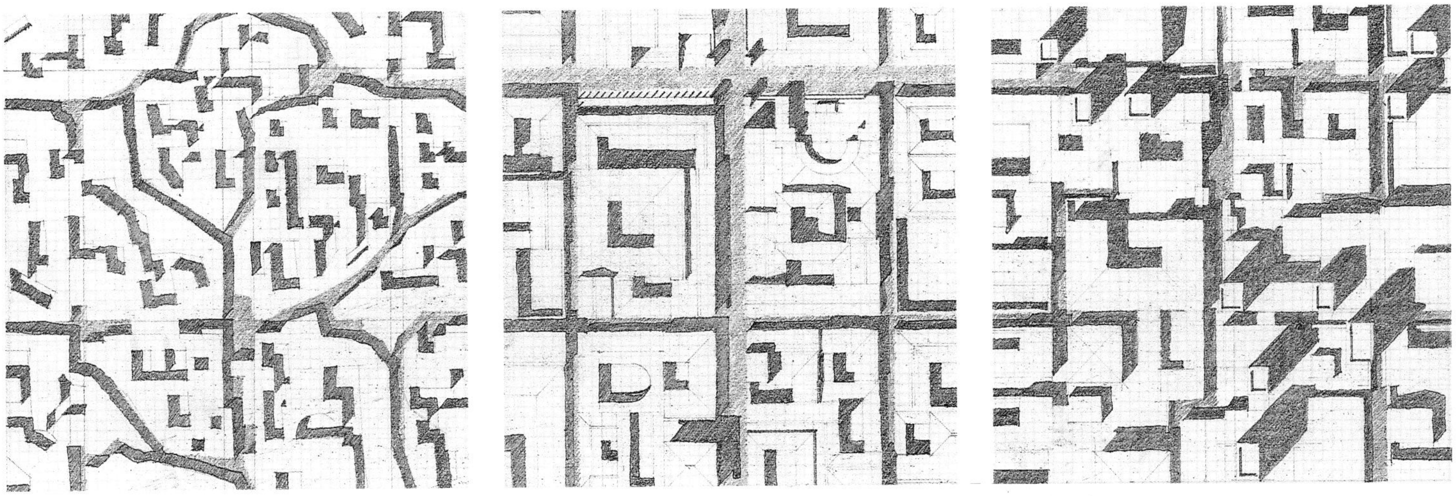

56–58 *Islamic and feudal Italian adaptations of pre-existing Roman towns are marked by characteristic differences in form and social context.* Center: *A gridded plan typical of the colonial settlements planted by the Roman Empire throughout the Mediterranean.* Left: *In its reconfiguration by an Islamic population, streets are replaced by a web of alleys that organize residential quarters common to a single tribal or ethnic group.* Right: *A modification of the same town plan in medieval Italy would see city blocks fused together to form fortified feudal enclaves crowned by defensive towers.*

socially exclusive units. The Roman grid is outer-related: the Islamic "block" is involuted. So in Roman gridded towns inherited by Islam—Damascus, say, or Mérida in Spain—the open space of the streets and public places, which now seemed extravagant, was reduced through progressive infill; through-streets were curtailed; blocks were merged together into solidly built superblocks; and an inward communication system was installed in this dense fabric, the principal element of which was the cul-de-sac serving its immediate occupants.

A similar reordering of Classical grids through new residential arrangements
58, occurred in the West, most conspicuously in Italy. It was triggered by the noble
60, families who moved into the cities and set out to reproduce there the fortified
111 strongholds of their rural residences. These compounds brought together units of disparate real property around inner courts, obstructed intervening streets, and sealed themselves along the periphery. The families made defensive alliances with neighboring noble houses, forming semi-autonomous, nucleated wards bristling with defensive towers. One of the main tests of nascent communes, or self-governing city states, in the later Middle Ages would be to crack open these private pockets and reclaim the streets and public places in the name of the entire citizenry.

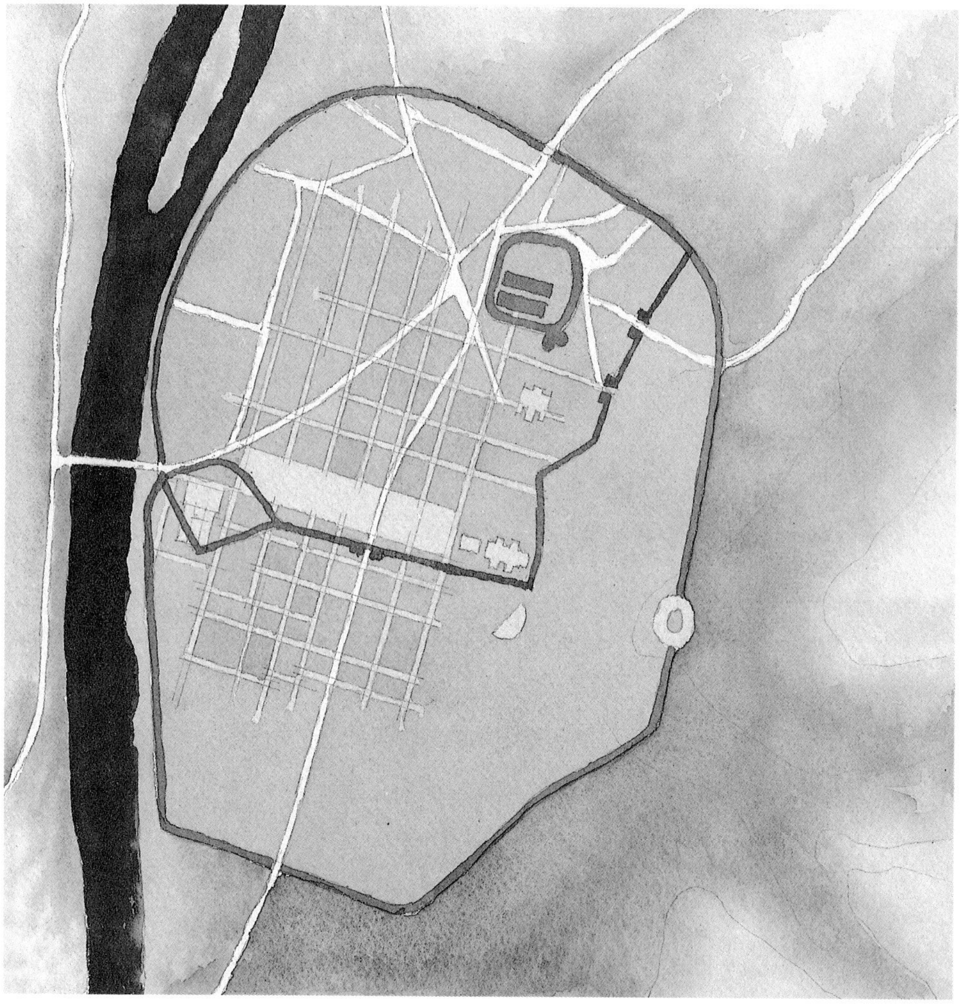

59 The superimposition of a medieval agrarian settlement pattern over a Roman grid in Trier (Germany). The Roman city's rectangular forum and strictly orthogonal street plan was initially circumscribed by an expansive circuit of walls. By the 12th century a greatly contracted Trier had redrawn its defensive perimeter, excluding about a third of the area formerly enclosed. The great Roman public institutions shown in white—thermae, *amphitheater, and forum—were abandoned, their ruins appropriated for private use. The focus of the medieval settlement shifted to a fortified cathedral complex in the northeast corner of town and the market situated just outside the sanctuary's gate. The revised street plan, completely replacing the previous grid, is a collection of radial paths converging on the cathedral market. (Plan after Böhner)*

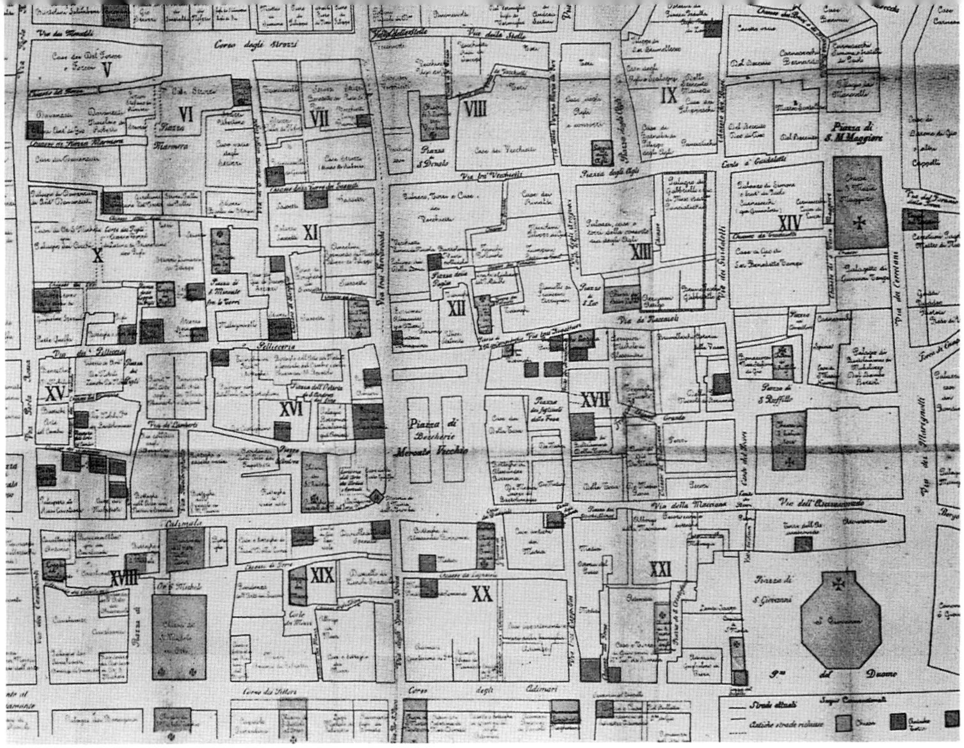

60 Florence (Italy). Medieval readjudments to the ancient Roman grid are evident in the catasto *(cadastral) plan of 1427, reputed to be Europe's first cartographic survey made specifically to assess private property for tax purposes. In this detail of a redrawn version of the plan, the octagonal Baptistery appears bottom right.*

Third, *the impact of new public foci on the urban fabric.* Traffic flow, like running water, will forge its own course: a castle, a cathedral, a bishop's palace—the anchors of post-Roman urban life in the West—will tend to pull the circulation net toward themselves. Concurrently, earlier streets that had led to foci once important but now of no relevance will decline or atrophy. Within the measured system of the Roman grid, these pressures of emphasis, allowed to have their way, will cause permanent dislocation.

In terms of delineating a hierarchy of movement to match the geography of public points within the city, the grid has obvious limitations. The main expedients are the relative width of streets and the setting up of favored spots within the rules of orthogonal design. The cross-axial scheme, and the placement of the civic center *110*
close to the crossing, was one way for Roman urban design to make amends for the routine univalence of passage in their implanted checkerboards. In the process of medievalization, however, this hierarchy was imposed against the grain of the Roman blocks.

In the West, wherever the medieval market adopted the Roman forum and the bishop's palace and the cathedral stood in this same area, the continuity in the nucleus of the town minimized dislocations due to shifts in accent. In the case of Trier in Germany, on the other hand, the Roman grid was completely ignored *59*
when, after a long period of shrinkage and social regrouping, several village-like settlements within the walls, formed around important manors, were linked with the fortified cathedral precinct close to the Porta Nigra, the Roman city gate to the north. The Roman marketplace, outside the south gate, was abandoned, and the main action of the restructured town moved to a marketplace immediately outside the gates of the cathedral precinct.[6]

It is enough to remember, then, that the maze of Mérida was once a planned Roman city, and that the grid of historic Florence we now prize as a Roman survival had to be energetically recreated in the late Middle Ages after its Balkanization by *60*
contentious feudal factions—it is enough to remember these fluctuations of urban form to be dissatisfied with simple formulas about planned and unplanned cities.

THE EVOLUTION OF "ORGANIC" PATTERNS

The fact is that no city, however arbitrary its form may appear to us, can be said to be "unplanned." Beneath the strangest twist of lane or alley, behind the most fitfully bounded public place, lies an order beholden to prior occupation, to the features of the land, to long-established conventions of the social contract, to a string of compromises between individual rights and the common will.

Power designs cities, and the rawest form of power is control of urban land. When the state is the principal owner, it can put down whatever pattern it chooses. This was true of the royal cities of ancient Persia, the imperial capitals of China, and the Baroque seats of European princes. It was true of company towns, and it is still true in the Soviet Union and the socialist countries of Eastern Europe where the rights of private property were severely curtailed. The planning that undisputed authority of this sort promotes is total, the urban form unambiguously legible.

In the long history of cities from Western Asia and Mesopotamia to the new towns of today, this exercise in totalitarian design has limited currency. The vast bulk of the world's cities do not go back to such single-minded beginnings. The power that comes of owning urban land is, as a matter of course, broadly shared, and therefore city-form is a negotiated and ever-changing design. This involved, continuous process sometimes may start with and sustain regular plans. More commonly, the urban diagram is intricately wrought, difficult to read, and since the forces that engender it are many, it may not always be explicable in every detail.

There are as many such distinctive diagrams as there are cities that inhabit them. No two are exactly alike. If the term "organic" be a convenient reference for this prevalent urban configuration, then it has reason enough to be around. If, on the other hand, there is a "biological" reality that is being implied or posited, it is best to reckon with it directly.

CITIES AS ORGANISMS

The notion of the city as an organism is not very old. It is related, of course, to the rise of modern biology, the science of life, and that does not antedate by much the mid-17th century. On the one hand, visual parallels between some organisms and some town-plans were hard to resist; you could see the venation of leaves in Muslim medinas, the pattern of tree rings in the ringed expansions of a town like Nördlingen or Aachen. On the other hand, the pairing of human organs and elements of urban form on the basis of functional similarities satisfied a simple urge of animation: it affirmed the primacy of urban *life*. Open spaces like squares and parks were the lungs of the city, the center was the heart pumping blood (traffic) through the arteries (the streets)—and so on. This literal affiliation differed from Renaissance humanistic imagery that ascribed to good, that is planned, non-organic, urban form human properties, as when Francesco di Giorgio states in his *Trattato* that "The
61 relation of the city to its parts is similar to that of the human body to its parts; the streets are the veins."[7]

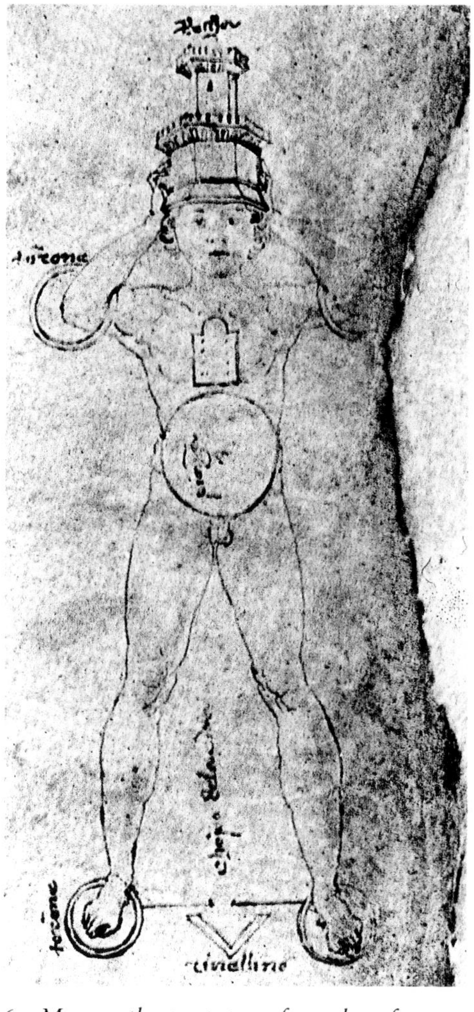

61 Man as the prototype for urban form, from Francesco di Giorgio Martini, Trattato dell'architettura, *late 15th century.*

Recently, this biological analogy had a startling revival based on economics. The urban lot or dwelling-place, in this model, functions as the cell; things like the port, the banking district, the industrial plant and the suburb are organs or specialized tissues; and capital, whether in monetary form or in built form, is the energy that flows through urban systems. "Even prior to the great age of capitalism, all urban growth arose in a capital accumulation process." In its material form, capital accumulation brings about changes in urban spaces; we can think of it as the net balance of destruction (depreciation) and construction.[8]

Two other aspects of organisms, their structural logic and their pathogeny, have been considered apposite to the behavior of "organic" cities. Plants and animals have definite boundaries and self-regulating systems of growth; they are subject to dependable processes of change and adjustment, and revisions in their form are the direct result of functional requirements. The same, it was argued, is (or should be) true of organic cities. And these cities, again like organisms, are subject to sickness and decay. There is a persistent strand of urban literature in the 19th century that posits the interdependence of the built environment and the physical and social health of the inhabitants. The villain in the pathological deterioration of the urban fabric that much of this literature decries is the Industrial Revolution, and the proposed action is to abandon the sick, overcrowded cities as dead, or to eradicate their "infected" parts, namely, the slums.

For our present purposes, these insistent comparisons are of little help. Their application to the design of modern cities, a favorite resort of Garden City advocates, comes across as disingenuous. In fact, the planned "organicism" of the Garden City and its affiliates contradicts biological behavior by insisting on the separation of functions and by treating them hierarchically, by predicating optimum sizes for cities, and by resisting change and the notion of continuous growth. The confusion stems from the fundamental inaptitude of the organic analogy. As Kevin Lynch correctly pointed out, "Cities are not organisms. . . . They do not grow or change of themselves, or reproduce or repair themselves."[9] It is human purpose and human willfulness that drives the making of cities.

On the question of "organic" city-forms, which is germane to this discussion, we must also reject any assistance from the world of biology. A study of true organic form proves that the atomized behavior of the elementary particles is forcibly restrained by an overarching discipline. In the words of Paul Weiss, "In nature the same over-all effect can recur with lawful regularity, although the detailed events by which it is attained will vary from case to case in ever novel constellations."[10] There is no evidence of any such lawful regularity at work in "organic" cities. This biological "order in the gross, and freedom, diversity, and uniqueness in the small," if it is at all pertinent to urban analysis, either recalls city-content (rather than city-form) in that, as Weiss notes, "a community can retain its character and structure despite the turnover in population from birth, death, and migration"; or else might be said to find a better echo, perversely, in the *planned* city-form, since it is often the case with regular plans like grids that the building activity within each block is of a great diversity while the total pattern remains unaffected.

THE ROLE OF TOPOGRAPHY

What, then, determines the seemingly idiosyncratic shapes of evolved or generated cities?

The most widely acknowledged causality, the natural landscape, rings true because it is visually the easiest to grasp. In some parts of the world, Latin America for example, the siting and spread of human settlements respond so fatefully to the sculpture of the land that it is impossible to isolate the urban experience from earth-induced affects. The lasting memory of Rio de Janeiro is always bound up with the hills, the mountains and the bay that have so thoroughly conditioned its shape during its three-hundred-year history.

More precisely, we can single out repetitive conduct on the part of those cities
62 mindful of the hints of their natural landscape. River towns might acknowledge the
flow of the course with responsive streets along one or two banks. The sea too
provides some choice design opportunities. Natural harbors with sweeping
63 backdrops will suggest suitable street-sweeps: Halikarnassos was famous in
Pl.5 Hellenistic times for its theater-like shape; Naples and Valparaiso, Chile, are
modern pendants. The defensive merit of craggy sites advertises itself throughout
urban history. The city-form so ensconced reacts boldly or sympathetically, with
devices like stepped streets and contour paths. In ancient towns like Idalion (Cyprus)
64 or Troy, the defensive wall closely followed the salient contours of the ground, and
the building blocks and street lines reflected the ins and outs of this complicated
outline.

Italian hill towns have always been a favorite demonstration of the evident fit
between the human-made and the natural. Studied clinically, these towns prove that
they have adopted one of several configurations depending on the character of their
65 perch. If the site is a ridge, the town will have a linear shape usually fixed with
architectural accents like castles and churches at one or both ends, or along one side

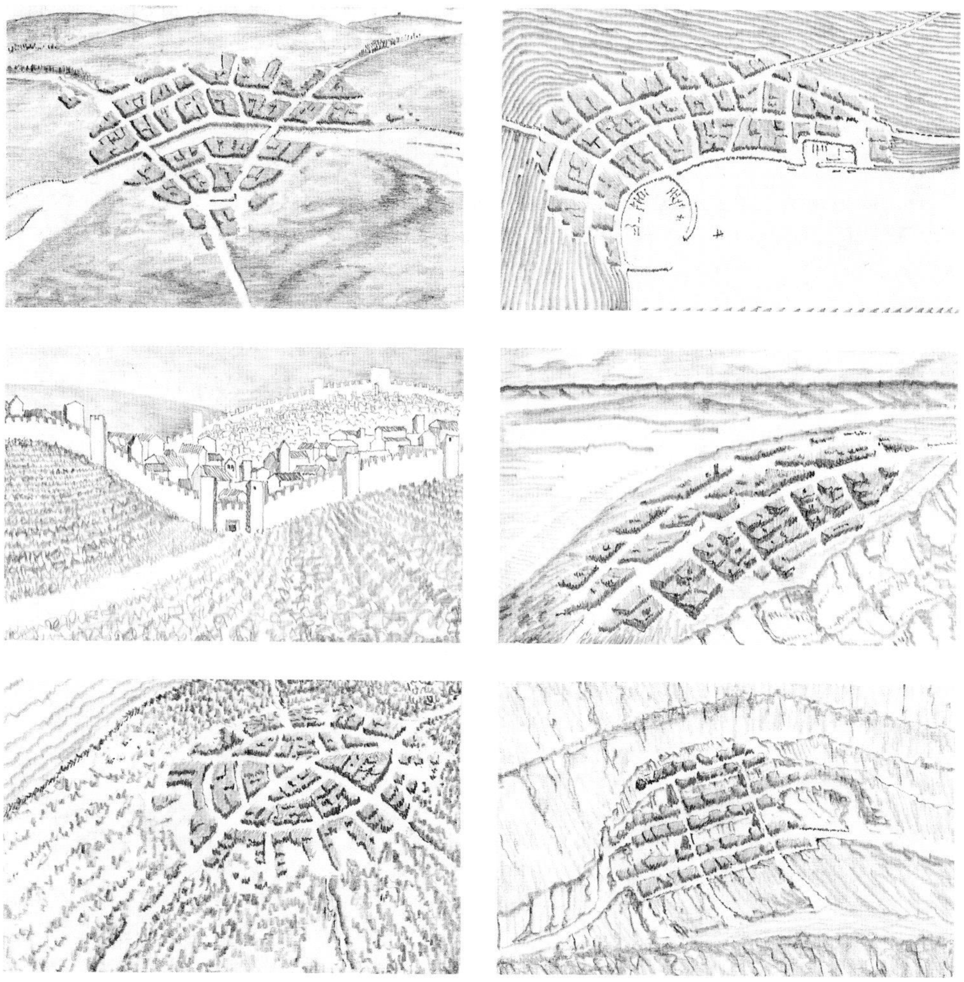

Topography as a determinant of urban form:

62 *Riverine settlement*

63 *Natural harbor*

64 *Defensive site*

65 *Linear ridge*

66 *Hilltop town*

67 *Sloped terrain*

of the ridge. Other main roads will run parallel to this spine further down the slope.
Tributaries will strike out in the direction of principal neighboring cities, giving us
the tentacled form of towns like Perugia. On round, domical hill sites, the main 66
buildings are likely to be at the top; and the streets, descending concentric circles.
Arrayed upon a steep slope, the town will have the terraced composition of Assisi or 67
Gubbio. *Pl.11*

All of these postures have universal currency. At the same time, we have to remind ourselves that the linear town and its blueprint, the rib plan, are as much at home on level ground as along land folds. The same holds for rounded city-forms, whether the wavering street system tends to a concentric or radial disposition.

Going back to the beginning, to Mesopotamia and Egypt, we must remember that sites of irregular cities like Ur and Thebes were flat. Most Mesopotamian cities were built in the flat mud plains of the Tigris and Euphrates, and one of the standard interpretations of the ziggurat form is that it was intended, by the early inhabitants whose original homeland was the mountainous region of the Caspian Sea, to simulate natural peaks. In Thebes the flat Nile bank hosted the lively tangle of the residential quarters, while the tossed topography of the western slopes was the setting for formally planned units (the mortuary temples).

We must therefore, at this stage, broaden our exploration of irregular city-form in two directions. First of all, a more refined reading of topography is needed than the generic themes of hills and valleys and rivers; and secondly, attention must be paid to the subject of pre-urban land division, which is obviously related to topographical incident, but goes further to involve culturally defined issues like patterns of ownership, farming practices, and the disposition of common fields and pastures.

The start of an irregular city plan is often due to a small number of topographic
peculiarities. In the case of Boston, for instance, these were the Shawmut peninsula 51
with its eastern coves and the narrow Neck to the south. There is nothing instinctive about the process of converting such peculiarities to an urban fabric. While some landscape features may be embraced and exploited, others may be rejected. The three-humped high ridge that rose through the center of the peninsula had little direct consequence for the early form of Boston, and survived only in the much reduced eminence of Beacon Hill.

Seen in the aggregate, there is perhaps as widespread a tendency in city-making to *amend* the natural landscape as there is to work with it. Hundreds of past cities were lodged in cleared forests and on land reclaimed from swamps and bays. To fit their public buildings, connect points of consequence directly or dramatically, and enhance their functions and beauty, hilltops were levelled and canyons filled in, rivers were diverted and inlets dammed.

These actions are too decisive, too arduous, too demanding of communal effort
to result in anything but planned bits of urbanism; but we must not assume that
"planned" here is inevitably synonymous with formal rigor or strict regularity. Both
Venice and Machu Picchu, in unique and ingenious ways, designed the land on 73
which they sit—the one by solidifying a lagoon, the other by steeply terracing *Pl.10*
vertiginous heights. Neither has submitted its spectacular groundwork to a readymade urban convention. Venice is liquid filigree; Machu Picchu, in the words of George Kubler, "a patterned blanket thrown over a great rock."[11]

The most celebrated redesign of nature, at least in the Western world, has taken place in the Netherlands. "God created the world," as the old saying has it, "but the Dutch made Holland." For centuries the inhabitants of this waterlogged tip of Europe have battled the fury of the sea and the flooding of rivers, building dikes—some, like the diking of the Zuider Zee, of heroic proportions—damming and

reclaiming tidal marshes, readying for settlement the belts of *geestgrond*, the land behind the coastal dunes.

A small number of Dutch cities stand on naturally high ground—islands, the confluence of rivers, or the solidified sand dunes and peat bogs of the *geestgrond* (Haarlem, Alkmaar). The oldest parts of such towns are the only ones that have the "organic" look of medieval towns in the rest of Europe. Elsewhere, the ground had to be drained, consolidated and raised above the level of the surrounding countryside before building could commence.[12]

The earliest artificial sites, predating Roman occupation, were the *terpen* or *wierden* along the northern coast and in Zeeland. These were mounds of mud painfully piled and rammed to a height that would clear the rise of the tide and of seasonal floods. (For towns built on *terpen* see below, pp. 163–64.) In the Middle Ages, trade attracted urban development along rivers and inlets, to sites which were highly vulnerable. Two kinds of town layout met the challenge: dike towns and dike-and-dam towns.

68 Sloten (The Netherlands). This Friesland dike town was founded at the intersection of a waterway and an overland route, marked by a bridge in the center of town, and chartered in 1426. The stellated fortifications with their defensive moat are a late 16th-century addition.

Dikes were broad enough to carry a road at the top; buildings stood on the slopes and on the lower ground protected by the dike against flooding. If the waterway were narrow—a canal, say, rather than a broad river—the dike town would stretch along both banks, which sometimes took a gentle curve. Towns like Sloten, *68* Nieuwpoort and Schoonhoven were established where a land route crossed a waterway, with some prominent landmark like the town hall placed at the crossing.

Even more typical is the town started where a river or a creek was dammed. This is how Amsterdam got under way, after a modest beginning as a dike settlement where the Amstel flows into the sea. A dam across the river above the small settlement *136* turned the downstream portion into an outer harbor. Diked canals diverted the flow along two sides, allowing for an inner harbor upstream and stable land for the extension of the town between the riverbed and the canals. The prized central space of the dam in such towns received important public buildings like the town hall, the weighing hall, or a church.

In the so-called water towns, or *grachtenstad*, built on land reclaimed from marshes or lakes, the layout is more regular but not uniform. Streets, principally canal-streets, were kept narrow, the building blocks were long and narrow too, and a broad moat enclosed the area. Since the water town was usually a later expansion of a *terp*, a natural citadel (*burcht*) or a dike town—Leiden is a good example—it occupied previously cultivated land whose patterns it absorbed. The field drainage ditches became the canal-streets, and the fields themselves gave the boundaries for *247* the elongated blocks. To the extent that this pre-urban pattern was orderly, which in this hard-earned ground was almost always the case, the water town reflected this order.

LAND DIVISION

The study of the process whereby an antecedent rural landscape translates itself into urban form has hardly begun. And yet pre-urban land division may well be the most fundamental determinant for the irregular city-forms of all ages. The main problem is that it is very hard, when not actually impossible, to reconstruct this initial landscape either through field work or documents. Field work can discover surviving old village nuclei within the suburban extensions of towns, but that phenomenon is rare, and the results do not lead us very far.

To establish a more pervasive documentation, our best shot is in more recent history. In England, for example, the common lands and open fields surrounding towns since the Middle Ages were in some cases not finally enclosed and alienated to individual ownership until the mid-19th century. When these large holdings were transformed to a belt of urban extension, the network of streets largely followed the medieval footpaths and furlongs of the old open fields.

One line of research is to superimpose tithe maps—based on land surveys made after an Act of 1836—and the extremely detailed maps of towns drawn to a uniform scale in the 19th century for the Ordnance Survey (which, like the Sandborn insurance maps in the United States, are a mine of information for urban history). By matching segments of the two it is possible to show how the pre-urban cadaster of Leeds, for instance, determined subsequent urban form. Generally small holdings *69* and a fragmented pattern of ownership led to small terraces of four to eight house units; these change alignment frequently, and so create a variegated, seemingly quirky design. With larger holdings, it is possible to have more regular terraces and a more systematic layout of streets. Even here, however, since no attempt is made to

69 *Potternewtown, north of Leeds, is a patchwork of terrace housing blocks. The development pattern becomes less arbitrary when it is compared with the area's early 19th-century street plan and property boundaries, shown respectively as wide and narrow dotted lines. (Base map reproduced from the 1922 Ordnance Survey map, landholdings plot after Ward)*

establish continuities between neighboring developments, the overall effect can suggest the evolved "organicism" of irregular towns.[13]

Only in relatively recent days did the rural landprint of England become obscured, as the arbitrary, traffic-engendered course of new arterial roads affected the orientation of the city-patterns in their immediate vicinity.

Without accurate records of this sort, the analysis of rural–urban continuities cannot pretend to be conclusive. Speaking generally, we can aver this much. In the early stages of settlement, the occupation of land commonly takes place without the benefit of a formal land survey. Fields, meadows and pastures have irregular boundaries, and the main lines of this division demarcate large pieces of land for common use. When this agricultural land finds itself in an urban situation, these main lines become streets, and the land parcels begin to be subdivided.

Agrarian law in many ancient cultures is based on the principle of the indivisibility of land. Once a town gets going and the circuit of walls decisively restricts outward spread, however, new legal and administrative measures are developed to expedite the subdivision of once common lands into building plots. Sealed within the walls, land grows precious. Congestion becomes endemic. The precincts of palaces and temples remain untouchable. The rest is divided between the public land of streets and markets, and private land. Public land is always under pressure. Streets are kept narrow, and there are no public squares or urban parks. In the cities of the ancient Near East and Egypt, the public square is usually the ample court enclosed within the temple precinct.

The two methods of land division—the practice of measuring by metes and bounds (fixing boundaries in relation to natural features), which yields "organic" patterns, and division according to a survey done with proper instruments (see below, p. 127), which establishes orthogonal relationships—are both old. Obviously the pointing and pacing techniques came first in every instance, but from the early periods of urbanization both methods were used simultaneously by the same culture. The orientation of Egyptian pyramids or Mesopotamian ziggurats is so precise that it was surely achieved with the use of instruments and computations. Yet these precisions coincide with the "organicism" we see in residential fabrics which may well go back to a more distant, practical mode of field division. Again, in 17th-century colonial America, the English used the headright method of land distribution in the South, where individual plantations were claimed before a thorough land survey had been made, whereas New England townships were surveyed and delimited ahead of time.

Colonialism disrupts the passage from a rural to an urban landscape which is the benchmark of continous human settlement. The colonial power can, out of hand, wipe away past land tenure systems, and the social and legal systems they support, opening the way for formal planning. As the French Minister of Colonies wrote in 1945: "There, space is free and cities can be constructed according to principles of reason and beauty."[14]

Settlement geography is sometimes wedded to traditional practices of cultivation. These practices, in turn, become established because of the particular topography of the land under cultivation and the related systems of irrigating it. A vivid instance is the street web of cities in Iran. Far from being "labyrinths of twisted alleyways"— *Pl.9*
the common perception of Islamic urban form—cities like Yazd can be shown to possess a roughly orthogonal pattern oriented away from the cardinal directions. This orientation cannot be explained in terms of climate or religion. The Iranian house may indeed be sited to maximize summer breezes and winter sun, but where street patterns veer away from optimum seasonal axes, houses follow suit. As for the mandatory orientation of the mosque toward Mecca, its particular angle does not routinely establish the direction of major streets.

The answer lies, as Michael Bonine has pointed out, in the nature of the irrigation system. When the topography is irregular, so is the system. In uniformly sloping terrain, however, the dominant lines form a roughly rectangular network oriented in the direction of the steepest slope. These lines consist of the *qanat*, the underground conduit that taps water for settlements and fields; the *jub*, which is the surfaced channel of this conduit at ground level; and a usable path or road that runs alongside the *jub* and separates it from the rectangular plots surrounded by high mud walls. Village houses are strung out in a line parallel to these watercourses. When the cities extend into the countryside, they simply take over this arrangement. "Topography and water," Bonine concludes, "thus constitute the elementary principles of Iranian settlement geography."[15]

SYNOECISM

The administrative coming together of several proximate villages to form a town, what Aristotle calls "synoecism," is repeatedly attested to in history. Such administrative arrangements have physical consequences, and given the nature of the units

being merged, that is, traditional villages, the result is bound to be "organic." There
31, are exceptions. At Teotihuacán, the communities were held together by a cere-
32 monial complex, a "nucleating center" in the urban geographer's jargon, which
eventually generated, and forced upon this loosely gathered group of rural villages, a
strict geometric organization.

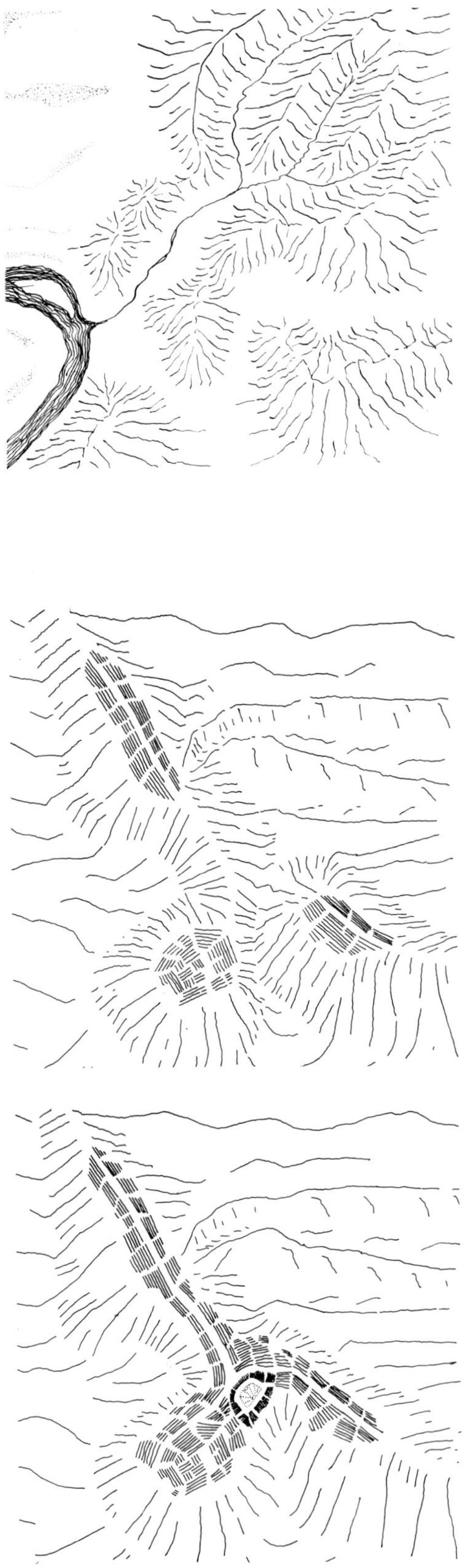

Recent scholarship has been identifying a form of settlement coexistence that needs to be distinguished from synoecism, or in some cases to be considered only a first phase of it. Cities of the floodplain along the Middle Niger in West Africa from the first centuries BC, for example Jenne-jeno and Shoma, and the much earlier urban sites in northern China like Zhengzhou, consisted of a cluster of residential communities in close proximity, each physically discrete and socially specialized according to occupation or status. There were no centralized institutions and no monumentality, as the communities avoided assimilation into a single entity. And yet these corporate groups that transcended bonds of kinship—fishermen and metalworkers, peasant farmers and elites—not only interacted purposefully, but also provided services and manufactures to their hinterland. That this urban structure is an alternative to the Sjoberg model of the pre-industrial city with its centralized elite, its temples and palaces, is only now being recognized.[16]

Synoecism can come about in two ways. People may leave their villages to move to a new town set up to absorb them; in early Mesopotamia and Iran, for example, the emergence of towns was accompanied by the desertion of other settlements in the immediate vicinity. Or else the villages themselves may merge to form the town. I am concerned with the second of these.

For Aristotle, synoecism—literally "living together"—is a political transaction. It enables people to transcend their tribal/pastoral ways, and join up in a pact of self-government. The decision to go urban is not the result of clearcut technological advances or a strategy to reap a finite advantage like trade: it springs from a conscious desire to replace the common law of tribe and clan with the free, durable institutions of the *polis*, the setting for experiments in democracy and the rule of equals. "When several villages are united in a single complex community," Aristotle writes, "large enough to be nearly or quite self-sufficient, the *polis* comes into existence."

Aristotle's definition of synoecism suggests that it is by the common decision of the villages that their territories are conjoined into a single administrative entity. In practice, these unions seem often to have been involuntary and to have been resisted strongly. The beneficiary often happened to be a ruler or an institution of some kind. It was the bishops (later archbishops) of Novgorod, for example, who directed the merger of that city.

Let us recall some celebrated cases of synoecism.

Athens started as a Mycenean citadel on the Acropolis. According to tradition, it was Theseus who brought together this citadel and the surrounding villages, and made the new city the head of a political union of the demes, or independent townships, of Attica. Here is how Thucydides describes the event:

> [Theseus] abolished the councils and magistracies of the minor settlements [of Attica], and established them in the single council chamber and town hall of the present city. Individuals might still enjoy their private property as before, but they were henceforth compelled to use Athens as the sole capital.[17]

The original *agora* (civic center) was on the northwest slope of the Acropolis. By the 6th century BC it had moved to a location more central to the new urban consortium—a flat open space further north, which had been a major cemetery.

70 opposite *Early Rome, ca. 650* BC. *Rome's famed* Septimontium *(seven hills) were the sites of at least three Iron Age settlements which eventually coalesced as a single city with the low-lying Forum as its center.*

71, 72 opposite, below *At the Tuscan city of Siena (Italy), as in Rome, the initial settlements were hilltop communities. These similar topographic circumstances yielded parallel results in terms of urban form: the low saddle of land between two of the original settlements became the site of Siena's central square, the Campo (see Ills. 1, 76).*

The process of synoecism was completed in 431 BC when Pericles brought the countryfolk of Attica within the walls of Athens when the Second Peloponnesian War broke out.[18]

Athens celebrated the legend of her origin in the festival of the Synoecia—as
Rome celebrated *its* synoecism in the annual feast of the Septimontium. In Rome, *70*
Romulus's settlement on the Palatine joined together with several other hilltop villages on the Esquiline, the Caelian, and perhaps the Capitoline, some time in the 8th century BC. They drained and levelled the swampy valley that separated them and which they had used for pasturage and burial, and turned it into a community center—the Roman Forum.

From the early Middle Ages, we have the special example of Venice. Its origin is as *73*
one of a group of lagoon communities that had sought refuge from the turbulence of the post-Roman period in this secluded body of water. In the early 9th century the head of the lagoon province moved his residence from what is now the Lido to what became the Piazza S. Marco, on one of a central core of small, irregularly shaped islands which were then consolidated—the specific process giving us both the labyrinthine nature of the city-form and its water streets.

Three more medieval examples, from Italy and Russia. Viterbo, legend has it, was the outcome of a union in the late 8th century ordered by Desiderius, the last Lombard king. It brought within a single wall the hamlets of Fanum (Volturna), Arbanum, Vetulonia and Longula, and you can still find the acronym "FAVL" on the
seal of the city. Siena dates from about the same time—the union in this case of three *71,*
communities, the bishop's castle-town of Castelvecchio (the cathedral quarter now *72*
known as Città), the hilltop settlement of Castel Montone (now S. Martino) to its east, and the linear settlement along the ridge of Camollia to the north. This explains the inverted Y which characterizes the shape of Siena to this day. The bonding of these three units to the open space between them by means of three directional

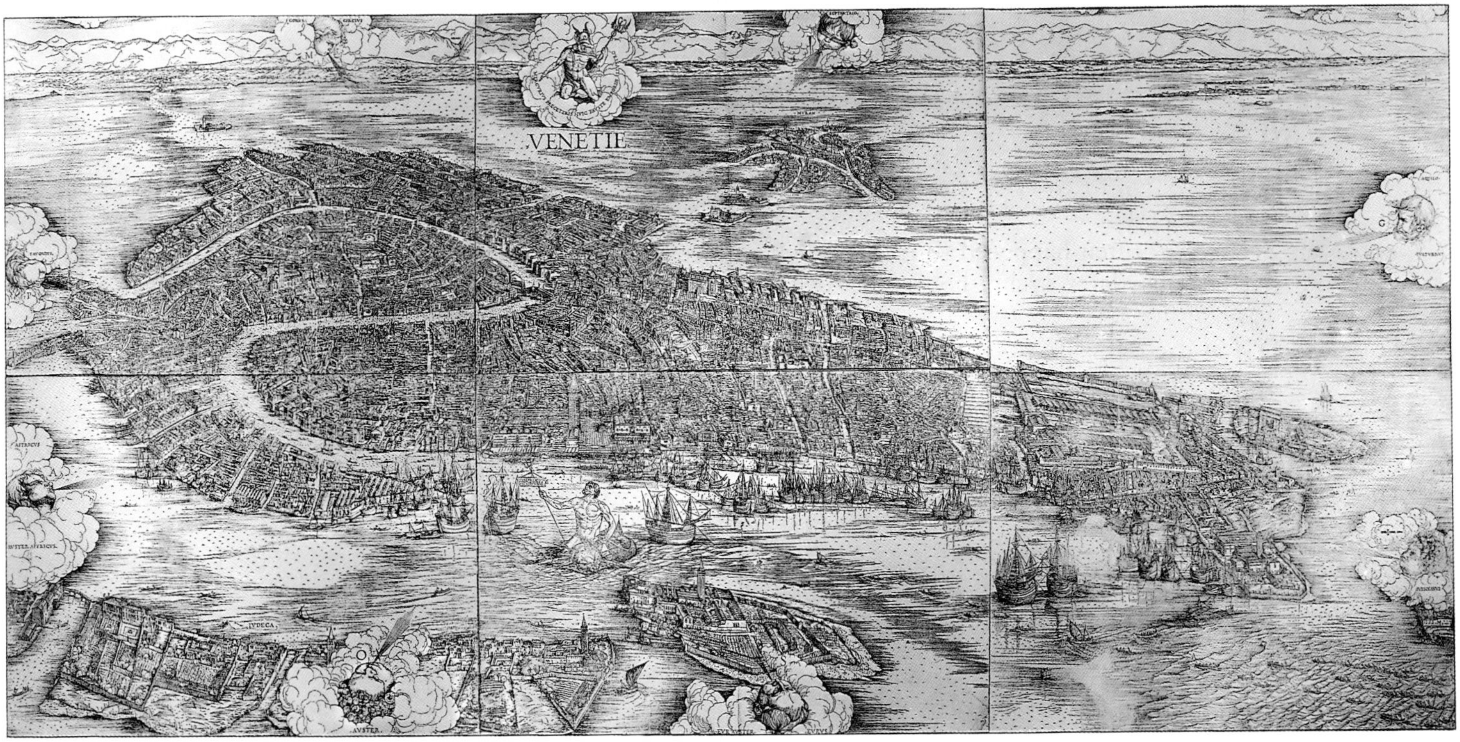

73 Venice (Italy). The powerful port city depicted by Jacopo de' Barbari in 1500 was formed through the consolidation of independently founded parish communities around the market place of the Rialto. About sixty of these parishes existed by 1200, each with its own market square, religious festivities, and local customs.

1, arteries, and the transformation of this open space into the communal center for *76* the town (the Campo), took several centuries. Novgorod also started from three separate settlements which were united probably some time in the 10th century. This may be the explanation of many other Russian towns which appeared quite suddenly beginning in the 10th century, in an area that had known no towns before that time with the possible exception of Kiev.

Synoecism is not a process peculiar to the West. In Burma, the great ceremonial center of Arimaddana (Pagan) was born of the union of nineteen villages some time before the 9th century AD. In South Asia, the city of Calcutta grew out of a cluster of villages on the banks of the river Hugli. The British East India Company purchased the rights over three of the villages in 1698, and in this area the town developed, with the white settlement around the fort built by the British and the native population outside. Islam, especially Muslim Iran, also has examples to show. Kazvin, Qum, Merv, Kazerum were all founded by the enclosure of a number of villages. Again, traditional black African cities until the coming of the Europeans were groups of village-like settlements with joint urban functions. The cities were very spread out, and retained the physical characteristics of their rural origins. They consisted almost entirely of one-story structures; the standard housing unit was the residential compound, and these compounds were located with no particular concern to align themselves with the streets.

This random sample would indicate that, indeed, synoecism is beginning to prove itself as one of the commonest origins of towns coming out of a rural context, along with one other process—the cohesion of an urban core around an important institution like a religious center or a fort. The form of a synoecistic city absorbs the shapes of the original settlements, along with their road systems. The open spaces that existed between the settlements are filled slowly, and retained open in part as markets and communal centers. A recent example: the Sudanese Muslim city of Al Ubayyid was made up of five large villages separated by cultivated areas; these the Ottoman regime of the 19th century partially filled in with barracks, mosques, a prefecture building, and government workers' housing.[19] In rare instances the establishment of a market serving several settlements may be the instigator of synoecism.

THE LAW AND SOCIAL ORDER

Much of what I have said so far on the evolution of "organic" patterns is earth-bound. Topography, land division, synoecism—these are all physical determinants of irregular city-form. It remains to speak briefly of urban improvisations based on social structure and the limits of public control.

The model of the traditional Islamic city has to be invoked once again. Neighborhood cohesion based on kinship, tribal affiliation or ethnicity was strong *53–* enough, I suggested earlier, to rearrange an inherited pre-Muslim grid of Greco-*56* Roman origin, and fuse and introvert its checkers into exclusive superblocks. When the city was not restrained by such prior abstraction, it carved its self-regulated residential maze with uninhibited purpose. The design of these superblocks might be fitful, but the social intention it served and demonstrated is enduring. It was valid in Islamic Spain and Islamic India, in the 9th century and the 19th. This explains the generic quality of Old Delhi and the medinas of Marrakesh, Aleppo or Tunis, which makes them almost interchangeable to the Western visitor, while for the people who live there each one possesses precise specificity.

74 A street in Baghdad (Iraq), with houses jettied out over the narrow public thoroughfare.

How was this privatized urban order wrought? The main thing to remember is that city-form was allowed to work itself out subject only to the respect of custom, ownership, and the Muslim's right to visual privacy.[20] You were not told what to do, what kind of city to design; you were only enjoined from doing things that threatened accepted social behavior. The concern for privacy, for example, determined where doors and windows would go on building fronts and how high buildings would rise. Visual corridors were consequently avoided, whether at the fine scale of a cluster of houses, or in the broader sense of urban vistas. More basically, this concern asserted itself in the introversion of the house, the appearance toward the street being unimportant. At the same time, the traditional grouping of attached courtyard houses expressed a degree of interdependence among neighboring structures having to do with legally arbitrated matters like party walls, the maintenance of cul-de-sacs, and the like.[21]

The primacy of the residential fabric, and the comparative weakness of the public space of streets, could not support an artificially pristine layout; rather, the public space was continually negotiated and redefined, as the buildings pushed out and over, interlocked and diversified. The room that bridged a street or a cul-de-sac was *74*
one common device used. All this improvisation was encouraged by the overriding principle that older uses and established structures had priority over new uses and structures. Radical urban renewal was out of the question: urban repair, that is, piecemeal changes to the extant fabric, was the customary procedure.

I am of course oversimplifying. Though much in this process depended on implicit conventions informally established and observed, and an uncontested building vernacular, there were also written building codes of local currency (though little is now known about them), and universally applicable religious law. This law derived from the Qur'an and the body of traditions called Sunnah. During the first three Muslim centuries it had been elaborated in a large body of literature addressing all aspects of public and private life, including questions relative to buildings—and therefore to city-making. The purpose of the latter, as with all religious law, was to adjudicate actual conflicts; the result was an extensive construct of precedent, with some degree of local gloss, having to do with things like temporary structures, boundaries, protrusions, heights, and uses.

General rules were few. The minimum width for public streets—7 cubits ($10\frac{1}{2}$ feet, or about 3.5 m.)—was established in a saying of the Prophet: this dimension allowed two fully laden camels to pass freely. Religious law agreed on a sensible minimum height, also about 7 cubits, set by the unobstructed passage of a person riding a camel. The planting of trees in a public right-of-way was disallowed. The cul-de-sac was considered to be common property—owned jointly by all occupants whose houses opened onto it. Standard building types for the public life of the city were the major mosque, local prayer facilities, schools, burial places of holy people, markets, merchants' quarters, baths. They too, like the residential tissue, locked together in interdependent systems expressive of social conventions.

The labyrinthine medina proves to be quite rational after all. To cite Old Delhi as an example: the primary streets carry the bazaars with the large retail and wholesale outlets. Production, storage and service centers are immediately behind, set in the clearly defined residential neighborhoods or *mohallas*. Secondary streets run as spines of commercial and residential activity through the *mohallas*, and can be closed off by doorways at their connections with the primary streets. Dead-ending tertiary streets, closed to general circulation, penetrate the cores of the *mohallas*. At the junction of two or more streets, modest expansions, called *chowks*, provide *94,*
some breathing room in the crushing density of the town.[22] *95*

If the outcome of this rational organization is not a formal layout, it is because it did not start as one, and there was no prescriptive guidance to steer it into a pure, geometrically unadulterated outline. The traditional Muslim city did not exercise methodical supervision over the city-form, because government, in the sense of the chartered cities of Classical antiquity or medieval communes in the West, was foreign to its nature. Citizens were allowed considerable latitude to exercise their personal rights in the treatment of their property. The structure of the city-form—the integration of uses, the concatenation of passages and nodal points—could possess the sort of coherence demonstrated by Old Delhi, and this in the absence of municipal authority to police and articulate public space, only because the social structure was well formulated, and tradition stood as the guarantor of a consistent *modus operandi*. Without the force of tradition and a consolidated social agenda, unsupervised city-making will succumb to disorder.

Notorious exhibits of this principle are everywhere around us. The modern industrial/capitalist city may not have invented abusive growth, but it has practically enshrined it. We could do no better than read Friedrich Engels's *Condition of the Working Class in England* (1845) to bring alive the first episode of disorderly settlement in major industrial centers like Leeds, Birmingham, Bristol and Liverpool. The trail would then lead to speculative development on the fringe of the metropolis, like the Paris *lotissements*, especially after the Great War where tracts were subdivided and sold without any provision for services or even roads, and the houses built were disciplined by no guidelines whatever. The last episode is of our own making—the ubiquitous squatter settlements of the last fifty years.

Disorder is a condition of order—unlike chaos, which is the negation of it. Disorder is provisional and correctible. As Rudolf Arnheim put it, "in any situation as much order will obtain as circumstances permit."[23] The range and history of squatter settlements document stages of disorder. These unauthorized, unregulated patches of urban growth are seen by their inhabitants neither as temporary shelter nor as the equivalent of urban slums, which are decayed shells of once superior housing. To them, rural migrants who mean to stay, these are permanent settlements alive to the pride of ownership and the ambition of self-improvement.

"ORGANIC" PATTERNS

The origin of many cities is humble; their form, insinuative and gradual. Where once there were fields and steep pasture land, streets will materialize and link up, tightly girded public places will ensconce collective life, and the spread of houses will thicken and mesh. The buildings will climb the slopes and take the bends as best they may. In time these natural arrangements will turn self-conscious. Terracing will suggest institutional and social hierarchies. The wending street will be exploited for its visual delights, its harboring volumes, its intricacies. We will then expect adventurous city-makers to recreate these effects where there is no innate cause to do so. The picturesque suburb is the city's retrospective celebration of its natural origins. And, too, a conjuring of virtues past. The belief that sustains modern nostalgia for the irregularities of "townscape" is this: that "organic" patterns once ensured social cohesion, and encouraged a spirit of community which we have washed away down the boulevards and expressways of the traffic engineer's town.

Pl.9 Nowdushan (near Yazd, Iran). The town plan is conditioned by the rural system of irrigation ditches.

Cities shaped by topography

Pl.10 above *Machu Picchu (Peru). The Inca city created a perch for itself high in the Andes by means of spectacular terracing.*

Pl.11 opposite, above *Gubbio (Italy) climbs up the side of an Umbrian hill. This is the town center, with the crenellated Palazzo dei Consoli on the left, facing a piazza jettied out on vast arches.*

Pl.12 opposite, below *In Prague, the ascent to the castle is made along the sinuous street called Nerudova.*

Pl.13 Free enterprise citymaking: in Rabat (Morocco), a precarious hillside shantytown rises toward a more permanent development of self-built housing.

Pl.14 left *The planned picturesque: the garden suburb of Glendale (Ohio), begun in 1851 to the design of Robert C. Phillips. This detail shows the winding streets, detached houses standing in lots of varied size and shape, and generous planting.*

They start out as shantytowns on unoccupied land at the distant edges of town, or in centrally located areas too difficult to develop, like steep slopes, canyons, garbage dumps. At this stage they have the look of refugee camps—no vegetation; no services; open trenches for sewers down rutted, unpaved streets. The building materials are what comes to hand or can be scavenged, mostly cardboard and scrap metal. Even then these shantytowns may not be innocent of intuitive design. In the squatter settlements of Zambian towns, Lusaka for example, village patterns surface in the prevailing confusion—units of about twenty huts around a common open space, and a physical grouping that approximates a circle.[24]

The process of upgrading begins instantly and never stops. Houses are made permanent in spurts with bricks and cement blocks. In the *barriadas* and *favelas* of Latin America, bright paint cuts the edge of tawdriness and exorcises despair. "Many houses have unfinished rooms or second stories, and a wild variety of fences abounds." As the settlement matures, order will inevitably tip the scales. There will be respectable self-built housing on a par with low-grade commercial construction; shops and schools; fully paved streets complemented by lighting and proper sewerage.[25] Lima's San Martin de Porres, begun as an invasion in 1952, had grown to a community of 75,000 inhabitants within fifteen years, its main street a divided paved highway flanked by three-story buildings.[26] *Pl.13*

THE STRAIGHT AND THE CURVED: DESIGN ALTERNATIVES

Before the modern period, it is hard to find evidence that the "organic" city form was appreciated as a rational choice. Cities were that way because they grew to be that way. Designing cities, as a conscious exercise, assumed some degree of geometric order. So it would seem. Nevertheless, urban thinking may not have been altogether clearcut. Aristotle paused to think on the matter. Always curious about the facts of things as they are, he saw advantages in the irregularity of old towns in military terms, while he championed the new-style urbanism of Hippodamus of Miletus.

Alberti, more of an empiricist than his reputation as the arch-theorist of early Renaissance architecture would allow, revived the defensive argument, and amplified it to support cul-de-sacs and alleyways. In *De re aedificatoria*, he wrote:

> The ancients in all towns were for having some intricate ways and turn-again streets, without any passage through them, that if an enemy comes into them, he may be at a loss, and be in confusion and suspense; or if he pushes on daringly, may be easily destroyed. [iv.5, Leoni translation]

But Alberti went further. There were health benefits to keeping streets narrow and turned. The Emperor Nero's legislation for a *nova urbs* may have tempered the twists of Rome, but we have it on the authority of Tacitus, Alberti observed, that the widening of streets "made the city hotter, and therefore less healthy." In narrow winding streets the air is more bracing, breezes and some sun will reach all the houses, and the force of "stormy blasts" will be broken.

On the subject of urban design, Alberti granted the appropriateness of the "organic" plan for hilly sites, but also more generally for small towns or "fortifications." This was not only a matter of common sense, but also of beauty.

The descriptive passage is rather remarkable for its esthetic acuity, and deserves to be quoted. In such towns

> it will be better and as safe, for the streets not to run straight for the gates; but to have them wind about sometimes to the right, sometimes to the left, near the wall, and especially under the towers upon the wall: and within the heart of the town, it will be handsomer not to have them straight, but winding about several ways, backwards and forwards like the course of a river. For thus, besides that by appearing so much longer they will add to the idea of the greatness of the town, they will likewise conduce very much to beauty and convenience, and be a greater security against all accidents and emergencies. Moreover this winding of the streets will make the passenger at every step discover a new structure, and the front and door of every house will directly face the middle of the street; and whereas in larger towns even too much breadth is unhandsome and unhealthy, in a small one it will be both healthy and pleasant to have such an open view from every house by means of the turn of the street. [iv.5]

It seems clear from this passage and others that Alberti, though he favored in principle a geometrically organized city form, responded with appreciation to familiar north Italian cities, many of which did not originate from, or had since lost the definition of, a Roman grid. These cities had a dense, intricately woven pattern
1 of run-on, attached, or closely contiguous residential units, held down by a handful of monumental landmarks, and firmly enclosed, purposeful public spaces. Prospects were closed and varied. The squares had unmatched sides, in both plan and elevation. The lots, narrow and long, thickly crowded these squares and the principal streets at the center, while the fabric thinned out at the city edge, and even dissolved into green. There was a convergence of streets onto markets and cathedrals, city gates and bridgeheads.

75 Duccio, detail of Christ before Pilate, *from the* Maestà *in Siena Cathedral, completed 1311.*

ORIGINS OF THE PLANNED PICTURESQUE

That these late medieval cities were far from being unguided in their appearance has been a documented thesis of recent scholarship. We have ample knowledge of the existence of vigorously enforced building codes, and regulations that were intended to insure the integrity of public spaces. But urban legislation and practice sometimes also display sympathy for the niceties of the energetic, cohesive cityscapes they were meant to tame.

Siena, for one instance, showed a determination to complete and polish the more informal physical arrangements of its early history, and to codify their effects. The city council was at pains in 1346 to insist that

> it redounds to the beauty of the city of Siena and to the satisfaction of almost all people of the same city that any edifices that are to be made anew anywhere along the public thoroughfares . . . proceed in line with the existent buildings, and one building not stand out beyond another, but they shall be disposed and arranged equally so as to be of greatest beauty for the city.[27]

And whereas its neighbour and mighty rival Florence had begun to campaign for streets that were "pulchrae, amplae et rectae"—beautiful, wide and straight—in proto-Renaissance solicitude for visual clarity, and also in the hope of re-establishing the orthogonal lines of Roman Florentia, Siena cherished the esthetic of Gothic curves. The three major spines that strapped the *terzi* to the Campo were paved in brick, to highlight their sinuous congress, and so was the Campo, the point

76 *Siena (Italy), Via dei Banchi di Sopra. The sweeping catenary curves of the thoroughfares that serve as Siena's connecting spine (see Ill. 72) may reflect a Gothic design preference. These sinuous geometries can also be found in renderings of drapery in Sienese paintings of the same period, like the one shown* opposite.

of their convergence; and when the city remade the bifurcation of the Via dei Banchi di Sopra and the Via dei Banchi di Sotto, in the first half of the 13th century, it estheticized the flowing curves in an urban equivalent of tracery or the rhythmic 76
drapery folds of the Gothic artist. 75

Even after the entrenchment of Renaissance design theories, a backward-looking urban esthetic stayed close to the surface, especially in the colonial experience. The first Spanish towns in the New World, with the exception of Santo Domingo, were not gridded, nor were Portuguese Goa and Rio de Janeiro. Alongside the formality of Louisburg and New Orleans, the French tolerated cities like Quebec which grew, as John W. Reps put it, "like a replica of some medieval city."[28]

How much of all this irregularity was sought after is hard to tell. One routinely invokes topography, of course, or permissive settlement habits. For every Boston, on the other hand, there is an Exeter, New Hampshire, or Woodstock, Vermont, where
peculiarities of irregular urban form seem studied. At Exeter, founded in 1638, one 77
main street followed the riverfront, the other struck inland in the direction of what is now the Philips Exeter Academy; at the intersection, the space was widened into a public place. At Woodstock about 130 years later, streets converged at either end of town, enclosing an irregular elongated green. (Local tradition saw in this green the shape and dimensions of a ship commanded by one of the town fathers.) "Did this irregular pattern of the Woodstocks and the Exeters of New England come about through overall village planning?" Reps asks. "The answer here must be tentatively

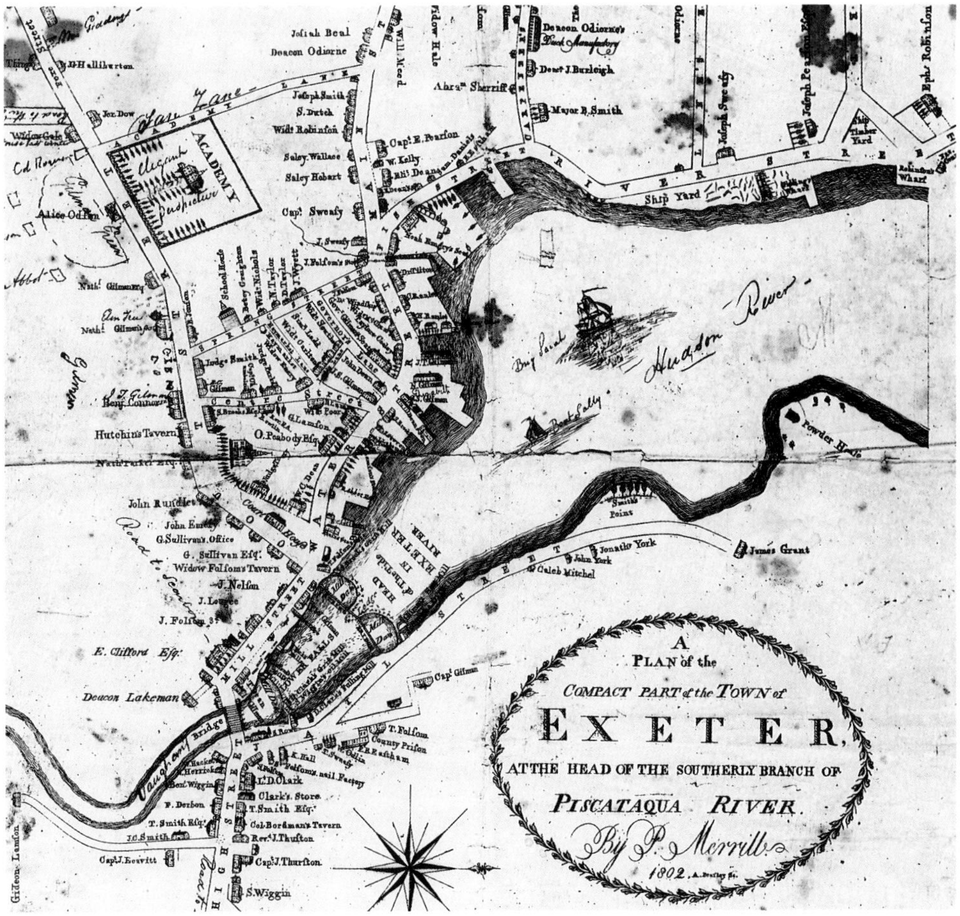

77 *Exeter (New Hampshire), engraving after P. Merrill, 1802. The layout combines routes of varied widths and geometries to create a harmonious townscape that suggests some degree of intentionality in the "organic" design.*

and cautiously in the negative."[29] But if these effects were not planned, ours is the burden to explain why and how they came to be.

The decisive swing toward an open, reasoned endorsement of non-geometric urban design came in the later 18th century. The revolt was against Renaissance theory and practice—the belief in the undeviating street prospect and the measured, uniform order of the street layout. For three centuries, Europe and its colonial outreach had been responding to the imperatives of the perfectly ordered city. To Renaissance thinking, the old accretive towns seemed obsolete, beginning with their towered defensive curtains and their patchwork streetscape. In the 17th century Descartes summed up the case against them:

> Often there is less perfection in works composed of several separate pieces and made by different masters, than in those at which only one person has worked. . . . So it is that these old cities, originally only villages, have become through the passage of time great towns, and are usually so badly proportioned in comparison with those orderly towns which an engineer designs at will on some plain, although the buildings, taken separately, often display as much art as those of the planned towns or even more.

But by 1750 the attraction of total urban design was coming into question, along with the authority of the Classical language of architecture. This change of heart shows best in England. There, it stages its alternatives, first, in the non-urban format of the picturesque garden. In town-planning proper, anti-Renaissance incursions that stand out prominently are of two kinds: combinations of curved urban settings and landscaping, as at Bath; and streets defiantly lax in terms of the Classical canon,
78 with jogs and unmatched elevations, John Nash's project for Regent Street being the best-known instance.

What was of key importance, however, was the Gothic Revival. The architectural aspects of this seditious movement have been exhaustively analyzed; not so with the concomitant rediscovery of medieval settlement patterns, primarily the imagery of villages and small rural towns. In practice, this retrospective view inspired two disjunctive offspring, one for the affluent and the other for those of stringent means. But the picturesque suburb and the industrial village recall for us the henceforth irrepressible promotion of a planning esthetic that is the modern affirmation of the eternal incidence of "organic" patterns.

Early industrial model villages, aspiring to entrap the virtues of the traditional English village along with its form, were tried out first in the wool centers of Yorkshire. The choice of a picturesque layout for workers' housing remains rare in the 19th century. Two late examples, sponsored by philanthropic employers, are
79 famous. Port Sunlight, near Liverpool, goes back to 1887; it was built from 1892 onward. Bournville near Birmingham, the brainchild of the Cadbury brothers, the chocolate manufacturers, starts a few years later; there, the curve was only gradually introduced. The plan of Port Sunlight was dictated by the creeks which penetrate the site from the Mersey. It was here that the "superblock" idea was first introduced, that is, the idea of having houses turn their back on main streets and look inward toward a green from which traffic is altogether excluded.

The picturesque suburb launched a more extensive, but equally exceptional,
80 reign. Bournemouth in Dorset has claims to primacy. More resort town than suburb, it started in the 1830s. The planners abandoned the conventional terrace form along a street grid, in favor of a curvilinear road scheme supporting self-contained villas in their own grounds. The guiding thought was the nature of the site. As Decimus Burton, chief architect after 1842, put it:

78 London's Regent's Park and Regent Street. The picturesque asymmetries of John Nash's early 19th-century design are the result of his masterful knitting together of new and existing streets. Planned as a means of linking the new Crown estates in Regent's Park (top) with the administrative seat at Westminster, Regent Street is a rare English example of the use of royal prerogative to mandate urban renewal.

79 *Port Sunlight (England), original town plan. The brainchild of soap manufacturer W. H. Lever, Port Sunlight was highly influential in popularizing the irregular street plan and neo-vernacular architecture that found their apotheosis in English Garden Cities. The picturesque layout seen here was amended beyond recognition in 1910 by the insertion of a broad mall and a hemicycle of radial lanes, both inspired by America's City Beautiful movement.*

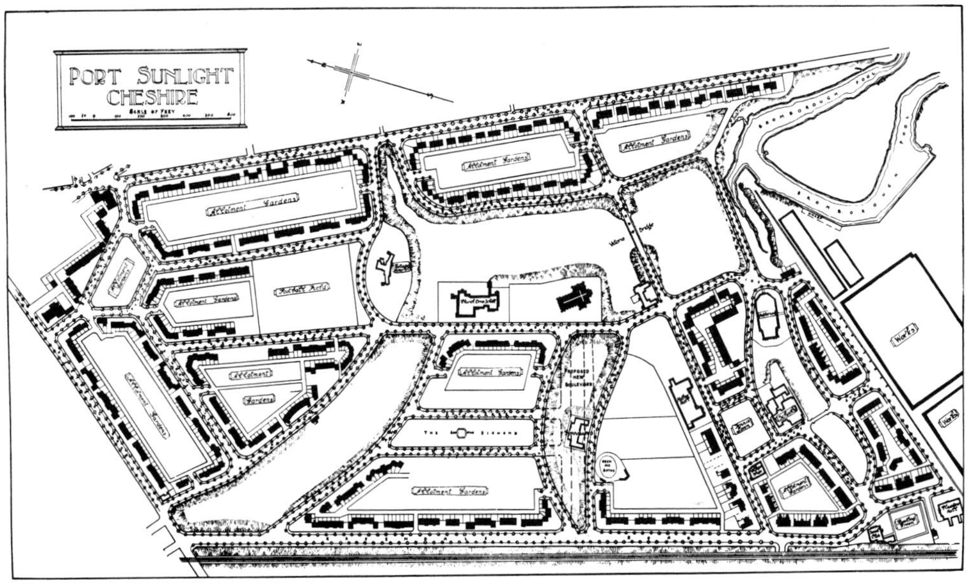

80 *View of Bournemouth (England) with Westover Villas and Bath Hotel, ca. 1840. Like other fashionable Victorian resort towns, Bournemouth's planning emphasized urban design features that would become synonymous with Garden City planning: districts reserved for purely residential use, gently curving roads, and a preference for detached houses.*

> The wooded valley through which the Bourne runs to the sea is and must always constitute the principal object in the landscape. . . . As a general principle in designing a building plan for Bournemouth, formality should be carefully avoided.[30]

In the United States, the picturesque suburb learned from the example of England, especially the 18th-century English garden, and the landscaped cottages of J. C. Loudon as reinterpreted for an American audience by Andrew Jackson Downing. Local inspiration came from the rural cemetery and the urban park, beginning at mid-century with Central Park in New York. To its chief creator, Frederick Law Olmsted, the park was an idealized rural landscape in the center of town that acted "in a directly remedial way to enable men to better resist the harmful influences of ordinary town life and to recover what they lose from them." What is important here is that the planned picturesque in the Anglo-American discourse becomes firmly identified with a non-urban imagery, and the excitement of the urban park derives from its clash with the quintessential American city-form, the grid. We have in this juxtaposition something of the reverse of what prevailed in ancient Mesopotamian cities. There, the formally planned precincts of temple and palace were played against the "organic" pattern of residential areas. Here, in New York, an "organic" park is intended to highlight the artificial formality of the overall grid, condemned by Olmsted as "the epitome of the evil of commercialism."[31]

Pl.14 The first American picturesque suburb is probably Glendale, Ohio, founded in 1851. The designer was Robert C. Phillips. Here too, as in Bournemouth, landscape features proved suggestive. Phillips took advantage of the contour of the site to lay out a scheme of winding streets which allowed for irregular lots of one to twenty acres (0.4–8 ha.). But in the end topography was incidental to the esthetic. If it was
81 there, it would be exploited; otherwise, it had to be created. At Riverside, Illinois, in 1869, Olmsted took a piece of flat prairie land and changed it into a romantic landscape. Thousands of trees were imported. A fluent system of curved streets was inscribed. Curved streets "suggest and imply leisure, contemplativeness, and happy tranquillity," Olmsted wrote, in contrast to straight streets which implied "eagerness to press forward, without looking to the right or left." Riverside was called "a suburban village," and openly touted as being for "the more intelligent and more fortunate classes." Indeed the Olmstedian residential development, always exceptional within the overwhelming rectilinearity of suburban tracts, became the

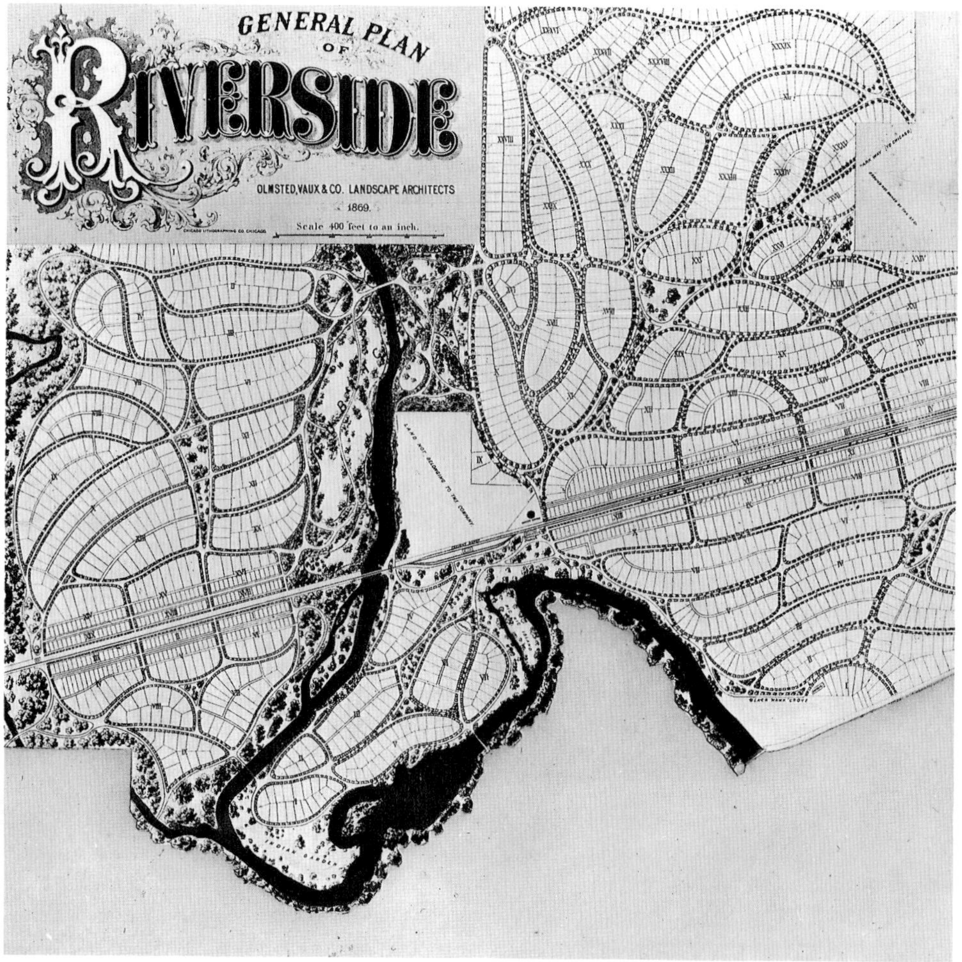

81 Plan of the suburb of Riverside (Illinois), 1869. Frederick Law Olmsted and Calvin Vaux were famed for their collaborative work on New York's Central Park at the time they received the commission to plan a suburban real estate venture 9 miles (14.5 km.) from Chicago. Their design for Riverside borrowed heavily from the vocabulary of the park landscapes. The curved, tree-lined residential streets bracketing the town's commuter railroad helped to define a new precedent for the suburban landscape.

province of well-off white Anglo-Saxon Protestants, to the covenanted exclusion of all other types of Americans—Blacks, Jews, Italians, and other ethnic groups that joined the melting pot in the course of time.

It is a strange twist that "organic" patterns in antiquity and the Middle Ages were intricate frames where the rich and poor were woven together. The organic of the modern suburb is exclusive: this is a private world peopled with one's own kind. It is also perversely insistent on an anti-urban message, as if curved streets had not been a millennial feature of great cities—of Athens and Rome and Siena and Nuremberg. This message is rooted in the merits of low density and the social pre-eminence of the detached single-family house.

In that sense, the picturesque suburb is considered vastly superior to city-form, which is seen as noxious both in its density and its insensitive, mechanical layout. If cities are to be "organic," they can only do so with benefit by being given a suburban layout. At the very least, a distinction should be made between business and residential districts. As the planner of northern Manhattan and the West Bronx wrote around 1870,

> The regions destined to be occupied for commercial and manufacturing purposes, it is desirable should be developed by streets and blocks of rectangular forms, so as to give the greatest facilities of communication and for utilizing the ground by compact occupation. The districts occupied for domestic purposes . . . must necessarily, to a large extent, be treated in a different manner, being governed, in this respect, by the exigencies of the topography.[32]

Such distinctions became more feasible in the United States as zoning—first *de facto*, then, since the 1920s, *de jure*—brought about the separation of residence and workplace, and created the possibilities of exclusive, single-purpose urban divisions. Even so the forces that nourished the exclusive early Downingesque or Olmstedian suburb were turned back by the speculative mentality that reigned in the great majority of planned housing developments or subdivisions and new towns. In 1873, Olmsted tried to sell the Northern Pacific Railroad an elegant "organic" plan (similar in its block shapes to that of Riverside) for its new town of Tacoma, Washington, a plan that exploited the topography of the site. But it was totally unsuitable for quick real estate profits, and so it was rejected. A contemporary source explained:

> [It was] the most fantastic plan of a town that was ever seen. There wasn't a straight line, a right angle or a corner lot. The blocks were shaped like melons, pears and sweet potatoes. One block, shaped like a banana, was 3,000 feet [ca. 900 m.] in length and had 250 plots. It was a pretty fair park plan but condemned itself for a town.

GARDEN CITY PARADIGM

All this precedes Ebenezer Howard—the author of the 1898 book *To-Morrow, A Peaceful Path to Social Reform*, retitled in the second edition of 1902 *Garden Cities of To-Morrow*. Howard had spent some years in Chicago before he wrote his book. He witnessed the frightening congestion of the modern city there and in his home base of London, the fierce speculative drive that shaped a dense aggressive center, and the unlimited sprawl that capitalized on the attraction of these dense centers of commerce and banking. Beyond the ragged fringe you might begin to encounter the sprawl of the next town, in a sort of regional ooze that a Howard disciple, Patrick Geddes, was to call "conurbation." The country was driven ever backward, away from the reach of the citizens.

Howard's solution was this: a limited company would acquire a tract of land in the country big enough for a community of 30,000. Private speculation being thereby eliminated, buildings would be spread out, and open space liberally provided for. The community would always be kept small, so the countryside would be within reach of everyone. The town would have its own industries and businesses and a ring of farms. The benefits of town and country would thus be combined. To limit the size of the town, one would circumscribe it within an unassailable greenbelt. The Garden City would have "all the advantages of the most active and energetic town life with all the beauty and delight of the country." Olmsted had said much the same thing earlier about the picturesque suburbs he was designing. Howard and his followers, however, combatively stressed that Garden Cities were not suburbs dependent on an old city but self-reliant communities with their own pool of resident jobs and their own apparatus of administration, culture and services.

193, Howard's famous diagrams belong in Chapter 3. He certainly did not specify
203, curved streets and cottagey houses for the Garden City. But the application of his
204 ideas settled for the kind of planned picturesque we have been surveying here—a small number of standard house types, mostly medievalizing but also neo-Georgian, grouped to form streets of great variety. The chief originators of this idiom were Raymond Unwin and Barry Parker, the planning team for the first Garden City—
226 Letchworth, in Hertfordshire, 80 miles (130 km.) north of London on a main railroad line, begun in 1902. The specific physical precedent—the superblocks, the individual gardens, and so on—came from the early industrial model villages of
79 Yorkshire already mentioned, and from Bournville and Port Sunlight. The road
82 system made use of the existing country lanes, and many existing natural features were preserved.

On the issue of density, "Twelve houses to the acre [0.4 ha.]" was Unwin's motto. Today when the 60-by-100-foot (18 × 30 m.) lot, or one-seventh of an acre, is the absolute minimum accepted for detached houses in the United States, and a quarter-acre is not untypical in many suburban developments, that provision may not seem particularly revolutionary. But this was eighty years ago, when the density of the industrial town was inhumane, and the greed of the developer worked largely free of today's legal restrictions. Fewer than twelve houses to the acre would not suit Unwin either. He wanted an arrangement that would promote community. What mattered was not alone a look of curvilinear intricacies; rather, it was the grouping and density of the individual houses in relation to the street system that would create the picturesque character of the Garden City.

The main invention from my point of view was the independence of the building line from the street line. The block system of land division was rejected. The houses turned on their lots, to catch the sun and view. The blocks were irregular, and the houses were grouped around blind alleys, frequently T-shaped. What Unwin was most interested in was to create a series of street pictures. And in this his inspiration went beyond the native English village; it went to German medieval towns and the visual delights they nurtured. He tried to combine the Anglo-Saxon penchant for the single-family house with its individual garden and the exciting volumetrics of old European towns.

The shape of the first two Garden Cities —Letchworth and Welwyn—was certainly not pure. In fact, the effect of formal Beaux-Arts urbanism, without its
226 overbearing monumentality, can readily be seen in the composition of the town center. In the first two decades of this century, the integration of "organic" and Beaux-Arts components was widely attempted. But a basic premise of the Grand Manner of urban design, that a hierarchical order of streets must exist both for

82 opposite *Letchworth (England), low-rent housing on Rushby Mead, ca. 1908. Planners Barry Parker and Raymond Unwin made a complete break with the standard English working-class environment of dreary bye-law terraces to create a street network of striking character and variety in Letchworth. Existing trees were retained through meticulous positioning of roads and buildings, and new foliage was introduced with a lavishness previously reserved for capital cities or holiday resorts.*

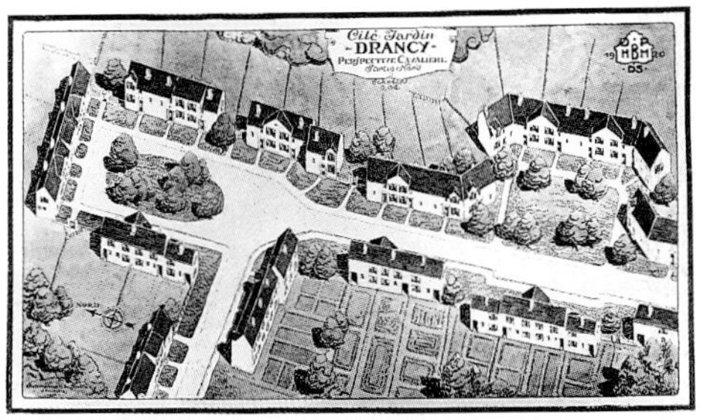

83 The Cité-Jardin of Drancy (France), 1920. Drancy was one in a series of satellite communities planned by the Office Public de la Seine to decentralize the population of Paris. Architects Bassompierre and de Rutté faithfully reproduced the Garden City models pioneered by Unwin and Parker in England a decade earlier.

representational purposes and for the smooth flow of traffic, was entirely alien to the thinking of Unwin. He wrote:

> The less area given over to streets, the more chance one has of planning a nice town. To be obsessed with the idea of planning for traffic is a mistake. One rather plans to avoid all needless traffic as far as possible.

The popularity of the Garden City as a principle of planning was its extreme flexibility, its relatively easy ensconcement into any ideology. The concept might travel along with that English form of "medieval" street flanked by cottages that Unwin and Parker popularized, or it could be separated from that form altogether and wedded rather to medium- and high-rise apartment buildings, and even to more regular layouts.

In France, proponents like Georges Benoît-Lévy and Henry Sellier presented the Garden City as the great alternative to the anarchic speculative sprawl of *lotissements.* With the collapse of the traditional private market in house construction after the First World War, Sellier, then in charge of housing for the Paris area, consciously adopted the Garden City as the model for the work of his office—the Office Public de la Seine. The first projects were in the spirit of 83
Letchworth. Then a higher density was introduced. Chatenay and Plessis show both phases: planned in the English manner, by the early Thirties they begin to replace individual houses with four-story blocks of flats.

The Garden City (*gorod sad*) seemed an attractive ideal in Russia as well after the terrible destruction of the Revolution and the Civil War. A Russian translation of Howard's book existed since 1911, and an early, rather literal, application of his diagrams appeared in a book by Vladimir A. Semionov of 1912 to illustrate the project of Prozorovska, a community for railroad workers. With the Bolshevik takeover of 1917 and the immediate abolition of private property, one of Howard's main premises, communally held land, was fulfilled. From 1925 on, when reconstruction could begin, the debate concerned choices between small houses and large apartment blocks; then it shifted to a rural–urban confrontation between those who favored dispersal and those who insisted on the retention and reinforcement of the existing urban centers. By 1932 dispersal theories were rejected. Official sources labelled Howard "a petit-bourgeois intellectual," and asserted that to do away with the old towns would be tantamount to "the disappearance and liquidation of the state."[33]

There are several things that kept the United States from embracing the Garden City ideal. It was almost impossible for the American system to tolerate communal ownership, or the controlled use of one's property. That smacked of socialistic or communist conspiracies. It was also almost impossible for America to accept a settlement pattern that was prejudiced against traffic, especially automotive traffic after 1920. So the American flirtation with that school of urban form was tentative in the extreme. But the garden *suburb*, American style, held a continuing attraction. Once the taste for the picturesque and for revivalist pluralism had subsided in the 1880s with the Beaux-Arts-inspired American Renaissance and its urban pendant, the City Beautiful movement, Olmsted's urban influence was largely confined to parks and park systems, and to the landscaping component for hundreds of urban projects in the Grand Manner. But the planned picturesque of Riverside lived on in

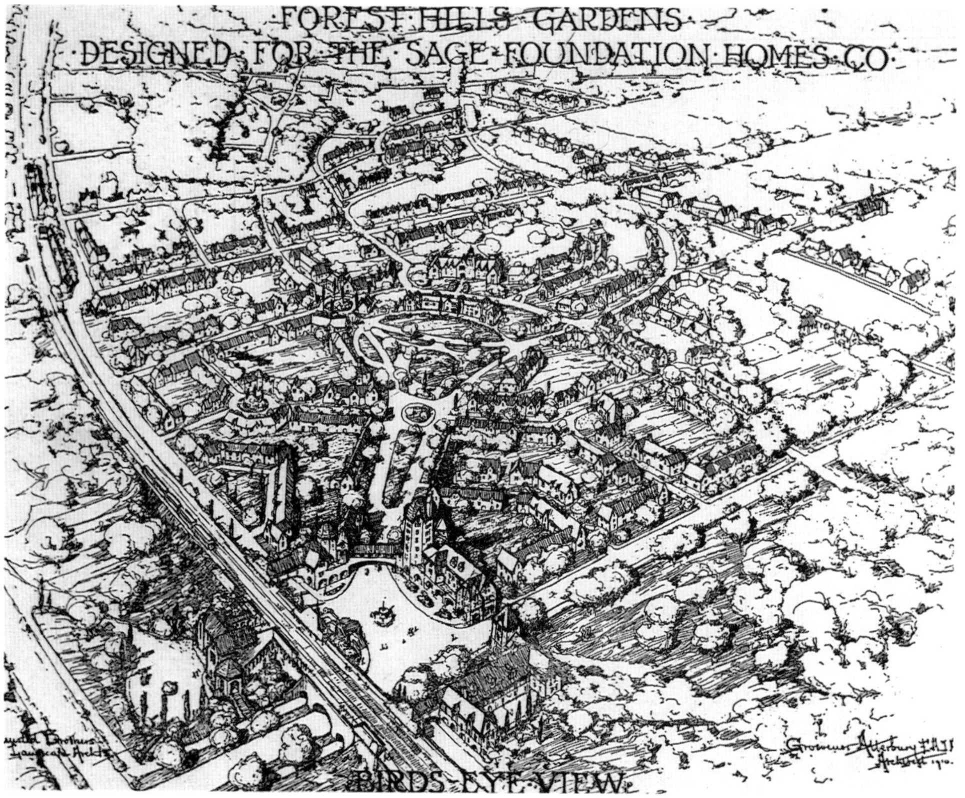

84 Forest Hills Gardens (New York), 1910. Designed by Grosvenor Atterbury and the Olmstead Brothers as a model workers' community, this is the most English in inspiration of America's early planned suburbs.

85, 86 Radburn (New Jersey), designed in 1928 by Clarence Stein and Henry Wright: pedestrian underpass and aerial view of the development under construction ca. 1930. Conceived as a "town for the motor age," in the words of Stein, Radburn combined elements of English Garden City planning with nearly absolute segregation of pedestrian paths from automobile traffic.

upper-class developments, where the now permissible conspicuous grandeur of the mansions, what we might call the Millionaire's Row complex transplanted to the suburbs, tended to overwhelm its effectiveness. The houses were often too big and ostentatious for the playfulness of the sinuous street and the layers of tree-lining.

Still, there are some memorable successors to Glendale and Riverside, for example, the Country Club District of Kansas City by J. C. Nichols, and Forest Hills Gardens in Queens along the main line of the Long Island Railroad. Both were *84*
started before 1915 and both were very early examples of restrictions by common consent, which included control of land use, minimum cost of dwellings, setback lines, building projections, free space, billboards, and of course racial and ethnic restrictions. Forest Hills was sponsored by the philanthropic Russell Sage Foundation which "abhorred the constant repetition of the rectangular block in suburban localities where land contours invite other street lines." It was meant for deserving families of modest means for whom "homes could be supplied like those in the garden cities of England." Even though this suburban estate was within the boundaries of New York City, it distorted the lines of the grid, with most streets evoking, in the words of Olmsted, Jr., who drew the master plan, a "cozy domestic character . . . where the monotony of endless, straight, windswept thoroughfares which represent the New York conception of streets will give place to short, quiet, self-contained and garden-like neighborhoods, each having its own distinctive character"[34]—in other words, Unwin's series of street pictures.

The garden suburb also made inroads in two other contexts. The reluctant Federal program for industrial worker housing toward the end of the First World War, sponsored by the Emergency Fleet Corporation, produced some model communities like Yorkship Village in Camden, New Jersey; Union Park Gardens near Wilmington, Delaware; and Buchman Village in Chester, Pennsylvania. And in the early Twenties, some private industries adopted this looser suburban format for their labor force in housing schemes like Goodyear Heights in Akron, Ohio, and the Billerica Garden Suburb for the Talbot Mills in Massachusetts. Under both Federal and private patronage, the arrangement was basically a suburban grid with some curves, and the point was insistently made that although the lots were not of uniform dimensions, they "in no case are of unusable irregularity."[35]

85 Then came a landmark design, the community of Radburn in New Jersey, of
86 1928, by the American Parker and Unwin—Clarence Stein and Henry Wright. English and American essays for the planned picturesque now began to coalesce. Radburn was designed for 25,000 people, and divided into three villages, each with its own elementary school and internal park. The grid was unequivocally rejected. Each village was subdivided into superblocks of about 40 acres (16 ha.), with pedestrian underpasses between blocks. The greenbelt principle of the Garden City was abandoned, but a scaled-down version of the industrial component, which was such a key element in Howard's thinking, did survive until 1986. Instead of public landholding, individual ownership was embraced. And the car's presence was perforce recognized.

A tremendous amount of propaganda was generated for this type of community on the part of an intellectual elite that included eloquent and passionate spokesmen like Lewis Mumford. The propaganda was enough to carry the day for a while during the New Deal. It played a part in the decision of the Federal Government to venture yet once more into sponsoring low-cost housing directly instead of through subventions or incentives. The so-called "Greenbelt Towns" are surely one of the most curious chapters of modern American urban history, and the closest the United States came to Howard's model. These towns did indeed have a greenbelt, at least at the beginning, and also corporate ownership, namely the Federal Government. The idea was sold to a hostile public as a rural rehabilitation program, and three of these towns did get built. Greenbelt, Maryland, and Greenhills, Ohio, adopted the superblock, the cul-de-sac, the traffic-free inner streets. The third, Greendale, Wisconsin, rebelled against this un-American preciosity, and modelled *it*self after Colonial Williamsburg. A fourth town on the Radburn model, Greenbrook, New Jersey, was blocked in the courts and never built. At any rate, the Government sold the towns after the Second World War, as it had the likes of Yorkship and Buchman after the First.[36]

But the Federal example had more far-reaching consequences. It is perhaps more because of official policies than the exclusivist rhetoric of the Mumford axis that after the Second World War the basic real-estate developer's street form began to change, from a dogged, unthinking reliance on the rectilinear grid toward curvilinear inflections. Part of this undoubtedly had to do with the increasing volume and speed of street traffic, which made it necessary to choose street patterns that would differentiate between one kind of traffic and another, and eliminate points of conflict. So the planning profession came to accept the notion that there should be roads for fast traffic, and others for local use laid out as loops and cul-de-sacs; long blocks, if not superblocks; and three-legged T-intersections that reduce traffic conflict points.

Radburn was the first to use this so-called functional street plan. But it was the Federal Housing Administration, organized in 1934 to provide mortgage insurance to local banks for loans on privately built housing, that set out both construction standards and desirable street patterns, to make sure that the housing was marketable and the risks were kept down. The official pamphlets had titles like
87 "Planning Profitable Neighborhoods" and "Successful Subdivisions," and they heavily favored curvilinear adaptations of the street grid and T-intersections. Seward Mott is usually credited with this official picturesque, and his inspiration
81 may well have been classic picturesque suburbs like Olmsted's Riverside, or Forest
84 Hills Gardens.[37] The Radburn exemplar, not very influential in its country of origin

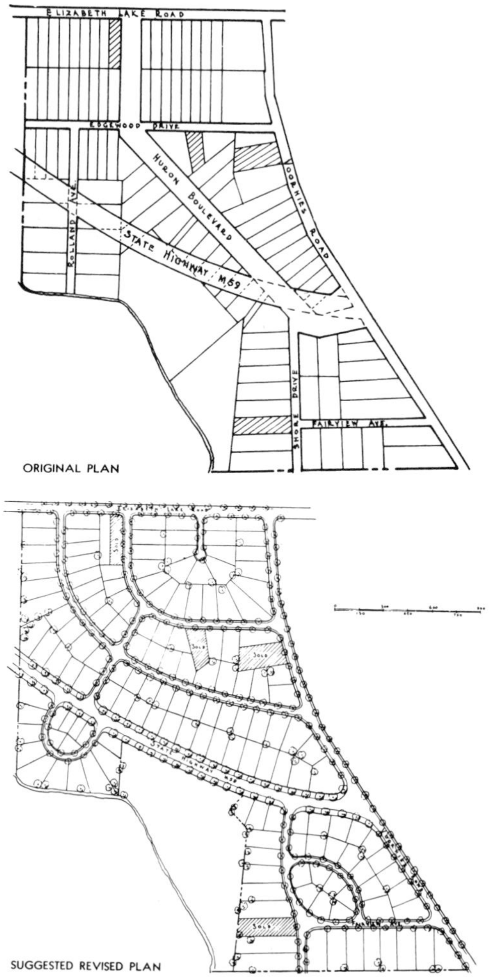

87 Original and revised plans of a speculative subdivision from the 1938 brochure "Planning Profitable Neighborhoods." When the Federal Housing Administration was established in 1934 no-one could have predicted the power it would come to wield in shaping America's built landscape. By establishing minimum design standards favoring curvilinear street formats, the FHA virtually assured the nationwide replication of "organic" townscapes during an era of explosive suburban growth.

88 Palm City (Florida). Suburban development was revolutionized by mass-production techniques in the late 1940s. The advent of new construction materials, power tools, factory preassembly of house components and specialization of skilled labor has transformed suburban developers into builders of instant cities. This snaking row of detached homes stakes a claim on the century-long tradition of curvilinear suburban street-scapes while revealing its assembly-line production.

beyond the Greenbelt experiment, would become instead a standard point of reference in Sweden and in Britain's New Town program after the Second World War.

In the United States the postwar era failed to adopt official policies for the design of whole housing developments. Instead, the design of the streets came to be governed by more and more detailed regulations which prescribe uniform setback lines, uniform side yard, rear yard and lot sizes, all decided on the basis of the individual lot. Hence the numbing monotony of most American developments. And since the developers themselves now usually have to build the streets and provide the services, rather than expect the relevant municipality to supply these as before,
89 developments tend to be small, scattered, and randomly shaped, creating a kind of accretive picturesque around an irregular rural road net. Sometimes the contorted pattern has the look, in plan at least, of medieval Cairo. To this speculative process add the esthetic fad of the cluster plan, which became popular in the Sixties, with land left around artfully grouped houses as permanent open space, and the unfinished history of the "organic" city-form will start nudging present-day practices.

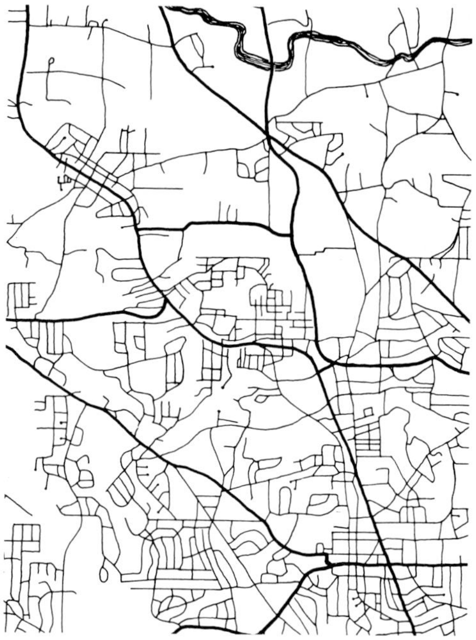
89 Patchwork suburban road network outside Atlanta (Georgia). (After Tunnard)

CONSERVATION AND THE LESSON OF HISTORY

Continental European involvement with the planned picturesque since the late 19th century constitutes a separate story. Central to this story is the Continent's own version of neo-medievalism. While England was looking to its traditional villages and their cottage architecture and learning something about urban living in easy contact with nature, Europe found comfort in its storied medieval towns for its own recipe against the effects of the Industrial Revolution on city-form—the ugliness, the dehumanization and the fraying of social bonds, the sacrifice of urban values to speculative profit and to efficient traffic. Demolitions in the old towns had become endemic after mid-century as straight thoroughfares were cut through compact medieval fabrics to link up more easily with the proliferating suburbs. In the suburbs themselves, comfortable access began to be set as a prime criterion of the good life. Common people and cultural critics alike looked with increasing distaste and alarm at the new breed of technocrats—traffic specialists and municipal administrators—who unapologetically gutted historic cores for the sake of circulation. *Eventrement*, evisceration, was the term popular with the most famous "demolition artist" of the
90 time, Baron Haussmann, whose comprehensive redesign of Second Empire Paris set new limits of radical urban intervention. While he and his brood opted for mechanical efficiency, the opposition mounted a cultural, social and historicizing defense of the old towns.

Most of the energy of the latter group went at first toward preventing the destruction of noteworthy buildings. These the technocrats also claimed to respect, as they cleaned away the accretions of time and isolated the monuments in large open spaces at the ends of vistas. But in Germany the issue was being changed to one of contextualism, and this along two fronts.

The first front is primarily esthetic, and is best represented by Camillo Sitte (1843–1903) and his book of 1889, *Der Städte-Bau nach seinen künstlerischen Grundsätzen* (*The Art of Building Cities*, or more literally "City-Building According to Artistic Principles"). The esthetic superiority of picturesque old towns to geometric modern street plans had been championed before Sitte. In the 18th century I. P. Willebrand, in his book of 1775 on the esthetics of planning, *Grundriss einer schönen Stadt* (The Layout of a Beautiful City), praised the physical form of old towns. A century later

90 Part of the Haussmannization of Paris, seen in a wood-engraving of 1858: a dense web of 13th- and 14th-century streets on the Left Bank makes way for the straight Rue des Ecoles.

the Prussian military hero Helmuth von Moltke wrote of his preference for the picturesque streets of Vienna over the rigid new extensions of Berlin. And the cultural critic Wilhelm Heinrich Riehl in a book which came out in 1854 stood up against "current building regulations in the layout of streets," Sitte's commentator George Collins explains, "saying that a picturesque effect could be attained by following the natural path of a stroller's feet. Such a graceful curvilinear trajectory is observable in the villages and is 'an honor' to imitate."[38]

But Sitte developed this appreciation into a theory of city-form. He argued against "the affliction of inflexible, geometric regularity," against Haussmannesque scale, against the mania of huge squares with monuments to this and that centered in them, against grand vistas focused on obelisks and equestrian statues. He made a careful study of urban form, especially of the medieval towns of his own country which he knew and loved, praising them for their "natural sensitivity." What is even more notable, he associated the vital irregularities of these city-forms not only with visual interest, but also with wholesome social use. Cities were agglomerations of buildings and of people, the bond between them evolved and sustained through time: neither must be segregated into classes, or zoned as to use and behavior. There is a gradually developed harmony between public buildings and their physical context. Urbanism, according to Sitte, is precisely the science of relationships. And these relationships must be determined according to how much a person walking through the city can take in at a glance. Streets and squares must be considered in three dimensions, as volumes. "The ideal street must form a completely enclosed unit." It must avoid bilateral symmetry; it must avoid cross streets that come into it at regular intervals and at right angles to its line.

91 Brussels, Marché aux Poulets; from L'Art de bâtir les villes *(1902). The French edition of Camillo Sitte's treatise on city building reduced the author's argument for enclosed urban space to a singleminded celebration of medieval town form. The illustration is from a chapter on street design added to the book by the translator, Camille Martin.*

Sitte did not himself advocate the use of medievalizing streets in town extensions. His book was equally positive about Greco-Roman urbanism, and about the great Baroque tradition of the German princes. The issue for Sitte was not the particular morphology of the container, but the quality of the contained—the space. The dogmatism of curvilinear patterns was fostered by his disciples, whose picturesque suburbs and city extensions of totally arbitrary design enflamed the criticism against Sitte. Formal planning had rules, the critics maintained; informal planning has to be largely intuitive. In fact, this German picturesque was indebted to English models
93 as much as to Sitte. The estates—Hellerau near Dresden (1908), Munich-Perlach,
92 Staaken Garden Suburb in Berlin, and Falkenberg, also in Berlin, by the young Bruno Taut (1912)—were more irregular and asymmetrical in street plan than Port
79 Sunlight or Letchworth, but the simple, quietly designed houses adhered to the street line. The houses were spaced closer together, and had unbroken ridge lines and deep roofs. The taste for garden suburbs lived on after the First World War as the Krupp dynasty of arms manufacturers, for example, in their workers' housing at Essen, continued to promote the Anglo-picturesque over the geometric.

Sitte's example was more helpful within the old cities than in the modern periphery. At the same time that the defense of the small incident, the twisted street, the rounded corner, the little planted oasis unexpectedly come upon, the long unbroken street front free of the dissection of geometricized blocks, was being used to make the point that modern planning of new quarters could be more inventive than profit-minded speculative geometry permits, it was also used to show that minor adjustments in historic cores were more to the point than massive demolitions. In Brussels, mayor Charles Buls rose up as champion of his city's old quarters. He addressed the prevalent esthetic question—whether medieval cities are beautiful, that is, the product of premeditation—and conferred upon them a special character. He wrote in the opening lines of his *Esthétique des villes* (The Design of Cities), of 1893:

> Old cities and old streets have a peculiar charm for all who are not insensible to artistic impressions. They may not be called beautiful, but they are attractive; they please by that beautiful disorder that here results not from art but from chance . . .

What accounted for the geometries of modern urban design was the professional's habit of arranging on the flat surface of the drawing paper symmetries which will never be experienced on the ground by the pedestrian once the scheme has been realized. At any rate, it is not a question of straight *or* crooked streets, Buls argued. Classical buildings demand an extended point of view, a vista, that would make clear the symmetry of their design; Gothic buildings need to have a closed perspective and a picturesque context.

After the turn of the century the cultural, historicizing perspective gained strength. Even Paris began to have second thoughts. Here is the Prefect of the Seine, Haussmann's successor in that office in 1909, in a report to the municipal council, in effect rejecting the work of his illustrious predecessor:

> We must avoid the danger of a too rigid regularity, we must not imitate the insipid grid of American cities . . . nor sacrifice any more to the abuse of geometric

93 opposite *Munich (Germany), Gartenstadt München-Perlach, by Berlepsch-Valendas, 1909. This unbuilt project is of the "forced picturesque" school of planning that emerged from the teachings of Camillo Sitte. A contemporary reviewer noted with approval that although the garden suburb was planned for a flat forested site already "cut up by drives into a perfectly regular gridiron . . . these have by no means been allowed to influence the plan of the villages."*

92 Berlin, Gartenstadt Staaken, by Paul Schmitthemmer, 1914–17. Berlin's first garden suburb is a synthesis of British Garden City theory and German neo-medieval design.

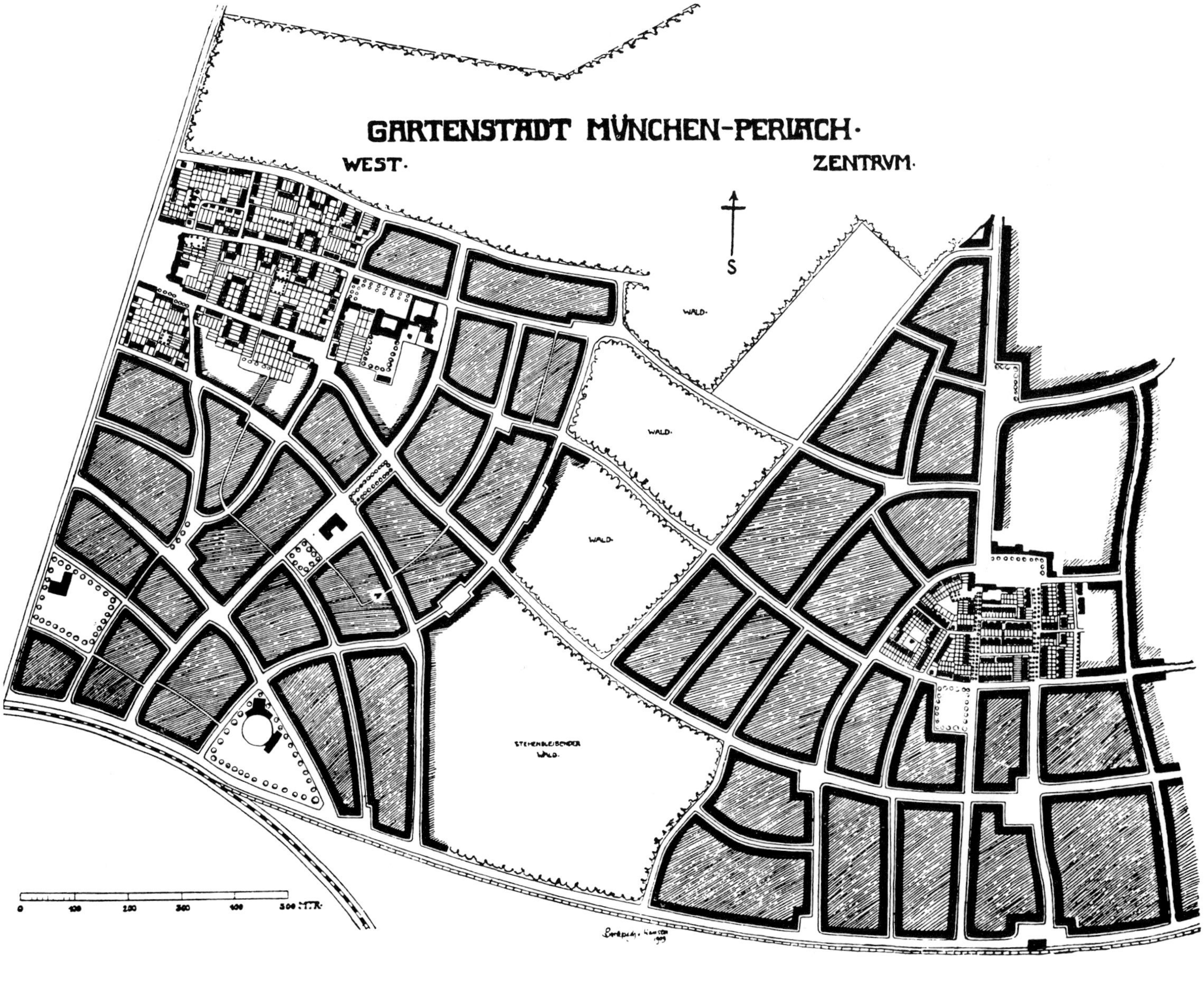

schemes the beautiful works of the past which have counted for nothing in the plans for alignment and expropriation.[39]

The change of heart in the French planning bureaucracy was most apparent in the African colonies. Military engineers had been ruthless in modernizing the medinas of Algeria, a French possession since 1830, and Tunisia, "controlled" since 1881. But when France proclaimed Morocco a protectorate in 1912 and appointed Marshal Lyautey to be resident general with full powers, a new conservative policy was immediately put in place. The age when all planning decisions for the colonies were made by the Ministry of War in Paris was over. Lyautey and his architect Henri Prost advocated separate development for the indigenous population and the European colonizers. Lyautey wrote: "Large streets, boulevards, tall façades for stores and homes, installation of water and electricity are necessary [for Europeans, all of] which upset the indigenous city completely, making the customary way of life impossible." So it was not a matter of protecting single monuments; one must "consider the totality of a quarter as an historical monument not to be touched in its lines and aspects."[40]

In a colonial setting this solicitude proved suspect. You could read into Lyautey's laudable declarations the brief for apartheid. But the concern for built contexts had other, even earlier, champions, whose motives, if not methods, were beyond suspicion. Their argument was far more than merely esthetic or broadly historicist. It rested on the notion that we are what we have built. The mindless destruction of our old fabrics erases our cultural identity.

The name of Patrick Geddes must always come first in this connection. In his early involvement with the Old Town at Edinburgh beginning in the late 1880s, with Dunfermline, and with Dublin between 1911 and 1914, he tirelessly promoted the idea of a civic survey—a comprehensive study of the geology, geography, economic life, and above all the history and institutions of the city—prior to any planning intervention. The survey would constitute "diagnosis before treatment." Then would come "conservative surgery." He wrote in *Cities in Evolution*, his great book of 1914:

> We must not too simply begin, as do too many, with fundamentals as of communications, and thereafter give these such esthetic qualities of perspective and the rest as may be, but, above all things, seek to enter into the spirit of our city, its historical essence and continuous life. . . . Its civic character, its collective soul, thus in some measure discerned and entered into, its daily life may then be more fully touched . . .[41]

In India, he tried to stem the *éventrement* mentality of British military planners, as Lyautey was doing in Morocco, endowed only with formidable powers of persuasion. He found beauty in the ragged tangles of the old towns, where narrow twisted lanes with earthen dwellings and main streets with stylish buildings formed
94 "an inseparably interwoven structure." The seeming chaos was of our own imagining—the product of the Western addiction to mechanical order; here instead we should see "the order of life in development." Reduce the number and width of
95 paved streets in residential areas, he urged, and turn the land saved into a chain of usable open spaces that will renew the values of social life. Have flexible plots that might be combined easily or subdivided. Undo as little as possible. And persuade the citizens to become involved, arouse civic enthusiasm, let them express their individuality, for streets will "look all the better for a certain freedom of treatment and rivalry between the houses."

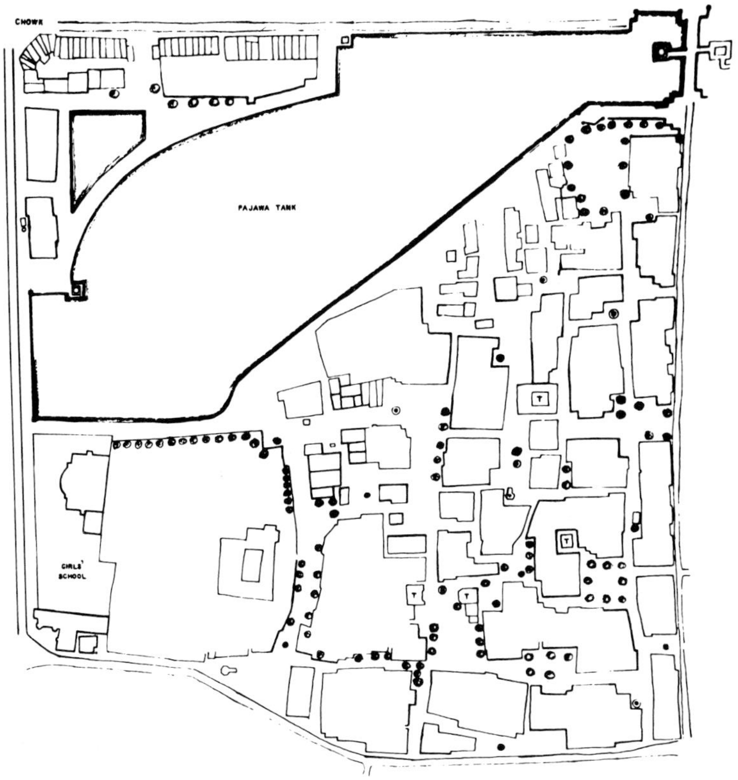

94, 95 Balrampur (India), renewal project, from Patrick Geddes's Townplanning in Balrampur *(1917). Geddes's theory of conservative surgery envisioned retaining the feel of a native settlement pattern while improving hygiene and traffic flow. His plan for Balrampur minimizes demolition through carefully plotted street expansion. Climate and local customs are also reflected in the provision of scattered tree-shaded* chowks, *the mid-street openings that harbor public life in traditional Indian cities.*

This slow, small-scale, participatory Geddesian approach had very little effect on the real world of planning. His teaching was soon absorbed by the Garden City movement, itself still an effort of the fringe. But his doctrine of preserving and rejuvenating historic centers was installed, without his help, in at least one European country—Germany. By the end of the 19th century, the goal of conservation there began to be identified as the urban skyline, the *Stadtbild.* Towns like Hildesheim, Rothenburg, and Lübeck passed strict urban conservation laws in the opening years of this century. Conservation, furthermore, was fervently being equated with nationalism, with *Heimatschutz.* This cult of the homeland was to survive the socialist upheaval of the Twenties, to emerge as a major planning directive of the Nazi regime. While in the big cities of the Third Reich Speer and others were installing the Grand Manner of Paris and Vienna, the ideal concept of "das Volk" was being applied to rural new towns. The medieval epoch was the purest, the theorists held, a time when Germany was free of foreign and cosmopolitan influences. Physically, this independence was expressed in the gabled-roof house, and in the medieval townscape which embodied a principle called, of course, "organic." The streets of medieval Nuremberg, wrote one planner, "like the ingenious rib structure of a leaf, satisfied the traffic requirements of the medieval city"—and the same configuration would serve the Nazi rural town. The ideal form 96
would be circular, in emulation of classic medieval cities like Nördlingen; the circle was to be stretched and molded to the contours of the landscape. A cross-axis organized traffic and made a special place for the political center. Where market and cathedral had been, the new towns would be fixed by Party buildings. The houses must nestle in the landscape; and the streets must also conform to land contours. They could not be a grid, but must "grow from the soil . . . be one with its natural form, the specific geomorphological surface relief."[42]

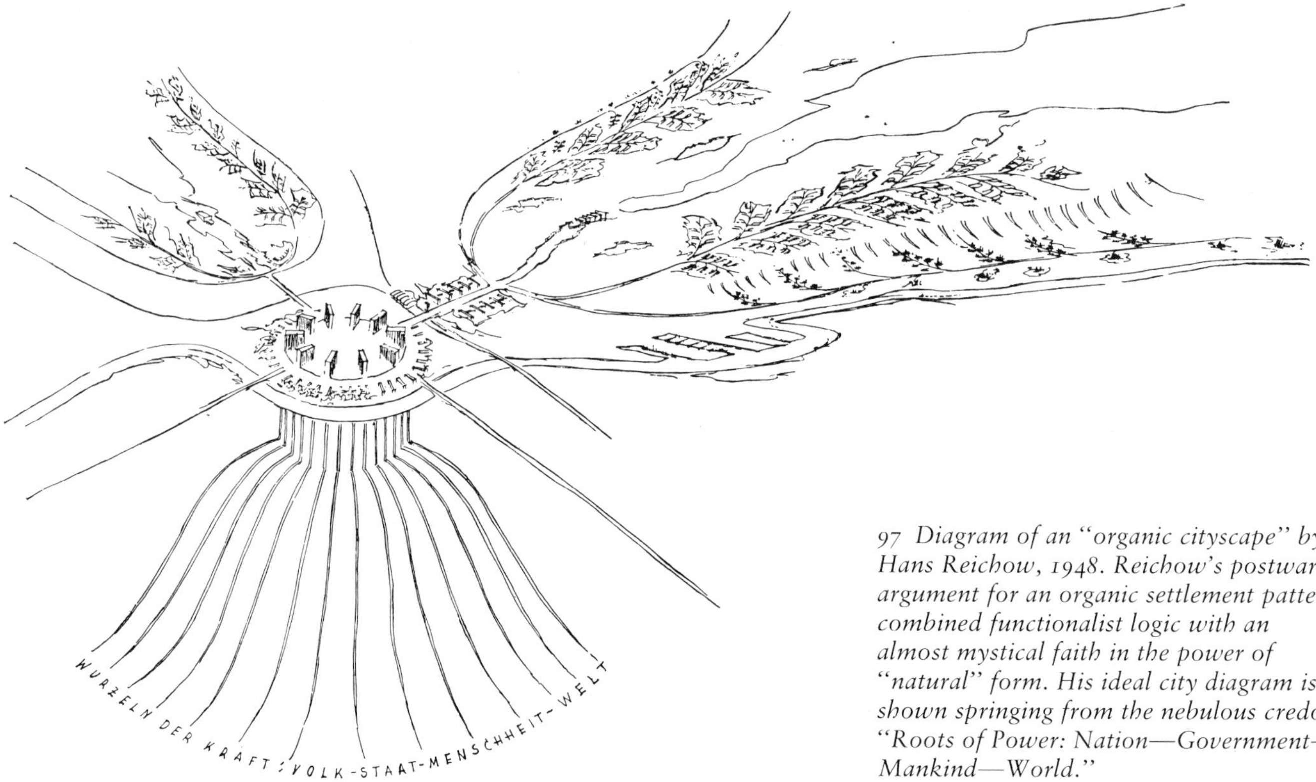

97 Diagram of an "organic cityscape" by Hans Reichow, 1948. Reichow's postwar argument for an organic settlement pattern combined functionalist logic with an almost mystical faith in the power of "natural" form. His ideal city diagram is shown springing from the nebulous credo: "Roots of Power: Nation—Government—Mankind—World."

96 opposite *National-Socialist new town project, 1938. This model by Grosser and Schürmann for a town of 20,000 inhabitants was one of several projects displayed at a city planning exhibition held in Frankfurt (Germany) a year before the onset of the Second World War.*

The passage of "organicism" into the post-1945 era was made through the long career of Hans Bernhard Reichow. Under the Nazi regime Reichow was city architect of Stettin, and adviser to the planning establishment of Hamburg. After the war he was employed by the West German Ministry of Housing for which he designed many settlements. In the war years, Reichow set out to extend the scope of "organic" imagery from the small rural town to the post-industrial megalopolis. He *97*
had in mind, first of all, the rebuilding of the major German cities, laid waste by bombs. This is the object of his 1948 book *Organische Stadtbaukunst, organische Baukunst, organische Kultur* (Organic City-Planning, Organic Architecture, Organic Culture). The metaphors are familiar—the branching of a tree, the structure of a leaf, the human lung. Reichow condemns all "inorganic" city-forms—be they simple grids, or products of the Grand Manner—as static. He faults advocates of linear cities for presenting this model as a complete urban solution. In itself the linear city is incomplete, but as an appendage of the organic city, one of its branches as it were, it works well. City expansion is organic when it occurs along radial lines without losing centripetal power. To close a radial scheme with a ring road is unnatural. The city will stop growing when it has filled its natural space. The "freedom of appearance" is a precondition to all natural beauty.

What the heart of the book represents is, in fact, the new thinking in the Nazi planning circles after 1940. The traditional Party doctrine of ruralism, with its fixation on the single family dwelling, was rather abruptly discarded when the rain of bombs over German cities brought home the urgency of future tasks—the rehousing of millions and the rebuilding of the urban infrastructure along more rational lines. Modernist tenets, once ostentatiously rejected, now seemed acceptable. Plans now called for a massive program of large apartment buildings, composed of standardized units (*Reichstypen*) and set in green parks; reliance on prefabrication; the functional separation of industrial and residential sectors. The new city would thus be fully modernized, but without totally forgetting its "organic" roots. There would be greenbelts surrounding the cities, and housing blocks were to be arranged along gently curving broad streets.[43] This is Reichow's agenda—to soften Modernism and bring it in line with the new Nazi policies.

98 Römerstadt, near Frankfurt (Germany), by Ernst May, 1927–29.

MODERNISM AND THE PLANNED PICTURESQUE

The destinies of Modernist urbanism and the Garden City movement had been entangled before. We can dismiss as a mere curiosity Le Corbusier's juvenile attraction to the picturesque, which led him to write a Sittesque urban tract and design a garden suburb for his birthplace of La Chaux-de-Fonds in Switzerland, complete with curving roads and gables, before he started raging against "the pack-donkey's way."[44] Ernst May's example is more to the point. He had trained under Unwin, and worked on Hampstead Garden Suburb. When he was installed as head of Frankfurt's housing authority under a socialist administration, he saw his first *Siedlungen*, those estates that became icons of the early Modern Movement, as Modernist interpretations of the Garden City. This claim was especially credible in
Römerstadt on the Nidda River, with the gently curving streets matched by the *98*
sinuousness of the exceedingly long housing blocks. But soon, here in Frankfurt as elsewhere in Weimar Germany, Modernist housing estates adopted a doctrinaire

schematism based on pseudo-scientific rationales like "heliotropic" (sun exposure) formulas.

After the Second World War, the triumphant return of Modernism brought an end, for a while, to the appreciation of the historic picturesque of European cities and the planned picturesque of Garden Cities and their offshoots. Nowhere else besides England did the Garden City become the official solution to postwar urban problems, and even there the ideal of Ebenezer Howard and the practice of Unwin reached out to marry Modernist building types like highrise housing slabs and the Modernist vision of "the city in the park." The policies of slum clearance and "urban renewal" seemed determined to finish the work of the bombs. Where Modernists had their way, the concern for context became an irrelevancy. The street pattern of a whole historic district of the City of London was erased under the Barbican; at Metz an old quarter was destroyed where houses went back to the 13th century.

The reaction of the Sixties, in terms of our present theme, took two separate paths. One led to an internal critique of Modernist urbanism; the other pointed back toward history and the surviving scraps of our urban past. Each within its own context reopened the ancient debate of "organic" patterns and reaffirmed their validity.

First, members of a loose international group of young Modernists known as Team X stood up against the arrogant internationalism of their elders. They saw themselves as pioneers of a new revolution. Since the Renaissance, they argued, the dominant thinking in urban design had been one of pre-planning and pre-fixing cities. Through the 18th century, ideal plans and single acts of design like Versailles or Washington guided our vision of cities. Regulating plans of the 19th and 20th centuries perpetuated the notion of city-form under prior control. And it was this fixed, formal organization that ruled the urban work of Modernist masters like Le Corbusier and Ludwig Hilbersheimer (see "The Grid," below, p. 155).

Team X proposed to adopt a fresh attitude that would see city-making as "organic process." The task was to fix a loose structure along which development could take place over time. The pioneering Golden Lane housing scheme conceived by Alison and Peter Smithson in 1952, and realized in Park Hill, Sheffield, in 1961, showed a rambling line of highrises which held aloft an elaborate pedestrian superstructure. Shadrac Woods, who masterminded a similar scheme as an extension of Toulouse, wrote of his project in terms of stems and webs, the classic imagery of the "organic" schools of urban design. The stem corresponds to a pedestrian street, and is served by public transportation. Housing is linear and plugs into the stem. Interconnected stems form the non-centric web, which develops peaks
100 of intensity through use. The plan of Toulouse-Le Mirail is reminiscent of some North African medina, and it is not without an element of irony that the quarter is now predominantly occupied by Algerian immigrants. But the physical reality of
99 what there is to see—huge multi-story housing slabs zigzagging across a barren site, and the scorned system of internal streets, almost wholly devoid of pedestrian activity, which threads them—makes a mockery of the designer's rhetoric that the city "is the domain of man on foot and seeks to respect his scale."

The other side of the coin was the resurgence of historic preservation, dormant under the vehement ahistoricism of the Modernists, and of the "townscape" esthetic. On the issue of the old city and its updating, the mood began to shift dramatically. In France, in 1962, an act was introduced by André Malraux, then Minister of Cultural Affairs, with the aim of protecting historic urban cores from the onslaught of renewal. The act established the concept of the *secteur sauvegardé*,

99, 100 Toulouse-Le Mirail (France): plan of the new town with the city of Toulouse, and a view of the apartment slabs from one of the internal streets. Candilis and Woods's design for an urban extension for 100,000 inhabitants occupies almost the same area as its host city of Toulouse. It is the most extensively realized application of the "organic" city-building process championed by the group of urbanists known as Team X.

and saved, among other endangered neighborhoods, the Quartier des Tanneurs in Colmar with its half-timbered houses and narrow paved lanes which had already been evacuated and was awaiting demolition. This "Loi Malraux" was the forerunner of the National Historic Preservation Act of 1966 in the United States, and England's Civic Amenities Act of 1967 which introduced the concept of "conservation areas."[45]

Townscape literature was an English phenomenon. Part Garden City and part Sitte, it began with Frederick Gibberd's *Town Design* of 1953, written when he was involved with the design of Harlow New Town, and Gordon Cullen's influential *Townscape* of 1961. Cullen defined town-planning, much like Sitte, as "the art 101
of relationships," and focused his analysis of historic fabrics on serial vision, awareness of human scale, and what he called "content," which partook of mystery, relief, immediacy and other comparable sentiments. A strong emotional element buttressed the authority of the townscape school. This was supplied by a considerable popular movement to reconstruct the war-ravaged old cores in a semblance of their former shape, in defiance of the radical policies of Modernism. The medieval street network was hard to bring back, but where they survived the shells of old buildings—in Warsaw, in Dresden, in Leipzig—were lovingly recreated, or else surviving portions were incorporated into the modern layout, with some poignantly picturesque street effects.

Today, after the terrifying Twenties and Thirties, when the old towns were attacked by Fascist/Nazi *grandezza* on the one hand and Modernist fanaticism on the other, after the Fifties and Sixties with their frenzy of urban renewal that devastated our city centers, we are learning to accept the wholeness of our cities.

CASEBOOK: SERIAL VISION

To walk from one end of the plan to another, at a uniform pace, will provide a sequence of revelations which are suggested in the serial drawings opposite, reading from left to right. Each arrow on the plan represents a drawing. The even progress of travel is illuminated by a series of sudden contrasts and so an impact is made on the eye, bringing the plan to life (like nudging a man who is going to sleep in church). My drawings bear no relation to the place itself; I chose it because it seemed an evocative plan. Note that the slightest deviation in alignment and quite small variations in projections or setbacks on plan have a disproportionally powerful effect in the third dimension.

101 A page from The Concise Townscape *by Gordon Cullen (1971). The British school of townscape theorists rediscovered the perceptual pleasures of a city fabric marked by the complexities of incremental growth. Cullen's notion of "serial vision" represents one attempt to distill design guidelines from pre-modern urbanism.*

It is with this acceptance, once more as in Ur and Thebes, imperial Rome and Haussmann's Paris, of all kinds of urban space, the grand and the incidental, that the arguments of Rob Krier's *Urban Space* (first published in 1975) and Colin Rowe's *Collage City* (1978) capture our imagination, and make us trust in the power of our collective urban heritage.

How are we to use our new understanding as we take our turn in renewing the fateful cities that have served us so long? In the first place, we must renounce all selective prejudice against the past, against this or that environmental order. The orgy of destruction sanctioned by the Modernists, a direct result of their contempt for cultural continuities, should give us no license now to hate back. At the same time, in the history-affirming mood we are determined to enjoy, we should be careful not to revive the artificial dichotomies of urban form—"organic" as against "planned"—by setting up medievalizing and classicizing camps. Sitte, Buls,

Geddes—they all knew better, and so should we. So Krier's warning that there can be no modern resurrection for the evolved organicism of the Middle Ages is misguided.

> There is a widespread and naive view prevalent among art historians as well as the general public that . . . irregular or "organic" architecture is more beautiful than a group of urban buildings planned synchronically. . . . The great popularity of medieval squares is rather more rooted in the fact that, first, they are squares of a type which no modern town could imitate, and second that they are surrounded by fine architecture. Our age cannot compete with the past in this area either.

True. But the same holds for the Renaissance and Baroque past. We cannot bring back the pre-industrial world, any of it, much as we might yearn for it. We should be content with saving as much as we can, to know what we once had—and to add our own pieces sympathetically to this collective artifact, with a feeling and love for the whole. The sympathy has to transcend mere visual appeal. Once again we must question Rob Krier's claim that, in looking at the typology of old streets and squares, we should stay exclusively with form. Symbolism is short-lived, Krier insists: function may change: what is eternal is "the poetic content and esthetic quality of space." But urban form is an incident of history; we are indeed what we have built. On this score it is wiser to hold on to Patrick Geddes' idealized evolutionary historicism, and remember with him that current development in any city must heed the circumstances of history, geography, and the needs of the present. For the rest, if we can only admit "organicism" as an abiding principle of thought, and of design which is a venerable branch of thought, we will be safe from talk of "unplanned" cities—and deprived of the dubious justification to "plan" them.

2 · THE GRID

PREAMBLE

The Pack-Donkey's Way," Le Corbusier decreed in his 1924 book on urbanism, "is responsible for the plan of every continental city." He meant the "organic" patterns reviewed in the last chapter. The pack-donkey "meanders along, meditates a little in his scatter-brained and distracted fashion, he zigzags in order to avoid the larger stones, or to ease the climb, or to gain a little shade; he takes the line of least resistance." That cannot be the way of humans. "Man walks in a straight line because he has a goal and knows where he is going."[1] The British architect Sir William Chambers had said much the same thing two centuries earlier: "on a plain where no [im]pediment obliges . . . it cannot be supposed that men would go by a crooked line, where they could arrive by a straight one."[2]

Man walks in a straight line, so this argument runs, and peels off from it at right angles when he needs to. The frequency of these cross streets is his own decision. Topography has little to do with it, especially on a level site. This simple, rational order of pacing the land—streets set at right angles to one another—is the first step in settlement planning.

102 The southern tip of Manhattan Island, to 34th Street (photographed in 1963). New York City is a demonstration of the effectiveness of the grid as a vehicle for urban expansion. The original Dutch settlement at the point of the island developed around a simple network of lanes and canals. In the late 18th century the city spread northward in a jumble of independently platted grids as meadows and marshes were converted into profitable real estate. The Commissioners' Plan of 1811 standardized the framework of the city by etching a monolithic street grid across the remainder of the island (see Ill. 118). The change can be seen here about two-thirds of the way up the image.

THE NATURE OF RECTILINEAR PLANNING

The grid—or gridiron or checkerboard—is by far the commonest pattern for planned cities in history. It is universal both geographically and chronologically (though its use was not continuous through history). No better urban solution recommends itself as a standard scheme for disparate sites, or as a means for the equal distribution of land or the easy parcelling and selling of real estate. The advantage of straight through-streets for defense has been recognized since Aristotle, and a rectilinear street pattern has also been resorted to in order to keep under watch a restless population. Refugee and prisoner camps are obvious settings. *165*
The grid of the *barrio* of Barceloneta may appear less strict now that the citadel of *152*
Philip V, who conquered Barcelona in 1714, is gone; but the siting of this planned *barrio* on a spit of harbor land outside the citadel's bastions, and the direction of the fifteen straight streets of long, narrow blocks, was an intentional strategy that

permitted surveillance of these "people of the sea" whose old houses had been demolished to make room for the citadel.

Yet, ubiquitous as the grid has always been, it is also much misunderstood, and often treated as if it were one unmodulated idea that requires little discrimination. Quite the contrary, the grid is an exceedingly flexible and diverse system of planning: hence its enormous success. About the only thing that all grids have in common is that their street pattern is orthogonal – that the right angle rules, and street lines in both directions lie parallel to each other. Even this much is not immutable; the
155 system can curve around irregularities on the ground without betraying its basic
Pl.18 logic.

Two singular, and well-preserved, grid schemes from unrelated cultural contexts—Sung China and Colonial America—should demonstrate the wisdom of studying this urban commonplace with particular care.

Suzhou, an ancient Chinese city in southern Jiangsu province, was thoroughly overhauled under the Sung Dynasty, and its extraordinary new design survives on
103 record in a beautiful stone engraving prepared in 1229. The planning is indeed orthogonal, but the overall pattern is of a supple rhythmic complexity free of dogmatic symmetry, continuous straight lines, or uniform divisions into blocks. Yet both in terms of a dimensional order and in the consistent articulation of a spatial structure, the plan was clearly premeditated, and executed according to precise calculations of measurements and levels. The street lines throughout the city were paralleled by a system of canals: 6 canals ran north–south and 14 east–west. Some 300 bridges crossed these canals, artfully grouped at junctions. The double network of transportation was enlivened by frequent cranked intersections and zig-zags. In shape the city was a walled rectangle about 4.5 by 3 miles (ca. 10 by 5 km.). But the frame had projecting sections mindful of the topography, and three corners of the wall were splayed to go with the direction of the water flow in the canals. Five gates were situated asymmetrically around the periphery. The focus of the city was the large walled and moated enclosure of the government complex; it lay southeast of dead center. All public buildings formed sealed compounds of this sort, their high walls reinforced, in the case of the most important institutions, with a band of water. North of the government complex, residential strip blocks provide the only passage of relative uniformity in the plan. They are divided into long narrow plots, with the house fronts lined along a street and the gardens walls at the back lined along a canal.[3]

104 Savannah, in the new colony of Georgia, was laid out in 1733, the unwalled core of a sophisticated regional plan. The city grid was organized into wards, each with its own square measuring some 315 by 270 feet (96 by 82 m.). On the east and west sides of each square, lots were set out for public buildings like churches and stores. The other two sides were divided into forty house lots. Darby Ward, with its Jackson Square, was the first to be built, and became the center of town. "Ward" of course is a political term. The plan was the blueprint of a political system. Ten freeholders formed a tything: four tythings made up a ward whose political officer was the constable. The tythings were grouped in two rows of five house lots, back to back, sharing a lane or alley. Since the houses all faced along east–west streets, the wards were united visually, as they were interdependent socially in the shared use of public buildings and the like. So the inner-oriented ward system around squares also had a street-oriented linear reading. The streets linking the squares and the squares themselves were tree-lined fairly early, while the north–south thoroughfares and the small streets within the wards remained treeless. The ward unit was repeatable, and Savannah extended its primary pattern unvaryingly well into the 19th century.

103 Suzhou (China), rubbing of a stone engraving of the city plan, 1229. The parallel system of streets and canals is accurately depicted, with fainter lines representing waterways. A rope-like pattern just outside the walls represents the surrounding canals.

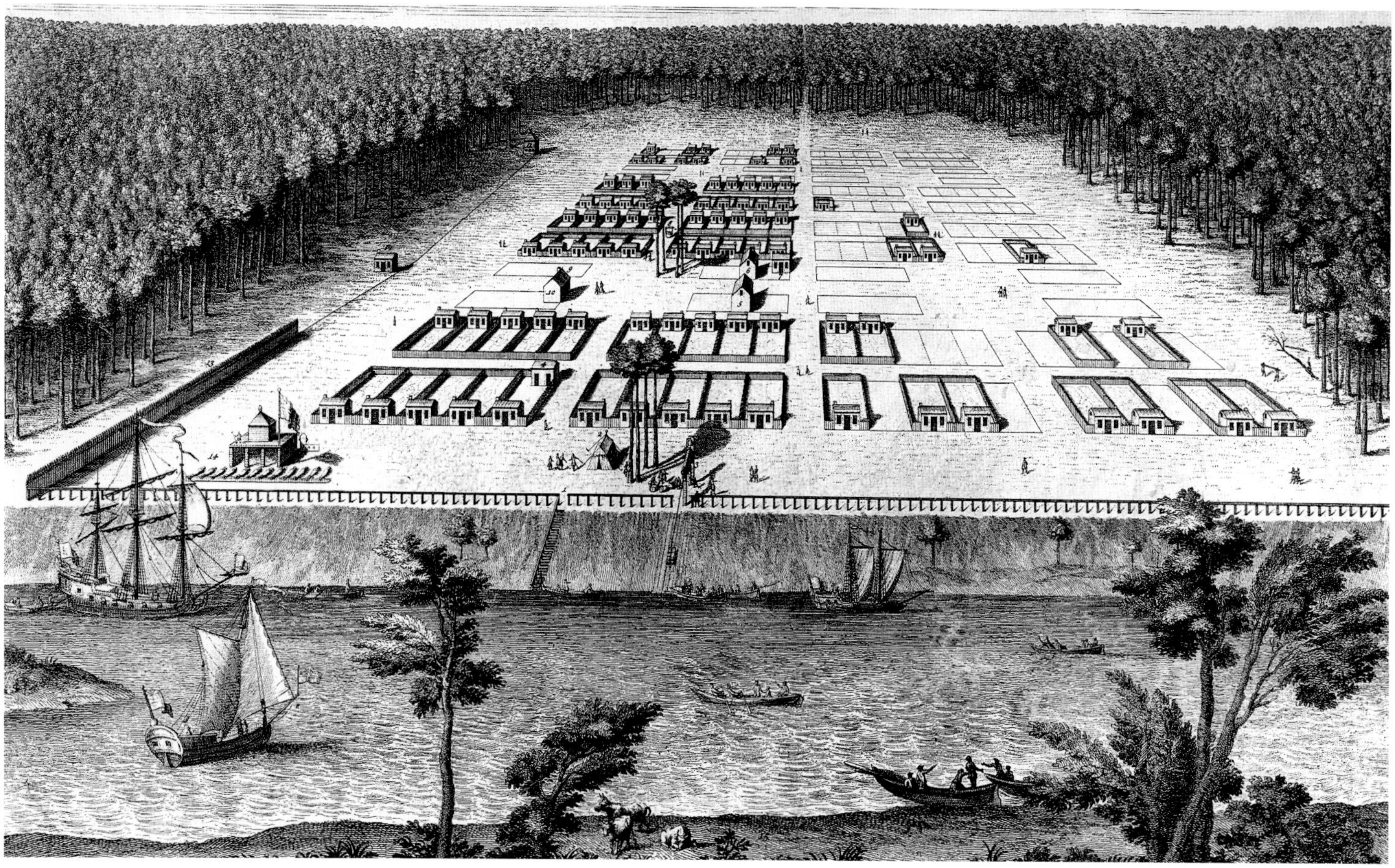

This arbitrary choice of two intricate rectilinear plans points up the scope of the historical analysis that follows. Some of the issues that have to be taken into account are the following:

1. the size and shape of the blocks, and their internal organization
2. the open spaces and their distribution
3. the accommodation of public buildings
4. the nature of the street grid, that is, whether any emphasis is created (by stressing a cross-axial focus, for example), or whether a systematic distinction is made between primary and secondary streets
5. the termination of the grid: open-ended? fitted into a walled precinct? locked into a system of city gates?
6. the relation of the grid to the surrounding country and the features of the topography
7. most critically, the effect of the grid in three dimensions, for example, Manhattan versus a small railroad town

All of these points are not only essential to conduct a discussion of form: they also go to the heart of the motivation of grids, the kind of life the grids are designed to play host to.

In addition, the subject is crowded by impure, composite, or other sorts of hybrid uses of the grid. I might single out:

104 "A View of Savannah [Georgia] as it stood the 29th of March, 1734," engraving by P. Fourdrinier after Peter Gordon. The pattern of Savannah's wards and tythings is evident in the rough pine cottages and fences shown a year after the settlement was founded.

1. loose approximations, where the lines are not strictly parallel or the angles strictly right (a good many of the medieval *bastides* fall into this category) *Pl.16*
2. gridded extensions of "organic" city forms (e.g., Berlin, Çracow, etc.) *253*
3. gridded additions to an original grid plan (e.g., San Francisco, New Orleans, *232* Turin) *134*
4. grids combined with other geometric planning principles, most commonly diagonal avenues, as in the famous instance of L'Enfant's Washington, or in the *208* 18th-century scheme for St. Petersburg
5. the curvilinear grid of the modern residential development

THE GRID AND POLITICS

Generally speaking gridded towns serve most of the purposes of towns *per se*: defense, agricultural development, trade. There is little premeditation in the choice of this street layout beyond the fact that it is, for certain periods in history, the most practical way to plan new cities. This was the case, for example, in the later Middle Ages. So when the philosophers and Church fathers insisted that the founding of cities was the duty of pious sovereigns, the model that stood before them had to be some type of orthogonal planning. Francesco Eiximenes, the Catalan philosopher of the 14th century, in the description of city-form he gives in his *Crestià*, recreates a generic version of the Classical grid.[4]

Simple equations common to surveys of Western urban history—the grid with democratic societies, and the Baroque esthetic with regimes of a centralist structure—are easily overdrawn, not to say fundamentally misleading. They do not account, for one thing, for the extensive use of the grid by absolutist powers like Spain and France in their colonial enterprises.

The grid has served the symbolic needs of the most absolute governments, China and Japan chief among them. The Chang'an of the Tang dynasty ranks among the *174* strictest of grids, and its example was exported to Japan to guide the planning of Heijokyo (modern Nara) in the early 8th century (see below, p. 175). In the first *139* centuries of Chinese imperial history, the administrative capital was an act of total creation; it was a place of enforced residence under political control. The city symbolized power, and was in the service of the needs of power. The orthogonal plan froze the spatial structure to reflect an unalterable hierarchy: it put in isolated urban envelopes the palace precinct, administration, religion, and housing according to class. Trade was of secondary concern and was strictly regimented within the political grid. That is what makes Suzhou fascinating. Its sprightly grid is *103* a vivid record of that slow loosening up of the Chinese administrative city after the 10th century, and the acceptance of commerce and pleasure as constituents of city-form.

These are famous episodes which, because of the remoteness and insularity of their cultures, are treated as exceptions to mainstream urban history. But the political innocence of the grid in the West is a fiction. In the early Greek colonies, for example, the grid, far from being a democratic device employed to assure an equitable allotment of property to all citizens, was the means of perpetuating the privileges of the property-owning class descendent from the original settlers, and bolstering a territorial aristocracy. The first settlers who made the voyage to the site were entitled to equal allocations of land both inside and outside the city walls. These hereditary estates were inalienable; the ruling class strictly discouraged a land market. The estates were huge, as much as $2\frac{1}{2}$ acres (1 ha.) for some families. They were then subdivided by the owner. Within the city, private land could only be used for housing. Any alienation of land, or any agitation for land reform, was severely dealt with, and could be punishable as for murder.[5]

Centuries after Chang'an and Heijo-kyo, the special arrangement of public buildings and other planning devices could still be used to cast a grid unmistakably in a mode that celebrates centralized political structure. Take Brest in Brittany, one of four new port cities sponsored by the administration of Louis XIV as part of a calculated extension of French sea power. The 1680 scheme of Colbert's engineer Sainte-Colombe was "a regimented, unbroken, unembellished grid pattern of blocks," as the student of these cities, Josef W. Konvitz, describes it. Next year Vauban introduced some improvements—specifically, the insertion of a unified composition of church, market and formal residential square, which distinguished this grid as a government creation. By placing this monumental episode between the city and the arsenal, Vauban effectively expressed that the new Brest was a royal initiative—without having to resort to great Baroque diagonals and the other obvious apparatus of absolutist planning. The *place d'armes* of French colonial plantations in America, situated on the waterfront and meant to carry an assortment of institutional buildings (palaces for governor, bishop and intendant, barracks,
6 hospitals, etc.), similarly marked the simple linear grid of New Orleans or St. Louis as a royal undertaking.

By the same token, to say that Holland's use of the grid in the 17th century represents "Calvinist dogmatism and democratic equalitarianism," as E. A. Gutkind does,[6] is to attribute simple political messages to an urban diagram that was largely motivated by matter-of-fact economic considerations. The Dutch furthered a pragmatic bourgeois mercantilist culture, to which Baroque diagonals and formal places marked by equestrian monuments were irrelevant.

The fact is that egalitarianism is no more natural to gridded patterns than to any other urban form. However noble the original premise, inequities will creep in sooner or later. In accordance with the free society they promoted, medieval new towns had honorable intentions about the equality of their parcels. The smaller lots
Pl.16 on the market square in a town like Villeneuve-sur-Lot were intended to make amends for the advantages of this privileged situation. Towns on hilly terrain were so laid out that every settler would encounter the same conditions in relation to the slope. But half-lots materialized soon enough, and select inhabitants were given the chance to build on double or triple lots.

The most persistent belief that urban grids represent an egalitarian system of land distribution is expressed in the context of modern democracies, principally the United States. The point is made regularly that grids, besides offering "simplicity in land surveying, recording, and subsequent ownership transfer," also "favored a fundamental democracy in property market participation. This did not mean that individual wealth could not appropriate considerable property, but rather that the basic initial geometry of land parcels bespoke a simple egalitarianism that invited easy entry into the urban land market."[7] The reality is much less admirable. The ordinary citizen gains easy access to urban land only at a preliminary phase, when cheap rural land is being urbanized through rapid laying out. To the extent that the grid speeds this process and streamlines absentee purchases, it may be considered an equalizing social device. Once the land has been identified with the city, however, this advantage of "the initial geometry of land parcels" evaporates, and even unbuilt lots slip out of common reach. What matters in the long run is not the mystique of grid geometry, but the luck of first ownership.

It may be that the most genuinely egalitarian use of the grid came most naturally to religious confraternities. Two celebrated cases will make the point.

The first is a late outcome of the great schism in the Catholic Church. After the repeal of the Edict of Nantes in 1685, over 200,000 Huguenots fled from France. They settled and founded towns and suburbs in Protestant Germany, and in England, Holland and Switzerland. All the towns had the same form: a regular street grid on a square site, uniform houses of identical shape, size and color, a small church, and identical manufactories. Among the best known Huguenot settlements are Karlshafen near Kassel, and Erlangen in the territory of the Margrave of Ansbach.[8] Here unequivocally the sameness was meant to express the social equality of all inhabitants.

So it was with the Mormons two centuries later. God informed these followers of the Church of Jesus Christ of the Latter Day Saints, through Joseph Smith, that the Second Coming would take place in America at a "perfect time and place," and that their mandate was to prepare a fitting city for this millennial event. In 1833 Smith drew up a scheme for the ideal Mormon city, known as the "Plat of the City of Zion." The Plat was one square mile (2.6 sq. km.) in surface, divided by a grid of streets. The dimensions were ample. All streets were to be 132 feet (40.25 m.) wide, the building blocks 10 to 15 acres (4–6 ha.). The houses, to be built of brick and stone, were to be set back 25 feet (7.6 m.) from the street line. The plan would grow infinitely as the faithful increased. All property would be deeded to the Church, and one would then be assigned an inheritance or stewardship—a farm, a store or shop, a ministerial mission.

The Mormons laid down the Plat of Zion twice (at Caldwell County, Missouri, and Nauvoo, Illinois) before their final stop, in the valley of the Great Salt Lake. Salt *105*
Lake City grew fast, around the Temple erected in one of the central squares. Beyond the monumental checkerboard sheltered by the Wahsatch Mountains stretched the garden and farm lots, also within the lines of an undeviating grid. The houses were built at the corners of their spacious plots, grouped in fours at street intersections. The successor of the square city of the Levites described in Numbers and Leviticus, and of Ezekiel's square city of Jerusalem, spread out in the Territory of Deseret, in the primordial rockscape of Utah. The Latter Day Saints were ready for the Second Coming.[9]

105 Salt Lake City (Utah), detail of a bird's-eye view from the north by E. S. Glover, 1875. The Tabernacle is near the center, with a large curved roof.

"BETTER ORDER" OR ROUTINE

Historically, the grid has served two main purposes. The first is to facilitate orderly settlement, colonization in its broad sense. This involves both the acquisition of distant territory—by the Greeks in Sicily, Spain in the New World—and the settlement of reclaimed or newly opened-up land, as happened in the Spanish peninsula with the *reconquista* or in the American Midwest after about 1800.

The other application of the grid has been as an instrument of modernization, and of contrast to what existed that was not as orderly. Romans tidied up native Iberian or Germanic settlements this way. In the Renaissance, princes extended the fabric of their medieval cities with exemplary gridded quarters; Ercole d'Este's addition
251 to Ferrara designed by Biagio Rossetti at the end of the 15th century is an early example. A royal decree of 1628 provided that all existing towns in Finland were to be reshaped as grids, so that they could be brought into "better order," and all new towns were to be cast in this same mold.[10] Modern Europe used the grid for new quarters next to the native cities of its colonial empires—in Cyprus, Morocco, or Vietnam. Newly established modern nations updated their territory with the help of the grid—witness 19th-century Greece after Independence and the contemporary versions of ancient cities like Corinth or Sparta. The Modern Movement developed its own basic grid, to serve as matrix for a revolutionary new way of planning or replanning cities in different countries and climates. Lucio Costa's plan for Brasilia, the new capital of Brazil, was said by him to be a perfect example of Modernist
153 principles. Chandigarh too, except for the famous group of civic buildings by Le Corbusier, is an anonymous Modernist grid in sharp contrast to the congested
94 tangle of the old cities of India.

The actual motivation for the grid has also varied. It served military arrangements (Roman *castra*, British cantonments), religious covenants, mercantile capitalism (railroad towns), and industrial planning. This versatility of program within what it is possible to see as a simple-minded, uninspired, unvarying formula has brought the grid many detractors. Advocates of the Grand Manner, from Baroque urbanists to the theorists of the City Beautiful movement in the United States, have faulted it for its timidity and its failure to provide distinctive sites for public buildings. Those who defended the visual interest and social richness of the old European towns could think of orthogonal planning only as a symptom of a primitive state of culture, or proof of the impoverishment of the urban experience in modern times. Charles Dickens, during his visit to the United States in 1842, complained that Philadelphia was "distractingly regular. After walking about it for an hour or two, I felt that I would have given the world for a crooked street."[11] Compared to the old core of Belgian cities, the reformist mayor of Brussels Charles Buls wrote in 1893, the modern additions with their streets running parallel or perpendicular to each other have "the character of an artificial crystallization, dry, mathematical."[12] And Camillo Sitte's slightly earlier appraisal of the Jeffersonian gridding of America was none too kind:

> This [division] is obviously due to the fact that the terrain was not well-known at the time and its future development could not be predicted, since America lacked a past, had no history, and did not yet signify anything else in the civilization of mankind but so many square miles of land. For America, Australia, and other unopened lands the gridiron plan may for the time being still suffice. Wherever people are concerned merely with colonizing land, live only for earning money and earn money only in order to live, it may be appropriate to pack people into blocks of buildings like herring in a barrel.[13]

This prejudice against the grid was nurtured by American planners and scholars in more recent days. The grid was an easy target for Garden City apologists like Lewis Mumford, for formalist urban historians who could appreciate the beauty of Savannah's pattern but saw no merit in the mean layouts of speculative towns, and for social historians eager to make the grid synonymous with greed and the unfeeling, mechanized production of mock-communities.

But of course to blame the grid for the shallowness and callousness of urban experience is surely to miss the point. Any grid holds the potential to become a beautiful city over time depending on how it is fleshed out. The architect, the social planner, the politician, the residents themselves have their chance once the two-dimensional diagram is in place. If grids serve up a routinized, alienating urban setting, it is largely because of what was allowed to happen or was not encouraged to happen after the initial lines were drawn.[14] Without collective control even model grids like Savannah's will quickly squander their initial advantages. With care and imagination, the initial sameness of the most prosaic of grids may become the matrix within which interest, diversity, and human richness can be provided for. And of course the original intention for the grid can itself ensure against tedium and trivialization. Against the profit-mongering of speculative towns we can pit communitarian experiments. The grids which Mormons planted along the trail of their persecution, though on paper no more enticing than the speculative diagrams of land development and railroad companies, were resonant with the force of faith. Perhaps it is indeed time to stop condemning the grid plan out of hand as "dull-witted, unesthetic, and somehow speaking of a lower use of man's intellect," and to see it rather as "one of the great inventions of the human mind."[15]

HISTORICAL REVIEW

Who invented the grid? Given the chapter's preamble, this is perhaps an unnecessary question; it is rather like asking who invented the right angle, that is geometry, and in fact that word carries in it the seeds of the grid's popularity, indeed inevitability. Geometry is a theory of space, and of figures in space; it is an order of lines and angles, and in terms of city-making one of the simplest ways of making order is to have horizontal and vertical coordinates in orthogonal relationship to one another. But geometry, from the Greek word *geometria*, means literally "earth measurement." So the grid applies to country and town, to fields and streets, and at its most basic it divides an undifferentiated stretch of land into regular, measured plots.

THE GRID IN THE ANCIENT WORLD

In both the urban and rural spheres, the Egyptians had a venerable tradition. The Old Kingdom worker villages at places like Giza had primitive grids, because that is the best and quickest way to organize a homogeneous population with a single social purpose. As for the field division of the arable Black Land on either side of the Nile, re-established after every flood, orthogonal planning came naturally because the strip was featureless: the river was a great linear axis running north–south and everything had to run alongside it or at right angles to it, in the direction of the rising and setting sun.

The genuine urban grid makes its appearance in pre-Classical antiquity in at least two regions of the ancient world. Mohenjo Daro and Harappa in the Indus Valley,

which came to a mysterious end about 1500 BC, had a citadel on the western edge of town and blocks of roughly equal size. A distinction was made between principal streets (as much as 20 to 30 feet—6 to 9 m.—wide) and the alleys onto which the houses looked. A carry-over of this planning tradition into the later phases of Indian history cannot be demonstrated. There is precise information, however, about the theoretical design of Hindu cities on a modular grid in texts like the *Manasara*, a section of the *Silpa Shastra*, probably of the first century BC but reliant on much earlier sources; and as far back as 1000 BC *Vastuvidya*, the occult doctrines of city-
181 making and architecture, provided for geometric urban mandalas that included rectilinear formulas.

The other archaeological region is Mesopotamia and Assyria, cities like Babylon and Borsippa. It seems certain that a trend toward regular cities started from the 9th century BC onward in Assyrian dominions, but at Babylon the grid goes back to the time of Hammurabi about 2000 BC even though the visible street pattern that has been recovered dates back only to Nebuchadnezzar in the 6th century BC. Herodotus describes Babylon as "intersected by straight streets, some parallel and some at right angles to the river." Early grids in this part of the ancient world include that for Megiddo II, after the Assyrian conquest, which can be dated at 915 or 732 BC.[16]

Yet none of these early uses of the grid which have left their mark can be called a coordinated system: public and residential buildings have not been worked out together, and blocks have no coherent logic except insofar as this is determined from inside out, from an inner court and the rooms around it, until the public space of streets and alleys is reached. So planning here actually consists only of laying out the main streets, and allowing for the formal arrangement of public complexes like temples and palaces. The real achievement is Chinese and Greek. It was in these two unrelated cultures that the city itself became the formal planning unit, within which individual buildings must find their appropriate place.

The Chinese grid was a political diagram, as we saw, reserved for administrative capitals. The known instances are late, but ritual formulas for the laying out of planned imperial cities on a rectangular basis existed in the late 1st millennium BC. (See "The City as Diagram," below, pp. 174–75.) The Greek use, on the other hand, was less compulsive, more pragmatic, even though it was not wholly without political intent.

The Greeks seem to have latched on to the grid in their colonizing efforts as early as the 7th century BC. Colony is *apoike* in Greek, an emigration, an "away-home," not a mere tributary like the modern colonial cities of the Western powers. If there was an increase in an urban population beyond what the countryside could bear, a colony was sent out. So Corinth spawned Syracuse in Sicily, and Syracuse spawned Acrae and Camarina in an ever westward expansion. The population of these cities was usually small, about 5,000. By 600 BC, in the western half of the Mediterranean, Greece was colonizing what is now southern France, Sicily and southern Italy, Libya, and Spain. Here, in the colonies, there was no prior Greek village structure that had to be respected, no ancient Greek sanctities. So there was no justification for the making of "organic" cities through synoecism or other processes of assimilation, as had been the case in the homeland. Prior land division did not have to be respected. In the colonies the land was culturally and ritually blank—from the Greek point of view of course. You brought your gods and their cults, and institutions like the agora, that premier symbol of self-governance, and the concept of the *polis* (city-state) itself.

These new lands were very different from mainland Greece and the Aegean islands. There were smooth, long beaches, ample plains. Still, in the beginning, the implanted cities had a rather loose arrangement, with public space set aside for the temples and the agora, and the remaining land inside the walls assigned to the first generation of settlers. By the 7th century the grid makes its appearance as a planning device in places like Smyrna and Olbia in the East (obviously not independently of prior Near Eastern example) and in some of the Sicilian colonies, and it signals a major reorganization of these first estates. The change from a random to an orthogonal system can be seen in Megara Hyblaea on the east coast of Sicily.

The division of the Greek grid was by strips rather than blocks, and the city walls wrapped themselves loosely around it. A major rethinking of these early layouts, which were based on practical surveying methods, came with Hippodamus of Miletus in the 5th century BC. Aristotle writes that Hippodamus discovered "the divisioning of cities," that he laid out the Athenian port city of Piraeus, and that "he was the first man of those not actually involved in politics to make proposals about the best form of constitution." Aristotle, describing the ideal city, endorses this urban blueprint of the Miletian thinker when he says, "The arrangement of private houses is more pleasant and convenient for general purposes if it is clearcut, in the modern Hippodamean fashion."[17] Now since Hippodamus could not have "invented" the grid, one possible interpretation of Aristotle's words is that he advocated a special instance of it (see below, p. 127), and combined it with a social theory of urbanism. Indeed Hippodamus, it would seem, proposed a political system "whereby the population of the town was divided into three classes—craftsmen, farmers, and soldiers—and the land divided into three portions, the first sacred, the second public (to support the soldiers), and the third private (to be owned by the farmers)."[18] The master plan of Hippodamus's home town of Miletus envisaged a *108*
population much larger than his prescription of 10,000. The total enclosed urban area is 250 acres (ca. 100 ha.), allowing for orderly growth. This too is different from pre-Hippodamian practice where all the land of a colony was divided and distributed by the original team, and later arrivals simply had to do without.

The 5th century BC was a very active period of city-making for Greeks. Old cities razed during the Persian Wars, including Miletus, needed to be rebuilt, and new colonies were founded for political and commercial reasons. The revitalized grid of Hippodamus spoke to this need. By the next century the popularity of the grid was at its peak. It was applied even to unsuitable terrain, as at Priene, laid out on a steep *120,*
slope. And with Alexander's conquests, the grid spread all over the ancient world as *214*
far as Persia and Mesopotamia.

Two categories of new towns were now initiated: *katoichiai*, which were military settlements (e.g., Dura Europos), and *kleruchiai*, legitimate offspring of mother cities. Frequently the preferred sites were along old trade routes or in places with commercially viable harbors. There is some evidence to support R. E. Wycherley's reference to "the mass production of new hellenistic cities": Antioch, its port Seleucia Pieria, Apamea and Laodicea—all founded by Seleucus I ca. 300—have blocks of the same size, roughly 367 by 190 feet (112 by 58 m.).[19]

The new towns could at times be much bigger than anything Greeks were used to. Seleucia Pieria, for example, with a circuit of walls that exceeded 6 miles (10 km.), was larger even than Athens. Another Seleucia, on the Tigris, was said by Pliny to have 600,000 people. This Greek grid with its rational subdivisions was alien to the old cultures overwhelmed by Alexander. The people reverted to their pre-Greek habits as soon as the Hellenistic episode was over, and the grids were suitably remade. The tidy subdivision of blocks came undone, the open space of agoras was taken over by stalls and small shops. The transformation of Dura Europos on the *106,*
Syrian frontier is an excellent instance of this process. *107*

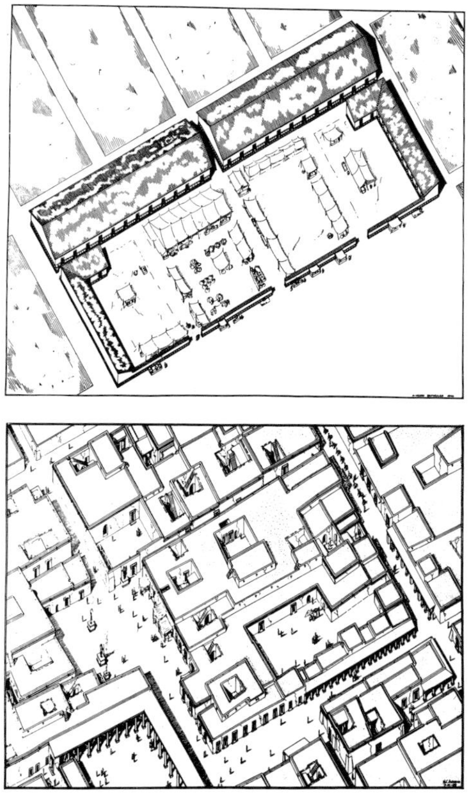

106, 107 Market at Dura Europos (Syria), as first built, ca. 300 BC, and as it appeared in AD 250. The agora of the Hellenistic colony occupied the equivalent of four of the city's blocks. During centuries of occupation the city center lost its formally configured public space, which was replaced by the dense warren of a bazaar. (After Ward-Perkins)

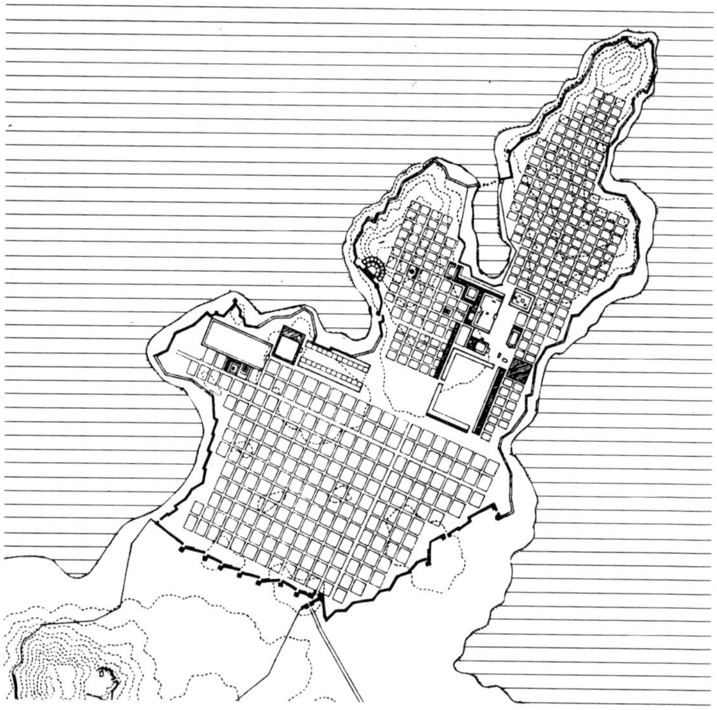

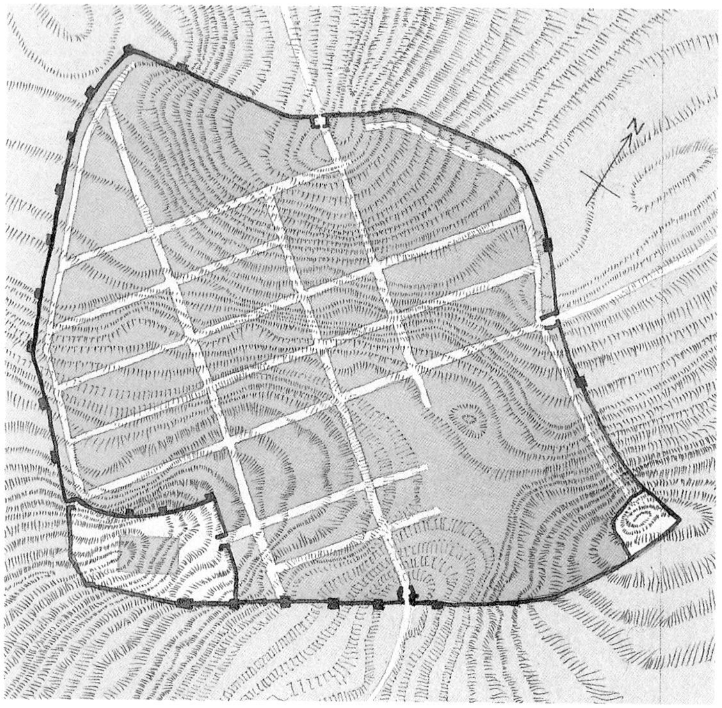

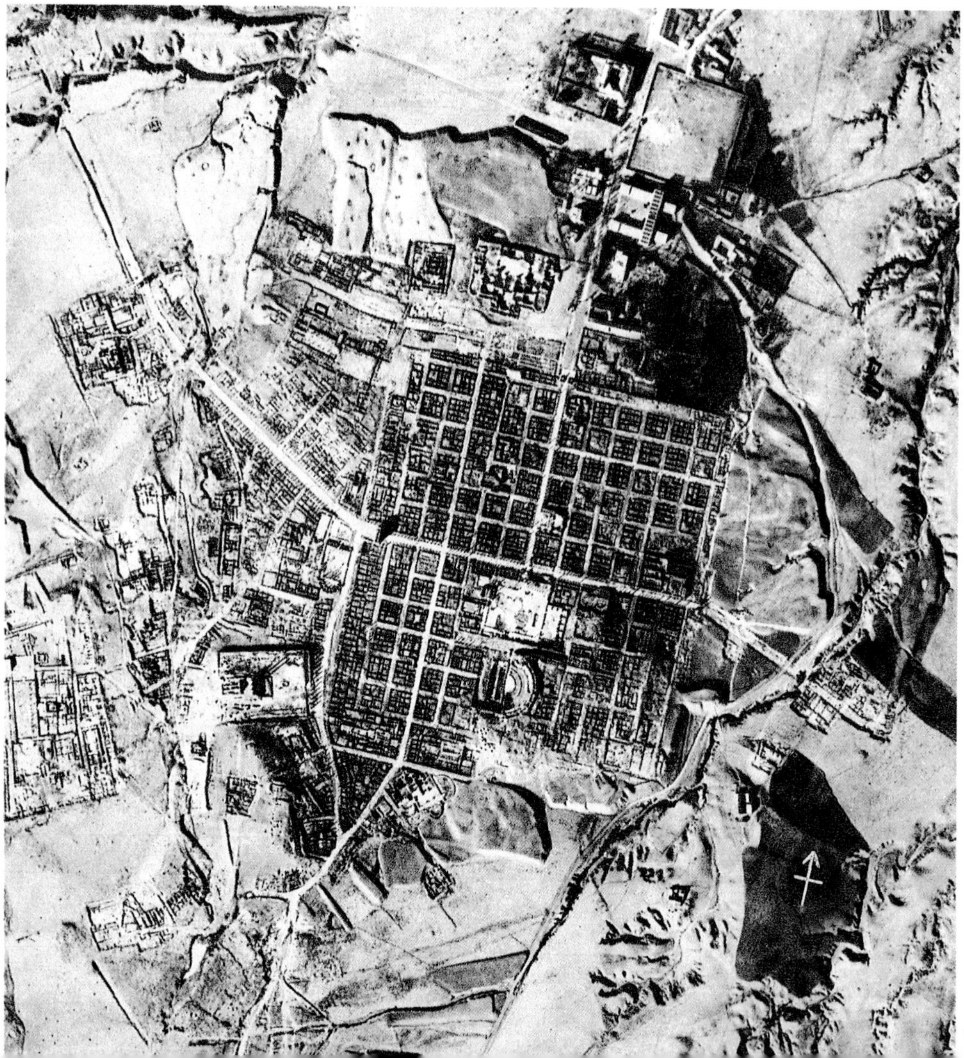

108 above left *A Greek grid: Miletus (Turkey), as refounded after the Persian sack of 479 BC.*

109 above *An early Roman grid: Cosa (Italy), founded in 273 BC to control the coastline north of Rome. Cosa's layout is an ingenious compromise between the rigorous topography of a defensive hilltop site and the advantages of an orthogonal street plan. The forum lay in the open space bottom right.*

110 left *The Roman grid at its most perfect, with square blocks and rectilinear enclosure: Timgad (Algeria), founded in AD 100. Just below the central crossroads are the forum—around which the grid changes scale—and the amphitheater. (The original layout soon proved inadequate for the colony's growing population. Defensive walls were demolished and replaced with a circuit of streets, encouraging the erratic pattern of urban sprawl that later enveloped the town.)*

Turning to the Roman world, the long tradition of gridded towns there, and the
progressively rigid application of the scheme, can be dramatized with a comparison
between Cosa, founded in 273 BC, and Timgad (Thamugadi, Algeria), founded in
100 AD for a colony of military veterans. Cosa was the first of the early Italian 109
colonies (*coloniae*) of the 3rd and 2nd centuries BC. The word *colonia* derives from
colo, *colere*, meaning "to farm"; a *colonus* is a farmer. One purpose of Roman
colonies was settling veterans of wars; the other was control of the conquered
territory. Cosa, situated on the summit of a rocky promontory, heeds the
topography to the extent that the *arx* or capitol is placed at the highest point, in the
south, and the forum in the most level spot near the southeast gate. The strip blocks
and loose-fitting city walls conform to the Greek model.

But it was when, in their systematic conquest of Italy, the Romans pushed out of
the mountains of the central region and onto the broad plains of the Po Valley that
Greek and Etruscan precedent was superseded. By the time of Pavia and Verona, 111
both founded in 89 BC, and Aosta (25 BC), the Roman grid had developed its own
identity—a more unitary plan with large square blocks, a tight mural frame locked
into the lines of the grid, and the forum placed on or beside the crossing of two major
axes. As the young empire spread outward in the 1st century AD, many gridded
towns were planted at critical sites in Gaul, Britain and North Africa. Timgad is one 110
of the purest in form—and the best preserved. The grid of Timgad measures about
380 yards (355 m.) on each side. It consists of four parts of 36 blocks each, 144 blocks
in all, of which 11 are eaten up by the forum, 6 by the theater and 8 by the baths.

111 Verona (Italy). The classic square-block plan of the Roman settlement founded in 89 BC can still be made out in the city today. In the center, the spindle-shaped Piazza Erbe marks the site of the forum. The oval amphitheater lay outside the walls. Typically, the blocks have often been joined together in pairs (cf. pp. 48–51, 147).

When new public buildings were needed, they developed outside the grid. Indeed, the Roman imperial city in its final two centuries relaxed into a much more flexible, impure orthogonality (described in "The Grand Manner", below).

The role of the military is extremely important. It was the growth of a professional army, stationed permanently overseas, that led to the establishment of a
164 standardized fort plan, and this in turn significantly influenced the design of new provincial cities during the late 1st century BC and the 1st century AD. The reverse is sometimes also argued—that the inspiration of these legionary camps must have come from the layout of early cities which preceded them. Polybius, writing in the 2nd century BC, suggests as much when he describes the Roman camp as "a square, with streets and other constructions regularly planned like a town."[20] At any rate, there is a similarity, as is evident in details of city plans like those of Aosta and Turin. Evidence of direct transference is also forthcoming, for example the recent discovery that at least three Roman military colonies in Britain—Colchester, Gloucester, and Lincoln—were converted from antecedent fortresses, retaining the same street alignments.

To the Romans of the late Republic and the early Empire, the grid represented the New Order. It was not wasted on small local towns in the provinces, which could remain "organic." But colonies, capitals of provinces (*municipia*), and capitals of *civitates* where the administration of each Gallic nation was centralized had to be gridded. In Britain the new towns started out as grids; in Gaul, the early free-form settlements of the Roman occupation were straightened out later at the cost of much clearing and levelling.[21]

As a rule, town planting was the State's prerogative, and its responsibility as part of broad administrative policy. These official plans were straightforward, and sometimes standardized. Verona and Pavia had identical grids, and blocks of equal size. Where private benefactors or local authorities became involved, cities were rarely contented with such prosaic regularity. The Emperor Septimius Severus spared neither purse nor talent to rebuild the city of Leptis Magna, his place of birth in North Africa. When his architects were done, the two extant gridded units had been welded together and extended in ingenious improvisations.

NEW TOWNS IN THE MIDDLE AGES

At the end of the Classical world we lose track of the grid for several centuries. The old gridded Greco-Roman cities lose their physical integrity or disappear altogether. The theory that in England the Wessex kings used a simple grid in the setting out of their principal *burhs* is problematical. When orthogonal planning definitively returns in Europe, it is from about 1100 on, and in two different contexts. One is the creation of new towns; the other is the use of the grid for extensions of earlier, mostly "organic" city forms, for example Massa Marittima, or the quarter of Borgo Ognissanti in Florence developed by the Cistercian abbey of S. Salvatore at Settimo in 1320–35. At Massa Marittima, the extension dates from about 1228; it is marked by a tower with an inscription that says "principium et decus nove urbis" (new foundation and ornament of the city). At about the same time comes the expansion of Fano and Gubbio, and the quarter north of the traders' suburb at Troyes. This process creates a big new scale compared to the straggled medieval fabric.

The new towns were located in three general areas of Europe:

1. Southern France, northern Spain, England and Wales. Here we find towns founded by the royal houses, by powerful noblemen like Alphonse de Poitiers, count

112 Aigues-Mortes (France). Founded as a stronghold from which to launch expeditions to the Holy Land, Aigues-Mortes was the port from which two disastrous crusades were dispatched: those of 1248 and 1270. As the city walls rose, financed by royal subventions, the economy boomed and houses filled the new town's skewed grid. But with waning enthusiasm for crusades and the silting up of the town harbor, Aigues-Mortes drifted into obsolescence and decay.

of Toulouse, and by other lords and abbots. In France especially, it came to be expected of a lord of the first rank that in addition to his castle, monastery, and hunting ground, he would be the owner of a new town or *bastide*. (The term derives from medieval French *bastir*, to build; the Latin origin is *terrae bastitae*, rural landholdings with built-up property.) Defense, agriculture and trade were the motivation, and the towns were usually an agency of settlement on land reclaimed from the forest or otherwise cleared, and of repopulation. In Spain these towns were linked with the readjustments required of the Christian kings in the process of the *reconquista*. Southwestern France, especially the area on either side of the Garonne Valley, was being contested all through the 12th and 13th centuries between the French king and his vassal the count of Toulouse on the one hand and the English king on the other. Both sides planted *bastides* to secure their claims. In the early 13th century the crusade against the Albigensian heretics (1208–28) was followed by town-planting intended to bring in right-thinking inhabitants to offset this native movement. Aigues-Mortes, on flat marshy land by the Mediterranean, founded by Louis IX (St. Louis) in the 1240s in connection with the Seventh Crusade, is a famous example.

124
112

2. Switzerland, Austria, and Germany east of the Elbe. This includes the towns of the
Pl.18 dukes of Zähringen, imperial towns under the patronage of the Holy Roman Emperor himself or his lieutenants, and settlements founded by the crusading
113 Teutonic Knights in the eastern expansion of Germany. By and large, this area had the largest number, and the most carefully planned, new towns.

3. New towns founded by the city-states of Italy. In this category, a prime goal was to disengage serfs and village folk from allegiance to landed magnates and readjust their loyalties to the political system of the city-states. Among these were Novara (which founded Borgomanero in the first third of the 13th century), Siena (Montereggioni), Lucca (Camaiore, Pietrasanta), and Florence (see below, p. 128).

113 Chełmno (Poland). A straight street is terminated by a Dominican church and flanked by a 19th-century Gothic Revival watertower in this new town founded in the 13th century by the Teutonic Knights.

There must have been perhaps as many as one thousand new towns in all three areas by the later Middle Ages, which would more than double the number of extant towns in Europe. And the catalogue is not exhaustive. There were *bastides* in the Netherlands as well, for example, all of a rather late date. They included Vianen,
133 Culemborg, Montfort and Helmond, belonging to a category where the town is supplementary to the castle, as was the case with the towns built by Edward I in
50 Wales, while others were sited independently of the castle—Elburg, Naarden, Kortgene—as was the common practice in England and France. There is reason to believe that it was Count Floris V of Holland (1256–96) who, having witnessed the town-building activities of St. Louis, Alphonse de Poitiers, and Edward I of England, initiated the series of Dutch *bastides* with Brouwershaven and Arnemuiden in the Zeeland islands, both in the 1280s.[22]

In all this activity, even before the famous proto-Renaissance of Florence, there was some awareness that with the newly planted towns one was reviving Classical precedent. The Emperor Frederick II made specific mention of this revival in his inauguration in 1247 of Vittoria, near Parma in Italy, and he traced the perimeter of the town with a plough in imitation of the *sulcus primigenius* of the Etruscan/Roman town-founding ritual. But this was more a literary than a physical inspiration, since there were no pure Roman grids around to emulate. We are told that, during an imprisonment, one of the Zähringer dukes studied the plan of Cologne, which had preserved parts of its Roman layout, but it is hard to assess the importance of this precedent on the subsequent town-planning activities of the Duke, who, after his release, founded Freiburg-im-Breisgau (1119), Murten, and Rottweil (1120).

Defensive and economic policies may account for *bastides*, but the encouragement of religion is a factor that cannot be ignored. The princely obligation to found cities is a recurrent theme in medieval literature. The central text must be Thomas Aquinas, from about 1270: "The city is the perfect community . . . and building cities is the duty of kings." The first part of this, the exaltation of the life of the city, had a long medieval history since Isidore of Seville (6th–7th century) and Hrabanus Maurus (8th–9th century).[23] But Thomas goes further and argues that, for a variety of reasons, city life is preferable to all other modes of living. Communal existence makes it possible to extend help to one another, and to share mental tasks, with one person making discoveries in medicine and others in other things. But above all city living leads to virtuous living; cities are necessary for the virtuous life, which means the knowledge of God. Since the role of Christian kings is to lead people to God, they must build cities. "The most powerful nations and the most illustrious kings acquired no better glory than comes of founding new cities, or associating their names to cities already founded by others."[24] The process of founding a town is the royal equivalent of the creation of the world, and so the prince must make all the important decisions: choose the site, assign places to the church, the tribunals, and industry, and group inhabitants by occupation. This pious act of kings has the potential of creating the ideal city. Thomas himself did not talk about the shape of this city; he might have if his book on rulers, *De regimine principum*, had not been left unfinished. He was familiar with the passage about Hippodamus through Aristotle, his principal inspiration, and it is not unlikely that he would have used it as his source on this subject as well.[25]

THE RENAISSANCE IN EUROPE

The two centuries between 1500 and 1700 in Europe are not primarily noteworthy for new towns. Urban growth was concentrated in large cities and in cities that became large, and the grid, now given the Renaissance *imprimatur*, appears regularly in extensions of extant towns. A few examples of new settlements are those founded in the early 16th century in the devastated countryside of southern France between Grasse and Nice, which could not recover from the Black Death and its turbulent aftermath, by the Benedictine abbey of St.-Honorat of Lérins—Vallauris (1501), Mouans-Sartoux (1504), and Valbonne (1519). Vitry-le-François on the Marne, built for François I from 1545 onward, shows the grid locked in the embrace of the new bastioned wall developed in response to a war technology based on artillery.

The only major fields of new plantations in these two centuries, 1500–1700, were Sicily, Scandinavia, and the New World. In Sicily scores of feudal towns were laid out by aristocrats who owned land in remote unsettled areas in order to lure a resident peasant population there, e.g. Vittoria (1607) and Montevego (1640). Between 1620 and 1650 alone 25 such towns were founded. Mostly, these had a simple grid plan with a single large open space in the middle. Occasionally, and especially in the rebuilding of old towns after the devastating earthquake of 1693, a more adventurous grid scheme, inspired by projects in a new crop of architectural treatises, would be attempted.

City-making in Scandinavia during the 17th century is also a story of epic proportions, involving the bitter rivalry of Denmark and Sweden over trade in the Baltic and the North Sea. Many of the new towns were ports intended to capture trade, and develop an economic base for the two empires; others were defensive outposts. Under Christian IV (1588–1648) Denmark's sphere of dominion took in Norway, part of Schleswig-Holstein, and Scania, the southernmost province of modern Sweden. Under Gustavus II Adolphus and his successors Queen Christina and Charles XII (d. 1718), the Swedish Baltic empire pushed far into German, Russian and Finnish provinces. So the program of defense affected all new towns, since these were often in alien territory and were strongly resisted by the native population.

Around 1600 systems of bastioned curtains improved over several decades were universally subscribed to. This meant that cities, old and new, were encased in an
elaborate, often star-shaped, ring of pointed low-spreading bastions with an *20*
enormous physical reach. Within this ring, the vast majority of the new towns were straightforward grids; a few towns adopted radial-concentric street systems inspired
by Renaissance projects of ideal cities like Filarete's Sforzinda, as subsequently *183*
reinterpreted by military engineers for the artillery age. In Scandinavia, the initial impetus was to stay with the simpler, practical grid.

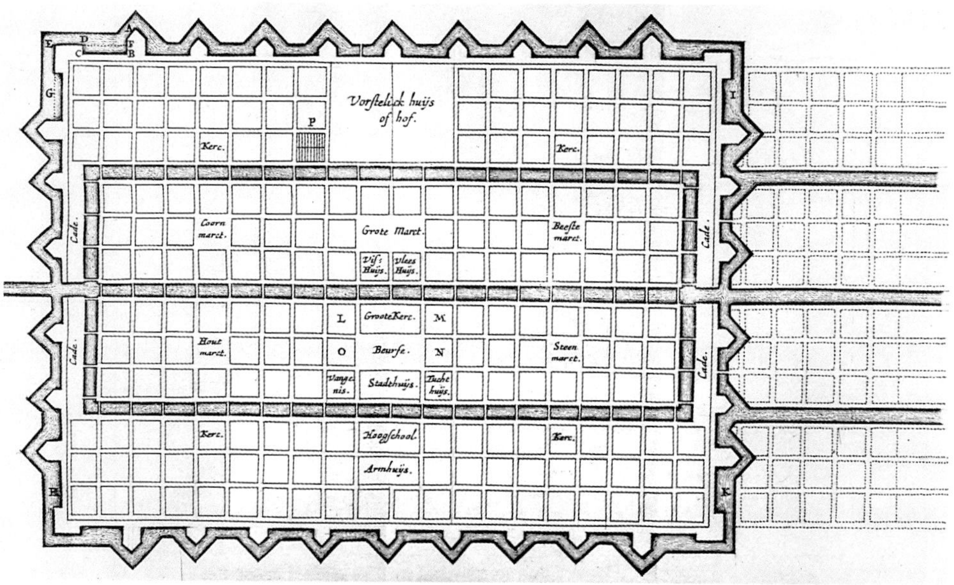

114 Ideal port city plan by Simon Stevin, 1590. The formal geometries of Renaissance urban theory are wed to Dutch pragmatism in Stevin's gridiron plan. Canals are woven into the fabric of the city for both economic and defensive purposes. The palace compound along with important public buildings and their plazas occupy a central band of blocks, while neighborhood churches and markets are uniformly disposed through the city. Provisions for expansion are also demonstrated in an extension of the matrix of streets and canals, to the right.

The main urban theorist of the North was Simon Stevin (1548–1620) of the Netherlands. His specialty was the planning of port cities; his models were real cities
135 like Antwerp and Amsterdam. The key to their prosperity was the waterfront; and canals were clearly the way to stretch out the commercial advantages of the actual
114 harbor. So Stevin settled for an extendable grid bounded by canal/walls and cut through by several interconnected longitudinal canal streets that could be continued beyond the walls. In this way the grid could stretch out on new annexed land, and suburbs could be strapped rationally to the city center.

Dutch practice influenced the city-making of Denmark and Sweden on either side of the Sund Strait. The new district of Copenhagen, Christianshavn, begun about 1640, was very much in the Stevin mold. The Swedish campaign for new port cities began in the 1620s under Gustavus II Adolphus, who had briefly corresponded with Stevin. Gothenburg, the first major Swedish site, followed Stevin's prescriptions, and so did the extension of Jönköping.

Then Swedish planners made an about-face. Even as early as the 1640s, when Stockholm was being replanned, canals were deliberately omitted from the gridded designs because they called to mind Dutch mercantilism, and were therefore unsuitable for the royal capital. Thereafter the fashion was for ideal plans of radial-concentric form. In the royal Swedish circle Eric Dahlberg started the trend after traveling in Italy in the 1650s; Nicodemus Tessin the Younger visited France in the 1670s, and embraced the new urban design of the French Baroque at the expense of the practical Dutch style. Examples of their work are the projects for the towns of Landskrona, Karlskrona, and Karlsborg.

By this time the new esthetic of Baroque urbanism was transforming European capitals. It was based on the dynamism of the diagonal, and came to be associated with absolutist states. In the debates for the rebuilding of London after the Great Fire of 1666, the exuberant new Baroque esthetic and the trustworthy grid clashed in public. On the one side there were the urban constellations of Wren and John Evelyn, on the other the grids punctuated by squares of people like Richard Newcourt, which Mark Girouard characterizes as the product of the land surveyor and the real estate dealer, "easy to lay out and easy to sell."[26]

But there is also the issue of message. When we bemoan the obtuseness of the English in missing the chance to have a great plan like Wren's or Evelyn's for their capital, we cannot altogether set aside the question of appropriateness—the fact that Baroque city-form had developed connotations of political centrality, and that the place of the king in the English scheme of things was very much in the public mind during those decades of the later 17th century. Besides, the near impregnable structure of private ownership under English law doomed any project for the wholesale remaking of the City.

PASSAGE TO AMERICA

More than one hundred years later, a similar clash over the design of Washington,
D.C., also centered on the question of appropriateness. There was Jefferson's
famous little grid, and L'Enfant's fury over its timidity (see below, p. 209). The grid 209
lost, and the Frenchman's splendid imperialist diagram won the day. But Jefferson's 208
victory was bigger, for he went on to subject the rest of the nation to a relentless
gridding which permanently affected the structure of American space. 132

The grid had long been at home in colonial America. The pert river grids of New
France like St. Louis or New Orleans are to be contrasted to the parish towns of the 6
St. Lawrence River which resisted the centralizing efforts of Paris officialdom, and assumed rather a carefree look. Even with clear attempts at directing the growth of cities like Quebec and Montreal, the lower towns by the river still demonstrate a flexible adaptation of stretches of straight line to topography, and a varied use of blocks.

The Spanish episode also has a formal and a casual side. The first cities on the coast of Colombia were unplanned, for example. But soon the grid took over and
remained the norm. The first planned settlement, Santo Domingo (Hispaniola) in 115
the West Indies, was laid out in 1493 on a more or less regular grid pattern. The most important cities of South America—Quito, Lima, Buenos Aires, Bogotá, Santiago

115 The Laws of the Indies *grid as a port city: Santo Domingo (Dominican Republic) in 1586, shown under siege by the English troops of Sir Francis Drake.*

116 The Laws of the Indies *grid as a farming town: a colonial village in Peru's Colca River Valley.*

de Chile, Valparaiso—were all founded in the decade between 1534 and 1544. Town building went on into the 18th century when the *pueblos* of San Antonio in Texas, 119 Galvez in Louisiana, and San Jose and Los Angeles in California were laid out. Dozens of provincial capitals, mining and processing towns, and Indian settlements were planted during the first century or so. The plan did not change, regardless of the function of the town. Port cities like Cartagena (Colombia) were laid out in the same way as agricultural centers. As Konvitz put it, Spain's "legalistic, programmatic approach to city planning avoided particular distinctions among cities and identified the functional aspects of planning with its administrative control, and, so, with uniformity."[27]

Officially the towns in New Spain, called *pueblos* or *villas*, were designed according to directives emanating from the Spanish court. In 1573 these were collected under Philip II in a document known as the *Laws of the Indies*, a genuine product of Renaissance thought. Its inspiration is ultimately the Classical treatise of Vitruvius, which had been translated into Spanish first in 1526, with a Latin edition dedicated to Philip being published in 1582. But it is surely also legitimate to see these American towns as a continuation of the long medieval history of *bastides*. From Spain itself, the planners in America retained the division into *barrios* (administrative precincts or wards), the religious and social life of these *barrios*, each with its own chapel, and the naming of streets on the basis of occupation and guild activities. Whether anything was contributed by the example of native pre-Columbian urbanism is an unresolved debate. The plan of Tenochtitlán, the great Aztec

predecessor of Mexico City, had a cross-axial structure with a central plaza, but the *Pl.7*
shape of its residential blocks is uncertain. The orthogonality of pre-Inca Chanchan on the Peruvian coast was a matter of large rectangular citadel-compounds of varying size assembled with no transparent overall design. The same "intersquared" plan characterizes the Inca capital of Cuzco, but other Inca cities come closer to a regular gridded layout. At Ollantaytambo rectangular blocks of roughly equal size are bisected transversely by a solid wall into identical halves.[28]

The grid with two main axes intersecting, and the large public square at the *116*
intersection, were standard. This *plaza* is the key to the entire settlement; its size regulated the makeup of the grid. The blocks immediately surrounding the plaza were divided into four equal sections (*solares*) and assigned to the leading settlers. Sometimes the blocks were oriented with their corners facing the cardinal points at such an angle that prevailing winds might not sweep the length of the town—as recommended by Vitruvius.

The *Laws of the Indies* did not affect two other types of settlements: the settlements for Indians—the *reducciones* of the Jesuits, the missions of the Mendicant fathers—and the *presidios* or military establishments. These too, however, followed a rectilinear plan more often than not. The distinction between the three types of communities—*pueblos*, *presidios*, and Indian towns—often disappeared in practice, especially after 1600.

The colonizing efforts of England in the New World also made use of the grid. In New England, which was township-oriented from the start and where the land was surveyed and delimited ahead of settling, the strict grid pattern is almost unknown. New Haven's crystalline plan of nine equal square blocks from which issued an *117*

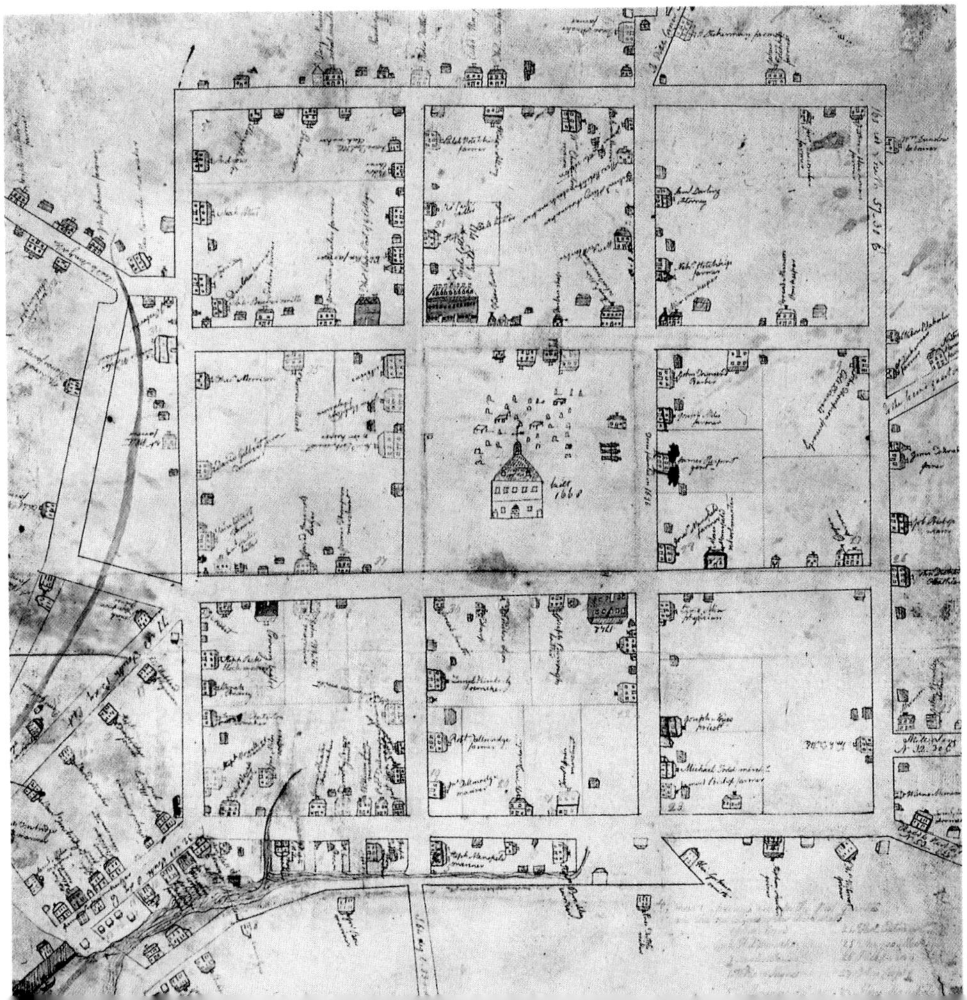

117 New Haven (Connecticut), plan drawn by James Wadsworth, 1748.

array of straight radial roads, with a tenth "tail" block linking up with the harbor, was an exception. The plan—the town was settled in 1638—may have been made in advance in London, or in Boston where the company first landed. It might be explained by the ambition of the colony, which set out to be an independent jurisdiction intent on controlling the whole of Long Island Sound. These dreams collapsed in twenty years, and New Haven became a small farming community belonging to Connecticut.

147 In the Middle Colonies, Penn's Philadelphia for a Quaker population was famous. But further south, the English colonies did not develop an urban structure in the 17th century. Virginia and Maryland were given a number of small unsophisticated grids, in accordance with the New Town Acts passed at the direction of the Crown. These towns—Yorktown is an example—were intended to serve as ports of entry, and as such they were resisted by planters and traders. With the introduction of West Indian tobacco to Virginia farms, and the arrival of slave labor, the rural character of the region seemed sealed. The only exceptions were Jamestown, Williamsburg where Virginia's capital was transferred in 1699, and Annapolis
217 which became the capital of the colony of Maryland (see "The Grand Manner," p. 221).

By the 18th century, however, Southern resistance to urban centers had weakened. In the newer colonies we see the rise of port towns like Charleston and
104 Savannah. When in 1785 the Congress decided, at the prodding of Thomas
132 Jefferson, to conduct a national land survey, it was in one sense merely extending the well-established rectilinear urban habits of late Colonial America to the unsettled territories. But of course the lands now opened up for settlement dwarfed all Colonial imaginings, and the ideal of equal shares of land as the guarantor of liberty and universal franchise became the true test of the American revolution.

THE GRID

Orthogonality is a manner of creating urban order, not a simple formula of urban design. If the urban grid is ubiquitous in the history of cities, it is neither standard nor predictable. On flat terrain, it is the sensible method of land division. But the grid will as readily climb hills or curve its lines to fit a river bend. The approximations and quirks may have natural causes, but they may also be fostering a calculated political and social structure; or else, as in the emblematic configuring of Sabbioneta, be altogether willful. The blocks that, at their least inspired, line up as real-estate parcels may also group themselves into wards, stretch into narrow strips of burgage plots maximizing street frontage, or be internalized through landscaped courts as in Berlage's Amsterdam. The virtue of the grid is, in fact, its unending flexibility. Tailor-made for moderate urban scales, it is able to ingest the superblocks of the modern metropolis. At home in simple initial settlements, it can extend almost indefinitely to make greater Chicago or the conurbations of Lima or Buenos Aires.

Pl.15 Chicago (Illinois), detail of a bird's-eye view by Currier & Ives, 1892.

Variations on the grid

Pl.16 above *Villeneuve-sur-Lot (France) has as its core two medieval* bastides: *the older one, on the far bank, is a regular grid built on virgin land; the one on this side, taking in an existing village and castles, has a more uneven texture.*

Pl.17 left *Sabbioneta (Italy), begun in the 1550s. Its distorted orthogonal layout has been called a "Mannerist grid."*

Pl.18 opposite *Bern (Switzerland), founded by Duke Berchtold V of Zähringen in 1191. The medieval core, a flexible grid, runs along the central ridge. (A new bridge, bottom, has broken open the end of the city; the old bridge survives beside it.)*

Pl.19 H. P. Berlage's rendering of the final version of his plan for Amsterdam South, 1915. He projected a syncopated grid of large housing units enclosing courtyards, their scale and general uniformity intended to eliminate class distinctions. Bottom left is the railroad station, at the head of a trivium of three radiating streets.

The National Land Ordinance ensured that the urban blueprint for most of the
United States would be the grid. For a century or so, until the borders were finally
closed, gridded towns almost unexceptionally dotted the breadth and length of the
continent between the old Colonial band of the eastern seaboard and the Pacific *Pl.15*
Ocean. The grid became the standard for new sections of old towns as well—
Boston, Baltimore, Richmond—but nowhere more fanatically than in New York,
where a three-member commission planned the whole of Manhattan as far as 155th *118*
Street in the form of identical blocks, unrelieved by public open spaces. At the time
New York had extended only as far as 23rd Street. The Commission's report of *102*
1811, with L'Enfant's recent plan of Washington in mind, dismisses "those supposed *208*
improvements . . . circles, ovals and stars," and states flatly "that a city is composed
of the habitations of men, and that strait sided, and right angled houses are the most
cheap to build, and the most convenient to live in."

What was new in this attitude, and a significant shift from the application of the grid in Colonial days, was that the social value of urban land, that dominant view of the past that an urban parcel did not realize its true purpose until a building had been put upon it, was swept aside. Another way of putting it, following Peter Marcuse, is that the 1811 plan of Manhattan represented the abandonment of the Colonial *closed* grid for the *open* grid of the new era of the Republic. The closed grid is essentially a pre-capitalist concept. It is seen as having firm boundaries, and a definite design within this fixed frame. The boundaries might be walls, or features of topography; they might be determined by public buildings placed at the extremes of the major axes; or the grid might be encircled by common lands and allotted farm plots which cannot be sold. This last is the prevailing form of enclosure in the unwalled grids of Colonial America. The open grid is predicated on a capitalist economy, and the conversion of land to a commodity to be bought and sold on the market. The grid is left unbounded or unlimited, so it can be extended whenever there is the promise of fast and substantial profit. In this state of affairs the grid becomes an easy, swift way to standardize vast land operations by businessmen involved in the purchase and sale of land. Public places, parks, and any other allocations that remove land from the market are clearly seen as a waste of a profit-producing resource.[29]

This is how New York's Commissioners justified their decision not to provide public space in their 1811 plan. Manhattan Island was embraced

> by those large arms of the sea which . . . render its situation, in regard to health and pleasure, as well as to convenience of commerce, peculiarly felicitous; when, therefore, from the same causes, the price of land is so uncommonly great, it seemed proper to admit the principles of economy to greater influence than might, under circumstances of a different kind, have consisted with the dictates of prudence and the sense of duty.

In plain words, when there is the chance of making money from urban land, the claims of the public good will be set aside.

Actually, the city of New York had practiced its Commissioners' gospel much before the notorious 1811 plan. At one time, New York owned all of Manhattan Island except for the little that remained in private hands south of Wall Street. The Dongan Charter of 1689 had legalized this general ownership. Almost immediately, however, the city fathers started alienating this public trust to fill the treasury coffers, and the sections to be auctioned off were routinely laid out on a grid for easy sale. As late as 1796 the city surveyor Casimir Goerck surveyed a substantial strip of land running up central Manhattan, and subdivided it in a rectilinear system. Now

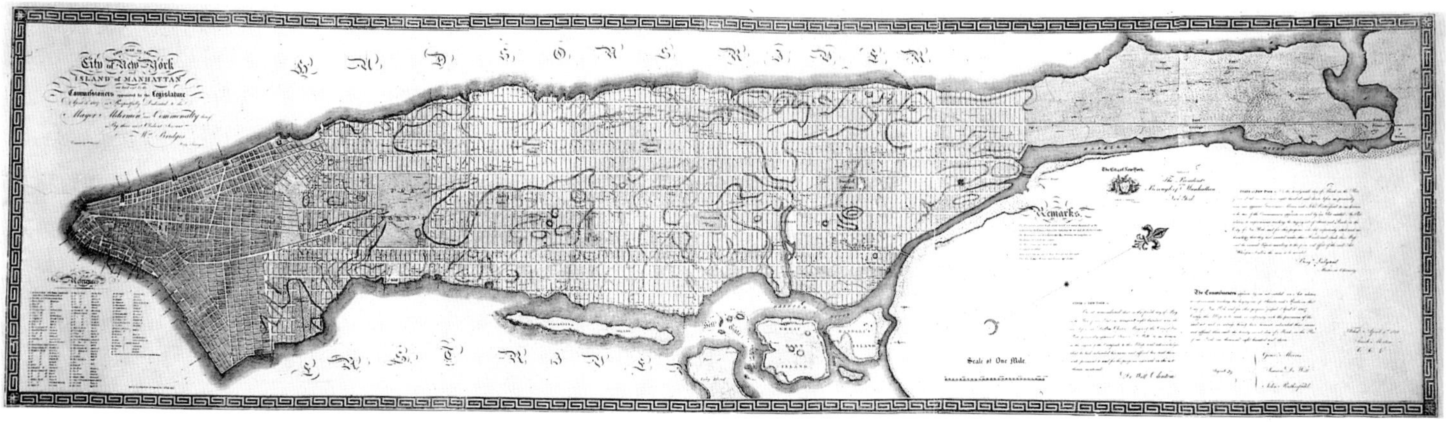

the Commissioners were merely applying these lessons unsentimentally and without exceptions.

It is instructive to observe this new attitude at work in the West, when California became American territory after the Mexican War of 1846–48. Under the Spanish system, land was the inalienable patrimony of each family (strictly speaking the family did not own the land outright, but held it in a kind of perpetual custodianship from the Crown), and there were centrally situated public open spaces and ample common lands for everybody's use. Under the Americans, this enduring social structure of the *pueblos* was replaced by laissez-faire planning. The promenades along the river or the ample plaza in the center of town became targets of development. The new municipal administrations allocated for community use only those parcels of land that could not be sold or given away. Common lands, set aside at the very beginning for the permanent benefit of the community, could now be disposed of by the city fathers as they saw fit. The *Laws of the Indies* considered town and country to be one working unit. American law considered the two subject to separate jurisdictions. Land taxes, unknown during Spanish and Mexican rule, facilitated the collapse of the rural aristocracy, and the acquisition and subdivision of its patrimony by the new ruling class of United States businessmen. All around the
119 original city-form, the grid spread out unchecked. It felt no obligation to continue the original Spanish schemes, nor did the American administration have the power to lay down an overall plan for this urban periphery before it was dismembered by hundreds of land speculators and home builders.

Speculative gridding did not require much finesse. As Lewis Mumford put it:

> An office boy could figure out the number of square feet involved in a street opening or in a sale of land. . . . With a T-square and a triangle . . . the municipal engineer could without . . . training as either an architect or a sociologist, "plan" a metropolis.[30]

The worst offenders were the railroad companies. The beneficiaries of vast land grants from the Federal Government, especially after 1862, they laid out hundreds of towns along their tracks, often on a standard plan, as a means to land speculation and the capture of national traffic. There were far too many of these would-be towns, as competing railroad companies divided the territory. Private proprietors followed the railroads and added their own trackside towns. The commonest rationale was to create shipping centers for farmers, to get their grain to mills and to main markets. The rate of failure was high. For every proposal filed at the county courthouse, there was the chance within a short period of time of a request for

118 New York City, Commissioners' Plan of 1811. Although the notion of gridding an area many times larger than the existing city (far left, and see Ill. 102) seemed presumptuous at the time, the Commissioners showed great foresight in their grasp of New York's potential for growth. The plan's deficiencies in other areas, such as provision for public open spaces, sites for public buildings, and the paucity of avenues stretching the length of the island, have created intractable problems for the city.

119 Plan of Los Angeles (California), ca. 1875. The central plaza of the Spanish pueblo *is framed in the crosshairs of the plan, its irregular plots of agricultural land below and to the right. A first gridded extension of Los Angeles was mapped by Lt. Edward Ord in 1849, a year after the town came under American administration. It brackets the* pueblo *to the north and south. The town surveyed its remaining undeveloped land in 1853, dividing it into a supergrid of large parcels framed by broad streets.*

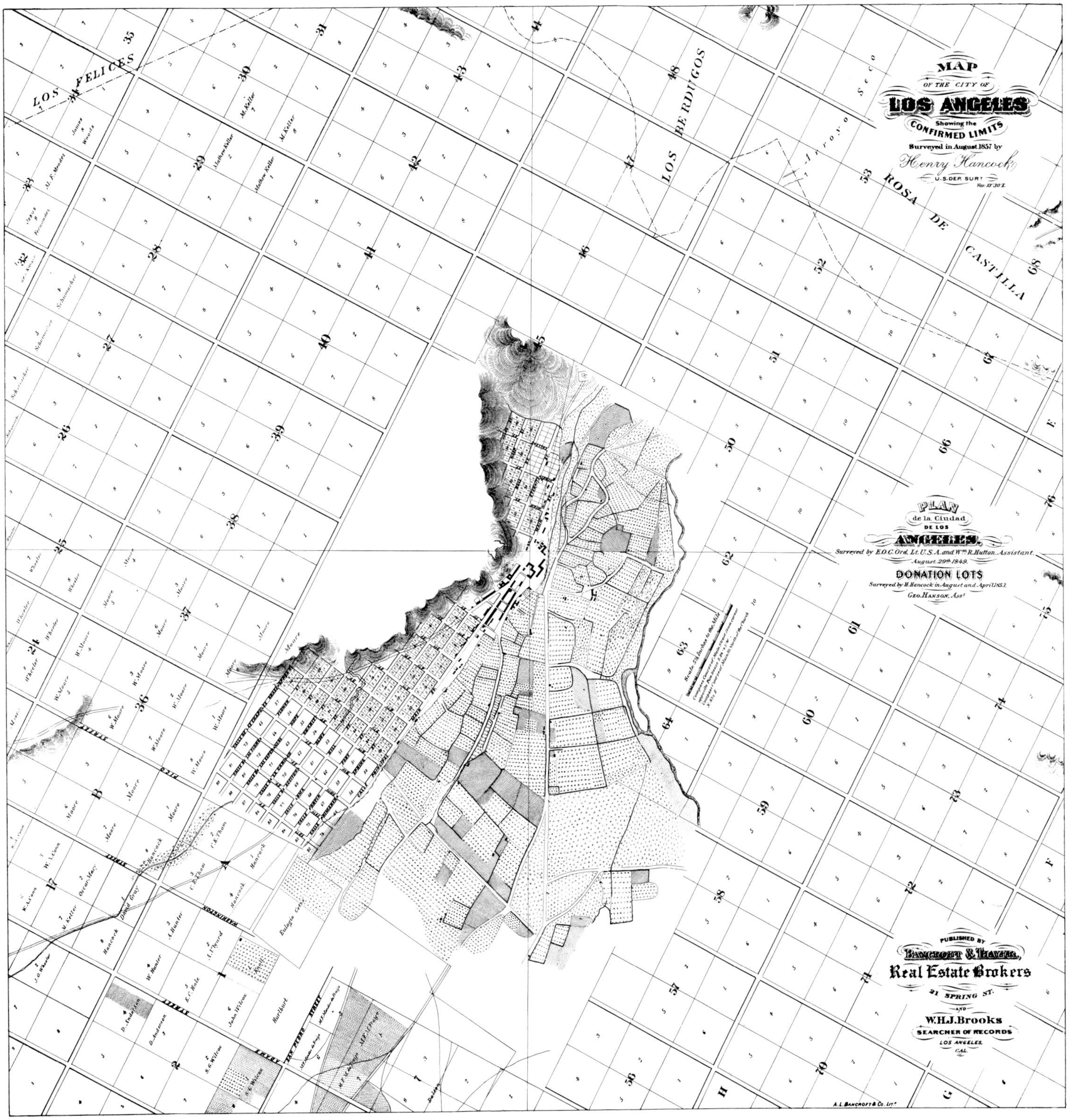
MAP
OF THE CITY OF
LOS ANGELES
Showing the
CONFIRMED LIMITS
Surveyed in August 1857 by
Henry Hancock
U.S. DEP. SUR.
Var: 13°30' E.
PLAN
de la Ciudad
DE LOS
ANGELES.
Surveyed by E.O.C. Ord, Lt. U.S.A. and Wm. R. Hutton, Assistant.
August 29th 1849.
DONATION LOTS
Surveyed by H. Hancock in August and April 1853.
Geo. Hanson, Asst.
PUBLISHED BY
Bancroft & Thayer,
Real Estate Brokers
21 Spring St.
AND
W.H.J. Brooks
SEARCHER OF RECORDS
LOS ANGELES,
CAL.
LOS FELICES
LOS BERDUGOS
ROSA DE CASTILLA
A.L. Bancroft & Co. Lith.

vacation, the legal procedure that cancelled the town and allowed parcels to be resold to area farmers.

These new grids of the 19th century for the most part had no more than 30 to 60 blocks, with 6 to 16 lots per block. Town plans were often standardized, varying only in their extent. One company might settle for blocks of 300 square feet (28 sq. m.), for example, with lots 140 feet (42.5 m.) deep. The plan had two linear axes, one of them the industrial axis along the tracks with the station, the grain elevator, coal sheds and water towers, the roadmaster's house, and a trackside park with a bandstand; the other, the commercial axis along Main Street. Sometimes the two coincided, or else they were set at right angles, or in the form of a T with the railroad line as the bar. If the railroad passed by after the grid was laid, the street plan might be realigned to give prominence and convenience to railroad business. In Galva, Illinois, the railroad lines cut diagonally across the gird.[31]

This speculative orgy of urbanization was not restricted to the United States. Elsewhere in the world where immense tracts of land were being opened up thanks to the railroad, the story repeated itself. Countries like Argentina in Latin America had a very similar record of alienating public lands to private interests. Mechanical and open-ended grids like those for Bahia Blanca and other 19th-century Argentinian new towns are the parallels of processes in the North that produced
Pl.15 the phenomenal gridded spread of Chicago.[32] In Australia and New Zealand, on the other hand, the simple town grids were framed by parkland not open to development, and the later suburbs that grew beyond this greenbelt had their own encircling green.[33]

LAYING OUT THE GRID

The word "grid" as it has been used so far in this chapter is a convenient, and imprecise, substitute for "orthogonal planning." "Gridiron," in the United States at least, implies a pattern of long narrow blocks, and "checkerboard" a pattern of square blocks. These are the two commonest divisions of a grid plan. The basis of a true checkerboard is bound to be modular, since the quadratic units produced by the coordinates are equal. A gridiron may prove to be modular or not, depending on the regularity of the long narrow blocks and the relation of their size to the public buildings and open spaces.

True checkerboards are rare. One thinks, in chronological order, of the unfinished Urartian town of Zernaki Tepe in eastern Turkey (8th century BC); early
111 Roman colonies in northern Italy such as Verona; Kyoto; a smattering of medieval
115 planted towns like Lalinde (Périgord, France); the towns of New Spain; the initial
152 schemes of American towns like Omaha, Nebraska; and Cerdà's Barcelona. Rectangular blocks are much commoner. But as a rule, a grid plan will contain a mixture of different-size blocks, if not initially, then through units added after the fact.

But the street grid and block pattern, the object of primary concern for historians of urban planning, do not in themselves explain the character of the city-form. At the time that this over-all grid is laid out, a second, more detailed grid is put in place—that of plot parcels within the block. Decisions affecting allocation of land to owners or renters need to be made before, or at the same time as, the drawing of the street lines. If in the city's history the street grid is likely to endure longer than this closer-grained, and less visible, division, it is because streets, as public space, are under official scrutiny while private parcels can stage their own internal transformations. Nonetheless, street grid and plot grid will always interlock and be interdependent.

Two other important considerations affect the quality of gridded urban form. The shape of the land is one of them; the technology of surveying and its relative sophistication at a given time and place is the other.

ON THE SITE

As always, one begins with the land. Where the land is flat, the grid is on its own. This is the closest the city planner will come to a blank sheet of paper. On level ground a standardized format can be painlessly repeated. The planning agency may indeed decide to create a level site, filling in depressions and shaving off swells. Roman towns in Gaul, it has been observed, "demonstrate a quite remarkable disdain for existing features, either natural or manmade. The demand was for a virtual *tabula rasa* . . . [so that] the new city could be shown in a condition of 'perfect horizontality'."[34]

Even on flat land, gridded settlement patterns may reflect the broad physical facts of the site. River towns, for example, will tend to run their main streets parallel to the waterfront, with a small number of connecting cross-streets. The *bastide* of Castelsarrasin on the Garonne in southwestern France is a case in point. Later, the river ports of colonial France in North America, grids of long and narrow shape, *6* exemplified more formal castings of this sympathetic street alignment.

The incidence of a pure, uncompromised grid over rolling topography is rare. The most celebrated instance from antiquity is Priene's well thought-out grid, from *120* the 4th century BC. The original town had been at the mouth of the Meander which

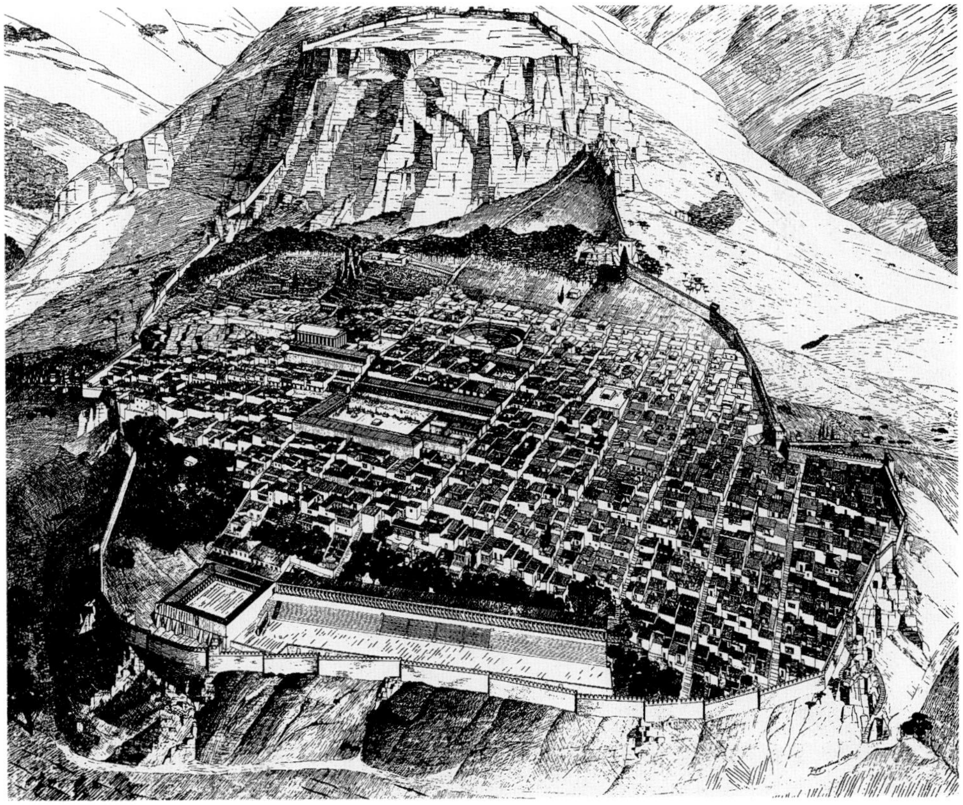

120 Priene (Turkey), reconstruction of the town in the mid-4th century BC: an application of gridiron planning to a topographically improbable site. (After A. Zippelius)

had silting problems. The new city, meant for a population of about 4,000 people, was built on high ground at the southern end of a spur sloping south, east and west. The city blocks were terraced like the seats of a theater along the main east-west streets, and the north-south streets for pedestrians were cut into steps in places. At medieval Lübeck, the disregard for natural topography can be rationally explained. The city was surrounded by the River Trave, the city core was along a ridge at the high point of the site, and straight streets down the slope were the shortest distance between the
121 center and the river piers. Modern instances like San Francisco are speculators' shortcuts; the challenge of coping with lots on slopes is passed on to the buyers.

121 The grid of San Francisco (California) marches with equal measure across infilled bay land and up the steep side of Telegraph Hill.

The common rule about street grids is to seek a compromise between natural irregularities and the abstract rigor of the right angle. We need look no further than medieval new towns to find a wealth of intuitive and expedient adjustments of reticulate city-form to the facts of local terrain. Among hundreds of *bastides*,
112 uncompromised grids like Monpazier and Aigues-Mortes in France and Flint in Wales are extremely rare. They occupy level ground, and are usually framed by the rectangle of city walls. The majority of new towns never were fortified, and not being so delimited at the start, their overall appearance was frayed at the edges. They
133 sat on uneven terrain, sometimes next to an extant castle settlement which had chosen its rough perch advisedly. For the most part, therefore, the layout was the product of "a primarily local, empirical approach in which a general familiarity with the bastide form was adapted to the exigencies of local conditions."[35] Ridges yielded simple linear grids of one main street and a parallel set along the slopes (e.g., Villefranche-du-Queyran, St.-Pastour). On rounded hilltops, the annular plan which would have resulted from "organic" growth was simply squared (e.g., Donzac). The planners of New Winchelsea gridded as much of the hilltop as they could, and left the irregular edges for odd-shaped house lots and grazing ground. Beaumont acknowledged the shape of its hill-back by bending the grid blocks north of the marketplace so that they are a few degrees out of line with those to the south. Prior settlements and major roads affected the new town to the extent that it was expeditious and economical to conserve street surfaces. The two *bastides* of Villeneuve-
Pl.16 sur-Lot, built on opposite banks of the river ten years apart, demonstrate this dependence: the older town on the right bank, built on virgin ground, is quite regular; its companion on the left bank, where a village and two strongholds of the lord of Pujols already existed, has a much looser form with large angular blocks.

As regards the general orthogonality of these hundreds of plans, it is well to remember that this was the only option for rational urban design open to the Middle Ages. It was the only system that facilitated the calculation of area and the coordination of parts. Until the Renaissance, planners did not have the instruments to construct mathematically accurate maps of geographic or urban forms. "In the Middle Ages," David Friedman writes, "it is only on an orthogonally articulated plane that the precise location of a point could be known."[36] Siena's planned organicism, remarked upon in the last chapter, was achieved within an extant scheme. Out in the open, this was a different story. It was only during the Renaissance that the possibility opened up to survey and record geographic features and irregular city shapes.

SURVEYORS AND THEORISTS

The simplicity of marking out an orthogonal street pattern made the grid a feasible city-form even for technologically unsophisticated cultures. The training of those who did the actual division on the site could be fairly basic. The tools remained in

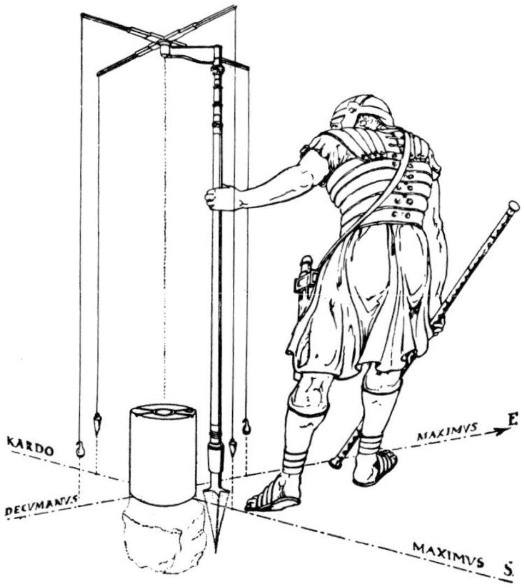

122 A Roman agrimensor *using a* groma *to survey land (Drawing by P. Frigero)*

use for long spans of time, with periodic improvements that made their performance more accurate. Ropes and pegs marked straight lines at all stages of history. Alberti's *hodometer* or "road-measurer" was described in Vitruvius fifteen hundred years earlier: an ordinary cart wheel of known circumference, the revolutions of which are recorded automatically.

Egyptians could determine the horizontal and the difference in height between two points. They had a simple sighting instrument, and used a primitive form of the transit, called *groma*, which was passed on to the Greeks and Romans and remained *122*
the standard land-surveyor's instrument until improved versions were developed in the Renaissance. In this transit, one of the lineals was used for sighting a main direction, and the other to determine the direction in the field at right angles to it.

In Greek colonial enterprises, the *horistes* was a key member of the original expedition; the word literally means the establisher of boundaries (*horoi*). He was a man of practical skills. The division was done in long narrow strips.[37] Diodorus in the late 1st century BC describes the founding of a colony: first, the ritual consultation of an oracle (the religious component); then, the location of a spring (water supply); the building of a city wall (defense); the laying out of a grid of broad avenues or *plateiai* (for Thurii which he is describing, there were four in one direction and three others at right angles to them); and after this primary order, the subdivision into narrow blocks for houses, served by lesser streets called *stenopoi*, basically footpaths between lots. The houses fronted on *stenopoi*, public buildings on *plateiai*. The blocks were 100 by 300 feet (30 × 90 m.). A portion of the city was strictly reserved for civic and commercial buildings; some economic activity was also incorporated in the residential zones. As for public buildings, the temples sometimes fitted the grid and sometimes were oriented independently (e.g., Agrigento, Paestum), presumably for religious reasons. The theater often took advantage of a natural slope for the arrangement of seats.

The case of Hippodamus of Miletus is puzzling. We have no working details for the system attributed to him, but what distinguished it, it seems fairly certain, was the fact that it relied on a theoretical formula of geometry, more so than the purely technical (and empirical) practice of land surveyors, and that it was carefully adjusted to the specific demands of the site. If we can judge from Piraeus, the system involved the division of the territory into sectors, each with its own rectilinear street pattern; the setting aside of public areas, delimited by boundary markers, for specific public functions; and provision for the placement of public buildings. From the example of Rhodes, to the extent that its ancient street pattern can be reconstructed, we might deduce that the Hippodamian geometric system had a triple order of division. The largest element was a square of which the sides measured one *stadion* each (a variable unit of about 600 feet or 180 m.). Each of these squares was quartered to produce squares one-half *stadion* to a side; and each of these was in turn divided into six parts to form rectangles measuring 100 by 150 feet (30 by 45 m.). Whether the system became established as a school of urban design after the death of Hippodamus, or simply refined the *modus operandi* of the common surveyor, is impossible to say.

We know a lot about the training of Roman surveyors. It involved knowledge of arithmetic, geometry, and law. On the whole they worked with squares and rectangles, and applied triangles, which they used not for surveying by triangulation but for things like finding the width of a river without crossing it and possibly for calculating height. Other instruments of the trade were the set-square, of most use to building surveyors, the water-table to establish precise horizontality, the portable sundial which helped with orientation, and of course measuring-rods and chains.

There was no strict separation between planned cities and the rectangular land survey of the agricultural land around them, nor between surveyors of rural land and military, or urban, surveyors.[38] It was customary to set up a *groma* in the center of a military camp.

Until the Renaissance, rectilinear layouts were generated by simple rotes of surface geometry. The surveyors knew how to create a perpendicular to a given line on the ground, and so establish the two coordinates to which parallel survey lines could be drawn. In many *bastides*, the Pythagorean triangle with sides of 3-4-5, which permitted the tracing of right angles with the help of a cord of 12 knots, was widely used. More complicated patterns based on constructive geometry, quite familiar in the design of Gothic cathedrals, could be transferred to the field but were not. In other words, the laying out of cities was not looked upon as an elevated problem of architectural design.

124 One case that does submit to analysis is Grenade-sur-Garonne, founded about 1300 by the seneschal of the king of France in the county of Toulouse. The plan is a late version of the town type developed by the planners of Alphonse de Poitiers around 1255 (see pp. 108–9), examples of which are Ste.-Foy-la-Grande on the Dordogne, Montréal-de-Gers, and Edward I's Monpazier. In this type the central feature is the intersection of two pairs of streets parallel to one another and at the same distance apart. The square they enclose is the market. Typically the blocks of these central strips are square, whereas the rest of the plan uses rectangular
123 blocks. The geometric basis of the Grenade plan is evident in the position of the general survey lines by which the town was laid out. It is the system of rotation described in the early 13th-century "Sketchbook" of Villard de Honnecourt, applied for the first time to a town plan. This is how it works. The distance between the pairs of primary survey lines, the axes that define the central file of square blocks, is 210 feet (64 m.). This was a primary decision of the town plotter. Then he took the diagonal of a square 210 feet on a side, which is 297 feet (90.5 m.), and used it to establish the distance between the main axes and the first secondary axes. This process, repeated, gave the sizes of the blocks in the outer section of town.[39]

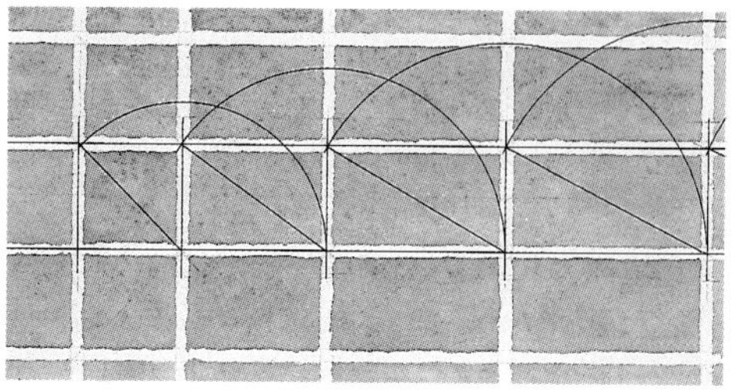

123, 124 Grenade-sur-Garonne (France), a bastide *founded ca. 1300. The varying grid reveals a complex formal logic: the length of each block is derived from the diagonal measure of the one preceding it in the series.*

THE TOWN PLANNER AS ARTIST

Is there any evidence, for the period before the Renaissance, of Gothic masters with knowledge of advanced theoretical geometry, masters associated with cathedral workshops, taking up the town grid as an *artistic* problem? David Friedman has argued just such a case in his recent book on the Florentine new towns of the 14th century.[40]

These towns—San Giovanni, Terranuova, Castelfranco, Pietrasanta and Scarperia in the upper Arno Valley, and Firenzuola in the Apennine region—were located in the countryside north and east of the mother city. They were laid out on
4 flat ground, and one basic scheme applied to all of them. The dominant long axis was usually a section of the major road on which the town was located; an extended piazza was laid at right angles to this. A defensive wall gave the settlement finite dimensions from the beginning. A road within the walls, intended for the movement of troops along the defensive perimeter, was second only to the main street in width. Finally, there were four equivalent neighborhoods at the corners, each with its own internal cross-axis.

It is Friedman's opinion that this scheme, in contrast to the constructive geometry
125 familiar to Gothic design, represents a sophisticated use of sine geometry, specifically trigonometry. Sine functions are related to the geometric measurement

of the circle, that is, to arcs and chords. That sine geometry may have been the basis of the Florentine plans is suggested, among other things, by the fact that block depths diminish from the center out, the deepest facing onto the main street, followed by three progressively shallower blocks all retaining the same width. It is not likely that this gradation represented a social hierarchy. Magnates were specifically excluded from the new towns. So the progression is largely an abstract one of geometry.

If sine geometry was indeed used here, it would constitute a unique case in medieval urban design. Sine geometry of an advanced theoretical application had traditionally been associated in the Middle Ages with astronomical studies and with the measurement of terrestrial dimensions. It was manifested in two things. One was
126 in mariners' charts that provided practical navigational information based on direct
observation of the earth's surface with the aid of scientific instruments. These
portolan charts, as they were called, have a characteristic pattern of radiating lines
130 forming a web over their surface—a pattern associated with the rose of the winds,
which in turn was part of the fully developed magnetic compass—and many sets of
parallel lines which yield a proportional system comparable to that of the Florentine
new town grids. The other application of sine geometry was in planispheric
127 astrolabes, with their sighting rule (the length of the disc's diameter and pivoted at
its center) used for taking observations. A simpler instrument derived from the
astrolabe was the quadrant, and both astrolabe and quadrant were known in Europe
as early as the 11th century.

125 The Florentine plans use the sine pattern of portolan charts and astrolabes,
and chord tables like those of Leonardo Fibonacci's *Pratica Geometriae* (Practical Geometries), written in Pisa around 1220. With these tables, the surveyor would actually have no need of astrolabes and quadrants. Traditional tools of surveying—the line or rod and the simple instruments for measuring right angles—would do the job. The surveyor need only lay down a baseline, the axis of the town's main street, and then strike a line perpendicular to this axis. Then, measuring out the chords of 11, 22, 33, 44, and 55 units of arc adjusted to an appropriately sized circle, he would fix the limits of the five units on either side of the town. Survey lines set out from

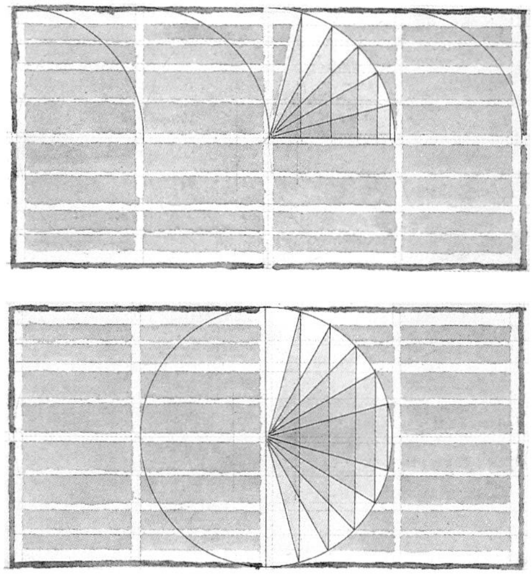

125 *The geometry of the receding block depths found in the grid of Terranuova (Italy), a Florentine new town founded in 1337, can be reconstructed as the product of the radius of a circle, inscribed in the four-square center of the plan, as it is rotated in successive 15° increments* (top). *Although this description can account for the plan, it is probably not the method that was used by the city's surveyors. A more likely explanation is that Terranuova's designers took the dimensions of the town plan from numerical entries in trigonometric tables derived from measurement of the chords of a circle.*

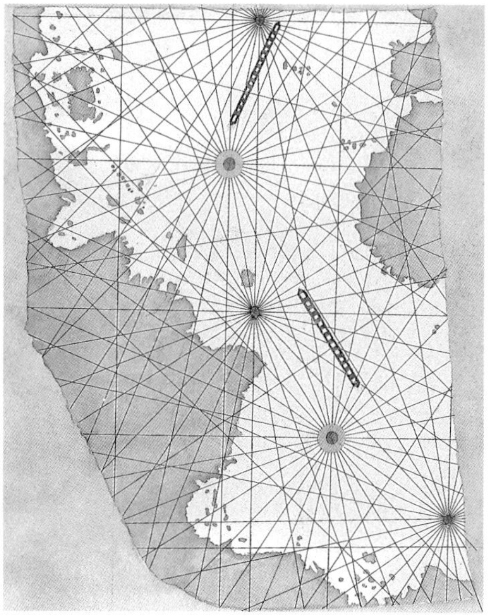

126 far left *A portolan chart, based on a map of America and West Africa according to Piri Ra'is (16th century).*

127 left *An Islamic astrolabe.*

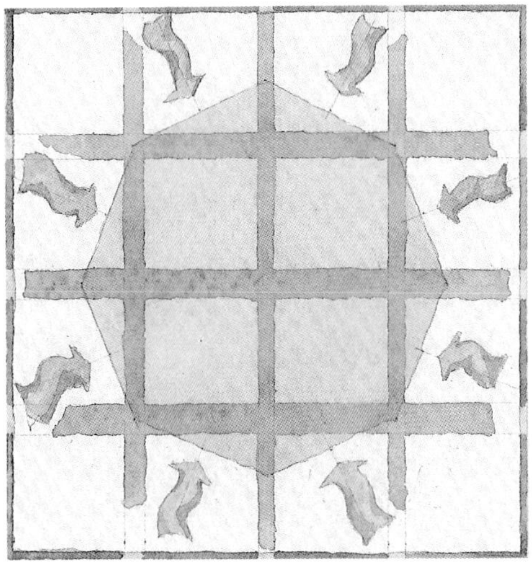

128 Wind rose and street system, after Fra Giocondo.

these points on the perpendicular axis parallel with the base line would complete the skeleton of the plan. But the main decisions came prior to this and they were the critical ones. Someone had to calculate the size of the circle; someone projected the chords of arcs 22, 44, and 55 66ths of the circumference to get the remaining dimensions. That someone, Friedman argues, was the Designer.

This conscious artistic creation of Florentine designers that reached beyond practical tasks of surveying and parceling presaged the Renaissance attitude that a city, like a major building, should be the product of architectural design. In the next century Alberti and others would equate a city with a palace. "The principal ornament of a city," in Alberti's words, "is the orderly arrangement of streets, squares, and buildings according to their dignity and their function." Beginning with Filarete's Sforzinda, Renaissance architects projected ideal cities with fixed *183*
perimeters and fully composed parts. In them the use of circle-based geometry as a proportioning device in urban design is clear.

One of the earliest instances is in Fra Giocondo's 1511 edition of Vitruvius, where a woodcut illustrates Vitruvius's famous passage about orienting a city's streets in *128*
such a way that none of them would face the major points of the compass, from where the strongest unhealthy winds were thought to blow. The woodcut shows an orthogonal street system made of 16 square blocks. On this plan an octagon is superimposed, each of its sides representing one of the winds and none of them running parallel with any of the streets. What is novel in Fra Giocondo's drawing, however, is that this geometric figure of the wind rose is coordinated with the streets, the size of the blocks, and the size of the town. Here we have an original Renaissance contribution for which there is no basis in the Vitruvius passage. Something like this coordination of circle-based geometry with a grid was what had determined the precocious design of the Florentine new towns two centuries earlier.

In making this drawing, it is likely that Fra Giocondo had in mind the ancient plan of Naples, the Greek Neapolis.[41] Like that, his street system shows three horizontal streets wider than the vertical ones.[42] As rebuilt at the end of the 5th century BC, modern field work has shown, Naples had three long streets a *stadion* (in this case about 607 feet or 185 m.) apart from one another, and 20 cross-lanes at regular $121\frac{1}{2}$-foot (37-m.) intervals. So the house-blocks had a proportion of 5:1. The lines of this scheme still survive in central Naples. The long streets slope gently toward the east, which is the only wind direction considered healthy by Vitruvius and his sources. The cross-lanes are steeper, facing south to the harbor. But in both directions the streets are 22.5 degrees from the meridian or the longitudinal compass line, which is what Vitruvius's prescriptions suggest as the proper way to site a city's streets.

In another drawing attributed to Fra Giocondo an ideal version of the original *129*
Naples plan seems to be shown, with a circle or wind rose in the middle divided into 16 points. Two of the points correspond to the middlemost longitudinal line of the street pattern, and two to one of the transverse lines that stand for the cross-lanes. We know that Alfonso II, Fra Giocondo's patron in Naples, had an active interest in Classical antiquity, and some attempts were in fact made during his reign to revive the Greek plan of Naples by extending the long streets and opening up and clearing all the lanes. The drawing is probably related to that process of resurrection.

These urban diagrams of Fra Giocondo, besides confirming the new bond between street grids and circles, are important for another reason. They belong in the development during the Renaissance of a new way of representing cities graphically—namely, as an ichnographic or ground plan, the sort of thing we take for granted as a city map today. The more common renditions of cities, in oblique projection or in bird's-eye view, were related to the invention of Renaissance one-

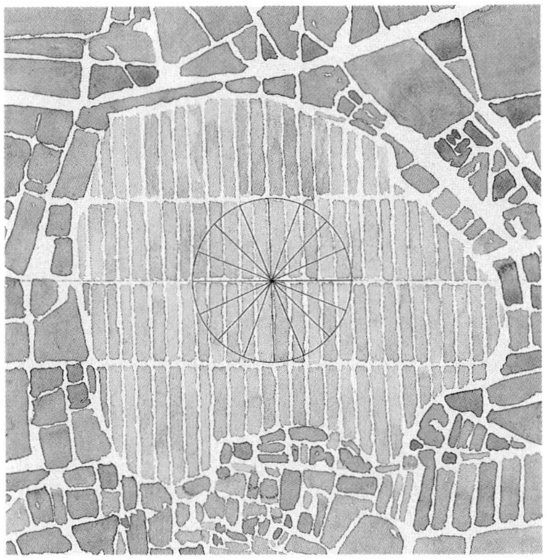

129 Wind rose superimposed on the street grid of ancient Naples, after a drawing attributed to Fra Giocondo.

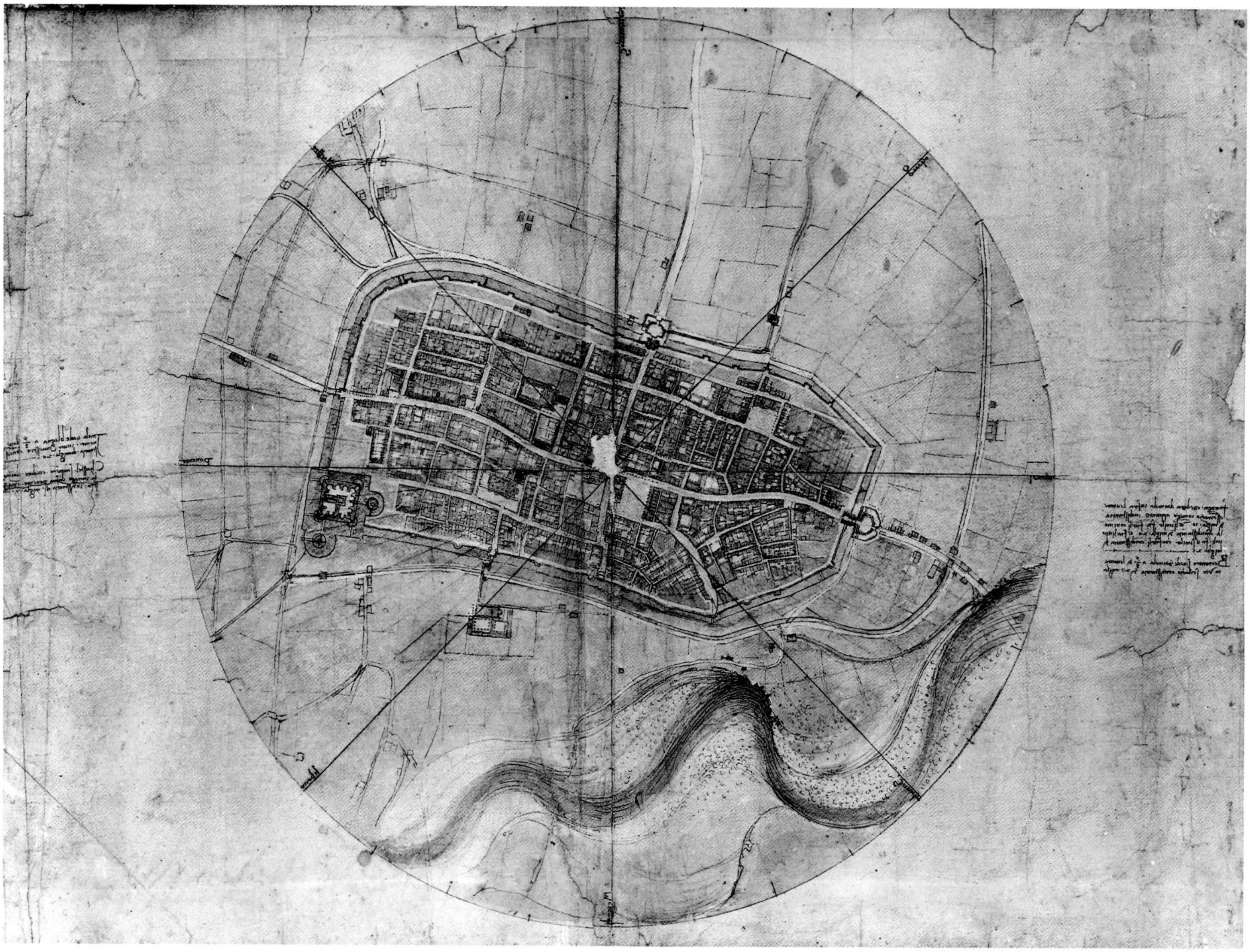

130 Plan of Imola (Italy) by Leonardo da Vinci, ca. 1503. This, the earliest ichnographic plan of the Renaissance, is set within a large circle divided into eight wedge-shaped sectors. The circle's spokes are labeled with the names of the eight winds. These clues reveal the secrets of how the plan was produced. An early surveyor's transit developed by Leonardo consisted of a circular disc divided into eight parts, with a compass at its center. The transit was set up to align magnetic north with the north wind, thus assuring a constant reference for observations taken from various points.

point perspective, which gave artists the ability to represent three-dimensional space
130 on a flat surface. The ichnographic plan, on the other hand, shows the city from an infinite number of viewpoints, all perpendicular to each topographical feature. Unconcerned with actual appearance, this highly complicated abstraction reduced the city to a two-dimensional record of solids and voids. And this ground plan, known to the Romans but abandoned in the Middle Ages, became possible again only with the development of advanced surveying techniques and instruments during the course of the 16th century.[43]

What is important to stress is that the new scientifically surveyed plan, and the contemporaneous development of mobile artillery, led to viewing cities as ideal diagrams. Cities began to be studied with detachment, as patterns into which all elements can be entered to form a perfect scheme. New treatises disseminated these patterns, which included artful variations of the grid. Most influential of these treatises were Pietro Cataneo's *I quattro primi libri di architettura* (1554) and
5 Vincenzo Scamozzi's *L'idea della architettura universale* (1615).[44]

131 Aerial view of Lugo, near Ravenna (Italy). The ancient Roman agricultural grid produced by centuriation remains inscribed on the countryside of the province of Emilia Romagna in the pattern of field boundaries, roads, and drainage ditches. (North is to the right.)

COORDINATED SYSTEMS OF TOWN AND COUNTRY

The centuries following these critical developments in urban design brought forth the most articulate and elegant exemplars in the grid's history, at least in the West—Avola and Turin, Richelieu and Neuf-Brisach, Mexico City and Savannah. Street widths, block rhythms and open spaces were calculated in concert; the habitually non-centric orthogonal array was punctuated with definite points of emphasis. In the colonial epic of the Americas, the urban grid was routinely lodged in a comprehensive regional plan which extended the structure of rectilinear space to vast rural jurisdictions.

RURAL GRIDS

The control of their countryside has always been a main worry of cities. A program of colonization or land reclamation is particularly dependent on the equitable distribution of agricultural land if it is to attract settlers. This often entails a large-scale grid of some sort. The two rectilinear systems of town and country are likely to follow similar rules applied at different scales, and the same units of measurement.

In early imperial China this unit was the *li*, which roughly corresponds to the Greek *stadion* (ca. 600 feet/180 m.). The rural grid divided the cultivated fields, with eight families in each square. The square was actually divided into 9 parts; the lord collected a tax from the cultivation of the ninth part. The relation of this agricultural division to a military system of conscription is unclear, but the fields were grouped into multiples of 5 for that purpose. In Japan, the *jori* system, introduced in the 7th century in connection with a new political order, was intended to ensure the equitable distribution of rice lands. The main squares measured roughly half a mile (800 m.) to a side. These were subdivided into 36 equal squares called *tsubo*, and each of these was further cut up into 10 strips, modest portions of land that were allotted by the State to the cultivators on a periodic basis. The outlines of the *jori* system are still in evidence today in parts of southern Japan.[45]

Roman land survey followed several methods, of which the commonest was centuriation. Two axial roads at right angles to each other started the survey; then *131*
field tracks (*limites*) were driven parallel to their course until a grid of squares or rectangles had taken shape. The squares measured 2,400 feet (some 730 m.) per side, and they were meant to contain one hundred small holdings (*centuriae*). The standard centuriation measure was the *actus* (120 feet/ca. 37 m.).

In the French *bastides*, a triple system of land division prevailed. Settlers received building lots called *ayrals* (between ca. 1,000 and 3,300 square feet, or 100 and 300 sq. m., each), vegetable gardens called *cazals* (6,500 to 7,500 square feet, or 600 to 700 sq. m.), and arable land for fields and vineyards called *arpents* or *journaux* after the units of measurement (about two-thirds of an acre/0.25 ha. per settler). These allotments formed three concentric zones. The urban parcels stretched to the limits of the town, or the walls if they existed. The gardens were within or immediately outside the walls. Arable land and pastures might not always lie adjacent to the town.

When the Spaniards arrived in the New World, land management was practiced on a regional basis. The jurisdiction of the original colonial cities was extraordinarily large. The territory of Asunción stretched for some 300 miles (500 km.) in every direction: the whole of present-day Paraguay thus belonged to this one city. Land tracts were generally square, 10,000 *varas* or $5\frac{1}{4}$ miles (8.5 km.) on each side; these tracts were called *sitios*. The town proper was in or near the middle of the tract. Around the town, on one or more sides, were the *ejidos*—common lands reserved for the enlargement of the town. Then came farming plots, most of them allotted to the original settlers, some reserved for latecomers, and some rented out to produce income for community purposes. There were also common pasture lands and common woodlands. Each settler got a farming plot and a house lot in the town. The land could not be sold. The similarity here to the ancient Greek practice in Sicily is obvious. I should also note that the land division pattern of the farmland—a large grid—made it possible to integrate the later urban development and the original town core, since the town grid could be systematically extended, and fitted into, the larger grid of the countryside. In South America, streets of 19th-century extensions are dead-straight continuations of the original grid lines, sometimes (as in Buenos Aires) stretching out for as long as 10 miles (15 km.). Only since the First World War have suburban streets in more irregular patterns appeared.

The colonial experience of the English in North America had its own rural/urban order. Savannah, to take a celebrated case, was conceived as part of a regional plan. Beyond the town limits were garden lots (half-squares in the form of triangles), and further out still, larger plots for farms of major contributors. In New England the pattern of farm fields, like that of the towns themselves, did not aspire to a disciplined grid.[46] Towns were organized as nucleated villages, a cluster of house lots around the common, or along the spine of a single street. Less commonly we get a compact "squared" town, like Cambridge in Massachusetts, or Fairfield and Hartford in Connecticut. In the South, holdings were isolated, and the settlement
132 pattern diffuse. Then after 1785 came the National Survey, to which I have already referred. The townships measured 6 by 6 miles (9.7 by 9.7 km.). Every other township was subdivided into plots one square mile, or 640 acres (260 ha.), in area, called sections, and the 36 sections were eventually broken down further into more
131 manageable halves and quarters. The distant precedents were Roman centuriation, the *sitios* of New Spain, the Japanese *jori* system, and the land division applied by Dutch engineers to land reclaimed from the sea (*polders*). In all these cases the survey adjusted to topography. Only the National Survey of the United States was strictly oriented to the points of the compass.

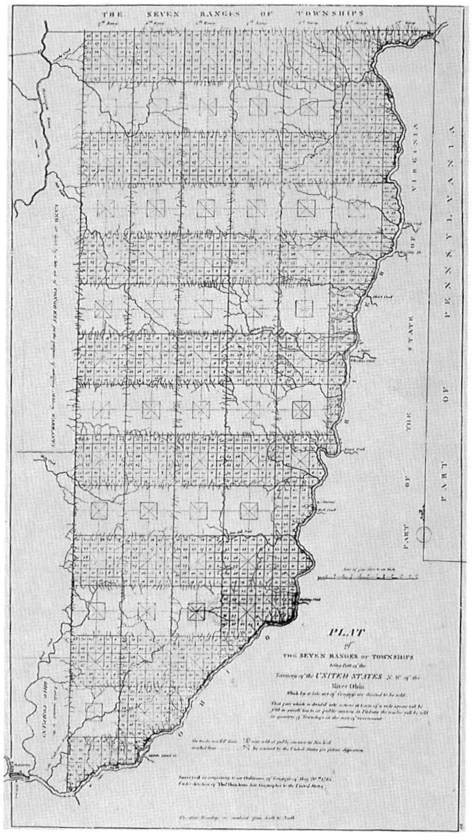

132 "The Seven Ranges of Townships," Ohio Territory, 1796: a plan of the first townships surveyed according to the national ordinance of 1785. Note the strict north-south orientation of the square grid.

But the unit of the square township basic to the Survey was quite familiar in the Colonies north and south by the late 18th century, and so Jefferson could find convenient models at home. As early as 1684, William Penn had declared: "Our townships lie square; generally the Village in the Center." Sir Robert Montgomery's Margravate of Azilia, planned in 1717 for what was to become the colony of Georgia, was based on 640-acre squares, with the town in the center, four square commons at the corners, and all around square plantations one mile (1.6 km.) to the side. In North Carolina the 640-acre section was common from the start. During his expedition against the Ohio Indians in 1765, Henry Bouquet's proposals for frontier settlements of 100 families specify as follows: "Lay out upon a river or a creek, if it can be found conveniently, a square . . . a mile on each side. That square will contain 640 acres." Of this area, 40 acres (16 ha.) were to go for streets and public uses, 50 (20 ha.) for houses (at half an acre—0.4 ha.—to the house), and the rest for 100 cultivating lots of 5.5 acres (2.2 ha.) each.[47]

The Jeffersonian gridding of America was based on the notion of "freehold", by which was meant property of a certain size or value, or that produced a specified taxable income. This is to be distinguished from leasehold, which signifies a condition of tenancy. Freeholders had political rights. They were enfranchised: they could hold office or they could vote. Property is the key to citizenship and suffrage. In the Colonial period freehold qualification was about 50 acres (20 ha.). Jefferson wanted Americans to have more. At the time of the Survey, most of the Thirteen Colonies had abandoned the literal sense of freehold for a tax equivalent. So Jefferson was being conservative. But his dream was to make of all Americans (white males at any rate) citizens with voting rights on the strength of being landowners. The National Survey grid has been considered, in that sense, the equivalent of the Constitution.[48] Under the circumstances, it was providential that the Constitution was indeed enacted, for the Jeffersonian land democracy, like almost all such experiments of history, proved exceedingly short-lived.

GRIDDED EXTENSIONS

The existence of a coordinated array of town and country did not ensure an orderly extension of town grids into the surrounding territory. As a rule, only when city authorities had the power to oversee the development of the suburban region could gridded extensions obey a coherent design and establish rational links to the urban core.

The suburban grid could be appended to an "organic" town, or to an original grid. Some *bastides* were gridded extensions grafted onto earlier castle towns.
Culemborg in Holland is a good instance. The old nucleus dates from the early 12th *133*
century, the castle from 1271, the "Nieuwstad" to the southwest from 1385–92. A street stretches from the marketplace in the old town, through the south gate, across the drainage canal and into the new town, strapping the two urban units together.[49]

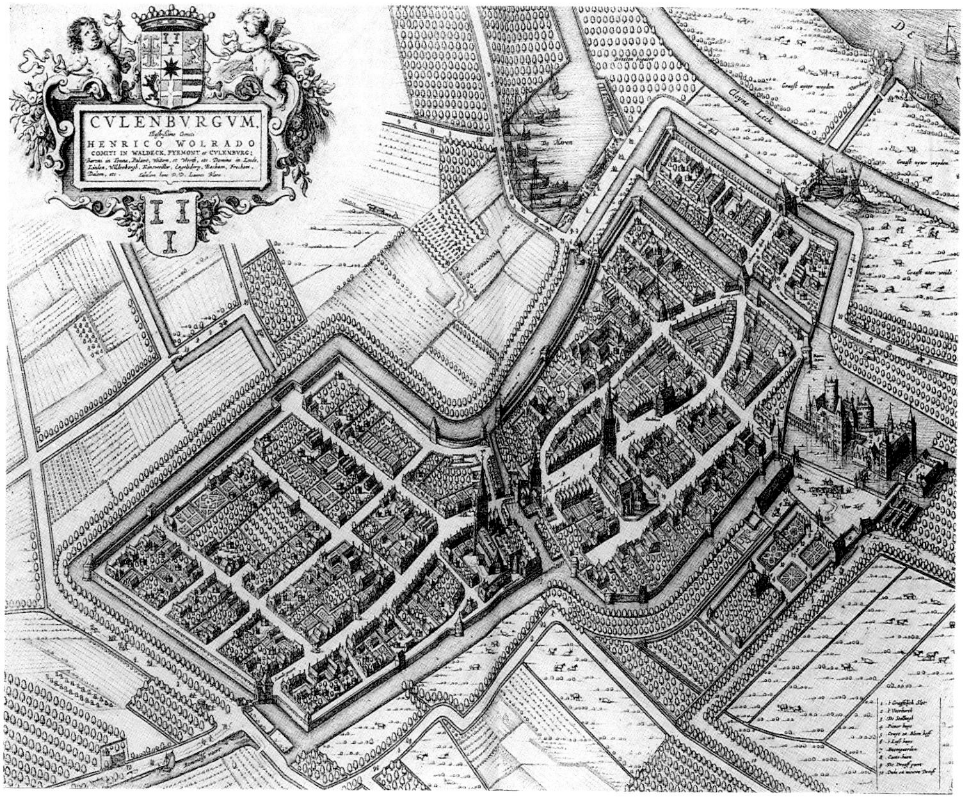

133 Culemborg (The Netherlands), bird's-eye view by Johannes Blaeu, 1648. The older town, on the right, has a variety of spindelform *plan (cf. Ill. 138).*

This is the standard device of junction, both between an "organic" core and a subsequent grid and between two grids of separate date. Examples at random would include Le Havre, where the main axis of the old town is extended into the gridded *ville neuve*, and Renaissance Ferrara where linear connections are made between the old market and the piazza of the Herculean Addition. If the gridded extension came after the old town had received bastioned walls, the problem of grafting was more
253 difficult. Berlin and its 17th–18th century additions of Dorotheenstadt and Friedrichstadt are a case in point; despite the strong cord of Unter den Linden, the
151 gridded suburbs could not mesh with the medieval core until its walls came down.

134 Turin is the most lucid demonstration of an original gridded town of Roman descent able smoothly to graft on later grids. Having been chosen to be the capital of Piedmont under the Savoy dynasty, Turin added no fewer than three gridded quarters to the old Roman core—a group of 12 new blocks outside the walls to the south in the early 17th century, an eastward extension to meet the banks of the Po beginning in 1673, and finally an addition to the west in 1712. In its last stage, the city had achieved almost an oval form. With its multiple piazzas, it now more closely resembled the ideal city of Renaissance theorists. The blocks of the later grids were larger than those of the Roman core. This was due in part to the Renaissance ideal of an urban residence—a large, regularly massed *palazzo*, more representative of the new urban nobility (State officials and the like); another factor was the possibility of allowing convents, which now assumed the State's burden of charity and education, to develop some of the generous block they were assigned as rental property. Along the Via Porta Nuova, the first gridded addition where the blocks measured about 400 by 280 feet (ca. 120 by 85 m.), the desire to develop a commercial strip determined a somewhat different block design—narrow fronts with small shops at ground level and residences above; a narrow alleyway cut longitudinally through the blocks to allow access to suppliers through the backs of the shops; and small warehouses or storage units in the internal courtyards of the blocks. The street linkage is not mechanical: some of the lines of the Roman grid are continued or slightly jogged, while others are suppressed as a single block in the newer grid takes on the width of two in the old section.

135, Amsterdam is a special case. This great northern port, which always exercised a
136 remarkable element of public control over city-form, borrowed the best of the "organic" system and the grid, to ensure a rational, long-range development. A major master plan launched in 1607 increased its area fourfold. The city had started in the 13th century, as we saw in the last chapter, with a sea-dyke along the south side of the Ij estuary and a dam across a little stream called the Amstel. Ditches were built parallel to this line of estuary and the Amstel, to the east and the west of the settlement—two sets of them between the end of the 14th and the middle of the 15th century. These converged south of town, and houses were aligned along them and along the river itself. The 1607 plan simply took the canals that then formed the city's edge, and retraced them in three encircling canals across empty land. The first of these—the Heerengracht—was built over the bastioned walls of 1593, and the two others ran parallel to them. Each of these canals was to serve as the new city edge during successive enlargements of the urban core. So you had both an overall extension plan, with land uses determined from the start, and the possibility of construction in stages. The narrow strips between the canals were gridded, but because of their concentric disposition a good proportion of the blocks were trapezoidal. The city itself decided the position of the three canals, but the development between them and the new walls beyond was left to private enterprise. On the western section of this area, a workers' district was laid out (the Jordaan),

134 Turin (Italy) at the end of the 17th century, showing the Roman core (at lower right within the fortifications) and successive gridded extensions.

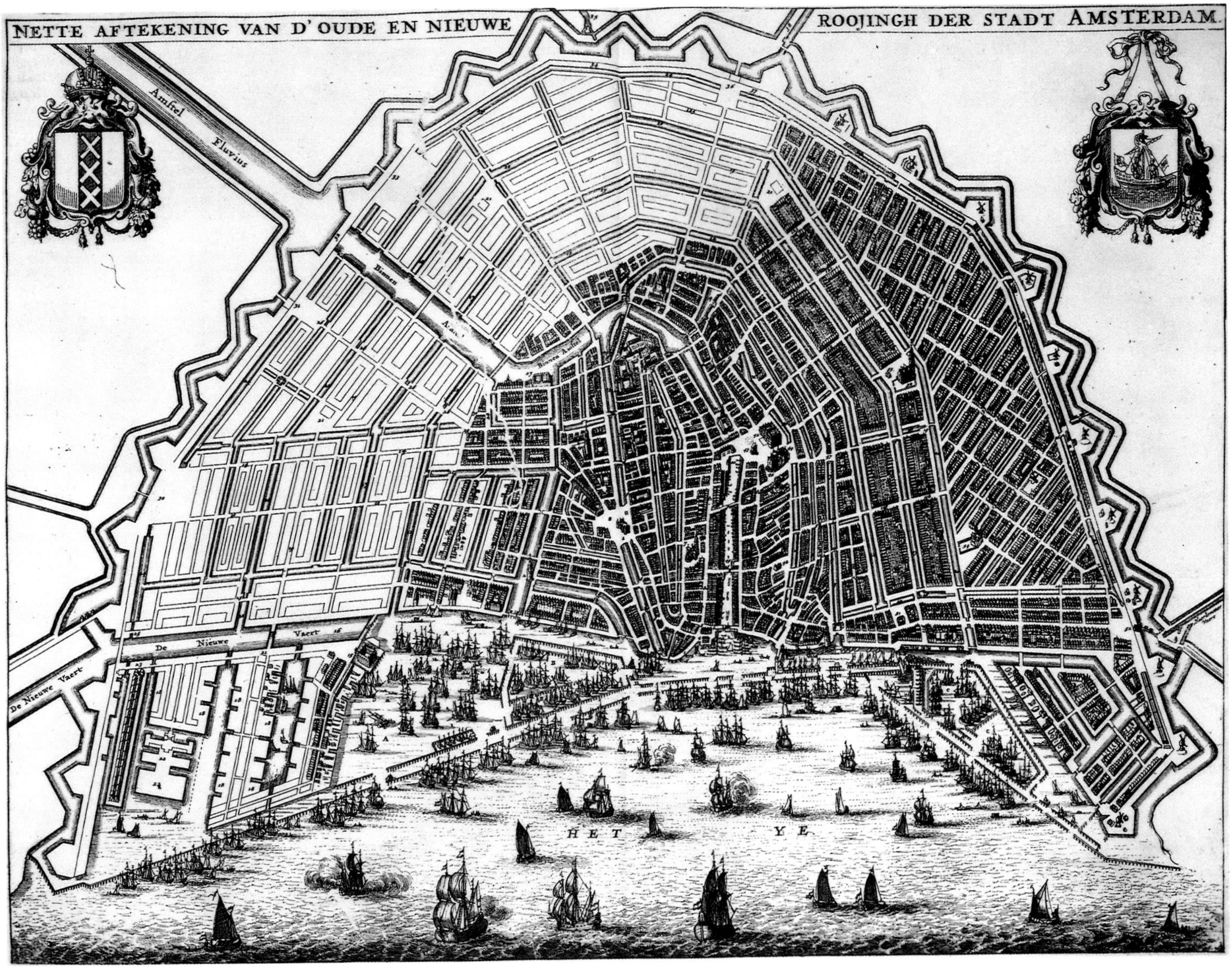

135, 136 Amsterdam, bird's-eye view by C. Anthonisz, 1536 (right)*; and plan of built and proposed city extensions, 1663. Until the early 17th century, Amsterdam grew as a series of artificial embankments running parallel to the initial dike of the mid-13th-century village on the River Amstel. The destruction of Antwerp by the Spanish in 1570 transformed Amsterdam into the region's leading port, and created commensurate pressures for expansion. The 1607 extension plan proposed a fourfold increase in the city's ground coverage within a framework of grids built on landfill.*

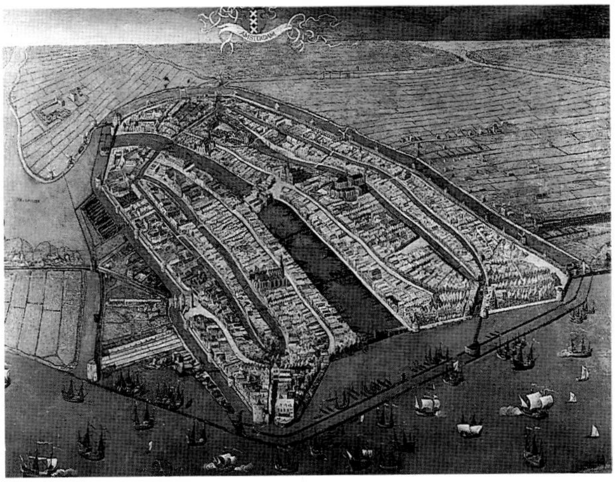

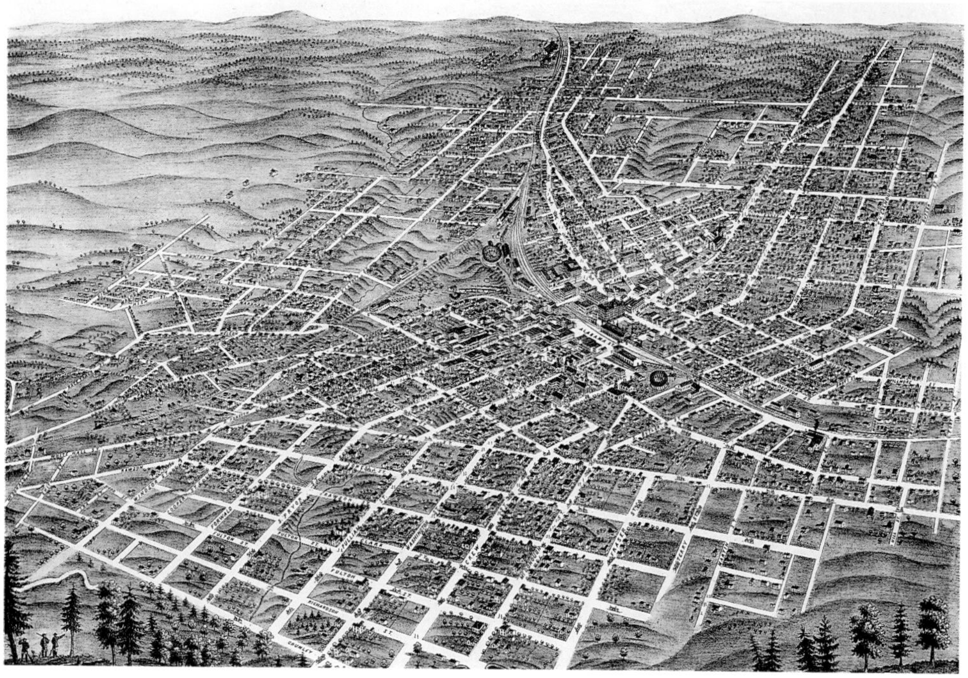

137 "Bird's Eye View of the City of Atlanta the Capitol of Georgia," lithograph by A. Ruger, 1871. Atlanta, like many other 19th-century American cities, developed as an uncoordinated patchwork of grids laid out by independent private speculators.

with housing, tanneries, woolen and velvet mills, and dye works. Its street grid, laid over existing paths and ditches, was aligned obliquely in relation to the new canals.

Without the centralized authority of cities like Turin and Amsterdam, or of German municipalities in the modern period, gridded extension degenerates into a patchwork of small developments that meet at ownership boundaries of rural holdings. *137* This is the common reality of American city growth, rather than the uniform 1811 grid of Manhattan. The impression of an "infinitely extendable grid" is in most cases indebted to the streamlining of this *ad hoc* patchwork by the traffic engineer's "supergrid" of through-streets assembled for the automotive age.

THE CLOSED GRID: FRAME, ACCENT, AND OPEN SPACES

Open grids with laissez-faire planning cannot aspire to a coherent design. To achieve a formal structure, the limits of the town would have to be determined at the time of origin.

THE WALLED FRAME

A walled enclosure is the most obvious, but not the only, means of delimiting. Conversely, the city wall where it exists may or may not be integrated with the street grid. The reason is evident: street grid and wall circuit have different demands placed upon them. As the primary system of defense, the wall must ensure its own survival under attack; its design has this issue to consider before all else. The grid within organizes civil life—the deployment of houses and their relation to the market, the distribution of public buildings and open spaces. In rough terrain, the walls will seek

138 Prototypical medieval new town with spindelform *plan.*

to maximize the advantages of natural features of defense. In such cases they will rise and fall where the street grid cannot or need not follow.

This is the case with towns of Classical antiquity like Neapolis (Naples) and Priene, Cosa and Alba Fucens, whose orderly street grids must somehow adjust to an *109,*
irregular *enceinte*. The main concern is with access to the town gates. Where *120*
coordination is possible without jeopardizing the needs of defense, several of the streets will be extended in a straight line until they reach the gates. Otherwise, streets will hook up less directly, or they will stop altogether short of the walls, forcing inhabitants heading out in certain directions to traverse an unplanned no-man's-land. In most medieval new towns the wall, when it exists, closely hugs the laid-out area to reduce the crippling cost defenses entail. The city-form concentrates on a rationally designed center around the square, and reaches out to meet the walled edge with distorted blocks that fit the pomerial space. Sometimes the streets parallel to the main axis will curve gently at the two ends, and meet that axis at terminal *133*
gates. This is the *spindelform* plan, so called on account of its similarity to a *138*
weaver's bobbin. The purpose is to hold down the number of entry points into the city. Typical cases are Brunswick Altstadt and Hamm. A rare Italian example is Montevarchi, founded some time in the first half of the 13th century by the Guidi, counts palatine.

When the town lies on a level site and the defense therefore must be entirely manmade, the conditions are favorable for an urban design that meshes street grid and town wall. Since army camps out on the field often had no other option than to invent their own artificial environment, some of the best solutions of the walled grid originated with military engineers. The Roman foursquare *castrum*, standardized in *164*
every detail during the late Republic, was one of these solutions. Whatever it learned of the principles of rectilinear urban design, it made its own—and then it was the city planners' turn to emulate its formulas.

The Roman camp had two parallel streets, the *via principalis* and the *via quintana*, at right angles to a major cross-axis. The walls were carefully coordinated with these main streets through gates. The particular divisions of the camp—stacks of long barracks buildings for the men, a thin row of units for the tribunes—yielded uneven block widths. These street rhythms were then transferred to cities that grew directly out of camps, like the British cases already mentioned, or cities like Aosta and Timgad that emulated the camp pattern. *110*

The success of such coordinated urban systems depends on a compliant street grid. If that has its own design rationale, there will be conflict. In the Florentine new towns, the staggering of street intervals was one such difficulty. In the plan of San Giovanni, the earliest of the new towns, the towers of the wall were coordinated with the street plan: every street ended in a tower. But the distances between towers and streets were influenced by very different considerations. Street frequency had to do with lot sizes and the length of blocks, so it was variable. Towers were situated in relation to the range of weapons and the accessibility to all parts of the wall, at a distance that ideally remained the same. At San Giovanni, tower spacing was compromised by the uneven spacing of the streets. So in later plans the coordination of towers and streets attempted here was abandoned.

With the advent of the bastioned defenses in the 16th century in response to artillery warfare, the total independence of the city wall from the street grid became inescapable. The most effective bastioned curtain was a polygon; any dovetailing of this shape to the orthogonal rules of the street grid was bound to be ineffectual. At the very least, it gave rise to blocks of peculiar shape adjacent to the inner perimeter of the walls, as in the projects of Cataneo and Scamozzi and built emulations of them *5*

145 like Avola. What was predicated by the geometry of the bastioned wall was a radial-
159 concentric street system, which however had its own problems as the organizing diagram of civilian routines. So the street grid and the bastioned wall coexisted without interlocking. With the phenomenal expansion of this defense system during the 17th century, the scale of the periphery crushed the sheltered grid and reinforced its alienation.

STREET RHYTHMS

Whether restricted by its own defensive armature or by consensually set up natural barriers like farm fields and common lands, a closed grid to some extent composes itself. Some of the elements at the disposal of the designer are rhythmic arrangements of streets, the creation of a strong center, and the disposition of open spaces.

Street rhythms are variously generated. The designer might scan unequal street widths, or unequal street intervals. In the division of many grids, the interweaving of main streets and alleys can have its own rhythm, and variations in the size of the blocks will directly affect the distance between streets. In the railroad towns of the United States, the business spine of Main Street had the maximum width (usually 100 feet, or 30 m.), important cross streets came next (80 feet, 25 m.), and the intimacy of residential streets was ensured with widths that did not exceed 60 feet (18 m.). Symbolism of another sort distinguished several street widths in Chinese
139 imperial grids like Chang'an and their Japanese imitations. We see this best at Heijo-kyo (Nara) in Japan, laid out about 710. The north-south axis leading from the south city wall to the main palace gate was the widest single street in the layout, and

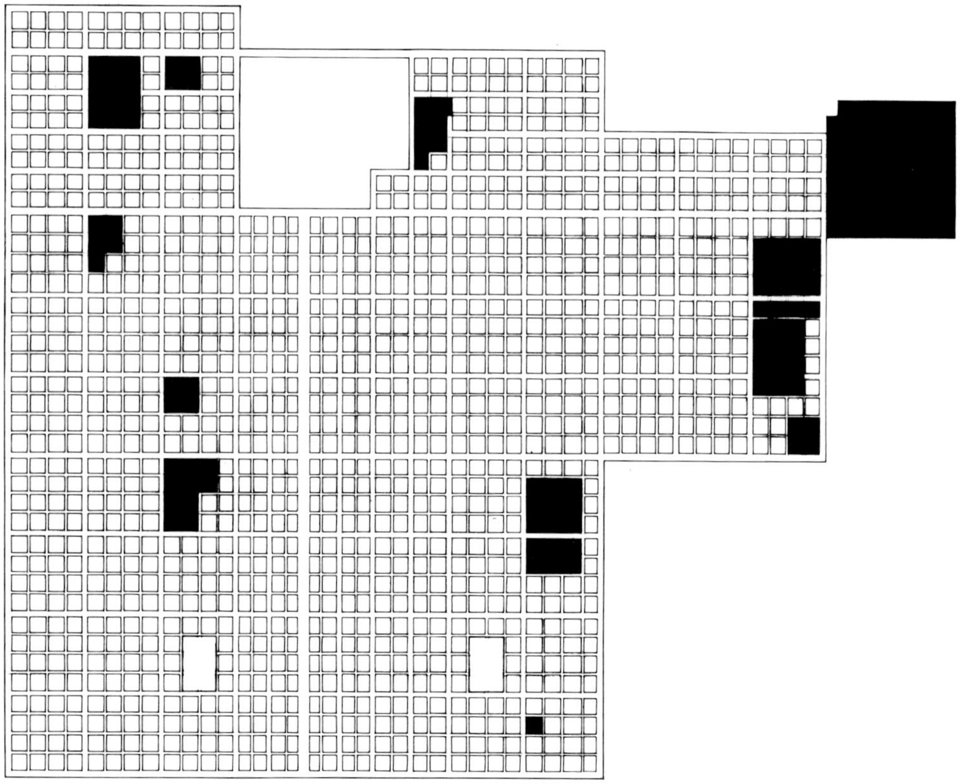

139 Heijokyo (Nara, Japan), founded in AD 710. Laid out with the Chinese imperial city of Chang'an as a model, the block sizes and proportions may have also been influenced by the pre-existing grid of agricultural land divisions. The white area at the top is the palace; temples are shown in black. (After Suzuki)

divided the city symmetrically into eastern and western halves. Next in breadth were streets that defined a larger palace quarter comprising the entire north section of the town, and ranges of privileged blocks for court officials on either side of the main north-south axis. A uniform minimum width was reserved for the common residential grid, with all the streets lined with willow trees. The lowest in the street hierarchy were the alley grids that divided each block into 16 squares.

But the course of the streets themselves can be made eventful, as in the case of the Sung redesign of Suzhou. In this and other Chinese grids, T-intersections are *103* intended to thwart the progress of evil spirits. An invading force trying to overrun the city, evil spirits of another kind, would be likewise hampered.

T-intersections are also encountered in the West. In the medieval *bastide* of Beaumont, for example, most streets are interrupted in the east-west direction. The reason is unclear, but in other *bastides*, for example Lamontjoie and St.-Clar, the aim seems to be to create closed-circuit roundabouts which will cut down the total number of streets without detracting from the symmetry and geometric esthetic of the plan. The T-system, perhaps intended to break the rigidity of the grid layout, can also be seen in Penn's Philadelphia (the Rittenhouse Square area). Modern-day planners praise the T-intersection for reducing the danger of head-on collisions and providing vistas for interesting or important buildings.

But Sabbioneta is the most flagrant, and intriguing, exhibition of this device. The *140*
town originated in the 1550s when the modest settlement around the family *Pl.17*
stronghold or *rocca* of Vespasiano Gonzaga Colonna began to be redone as a model city on the designs of Domenico Giunti. A few years earlier, in 1549, another Gonzaga had put Giunti in charge of the urban development of Guastalla. Both are basically citadels with powerful fortifications and a *rocca*, two gates, and a rather

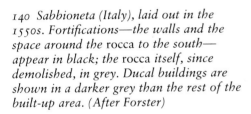

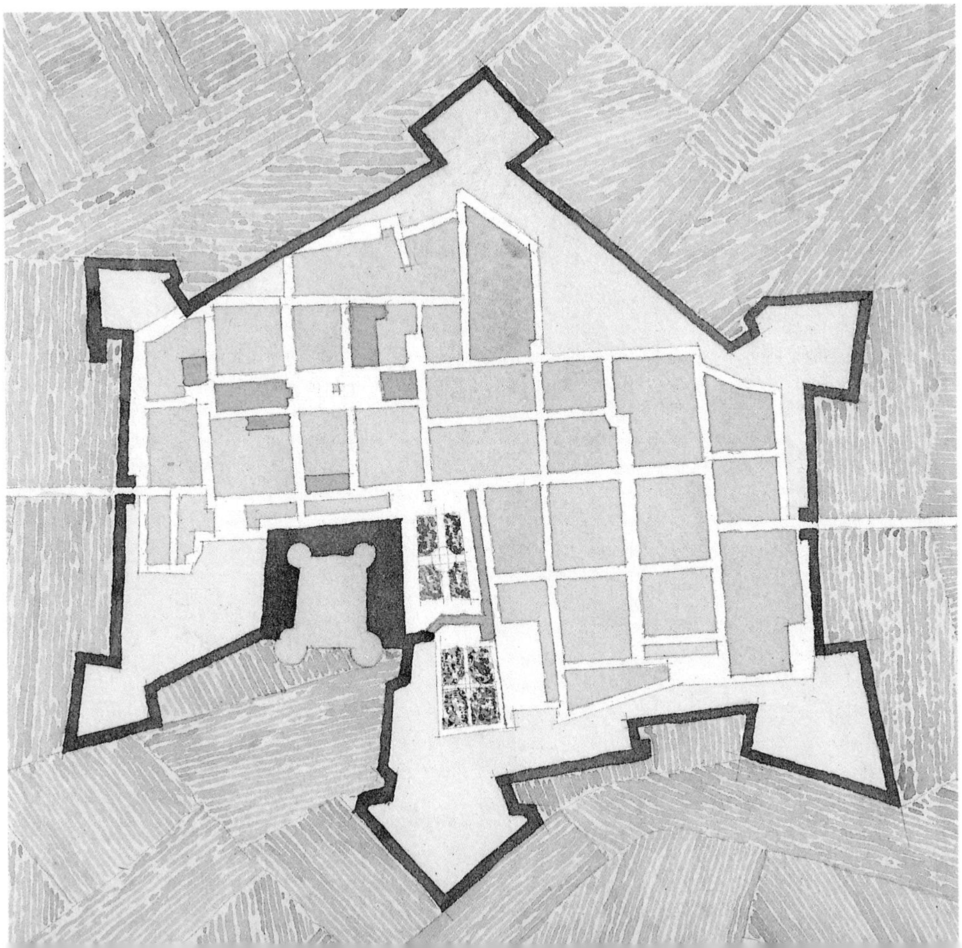

140 Sabbioneta (Italy), laid out in the 1550s. Fortifications—the walls and the space around the rocca *to the south—appear in black; the* rocca *itself, since demolished, in grey. Ducal buildings are shown in a darker grey than the rest of the built-up area. (After Forster)*

eccentric street grid. The two gates are connected with the longest straight street of the scheme, but it breaks twice at right angles before linking up with them; a perpendicular cross street in both cities ends in a trap at either end; and so on.

There is no doubt that these erratic street lines at Sabbioneta were intentional. We have many of the original corner blocks used in marking the streets to prove the point. But what purpose was being served? It may be possible to explain the street scheme as an attempt to separate several functional spheres: the private ducal realm; the public ducal realm; the area of habitation and production; and the center where all three meet. Kurt Forster has done so, but he has further claimed that the plan of Sabbioneta must be interpreted, in the last analysis, as a Mannerist application of the grid. The standard art-historical exegesis of Mannerism is as an iconoclastic style which creates its tensions through tampering with the rules of High Renaissance ideal form. As Mannerist painters disproportionately elongated their figures, canted Renaissance perspective into willful diagonals, and built disturbing imbalances in their compositions, so Gonzaga and his architect, in the realm of urban design, indulge in Mannerist play by setting up a grid in order to break it. Forster points out that the labyrinth was the Gonzaga emblem, and Vespasiano may have wanted to express it urbanistically.[50]

The most emphatic way to create a focus in a gridded plan is to have two axes—north-south and east-west—cross each other at the center, and to mark the crossing with a public square. This is what distinguishes Greek from Roman grids. The latter tend to be more centralized, commonly by means of a cross-axis, with the forum and other public buildings making a civic center at or close to the crossing. This perfect
110 cross-axial arrangement is rare (e.g., Timgad). More often the crossing is off-center, or one or both of the arms of the cross stop short at the forum or are split in two there (e.g., Silchester, Trier, Paestum). In the modern literature these main streets are called *cardo* (north-south) and *decumanus* (east-west), for which there is no solid ancient authority. In antiquity those terms applied to the main coordinates of centuriation, the land surveying system of the countryside, and only when the *cardo maximus* and the *decumanus maximus* of the centuriation pattern, whose orientation often responded to topographical features like river and land contours, correspond exactly to the main cross-axis of the city can the terms be properly transferred. But this is not always the case. In Roman Florence, for example, the lines of the town grid, oriented to the points of the compass, did not coincide with the coordinates of the centuriation.

In the eastern territories of Rome, the emphasis was achieved by one axis alone, usually lined with porticoes, that ran the full length of the city. We see it in the towns
Pl.20 of Termessos, Perge, Side, Palmyra and Damascus. In Seleucia on the Tigris, this main street, which was actually a canal, terminated in a piazza at the south end. The fully developed colonnaded street is not earlier than the time of Augustus. At Antioch it marked the edge of the Hellenistic city. The idea of supplying the main street with colonnades is sometimes credited to Herod the Great.

The Roman cross-axis survived in the plans of some medieval towns like 12th-century Chester in which the monk Lucian (inevitably) saw the symbolism of the Cross.[51] The medieval version of the cross-axis appears independently in most of the new towns except for those with an elementary linear grid. Even within that
141 category, an important variant is the so-called *Strassenkreuz* (cross-street) scheme where two market streets intersect at the center of the plan. Villingen and Rottweil, two foundations from the 1120s traditionally associated with the dukes of Zähringer, would be good early instances but they may in fact be an elaboration of a century later, after the extinction of the Zähringer line in 1218, when the towns had

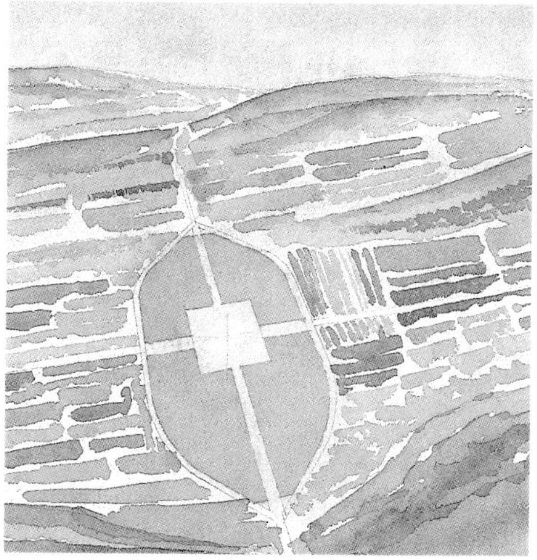
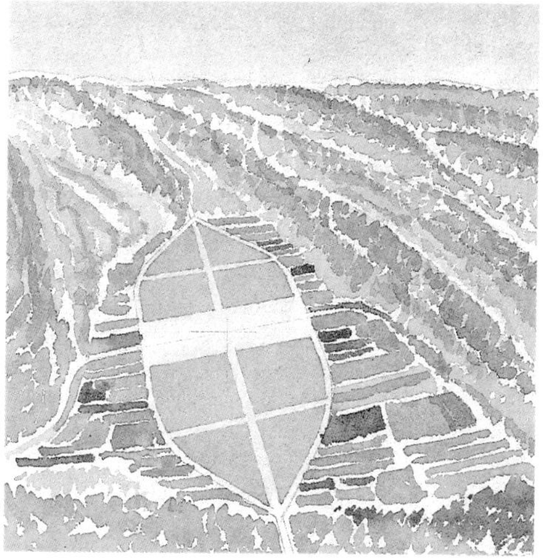

141 Cross-axial streets as marketplace: Strassenkreuz *town plan.*

142 Central market square: Rechteckplatz *town plan.*

143 Wide cross-axis as marketplace.

passed to Frederick II, the Hohenstaufen emperor. Indeed this cross-axial type is extremely rare in the 12th century, much more frequent in the 13th. Examples are towns in Swabia probably influenced by the planners of Frederick II, like Kenzingen founded by Rudolf II of Uesenberg in 1249, where the two axes of the cross have very different widths (the shorter being the wider); and towns laid out for the Wittelsbach dukes of Bavaria who were tied to the Hohenstaufen through marriage, e.g., Landau on the Isar (founded in 1224), Kelheim (ca. 1231), Deggendorf (shortly after 1242), and Neustadt on the Danube (between 1260 and 1270).

THE DISTRIBUTION OF SQUARES

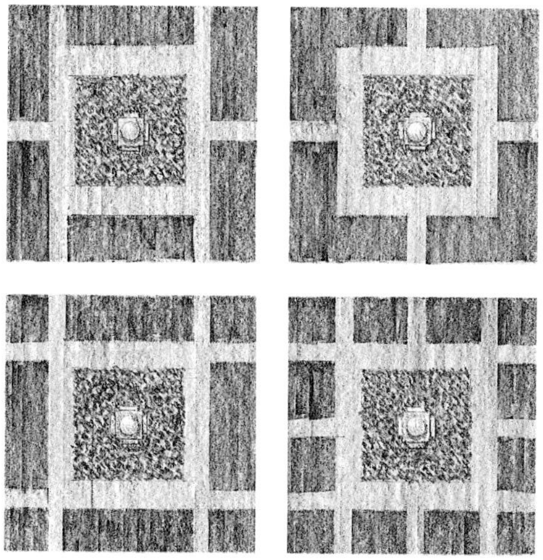

144 American courthouse square types (clockwise from lower left): block square, Harrisonburg square, Philadelphia square, four-block square.

The crossing acquired a proper square in Austria, in the so-called *Rechteckplatz* *142*
(right-angle square) type. This market square was sometimes extended perpendicular to the direction of the main streets of the linear grid. Radstadt in old Carinthia, *143*
and Venzone now within the limits of Italy, are two examples. The advantage here is that the square can be stretched out in concert with the growth of the rest of the city. The type will be transmitted to Tuscany, and will appear in the Florentine new *4*
towns of the 14th century. Here in Italy, however, the Roman heritage may also play a part. The probable model for the transverse piazza in Pavia, part of a late-14th-century redoing of the city, was Verona's Piazza Erbe, a genuine survival of the *111*
rectangular Roman forum from the city's original layout.

In the region of French, English and Spanish *bastides*, the central market square relates to the grid in two distinct ways. Sometimes it takes up a single block in the middle of the grid, and is approached at the corners along the four streets that define *124*
the block. Less frequently the market sits at a genuine crossroads, in which case it is approached axially and pushes its closed corners into four city blocks. But the two variants have a currency beyond the Middle Ages. The *Laws of the Indies*, for example, prescribed that the central plaza have streets coming into it both at the *116*
middle of each side and also at the corners—a composite formula rarely followed in practice. In county capitals of the Midwestern and Southern United States, the central square with the courthouse in the middle of the open space has four different *144*
approach types: in the so-called "block square," the streets run along the sides of the square; in the "Harrisonburg square," there are two additional streets emanating from the middle of two opposite sides; the "Philadelphia square" follows the axial arrangement with the closed corners; and the "four-block square," as the name

implies, takes up four blocks of the street grid, and therefore reproduces the formula set down for New Spain.[52]

The urban projects in the treatises of Cataneo and Scamozzi popularized the multicentered grid. Held in its bastioned polygonal hoop, the grid is punctured with seriated squares—a principal square in the middle and a ring of other subsidiary ones of varying sizes in some symmetrical distribution. It is the relationship between these squares that gives unity to the grid, rather than the mesh of the grid blocks itself. The blocks vary in size in order to correspond to the main and satellite squares.

The ideal grids of Cataneo and Scamozzi were applied to real towns, among them
147 Charleville northeast of Reims (built 1608–20), Penn's Philadelphia, the new towns of Sicily like Avola and Noto, 18th-century towns like Versoix and Carouge in France, and further afield, the Portuguese town of Daman on the Indian coast. Avola
145 is paradigmatic. It was designed in 1693, following the great earthquake, by Fra Angelo Italia, a Sicilian architect who was obviously looking at Cataneo's book. The town has a hexagonal grid plan, a shape not unacceptable to contemporary fortification theory—as Vauban's Neuf-Brisach (1698) and Montdauphin (1692–93) prove. The five squares are organized as a cross, with the largest at the intersection and the others as terminal features of the arms. The symmetry is reinforced in the paired rhythm of the six churches in the town, their locations balanced bilaterally in relation to one of the main axes.[53]

In all these ideal grids, both projected and executed, the main square in the center is the key to the composition and the social structure of the town. Scamozzi specifies that the prince's palace is to be prominently located on this square, as well as the headquarters of the Church. The satellite squares are intended as market-places. But there are also post-Renaissance grids which explore alternatives to such canonical
146 centrality. At Richelieu, a rectangular city with traditional curtain walls, a "Grande Rue" oriented north-south in the long direction of the rectangle connects two terminal square *places* of identical size. The northern one of these is exclusively

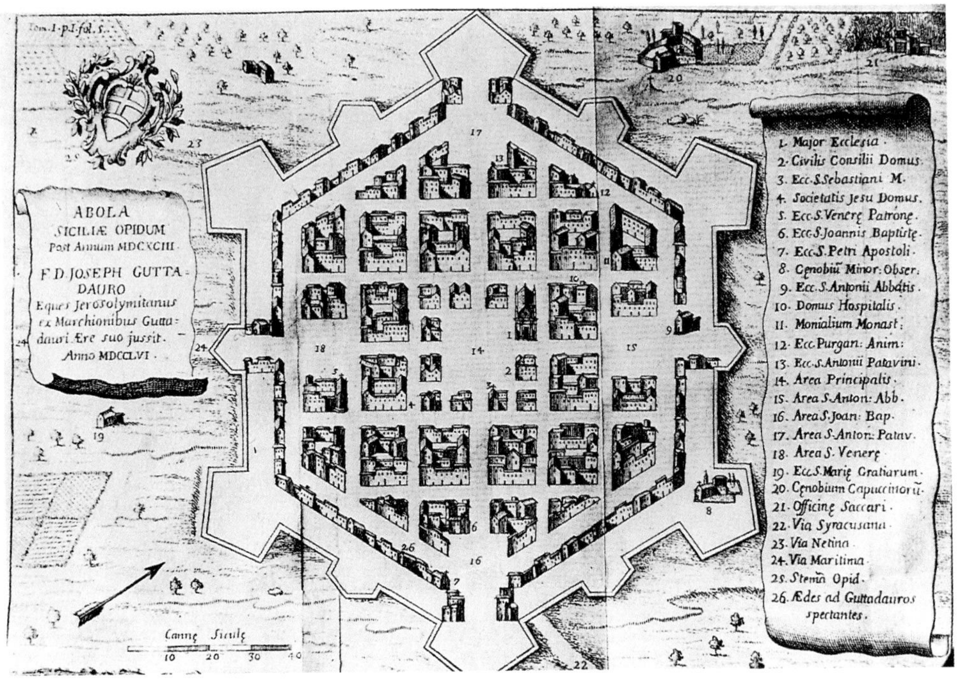

145 *Avola (Sicily), plan from V. Amico,* Lexicon Topographicum Siculum *(1757). For the Viceregal governors of Sicily, the opportunity to realize an ideal gridded city came in the guise of the disastrous earthquake of 11 January 1693. The demolished hill town of Avola was rebuilt on a flat coastal site with all of the latest town-planning features: a rigidly symmetrical plan, low earthen ramparts rather than defensive walls of stone, and wide straight streets.*

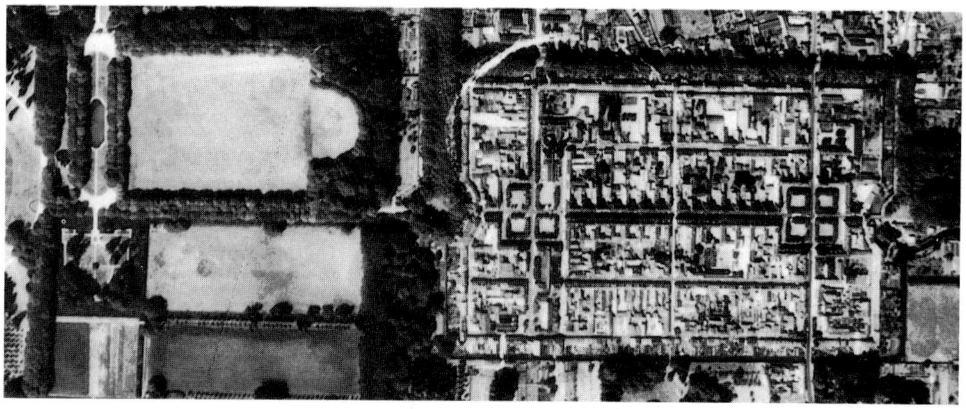

146 Richelieu (France), designed by Jacques Lemercier in 1628 for Cardinal Richelieu. The coordinated design of town, château, and garden represented a realization of the Renaissance town-planner's dream. The château, which occupied a site on the south—in the square plot at the far left of the photograph—was demolished in the 1820s.

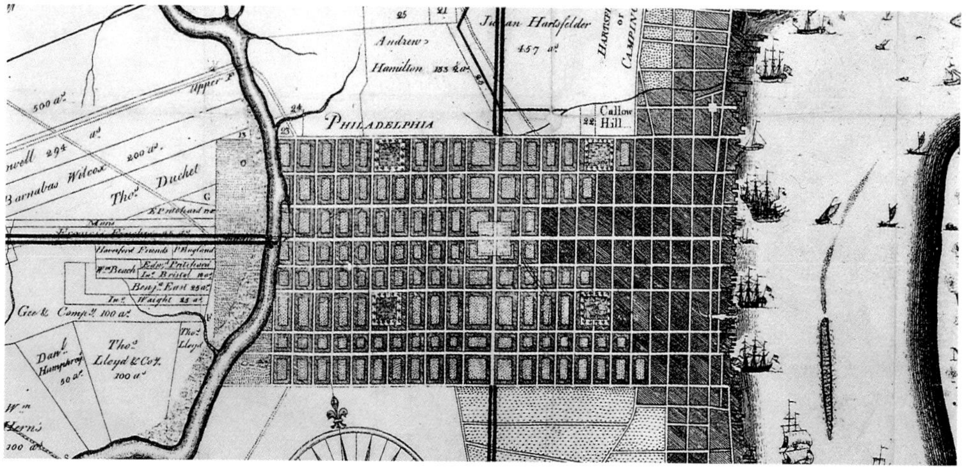

147 Philadelphia (Pennsylvania), plan drawn by John Reed, 1774. Laid out by William Penn in 1683, Philadelphia was the first large American city to be configured as a gridiron.

residential; the other is the true center of town, with the church and market hall facing each other across the open space. There is also a town hall, but no princely residence, since the Cardinal's castle lay in a park just outside the southern city gate.[54]

If the original plan of Savannah and its system of wards around six individual 104
squares might seem to echo Cataneo, the equal size of the squares and their alignment in two rows rejects the centrality and hierarchy which are his trademark. The sources of this elegant design are unclear. There was at least one plan for the reconstruction of London after the Great Fire of 1666, the one by Richard Newcourt already mentioned, which showed five squares in the Cataneo mode, and block-size wards with their own inner squares at the intersection of alleys. But this obscure image does not go much beyond a crude diagram. The model closer to hand which is often evoked, Penn's plan of Philadelphia, is not in my opinion comparable.

As a two-dimensional plan, Philadelphia clearly belongs with the Cataneo brood. 147
But it is special in ways not evident from the plan. The two principal streets crossing in the middle at a public square were 100 feet (30 m.) wide, and the rest half that much—an extremely generous arrangement for its time. The four smaller squares were designated as recreational parks. And the residential blocks were themselves ample and idyllically underbuilt. Penn's memorandum of 1681 giving instructions for the founding of the town says in part:

> Let every house be placed . . . in the middle of its plat, as to the breadth way of it, that so there may be ground on each side for gardens and orchards, or fields, that

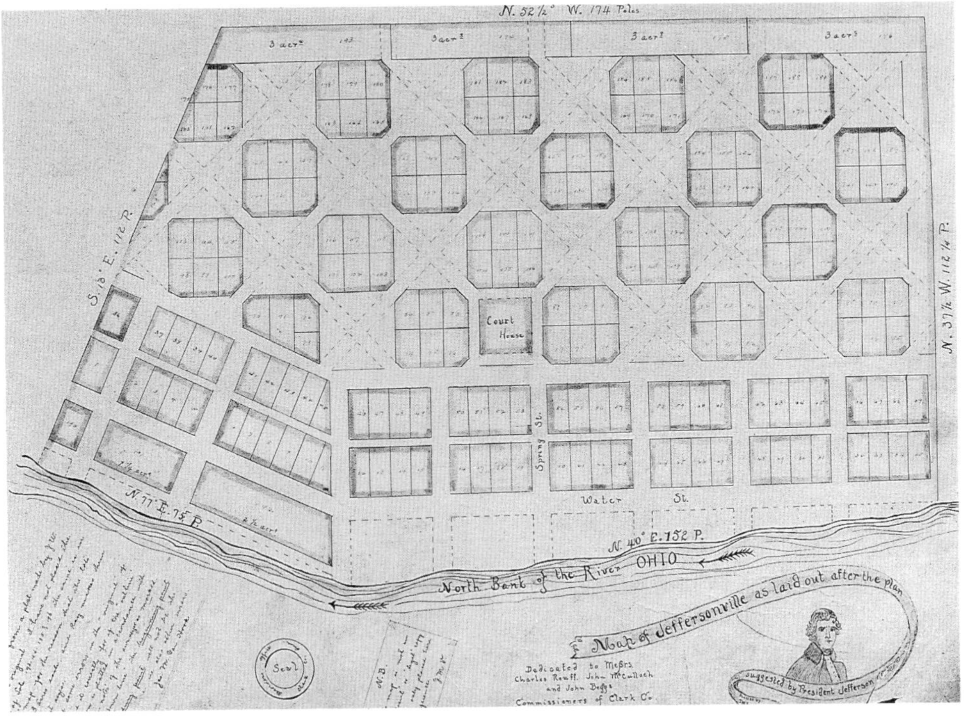

148 Plan of Jeffersonville (Indiana), after J. W. Ray, 1802.

it may be a green country town, which will never be burnt, and always be wholesome.

In fact, there is very little of a public nature in Penn's scheme; the only commercial consideration, for example, is a vague reference to the "place of storehouses." There is also no articulated urban center, nothing like the centrality of New England townships around the Puritan meeting house. Penn was a Quaker, we need to remember, and the Quaker community was free of a fixed ministry or a fixed place of worship. So in a way Penn's Philadelphia was much like the planned estates of 17th-century London, not a city so much as a residential district. As soon as Philadelphia was no longer in the total control of the proprietor, this gracious Quaker settlement was under pressure to adjust. Other cultural values besides those of Penn and his correligionaries came into play. The public parks were encroached upon; the generous blocks became crowded.

One late attempt at balancing the grid with public open spaces in the spirit of
148 Savannah ought to be noted—Jeffersonville, Indiana, on the Ohio River. The plan, based on a scheme devised by Thomas Jefferson about 1800, had an alternating pattern of open squares "in turf and trees" and subdivided blocks. Jefferson's rationale was prevention of yellow fever, a disease of epidemic proportions at the time. Diagonal streets cutting through the open squares were introduced into this scheme by the man who actually laid out the town, one John Gwathmey; this was
208 presumably meant to update the plan in line with L'Enfant's Washington, thereby in a sense re-enacting Jefferson's contest with L'Enfant over *that* city's form. This strange amalgam produced two superimposed grids—that of the city blocks, and another of the street system at an angle of 45 degrees to the first. (This same hybrid, but without the squares, will reappear at the end of the century in the original plans of two major Argentinian cities, La Plata and Belo Horizonte.) Within fifteen years of its founding, Jeffersonville was redesigned as a conventional grid. The ingenious

Jeffersonian system was used again a few years later for Jackson, the new capital of Mississippi, but there too the open squares were built over in time.

BLOCK ORGANIZATION

As the basic unit of orthogonal planning, the block and its structure in three dimensions give the urban grid its character. The common historical terminology for these blocks refers to islands—*insulae*, *îlots*, etc. First at New Salisbury (Wiltshire) they were called "chequers," which "shows that the chess-board analogy had not escaped its planners."[55]

At a simple, quantitative level, the notable features are the size and the density of the blocks. Neither remains fixed for all time. The larger the block in the initial grid, the more it is likely to be cut across by new "breakthrough" streets; the more open space is enclosed within the block, the greater the likelihood, with an increase in population, for a shift to buildings of higher density. The distribution of people was variable from the start, depending on the economic value created by land use. The edges of medieval market squares and their street extensions, and pier streets in ports like Lübeck, were more thickly crowded with narrow lots than blocks removed from the commercial action. In the United States, many grids provided for higher lot densities along railway, wharf and courthouse square peripheries.

The size and shape of the blocks were of course directly related to the number and shape of the lots into which they were subdivided. The strip blocks of Greek grids had four to ten attached back-to-back houses. At Olynthus the uniform blocks, each measuring 120 by 300 feet (37 by 90 m.), were subdivided longitudinally by an alleyway. At Priene the blocks were 120 by 160 feet (37 by 49 m.), and subdivided *120* into four or eight houses each. This squarer format is more in line with later Roman practice, where moreover the blocks tend to be quite large. Florence, for example, had blocks of some 645 square feet (60 sq. m.) each. In Aosta, they measure 230 by 260 feet (70 by 80 m.); in Winchester they are 440 feet (135 m.) on each side. To accommodate the forum, whose proportions were variable, there was often an alteration of the block rhythm and block width in its vicinity. Roman blocks had a *110* fairly free range of uses: they could be occupied by shops exclusively, or by apartment blocks as at Ostia, or by single-family atrium houses with ground-story shops. But since in most cases occupancy of these blocks was predicated on single-story or two-story buildings that opened onto interior courts, these proportions worked well. The tall, narrow, street-oriented rowhouses of the later Middle Ages were not very well accommodated in such blocks. Where the Roman grid underlies a medieval town, the original blocks will often have been consolidated in pairs and *60,* subdivided lengthwise into strips. *111*

The change from a division into squares or wide rectangles to a pattern of strip parcels has also an inherent medieval history, independent of Roman survival, and is a constituent in the genesis of the merchant's and craftman's city of the later Middle Ages. The urban shift from an agricultural to a commercial economy was in full swing by the end of the 12th century, from Flanders and North Germany to the Sicily of the Hohenstaufen. The process has been documented at Bern, a Zähringer *Pl.18* foundation. Typical of all the original Zähringer towns was the division into a set number of farm yards (*areae*) allotted to the founder's dependents. Each member was assigned one yard to be divided into lots for houses (*casalia*). The dimensions of the yards were variable, the standard proportions being 2:1 and 3:5; the long side was parallel to the street. The number of lots was also variable—3, 5, or 7. In the early stages, the yard had judicial and tax functions. The houses sat back from the street, which was therefore not fully enclosed. This basically rural system was slowly pushed aside from the mid-12th century, as strip lots redefined an urban framework suitable for a merchant economy, with the agricultural component now clearly secondary. The proportions of these new parcels could be extreme: 13 by 150 feet (4 by 46 m.) in Basel, 23 by 175 feet (7 by 53 m.) in Bern, and 23 by 213 feet (7 by 65 m.) in Geneva. The tall narrow houses, pushed up to the building line, remade the character of the streets.[56]

In new towns or town additions of the later Middle Ages intended for trade from the start, long narrow blocks accommodated a tight series of deep parcels with narrow street frontages. These so-called "burgage plots" bring home a basic truth about block and lot dimensions—that they are determined at the outset by the type of buildings and uses intended to occupy the town parcels. Italian urban geographers have coined the term *tipo portante*, or "leading type," to refer to this standard form of urban construction on green-field sites at the time of the grid's initial marking. In the case of the burgage plots, the house front would be flush with one street, and the back lot would be a produce garden and animal yard; outbuildings would be pushed to the edges of this open space and along the short back end. As a result, the same street might be lined with both houses and outbuildings. In a "double-loaded" block, two rows of houses front on proper streets and the outbuildings, pushed to the center of the block, sometimes border a dividing alley that is no more than a footpath. It is not uncommon for a row of burgage plots, in the course of time, to become a double-loaded block by abbreviating the gardens and having new houses take up the back ends.

The elongated plot with its narrow dimension fronting the street, characteristic of a time when agricultural uses were a necessary side of urban life, still found a place in the settlement patterns of the 19th century. In Łódź, Poland, a state-owned textile manufacturing town, the linen spinners' district was laid out in the mid-1820s as a grid of elongated plots, approximately 65 feet wide and 985 deep (20 by 300 m.), to allow the inhabitants to cultivate their own flax. At about the same time, the deep lot pattern was brought to South Africa by the Dutch *voortrekkers* (pioneers). Their gridded agricultural settlements had a free-standing Cape-Dutch house at the head of the deep lot, and an intensively cultivated yard at the back.

But in the 19th century such deep lot formations and their excuse—the mix of urban agriculture and trade—were exceptional medievalisms. The pressing need now was to supply rental housing for the industrial worker. In England, speculators busy exploiting this need for quick profits put up thin blocks of row houses on the cheap land at the city edge which created a skewed patchwork of grid patterns. In the North and the Midlands, they were usually "back-to-backs"—double rows with no intermediate space. This housing type emerged in newly industrialized medieval towns, where the burgage plot of the inner city was pressured to respond to higher residential densities. The long narrow yards behind the solid street frontage of houses and shops were gradually filled with a string of lean-tos that huddled against one yard wall, leaving a narrow passageway along the other for access and ventilation. Dozens of these jerry-built dwellings could be jammed into a single burgage plot, like the 420-foot (128 m.) long specimen recorded in Wakefield.[57] Beyond the saturated core, multiple-story back-to-backs were built on scraps of vacant land and in the narrow strips of small agricultural holdings that came up for development. This unwholesome grid of shabby dwellings looking onto streets no better than back alleys spread fast, and surrounded major industrial cities like Leeds and Manchester. In Liverpool gridded blocks of three-story back-to-back rows encased alleyways that provided the only access to mid-block "court houses."

149 Middlesbrough (England) displayed a dense patchwork of grids of bye-law housing, built in the later 19th century around the new Town Hall and square (lower left), as spectacular growth followed the discovery of iron ore locally in 1850: in 1869 the city was hailed as an "infant Hercules."

Social reform and urban development over the last century have wiped off the shameful landscape of back-to-backs. But the middle-class equivalent, the piecemeal grid of terraced rows that commonly defined the 19th-century commuter suburb all across England, is still intact. Its imagery owed a debt to both ends of the social spectrum. From the aristocratic Georgian terrace came the practice of subdividing suburban estates into *ad hoc* grids of blocks packed with unified rows of repetitive design: from it, too, the taste for class segregation. At the other end, progressive models for working-class housing, and the Public Health Act of 1875 which spawned the "bye-law street" with its minimum 40-foot (12 m.) width and the obligatory open space between rows, gave late Victorian speculative builders the excuse they needed to fix on a standardized formula of broad straight streets and monotonous rows of near-identical houses separated from their back neighbors by *149*
small gardens. The street layout was the developer's purview, the length of a terrace block only limited by the size of the estate at his disposal and his common sense. Rows of 800 feet (245 m.) and more were not unknown, especially along railroad tracks.

The 19th-century transformation of burgage plots into hidden warrens of slum housing in England had parallels near and far. Through a similar process, the long plots of Łódź tailored for the common textile worker were lined at the street edge with the fashionable residences of the industrial bourgeoisie, while their deep yards sequestered dark multi-story tenements built at the highest possible density on these expensive midtown sites. Colonial cities built on a deep-plot grid, like Pietermaritzburg, South Africa, and Paramaribo, Surinam, saw the familiar theme replayed in an ethnic context: Black servants could be inconspicuously housed in backyard shelters or barracks. In Washington, D.C., the block shape was different, but the social process much the same; in the later 19th century, in the shadow of the Capitol, the core of large dignified upper-class blocks concealed alley-ghettoes for immigrant Black families.

In the United States, the Colonial grid bequeathed to later periods a tendency for generous street, block and lot dimensions. Principal streets were rarely less than 75 feet (23 m.) wide. Typical of the range of lot sizes in the early grids are Savannah (60 by 90 feet, 18 by 27 m.), Mobile, Alabama (75 by 150 feet, 23 by 46 m.), and Marietta, Ohio (90 by 180 feet, 27 by 55 m.). A standard railroad town block size was 300 square feet (28 sq. m.), with lots 50 by 140 feet (15 by 43 m.). When population increased, the pressure to reduce these proportions by adding new streets and alleys was hard to resist.

In Philadelphia fragmentation got an early start. The ample blocks were cut through by very narrow alleys that slowly turned Penn's "green country town" into a city of tightly packed row houses and alley dwellings. This is deplored in the standard accounts of American urban history, and considering the congestion of the blocks and the eventual squalor of the alleys it does indeed constitute the degradation of a beautiful urban arrangement. But beauty of form must be weighed against social equity, seemliness against need. A different assessment of the Philadelphia case is certainly possible. Infill made home-ownership possible for many more than the low starting density would ever have permitted. And there was more. It has been pointed out that by 1930 some 50 per cent of Philadelphia's houses were owner-occupied. This was so because of the relatively low cost of houses; and that was so because of the highly efficient construction technique of cramming row houses into the grid. The city's building standards for foundations, walks and joists were considerably lower for narrow houses, so impressive savings were made in both labor and building materials.

New York City wrote the most telling chapter on the conflict between an original grid and modern urban densities. The 2,000 blocks created in the 1811 Commis-
118 sioners' Plan were subdivided into 25 by 100 foot (8 by 30 m.) lots, the narrow end toward the street. The Plan's failure to make any provision for midblock alleyways thwarted the potential for additional accessible units through subdivision. By mid-century lots sized for a single-family rowhouse with a back yard were loaded with tenement housing that covered 90 per cent of the site or more. The well-intentioned Tenement House Act of 1879 gave birth to what Catherine Bauer was later to call "probably the worst legalized building form in the world."[58] This was the
150 "dumbbell" tenement, so called from the shape of its floor-plan. It covered 80 per cent of its site with a solid building block, relieved by minimal air and light shafts along each party wall. By 1900, the city realized that the 25-foot (8 m.) wide lot could not carry such high densities and allow for decent standards of ventilation and natural light. The only solution was to assemble multiple plots for large buildings.

The situation went beyond housing. The changing scale of urban buildings in general was no longer consonant with established plot dimensions. In the industrialized nations, new building types of immense size—apartment houses, railroad stations, commercial offices and government ministries, department stores and warehouses—required as much as an entire block of the grid, even two as in the case of New York's Pennsylvania Railroad Station. In the United States, the relative newness of city grids eased this passage to metropolitan scale. The inexpensive residential *tipo portante*, the wood-frame house, was not a significant barrier to land-hungry institutions, so central business districts could spread out into the residential blocks at their periphery, where large building plots could be assembled at low cost.

Pl.23 The European case is more complex. The large blocks of Haussmann's Paris were
90 the result of radical surgery. Expropriation and demolition on a massive scale remade the urban block pattern, "demapping" the fine-veined system of medieval streets and lanes and merging plots to shape ample new building sites. These techniques were widely emulated across Europe in the late 19th century. Less traumatically, the new large blocks might be set down on undeveloped land at the

150 Model of a New York City block hypothetically redeveloped to maximum density with "dumbbell" tenements, 1900.

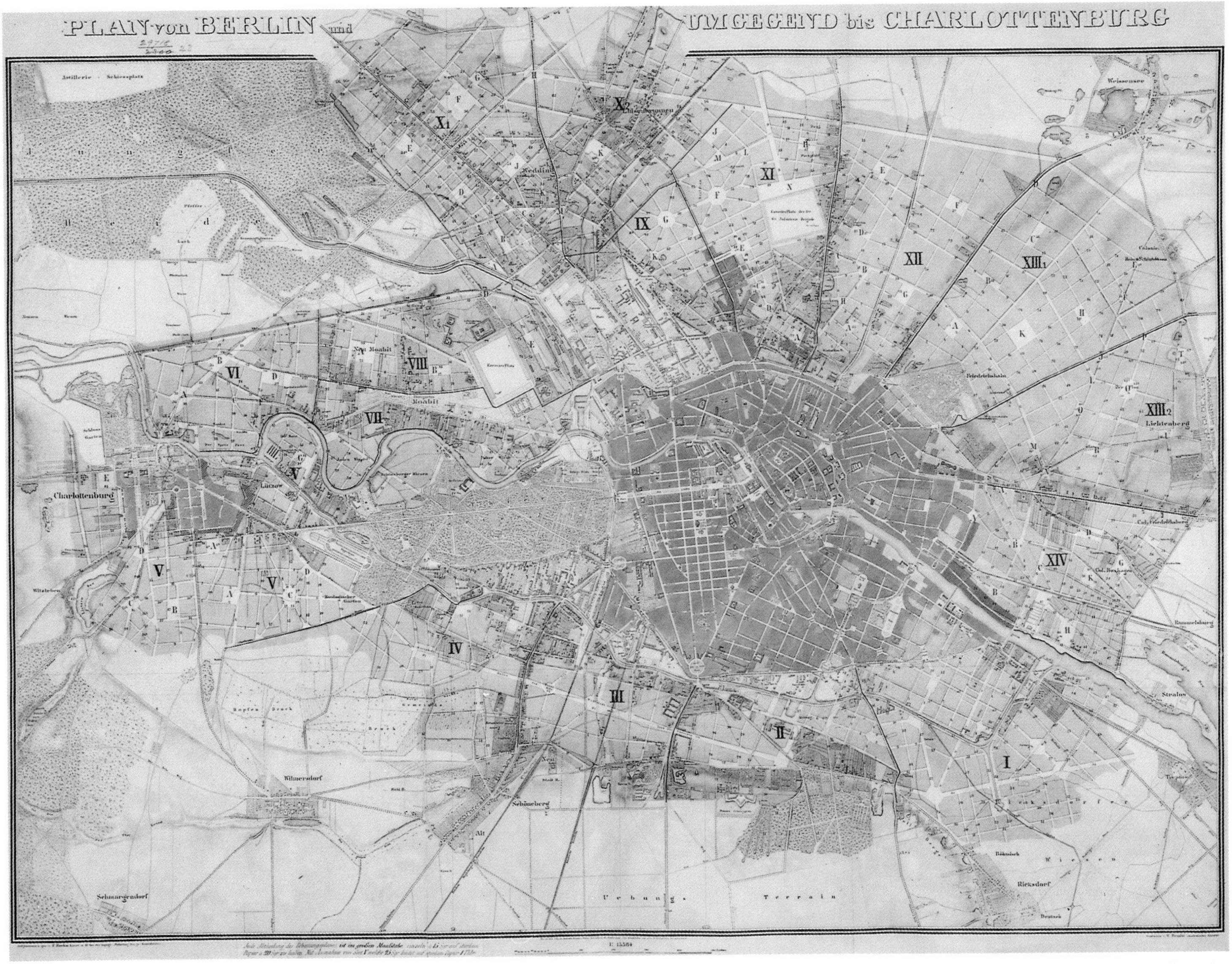

151 Plan of Berlin with new districts projected by James Hobrecht; lithograph by F. Boehm, 1865. (The existing city, shown in darker grey, includes the historic core and the adjacent 17th- and 18th-century gridded extensions of Dorotheenstadt and Friedrichstadt. The broad east-west street running across the grid is Unter den Linden, linking the Schloss to the vast Tiergarten; cf. Ill. 253.)

city edge. So Vienna used the vast expanse of the demolished fortifications for the superscaled public and residential buildings of the Ringstrasse. And the native son *Pl.4*
Otto Wagner, in his *Grossstadt* proposal of 1910, projected a broadly conceived grid *254*
of block-filling seven-story apartment houses which would encase and spare the historic center, and be infinitely extendable.

The model for this notion of the modern metropolis as a limitless, gridded city extension of stringently regulated private development went back to two actualized schemes from about 1860—the James Hobrecht plan for greater Berlin, and *151*
Ildefonso Cerdà's Barcelona plan intended as a prototype of urban extension for all of Spain.

Hobrecht took as his model the unexecuted urban extension plans of the 1820s by Peter Joseph Lenné, the Royal Director of Gardens under King Friedrich Wilhelm III. Lenné's audience was the aristocracy: he projected a minimum number of streets framing huge blocks that would provide space for expansive estates, which could later be subdivided in accordance with the owner's preferences. By Hobrecht's time,

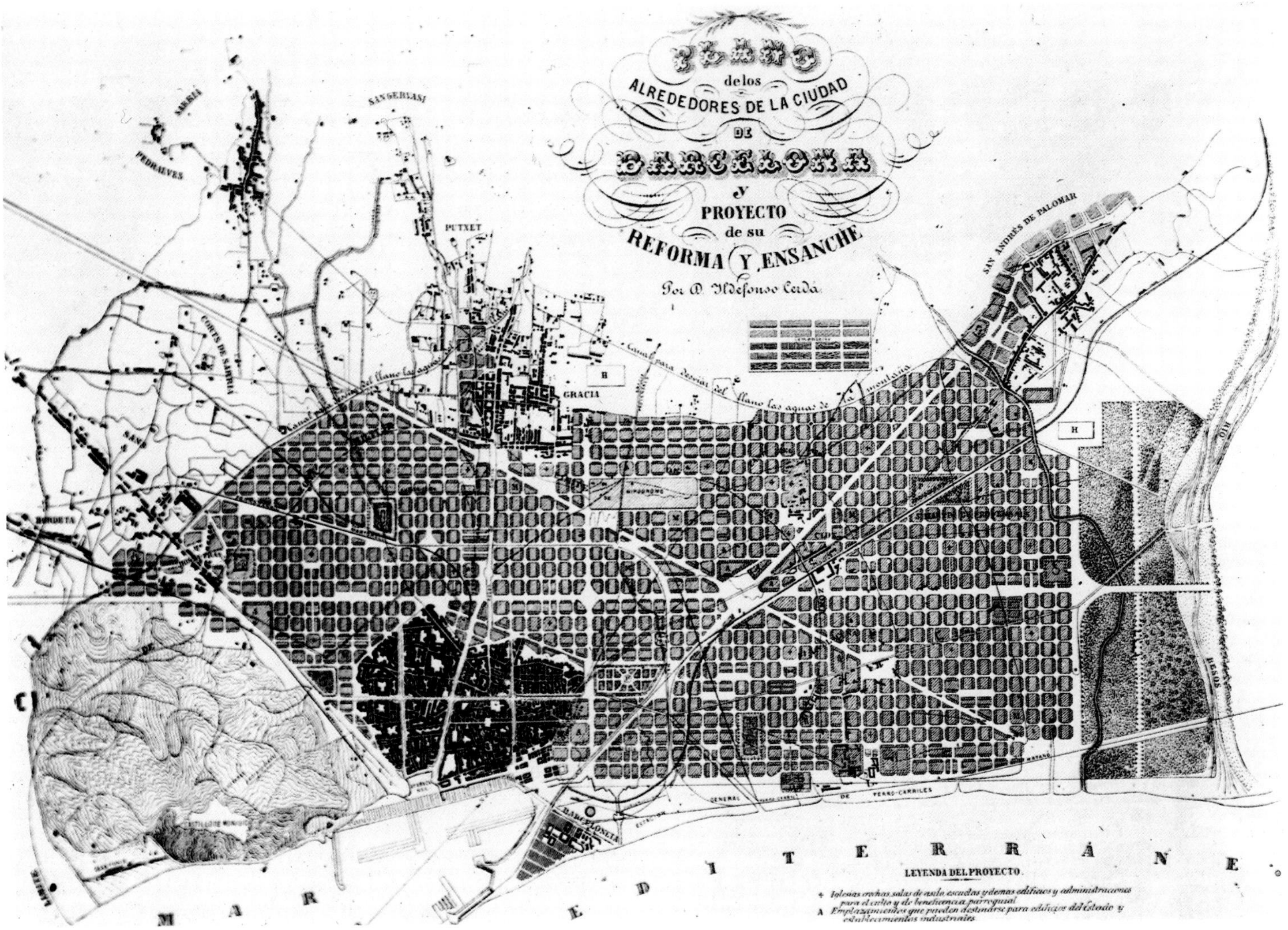

however, Berlin was a major industrial center. The pre-eminent need was now working-class housing. So the huge blocks in the Hobrecht plan, as large as 820 by 490 feet (250 by 150 m.), were packed with five-story *Mietskasernen* (rental barracks)—and damned the grid, in the eyes of a new generation of urbanists, as the perfect matrix of slum landlords and abusive congestion.

152 Cerdà left the old city of Barcelona intact, and spread an unvarying grid across more than 10 square miles (26 sq. km.) of flat land outside the medieval city walls. The streets were all of equal width, 20 meters (66 feet), and the square blocks had cut-off corners of a length that matched this street width. The buildings were also to be locked into this proportional relationship, being uniformly as high as the street was wide. To Cerdà, the squared block "is the clear and genuine expression . . . of mathematical equality, which is the equality of rights and interests, of justice itself."[59]

The stupefying regularity of this plan was relieved only by a few diagonal boulevards that formed a huge harsh "X" across the grid. But the monotony was deceptive. Most blocks were to be built up on only two sides, and not always the same two; the unbuilt remainder of each block was to be landscaped. These

152 Barcelona (Spain), plan of the city showing expansion planned by Ildefonso Cerdà, 1858. The irregular pattern of the medieval city core—the dark area at lower left—is shown sliced by a supergrid of (unbuilt) boulevards. The 18th-century grid of Barceloneta is on the triangular peninsula. The grid of Cerdà's extension, in which only two sides of each octagonal block were to be built up, fills the remainder of the city's coastal plain.

provisions made possible a kaleidoscopic variation of building and open space, from large quadrangles to linear arrangements of slab blocks prophetic of Modernism.

But Cerdà did not reckon with the forces of private ownership and the speculative market. He had set a four-story height limit for his blocks, and a 28 per cent surface coverage for building. But in the course of the century or so during which the Cerdà Plan was supposedly in effect, this Garden-City density quadrupled as all four sides of the blocks were built up, the height of units raised, and an inner courtyard space of indifferent conformation trapped in the middle. Today some of the blocks house structures of twelve stories over 90 per cent of the surface area. The ideal diagram, which reflected Cerdà's hopes for social egalitarianism, was distorted: the middle class colonized the great grid, banishing the working classes to the city's industrial rim and to rundown houses in the old urban core.

THE GRID IN THE 20TH CENTURY

The coming of the Modernist era marked the end of experimentation to salvage the traditional gridiron city through new building typologies. From the 1880s to the 1920s, protagonists of social reform—those, at any rate, who had not been converted to Garden City ideology—had championed the perimeter block as the answer to tenements. Enclosed blocks with large open courtyards were built in the 1890s as philanthropic projects in Berlin, to designs by Alfred Messel, and in New York by William Field and Sons. By 1910 this building type was being promoted by German reformers like Paul Wolf and Bruno Möhring as a benign alternative to Berlin's infamous tenement blocks, the *Mietskasernen* of Hobrecht's periphery. Finally, Berlage in his 1915 plan for Amsterdam South laid out a syncopated grid of *Pl.19* long courtyard-framing housing blocks with uniform façades, which were intended to obscure class differences. As realized in the Twenties, the district is a telling betrayal of Berlage's intentions. The housing complexes which took shape under the guidance of gifted architects like Michel De Klerk and Piet Kramer, the so-called Amsterdam School, were blocks of individualized design, idiosyncratic in massing and detail, eroding Berlage's careful delineation of separate courtyard and street volumes.

Time had passed Berlage by. For urban designers of a Modernist stripe, the grid could not serve as the frame for socially equitable development. Advocates of housing reform—Werner Hegemann in his scathing indictment of Berlin's tenements, *Das steinerne Berlin* (Stony Berlin) of 1930, and Catherine Bauer in her influential *Modern Housing* of 1934—represented the gridiron block as an intractable source of urban misery. Modernist ideologues condemned high density block development on the grounds that it denied tenants their inalienable rights to *Licht, Luft und Sonnenschein* (light, air, and sunshine). But the seemingly boundless increase in modern city traffic was perhaps the most persuasive indictment of the grid. It was now argued that the grid was essentially made for carriage traffic. The automobile had changed its character for the worse, turning city blocks into besieged islands. An estimate of 1933 claimed that the automobile had tripled the radius of the metropolitan area, and increased the daily traffic area ninefold.[60] The volume and speed of this traffic made streets extremely dangerous, especially for children.

All this provided the rationale for abandoning the grid as such, and embracing the idea of an inturned superblock bounded by major traffic arteries. Now the use of the

grid as a frame for separate communities, rather than as a means of organizing individual building lots, has non-Western precedent. In a number of cultural situations, the rigorous block structure forms the overall urban matrix within which a tracery of finer scale and more lively intercourse takes shelter. In Chinese imperial cities up to the 10th century or so the periphery of the large blocks was merely a screen—in the early Empire sometimes literally a wall—beyond which a complex
180 local organization prevailed. Similarly, the great square subdivisions of old Jaipur, of about one-half mile (800 m.) on a side, might best be called "sectors" rather than blocks. Within each one is a closer-grained and looser "minigrid" defining neighborhoods (*mohallas*). These neighborhood blocks accommodate 40 to 50 residential plots, and hold a homogeneous population based on caste, trade, or ethnic/religious affiliation.

The Modernist superblock has a different edge. In Europe, one common arrangement is to set freestanding terraces (*Zeilenbau*) in parallel rows, the long pared-down façades looking onto strips of greensward, the short end-faces, often blank, turned to the circuit of major streets that create a moat around the development. American advocates of the residential superblock had a specific social agenda: to build community spirit. The conventional street grid stranded residents on "rectangular islands surrounded by noise, dirt, fumes, and danger."[61] Denied easy access to a rewarding social life, city dwellers were depicted as isolated and anomic, afloat in a "great sea of despondency."[62] The solution was to promote social intercourse in superblocks designed as self-contained neighborhoods, each with its own shops, schools and community facilities.

An early formulation of these ideas was in Chicago around 1915. A competition sponsored by the City Club sought out innovative designs for the development of outlying portions of large cities—designs that would abandon the conventional grid and its small blocks for a unified treatment of parcels as large as a quarter-section. "The temperamental nervousness that characterizes us as a people must find an outlet in variety and not in monotony," a jury member wrote, "[and] this should be expressed by the foiling of . . . playfulness and charm against severity."[63] All the winning projects kept the rectilinear section roads as a stable frame, while introducing broad curves and a looser block structure. All emphasized landscaping, and focused their inward-looking parcel with public buildings like schools and churches.

But the first major policy statement of the "neighborhood unit for the family-life community" came in a 1929 paper by the sociologist Clarence A. Perry for the Russell Sage Foundation. Focused on a "community center" and endowed with a freewheeling system of interior streets, the Perry scheme generalized the select experience of American picturesque suburbs and English Garden Cities. Architects like Henry Wright, the American advocate of Garden City principles, went so far as to argue for a legal modification of the American grid as the matrix of land development.[64]

From the Thirties onward, American concepts of superblock planning became increasingly allied with theories emanating from the International Congresses of Modern Architecture, or CIAM. According to Modernist canons set down in CIAM's 1933 position paper known as the Athens Charter, traffic flow and its design was the primary determinant of city form. CIAM dogma focused on the incompatibility of the sleek new transportation technologies with the slowly evolved husks of existing cities. In practice, the Modernist alternative was a composition of freestanding buildings, set in a diffuse landscape of foliage and organized by a loose grid of high-speed arteries. In Detroit and Minneapolis planners had envisaged a maxigrid of this kind, as an adjunct to the gridiron of streets rather than its replacement, as early as the Twenties. In Detroit, the land was assembled "for a comprehensive system of 204-foot [62 m.] wide rights-of-way laid out in a grid at approximately three-mile [5 km.] intervals, supplemented by intermediate 120-foot [37 m.] wide major thoroughfares at one-mile [1.6 km.] intervals on the formerly 66-foot [20 m.] wide roads."[65]

A more comprehensive proposal to reshape the American gridiron came from a Chicago-based luminary of the Bauhaus diaspora, Ludwig Hilbersheimer. His "settlement unit," inspired by both American neighborhood unit planning and the more radical urban proposals of European Modernism, was predicated on the gradual transformation of the conventional gridded city through an orderly program of street closings and selective demolition. In the new pattern neighborhoods would be separated by park belts and made safe from traffic through the provision of residential cul-de-sacs as a part of an overall street hierarchy.[66]

In contrast to Hilbersheimer's accommodation of the historic settlement pattern, orthodox Modernist projects for high-speed maxigrid cities were plotted against vacant backgrounds. New towns held the best chance for unencumbered city-making of this sort; bombed postwar cities provided a less tidy but workable slate. The "Collective Plan" of 1946 for the reconstruction of Berlin, prepared by a group of Modernists led by Hans Scharoun, rejected the city's circular-radial traffic pattern in favor of a new metropolis built upon a high-speed grid system of 64 clover-leaf interchanges. Only the medieval core would be saved, as an urban museum; other fragments that had survived the war would be pulled down. Scharoun wrote: "Whatever remains, after the bombs and the final battle created a mechanical decongestion, gives us the possibility to organize an urban landscape [where] from nature and buildings, from the low and the high, from the narrow and the wide will rise a new vital order."[67] The plan was rejected the following year and Scharoun replaced by the conservative Karl Bonatz.

At Chandigarh (founded in 1951), the first Modernist city to be realized *ab ovo*, 153
the sophisticated residential pattern is characterized by the interpenetration of green

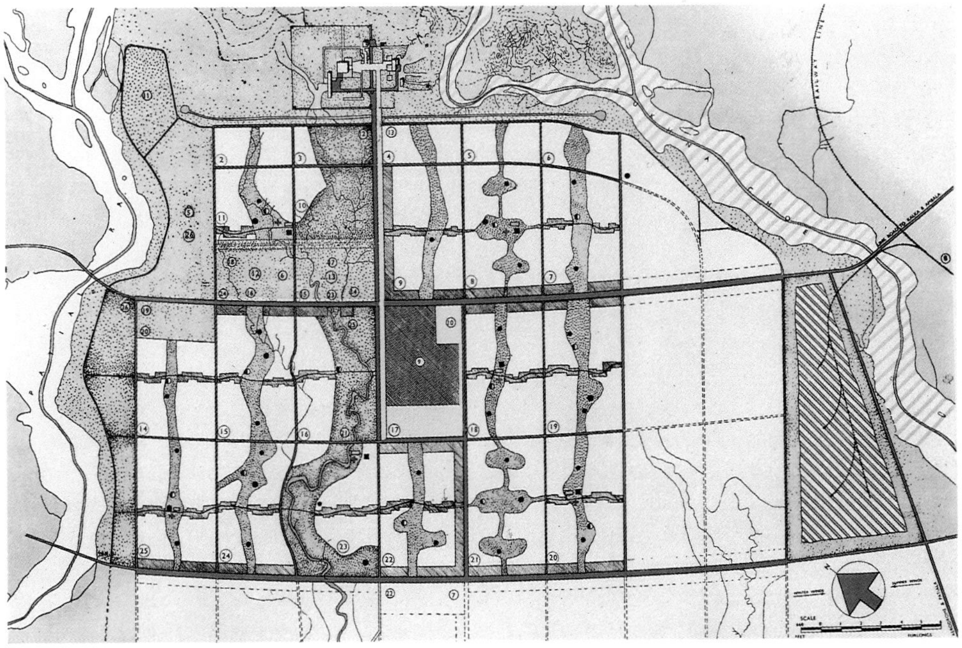

153 Schematic plan of Chandigarh (India), capital of the Punjab, designed by Le Corbusier in 1951. Market streets are shown running through the supergrid horizontally, parks vertically. The dark area in the center is the city's business district. The capitol complex is outside the supergrid at the top of the plan.

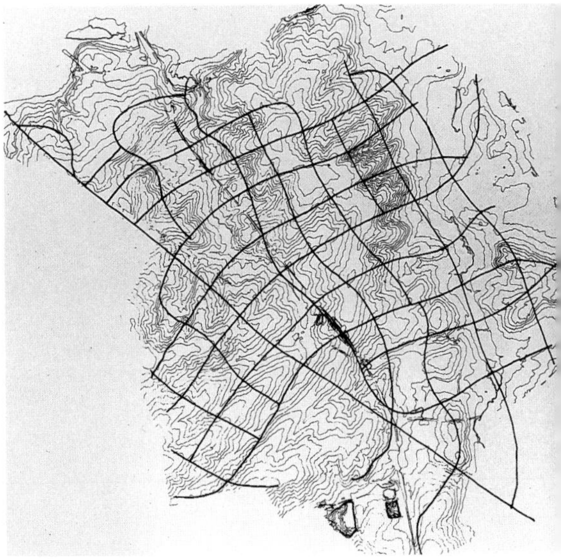

154, 155 Milton Keynes (England), aerial view of the town center drawn by Helmut Jacoby, and map of grid roads and land contours. Like other Modernist supergrids, Milton Keynes's loose weave of traffic arteries serves to delimit the boundaries of urban districts, rather than to define conventional city blocks. One such district, the city center, is configured as a rigidly orthogonal minigrid of streets, buildings, and parking lots nested within the supergrid of the primary road network.

landscape and a loose grid pattern of primary roads defining superblocks. The superblocks, or "sectors" as they are called, measure 800 by 1,200 meters (half by three-quarters of a mile) each, proportions based on the Golden Section. The blocks are controlled communities oriented inward, so that the primary traffic roads have little if any street life. Each block is bisected lengthwise by one major local through-street, the market street; together, these form a linear shopping system, Modernism's homage to the bazaar. The lines are not actually continuous from one end of the city to the other: mostly they are offset when they meet primary roads. At the same time, a central park system runs transversely through the blocks. In the crossing of two major axes is the civic center, as the forum would be in a Roman grid. But the true focus of the city is the Capitol, the heroic governmental complex by Le Corbusier comprised of the High Court, the Legislative Assembly, the Secretariat, and the Governor's Palace. It is designed on a huge module of squares measuring 800 by 400 meters (2,625 by 1,312 feet). Set against the awesome backdrop of the Himalayas, the buildings are scaled accordingly; the spaces between them are hardly negotiable on foot in the searing Punjab sun, even though the entire Capitol plaza was conceived as a pedestrian area, with motor traffic sunk below ground in trenches leading to parking areas.

154, The most thoroughly worked out Modernist grid of recent years is in Milton
155 Keynes (founded in 1967), the last of the English New Towns. This grid system is

made up of motorways defining one-kilometer (0.6 mile) squares, and it is far from being rigid. The lines gently undulate, at the same time that they rise and fall, in sympathy with the gently contoured land. Moreover the roads are bordered by thick tree-walls intended to absorb traffic noise. The imagery is hybrid: the picturesque green effects of the Garden City are made to civilize a rational grid, with the road engineers "trying in vain to give a useful structure a look of self-grown beauty."[68] There is no specific road center, and therefore the congestion of traffic that is inevitable in a centralized plan like Ebenezer Howard's original diagram of the 204
Garden City, subsequently respected in all the New Towns, is here avoided. The town center is in the nature of a shopping mall, and one of the motorways runs through it at upper-story level.

Within the grid squares, private development has a free hand. Both apartment blocks and detached houses are acceptable, and some of the squares are of course relegated to industrial and commercial buildings, to leisure and recreation. Despite the planners' espousal of mixed use, the Modernist dogma of breaking the city into "functions" prevails. A network of local traffic accommodates pedestrians and bicyclists. But the grid squares are not conceived as inturned "planned residential neighborhoods" in the Garden City mode. If anything the desire here is to revert to the open grid, and use the motorways and local streets to move freely over the entire city. At Milton Keynes, it might be fair to suggest, the experiences of Modernism and the Garden City are redirected to traditional ends.

Indeed, the crusade of the last two decades to bring back the historic city, conserve what is left of it and rehearse its lessons, also entails the recovery of the traditional block. The grid, in fact, never quite disappeared. The Modernist cityscape had displaced two other urban traditions that were now being reclaimed: the "organic" townscape with its picturesque effects and irregularities all within a system of spatial closure, of tight spatial sequences; and the Baroque townscape with its complete compositions, its visual drama, its showcasing of monuments in formal squares and at the ends of vistas, its scenographic hierarchies.

It is the great virtue of the grid, of its ceaseless usefulness, to resist both of these contrived urban experiences. Their champions hold as an article of faith that the complexity of social life requires complex street systems to seek its fulfillment. The premise of the grid is that city-form, as a tissue of lines on the ground, is the inscribed set on which our lives are played. How well we play on this set, what progress we register towards creating a decent and proud community, is in our hands. The proof of our intentions will be in the streets and public places as we shape them in our progress. The virtue of the grid is precisely in being a conceptual formal order, non-hierarchical, neutral, until it is infused with specific content. The grid is free both of *malerisch* incident and of ideological posturing. It is repetitive, homogeneous, even redundant. And because it is so, it calls us both to respect it and to complete it. Our task as designers becomes one of celebrating its commonality while teasing it into calibrations it does not promise as a two-dimensional plan on the ground. The grid carries no inherent burden of its own. The grid is what you make it.

3 · THE CITY AS DIAGRAM

CIRCLES AND POLYGONS

ARCOSANTI AND PALMANOVA

ONE of the popular tourist sites of Arizona lies northeast of Cordes Junction, *158*
60 miles (some 100 km.) due north of Phoenix. There, perched high on the edge of a remote mesa, is an odd assortment of unfinished buildings—like the ruins of an Indian cliff dwelling, one is tempted to say mindful of the area's history, except that these make no attempt to connect with the land on which they sit. It is more like an open-air market of architecture—intriguing fragments that do not relate to one another, but seem to share a common, obscure fate through their proximity and the austere grandeur of their desert setting.

This is Arcosanti, under fitful construction since 1970. Its mastermind is Paolo Soleri (1919–), born in Turin, an ascetic philosopher-architect and the inventor of "arcologies," of which these random scraps overlooking the canyon of the Aqua Fria River are an embryonic demonstration. He coined the word "arcology" to suggest an architecture responding efficiently to ecology; more precisely, it refers to Soleri's breed of the city of the future, contained within a single megastructure, and aiming to maximize social benefits and minimize costs of land, energy and raw materials. For Arcosanti the ultimate goal is to house 5,000 people in a single-structure solar-powered arcology 25 stories high; it will occupy only 14 acres on a 3,000-acre site (5.7 out of 1,215 ha.), the rest to be reserved for agriculture, recreation and beauty. The models and drawings of the Arcosanti vision are there to *157*
admire, and Soleri's fecund imagination has created many other sister arcologies on paper along with charters of their philosophy.[1]

But for now, after twenty years of toil, the crop is meager and hybridized. Instead of a single urban shell, there are single buildings. The Soleri language has by now become familiar—barrel vaults; circles; quarter-sphere apses; sweeping half-arches; frameless round window holes. The detailing is crude. The most conventional, and prominent, building is the information center which contains a restaurant and a gift shop. Visitors' fees are a main source of income to support construction: so are the bells made on the premises. The foundry, in fact, was one of the first structures to go up, along with the ceramic apse where the bells are exhibited, with its silt-cast ribs and hangers cast into the concrete shell. There are, besides, a music center, two units of minimal housing for the thirty-odd residents, and Soleri's own house. The north

156 Nahalal (Israel); moshav *founded in 1921, designed by Richard Kauffmann.*

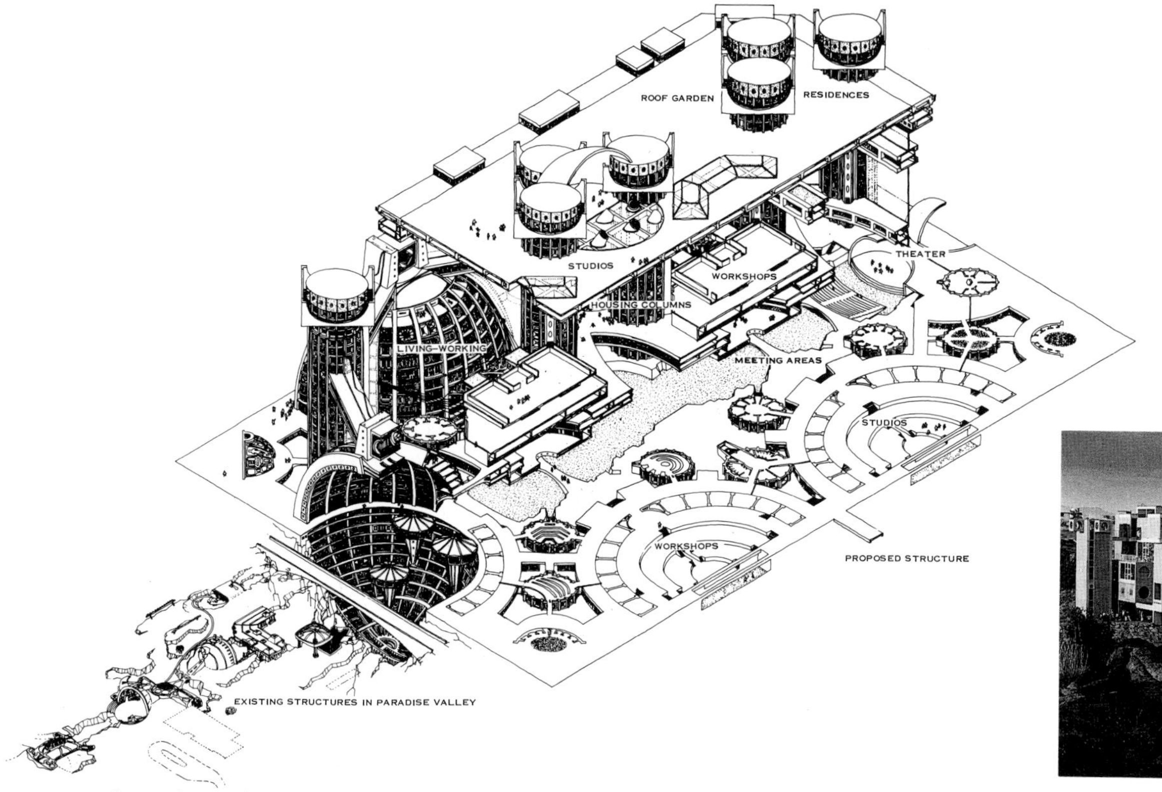

157, 158 Arcosanti (Arizona), axonometric view of the original scheme, late 1960s, and the site under construction.

and south vaults, open at both ends, were assigned no particular function, though things like the welding shop and the electrical shop find home there, and breakfast and lunch are served for the workers.

They are called "workshoppers," people with little or no construction experience, who pay to attend five-week "seminars" or workshops mostly consisting of doing unpaid labor. One of their number describes the breed, self-importantly, as "construction worker, new age visionary, monk-builder, consciousness pioneer, evolution's own awareness of itself." They live in a base camp down in the valley, while the residents use the housing in the arcology itself. In the future, Soleri's world will be classless. "The foundation of equity is . . . granted." But in these imperfect beginnings tensions have already surfaced. Some workshoppers see the residents as aloof hill-top dwellers, segregated from the camp. "They seem to consider themselves upper class citizens."[2]

Soleri is not concerned. Utopia is not possible today: it is for a distant time. Arcosanti is not a model society. It is merely the workshop of our urban future. The forms have to come first; slowly and incrementally, they will shape behavior. Function follows form. Or, as he puts it, "The instrument has a chronological precedence over the performance." When the age of arcologies has at long last emerged, however, there will be no slums, no crime, no ethnic segregations. "A social pattern is influenced, if not directed, by the physical pattern that shelters it. In a one-container system are the best premises for a non-segregated culture. The care for oneself will tend to be care for the whole."[3]

In Soleri's native country, some distance south of Venice, is a perfectly shaped
Pl.3 polygonal city frozen in its tracks for all of four centuries. It started life as a military
outpost of the Venetian Republic called Palmanova, lying on a main crossroads of
159 the Friuli district. First laid out in 1593, its bastioned curtain was completed in 1623.

159 Palmanova (Italy), as first designed in 1593, from Braun and Hogenberg's Civitates Orbis Terrarum.

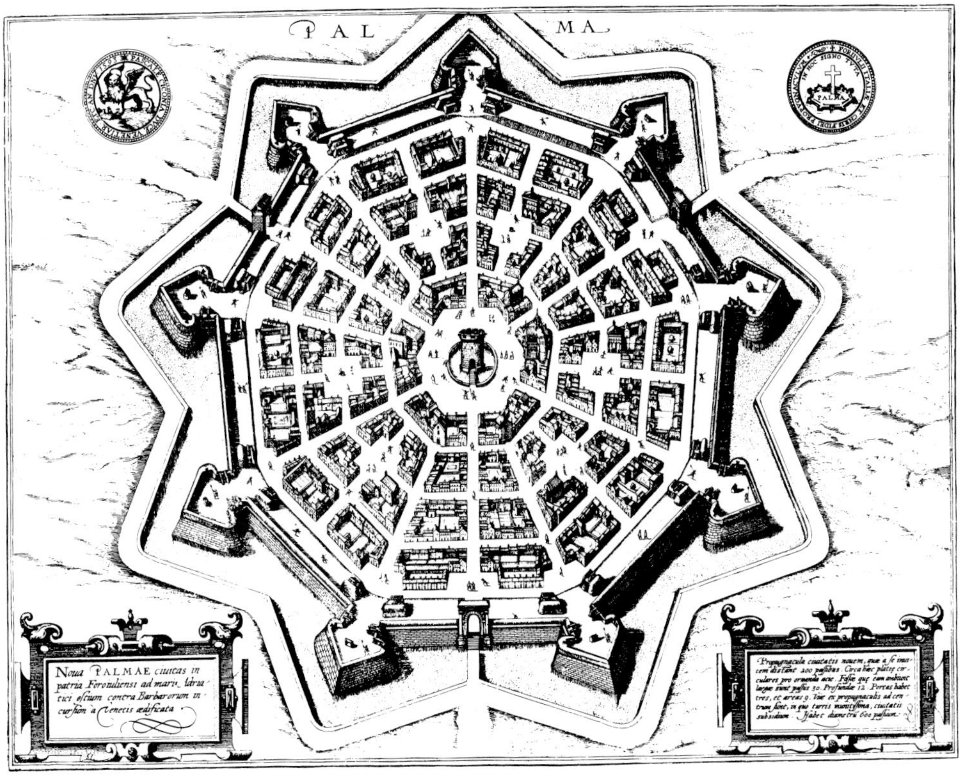

It was reinforced by a second ring in 1667—90, and then again in 1806—9, during the French occupation, a mighty third ring with an elaborate system of outworks was put in place. At every stage of its history, Palmanova's defenses represented the state of the art.[4]

Palmanova is the only complete radial plan to be built in Italy in the 16th century. In the choice of the site and the initial conception of the city-fortress, several distinguished military engineers and planners, including Scamozzi, collaborated. The frame is a nine-sided polygon, but the central piazza is a hexagon, and even then only three of the town's nine bastions are linked to it in a direct line. On the road just within the fortifications fronted the barracks of the mercenary troops—Greeks, Slavs, Germans—parade grounds, and arms depots. Mounted police on the outside, quartered at three stations, patrolled the perimeter against internal sabotage. The central piazza and the area around it was for the commanding officers and the native Venetian soldiers whose loyalty could be counted on. The piazza could be isolated and defended from the outside by sealing off the six radial streets that converged upon it. The area in between was the civil zone, with a number of additional radial streets that stopped short at the central military zone. The gates, of which there were originally only three corresponding to the main land routes, were in the middle of the curtains; streets connected them directly to the center, and small squares were placed midway.

Palmanova saw battle only once, when Venice engaged Austria in the war of Gradisca of 1615–17. Thereafter it played a deterrent role. Under the Austrians it served as a barracks town. It was finally abandoned as a military post in 1866, when Friuli was annexed to the newly instituted kingdom of Italy. It is still there today, near perfect and sad, proof of how suddenly single-purpose towns turn into anachronisms. There is now a desultory market of trinkets in the gravel-covered central piazza, and in the streets that radiate out from it a handful of inhabitants lounge in improvised sidewalk cafés preoccupied with the passing visitors. Their number, too, is small, mostly buffs of military architecture. The town has chiefly its ideal plan to show, and city-form in itself has never been a compelling tourist attraction.

The spherical compulsion of a would-be arcology in the Arizona desert: a sunburst for warfare in the Veneto. We are concerned in this chapter with this brand of inflexible city, planned at one time as a precise diagram of some presumed or promulgated order. Now behind all cities there is a strong formative will, ambition, the calculated and complex art of public association. There is choice—here and not over there; arbitrary decision—this big and no bigger; willful change—tearing down that and building up this. But in what I have called the "organic" pattern, at least in its pre-modern phases, we encountered a common-sensical, flexible order, accommodating topography, prior markings on the land, and the rhythms of living together in close quarters. And in the grid we hailed a simple geometric idea of great versatility. In contrast, cities here under discussion are single-minded visions of some determined individual or institution about how the world should function ideally, under the supreme direction of that individual or that institution, or else in accordance with some all-encompassing principle.

By their nature such cities often remain on a theoretical plane. There have been many more ideal cities on paper than on the ground. Or else they struggle, in the absence of centralized resources and political power, that is, without the State, to establish themselves and persevere, only to waste in the act of building. Arcosanti might yet prove the exception, but its short history is not propitious.

When they do get built, these ideal cities are often very short-lived in their pure state, being overtaken by reality, the way we really are and behave when we are not under rigid surveillance; or they are supplanted or ousted by a new ideal of total order. One can see no trace whatever, under the tangle of modern Hamadan in Iran, of the Ecbatana of seven concentric walls described by Herodotus. Rice fields have
139 overtaken the strict hierarchical geometry of Heijokyo (now Nara), the old imperial capital of Japan, save for some hamlets and the enclaves of temples. If Palmanova has come through more or less intact, it is not as a viable community but as an unwitting exhibit in a museum of ideal cities.

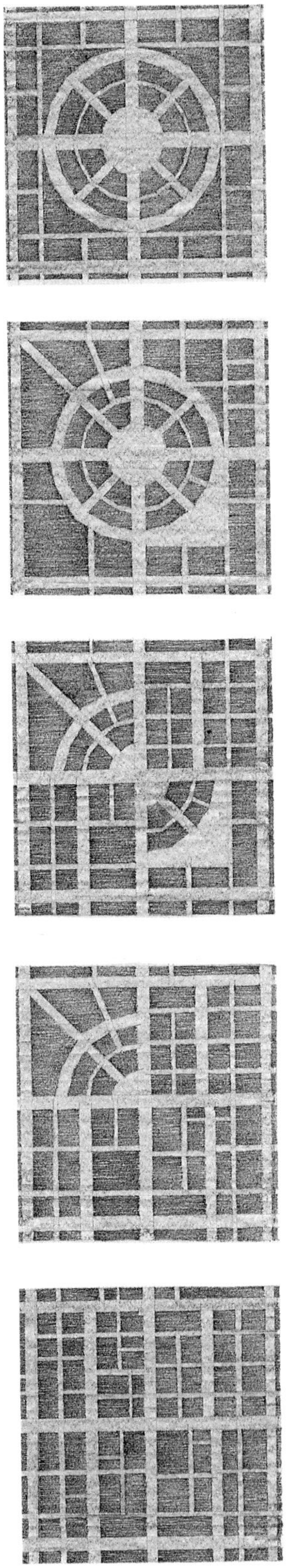

UTOPIAS AND IDEAL CITIES

By their nature, these cities are most often transposed into design in perfect geometric shapes, circles and focused squares and polygons of various kinds, and they obey rigid modes of centrality—radial convergence or axial alignment. But the temptation to see iconographic significance in every seemingly express spatial diagram must be resisted.

In the first place, urban history has not been spared whimsical geometries that are eminently negligible. Two California specimens are Corona, now absorbed within the eastern sprawl of greater Los Angeles, and Cotati, the "Hub of Sonoma County." The first, called "Circle City," was founded in 1886, and featured a circular "Grand Boulevard" enclosing an area one mile (1.6 km.) in diameter; but the area was filled with a routine speculative grid, and the farm pattern outside the circle was also prosaically rectilinear. Cotati's six-sided radial scheme of 1893 had to do with the fact that the proprietor, a Dr. Thomas S. Page, had six sons he wished to have streets named after.

160 opposite *The "squaring" of Circleville (Ohio): from top to bottom, the original city plan of 1810, and its condition in 1837, 1838, 1849, and 1856. (After Reps)*

The only other 19th-century American experiment with ideal form was Circleville, Ohio, on the Scioto River, a circular city with radiating avenues laid out *160*
by one Daniel Driesback in 1810. American, because it purported to base its circular core, with its circular plaza fixed by an octagonal courthouse, on a large circular earthwork created by Indian mound builders. But the circle was surrounded by a gridded square which was infinitely extendible. It soon ate up the middle too; within a few short decades the squaring of Circleville was complete. When James Silk Buckingham visited the town in 1840, a few years before he designed his own model town of Victoria, he wrote of it: *201*

> So little veneration . . . have the Americans for ancient remains, and so entirely destitute do they appear to be, as a nation, of any antiquarian taste, that this interesting spot of Circleville, is soon likely to lose all traces of its original peculiarities . . . The circular streets are fast giving way, to make room for straight ones; and the central edifice itself is already destined to be removed, to give place to stores and dwellings; so that in a century or less, there will be no vestige left of that peculiarity which gave the place its name, and which constituted the most perfect and therefore the most interesting work in antiquity of its class in the country.[5]

In the second place, a line needs to be drawn, in accordance with my own aims in these books, between utopias and ideal cities. A utopia does not have to be a city. Utopias are no-wheres. They are outside specificities of place and state, and vague about the kind of physicality their design codifies. Ideal cities exist in context. They are often intended to clarify the standing of a ruler in relation to his subjects and a wider circle of contemporaries, and they are dependent for their effectiveness on being fixed in place within a larger geographical frame and a prior cultural landscape. Even when they are free of political absolutism, purposely removed far away from a customary geography in order to start fresh, theirs is a structured response to a specific order found intolerable. Utopias, on the other hand, may be antidotes to nothing more precise than the pervading wickedness and injustice of humanity at large.

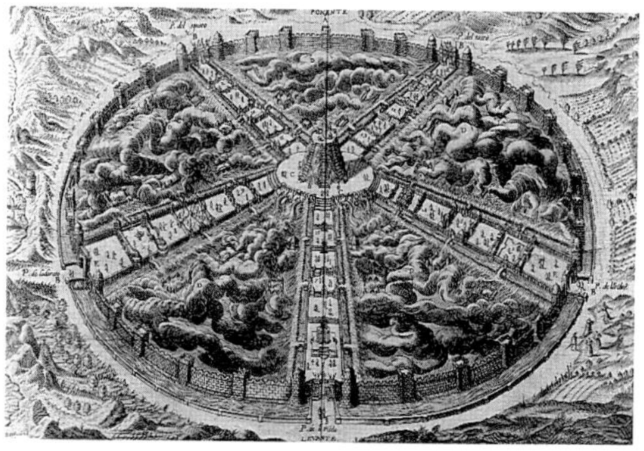

161 Bartolommeo Delbene, the "City of Truth," engraving from his Civitas veri sive morum *(1609).*

I am therefore not concerned *per se* with Thomas More's Amaurot, the capital of Utopia, or Tommaso Campanella's "Città del Sole," or Andrae's Christianopolis. These and other urban confections of philosophers feed on each other, going back to Plato's *Republic* and Augustine's *City of God*. Their understanding of the actual workings of cities is exceedingly innocent: from cities they learn nothing at all, borrowing only the diagrammatic rudiments of urban design, which means almost always ideal schemes like circles or centered squares, to accompany the tidy systems of their moral philosophies. Even more distant from urban reality are allegorical cities like Bartolommeo Delbene's City of Truth (published in 1609): based on *161*
Aristotle's *Nicomachian Ethics* and on the radial-concentric formulas of Renaissance urban theory, it depicts a round city wall with five roads of the moral virtues emanating from a center of intellectual virtues and cutting through the swamps of vice.[6]

Finally, there are "geometries" that come about through rational processes unrelated to the ideal-city phenomenon here under discussion. The concentric rings of Lucignano in Tuscany are the result of urban evolution, and Lucignano has a lot of company within Italy and out. Similarly, the rays of some old Dutch cities are due to their retaining the pattern of pre-extant *terpen*—artificial mounds of turf sods and clay made to avoid flooding by sea, which in pre-Roman and Roman times accommodated hamlets surrounded by small block-shaped fields. The

162 Takht-i Suleiman (Azerbaijan), Parthian sanctuary of about the 1st century AD. *The focus was the sacred fire called Adhur Gushnasp, which means "fire of warriors" or "royal fire."*

larger *terpen* had a circular road and ditch, with a radial arrangement of farms, and this is what accounts for the radial-concentric structure of towns like Leeuwarden or Middelburg.

On the other hand, two classes of idealized patterns engage our subject even though, strictly speaking, they pertain to pre-urban or non-urban landscapes. The first class concerns settings of faith. Prehistoric sanctuaries like Stonehenge, we have been discovering, fixed with great precision a cosmic diagram that guided human lives in accordance with celestial behavior. Since the motive of many ideal cities in antiquity was to recreate on earth the design of the universe, to use the urban plan as an intermediary between heaven and earth, the henges of Salisbury Plain or of Dacian Sarmizegethusa in modern-day Romania should be seen as setting up themes of reverberation. The same holds true, and more directly so, for those sanctuaries of
162 urban cultures like the Mazdean lake-sanctuary of Takht-i Suleiman in modern Azerbaijan with its enormous circular wall. The round cities of Persia cannot be dissociated from this religious example, any more than the symbolism of the seven planets in the Ecbatana of the Medes, and the twelve signs of the zodiac at Sassanian
182 Gur (Firuzabad), can be divorced from the magic preoccupations of their priests.

We cross into our proper subject, then, at the point when the primal urge to occupy the land with reverence and appease cosmic energies is extended into a general system in which the movement of all of us, not just of the sun and the moon, is charted on the ground. This comes about when a society functions under a finely articulated belief that one single human agency, a king or emperor or high priest, holds the key to cosmic harmony. He sits at the top of the human pyramid, and administers appropriate control that will make sure all things are in their place, and all of us are doing, in accordance with our station, what he has assigned us to do.

So an ideal city, unlike Stonehenge or Takht-i Suleiman, engraves a pattern of faith *and* government. The human agency at the top is in tune with divinity, communicates with the heavens directly or through ritual, or is at times himself divine. As an Assyrian proverb has it: "Man is the shadow of god / The slave is the shadow of man / But the king is god." In that capacity, the ruler uses the urban diagram to organize the entire population, which is itself diversified as befits a city, in terms of social strata that are keyed to his position. We will be lined up or zoned according to our occupations, perhaps our origins, or we will be distanced from the focus of the urban diagram according to some conferred status or rank that depends on the central agency.

The other class of incomplete but premonitory diagrams are those of social arrangement not informed by a centralized bureaucracy. There are the circular settlements, for example, of the Bororo of the Mato Grosso in Brazil, made famous by Claude Lévi-Strauss, who planned their villages with strict orientation to the four cardinal points, with the men's house and dance platform in the center of the circle, and spatial assignments that reflected the tribal and class structure of the village. The temporary tribal assemblies of the Cheyenne Indians chose a circular arrangement, and so did the Nguni in South Africa in their kraals which were circular protective stockades for home and cattle.

But what is missing in these from our viewpoint is the existence of an unchallengeable political authority that would make the diagram a record of a permanent, unchanging order. We know how, in some African villages, the death of a chief and the selection of a new one reorients the entire village away from the dead man's hut and toward that of the new chief. But the dynastic city is fixed for all time. This is what dynasties are all about. When there is a political upheaval and a new regime comes to power, it will have two options. It will either identify itself with the passing regime to establish legitimacy and continuity, or it will dramatize the break with the past by abandoning the dynastic city for one of its own.

But the same circle may inscribe without a major visual effort the passage from a consensual to a coercive social structure. When the kraal module of the Zulus is pushed to urban proportions in the 19th century, with a royal kraal in the middle and the huts of the warriors and their families arranged in four or five rows around this, we are within close range of Gur or the round city of Baghdad.

SPECIALIZED ENVIRONMENTS

THE DESIGN OF REGIMENTATION

163 Encampment of Assurbanipal, from a carving at Nimrud (Iraq). Cooks and servants are depicted preparing for the ruler's return. (After Layard)

Inherent in the stratification or the regimented behavior of their populations is the diagrammatic layout of some specialized communities like military camps, monasteries, and industrial towns. We need to acknowledge these as ideal cities in embryo, despite the artificiality of their associative net or their sometimes unresolved geometry.

Military camps and garrison towns readily fall into line because of the pre-established ranking and routines of their inhabitants. The crop is varied, but the tight structure of the environment stays constant. An Assyrian relief on an orthostat *163*
in the throne room of Assurbanipal's palace at Nimrud shows an army camp as two crossing roads inside a fortified circle. The Roman *castrum* had a rigid rectangular *164*
layout determined by two crossing streets, the *via principalis* and the *via quintana*, that led to four principal gates and divided the camp into four quadrants. Spanish *presidios*, on the other hand, had small houses for the limited number of soldiers, married for the most part, that were needed for the protection of settlements and the expansion of missions and *pueblos*. Even so, the simple mud houses, along with a whitewashed chapel, a "royal" storehouse and a guardhouse were lined around a square which served as parade ground, and the camp was enframed by palisade walls of adobe. Single men lived in barracks.

The components of a garrison are barracks for the rank and file, separate and less spartan quarters for the officers, an ordnance depot, a church, a hospital; in the contemporary garrison, clusters of houses for married officers, often a regular suburb, would be found outside the military diagram. Even when the garrison is not its own town but an adjunct to a civil settlement, it will remain faithful to its own spatial structure unrelated to the city-form at large. Cantonments of Indian towns during the British Raj are a case in point. Their strict formality is evident in surviving maps of cantonments like those at Berhampur and Peshavar.

To these coercive gatherings we can relate, from the experience of our own time, the planned concentration camp. The long barracks building is the principal unit of it as well, and the lining up of these standard units in parallel rows, at right angles to or facing access paths, forms the skeleton of the physical organization. The barracks homogenize the population, and obliterate pre-extant social distinctions. In Japanese prisoner-of-war camps like Camp O'Donnell during the Second World War, the process was ensured by breaking up company and battery organization, and putting men in barracks according to civilian skill.[7] Beyond this general resemblance in housing, and obligatory facilities like hospitals, latrines, and administrative quarters, the camp completes its layout as its aims dictate.

In the spring of 1942 ten "relocation centers" were built by the United States Government in the West and Middlewest for approximately 110,000 American citizens of Japanese descent living in the Pacific coastal regions. This large-scale evacuation of innocent civilians, unaccused of subversive activity yet placed under total military restriction, was considered an unusual opportunity for social experimentation. It was official policy to develop self-government within the centers and re-establish the economic independence of the internees. The lessons of this enterprise could then be applied later, in the opinion of high-ranking officials like John Collier, Commissioner of Indian Affairs, "in the government of occupied areas, in relief and rehabilitation and in the reestablishment of millions of displaced persons after the war."

Yet for all this high-sounding agenda, the centers adopted the familiar camp diagram. The largest of three centers built at Poston, in the Arizona desert, could stand as example.[8] It was intended for a population of 10,000, and it was declared ready to occupy in a matter of weeks after the start of construction. Mesquite and other forms of vegetation were cleared for several square miles, and on the hot desert dust shadeless blocks of barracks were erected as fast as beams, boards, tar paper

164 The Roman legionary fortress at Caerleon (Wales) was founded ca. AD 75 *and rebuilt in stone not long afterwards. It showed the standard headquarters plan, of a rectangle bisected by the* via principalis; *at the T-junction of that street and the* via praetoria *stood the headquarters building* (principia) *and general's quarters* (praetorium). *Barracks for the troops lay on the other side of the* via principalis *(foreground). At Caerleon, as at Verona (Ill. 111), the amphitheater stood outside the walls. Further outside lay the civil town, presenting a striking contrast to the diagrammatic fortress. (Reconstruction by Alan Sorrell)*

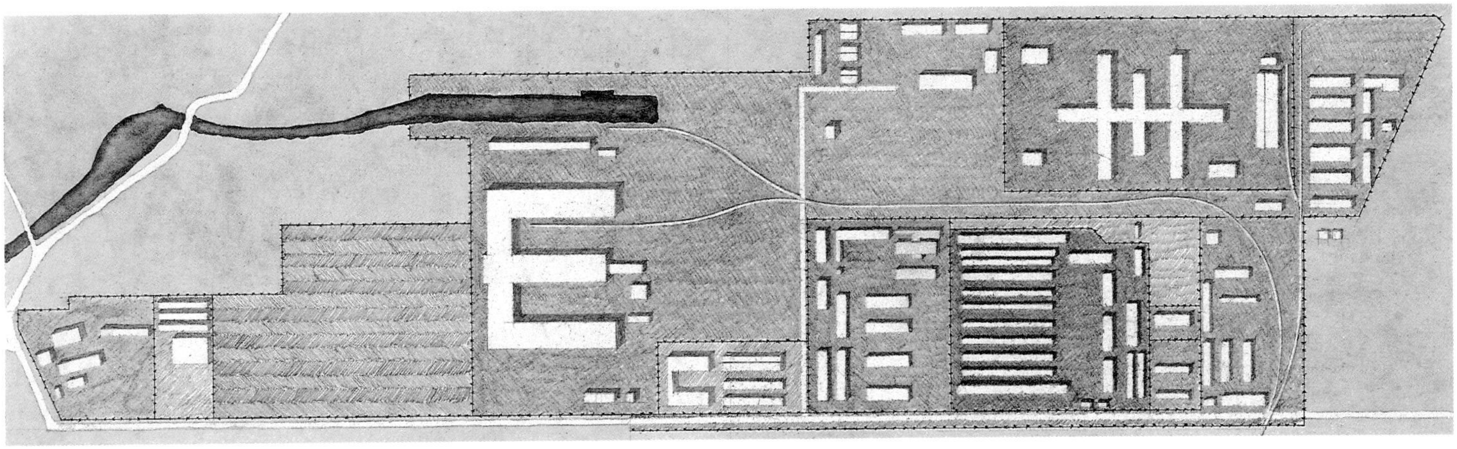

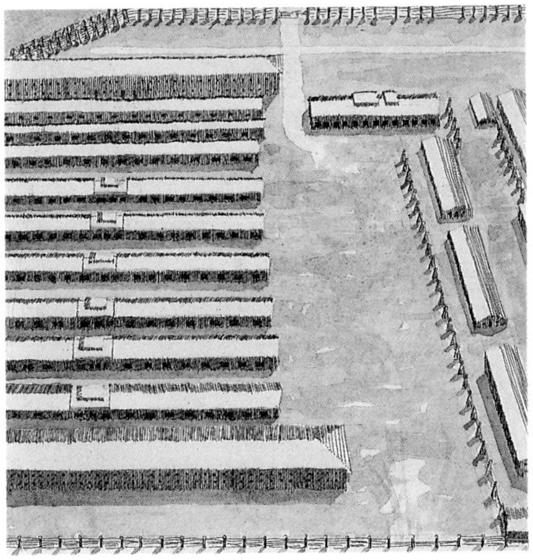

165 top *Hamburg (Germany), Neuengamme concentration camp and armaments factory. The site was originally a small brick works (extreme left); the vast expansion came after 1940.*

166 above *Close-up of the prisoners' area at Neuengamme with the range of barracks on the left.*

and nails could be hauled in by truck and trailer and freight car. Each block had 14 barracks, a recreational hall, a mess hall, latrines for men and women, and a laundry and ironing room. Besides the 36 residential blocks, there were also a 250-bed hospital, an administration area, and warehouses (which took up 4 blocks) for supplies that poured in. Two broad firebreaks ran through the blocks, and a central street with a canal running along some of its length had a dry goods store, a shoe repair shop, and an outdoor movie theater. The mechanisms of self-government set up by the War Relocation Authority, with a Community Council composed of representatives from each block to serve as liaison with the Project Director and a judicial committee established by the Council to oversee law and order, had no bearing on the physical diagram of the camp. Within this crude blueprint of order, many blocks organized specific activities—a sports center in one, woodcraft in another, drama in a third, Buddhist and Christian centers, a library, a police station. Poston proves the rule: in all "ideal" cities, the diagram will remain inviolate as long as its inhabitants are denied freedom of action.

The planning of Nazi concentration camps could be much more complicated—at least after 1940 when the task assumed staggering proportions and the streamlining of camp operations became imperative. At Hamburg's Neuengamme, a relatively small operation, the long rectangular camp site was served by a canal with port facilities running north-northwest, which hooked up to a rail system coming in along the east flank of the camp where the station was. To the south and west of this railway, occupying about a fourth of the camp grounds, were the quarters of the prisoners separated from those of their SS guards to the west. In plan there is little difference between the two, except that the SS barracks are fewer, smaller, and doubtless roomier than the long barracks buildings for the prisoners, each subdivided into two units, closely packed on one side of their camp. The buildings set at right angles to these barracks, of the same basic type, included, on the SS side, air-raid shelters and officers' mess; on the prisoners' side, sick bays, confinement shelter, a building with delousing, bathing, and death chambers, and east of these, three "special barracks" or brothels. On three sides of this residential core of prisoners and keepers were the ample areas for workshops and manufactories, principally a large brickfield and, on either side of the eastern railway line, an armaments works with its rifle range. The crematorium stood modestly at the northwest corner of the section of the works to the west of this railroad line.[9]

165, 166

In voluntary patterns of association like monasteries, rigor of place might seem inappropriate. But if men and women joined a monastic community by choice, thereafter they submitted to strict routines of daily life and unflagging supervision. The Order in question made all decisions affecting the organization and building of its monasteries, at least in the West, and uniformity was proof of submission. Sometimes, during the Carolingian Empire for instance, monasteries were considered State institutions, subject to central planning.

In the West under most Orders, the diagram starts in the middle with the church, which determines the main axis, and the cloister to its south. Then, in orthogonal relationships emanating from this irreducible core come the ancillary functions of the enterprise and accommodations for people who are novices, servants, and guests of the monastic community. In some cases the arrangements amount to sizeable towns. The ideal monastery of the time of Charlemagne, as an extant drawing shows, placed functional buildings—things like the drying kiln, the bake and brew house, and workshops—to the south of the central *claustrum*; animal pens along the west side; the abbot's house, the school, and guest lodgings along the north side; and to the east the infirmary, the cemetery and medicinal herb garden, and a miniature monastic frame for the novitiate with its own church. Beyond the bounds of the formal plant, hundreds of serfs and servants worked in the fields and orchards, supplying the needs of the monastery.[10] In the following centuries Cluny, the mother house of the Cluniac Order, and certain Cistercian foundations like Clairvaux grew to even more extensive proportions.

In the 19th century, the movement of communitarian socialism gave rise to hundreds of utopian plantations, especially in the United States. Without the monolithic structure of the monastic Orders, the great majority of these had an improvisational approach to the actual layout, inventing as they went along.
105 Mormon grids, and the odd proposal for a radical geometry like the use of centrally planned hexagonal blocks for Modern Times in New York State and Utopia in Ohio, are exceptions. Far more common are the loose assemblages of buildings that characterize Amana villages or Shaker communities like Hancock, Massachusetts.

But we must be cautious in our assessment. The perception of outsiders, in these cases, picked up the "disorder," while the internal discipline of the groups directly involved could identify their environment with a clear social design. For example, whereas visitors saw an Amana village as a simple line of houses on either side of the main street—hence the German name *Strassendorf*, "street village"—the communards themselves focused on the interior of the blocks and their network of "foot streets." Hancock, in its own terms, was able to define its organization through "the right-angle alignment of landscape boundaries and buildings, the hierarchical positioning of buildings according to functions, the distinctive shapes accorded to special functions, and the color coding prescribed by the Millennial Laws."[11]

Company towns of the 19th century, subject to unwavering schedules and owned and operated by hard-nosed profit-seeking individuals, were the obverse of communistic settlements whose modes of living, in truth, were intended to challenge the values of the new industrial society. For different reasons, the contributions of both groups to urban design could be expected to be marginal. The communards lacked resources and skills to invest in overall planning, and the evolving nature of their experiments quite often discouraged such planning. As for the industrialists, given their motives of self-interest and the centrality of routinized production, it would seem unlikely, on the face of it, that they would put much effort in the organization of their towns except for the plant and its dependencies. Most industrial enterprises were, in point of fact, improvisational, squalid settlements in the shadow of an efficiently and solidly built factory and the elegant residence of the owner or his overseer.

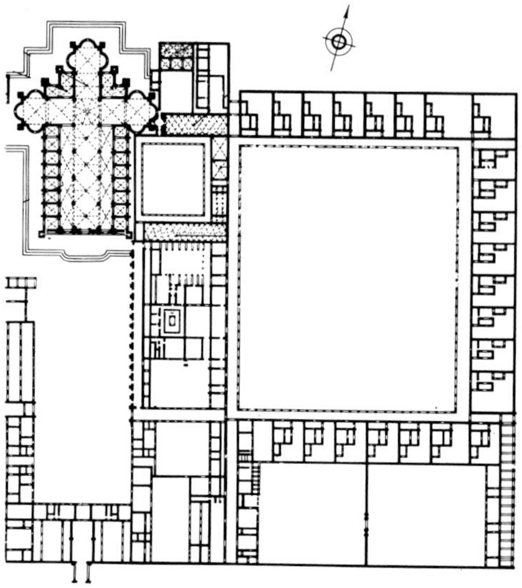

167 The Charterhouse of Pavia (Italy), founded in 1396 by Giangaleazzo Visconti, Duke of Milan, is planned with exceptional geometrical clarity. This detail shows the church (top left) and the great cloister, surrounded by the Carthusians' individual houses; between them lie the chapter house, little cloister, refectory, and ducal palace. To the left, not shown here, are stables and further buildings for guests and the secular activities of the monastery. (After Richards)

Most—but not all. The small scatter of model industrial towns, in Europe and the United States, make up a familiar roster: Saltaire in Yorkshire, Nadelburg south of *169*
Vienna, Pullman outside of Chicago, Port Sunlight on the banks of the Mersey near *79*
Liverpool, the Krupp works at Essen. They were made much of in their time and in the literature of modern scholarship. These model towns were the brainchildren of idealistic captains of industry who assumed a paternal role toward the population in their employ. They shouldered responsibility for the physical and moral well-being of the worker, and put their faith in design to keep him sober, upright and productive.

The three key points in the diagram of a model town were the plant, the church, and workers' housing. Other amenities figured in line with the owner's vision of his domain. Each town presumed to establish the prototype for the industrial environment at large. Almost all had hopes for the redemption of the working class, or rather, for the development of a working-class culture congruent with the interests of the employer.

Saltaire, the creation of Sir Titus Salt, a Congregationalist mill-owner, can stand *168,*
for the others because of the clarity of its layout and the rigor of its social contract. It *169*
was founded in 1851 in Yorkshire, near Shipley, for Salt's alpaca empire, and was completed by the late 1860s; it stood then in open country, but is now buried in the outskirts of modern Bradford. The admiring editor of the *Birmingham Post* wrote at the time:

> Saltaire is not a tortuitous [*sic*] collection of dwellings gathered by chance around the manufactory where their occupants are employed. It is the result of thought and design, the realisation of a great idea . . . It has at least shown what can be done towards breaking down the barrier which has existed between the sympathies of the labourer and the employer. . . . No finer picture could be imagined by the dreamer who would think of a probable future of progress for mankind, than that of a city where education is open to every child,—where labour is respected,—where intemperance is banished,—where the graces of life and the higher intellectual pleasures are open to the enjoyment of all,—and where misfortunes are tempered by forethought and kindness.[12]

Salt may well have been inspired by the model factory villages described in Disraeli's novels like *Coningsby* (1844) and *Sybil or the Two Nations* (1845), and their model sponsors—Mr. Millbank, for example, who saw in the rising industrial world a vast wealth "which was rapidly developing classes whose power was very imperfectly recognized in the constitutional scheme, and whose duties in the social system seemed altogether omitted"; or Mr. Trafford, who "with gentle blood in his veins, and old English feelings, imbibed, at an early period of his career, a correct conception of the relations which should subsist between the employer and the employed. He felt that between them should be other ties than the payment and the receipt of wages."[13]

The organizing principle of Saltaire is an ascending straight street, Victoria Road, that runs south starting at the bank of the River Aire. At this level area, the mill and the church face each other across the street, unequal in size but clearly paired as a unity. The church is aligned with the triumphal arch that forms the entrance to the mill's front office, and both buildings are made of a matching light stone "in the Italian style of architecture." Across the river is the park.

Moving away from this town center, past a line of shops, Victoria Road comes to another institutional cross axis. Set well back from the street are the "factory schools" on one side and the Saltaire Club and Institute on the other. These estab-

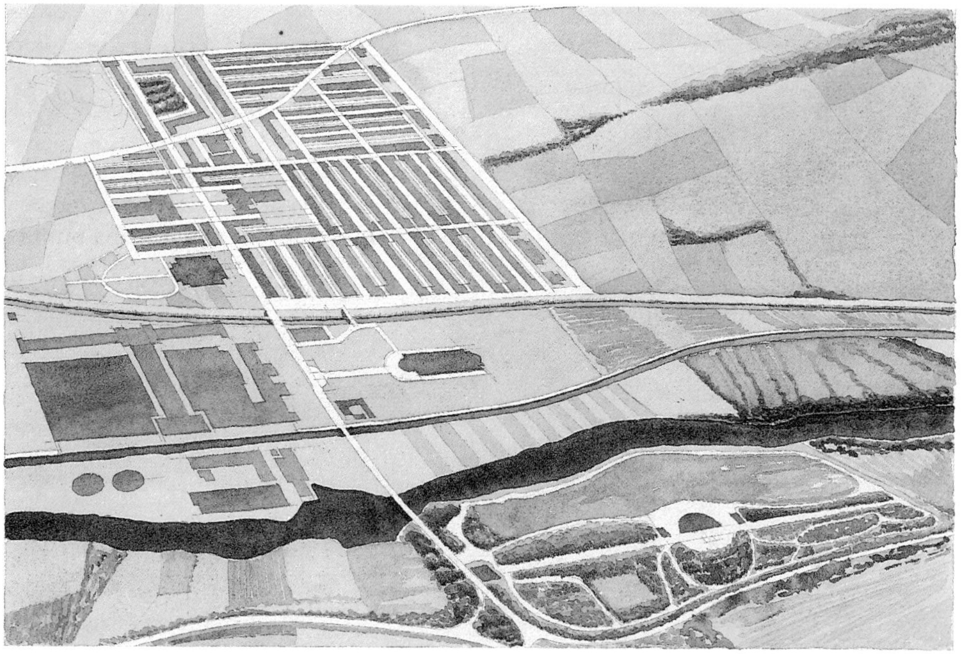

168, 169 Saltaire (England), plan and aerial view. The mills are in the foreground (lower left in the plan), opposite the church with its semicircular portico and domed tower. Victoria Road runs between them (toward the upper left in both plan and view). Further along Victoria Road, the large T-plan building with a tower is the Saltaire Club and Institute; just across the street are the "factory schools."

lishments provided for the intellectual advancement of the workers at various stages of their lives. The schoolrooms were cleverly fitted with a system of curtains that enabled boys to be separated from girls "and yet under the complete control of the master." The graduates would then embark on a lifelong course of learning at the Institute across the street, "a place to which you can resort for conversation, business, recreation and refreshment, as well as for education—elementary, technical, and scientific." The Institute also replaced the pub, since Sir Titus banished "beer shops" from his model town; it was "intended to supply the advantages of a public-house without its evils." The housing was neatly packed in parallel rows behind these monuments, on the west side of Victoria Road.

At the top of the hill the town axis was concluded with the almshouses and infirmary, the chief exhibit of Titus Salt's generosity and the bargaining chip in his covenant with the workers. The almshouses, resembling a line of attached Italian villas, could accommodate 60 elderly and infirm company folk out of a total population of over 4,000. Residents also received a modest pension. Admission was based on age and need and restricted to persons of "good character" as judged by Sir Titus and, after his death, a board of trustees. Applications were buttressed by written statements from a qualified doctor and a minister of the Gospel, and an affidavit of employment history. Far from being a comprehensive welfare program for the workforce, then, this selective charity rewarded tractable individuals who had demonstrated a lifelong dedication to the enterprise and the owner's dual standards of Christian virtue and scientific social knowledge regarding hygiene, recreation and the like. Workers who did not measure up, and their families, were banished from this paradise of industry, to face old age on their own.

HOLY CITIES

Since religion is the basis of pre-industrial society, all pre-industrial cities, it can reasonably be claimed, have a sacred dimension. What we are isolating in this section is those cities of concentrated sanctity whose physical organization displays a deliberate program of ritual intent. These are cities, like Mecca and Jerusalem, where particular religions place their origin; cities where the worship of principal deities is condensed, as with Amon at Thebes or Shiva at Benares (Varanasi); or cities where a king seeks to anchor his reign, as did Jayavarman VII at Angkor Thom, through the inscription upon the urban form of an elaborate cosmological conceit.

Not all holy cities wear their iconography in a legible design. It is impossible to find, in the tangled fabric of Benares, the manifold structure of the Hindu *Pl.1* macrocosm that justifies the more than one thousand temples and five hundred Shiva *lingams*. The assertion that around every important temple of the city there is a traceable street for circumambulation, and that these constitute religious planning, has not been verified. And yet in this first city to appear after the great cosmic dissolution (*mahapralaya*), according to Puranic literature, Hindu cosmography is charted through holy markers and the pilgrims' routes or *yatras*. The ideal diagram is of a series of concentric circles increasing in sanctity as one nears the center. These seven circles, representing layers in the atmosphere, are intersected at eight places by radials which signify the directions. At the fifty-six points of contact, there are shrines to the elephant-headed Ganesha, son of Shiva and Guardian of Thresholds.[14]

In some holy cities of South and East Asia, on the other hand, similar cosmic diagrams determined the plan from the beginning. These cities emerged in the

Middle Ages as an affirmation of the political power (and ritual purity) of kings. Famous examples are Pagan, the great capital of Upper Burma established by the
173 11th century; Angkor Thom, "The City of Gods," sacred focus of the Khmer
25 Empire; and the temple city of Madurai in South India, largely the product of the 16th and 17th centuries, and associated with the Nayaka dynasty and its founder Vishvanatha.[15]

The beginnings of this political process, perhaps as early as the 1st century AD, involved the adoption by many tribal chiefs of the concept of *deva-raja*, the cult of divine kingship, and its attributes—palace, throne, tiered umbrella, *lingam*—which were contained in the holy city.[16] As a symbol of his piety and power, the king built the holy city following ritual formulas contained in sacred texts like the *Silpa-Shastras*. Since this city was the covenant of the State to ensure contact between earth and heaven, the site was scrupulously chosen through geomancy. Temple and city were laid out in accordance with the same sacred diagrams. Both faced east, and were aligned with the four quarters of the compass. Four city gates corresponded to these cardinal axes. The main temple and the palace occupied the center. A series of concentric routes inscribing squares surrounded this core, and were used for car festivals involving the perambulation of important deities. The concentric streets had the names of those months in the Tamil year when the deities were taken in procession through the city. Along the streets, quarters were laid out for different castes and professional groups.

170, At Srirangam in South India, the spatial pattern appears in its purest. This pattern
171 (admirably analyzed by Jan Pieper) begins with the land at large. Srirangam is the first of four South Indian Vishnu pilgrimage sites. By visiting them in the prescribed sequence, the pilgrim in effect circumambulates the whole of the Tamil region. The city is also part of a linear sequence of holy places along the Cauvery River, sitting as it does on the "end island" of that river. This broad sacred geography is narrowed down to a Holy Field around the town, subdivided into several concentric zones. The innermost zone is marked by eight ponds or "tanks" (a ninth is inside the main temple) for the ritual bathing of pilgrims. By moving in the proper sequence among these eight markers, the pilgrim circumambulates the town three times. Closer still is a diamond-shaped forefield, fixed by two *ghats* or cremation areas, along the Coleron River to the north and the Cauvery to the south, and by two important extramural sanctuaries to the east and the west.

The city itself is composed of seven concentric walled enclosures, of which the inner four are the temple proper, while the outer three are residential quarters. A cross-axis runs through these enclosures in the cardinal directions, accented by gate towers or *gopuras* of decreasing height from edge to center. The first two ringroads outside the temple precinct (Uttira and Chittira Streets) are inhabited exclusively by the Brahmin class. Brahmin residences also take up the northwest and southeast corners of the third street (Adaiyavalanjan Street), while leaving the opposite corners for the lower castes—agricultural workers and peasants in the northeast, and artisans and servants in the southwest. With rare exceptions, no car festivals are allowed on this third street, and circumambulation, restricted to Uttira and Chittira Streets, is done only clockwise.

173 Built in a little over forty years, between 1181 and 1219, Angkor Thom set out to recreate the cosmic landscape that is shared by Hindu and Buddhist doctrine. A holy mountain where the gods live is the axis of the universe; it is surrounded by a series of lower continents and oceans, the habitat of humans and spirits. In a rigidly orthogonal ground plan and a lavish, ornate architectural style, Angkor re-enacts this sacred configuration. The Bayon in the center, the largest temple of the city, is

170, 171 Srirangam (South India): plan of the center of the holy city, and location map of the town and surrounding pilgrimage sites on the Cauvery River.

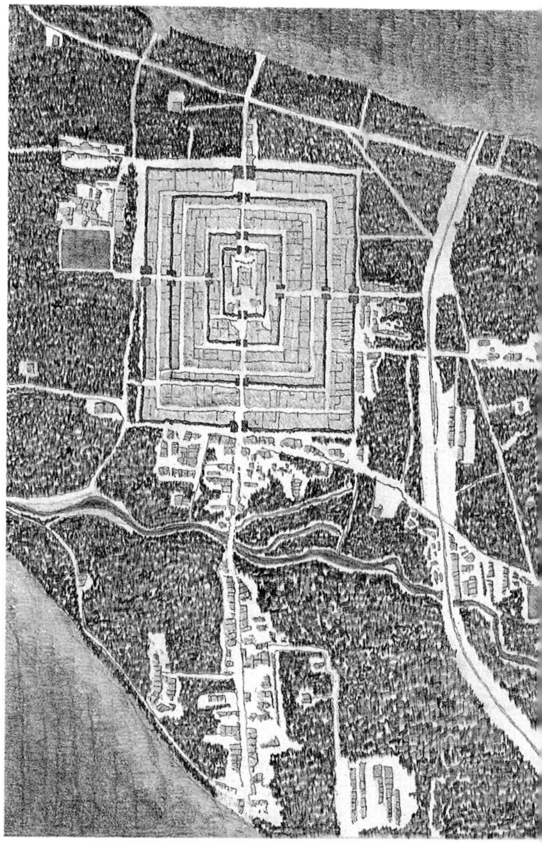

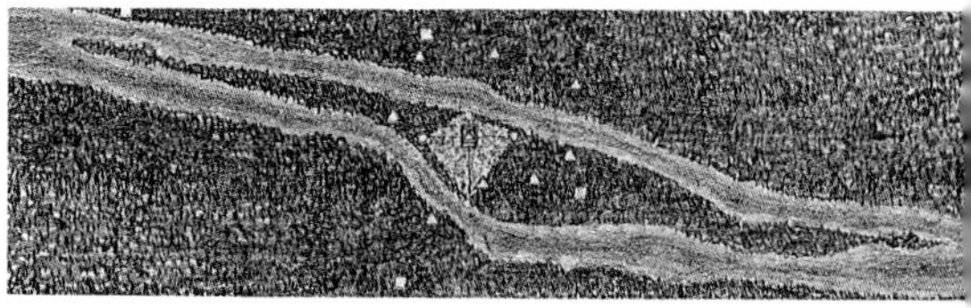

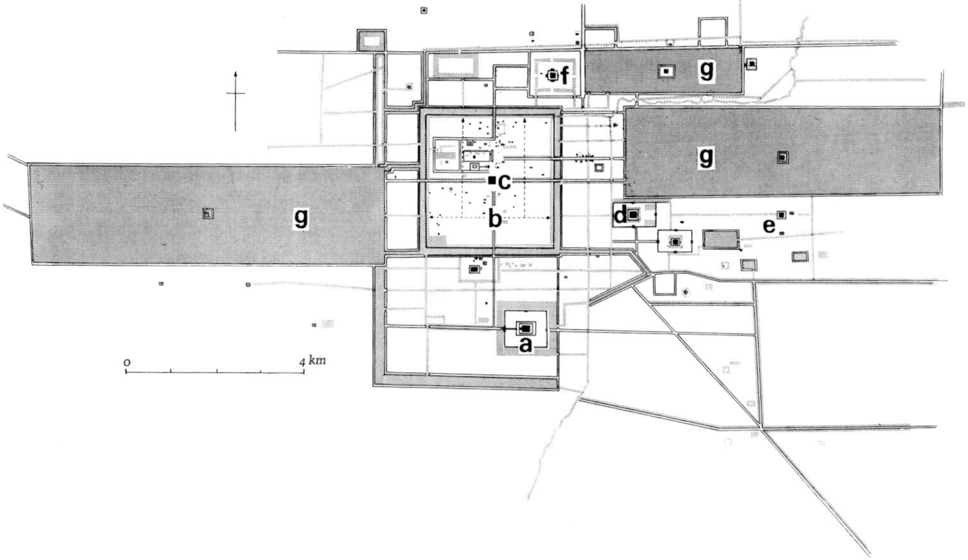

172 Angkor Wat (Cambodia), the temple seen across its moat.

173 Angkor Thom, diagram of the general layout: a *Angkor Wat,* b *Angkor Thom,* c *Bayon sanctuary,* d *Ta Prohm temple,* e *Pre Rup temple,* f *Preah Khan temple,* g *reservoirs.*

the mountain of the gods, Mount Meru. Surrounding it is the enclosure of the royal palace, followed further out by the walls and a wide moat, corresponding to the lower elements of the cosmological universe. The moat was crossed by five stone causeways. This royal city formed a square almost two miles (some 3 km.) on each side. The towers above the four axial city gates, directed toward the four cardinal points, had the same crowns of the fourfold faces of Lokesvara as did the gate towers of the central temple. Canals fed by two artificial lakes to the east and the west of the moat ran through the city, and also irrigated the area outside the walls where common people lived in dense villages separated by rice fields, and temples loomed above their square precinct walls. Most renowned was Angkor Wat, whose five *172*
towers symbolized Meru's five peaks. This surrounding population paid tribute to and serviced the temples and their cults in the thousands.

Such richly developed urban microcosms that seek to encapsulate the spatial structure of heaven find no parallel in the Christian world, or for that matter in the lands of classic Islam. The literature describing the physical aspects of heaven in both religions is comparatively poor. There are the four rivers of Paradise. There are selected *omphaloi* of the world, like the Rock of Abraham in Jerusalem. Not much to model a sacred city after. The imagery of the Heavenly Jerusalem itself is preponderantly formulaic.

One notable Christian response was to fashion a sacred urbanism out of specific geometric and numerological symbols. An early example was the Benedictine abbey of Centula or St.-Riquier in northern France, built in the the 7th and 8th centuries, which was attached to a small town of about 7,000 to form a holy city. The abbey, which no longer exists, was dedicated to the Trinity, and its layout was a rough triangle to underline this symbolism. Three churches at the points of the triangle were joined by walls and porticoes, a sort of extended cloister, as can be seen in a 1612 view that goes back to the 11th century. Seven hamlets nearby played a religious part similar to the seven pilgrimage stations in Rome. Knights, merchants and craftsmen lived in separate neighborhoods of the town.

From a much later period we have Scherpenheuvel, northeast of Leuven (Louvain). It was conceived in 1603 by Archduke Albert, the governor of the Catholic Netherlands, and his wife Isabella, as a seven-sided star-shaped town in honor of the Virgin Mary, the *stella maris*, at a site where there was an oak dedicated to her. As a place of pilgrimage, it was meant to combat the expansion of Dutch Protestantism. In the middle was a seven-sided garden that represented Mary as the *hortus conclusus*, with a pilgrimage chapel in the center where the oak had been. Between the heptagon of the garden and that of the bastions, the space was meant to be built up. A royal castle stood at the head of this space. Three processional routes crossed the walls through three city gates, and headed to the open countryside. "At the root of all this lay the idea," Braunfels writes, "that the security of the complex could be enhanced by the correspondence between the symbolic form of the star and the star-shaped fortification."[17] The defense wall was demolished in 1782, but the radial design is well preserved.

THE POLITICAL DIAGRAM

If the holy city affirms the centrality of faith and translates itself into a microcosmic heaven, the ideal city for secular authority might use the same diagrams to give visual primacy to the ruler and his military shield. In theocratic systems of government, or in regimes anxious to exhibit piety and assimilate the religious establishment, the temple, the church or the mosque will never be far from the seat of power. But the political diagram celebrates monocentric dominion: and its most expressive devices are the axis and the circle.

LINEAR SYSTEMS

Axial alignment is commonly used in association with an overall urban diagram that upholds its premises and highlights its effects. It depends on one of two inducements: cosmology, and physical and cultural topography.

China is the obvious place to explore the first of these. Chinese planners invariably emphasized the north-south axis, image of the meridian, to order their capitals. This was in coordination with a precise structure of thought regarding the universe and the place of the ruler within it. The earth in Chinese cosmology was a stable cube; the heavens were round. Space was conceived of as a series of imbricated squares, at the center of which lay the capital of the empire strictly oriented to the points of the compass. And in the fulcrum of the capital, the imperial palace commanded the main north-south axis, facing southward (as did all important buildings) in the direction of the Red Phoenix, of summer and fire. From the north came winter and destructive hordes. Its color was black, and the emperor faced away from it except when he addressed the gods or his ancestors.

Everything about the city-form, down to where a house was allowed to be in its *fang* or neighborhood and how large it was supposed to be, was set down in the official code, based of course on status. In the palace, in a calendar house called the Ming Tan, the emperor adjusted his behavior to nature's cycles, moving from hall to hall as the seasons changed and completing one revolution in the course of a year. This cosmic schema, called the Great Plan (*Hung fan*), came from heaven to the first dynastic emperor, a mythical character called Yu who invented surveying. Its basis was a ninefold square, which was also the composition of the Ming Tan. The fixity was not, however, final. Every time the capital moved, so did the center of the universe. We are talking, therefore, about an existential and not a geometric or geographic order. And the capital moved often. Every prince wanted his own capital, and so added to the one he inherited, or built another from scratch somewhere else.[18]

There were two basic models for the layout of new capital cities, if an extant old town was not pressed into service by the court. Both models existed in the first millennium BC. In fact, by the time of the first unified Chinese empire under the Han, about the time of Christ, there was a large body of lore and practices concerning city building. The square or rectangular form was established, as were the precise alignment of the city in the four cardinal directions, the "facing south," the separation into functional zones, and the placement of urban cults like those of the god of soil, of the imperial ancestors, and of heaven. Both capital models made adjustments to their ideal form in line with topographical conditions. The issue became especially relevant when the Chinese moved down into the Yangtze Valley and the mountainous regions further south and east, which, unlike the flat sites of the north in earlier times, made neat diagrammatic plans difficult.

The first model is represented by Chang'an under the Tang dynasty (7th–9th *174*
centuries). Here the imperial palace is at the north end of a central axis, as we have just described. The city lay on the bank of the Wei River in south central Shaanxi Province. In the Tang period, it had an outer wall of more than 22 miles (36 km.) in perimeter and a population of perhaps about one million. The prior town on the site, the Chang'an of the Western Han, was very much smaller; the common people lived just outside the city gates.

By the 8th century the plan of Tang Chang'an "had come to be a universal East
Asian symbol of rule."[19] It was imitated in Japan in Heijokyo (Nara) from 708, and *139*
other 8th-century Japanese capitals (Naniwa, Shigaraki, Kuni); and in the capital of the kingdom of Bohai, Longquan Fu (in modern Heilong Jiang). Heijokyo was slightly less than one-fourth the size of Chang'an, its grid delimited once and for all; but, unlike the Chinese model, it had no city wall. Heijokyo, the capital of the Empress Gemmei, was preceded by Fujiwara, projected by Temmu Tennō and built by his successor. This was occupied in 694, and was the first Japanese capital to be conceived as a unitary whole. The urban ensemble was divided into east and west halves by a longitudinal avenue, the Suzaku, with the palace at its northern end as in Chang'an.[20]

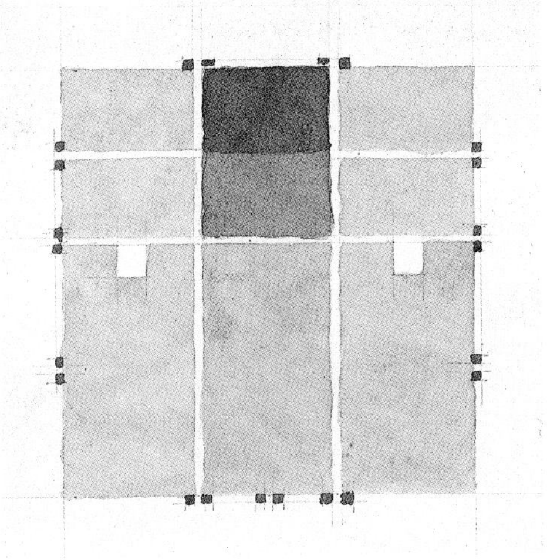

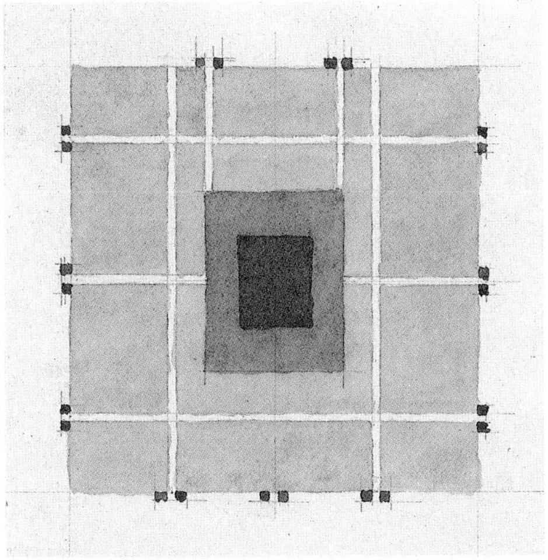

174, 175 The two ancient schemes for Chinese imperial capitals: the palace at center north backed into the city wall, as in Chang'an (top)*; and the palace in the center of the city, as in Beijing* (above).

In the other capital scheme, the palace is in the middle of the city; this is the case with *175*
Beijing, which of course is only a very late example. It would seem that it was Khubilai *Pl.2*
Khan, building his Mongolian capital of Dadu beginning in 1267, who revived this ancient type, after long disuse, so as to confer legitimacy on his non-Chinese regime. Beijing, built on the ruins of Dadu, merely retained the resurrected type. Indeed by the time the Sung took over Kaifeng as their northern capital in 960, Chinese capital cities had lost their cosmic purity, and served additionally as commercial and industrial centers, with shops throughout the fabric replacing the tightly controlled closed markets of a capital like Chang'an situated symmetrically on either side of the central axis. The southern Sung capital of Hangzhou, for example, was quite irregular. It was the conservative Ming dynasty in Beijing, inspired by Dadu, that brought back the rigorous townplanning practices of the classical cosmology.

The authority for the Beijing model resides in a text of the first century AD called *Zhou Li* (Rituals of [king] Zhou). The text declares that "it is the sovereign alone who establishes the states of the empire, gives to the four quarters their proper positions, gives to the capital its form and to the fields their proper divisions. He creates the offices and apportions their functions, in order to form a center to which the people may look."[21] The city begins with the building of a foursquare outermost wall, with three gates on each side. Major east–west, north–south arteries connect these gates, obstructed only by the second enclosure, the palace city in the center. Six subsidiary streets run north–south and six east–west. "The north–south streets shall accommodate nine chariot-ways." A temple for the imperial ancestors stands to the east of this city center, altars to soil and grain to the west, the ruler's audience hall to the south, and markets to the north.

Without such recondite systems of belief, the political axis is fixed by the location of the palace, and that is determined with an eye to the shapes of the land and, where the site is marked with artifacts of prior cultures or antecedent regimes, to the possibilities of symbolic connections. Let us take a giant leap here, from ancient China to early 20th-century Britain, and the new capital for her dominion of India. We will return to New Delhi several times in the following chapters. I am here concerned chiefly with the government axis. As Edwin Lutyens's initial layout had it,
176 New Delhi was organized about a great east–west avenue called Central Vista and King's Way. This led from the dominant Raisina Hill, on which would stand the domed Government House, eastward to Purana Qila or Indrapat (Indraprastha), the site of the oldest of several historic Delhis being superseded by this one of Britain.

207 The formal model was the Mall in Washington, D.C., with the Capitol at the head of the long green band and the Lincoln Memorial at the opposite end. But the symbolism was uniquely colonial British. In front of Government House, the

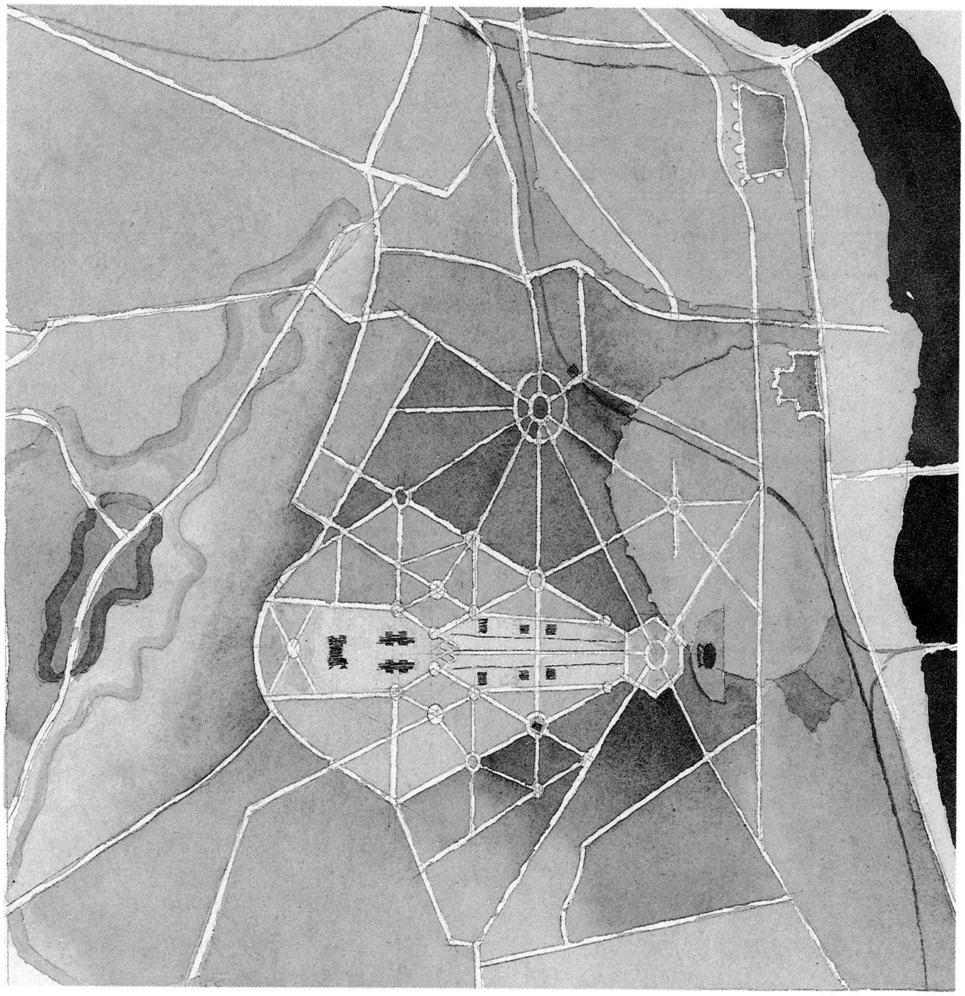

176 New Delhi, schematic plan showing the location of the east-west government axis (bottom center), Connaught Circus further north, and Old Delhi or Shahjahanabad with Delhi Fort by the Jumna River (top right-hand corner).

177 New Delhi, King's Way looking west toward the Secretariats and Government House, 1945. The occasion is a Victory Week parade.

viceroy's official residence, were lined the massive Secretariats forming a set of monumental propylaea to the Central Vista, and in front of these came the quarters for the Executive Council. Gazetted officers were housed immediately to the north and south, those with lower rank and less seniority being placed on the north side. In a radial pattern near the eastern end of King's Way, its center marked by a triumphal arch, were accommodated the princes of the "native states" of India. The progress *Pl.28* along the axis from east to west to reach the climax of the viceroy's residence was described, in the final report of 1913, in symbolic terms. "The imagination is led from the machinery to the prime moving power itself," Government House, which is not only the heart of the new city but "the keystone of the rule over the Empire of India; this is the place of Government in its highest expression."[22]

The east–west axis was traversed by Queen's Way, which was to have the railroad station at its north end (not built) and the Anglican cathedral at its south end. At the intersection four large buildings housing the Oriental Institute, the National Museum, the National Library, and the Imperial Record Office would frame a cultural plaza. To the west of Queen's Way, between the railroad station and the Secretariats, was the housing for the local administrators and the European clerks; further out were the quarters of the Indian clerks, and further out still, the "non-official" space for those too lowly in rank and status to qualify for a place in the Imperial City, namely, peons, sweepers and *dhobis* (washermen). So the hierarchical housing fanned out from the axis along radial avenues beginning with the residences of Deputy Secretaries, then Under-Secretaries, Registrars, Superintendents, then the higher ranks of European clerks, and beyond those the Indian clerks. The reporter of the Calcutta newspaper who asked "Would it not be kinder to put the senior and richer men who can afford plenteous petrol and tyres on the outskirts, while their subordinates walk to work?" obviously did not comprehend the premise of ideal cities or was too embarrassed to admit its logic.

In fact the axis of King's Way and the system of hexagonal grids within which it runs define an elaborate spatial structure based on race, occupational rank, and socio-economic status. Having been assigned to an appropriate area of this structure, your standing was more precisely indicated by the altitude and size of your compound and its proximity to Government House, the size of your dwelling, the width of the road on which it sat, the name of the road and of the area, and the number and index of the house type (e.g., Block 4, 1E).[23] An equally elaborate hierarchy was inscribed in the temporary setting of durbar camps, like the one arranged by Lord Curzon in 1903 to celebrate the coronation of Edward VII.

With its prejudice against monumentality and its belief in the irrelevancy of the traditional institutions of society, Modernism would seem an unlikely language for a power diagram on the model of New Delhi. This is what made the government axis
178 at Brasilia, the newborn capital of Brazil, iconoclastic as a product of the Sixties. On either side of a 200-meter (218 foot) wide mall the planners lined up ministries, all of them slabs of identical design perhaps to stress the symbolic equality among them. The two traditionally most prestigious ministries, Foreign Affairs and Treasury,

178 Brasilia, government axis looking east to the Plaza of the Three Powers. The cathedral is on the right, separated from the Plaza by one bank of ministries.

were given distinctive buildings closer to the head of the axis at the east where the Plaza of the Three Powers unites the National Legislature, the executive offices or Palace of the Planalto, and the Supreme Court. The Legislature complex sits astride the axis—an apparition of two white tower-walls that are the blind ends of the high-rise Secretariat slabs, flanked by two half-spheres, upright for the Senate and inverted for the Hall of Deputies. Moving down the axis, just west of the ministries, an equally dramatic form, circular and skeletal, rushing up to a spiky crown, represents the cathedral. Further west, on the opposite side, is the National Theater building—and then the axis is slashed across by the main traffic interchange of the city lifted up above the mall on a platform. The line of the axis, continued beyond the interchange, meets a television tower, and then the modest complex of the municipality, before heading out to the railroad station.

CENTRALIZED SYSTEMS

The other device for charting political order is to dilate the city form in bands of diminishing importance out of a center, rather than transfix it with one dominant axis. The two related variants here are the concentric and the radial.

1. Concentric organization

Concentricity implies the circle, but in city diagrams this is at best a relative matter. The castle towns or *jokamachi* of Japan, the symbol of an all-powerful feudal aristocracy taking over from a declining central government in the 16th–17th centuries, hardly show the geometrical purity of ideal cities, yet they are unequivocal diagrams of centralized power. Seat of the *daimyo*, the new feudal lord, these towns, among them Edo, Osaka, Tokashima, Kochi and Kumamoto, were focused upon the castle. *179*
Ranged around this keep were the residences of vassals in two belts, and between these and the keep, within the security of the main rampart and the inner moat, were the high officials. The second belt, for lesser vassals, was unprotected, except perhaps by an outer moat and sometimes an earthen barricade. At the edge of this outer belt lay a ring of temples and shrines; this formed a circuit of first defense controlling the main roads and the points of access into the city. Between the two belts of vassals resided the *daimyo*'s privileged merchants and artisans.[24]

Southeast Asian cosmologies combine the circle and its urban consequence, the centrally organized ideal city, with the square principle and its consequence, the grid. The most abstruse cultural manifestation of this interlock is the Indian *mandala* (chart).

The mandala is a mystical symbol of the universe in graphic form: it is circular and the center is the most important part, for in that lies eternity. Man is the center of his own universe, his own time/space, and from it he receives a cosmic consecration. But an absolute, extramundane order resides in the square, in which is manifest the supreme principle, Brahma—the geometric form assumed by the world of reality as it was defined at the creation. These ideal forms, the circle and the square, duly fixed by the cardinal points, could be divided at their perimeter by any number up to 32, yielding thus between 1 and 1,024 units or *padas*.

It was up to the priest to select one of these variants or mandalas as the basis for laying out a city. There was the urban mandala called the *swastika*; there was the *181*
cruciform mandala or *dandaka*; there was the lotus leaf or *padmaka*. Early town schemes are not now recoverable, except in the remote example of Shishulpargh in Orissa, a fortified city of the 1st–2nd centuries BC. But if surviving architectural books are to be believed, these schemes conformed to mandalas with as many *padas*

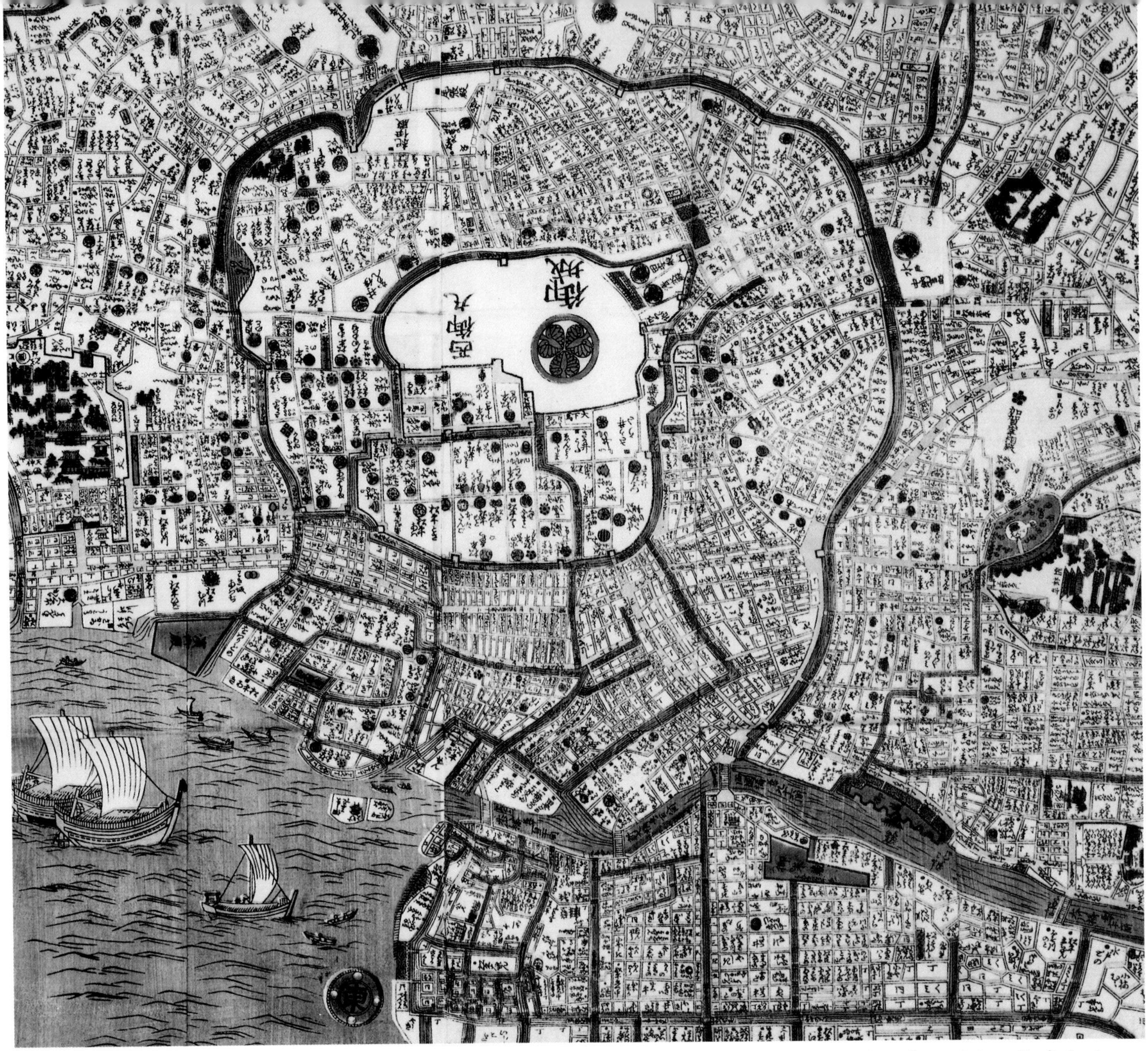

179 The daimyo *of Edo (Tokyo) in 1849, detail from a woodblock print. Edo was established in the late 12th century around the castle built by Edo Shigenaga, the governor of Musashi province. In contrast to the geometric clarity of Heijokyo (Ill. 139), Edo grew in an irregular but purposeful pattern expressing the warrior caste system typical of castle towns. By the early 17th century it was the seat of Japan's feudal government and, with a population topping 1,000,000, probably the world's largest city.*

180 opposite, above *Jaipur (India), nine-square plan based on an ancient mandala.*

181 opposite, below *Four of the town-planning mandalas described in ancient Hindu literature: circular form of* vastupurusha, swastika, dandaka, *and* padmaka.

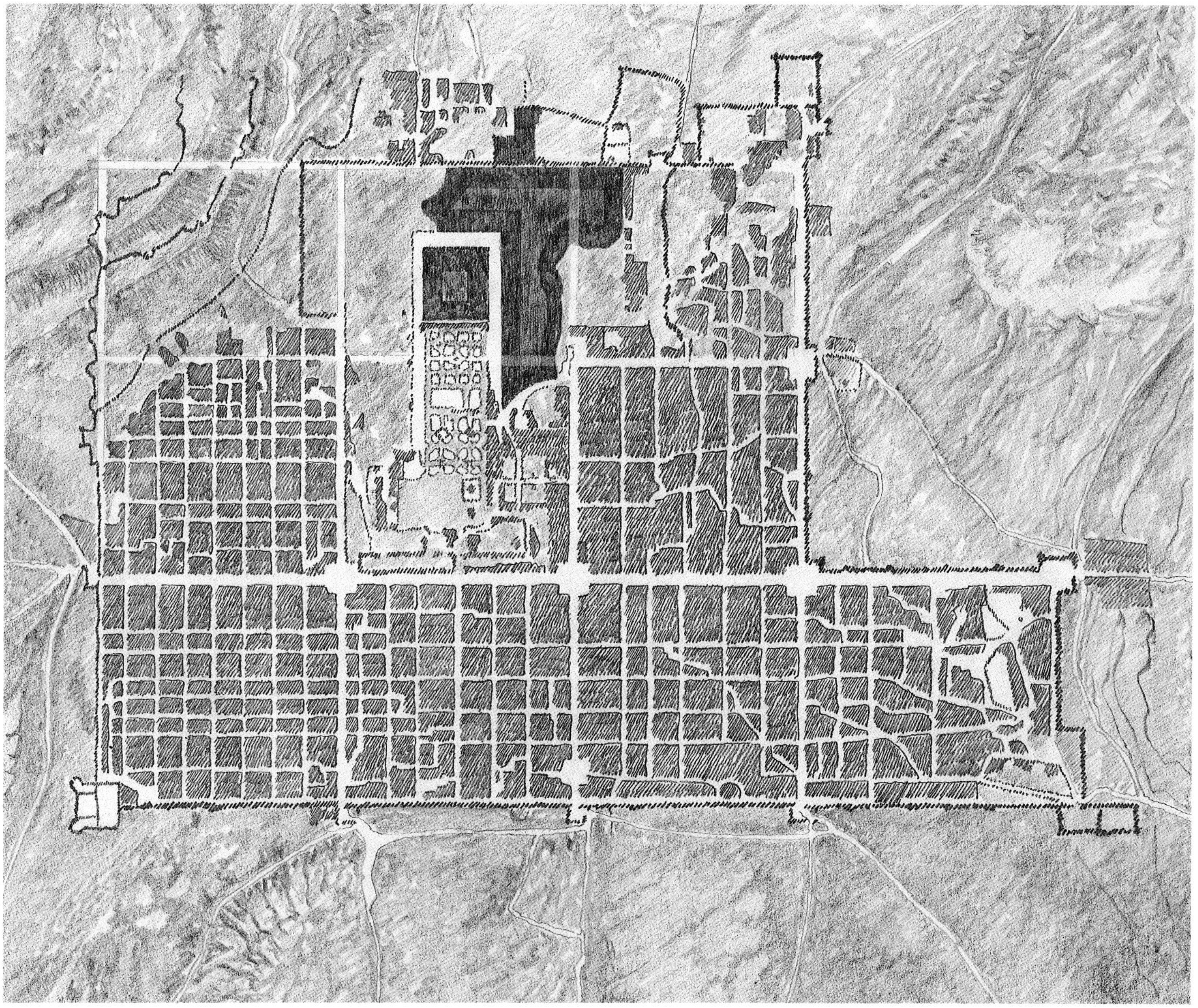

as there were to be residential quarters, and only within each *pada*, inhabited by members of a particular professional group, might a looser subdivision of alleys and footpaths be countenanced. The trace of abstract mandalas can be mapped, stretched out into real urban patterns, in cities like Kirtipur near Kathmandu (Nepal).

These ancient traditions of city-planning were consciously revived for political ends in Rajasthan by the astronomer-king Sawai Jai Singh (1700–1743) in laying out
180 his capital city of Jaipur, named after himself.[25] The nine-square diagram, corresponding to the *prastara* type of mandala, was adapted to the irregular site, with the northwest block shifted to the southeast on account of the Nahargarh Hills. The tilting of the grid in a northeast–southwest sense minimized adverse conditions of the region's harsh climate by avoiding the course of winds. The central square contained the palace complex and the observatory; the other sectors were residential with internal streets laid on an orthogonal pattern. There were three major north–south roads and one major road running east–west along a ridge. At the intersections, three large public open spaces called *chaupar*, measuring 330 × 330 feet (100 × 100 m.) each, were totally pedestrian and were surrounded by façades whose design was controlled. The palace of the king occupied the central position of Brahma in the mandala, and the observatory was a means of incorporating into the city the physical ability to make contact with the heavens, of which affinity the mandala was the symbol. In this practice Jai Singh might also have been linking up with a Muslim tradition in Transoxiana (modern Uzbekistan) where the Timurid ruler Ulugh Bey in the 15th century had an observatory erected in his capital city of Samarkand; and Ulugh Bey in turn was probably influenced by a still older local tradition represented by Koy-Krylgan Kale at Khwarazm on the Oxus River near Samarkand. This round city, dating from as early as the 4th century BC, functioned as a fortified tomb or temple and an astronomical observatory, or more accurately an astrolabic circle.

If we accept Sjoberg's classic model of the pre-industrial city, we could make a case for a broader universality of the concentric principle. Since the center according to this model is always taken up by government and religion and the residences of the elite, and the lower classes are relegated to the periphery, a concentric intent can be said to be present in every pre-industrial city, however disorderly its urban fabric.

In colonial towns this progressive social descent outward from the center was built into the innocuous orthogonality of a grid—or even looser spatial matrices. We have had occasion in the last chapter to analyze the gridded towns of New Spain planted in conformity with the *Laws of the Indies*. There, the central plaza and its vicinity was the preserve of the upper crust, families of pure Spanish blood directly traceable to the conquest; they made up the peak of a concentric declension that stopped with the mulattos at the city edge.

The New England equivalent of the *Laws*, the anonymous pamphlet of 1635 called "The Ordering of Towns," sets down a similar spatial hierarchy for an agricultural community. The author proposes a township of six concentric rings around the meetinghouse, which is "the center of the whole circumference." The houses that surround it form the first ring; then comes the ring of common fields, and the pastures for the livestock. This is the extent of the settlement, and will remain intact until the assured welfare of the colony allows further freeholds in a fourth and fifth ring. Beyond comes the wide circle of swamp and forest, two-thirds the area allotted to the settlers in the initial grant, which can be used but cannot be occupied. The assignment of land parcels according to each one's status and fortune reinforced a social hierarchy. When an irrepressible appetite for more land than the covenant permitted seized the children of the first generation, the spatial order came undone and the discipline of the township disintegrated.[26]

The convention that depicts the city and its territory as a series of concentric rings is older than the 17th century. The distant Classical source for the West remains Plato's Atlantis, where a central acropolis is surrounded by five circles of land and water. But it was the Renaissance that gave this formula a specific urban application, both in literary and in visual terms.

David Friedman has drawn attention to an early symbolic rendition of the Florentine state in a vault painting of the second half of the 14th century which makes a first step in that direction. Political emblems like the lily and the eagle are set in the center. They are surrounded by the arms of the sixteen geographic divisions of the city and the four quarters into which they were grouped. Then come two outer circles for the guilds, which are represented by their coats of arms, and again by images of their patron saints. The city walls make up a final ring—the only physical component of the real city in an otherwise emblematic diagram of spatial and political structure.[27]

In his 1403/4 panegyric to Florence, the humanist and chancellor of the republic Leonardo Bruni is much more specific. He describes the city and its territory as an ideal visual entity with the walls ringing the urban core and the town hall, the Palazzo Vecchio, at the center, "the castle of a castle." Beyond the walls come the suburbs, the rural mansions and estates, and around them the circle of dependent towns; "and this whole outermost region is enclosed in a still larger orbit and circle." We are clearly in anticipation of the Renaissance ideal of the "perfect city," and indeed an image of Florence from the last quarter of the 15th century faithfully *Pl.33* suggests Bruni's geometry of a circular walled city in an expanding perspective of rural settlements and distant mountains. But elsewhere in his panegyric Bruni reveals an older source of imagery for the concentric city diagram. "The city herself stands in the center, like a guardian and master," he writes; "towns surround her on the periphery, each in its place. A poet might well speak of the moon surrounded by the stars."[28] This astronomical metaphor recalls the practice in the Middle Ages of representing the structure of the Ptolemaic universe as a set of concentric circles. The late 14th-century example in the Campo Santo at Pisa includes the elements, the planets, the stars, and the nine grades of angels.

In the ancient world, where cosmic alliances with the sources of political power were perceived as the norm, there was no conflict between the circles of the heavens and the centralized emanation of princely authority. The Near East, that cradle of absolute rule, swung its urban circles without hesitation. Assyrians, and Persians after them, seem most at ease with these royal diagrams. The tradition is recorded by Herodotus. He describes Ecbatana (now Hamadan), founded in 715 BC as the capital of the Medes on a gentle hill in a plain in northwest Iran. It was perfectly circular, he says, with an elaborate system of seven concentric walls. Each was painted a different color to identify it with one of the planets, beginning with the outer wall which was white for Jupiter and ending in the middle with a silver wall for the moon and a gold one for the sun. The king and his entourage were in the center rings, then lesser officials in descending order. The common folk lived beyond the outer walls.

The tradition continued with the Parthians and the Sassanians. The cores of their cosmic cities have not been properly explored, but there is enough evidence to indicate that the circular form, with palace and temple in its center, was an intentional diagram of princely rule. Hatra was surrounded by two round walls, and had a large temple complex in the center. Another Parthian city, Darabjerd in southern Iran, enclosed within its perfectly circular wall two rock formations, with a castle on one and, most likely, a temple on the other. Nearby is Gur (Firuzabad), *182* the site of the first Sassanian capital, Ardashir-Kurra, built by the founder of the

dynasty Ardashir I (AD 226–240). The great circle can still be seen. Within, the city had a radial organization of twelve sectors named after the signs of the zodiac.

182 Gur (Firuzabad, Iran), Sassanian capital of the 3rd century AD.

2. Radial organization

The combination of concentric space and street rays that join center to periphery made sense in terms of circulation; but more to the point in political terms, the composite diagram was a strong visual projection of the all-pervasive nature of absolute power, while the radiating streets might also play a secondary role as dividers for some intermediary organization.

Imperfect specimens are widespread. Even in traditional African societies, wherever politically centralized systems develop the radial-concentric city makes its appearance. This is true of Asante, Yoruba, Hausa and Ganda. In the Yoruba city of Ife, for example, radial roads begin at the royal compound, and cut through several concentric roads to reach various provincial seats. These subsidiary compounds were situated at varying distances from the royal center on the basis of rank and social status; each chief assumed the responsibility of maintaining the road that led to his own compound.

9 The famous round city of Baghdad in the 8th century provides the classic Near Eastern examplar of the radial-concentric scheme. Also called Madinat as-Salam or the City of Peace, it was conceived by the caliph al-Mansur as the capital of the Abbasids, the second major dynasty of Islam. The design continued the royal tradition of Persia which Islam had conquered during the previous century. Baghdad is in fact on the River Tigris, a short distance east of Ecbatana.

No excavations have ever been conducted on the site of al-Mansur's city, but the literary sources are forthcoming.[29] In the center of the circle was a vast courtyard that held the ruler's palace, a mosque, and two buildings for the guard and the police. It could be entered by a very few, and then only on foot. Surrounding this circular courtyard were the residences of al-Mansur's children, quarters for his servants and slaves, as well as government agencies like the treasury, the arsenal, and the headquarters of the palace personnel. The gates of these buildings, originally opening onto the circular court, were soon shifted by decree to face outward onto a ringroad which separated the caliph's personal domain from a broad residential belt. Here lived units of his army, carefully selected to represent the ethnic and tribal elements of the Muslim domains. A double wall enclosed the city, penetrated by four gates only. The four arcaded streets that cut through the residential belt to connect the gates to the central court were used as limited markets for the residents of the royal city, until al-Mansur, fearing for his safety, moved the markets.

There is no comparable radial-concentric diagram of political power in the West during the Middle Ages. In the "organic" parallels that are sometimes evoked, like Nördlingen in Germany, the circle is the folding embrace of a loosely growing town, concentric ringroads represent the superseded walls in this progressive growth, and converging streets mean a short cut to the central market and the cathedral.

Classical antiquity is equally inhospitable to autocratic political diagrams. Where power was supposed to reside in the people, the "center" was the marketplace (the agora), and the acropolis or "head of the city" was a natural height occupied by the gods. There was no palace. In his ideal city of Atlantis, Plato put the acropolis in the middle surrounded by a circular wall: from it emanated twelve divisions, each housing a separate population group. In an ambiguous passage in *The Birds*, perhaps in praise of the Hippodamian system of orthogonal planning (see above, p. 105) Aristophanes seems to be rejecting a radial layout in favor of the grid.

> With a straight rod I measure out that so
> The circle may be squared; and in the center
> A market-place; and streets be leading to it
> Straight to the very center; just as from
> A star, though circular, straight rays flash out
> In all directions . . .[30]

But that is as far as the Greeks went with ideal cities. They did not build any, and neither did the Romans, since they must have seen the paradox between a radial scheme and a society of citizens at least theoretically equal.

What the Romans did with this political diagram was to find a functional rationale for it. Vitruvius mentions circular cities in passing, with this explanation: "Towns should be laid out not as an exact square nor with salient angles, but in circular form, to give a view of the enemy from many points." As for the radial scheme, Vitruvius explains it in terms of the prevailing winds. There were eight of these, and eight radial streets could so be struck from a center that they would avoid the assumed paths of the winds. Actually, as we saw in the last chapter, Vitruvius's point was not to create radial streets, but to use the wind rose to produce a "safe" *128*
grid. It was Cesare Cesariano in his 1521 edition of Vitruvius who interpreted the Vitruvian wind-rose passage literally as a radial city. This provided some support for the contention of Renaissance artists that their radial city plans were reviving long-forgotten principles of Classical urban design.

The logic was again derived from Vitruvius. In a totally different context, in describing the anthropomorphic qualities of Classical architecture, Vitruvius had proposed the circle and the square as the most perfect geometric figures by the striking imagery of a spreadeagled man whose extremities would touch the perimeters of these perfect figures. Italian Renaissance theory began to see radial design, or at least centrally-planned schemes, as the diagram of humanist perfection, and went further, in urban–political terms, to equate perfect social order with the humanist prince. So came about the transference of this discussion as justification of the radial city.

SFORZINDA'S EXAMPLE

183 Filarete's Sforzinda is first. It was designed in 1457–64 for Francesco Sforza, tyrant of Milan, and named after him, but was never built. The basic form was an eight-point star derived by superimposing two quadrangles in such a way that their angles are equidistant. This particular figure is in fact an ancient magic sign, and it was sometimes used in the Renaissance as a diagram that interlocked the four elements

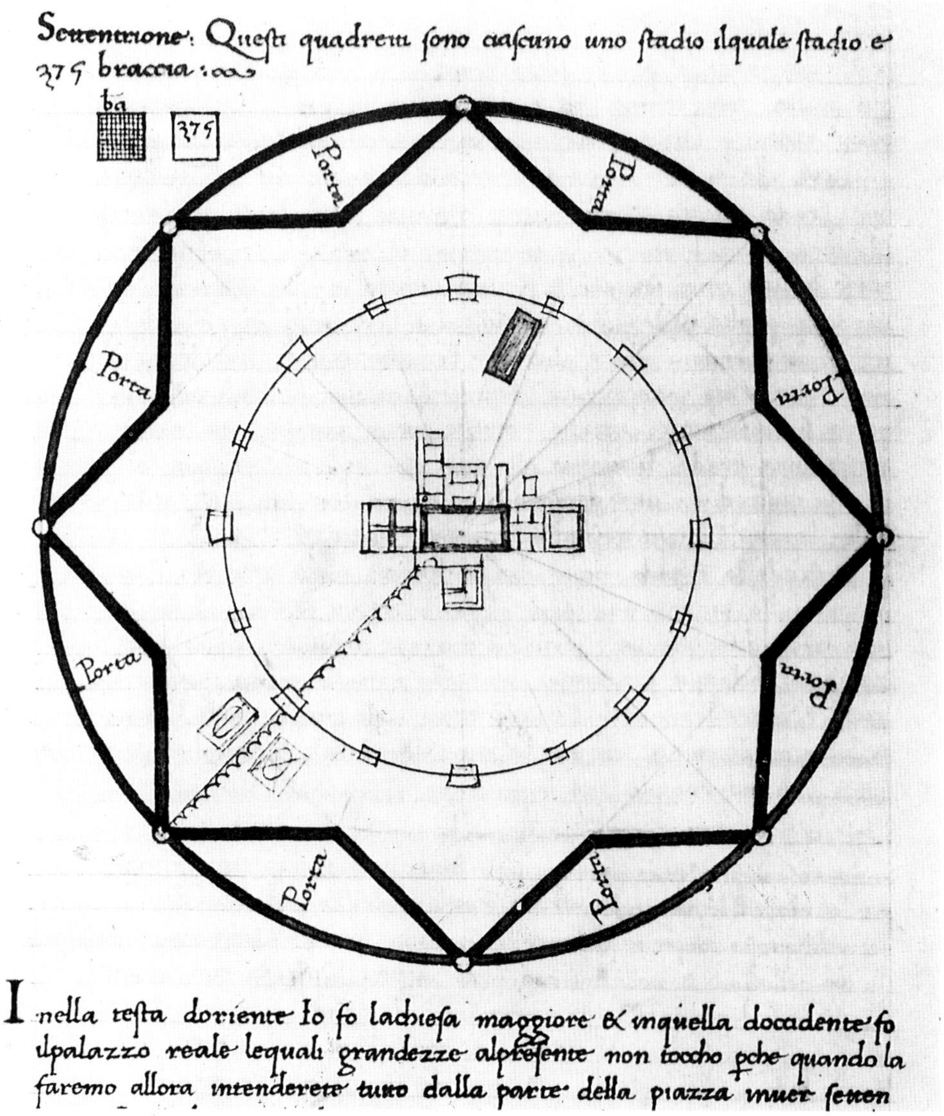

183 Filarete (Antonio Averlino), design for the ideal city of Sforzinda, ca. 1460–64.

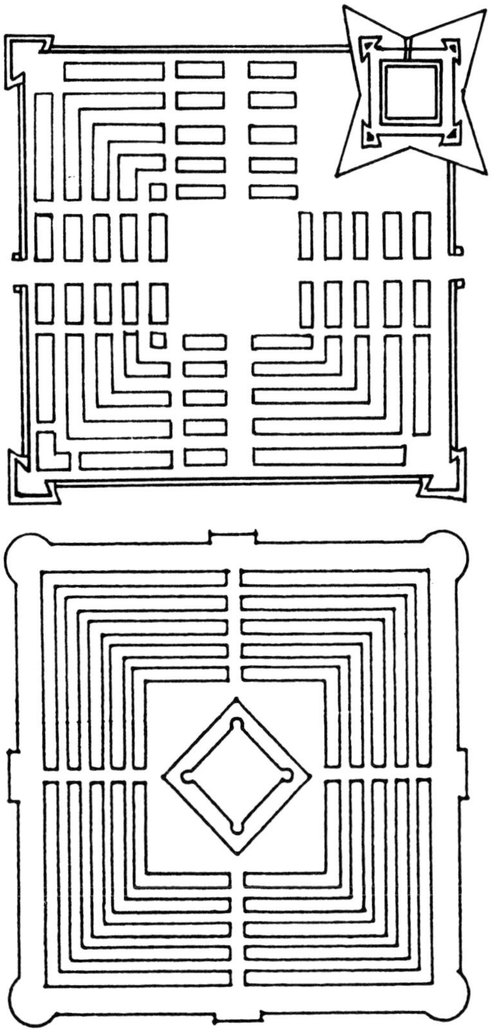

184, 185 Freudenstadt (Germany), founded in 1599, alternative designs by Heinrich Schickhardt.

and the four Aristotelian qualities—dryness, humidity, cold and heat. Filarete's expressed interest in magic and astrology makes extra-urban links of this sort probable.

In the fully developed scheme of Sforzinda, the gates were fitted in the inner angles of the star, and towers in the outer angles. There was a formal town center with a main open space, and sixteen subsidiary squares throughout the city for markets and churches. There were to be separate schools for boys and girls, and a ten-story House of Vice and Virtue, a bit like the Colosseum, with a brothel on the ground floor, lecture rooms, and an Academy of Learning higher up. Filarete's interest in this subject was live. He himself tells us that he had made a thorough study of representations of the Virtues and Vices, and it has been suggested that the radial design of his city might have profited from medieval diagrams of St. Augustine's Earthly City, where the circular shape is divided into compartments each of which contains a Virtue and the corresponding Vice, or even the allegory of the uncertainties of Fortune shown in the Middle Ages as a spoked wheel.[31] This first Renaissance radial city, then, might not be quite as free of medievalisms as we like to pretend.

Filarete originally planned to place a tower in the middle of his city: the idea of interrelated squares came later. The important buildings were all around the central square, which was actually a complex of three squares, one dedicated to the prince's palace and the cathedral, the others to merchants and their market. The buildings included a bank and a mint, a bath, and as a sop to the communal apparatus of self-governed cities (one imagines) a palace of the *podestà*, a key official of the medieval city-state. Filarete developed the buildings of this central complex in some detail, but he was much less certain of how it would hook into the radial street pattern. Every second street was to be replaced by a waterway. The residential sections were to include artisans' cottages and a small colony for workers.

Sforzinda introduces several themes which were to be exploited in future ideal cities.

First, for all its ties backward, Sforzinda is the archetype of the humanist city of the High Renaissance, where perfect form is the image of a perfect society. Sforzinda and its High Renaissance successors share that conflict between the ideal of a humanist view of life and the reality of despotism. Since their execution demands centralized power and the resources it can command, the perfect society has to be moored to the concept of the good prince. "The human race is at its best under a monarch," as Dante had said at the dawn of the Renaissance. "Monarchy is necessary for the well-being of the world." So the ideal city-form of the Renaissance could end up by rationalizing tyranny.

The perfect radial city as political diagram is rare in the flesh during the Renaissance, and when it occurs it can be strangely diluted. Freudenstadt in the Black Forest, one of these rarities, is a mining town. It was built for the Christophtal silver mine by Duke Friedrich of Württemberg, for workers who were Protestant refugees from Carinthia and the Steiermark. The shape is square, with a central open space, and successive projects for it by Heinrich Schickhardt, a German architect trained in Italy, are instructive, in that they show a consciousness about the political significance of the centralized scheme. In the first design (1596) Schickhardt placed *184*
the ducal residence in a peripheral location, at the northeast corner, in line with traditional medieval thinking. The Duke rejected this as "old-fashioned," and proposed a central location for the castle, set at an angle to the axes of the main streets. *185*
This second design was executed but the castle was never built. There is also a frivolous side to this final scheme. It seems it is really based on the board game of *Mühle*, the idea having occurred to the prince while he was playing the game.[32]

In Italy the centrality of the *signore*'s seat never quite attained the diagrammatic purity of Filarete's Sforzinda. Real towns with a long medieval history could only be wishfully coaxed into a semblance of the symbolically correct *signoria*. The centrality of the ducal palace at Ferrara was manufactured—by the remarkable expedient of doubling the size of the town, with a vast new quarter on the far side of the once peripherally situated medieval castle. At places like Rimini, the ducal residence remained at the city edge.

186 Karlsruhe (Germany). An original hunting tower of 1715 was replaced by a princely palace (1752–81) which became the focus of 32 radiating roads. Some of these run through the park-forest behind, while nine radials organize the town to the south.

In a replay of this political debate, a later new town devised a peculiar solution, where the prince removed himself by choice from the center. This is Grammichele in Sicily, built to replace the small community of Ochialà leveled by the disastrous earthquake of 1693. The patron was Carlo Maria Carafa Branciforte, prince of Butera and Boccella. The six-sided central space is overlooked only by the church. Radial streets extend beyond the polygonal urban core into five gridded neighborhoods or *borghi* with a formal square for each, and a sixth, larger, unit intended for the prince. It is at once a gracious gesture on the part of a reputedly enlightened ruler, this withdrawal to one side, and also a reaffirmation of the old feudal set-up of the town in front of its lord's isolated castle.

But reflected in Filarete's diagram is a second alternative of the radial power-city, and that is the scheme that was to become widespread in the 17th and 18th centuries after its brilliant application to the new court city of the French king Louis XIV at Versailles. These Baroque capitals combine radial-concentricity with axiality, in *238*
that all roads converge upon the royal palace, which responds at the same time to a *186*
grand, axial avenue that leads to the centre of its main façade. This avenue is often the middle prong of a dominant triplet of roads, or *trivium*. The city does not in fact surround the palace on all sides: the sector behind the palace is a royal park. The advantage of this scheme is that the royal person has the security of the old feudal arrangement of an independent defensive castle at the edge of town, as well as the centrality of a power-city. The palace grounds, furthermore, have room to expand, and in planning these grounds the ruler can indulge in the kind of Baroque amplitude that would be impossible in a fully circumscribed radial scheme. Indeed a characteristic of these capital cities is that their boundary is not fixed. The radial avenues shoot into the countryside in all directions. The grand axis, meantime, provides a hierarchical approach to the royal person that is direct, unique (in contrast to the true radial scheme where all the rays are presumed equal), and admissive of gradations.

Two other aspects of Sforzinda are premonitory. The moral tone of Filarete's commentary, and the provision for things like the House of Vice and Virtue, lead, beyond the Renaissance, to the geometric social diagrams of the modern period starting with Ledoux's Chaux, which I shall take up shortly. At the same time, *196*
Sforzinda can be considered to be the prototype of the functional city. Filarete models his city after Vitruvius's wind rose, thus guarding the population against the risks of harmful drafts. Filarete also hints at the military superiority of his design. And it is exactly this last aspect that would give the radial city an enormous popularity in the second half of the 16th century.

THE FUNCTIONAL DIAGRAM

THE LOGIC OF DEFENSE

The greatest interpretation of the radial scheme is, in fact, by Renaissance military engineers. The issue of fortifications is best taken up in a chapter on the city edge in my companion volume. The point that needs to be made here is that ideal schemes like Filarete's with a sociopolitical program were embraced after the mid-16th century with a defensive program in mind, where strategic considerations outweighed all others. But this did not happen until the design problems of Sforzinda were resolved, particularly by Francesco di Giorgio (1439–1501). He was

the first Renaissance architect and military engineer to articulate the ways in which a
187 radial system of streets, a bastioned periphery wall, and a public space in the center could be made to work together. He tried out variations where this central space is circular or polygonal, and where the street system has to be accommodated to a number of topographical situations. The placement of gates for the coming and going of the citizens and the defense of the bastions complicated the purely geometric resolution, as Francesco di Giorgio realized, and it is his effort to arbitrate in his designs between the needs of the inhabitants and the needs of artillery that makes him critical for the increasingly sophisticated experiments of the next century, as bastioned defenses took the place of the simple curtain walls of the past.
5 His influence is seen in Leonardo, Francesco Marchi, Scamozzi and others.

A main complication arose from the fact that the bastions had to defend their own circuit if they were to defend the city at large behind them. In that context, from a military point of view, the circle and the square, those standard forms of the ideal city, were equally unsatisfactory. The circle was inadequate because the military planner preferred to have straight curtains between two bastions, since only straight curtains permitted efficient defense by the flanks. They were also the cheaper to build. The square was the smallest and cheapest fortress to be had, but *it* was inadequate because it afforded the least flexibility to bastions which were forced to be blunt given the right angles of the corners, but which were least effective when they were blunt because they left little room for maneuver at the top of the platform and the sharp point was easily ruined by enemy fire. (See, e.g., Mariembourg in Belgium of 1542.)

A regular polygon was the best solution. The ideal plan was most effectively executed on flat, open plains unmarred by natural impediments. Bastions, the least protected parts of the defensive system, had to be linked to the interior by wide traffic arteries in order to be properly and quickly supplied in time of need. This translated into a radial scheme of streets setting out from a vast piazza and directly connected with the bastions. In Renaissance ideal planning, the spokes linked the center with the gates, and the center hosted important buildings like the church and the palace. But the center in these military polygons is empty and unpaved. At times of siege the commander would station himself there in a tower or raised platform that afforded an unimpeded view of the bastions. To see the improving quality of
188 these military towns, one need only compare Philippeville in Belgium, built by the Emperor Charles V in 1555 on the designs of the Dutch architect Sebastian van
159 Noyen, and Palmanova from the end of the century which was described at the beginning of this chapter.

Within a matter of decades after the inception of Palmanova, military techniques had advanced beyond the point when bastions were the dominant feature of the defensive system. Past this line of primary defense spread a panoply of outworks—semi-independent units like pincers, lunettes and ravelins, as well as even more distant forts—which isolated the town more and more from the surrounding countryside. The radial scheme of streets within could now be given up in preference for the simpler grid, since supplying bastions along straight access roads had lost its
5 urgency. Even before this point the grid was often inserted within a polygonal defensive wall, in the projects of Pietro Cataneo for example.

189, One late survival of the Palmanova model is Hamina in Finland, founded in 1723
190 astride the Turku-Viipuri road, on the neck of land between the sea and Kirkkojärvi Lake. Hamina actually replaced a 17th-century gridded town destroyed by fire. The new town was to be the cornerstone of the defense of the eastern border with Russia and was designed by the fortress commander Axel von Löwen. But it would also

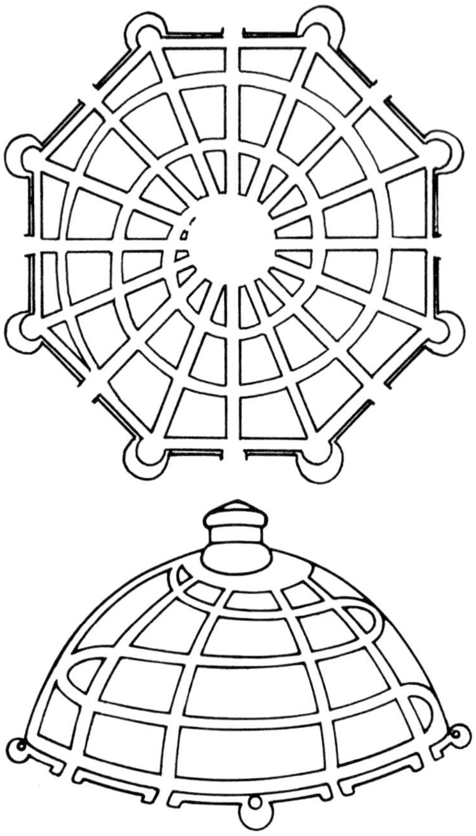

187 *Radial schemes imposed on hilly sites, by Francesco di Giorgio Martini, 1490s (after the* Codex Magliabecchanius*).*

188 *Philippeville (Belgium), original scheme of 1554 by Sebastian van Noyen. The fortifications were extended a century later by Vauban. Nothing of this elaborate defensive circuit can be seen today in the small modern city, but the radial street pattern and central square survive.*

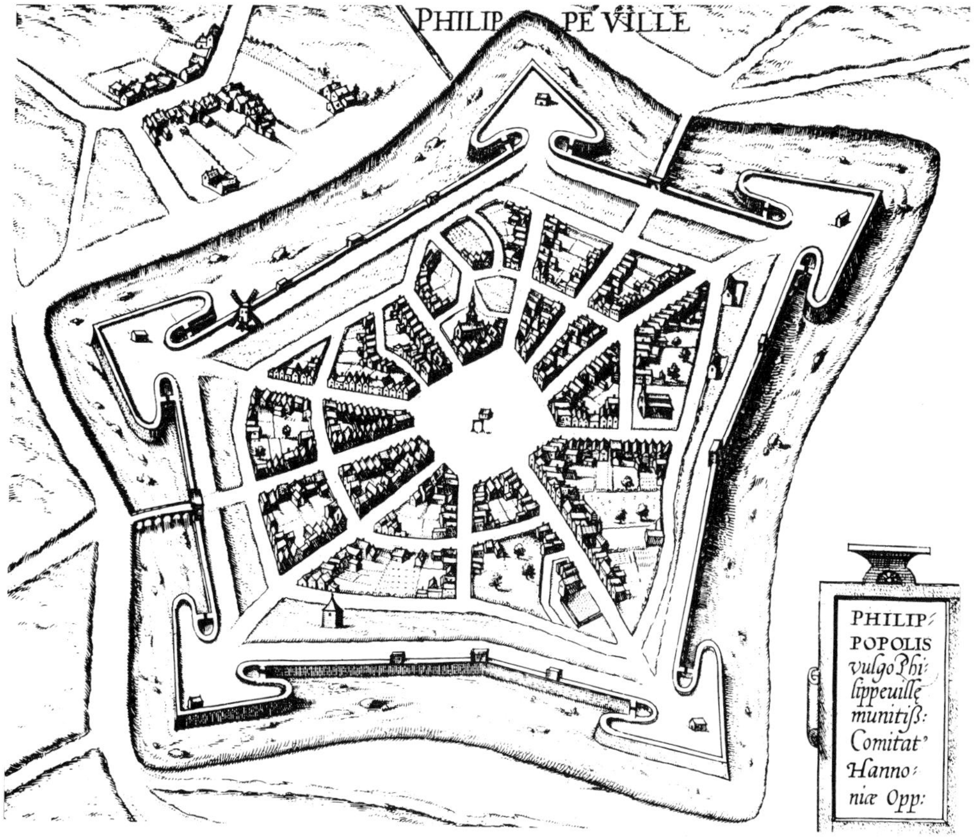

189, 190 *Hamina (Finland), founded in 1723; plan ca. 1750, and aerial view of the town center. The Town Hall stands in the middle; below is the Lutheran church; above, the round Greek Orthodox church—all three rebuilt in the 1790s and 1830s–40s.*

double as a trade center intended to complement Finland's leading trade center, Viipuri; and it would take over Viipuri's role as provincial capital. The shape could not be made perfect because of the narrow land-strip site, so the northeast side toward the sea had to be flattened. Nevertheless, there were eight radial streets, and two ring roads. Barracks were located at the ends of the radials, and the street running northwest was completely lined by military buildings. The rest of town was inhabited by burghers.

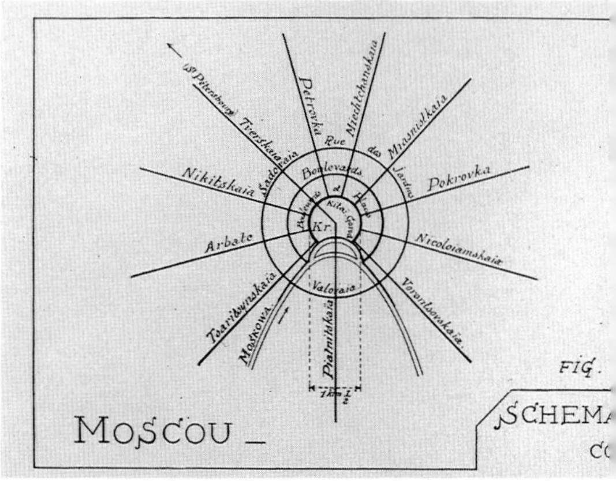

191 Schematic traffic diagrams of Moscow and Paris, from Eugène Hénard's Etudes sur les transformations de Paris, *1903–9.*

TRAFFIC AND RADIAL-CONCENTRICITY

The felicity of the radial-concentric scheme for convergent traffic had been apparent since the Middle Ages in the merchant towns with their central marketplace. But it was the widespread acceptance of the coach in the 17th century and the fast diagonals of Baroque urban design that opened a modern, post-military chapter for the radial city as a functional diagram. This fitness became an article of faith to traffic engineers and city planners with the transformation of the city center into the central business district of the modern metropolis and the entrenchment of rapid transportation systems. The railroad, streetcar, and automobile city made a coherent system out of radial traffic arteries and girdle streets. In the old fortified
Pl.4 cities, the walls were pulled down and converted into a continuous ringroad, while former direct approaches from the countryside into the city were rationalized into straight radial roads linking the fattened suburban belt with the center. The radial star or asterisk came to be seen, by many planners, as the best form for cities of moderate to large size. It became the favorite device of traffic engineers and their transportation plans, and it remains so to this day. The type is succinctly described by Kevin Lynch:

> There should be a single dominant center, of high density and mixed use, from which four to eight major transportation lines radiate outward. These lines would contain mass transit systems, as well as the main highways. Secondary centers are disposed at intervals along these lines, and the more intensive uses either cluster around these subcenters, or string out along the major lines. Less intensive uses occupy bands farther back from the main radials, and open green wedges take up the remaining space between the fingers of development. At intervals outward from the main center, there are concentric highways, which link the fingers together, but which are free of adjacent development except where they intersect the fingers themselves.[33]

Seductively logical at the level of theory, the star shape is hard to adhere to, especially in a capitalist economy. Without strong central control, the green wedges cannot be maintained as open land free of building. Continuous development may stretch along the concentric roads, and the danger that the center, as the object of all incoming traffic, may become overloaded is quite real.

The answer has been sought in two related propositions. One is to plan new cities with a number of small interrelated stars, in size somewhere between *rond-points* or roundabouts and the unmanageable radial-concentric metropolis. Walter Burley
192 Griffin's celebrated design of 1912 for the Australian capital city of Canberra epitomizes this approach, and has the distinction of having been built. The overall plan was held together by two giant axes related to the topography: the "land axis"
Pl.24 between Mount Ainslie to the northeast and Mount Bimberi to the southwest, passing through the two eminences which became Parliament Hill and Capitol Hill; and the "water axis" extending southeastward from Black Mountain along a

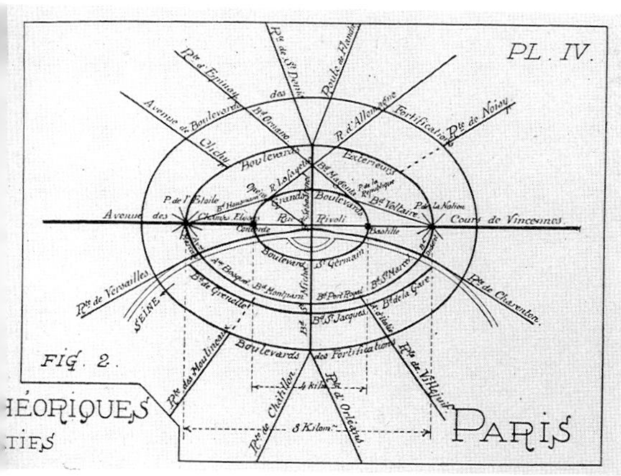

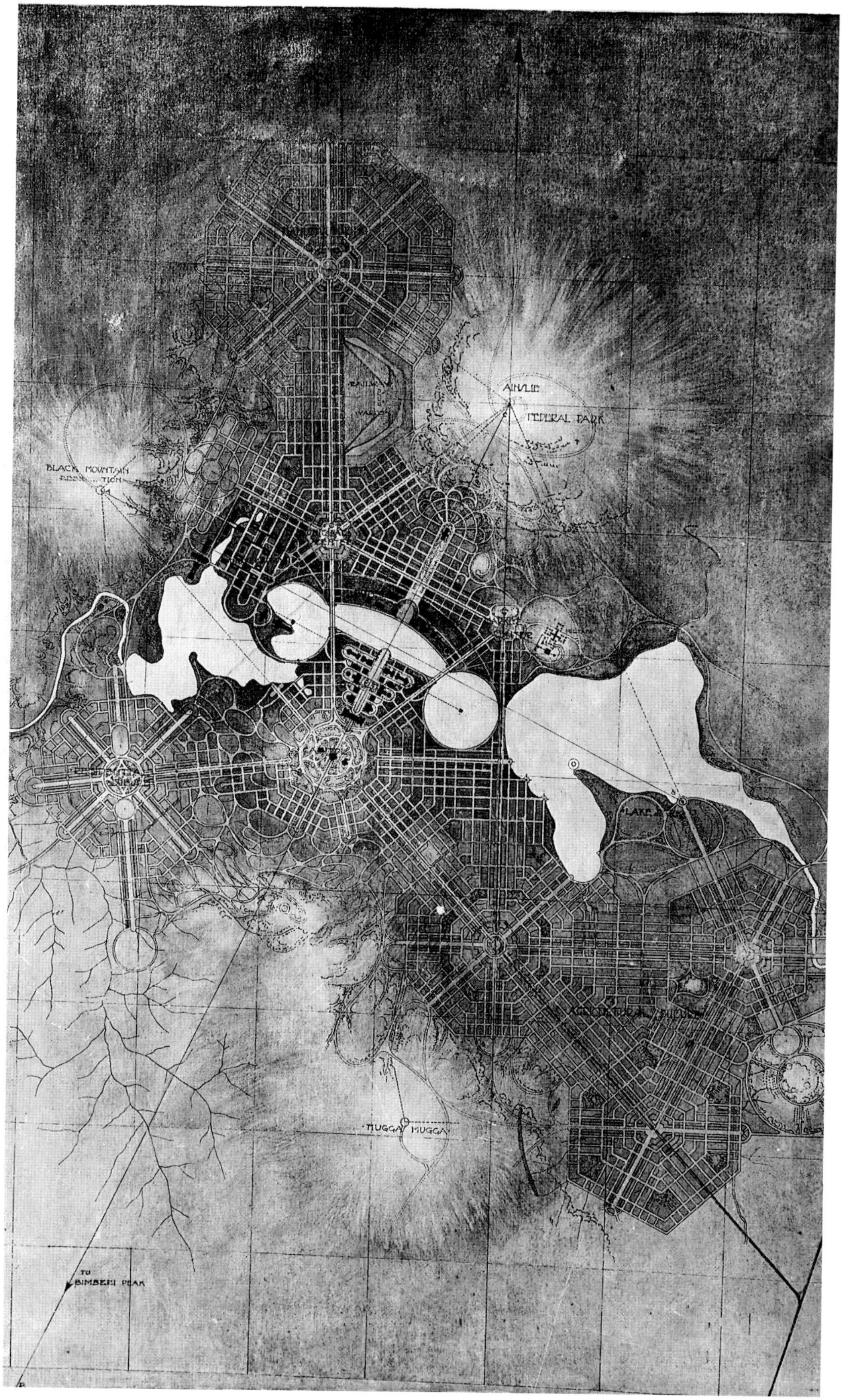

192 Canberra (Australia), plan, premiated competition entry by Walter Burley Griffin, 1912; ink on silk drawing by Marion Mahoney Griffin.

sequence of waterways to a large lake created by damming the Molonglo River. But all this is less evident than the constellation of sunbursts, or rather spider's webs, which characterize street intersections. In elegance the only worthy successor of this Griffin lacework is the unadopted plan for Brasilia by the Roberto brothers, entered in the national competition of 1957. It featured a cluster of seven units, each a self-sufficient town-size quarter for some 70,000 inhabitants, with others to be added as there was need. Within each quarter an aspect of the capital's functions—finance, arts, welfare services, communications and so on—was to be installed.

For the old metropolis, the proposed solution was the so-called satellite model. The idea would be to distribute at some distance from the central agglomeration a ring of satellite communities of limited size. These would be separated from the mother city by broad stretches of rural land, and keep their size intact within greenbelts of their own. In Lynch's summary: "The dominant center is maintained, as well as the general radial form, but growth is channelled into communities well separated from the central area, instead of spreading continuously outward along the radial arms."[34]

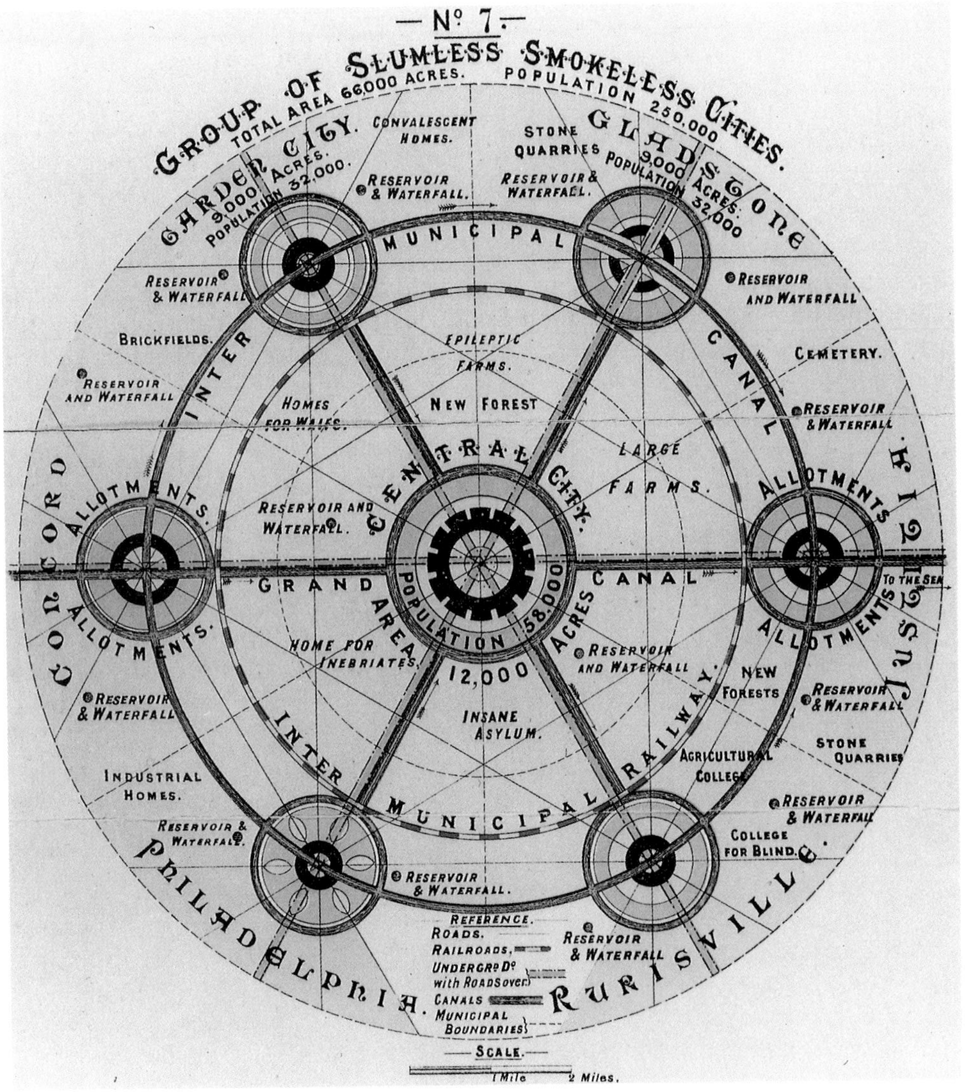

193 Diagram of "Social Cities" from Ebenezer Howard's To-Morrow: A Peaceful Path to Social Reform, *first published in 1898, and renamed in later editions* Garden Cities of To-Morrow.

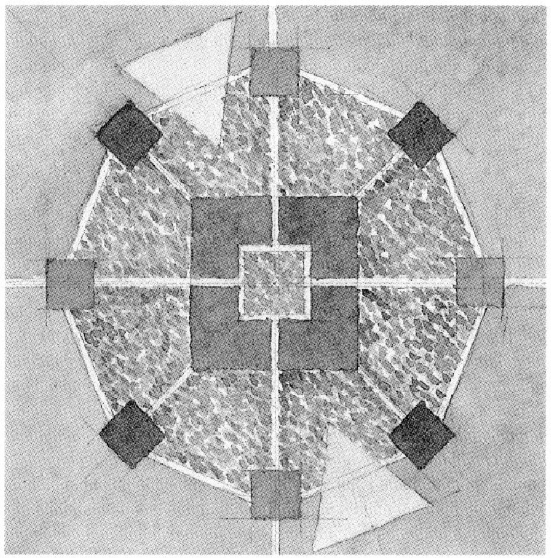

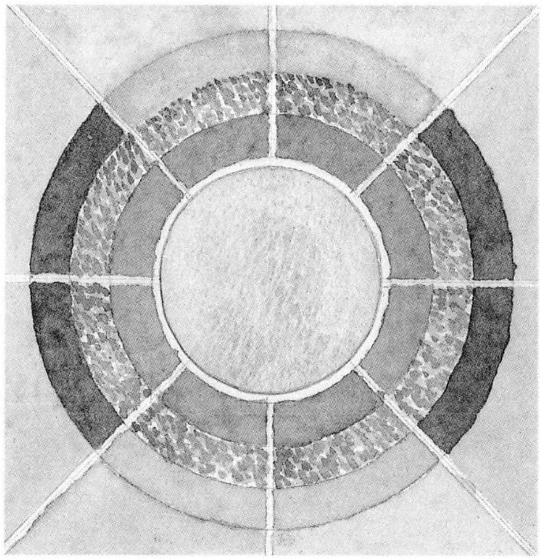

194, 195 Dispersal diagrams of the postwar period, after Ralph Lapp's Must We Hide? *(1949): the "satellite" city* (top) *and the "doughnut" city.*

If Ebenezer Howard was not the first to promote the concept of satellite cities, his exposition in *Garden Cities of To-Morrow*—first published in 1898 under the title *To-Morrow: A Peaceful Path to Social Reform*—was the most influential. His diagram "illustrating correct principle of a city's growth—open country ever near at *193*
hand, and rapid communication between off-shoots" became famous. It showed small circular cities (population 32,000) surrounding a Central City (population 58,000), and connected to it by spokes of railroad and to each other by main roads. It began to be replicated in projects of regional planning, even though Howard himself made clear that he was not proposing to have his cluster of cities "arranged in the precise geometrical form of my diagram." The diagram was refined by Raymond Unwin: he made clear that all indispensable institutions would remain in the center, with some residential districts for the people who work there. The satellite cities would each consist of four parts, one for industry and the other three for housing. In Germany, the architect Erich Gloeden worked along similar lines in the 1920s, but with this difference—that he no longer insisted on a primary center. The original settlement becomes equal to the new settlements around it, and the interrelated circular urban units are fully integrated with the open land. Each radial-concentric unit performs a different urban function. In a sense this co-ordinated system of settlements, to which others can be added in time, prefigured the multi-nuclear Roberto plan for Brasilia.

Many old cities became the subjects of these dispersal fantasies. Unwin applied his diagram to Greater London; Martin Maechler reduced Berlin and its territory to a diagrammatic orgy of overlapping circles; and the Capital Planning Commission of Washington, D.C., developed its own "Ring of Towns" assuming, the architectural critic Sibyl Moholy-Nagy wrote acidly, that "a hundred years later people would still believe in this lovely utopia, all evidence to the contrary, and surrender their real-estate holdings and speculation houses to the state or the center city for perpetual safekeeping of uncontaminated nature."[35] Indeed, England had to go much beyond the diagram when after the Second World War she adopted the principle of satellite garden cities as the central dogma of her national urban policy, the program of New Towns, which was steadfastly adhered to until recently. None of the thirty-odd satellites looked like Palmanova or Gloeden's sunburst settlements. Other nations have since forged their own versions of dispersal, although big cities continued to grow and the satellite cities themselves have rarely been able to stay within their prescribed limits.

For a while in the immediate postwar period, the dispersal theory found a peculiar market in the United States. Convinced of the inevitability of atomic warfare, Government agencies and semi-private think-tanks advanced proposals of preparedness which favored the shrinking of existing cities. All new development would be concentrated at a distance from them, thereby reducing "target attractiveness," improving the chances of survival, and incidentally bringing about a pleasanter and healthier urban environment. A book called *Must We Hide?* (1949) argued for a voluntary long-range plan that "should contemplate the spreading out of industry and residences into closely knit but not highly concentrated units." Two models were proferred. One was the widely known satellite city model, with the *194*
individual units separated by about 3 miles (5 km.). The other was the "doughnut city" model, in which the central business district was replaced by a park or airport, *195*
and business, light industry and residential areas were wrapped in bands around it separated by greenbelts of parks and golf courses and cut through by the spokes of rapid transit—the classic radial-concentric ideal city diagram baptized for the atomic age.[36]

THE SECULAR/SOCIALIST DIAGRAM

This last chapter of the ideal city is the product of the Industrial Revolution and its familiar accompaniment—the horrible congestion of the old towns, the plight of the working class. The motivation here is reformist, then, and not related to practical matters of traffic or defense or to the symbolism of the State. The apparatus is the same as that of earlier diagrammatic cities: concern for geometric purity, a special population (with an emphais now, in theory at least, on a classless society or on the working class), and visual control. In fact, there is an acute conflict between the authoritarian nature of the diagrams and the enunciated aim to have inhabitants participate fully in the design and life of their community—a conflict that we had seen much earlier in the rhetoric of Renaissance humanism.

What to put in the middle, therefore, becomes a touchy issue. What is a representative architectural symbol for the Fourth Estate, the workers and the peasants? And the other issue is the realization of these ideal schemes. No central power stands behind them that can command the huge funds and the labor pool needed to make such visions come true. On one side there are the beautiful, stereometric forms of the architects, often only remotely connected to use. Ledoux applies the circle to the city, the cemetery, and the cooper house. On the other side, there are the images of scraggly settlements, idyllic and touchingly underorganized, that are aspiring to that formal beauty. With the legal and financial realities being what they are in society at large, new lands, empty of precedent, are sought for these ideal communities—New Zealand, the United States, Algeria, New Caledonia. The names say it all: Harmony, Unity, Utopia, even an Owenite foundation called Mutual Co-operation. For the actual placement of them, orientation is unimportant in the sense of the cosmic diagrams. What is more important is orientation for reasons of health and wholeness—to avoid harmful winds, to catch the sun, to be at one with nature.

THE COSMOS OF WORKERS, CRIMINALS AND STUDENTS

The natural starting point is, of course, the Enlightenment. If the most obvious opening act cannot but be Ledoux's Chaux, of about 1775–80, there were lesser essays in the creation of a workers' cosmos that prove the pervasive 18th-century urge to rationalize and idealize the workplace.

The scale of San Gregorio da Sassola near Rome is modest, the enterprise is rural, but there could be no doubt of the new ordering spirit when the little village on the site was razed some time in the 18th century and rebuilt as a continuous oval for the communal life of a group of farming families. In the environs of Naples, the workers' colony of San Leucio founded in 1775 by Ferdinand IV for the State's silk industry was to be no mere center of production, but a social experiment in sympathy with Enlightenment goals of "good government" and a society rationally ordered. The physical example that came ready to hand was the radial-concentric ideal city of the Renaissance, but despite royal patronage the diagram was at the service not of the humanist *signoria* and its entourage but of the working class.[37] The impressive Neoclassical oval for the industrial community of Grand Hornu in the Borinage district of Belgium carries these noble sentiments of social harmony into the 19th century.

196 Chaux, like San Leucio, was under royal patronage, and was substantially advanced when the Revolution interrupted the projects of the Crown and made

196 Claude Nicolas Ledoux, project for the city of Chaux, ca. 1775, perspective view; engraving from his L'Architecture considérée sous le rapport de l'art, des moeurs, et de la législation *(1804). An alternative design, D-shaped in plan, was built for the saltworks, near Besançon in northeastern France.*

Ledoux an enemy of the people. It could therefore be built solidly, indeed monumentally, at least in part. The commission was for a model town for the royal saltworks, an ideal industrial community in the center of a regional plan that took in the river, canals for the deviation of salt water toward the site, the evaporation plant outside of town, and the forest that provided the wood for the drying process.

The original scheme for the town was a full oval defined by a tree-lined ringroad which was connected to the center by radiating avenues. Ledoux wanted the form to be "pure like that which the sun describes in its course." Public and private buildings extended beyond this ring on all sides. The church, for example, is outside the oval on the left. The spiritual and social, rather than the physical, welfare of the inhabitants predominated. There was no hospital, for example, but we read of something called a *Pacifère* where quarrels were to be settled peacefully, a Temple of Memory dedicated to the Virtue of Women, and the *Oikema* or house of sexual instruction in the form of a phallus—all of which recalls Filarete's Sforzinda with its House of Vice and Virtue.

Ledoux wrote: "Build temples to social virtue; support your ideals on the basis of a universal pact which challenges the qualities of the whole race to serve the well-being of all." The half of Chaux that was built gives an idea of the strict hierarchy that was to reign in this model industrial town. There were three classes of population—the officers headed by the governor, the employees in charge of locks and the wood supply and the clerical work, and lastly the workers. The governor was in the center building, along the diameter, which also included a chapel. It was flanked by the two processing buildings where huge stoves burned tons of wood day and night. The half-oval has a main gate on axis which grouped about itself the quarters for the guards, a prison and a bakery. To the right were the metal-workers—the blacksmiths, the coopers who made the barrels that transported the dried salt, and so on. To the left were carpenters and wheelwrights. There was living accommodation in these shop buildings, and more elsewhere on the site. Families were to have a single room each, and prepare their meals in common kitchens.

The central placement of the director and the peripheral disposition of his charges brings to mind Jeremy Bentham's "Central Inspection Principle" or "Panopticon." Bentham, a Radical philosopher, called his multipurpose device a "social invention," and it reveals chillingly the sinister side of Enlightenment order. It was now fashionable to speak of model societies as "inventions" – the community as a machine, as it were. Robert Owen wrote of his own model community design: "If the invention of various machines has multiplied the power of labour . . . this [his plan for a model community] is an invention which will at once multiply the physical and mental powers of the whole society to an incalculable extent without injuring anyone by its introduction and its rapid infusion." And this invention analogy carries all the way to the end of the 19th century. Howard called himself "the inventor of the Garden City idea," and compared his achievement with George Stephenson's work on the first locomotive.

The principle of the Panopticon is best described by Michel Foucault, who has also been its most eloquent interpreter:

> . . . at the periphery, an annular building; at the centre, a tower; this tower is pierced with wide windows that open onto the inner side of the ring; the peripheric building is divided into cells, each of which extends the whole width of the building; they have two windows, one on the inside, corresponding to the windows of the tower; the other, on the outside, allows the light to cross the cell from one end to the other. All that is needed, then, is to place a supervisor in a central tower and to shut up in each cell a madman, a patient, a condemned man, a worker or a schoolboy. By the effect of backlighting, one can observe from the tower, standing out precisely against the light, the small captive shadows in the cells of the periphery. . . . Visibility is a trap.[38]

As Foucault correctly assesses it, Bentham's mechanism "automatizes and disindividualizes power." Instead of kings, we have now an invisible but omnipresent authority in the center of the ideal diagram which can inspect and judge our behavior—and alter it. Bentham himself applied the idea to a penitentiary where a single jailer with the aid of mirrors could supervise 2,000 inmates. His brother Samuel used the Panopticon for an "industry house," and it could also have an application for other building types like schools and hospitals. In fact, as its inventor wrote, the Panopticon would be applicable "to all establishments whatsoever, in which, within a space not too large to be covered or commanded by buildings, a number of persons are meant to be kept under inspection." The size of space makes the literal application of the device impractical for cities, though from time to time a grim urban reality leads Bentham's way, as with Fascist projects for new native towns in Ethiopia. But the implications of panopticism for the structure
197 of society and its component parts were formidable. In prison planning the influence was direct.

197 Statesville (Illinois), panopticon cell house of the Illinois Penitentiary, by C. Harrick Hammond, 1919.

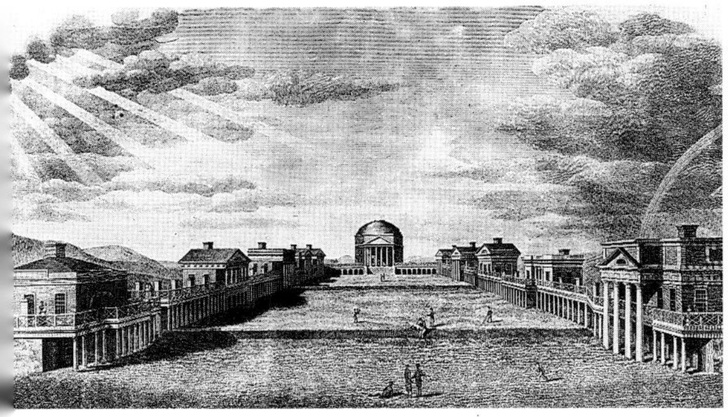

198 Charlottesville (Virginia), University of Virginia campus, by Thomas Jefferson, 1817; engraving by Benjamin Tanner, 1827.

But let us remember that the Enlightenment climate that produced the Panopticon also gave us Thomas Jefferson's University of Virginia, an "academical village" *198*
hierarchically organized, with ranges of pavilions to serve professors as house and classroom, and appropriate student housing linked directly to them. "Every professor would be the police officer of the students adjacent to his lodge," Jefferson wrote. This plan, with its broad mall and the domed library rotunda at the head of the axis, was rediscovered at the turn of this century, and was for a time very popular with American campuses.[39] But the Enlightenment spirit that could combine an ideal ensemble with the mechanics of surveillance had long been pushed aside by more pragmatic drives. Jefferson's scheme was attractive for the clarity of its *parti*, not for its social logic.

Campus planning is, in fact, one area where America contributes to the discourse of "the city as diagram." Since the campus was looked upon as an ideal community, unencumbered by, and preferably at some distance from, the real world, its planning gave opportunity, in America and elsewhere, for a variety of ideal schemes. The most graphic are, once again, those that rely on radial-concentric solutions. An English example abroad is the new campus town in Benares, India, called Malviyanagar and built in the years following the Great War. In the center of the half-circle, as in Ledoux's Chaux, is the governing power, in this case the administration offices; the colleges form a first ring, and after a green zone of playing fields comes the outer ring of housing for staff and students. The 13 radials, artfully locked into 6 semicircular arc roads, observe geometric purity rather than a deliberate symbolism of program.[40]

REFORMING URBAN SOCIETY

The inexorable congestion and disorder of the industrial metropolis during the 19th century, and the attendant physical and moral ills, spurred on new experiments in reformist urban design. Spurred on utopian thoughts about the rehabilitation of urban society, I should rather say, with matters of form given only a cursory, diagrammatic turn.

Three names stand out in the crowd: Charles Fourier (1772–1837), Robert Owen (1771–1858), and at the end of the century the champion of garden cities, Ebenezer Howard, whom we have already met. We need not dwell on the particulars of their doctrines; they are familiar enough, and not strictly material to a discussion of the city as diagram. These men, and other less influential reformers, had in common a passion to supplant the deteriorating old cities of the world with a system of fresh implants, small, sanitary and equitable, where the social classes would live in harmony and the bond with Nature would be reaffirmed. They decried the evil of private property, and advocated that the land of the new cities of the future be collectively owned. In varying degrees, they also espoused communal living, equipping their settlements with refectories, common kitchens, and dormitories. But they were no architects or professional city-planners. Beyond a simple picture of the general urban configuration, which some of them insisted was not binding or invariable, they were not always forthcoming about the precise shape of the daily environment or the nature of urban services. The models remained those of the past, especially the celebrated works of Baroque urban design. The modern twist was a fascination with the metal and glass architecture of railway sheds and exposition halls, which seemed perfect for the covered, climate-controlled streets and passages of the new towns and the great concourses of their class-abjuring population.

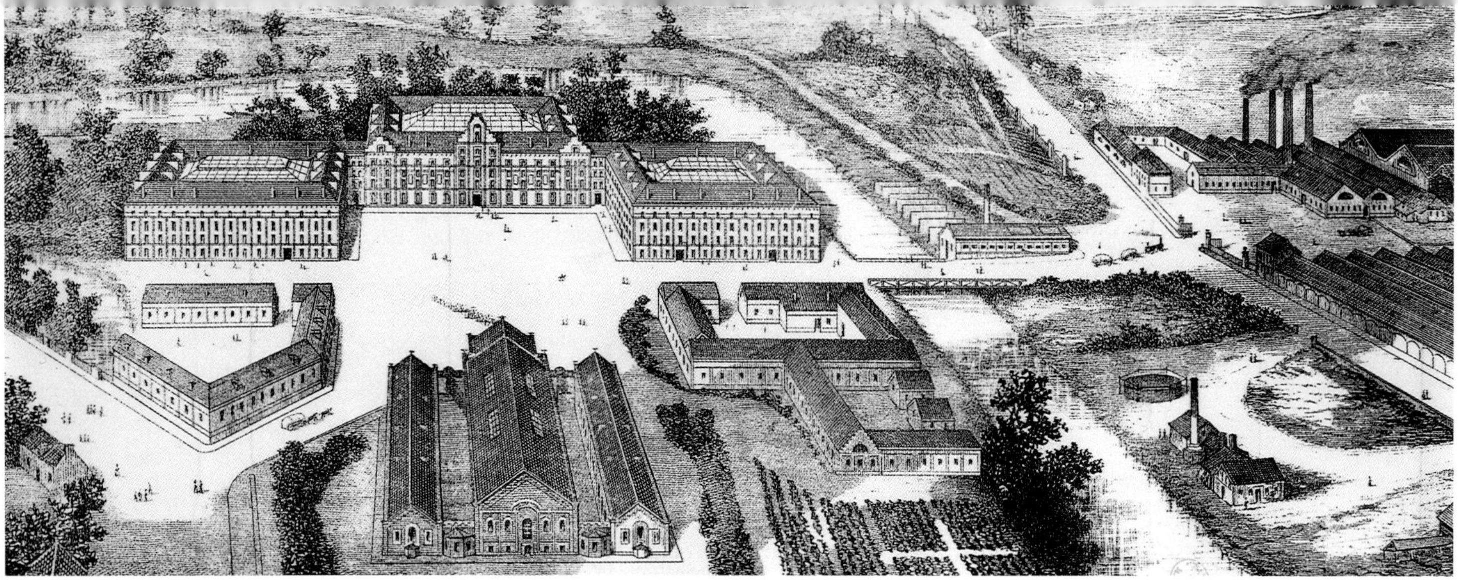

238 Fourier's model was the palace of Versailles, wrested from the *ancien régime* and made over to the People. He had also proposed a scheme for what he called the City of Garantism, which prefigured Howard by about sixty years. It was composed of three concentric bands: the commercial city at the centre, then the industrial city, and then an agricultural zone. The three bands were separated by hedges. Open space would double in the middle band and triple in the outer. But we know Fourier best from his "phalansteries," a massive collection of connected buildings like the palace of Versailles and its salient wings. Fourier described the complex as "really a miniature town but without open streets; all parts of the building can be reached by a wide street-gallery on the first floor." Each phalanstery would be for about 2,000 people of all races, classes, sexes and ages. A small version was actually built, at
199 Guise northeast of Paris, beginning in 1859. It was the brainchild of a young industrialist, Jean-Baptiste Godin, who ran an iron foundry. Before his death he turned the whole enterprise into a co-operative owned and managed by his workers.

Fourierism spread to Belgium by the mid-1840s—and then far beyond. Phalansteries were tried out on an island off the coast of Brazil, and on the hills outside Oran in Algeria. In the United States, Fourier was interpreted by Albert Brisbane, and became the prophet of Associationism. The followers believed in universal social reform without class struggle or government intervention. They also believed that a community of a certain size and organization would engender the right group harmony. Some forty-five Fourierist communities were started, of which the most famous were the West Roxbury Community in Massachusetts outside Boston, known as the Brook Farm Phalanx (1841), and the North American Phalanx in New Jersey. The last was La Réunion in Dallas County, Texas, on a high bluff overlooking the alluvial plain. There Victor Considérant, Fourier's most active disciple, was in charge, and he tried to stretch the Versailles parallel into a Baroque town plan, with a formal garden along the slope featuring parterres and cinquefoils, while Madame Considérant held court under the branches of her "cedar salon."[41]

None of these phalansteries made it. The often remote sites became endurance tests of frontier living rather than noble experiments of communitarian socialism. Communal living sharply conflicted with the long-entrenched sanctity of the American family. And, too, the absence of authority doomed planning; it was true here as it has been all along that without an empowered governing system there can be no organized development.

Owen went for the square. He had been a worker and then an owner in the spinning-mills of New Lanark, Scotland. When he set about to reorganize society, he

199 Guise (France), bird's-eye view showing the "Familistère"—the three linked buildings on the left within the bend of the river—begun in 1859. Unlike Fourier's phalanstery, this version housed families in separate apartments rather than communally. The factories are on the right; in the foreground are the workshops and the building containing the schools and theater.

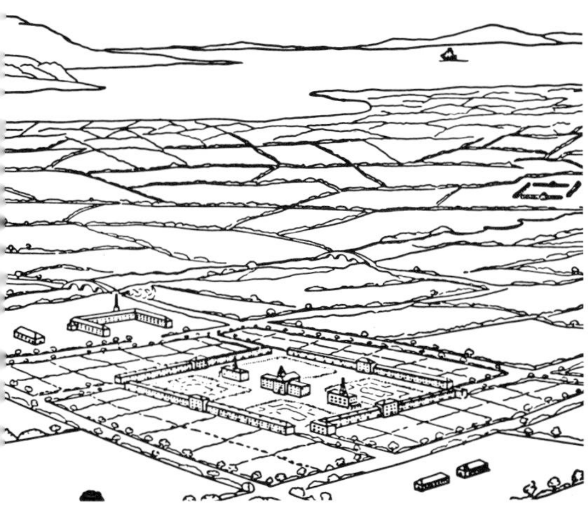

200 Robert Owen, "Project for a Village of Cooperation, with other Villages in the Distance," 1816 (detail).

201 James Silk Buckingham, design for the model town of Victoria, 1849.

thought of a series of small associations owning their land and living collectively to exploit it. The Owenite diagram had residential buildings on all four sides of his square—on three sides for married couples and children under three, and on the fourth side a dormitory for children over three. In the center of the square were the collective buildings: refectory, kitchens, schools. Beyond the square there were workshops and farms, and an occasional industrial establishment. Owen presented his ideas to Napoleon on Elba, and to Tsar Alexander I. His architect, Stedman Whitwell, presented a model of the Owenite city to President John Quincy Adams, and it was exhibited in the White House in 1825. Owen himself lectured to American audiences which included presidents and members of the Supreme Court and Congress. Owenite communities were set up at New Harmony, Indiana, where Owen and his family lived for some time; Yellow Springs, Ohio; and Valley Forge, Pennsylvania. 200

Owen's influence passed on to the English politician and traveler James Silk Buckingham, author of *National Evils and Practical Remedies* (1849). His model town was Victoria, named after the Queen, to be built in open country. It was meant to solve the problem of unemployment, and it was designed for 10,000 people. It had a quadrangular plan, with buildings composed in concentric rows, seven of them, tall in the center where the public buildings were and increasingly smaller toward the outskirts. This was, exceptionally and provocatively, not a socialist utopia, but a capitalist one. Members of government and wealthy citizens would have their houses in the center, while the poorest classes occupied the periphery. The reasoning was that it was for these poor folk that easy access to the country was most desirable. Covered galleries were added to the houses, to form inner streets. Hygiene was a prime concern—fresh air, light, washable clothes, and floors polished with beeswax which was said to generate "health-giving ozone." 201

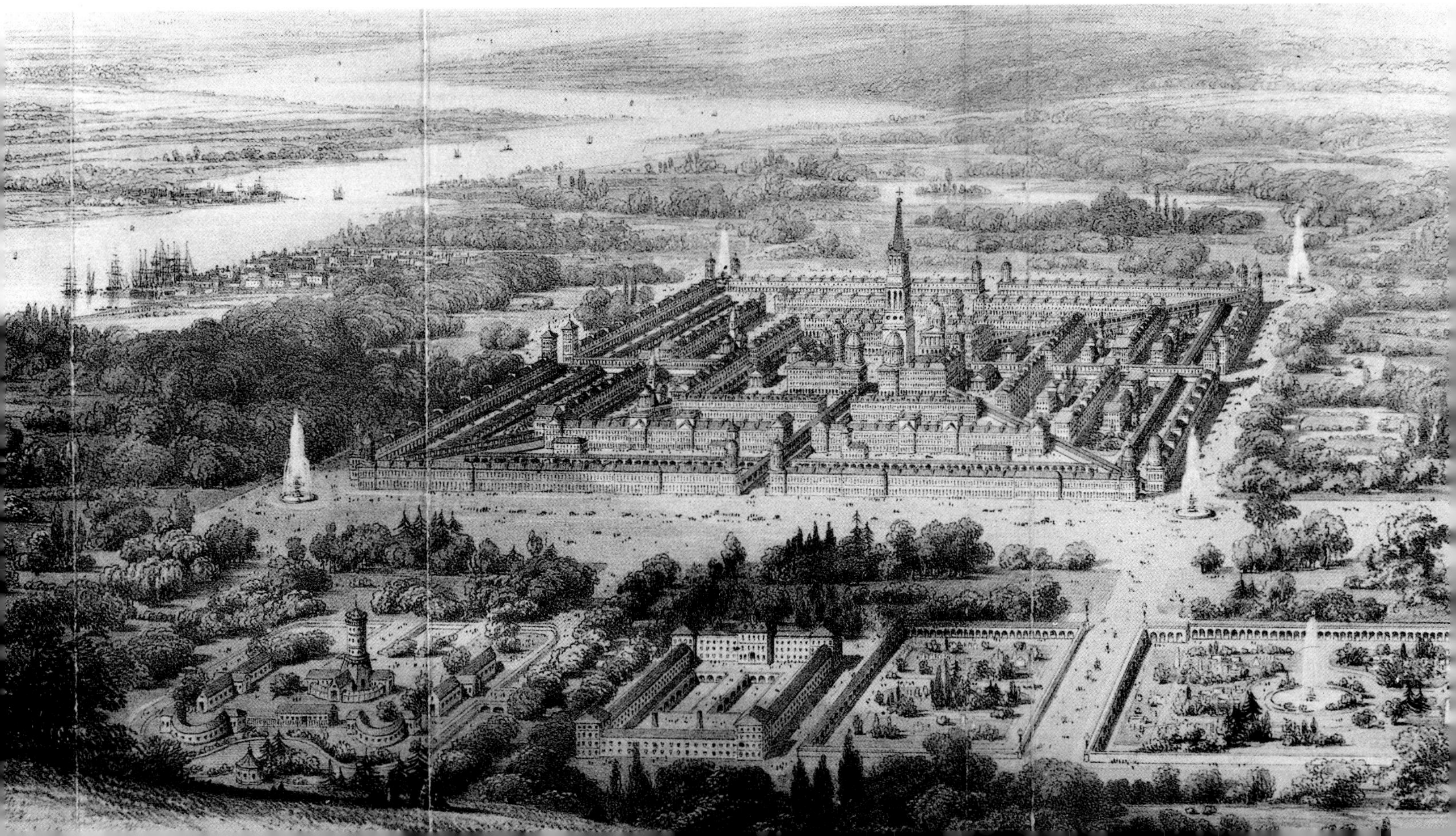

In the end the radial-concentric organization remained the most appealing. If
204 Howard was to renew its currency with the famous diagram for his Garden City, he had plenty of company. He doubtless knew of the Chaux-inspired Queen Victoria Town as described by Robert Pemberton, a pupil of Bentham, in his book *The Happy Colony*, meant for the colonization of New Zealand. Inspired by Pemberton's belief that "All the grand forms of nature are round," this envisioned ten concentric towns, each arranged around a community core that had a model farm surrounded by four curved iron-and-glass college buildings. The year was 1854, the memory of the Crystal Palace was fresh, and its light, skeletal architecture of prefabricated parts seemed the proper new look for a new urban future. The land was to be collectively owned. The size of the towns was modest—one mile (1.6 km.) in diameter, judging by the drawings for Queen Victoria Town.

This ideal vision for land settlement continued to inspire planners. Something about the round form, it would seem, unwalled and ringed by green, suggested a unified pioneering community, the will to endure, a defense against unchecked sprawl and the encroachment of cities. The first *kibbutzim* built on the newly
156 possessed land of Israel in the 1920s were concentric. Nahalal, designed by Richard Kauffmann, was actually a *moshav*, a cooperative agricultural settlement with private land ownership rather than a fully communal *kibbutz*. The town core with community facilities was separated from the residential belt and the radially expanding fields by a broad ring boulevard. Again, in the Sixties, a concentric model
202 town was built in the Brazilian interior near a hydroelectric plant, 500 miles (800 km.) northwest of São Paulo. Like Pemberton's Happy Colony, it had a model farm in the center, around which 12,000 worker families were to be housed in pie-shaped sections of curvilinear housing.[42]

Howard's place at the turn of the century remains unique. His thought was not original. He himself generously gave credit to his predecessors, calling the Garden City a "unique combination of proposals" already before the public. But his artless and passionate advocacy of an ideally balanced human environment where town

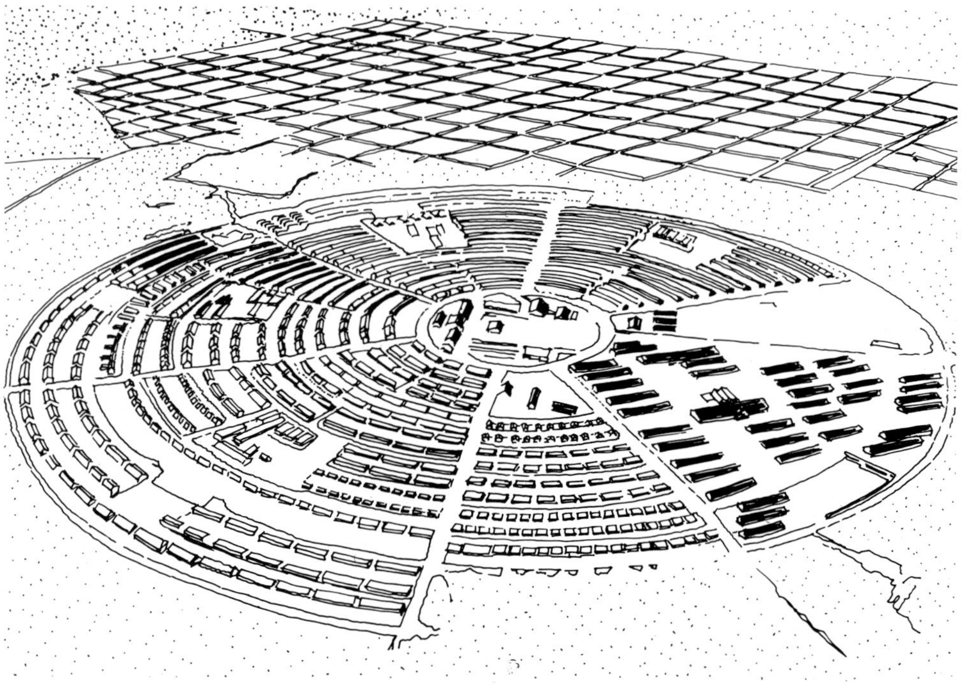

202 Vila Piloto—pilot town—of Jupaià (Brazil). This settlement for workers constructing the Urubupungà hydroelectric complex was designed to be transformed into a model agricultural community after the power station's completion. The cost of the town's upkeep, however, prompted officials of the state of Mato Grosso to refuse the construction company's gift. Half of the circle was eventually taken over by the Brazilian army, who promptly relinquished the other half to their bulldozers.

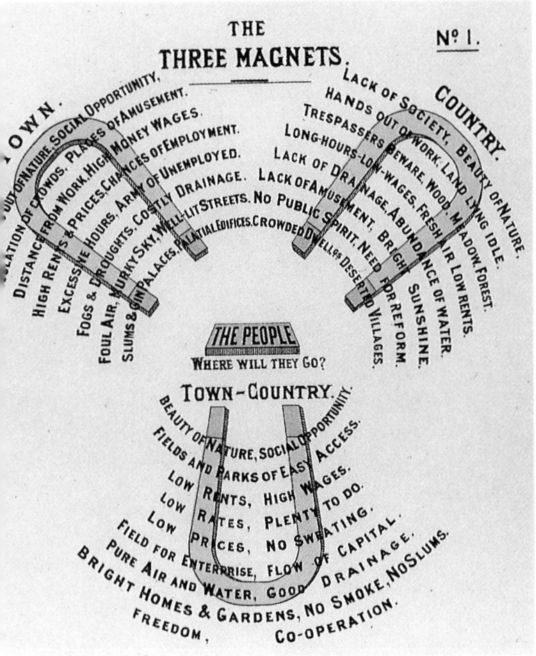

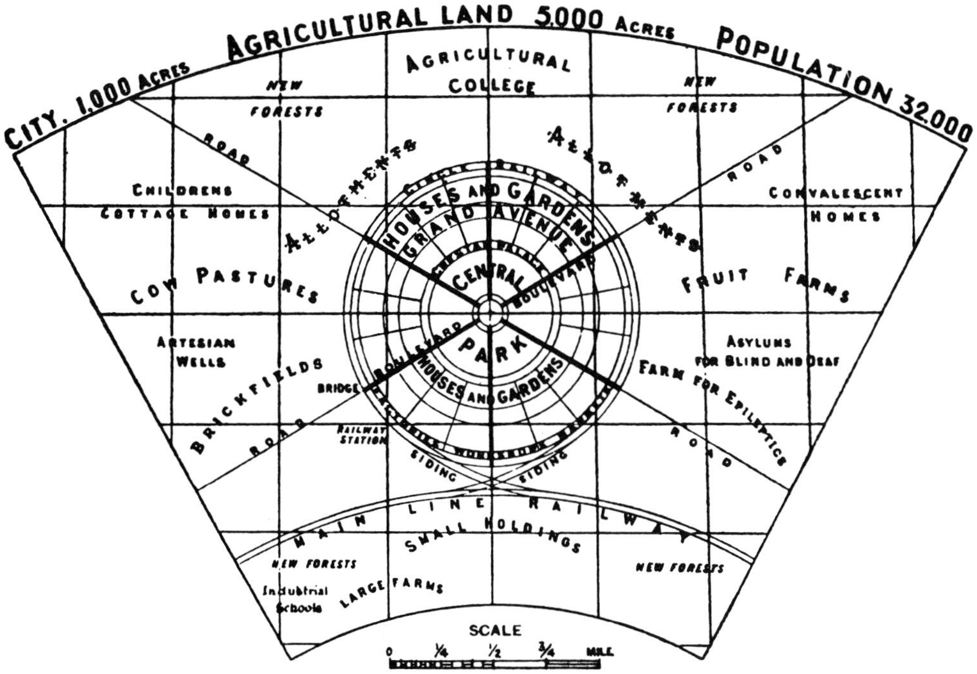

203, 204 Ebenezer Howard, diagrams of the Three Magnets and the Garden City, from To-Morrow: A Peaceful Path to Social Reform *(1898).*

and country met, which has already been introduced (pp. 75–76), had enormous appeal. It would be the closest we came to paradise on earth: "Beauty of nature. Social opportunity. Fields and parks of easy access. Low rents, high wages. Low rates, plenty to do. Low prices. No sweating. . . . Pure air and water. . . . Bright homes and gardens, no smoke, no slums. Freedom, cooperation." This was the magnet of
Town-Country, made to face the magnets of Town and Country both fraught with *203*
inconveniences and dangers. Howard provided particulars, trying to respond to people's queries and anticipate their objections. He detailed aspects of Garden City culture, from administration and expenditures to temperance reform. And then
there were those irresistible diagrams: the Three Magnets, the satellite circles *193*
bonded to Central City, and the layout of the Garden City itself, lucid, clearly *204*
labelled, and in its form reflective of a long line of sunburst cities, actual and imagined, from Gur to Karlsruhe. The labels were the familiar terminology of the Grand Manner. "Six magnificent boulevards" would separate Central City into wards, and would converge in a five-acre garden to serve the "civic spirit," surrounded by public buildings—town hall, museum, theater, hospital, library, concert hall. Past a generous central park came the "Crystal Palace," a covered shopping mall of obvious inspiration, and then Grand Avenue, a 420-foot (128 m.) wide parkway which would serve as an internal greenbelt. The round city would be encircled by a "main line railway," Howard's own acknowledgment of modernity, beyond the ring of allotments with its dairy farms on which would front factories, warehouses, and coal, timber and stone yards. Housing would stretch from Fifth Avenue, the circumferential street next to Crystal Palace, until First Avenue next to the industrial zone.

To give Howard his due, he insisted emphatically, as he had for his diagram of satellite cities, that this was merely a blueprint of an idea, not an actual city-form. "Diagram only," he wrote on his Garden City drawing in the second edition of the book (1902). "Plan cannot be drawn until site selected." But this did not prevent the diagram's being replicated in the most unlikely places. At Llano del Rio in southern

California, for example, a communitarian experiment was launched in 1914. The designer for the settlement was a self-trained architect, Alice Constance Austin. There had been the beginnings of a previous town on the site, called Almondale, with a radial scheme of its own: a small central grid, two ring roads beyond it, and radials extending out of both rings to the limits of the settlement's territory. But Austin paid Almondale no attention. She practically duplicated Howard's diagram for this remote site at the edge of the Mohave Desert. The automotive age had dawned and she allowed every family their car. Howard's railway now became a drag strip for cars, with stands for spectators on either side. All business traffic was put underground.[43]

Howard's was the last of the great 19th-century social diagrams, though certainly not the last socialist utopia. But the centrally planned ideal cities lost their elemental power of suggestion as the radial-concentric scheme slipped into the hands of traffic engineers, and led a vicarious life showcasing French casinos in Cabourg (ca. 1860) and Stella-Plage (early 1900s). Reduced to a fan-shaped plan, it appeared in the Russian additions to the old native cities of Central Asia (Tashkent, Samarkand, etc.) during the 19th century; but the center, the converging point of all the radial streets, was empty. The only noble impulse left to the modern world that made demands for ideal solutions was the sentiment of internationalism that came in waves on either side of the Great War.

International expositions were the main pre–1914 setting for displays of a world acting in harmony, and a number of exposition plans attempted to design this unison. The earliest to do so was the Paris Exposition of 1867, with its "véritable cité" in the Champ de Mars conceived by the architect Frédéric Le Play. A series of concentric covered galleries were intersected by radial lines which allowed for a double system of organization. Each concentric ring exhibited the same range of products from all participating nations; each radial segment embraced all the products of a single nation. Vienna in 1873 stretched a long gallery along the Danube with identical rectangular pavilions stacked at right angles to this axis and an immense rotunda in the middle—a Victorian version of Enlightenment "machines." But this sort of idealized unity would be abandoned as time went on, in favor of huge exhibition halls and a competitive assortment of national pavilions, each trumpeting its own independent message.

During the war years, hopes of an ecumenism of peace were encased in ideal projects for a world capital. The most grandiose was the collaborative effort of a wealthy American, Henrik Christian Andersen, and the accomplished Beaux-Arts
205 architect/planner Ernest Hébrard.[44] Their "world center of communication" would bring together the most gifted people of the world—religious leaders, scientists, artists—for the benefit of all humanity and the promotion of peace. In the middle of the composition was the Tower of Progress. It was ringed by the buildings devoted to medicine, agriculture and industry. Subordinate cores were dedicated to Olympic sports, the arts, and communications. The plan combined a grand linear axis and a series of spoke avenues emanating from the Tower to organize the other monumental institutions, among them a Temple of Religions and a Palace of Justice. The architectural style for the city would be the culmination of the entire history of architecture. There were of course no buyers. A postwar campaign to turn this improbably magnificent paper fantasy into the home of the League of Nations got nowhere. The workaday ecumenism lodged in Geneva and New York made do with much more modest, and diluted, settings.

205 *Frontispiece to* Creation of a World Center of Communication *(1913), by H. C. Andersen and Ernest Hébrard.*

THE PLANET AND OUTER SPACE

When the ideal city made its comeback in the Sixties and Seventies, its stage was no longer the political geography of nations. Hopes were directed toward the planet earth which is our common home, and the extraterrestrial settings opening up to our exploration. The flood of megastructural urban invention that swept in may seem in retrospect to have been nothing more serious than an upbeat exhibitionism of new technologies and the naive belief in their universal relevance. But there was a genuine mood to reverse our wasteful ways and forge a new compact with the natural environment and all its creature inhabitants. Projects came from all directions but shared the same vision of redesigning the planet. It mattered little if they originated with the Japanese "Metabolists," the French circle of Yona Friedman and Paul
158 Maymont, or Paolo Soleri, the Italian desert seer in Arizona. Metapolis and arcology, giant space frames, floating capsules and spool-shaped conocylinders—all ranged within the same imaginative field. The site might be specified—a city under the Seine, a floating settlement on a lake near the Tokyo Airport at Narita, an "arctic city" in Antarctica or Lapland—but the prevailing imagery was of a generic, even primal, sort. The new urban machines were to be set afloat on the seas, fitted into canyons and quarries, lifted on stilts above cultivated farmlands. And the shapes themselves were often primal—the Helix City of Kisho Kurokawa, the cubes and hexahedrons of Soleri arcologies.

That phase of radically remaking human settlement had a short span. Soleri alone persisted. He is still warning us against spread, and preaching the gospel of miniaturization which he props up on the thought of Teilhard de Chardin. It is the gospel of the progressive complexity of matter within progressively smaller frames. So his Arcoindian and Babeldiga, Arcosanti itself now in active gestation, prepare us for an urban life of tremendous density, thirty times and more that of Manhattan. Compression vitalizes urban existence: "clustering etherealizes."

But the newest frontier since the Moonwalk has been outer space. There too, on the moon and asteroids and the benign surface of Mars, our perfect shapes will usher in perfect societies, as they were intended to do at Chaux, at Fourierist phalansteries, at Happy Colony, New Harmony, and the New Towns of England. There especially, in outer space, too far away from our earthbound culture, from those encrusted restraints of land and time and season, to feel the clasp of place or the inescapable bonding of history. There where

> Temperature, humidity, seasons, length of day, weather, artificial gravity and atmospheric pressure can be set at will, and new types of cultures, social organization, and social philosophies become possible. . . . We will be in a position to invent new cultural patterns and new social philosophies, and then choose material conditions and community design to fit the desired cultural goals and philosophies.[45]

Perhaps. But the space colonies we have been able to conjure in the first flush are "earth-like landscapes [of] farms, hills, trees, grass and animals." The shapes we can
Pl.8 dream up are the old geometries of cylinders, spheres and the circular torus. The brilliant technology trips upon tradition: we travel millions of galactic miles out into space only to reach home.

So here, in obsolete fashions and strange built fragments on earth, and in the technological fantasies of colonies in space, the story of the ideal city is suspended. The cosmic diagram flickers at Sri Aurobindo in India, the recent ashram of a
206 deceased master. Its extension, the city of Auroville, swirls like a nebula; the core,

206 Model of the ashram-city of Auroville (South India).

with its Banyan and Urn and Matrimandir, is a cross between a radial city and a hallucination. Arcosanti lurches unsteadily, a monument-ruin to the ecology-minded Sixties and the monomania of a visionary architect. The future space colonies, the "Bernal sphere" and the "Stanford torus," incubate in NASA laboratories.

In the end, all ideal city-forms are a little dehumanizing. Life cannot be regimented, it seems, in the ways they would like, except in totally artificial units like monasteries and cantonments and concentration camps where inhabitants submit willingly or are constrained without choice. Left to its own devices, human nature is resistant to regimentation, while it may crave for order. What price liberty?

It is of course a question all non-centralized political systems must address daily, and fight for daily, in the making of their cities. Such systems function between extremes of total control and total laissez faire. We know it is not possible to have cities without any controls at all, even if we use them to keep the wrong businesses out of our neighborhoods or to prevent epidemics. Our daily urban diagrams are created, in fact, by zoning, economic pressures and the like. The question is whether "we" the citizens decide the nature and finality of the diagram, or whether we let "authorities" decide them for us.

Now it is easy for us to take charge if "we" are all the same class of people. As soon as we confront pluralism, our problems begin. Two options then present themselves. One of them is for a segment of this pluralist society to make itself the dominant controlling party. The other option is for a cohesive and empowered segment of society to make itself independent of the rest through incorporation. This has been a strong trend in the United States since the suburban movement became institutionalized a hundred years ago or so.

But the more homogeneous the urban population, the less we are entitled to talk about a city. The more segregated urban functions and urban groups, the less we are actually creating an urban community. The city as diagram, in the end, is the story of dreamers who want the complexity and richness of the urban structure without the problems, tensions and volatility. In dreams we expect this sort of gratification without dues or consequences. In real life, we know better.

4 · THE GRAND MANNER

PRELIMINARIES

It was some time in March 1791 that President Washington assigned Major Pierre L'Enfant the task of drawing up a plan for the new Federal capital. A short while earlier, L'Enfant and Andrew Ellicott, the first Surveyor General of the United States, had surveyed the area under consideration along the Potomac, which included the three small gridded towns of Carrollsburg, Hamburg and Georgetown. Thomas Jefferson favored a compact settlement for the capital, and in advising the President he sketched a modest grid at the confluence of the Potomac and the Anacostia where Carrollsburg was situated; and then he drew a second grid closer to Georgetown. 209

L'Enfant scoffed both at the scope and at the form of these proposals. On the first issue, he wrote the President that "the plan should be drawn on such a scale as to leave room for that aggrandisement & embellishment which the increase of the wealth of the Nation will permit it to pursue at any period however remote." As to the design, a grid might be suitable for flat ground "where no surrounding object being interesting it becomes indifferent which way the opening of streets may be directed." Yet "even when applyed upon the ground the best calculated to admit of it [the grid] become[s] at last tiresome and insipid." But the topography of the new capital was eventful—and the destiny of the new nation full of promise. What was called for was a design "laid out on a dimension," as L'Enfant put it about one of its avenues, "proportioned to the greatness which . . . the Capital of a powerful Empire ought to manifest."[1] Following the process whereby L'Enfant plotted and refined his great plan, and this is possible to do up to a point through extant documents and 208 drawings, gives us a clinical demonstration of the methods of a Baroque planner.

L'Enfant surveys the site not merely to verify the appropriateness of the location for settlement—looking, say, for the source of water, for the best paths of communication, for the direction of the winds perhaps—but in the interest of reading the topography for its design potential. He is rivetted by the commanding position of Jenkin's Hill, "which stands as a pedestal waiting for a superstructure," as Ellicott, L'Enfant's unwelcome collaborator and successor, said of it. It would be the pedestal for the United States Capitol. L'Enfant thinks of all such natural features in relation to public buildings and their hierarchy—the Capitol, the

207 Washington (D.C.), looking west from above Lincoln Park toward the Capitol, the Mall, and the Washington Monument and Lincoln Memorial.

President's House, the Supreme Court, and a number of lesser ones which he sees scattered across the site. And then he sees these buildings connected to each other grandly. In between is urban fill; a grid there would do fine.

The public spaces are themselves programmatic, not merely serviceable areas of concourse—market or administrative or recreational centers. Fifteen squares would represent the fifteen states of the Union, each with a suitable statue or another sort of monument in the middle making its programmatic identity clear. There are to be magnificent public walks, an equestrian statue of George Washington at the crossing of the axes of the Capitol and the President's House, and places of institutionalized culture like academies. The waters of the Tiber Creek are to be passed under the Capitol, and made to fall in a great cascade.

Here is how L'Enfant described his procedure when he first started work on the plan:

> Having determined some principal points to which I wished to make the other subordinate, I made the distribution regular with every street at right angles, North and South, east and west, and afterwards opened some in different directions, as avenues to and from every principal place, wishing thereby not merely to contrast with the general regularity, nor to afford a greater variety of sites with pleasant prospects, which will be obtained from the advantageous

208 Plan for Washington by Pierre Charles L'Enfant, 1791. The site of Lincoln Park (see Ill. 207) is marked by the letter "B."

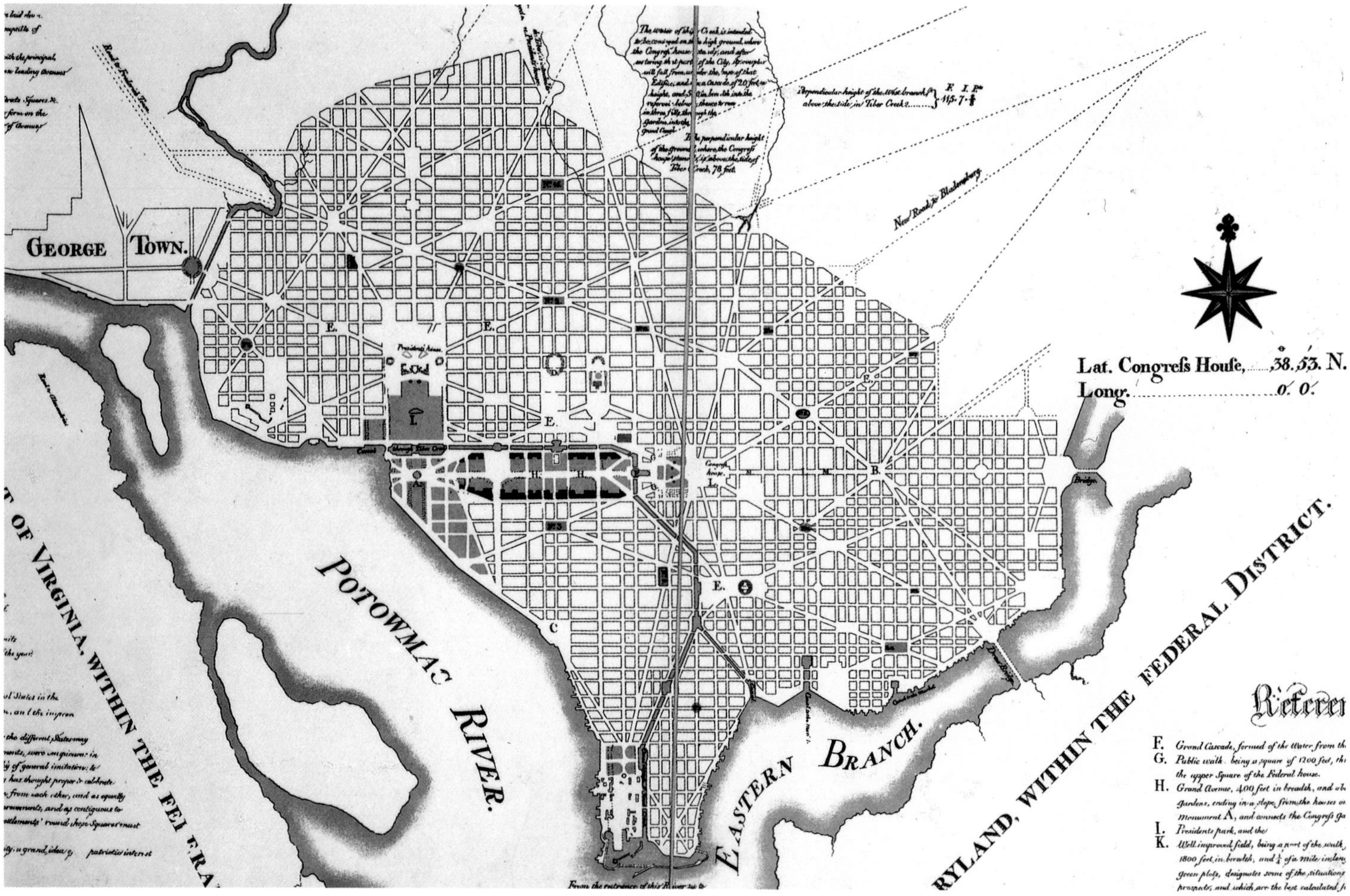

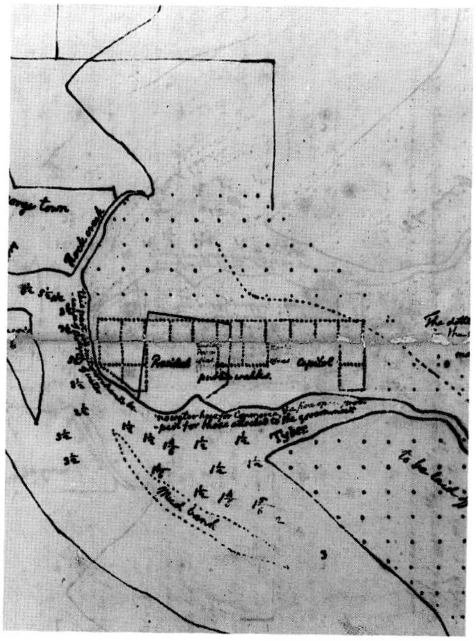

209 Thomas Jefferson's plan for Washington, 1791. The widely spaced dots represent streets in a future extension of the original compact settlement. Within the grid, three blocks are allotted for the President's house and gardens, and three for the Capitol. The two would be connected by "public walks."

ground over which these avenues are chiefly directed, but principally to connect each part of the city, if I may so express it, by making the real distance less from place to place, by giving to them [the principal points?] reciprocity of sight, and by making them thus seemingly connected, promote a rapid settlement over the whole extent, rendering those even of the most remote parts an addition to the principal, which without the help of these, were any such settlement attempted, it would be languid, and lost in the extent, and become detrimental to the establishment.

Let me enumerate some of the characteristics of the Baroque esthetic in urban design as these are revealed in L'Enfant's work:

1. a total, grand, spacious urban ensemble pinned on focal points distributed throughout the city
2. these focal points suitably plotted in relation to the drama of the topography, and linked with each other by swift, sweeping lines of communication
3. a concern with the landscaping of the major streets—"these avenues I made broad," L'Enfant writes, "so as to admit of their being planted with trees"
4. the creation of vistas
5. public spaces as settings for monuments
6. dramatic effects, as with waterfalls and the like
7. all of this superimposed on a closer-grained fabric for daily, local life

The advantages of this school of planning, as L'Enfant sees them, are expeditious and even settlement of the new city, smooth traffic flow, and visual interest.

HISTORICAL REVIEW

Behind L'Enfant's Washington plan stand over two hundred years of urbanism whose main invention is in fact the capital city, dwarfing all others around it, pushing its avenues out to the country so that entire regions are seen to converge upon it. Now L'Enfant knew one such Baroque capital, a total creation like his—
Versailles. Here he had spent his childhood when his painter father was *238*
commissioned to participate in the decoration of the Ministry of War. L'Enfant also knew the great tome Pierre Patte had published in 1765, in which he had imposed on
a contemporary map of Paris the competition submissions for a monument to Louis *210*
XV held in 1748. The choice of site had been left to the participants, and several had used the opportunity to propose urban solutions for large areas around their proposed monument. In one respect, then, the Patte plan was an exercise in submitting all of Paris to a multi-centered Baroque plan. L'Enfant was also familiar with the new capital of St. Petersburg on the Neva, which had started being planned
in 1703, and with Karlsruhe, a German Versailles with a sunburst of 32 radials *186*
around the palace of the Margrave of Baden-Durlach. The latter was included among a number of city maps which Jefferson procured for L'Enfant as the Frenchman had requested.

This European tradition of "magnificent distances," in Dickens's phrase about Washington, is, however, only one chapter in the history of what I have entitled the Grand Manner. The beginnings of this chapter reach back into the 15th century; its long afterglow stretches toward the present. But there is an earlier era when such

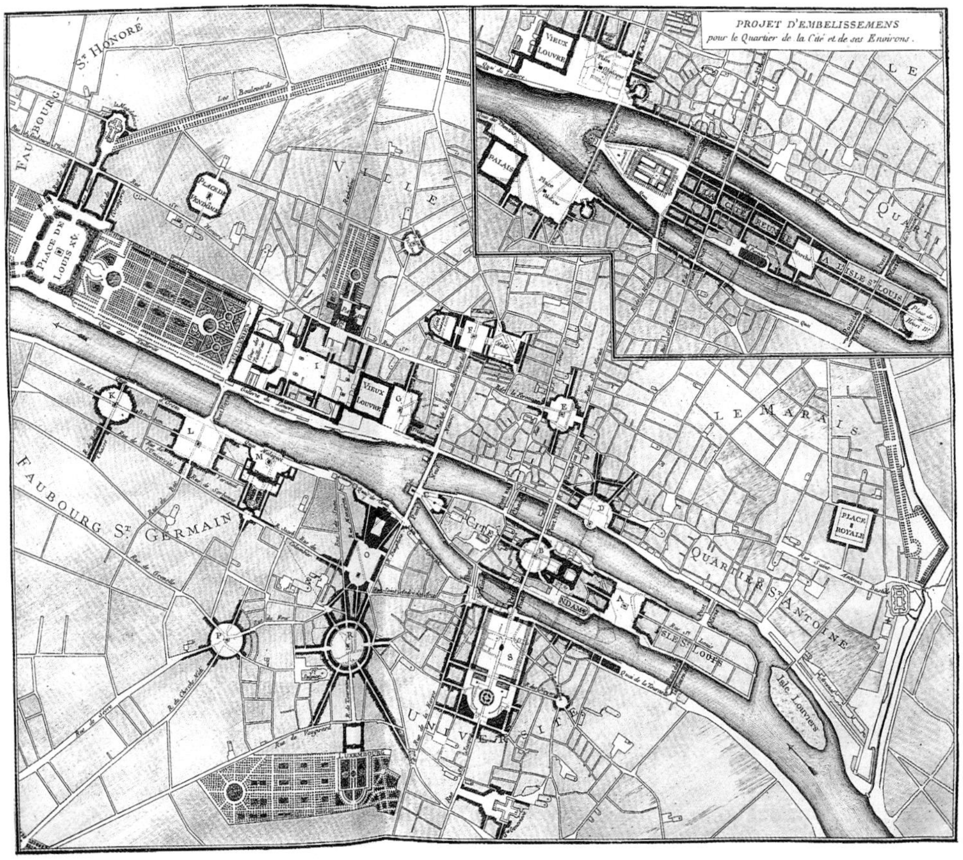

210 Plan of Paris on which are superimposed competition projects for the Place Louis XV, from Pierre Patte, Monuments érigés en France à la gloire de Louis XV *(1765).*

consummate theatricality, the conventions of a hierarchic and ceremonial urbanism, had made its appearance. Straight streets with continuously conceived elevations, vistas, urban platforms and stairs, and the negotiation of slopes with terrace architecture—all this has a story in the Hellenistic/Roman period. And we can go even earlier to Egypt, to the sphinx-lined avenues and axial processional arrangements of Luxor and Karnak, or the splendid terrace architecture of Deir el-Bahri.

ANTIQUITY

In pre-Classical antiquity, we cannot point to entire urban systems that could be called Baroque, in the manner of Washington, D.C. At issue, rather, is the introduction of some isolated elements of such systems into an urban form that is itself very different in spirit and intention; or else the accumulation of these "Baroque" fragments in one area, with no resolved coherence in terms of urban design, in other words, with no fixed master plan, as in a Greek acropolis, a ziggurat complex, or a Mayan site.

In the Hellenistic period, there is an important development. The planning of
211 Attalid Pergamon in the 3rd and 2nd centuries BC seems to attest to a distinctive
school of urban design which employs a sophisticated array of "Baroque" devices in a coordinated system. The city form of Pergamon, laid out on a narrow mountain ridge in western Asia Minor, is an integrated series of visual and kinetic experiences.

The main compositional feature is a set of terraces forming a fan of platforms on which public buildings are grouped. This terracing fortifies and makes monumental the design inherent in the natural contours. The great fan of five platforms that constitutes the upper town is riveted by the theater, which avails itself of the natural slope. The platforms are edged, along the ridge drop, with multistoried stoa units. A paved esplanade starting at the main city gate in the lower town connects the platforms, zigzagging up the hill in sharp bends.

It is sometimes maintained that this Pergamene manner of urban design had its initiation at another Asia Minor site, the Halikarnassos of King Mausolos, the native dynast of Caria, where the vertical, three-dimensional alliance of major building groups on a hilly site was given an early demonstration. This was in the mid-4th century BC or a little earlier. The city was arranged like an open-air theater around its bay (as Vitruvius put it), capped by a giant statue of Ares. The famous Mausoleion, the centerpiece of the composition, stood on a broad curving avenue half way down the slope. The agora was at the foot of the hill, by the harbor, and crowning the two extreme points of the bay, on high promontories, were a temple to Aphrodite and Hermes, and (where the crusader castle now stands) the palace of Mausolos.

But it is likely that the arrangements at Pergamon had a more dispersed, and cumulative, background.

We must, first of all, be mindful of the Eastern connection. The Ionian territory was quite susceptible to the cultural landscape of non-Greek states in Asia Minor and the Near East. Terraced monumental groups with buildings arranged at odd relationships to one another had a well-established place in this landscape, and though it is hard to find anything resembling the subtle interlocking in three dimensions we see at Pergamon, we should not dismiss the general impact of sites like the late Hittite citadel at Zincirli (Sam'al) in south Turkey (9th–8th century BC), with its Upper and Lower "Palaces," where fortuitous relationships are created by newer palaces with respect to the original government center.

The 4th-century BC Greek precedent itself has also to be considered—not the exceptional dramatic scenography of a site like Halikarnassos, but the component units of public architecture that shaped later Greek townscape. Several trends are discernible. The invention of new, complex building types of unconventional form, propped by an advanced building technology that could allow for adventurous

211 Pergamon (Turkey), Hellenistic capital of the Attalid dynasty; model of the upper town.

massing, is one of these trends. Another, stressed by Mario Coppa in his detailed account of Hellenistic urbanism, is the breaking down of closed architectural schemes, and the increasing acceptance of loosely interlocking parts. In this, and in the freshly rethought integration of monumental units with the quarters of housing, we have nothing less than a spatial transformation of the Classical Greek city.[2]

Whatever the impetus, Pergamon is still without peer as an articulate overall system of urban design—and this is the more remarkable in that the city form did not result from a master plan worked out at the beginning, but rather from the responsive efforts of several generations of planners and architects. Its lessons were widely disseminated. Aigai, as enlarged in the early second century BC, is clearly reminiscent of Pergamon, but there are a score of other towns of western Asia Minor that echo its effects. And the ways in which this Pergamene school interacted with, and reformed, Roman planning practices have yet to be sorted out.

For the Roman city, a recent book by William MacDonald provides us with an excellent visual analysis of urban design under the Empire.[3] The grid was old-fashioned by the first century AD. In its place, the Romans substituted an easy, flexible orthogonality. The city form was anchored to an armature of thoroughfares and open spaces that created an uninterrupted passage throughout the town. This scheme was never laid out at one time, but was shaped gradually, empirically, without theoretical rigidity. It was a matter of elaboration and extension. Obviously city planning had come first. The original settlement might have started as a military camp or a planted town, with a neat gridded cross-axial plan. The armature developed later.

The elements of this supple urbanism were mostly there, before the primacy of Rome. So of course was the Classical language, which is the medium used by Roman architects and planners to pull together their improvised urban effects. But the fluidity of Roman urban design is new. And it was honed into a reliable system, fitted to the particular circumstances of the site. A main road from another town met a major gateway in the circuit of walls. Once inside the walls, this road transformed itself into an urban avenue, moving through densely built up ground to the forum.
256 The avenue was paved and had sidewalks and covered porticoes.

Other standard features of the city form were public open spaces, placed usually athwart or beside a thoroughfare; stairs, commonly used in conjunction with terraces; hinge buildings like *exedrae* (curved recesses), *nymphaea* (fancy fountains), and other setpieces in the service of an art of concealment—making a virtue out of a clumsy joint, obscuring a sudden drop at grade, and so forth. Above all there was the panoply of public buildings—theaters, amphitheaters, temples, basilicas, libraries, public latrines, concert halls (*odeia*), and circuses. These were sprinkled all across the urban fabric, so that no neighborhood was without some public monument, and certainly none without commercial activity. The public buildings were tall, highly visible structures, and their arrangement along the urban armature allowed for their gradual revelation. How the Romans used this standard repertory of public buildings to effect what MacDonald calls "architecture colonization" has been noted by most students of the farflung Empire.

The Romans' rich bag of tricks that produced impressive urban scenography out of often imperfect geometries holds relevance for European urbanism of the Baroque epoch strictly so called, Baroque Rome to be precise. In fact, just as the architecture of Borromini is often said to be prefigured by Hadrian's Villa and the tomb façades of Petra, so the Rome of Urban VIII and Innocent X is prefigured in the provincial cities of the Roman Empire.

EUROPEAN BAROQUE

The roots of European Baroque are in the 16th century, and even earlier. In a fundamental sense this climactic phase of the Grand Manner is bound up with broad intellectual, political and technological developments, such as the Counter-Reformation, the rise of authoritarian, one-man rule, advances in astronomy, and the spectacular discoveries of hitherto uncharted corners of the world. The space conception of the European Baroque is consonant with the post-medieval repudiation of the static universe prescribed by theology—the world as a motionless exterior reflection of an inner order. With the Copernican shift from an earth-centered to a sun-centered universe, the world is now seen instead as infinite space, an object moving around the sun. This critical change, new developments in science and especially in mathematics, optics as well as astronomy, the new world of illusion in theater and theatrical spectacle, and the opening up of Asia and the Americas to European exploration are all aspects of the general cultural setting in which European Baroque urbanism was exercised. The dissemination of this cosmopolitan culture through artistic academies to which the rulers often belonged created an international audience for the Baroque esthetic. Artists traveled among the capitals, and books on architecture and cities were studied widely.

The European Baroque is, as I said, a phenomenon of capital cities. It served the tastes and representational needs of absolutism, which, speaking loosely, started with the rise of *signorie* in Italy in the 14th century and the resurgence of the royal houses in France, Spain and England during the next two centuries. The progress to autocratic rule swelled the population of capitals and in time their physical dimensions. There was, for example, the phenomenal transformation of Madrid, from a small village in the 16th century to a population of 170,000 in the next. Paris, Amsterdam, London, Copenhagen all followed in the same pattern. In the German states, residence-cities of local princes set resplendent examples of urban design. *13*
Now the label of absolutism is of course a feeble crutch. The term "Age of Absolutism" is too coarse a characterization that obscures wide differences in politics and society. Still, it was the ceremonial and political pretense of rulers that gave European Baroque its most flamboyant raison d'être.

Like the beginnings of one-man rule, the invention of a Baroque language of urbanism is inseparable from the Renaissance. In the old towns the rediscovery of the straight street, artistically conceived, surfaces as a conscious urban program as early as the 14th century, and even slightly earlier. It is then that in Florence the documents begin to speak specifically of the desirability of having streets that are "amplae, rectae et pulchrae"—wide, straight and beautiful. The street, it seems clear in this attitude, will no longer be thought of as the space left over between buildings, but as a spatial element with its own integrity. Within the Renaissance tradition, the buildings defining this street channel will tend to be viewed as independent entities. What the Baroque adds to this element of urban design is the sense of continuous planes, this by the end of the 16th century, and then, in the next century, of continuous uniform façades. Other Baroque features are also prefigured during the Renaissance. The designed square in the manner of a Roman forum is one example; the *trivium*, or the convergence of three radial streets upon a square, is another. Finally, we can plot imperfect efforts of a proto-Baroque concern to connect churches and other public buildings with straight streets, and so create constellations of monumentality. In Renaissance Florence, for example, a new pedestrian pathway system was put in place step by step, designed to link peripheral churches and squares to the Duomo.

It is in the Rome of the 16th century, culminating in the famous master plan of
Pl.21 Sixtus V (1585–90) and his architect Domenico Fontana, that the most enduring
themes of the Baroque tradition are first articulated. Here the *trivium* is invented in
the 1530s (see below, pp. 236–37); the notion of the vista finds its first coherent state-
257 ment in this same decade in Michelangelo's Strada Pia; the obelisk is resurrected and
starts its career as a striking spatial marker; and of course the overarching urban
principle of geometric order for its own sake becomes established.

THE GRAND MANNER OUTSIDE ITALY

After this impressive Italian lead, however, France appropriates the Baroque
esthetic after 1650, and develops it into a rational system of urban design. It is there
that the Grand Manner will enjoy an uninterrupted career all the way until the
225 Second World War, as the Champs-Elysées sequence alone, from Le Nôtre to
260 Haussmann and to the 1931 competition for the stretch from Porte Maillot to La
311 Défense, should make clear. The just completed Grande Arche at La Défense,
echoing the Arc de Triomphe $2\frac{1}{2}$ miles (4 km.) away on the same axis, brings the
tradition nurtured by Louis XIV and the two Napoleons up to the present, to the era
of the imperial presidency, of De Gaulle and Pompidou and Mitterand.

For it was always, in France at least, an urbanism of the State. In the 17th century
Paris was well on its way to being established as the political and social fulcrum of
Europe. The population of France had reached 20,000,000, making it the largest
European nation. The country's gift for centralized administration touched everything from government to architecture. The Grand Manner became institutionalized not only through royal patronage but also through the official educational
structure of the Académie and its successor, the Ecole des Beaux-Arts. It ranked in
the end as one of the country's prime cultural exports. It spread across Europe, and
240 lodged in the vastness of Russia with the remarkable creation of St. Petersburg. It
216 moved across the Atlantic in the "backwoods Baroque" of Detroit and the magis-
208 terial plan of L'Enfant for Washington, the most coherent demonstration of the
French school of urbanism until that time. And with the spread of colonialism in
the 19th and 20th centuries, the Grand Manner found an international setting as it
176 made over from scratch, or drastically remade, cities as farflung as Delhi and
192 Canberra, Chicago and Rabat.

The elements of the Grand Manner as they were codified in the 17th and 18th
centuries were few, but they could be as versatile as the Classical orders. The tree-
238 lined avenue is the most ubiquitous of them—and indeed the use of trees in uniform
rows to establish spatial boundaries was a prime French contribution to the history
of environmental design. Equally influential was the residential square, defined by
continuous uniform façades and fixed by a central monumental statue. The type had
243 its debut in the Paris of Henri IV with Place Dauphine and Place Royale (des Vosges),
and culminated a century and a half later with the non-residential Place de la
260 Concorde. By then it was everywhere.

But perhaps the most consequential aspect of the French experiments with the
Baroque esthetic was the ability to link the tree-lined axes, the *rond-points* (circus
244 or roundabout), the formal squares of distinct shapes playing host to radials of
variable length and obliqueness—to link all these into geometric constellations
suitable for whole new districts, or even entire cities. The city form of Paris was too
encumbered by its long history to benefit from the wholesale application of the
Grand Manner—at least until the spectacular pairing of Napoleon III and Baron
Haussmann two hundred and fifty years after the design of the first royal *places*.

But where the ground was comparatively clear, at Versailles, for example, or the 238
City of London after the Fire of 1666, or at Washington, the potential for such 212
comprehensive planning schemes was evident from the start. 208

If the Grand Manner is routinely associated with centralized power, we can readily see why. The very expansiveness it calls for, and the abstraction of its patterns, presuppose an unentangled decision-making process and the wherewithal to accomplish what has been laid out. When such clearcut authority cannot be had, the Grand Manner remains on paper. The City Beautiful movement in early 20th-
century America is a case in point. Daniel Burnham's magnificent urban visions had 235
more success in the subject Philippines than in his own homeland. Without the enabling political clout of an Haussmann or a Speer, Burnham could not remake Chicago or San Francisco into a City Beautiful. It is not an accident that Washington
was the only American city to celebrate the Grand Manner unequivocally, when 207
L'Enfant's moribund plan was revived and elaborated by the MacMillan Commission in 1902. This was the only city in the United States that had a centralized administration, however deputized, being under the direct authority of Congress. Elsewhere one could only resort to persuasion, and try to advance whatever fragments of the overall plan one could through the tangles of the democratic process. The most appealing fragments were public parks and associated boulevards and parkways, beautifications for waterfront leisure, civic centers, and civic ornaments like approach bridges and entrances (e.g., the Gateway in Minneapolis). At any rate, it was strictly in the public domain that the City Beautiful could exert some influence. The commissioned city plans had no legal force, and the courts would not support the exercise of eminent domain (compulsory purchase) over private property.

The presumption of absolute power explains the appeal of the Grand Manner for 229,
the totalitarian regimes of the Thirties—for the likes of Mussolini, Hitler and Stalin. 263
There is also no mystery in its popularity on the colonial scene, where it functioned as an appropriate instrument of imperialism. The pattern transported dominion and showcased it—at American Manila and British Lusaka, at Hanoi in French Indochina and Dire Daua in Italian Ethiopia. Set next to traditional Indian towns or the North African medinas of Tangiers and Fez, European new towns in the Grand Manner highlighted the difference between the "civilization" of the colonizers and the "retarded" old order of the indigenous population.

But this representational force alone could not account for the continued success of the Grand Manner through the 19th and 20th centuries. It is clear that the Baroque esthetic was endowed in stages with the blessings of modernity. The openness of the city form and the flow of fast-paced traffic, already important in the thinking of planners like L'Enfant who set out to make "the real distance less from place to place," were also pre-eminent modern concerns. At the same time, wide straight streets, open prospects, and the generous distribution of green reinforced the preachings of the increasingly vocal sanitation movement.

Now of course issues like modern transportation and a healthful urban environment will also be central to the proponents of Garden Cities and later on of Modernist planning. What the Grand Manner had over them in this respect was precisely its association with the great European capitals of the post-medieval centuries. Where the Garden City and Modernism downplayed or rejected a monumental public realm, the Grand Manner celebrated it. Where they singled out the residential component as the crux of the urban experience, the Grand Manner swept it into a comprehensive monumentality affecting the city form as a whole. The Baroque esthetic thrived as long as it did because, above all its other modern

attributes, it had become synonymous with the city as a work of art. It thrived because it could stage easily perceived, strong urban images that were at once modern and resonant with historical authority. This is what appealed to the City Beautiful movement in the United States, as Daniel Burnham, Charles Mulford Robinson, Edward Bennett and their associates sought to civilize the anarchic growth of the American city seized by the demon of commercialism and the unabridged tolerance for the laissez faire. And this, in the end, is what appeals to
Pl.30 post-Modern city-makers like Leon Krier and Ricardo Bofill.

PLANNING IN THE GRAND MANNER

In his report of 13 November 1666 presented to Charles II a few days after the Great
212 Fire along with "a survey of the ruines, and a plot for a new Citty," John Evelyn invokes three principles for his rebuilding of London: "beauty, commodiousness, and magnificence." If the first two refer to the famous Vitruvian principles of *venusatas* and *utilitas*, magnificence is the Baroque component par excellence. It supersedes utility, as we can tell from Evelyn's proposals for the harbor. In insisting on a noble waterfront, free of untidy landing stages, warehouses and yards, he was putting magnificence ahead of the productive vitality of the city. His proposal to move burial grounds from churchyards to the edge may strike us as a progressive pre-Enlightenment idea, as does his plan to situate slaughterhouses and prisons away from the center near some entrance of the City. But the list of activities he would banish includes "Brewhouses, Bakehouses, Dyers, Salt, Soap, and Sugar-boilers . . . Fish-mongers," etc., some of which would surely have been cause for extreme *in*commodiousness.

It is an urban grandeur beyond utility, beyond pragmatic considerations, that the
263 Grand Manner seeks to achieve, whether it is in ancient Babylon or in Nazi Berlin. And its instruments are heroic scale, visual fluency, and the luxury of building materials.

TOPOGRAPHY

The site comes first, and is studied with care. John Evelyn, before he gave London a modern plan, wanted to prepare a contour map describing accurately "all the declivities, eminences, water courses &c. of the whole area."[4] But this did not mean that the care was expended to develop a good working relation with the shapes of the land. On the contrary, these shapes were a challenge: they were to be dramatized where useful to the intentions of the planner, suppressed where they were not. The placement of public buildings and their visually meaningful interrelationships, and the possibility of exciting vistas are two of these intentions. So Fontana could boast,
Pl.21 for example, that Sixtus V "has stretched these streets from one end of the city to the other, and, not heeding the hills and valleys which they had to cross, but flattening here and filling in there, he has made them gentle plains and most beautiful sites . . ." So Evelyn, in his plan for London, thinks "fit to fill up, or at least give a partial level to some of the deepest valleys, holes and more sudden declivities, within the city, for the more ease of commerce, carriages, coaches, and people in the streets, and not a little for the more handsome ranging of the buildings."[5]

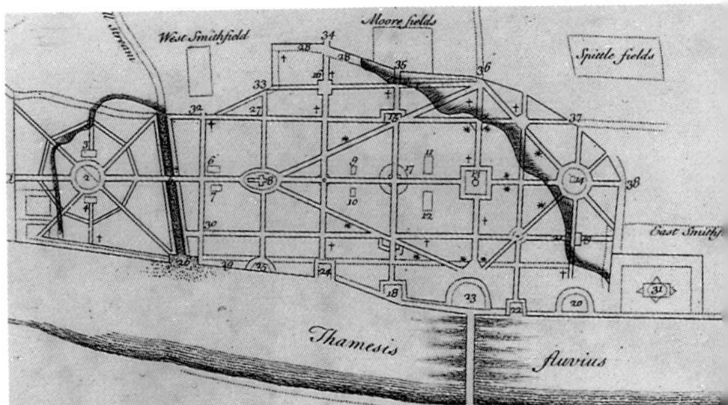

212 *John Evelyn, plan for the proposed reconstruction of the City of London, 1666, first version. St. Paul's Cathedral is set in an oval left of center, at the head of a* trivium.

213–215 Diagrammatic views of Delphi (Greece), Priene (Turkey), and Lindos (Greece), representing respectively the urban experience of an "organic" site, a grid, and a composition in the Grand Manner.

Three examples from Classical antiquity might clarify how the Grand Manner manages its effects differently from "organic" patterns or the common grid. At Delphi the processional experience derived from the irregular climb of the sacred *213* way and the aggressive positioning of treasuries, those symbols of rival city states, in relation to its natural rhythms. The temple of Apollo took its place against the mountain spur, its freestanding sculptural form shifting in angle and magnitude in the eye of the approaching pilgrim. Priene's inflexible grid, on the steep lower slopes *214* of Mount Micale, locked the temple of Athena in the rectangularity of its blocks, and forced visitors to approach it along a straight line, stepped in the north–south direction, level from the east or the west. In the case of the Hellenistic acropolis at Lindos, the rise has been thoroughly subjected to an architectural treatment of *215* terraces, grand stairs, and enveloping stretches of porticoes, all brought into line along a rigid axis. The experience as one climbs and moves through this monumental range of forecourts is of methodically revealed architectonic prospects which, having tamed and concealed the pleats of nature under foot, find use for them only as a distant backdrop.

We need to insist on the arbitrary nature of this brand of urban design. Geometric order is often its own reward, even when it has no specific support based on local conditions. Now of course there is always some official justification for what is imposed on the city form from above, and I shall soon be talking of some of these arguments in terms of the straight street. But the wilfulness is never explained away: indeed it is cherished.

Evelyn condemns the old London as "a City consisting of a wooden, northern, and inartificiall congestion of Houses"[6]—I think the word "inartificiall" here is very much to the point. The Baroque city is an artificial design, in the double sense of "concocted" and "full of artifice." When Judge Augustus Woodward drew up a plan for Detroit in 1807, after a fire two years earlier had swept through the frontier *216* outpost, he declared that "the bases of the town . . . shall be an equilateral triangle, having each side of the length of four thousand feet [1,200 m.], and having every angle bisected by a perpendicular line upon the opposite side." Each equilateral triangle would thus be divided into six right-angle triangles known as "sections." Why this was to be so the good judge did not explain. Edwin Lutyens's celebrated design for New Delhi, likewise, for all the other reasons to pay it heed, ultimately is *176* justified by his love of the equilateral triangle and the hexagon—that and the celebrated exemplars of the Anglo-American Grand Manner. As his colleague Herbert

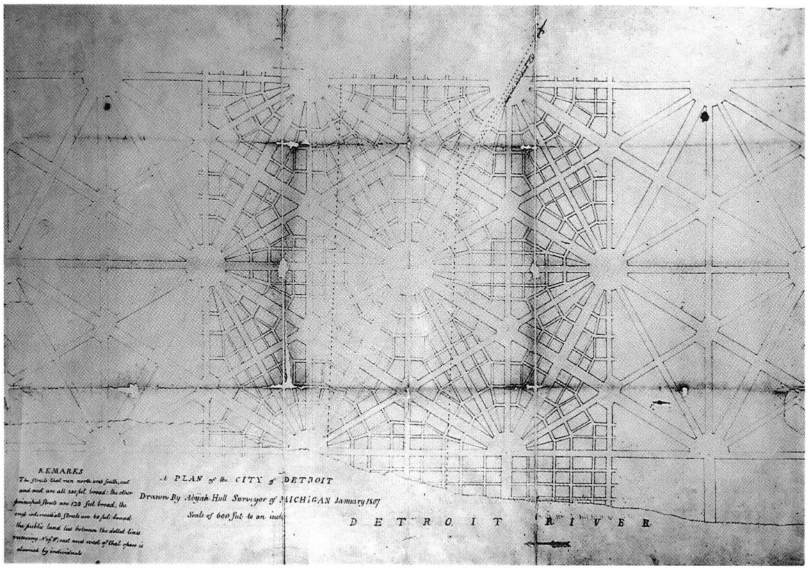

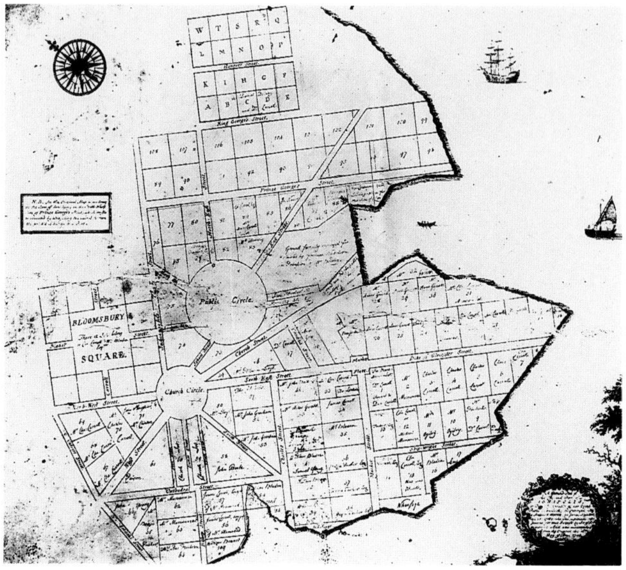

Baker put it in 1930, New Delhi's layout was "a noble development of the germ of
208 L'Enfant's plan of Washington and Wren's rejected design for the City of London."

That such inflexible arrangements come at a considerable cost to the extant order of things should be obvious. Outside of the built-up area, they disrupt the established pattern of property boundaries. In the city, the damage is to building stock. A *note douloureuse* of the time, reacting to the frenetic activity associated with Sixtus V's master plan, commented wisely: "Those poles placed throughout the city in straight lines across vineyards and gardens bring fear to the souls of many interested persons who are not unaware that, in order to make roads without turnings, many a neck has to be twisted."[7] The demolition of one's property, in the city states of Italy during the Middle Ages and the Renaissance, was commonly a punishment reserved for traitors. Now this punishment is meted out where there is no crime. A papal bull of 1480 already establishes the principle of expropriating and demolishing for the public good.

This unavoidable destruction is why so much Baroque planning is outside old cores. The impact was comparative—ample, visually cohesive fragments next to the
253 tight, picturesque accretions of the medieval fabric straitjacketed by its lumbering defenses. The same cannot be said of the modern period. Beginning with Napoleon the Great and the planners of his imperial cities, the notion that order in the Grand Manner must be imposed on the old cores gained momentum, until levels of unprecedented destructiveness had been reached with the Haussmannian *grands*
90 *travaux* in Paris of the 1850s and 1860s and the universal influence of their example.

There were two reasons for this license. On the functional side, the historic city, unable to cope with the new volume of traffic and the pressures of modern life, had to be opened up, and interlocked with the voraciously spreading suburbs. But for the régimes of Napoleon Bonaparte or Napoleon III, of Franco or Mussolini, the more serious issue was revaluation. History itself had to be staged and updated. The great
7 monuments of the past were to be disencumbered of their ramshackle hangers-on, new monuments celebrating the personality and political message of the current ruler had to be erected within this same hallowed frame of history, and representational connections made on location between ancient memories and modern triumphs. For this one needed room.

216 above left *Detroit (Michigan), plan by Augustus Brevoort Woodward, 1807. In the 1820s the city shifted from this triangle-based scheme to the familiar grid; most of the diagonal streets were abandoned.*

217 above *Annapolis (Maryland), planned by Governor Francis Nicholson in 1694. The scheme survives in this manuscript copy from 1748 of the version drawn in 1718 by James Stoddert.*

Indeed one of the requisites of the Grand Manner is expansiveness. For the magic to work, there must be adequate space for the effects of a proliferating geometry, of opening up, of boundless prospects that breach the city edge and shoot out into the countryside. We are struck, looking at Evelyn's plan for London and the equally *212* famous one by Sir Christopher Wren, with how cramped the Baroque devices seem in the tight envelope of the City. In executed plans of this sort, the constriction reduces the Grand Manner to rote mannerisms. That is the feeling one has of the Rondell *trivium* in Berlin's Friedrichstadt from the 1730s, or worse still, in Georgian *241* Annapolis, Francis Nicholson's capital for Maryland, where a clumsy assemblage of *217* grand Baroque effects is crowded into a tiny site—a large circle with the state house in the center, on the highest point; a small circle with the church in the center; and Bloomsbury Square. Even the pinwheel arrangement of the diagonals that take off from the large circle instead of running directly on axis with the center, perhaps an intentional esthetic choice, comes across as a distortion due to the compressed terrain.[8]

On the other hand, the system works beautifully not only in the sweeping field of a Karlsruhe or a Washington, but also within the limited confines of palace-parks like Nymphenburg in Munich, the Zwinger in Dresden, or Capodimonte and Caserta *218* near Naples. So it is not simply a question of how large the area is that is being designed in the Grand Manner. As always in matters of design, it is not absolute size that determines scale but the coordination of parts.

The relation of the Grand Manner to the radial schemes discussed in the chapter on "The City as Diagram" can be stated simply. Geometric planning schemes of the sort we are presently concerned with were also not innocent of symbolism, of seeing the city form as a diagram of some ideal order be it cosmic or political. But they were more openly concerned with visual delight. The plan of Sixtus V had its weighty, *Pl.21* symbolic interpretations. Caterva Foglietta, in a letter of 1587, points out that the crossing of the Strada Pia of Pius IV and Sixtus's Strada Felice "fa una bellissima Croce" (makes a most beautiful cross), the cross of Calvary; and Giovanni Francesco Bordino interprets the whole Sistine plan to be "in syderis formam" (in

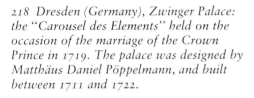

218 Dresden (Germany), Zwinger Palace: the "Carousel des Elements" held on the occasion of the marriage of the Crown Prince in 1719. The palace was designed by Matthäus Daniel Pöppelmann, and built between 1711 and 1722.

the shape of a star), with S. Maria Maggiore at its center—the five-pointed star being in fact a symbol of the Virgin. But at the same time, the planner himself, Domenico Fontana, can see the esthetic benefits of his design, when he writes of the new streets that "along their routes in many places there open views of the lowest parts of the city in varied and different perspectives. Thus beyond the religious purposes, these beauties provide a pasture for the bodily senses."

THE GRAND MANNER AS THEATER

The city as theater is not the exclusive preserve of the Grand Manner. In every age urban spaces—streets and squares—have served to stage spectacles in which the citizenry participated as players and audience. Urban life is nothing if not theatrical.

There are two senses in which the Grand Manner had a distinctive relationship to theater design and the general notion of theater. First, it emulated theater design in the creation of temporary environments for special occasions. Stage sets were a quick, legally uncomplicated, and economical way of realizing effects of urban design in the Grand Manner. Second, what the Grand Manner aspired to achieve was to turn the composition of urban spaces, the spatial experience of moving through streets and squares, itself into a spectacle. The atlas of plans and views commissioned by Duke Carlo Emanuele II of Savoy in 1682 to celebrate the projected transformation of Turin into an absolutist capital was entitled *Theatrum statuum Sabaudiae* (The Theater of the State of Savoy). Similarly, the 1665 volume of plates in commemoration of the Rome of Pope Alexander VII was entitled *Il nuove teatro . . . di Roma moderna*. Alexander himself refers to his redoing of the piazza of S. Maria della Pace as "Teatro della Pace"; he also refers to St. Peter's Square as "piazza del teatro di S. Pietro."[9]

The ancient correspondences are obscure, but it was Hellenistic practice as codified by Vitruvius in his three "scenes" that became the basis of Sebastiano
220 Serlio's three streets in his treatise on architecture: the "tragic" street of public buildings in the Classical style for the high life of kings and nobles, ending in a
221 triumphal arch leading out of the city; the "comic" or residential street for the ordinary life of shopkeepers and merchants—arcades and shops at ground level, apartments above, and a church tower completing the view, almost all done in the by then aberrant Gothic style; and the "satyric" street, a country path for bucolic activities and country sports. Serlio was following earlier designs by Peruzzi, who in turn may have derived them from Bramante. Later in the century, in 1584, Vincenzo Scamozzi completed Palladio's Teatro Olimpico in Vicenza by building three-dimensional versions of these three streets into the *scaena*, where the art of perspective takes over and unifies the street sides with devices like even cornice lines. We could say that Domenico Fontana's planning scheme for Sistine Rome is merely the introduction of the "tragic" street into the realm of urban design. In fact, if John Onians is right, we now can pinpoint a much earlier and more specific connection
219 between theater design and a real urban project. The Piazzetta of S. Marco in Venice as redesigned by Jacopo Sansovino in the 1530s may have been based, according to Onians's recent book, on Peruzzi/Serlio's "tragic" scene, which may have supplied the theoretical motive for replacing the extant Gothic buildings and their low-life connotations with the Classical forms of Sansovino's Library, Mint and Loggetta.[10]

From theatrical decor urban designers of the Renaissance and the Baroque absorbed renditions of Classical themes like triumphal arches, temple fronts, exedrae, and public statues on pedestals. From the same source they learned to apply

219–221 *A comparison of the Piazzetta of S. Marco in Venice and two of Serlio's street "scenes" for the theater, ca. 1537: the "tragic" scene* (left), *and the "comic" scene. Sansovino's Mint and Library are on the left in the photograph, and his Loggetta is at the base of the Campanile, partly concealed by the left-hand column.*

perspective to urban vistas, that is, by erecting architectural proscenia through which the vista could be seen, using continuous street planes to create the necessary directionality in depth, and fixing the vanishing point with a terminal marker. Besides convergence and symmetry, the stage designer could conjure an overall order through uniform street elevations. The connection is made by John Evelyn. In speaking of Paris, he says that in many streets the houses were built "so incomparably fair and *uniform*, that you would imagine your self rather in some *Italian Opera*, where the diversity of *Scenes* surprise the beholder, then beleeve your self to be in a reall *Citie*."[11]

Before such properties could be permanently incorporated into urban design, and, for that matter, long after they were, the improvisations of stage sets recomposed the reality of the extant urban fabric and readied it for state functions and ceremonial occasions. Façades along the route of a procession were transfigured with appropriate Classical screens; false perspectives painted in *trompe l'oeil* masked the picturesque medieval jumble of side streets; triumphal arches of stiffened cloth or plaster were put up at intervals to devise appropriate caesuras for the advancing cortege. Mock triumphal arches also blocked from view the spiky silhouettes of the medieval city gates.

Politically speaking, the dramatization of urban form was a function of autocracy. The new rulers of the Renaissance were the patrons of the revived Classical theater, and the chief movers in the official restructuring of urban space. From the 16th century to the 18th, the great majority of the new permanent theater buildings were within the grounds of princely palaces. The city itself was coaxed to acquire the look of an ideal theater environment in order to reflect the tempered dominion of the prince. Urban passages from the principal city gates to the ruler's residence were the most critical in the transformation of the old medieval fabrics.
222 The task was to create ceremonial thoroughfares that would centralize and fully control the urban experience of visitors from the moment they entered the city, and the conventions of the theater, especially perspective, helped to emphasize "the order imposed upon space by the political master of that space, the centrality of that master's vision, and the increasing insignificance of objects as they were located at greater distance from the position of power."[12]

With the decline of the Age of Absolutism, the identity of the master changed. The spaces of an abstract ideal city remained in use, or were freshly reinterpreted and extended, for the rituals of new dominant classes. In the 19th century the show went
223 middle-class. Haussmann's boulevards put on public display the new pastimes of a
248 fancily dressed café crowd, turning the entire city into a bourgeois spectacle. *Flânerie*, which has been described as "that eminently Parisian compromise between laziness and activity," came into its own.[13]

Predictably enough, the masters of socialism in their turn claimed the city for the masses, but after some experimentation they too settled for the same stage sets in the
224 Grand Manner, with some appropriate symbolic flourishes of their own. In the Stalin years, the urban designers of Eastern Europe openly acknowledged this debt. What was at fault was the laissez-fairism of the intervening century, the 19th, when individualistic housing practices condoned a picturesque esthetic—the hallmark of capitalist escapism. The state was absolute once again, and therefore the planning principles of the 17th and 18th centuries were the proper model. (It was understood, of course, that the Baroque state was an agency of repression and exploitation, whereas in the socialist state the people themselves had become the supreme architect.) "Nobody doubts," an East German architect wrote as late as 1955, "that with ensembles built around an axis in the fashion of Rossi Street [in Leningrad] and

222 *A princely avenue: Berlin, Unter den Linden, looking west; painting by Carl Friedrich Fechhelm, 1756. On the left is the Opera House, on the right the palace of Prince Heinrich, later the Humboldt University.*

223 *A bourgeois boulevard: Vienna, the Ringstrasse, 1873. The view is down Opernring, with the Opera House on the right.*

224 *A socialist* magistrale*: East Berlin's Stalinallee (now Karl-Marx-Allee); H. Henselmann, designer-in-chief, 1952–57.*

the Place de la Concorde [in Paris] one can attain the most splendid embodiment of socialist society."[14]

Long after the abandonment of Socialist Realism, which expired with Stalin, these words were to assume new life, as we shall see, in the housing estates of Ricardo
Pl.30 Bofill. With a socialist credo of building for the people and an almost literal dependence on the aristocratic forms of the 18th century, he has sought to deliver on his boast about his work: "each construction is a monument, each public space a theater."[15]

THE GRAND MANNER AND LANDSCAPE DESIGN

The propinquity between landscape design and urban design was a commonplace in the Age of Grandeur. The garden *allée* stood cousin to the tree-lined avenue, the *rond-point* graced park and city alike. It is impossible to write of the Grand Manner in the 17th and 18th centuries without a working knowledge of garden forms.

The ancient phase of our subject does not oblige in this respect. The visual proof is largely gone, of course, but even with what is left for us to study it is apparent that the urban effects of the Grand Manner did not rely on landscaping, and had no guidance from the art of the gardener. Trees and plants were at most accessories to public buildings; parks represented a paradisiac world apart from the stone order of *place d'armes* and ceremonial axis. The famous Hanging Gardens of Babylon greened a corner of Nebuchadnezzar's palace, and trees livened the upper terraces of the Mesopotamian ziggurat at Ur; but city streets and sacred precincts were innocent of formal landscaping. The more studied landscaping of Queen Hatshepsut's funerary complex at Deir el-Bahri aimed to recreate the homeland of the gods: the tamarisks and sycamore trees of the entrance forecourt, the myrrh trees for the terraces above, were an earthly emulation of "the paradise of Amon."

To witness the startling coincidence between the gardener's art and the "embellishment" of cities, we need to be transported to the late 16th century, with Italy as our first stop. It was then and there that landscape design began to assume an
236 architectural structure that approximated on a small scale the spatial possibilities of contemporary city form. Working with a relatively free surface area, gardeners were at liberty in the next half-century to experiment with overall patterns of spatial order which architects and engineers, confronted with the built reality of old cities, could only project in the abstract.

In France during the 17th century this coincidence was enhanced when suburban gardens pushed their formal patterns beyond their boundaries, suggesting ordinates for a disciplined city edge. At the same time, the transformation of the stiff architectural framework of bastions into landscaped promenades, most notably in
243 the Grands Boulevards of Paris, further narrowed down the difference between the design of gardens and the modern layout of urban stretches. To put it more accurately, a rational order for structuring space came to be applied uniformly to the open and the built landscape. And the acknowledged master of this new spatial art was André Le Nôtre.

In the next century, when established practice was spelled out as theory, the urban lessons to be learned from a master gardener like Le Nôtre were said to be, in W. Herrmann's summary, "how to straighten winding streets, rectify unavoidable irregularities of the ground, and arrange viewpoints."[16] The Abbé Laugier was picking up on this debate of his time when he pronounced the great Classical French
225 gardens and parks a paradigm for what cities like Paris could aspire to. "Let the design of our parks serve as the plan for our towns," he wrote in 1755. The

225 *Contrasting spatial orders: Paris's intricate pre-Haussmann street network (right) and the stellated arrangement of* ronds-points *and forest* allées *in the Bois de Boulogne (left); detail of the Cassine de Thury plan, 1744. The great axis of the Champs-Elysées is already marked as a tree-lined road, the Avenue des Tuileries, leading northwest out of the city and touching the northern edge of the Bois de Boulogne.*

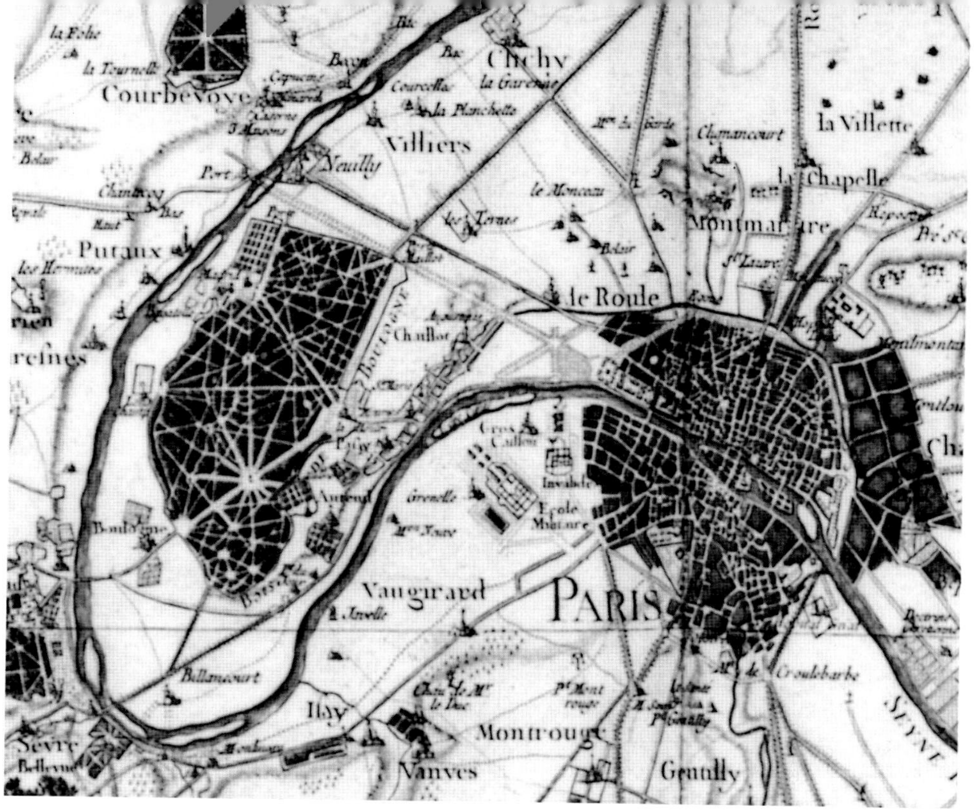

traditional city was indeed like a great untamed forest, to which the planner, like the landscape architect in his own realm, would bring a rational order. Laugier wrote:

> Paris; it is an immense forest, varied by the inequalities of the plain and the mountain, cut right through the middle by a great river, which dividing itself into many arms forms islands of different size. Let us suppose that we were allowed to cut and prune at will, what means could not be drawn from so many advantageous diversities?[17]

And his vision of the ideal entry into the capital—a grand avenue lined with multiple rows of trees, ending in a triumphal arch set into a radial scheme—sounds very much like the Champs-Elysées sequence, fathered by Le Nôtre, which was beginning to take on its classic shape by the mid-18th century. Behind the entrance gate, on the city side, would be a big square with three streets fanning out into the town.

By the century's end this French equivalence of landscape architecture and urban design becomes a commonly held belief among practitioners in Europe. The birth of the picturesque English garden in the second half of the 18th century, and its rising popularity on the Continent, and, through Downing and Olmsted, in the United States, could not undo this firmly held Baroque conviction that city form and the art of landscaping were inseparable. Alphonse Alphand, who laid out some of the finest Parisian parks under Haussmann predominantly *à l'anglaise*, also masterminded the landscaping of Haussmannian boulevards and *places* with the expert assurance of 248
an urban designer in the Grand Manner.

In America, picturesque parkscapes and the sweeping formality of Baroque urbanism coexisted more intimately within the broad context of the Grand Manner. Unlike the French position that urban design and landscape design share the same formal principles, the American Baroque esthetic merged two distinct urban experiences—the monumental network of streets and squares and the soft, romantic undulations of urban landscaping which derived from the tradition of the

226 *Letchworth (England), the first Garden City, laid out by Raymond Unwin and Barry Parker and begun in 1904. While the streets of private houses have an "organic" feel, the public realm reflects Beaux-Arts formal ideals.*

English garden and the more immediate experience of Olmstedian urban parks. Within the old pre-City Beautiful gridded plans like that of Manhattan, the insertion of a "Central Park" was intended sharply to juxtapose the reality of the standard American city order and the fundamentally anti-city concept of the park. The new City Beautiful plans, on the other hand, fused the two gracefully, since the
250 tree-lined boulevards and parkways greened the main city-form itself and bonded it to the recreational landscape of parks and waterfronts.

After the First World War, the English put their own gloss on this fusion, when the influence of Ebenezer Howard's gospel aligned the design concepts of the Grand Manner with those of the Garden City. New Delhi is both grand and gardenlike, but
226 so in its own way is Letchworth, the first Garden City. The stubborn discrimination in the British sphere between a public domain, where multistory buildings and monumental effects predominate, and a residential low-density fabric based on the single-family house made for a more variegated settlement pattern than in Continental Europe and its colonial outreach that accepted the apartment house as the residential norm. That is what sets New Delhi apart from French Tunis or Algiers.

THE DESIGN OF HEIGHTS

The formal creation and manipulation of heights, in order to locate public buildings above the setting of daily life, and to produce a sense of arrival, of dignified approach, is central to the urban experience of the Grand Manner. This is achieved in a number of ways.

Platforms. In antiquity, the ziggurats on which Mesopotamian temples sit, and the temple-pyramids of Meso-America, are the most extreme examples. In a more

227 Rome, the Spanish Stairs, by Francesco de Sanctis, 1723–25, looking from Piazza di Spagna toward the 16th-century church of the Trinità dei Monti at the summit.

228 above right *On the Capitol Hill in Rome, the stairs leading up to the church of the Aracoeli (left) are simply a means of ascent, but Michelangelo's* cordonata, *conceived in the mid-16th century as part of his redesign of the civic buildings on the hilltop, is carefully composed for dramatic effect. The effect is intensified by the double flight of stairs leading to the Palazzo del Senatore, on axis at the top. Etching by G. B. Piranesi, 1757.*

measured way, the stereobate of a Greek temple serves the same principle. A modern 277
example is the two-story-high podium of the Albany Mall (the Empire State Plaza) in upstate New York, on which four identical office towers sit.

Stairs. The complex of Queen Hatshepsut at Deir el-Bahri, the Hellenistic acropolis at Lindos, or any of the great classical Maya sites can be instanced here. At issue are 215
stairs whose size exceeds any reasonable need stairs might fill ordinarily. In effect, we have here a species of "inclined plaza." Modern examples would include Rome's Spanish Stairs or the main entrance staircase of New York's Metropolitan Museum 227
of Art.

Ramps allow access to heights for wheeled vehicles, and sometimes a less strenuous climb for pedestrians. They are often used together with stairs, to secure all options during ceremonial occasions. The *cordonata* leading to Michelangelo's Campi- 228
doglio is a compromise between a stairway and a ramp.

The cadenced climb in stages, with an artful use of landings, viewing points, and the alternating concealment and revelation of the terminal object, was a special gift of Roman designers. Even in a strictly axial composition, they were able to build in visual suspense. They did so by breaking up our headlong progress upward in a straight line with certain unavoidable diversions, as when the axial route was split into two channels at a landing, or a monument on the axis, an altar or a statue, forced us to move around it. The temple of Fortuna Primigenia at Praeneste (Palestrina) is an intricate study of such effects—and it is certainly behind Bramante's Cortile del Belvedere and Michelangelo's Campidoglio. If we concede to the latter the full scope of its conception, with the staired approaches from the level of the Roman Forum at the rear taken into account as well as the classic city-side rise of the *cordonata*, the sequence is a remarkable choreography of human movement through architectural means.

Two more recent instances, both in Russia, are of comparable quality. The giant stairway at Odessa, now known as the "Potemkin steps" because of the famous scene in Eisenstein's film *The Battleship Potemkin*, dates from 1837. It was designed to monumentalize the relation of the hilltop city and its harbor, replacing the patchwork of paths and wooden stairs. The sequence of stairs and landings was so contrived that "a person looking down the stairs sees only landings, while an observer looking up sees only steps."[18] At the top, the stairway locks into the majestic Primorskii Boulevard, laid out at about the same time, that runs along the city edge. At Kerch in the Ukraine, the goal of the great staircase is the mausoleum at the top of the hill that carries Mithridates' name. The sequence starts at the straits with a large octagonal open space, and the run of the stairs is broken by three terraces.

Modern descendants of these Baroque *Treppenstrassen*, having rejected the precious materials and the programmatic association with history, will tend to make a virtue of the mere technics of terracing, or will resort to landscaping and street furniture for a domesticated experience. In Kassel as rebuilt after the Second World War, the hillside from Scheidemannplatz to Königstrasse is scaled by a pedestrian shopping street whose line of terraces connected by steps and ramps has a broad median furnished with seats and planting, a fountain, and an open-air tea garden.

"BAROQUE" ELEMENTS

THE STRAIGHT STREET

The arguments for straight streets are at least as old as the Renaissance.

(1) The straight street promotes public order by doing away with the nooks and crannies of irregular neighborhoods, and thwarting the temptation to obstruct passage or to shield insurrection behind barricades. King Ferdinand of Naples was fond of saying that "narrow streets were a danger to the State."[19] About Via Alessandrina, opened in 1499 on the Borgo side of Rome, a contemporary source wrote:

> The architects decided to run a street straight from the bridge [of Castel S. Angelo] to the [Vatican] palace gate to give the palace an open perspective, free of obstacles, and in case of riots—as often happens in this turbulent Rome—one can get help quickly and defend oneself from the urban attackers.[20]

Similarly, the straight streets which relentlessly opened up the tangled stretches of
90 Paris in Haussmann's *grands travaux* were a response, among other things, to the
very real threat of violent civil disobedience. Napoleon III, after all, came to power
in the wake of the bloody Revolution of 1848. The new avenues were sometimes
referred to as anti-riot streets, and they were coordinated with barracks for the
permanent quartering of troops and police at all major crossroads, especially in the
259 working-class east end. Haussmann himself wrote of the Boulevard de Sébastopol:
225 "It meant the disembowelling of the old Paris, the quarter of uprisings and
barricades, by a wide central street piercing through and through this almost
impossible maze, and provided with communicating side streets."

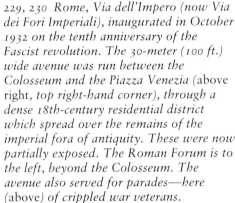

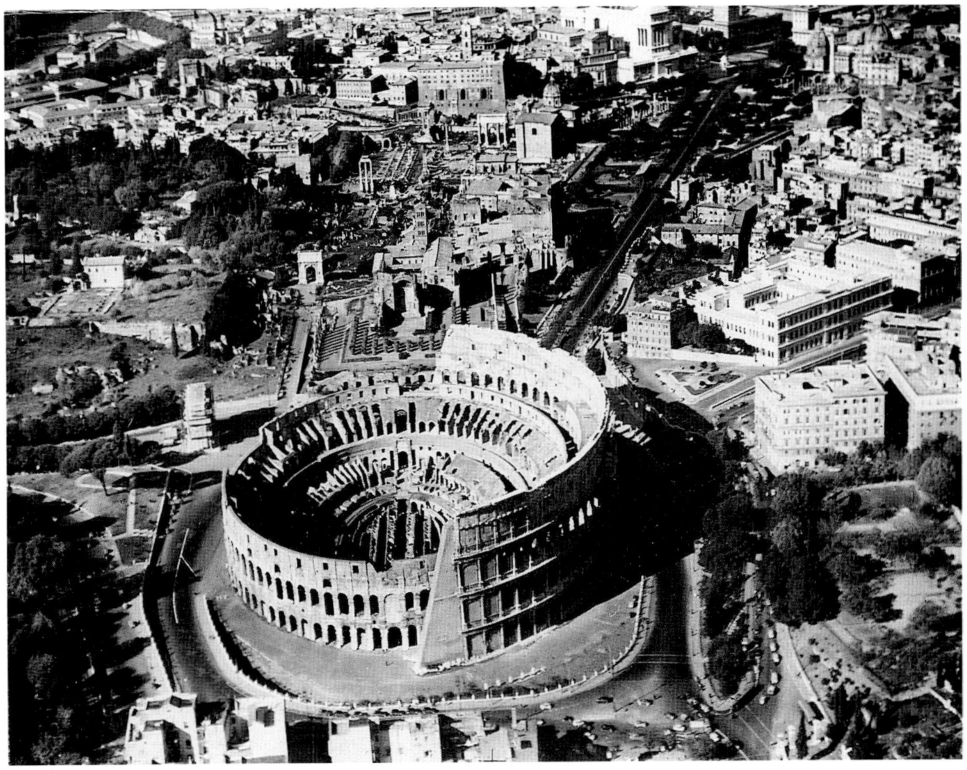

229, 230 Rome, Via dell'Impero (now Via dei Fori Imperiali), inaugurated in October 1932 on the tenth anniversary of the Fascist revolution. The 30-meter (100 ft.) wide avenue was run between the Colosseum and the Piazza Venezia (above right, *top right-hand corner), through a dense 18th-century residential district which spread over the remains of the imperial fora of antiquity. These were now partially exposed. The Roman Forum is to the left, beyond the Colosseum. The avenue also served for parades—here* (above) *of crippled war veterans.*

(2) The straight street has a practical superiority, in that it connects two points directly and so speeds up communication. The Via Alessandrina was officially explained as an aid to the movement of pilgrims. Fascist rhetoric made *la linea diretta* a metaphor for resolute decision-making—"the straight line that does not lose itself in the meanders of Hamlet-like thought"—and Fascist planners demonstrated the principle with brutal disregard of the extant settlement pattern when they ran the ramrod Via dell'Impero between Piazza Venezia, where the Duce *229,*
had his official residence, and the Colosseum.[21] *230*

The increasing popularity of straight and wide streets is directly linked with the surge in the use of wheeled carriages beginning in the 16th century. It can be demonstrated that a principal motive for the widening and straightening of streets in the Age of Absolutism was to ease the passage and parking of coaches in the old urban cores. The same considerations affected the laying out of new quarters.

The coach, namely, a carriage with a suspension system that cushions riders from the jarring of progress over an uneven surface, is thought to have originated in Hungary. Legend honors the primacy of a coach presented in 1457 to Charles VII of France by Ladislaus, King of Hungary. By 1530 the new Hungarian coaches had made their appearance in most European countries—an important object of status for the upper classes, especially noble women. Once the feminine associations of coach-riding, as against horseback riding, were overcome, the number of coaches increased rapidly—and so did the problems related to their movement and parking. In 1560, when London had two and Paris no more than three, Antwerp is said to have let loose on its streets over 500 coaches. By 1594 there were 883 coaches in Rome.[22] By 1636, Henry Peacham in London points to Paulsgate, Ludgate, Ludgate Hill, and "the Holborne-Conduit to the bridge" as "villanously pestered" by coaches, with the vehicles so thick at an aristocratic fête or the opening of a play that "you would admire to see them, how close they stand together (like Mutton-pies in a Cookes-oven) that you can hardly thrust a pole betweene."[23]

But of course, and related to the first reason given, the straight street also facilitates the movement of troops, and war machines like artillery. (It is interesting here to contrast the strategic advantages attributed to the "organic" city plan—that it confounds intruding forces and makes it easier to entrap them—and the open nature of the Baroque plan that gives the enemy no umbrage and gives defending forces free passage to points of trouble.) Again, the example of Haussmann is relevant here. The key word in his promotional efforts was circulation, primarily of normal daily traffic. But the extremely wide straight streets leading in from all the railroad stations were there at least partly for the benefit of bringing in soldiers when needed.

Finally, (3) the straight street can direct the social and practical advantages it possesses into a discourse of ideology, and with a suitable coding of architecture and decoration it can impart a powerful representational message. I shall have more to say on this further on.

THE "BAROQUE" DIAGONAL

When the straight street is run sufficiently contrary to the grain of the extant urban fabric or the gridded matrix of a new plan, we talk of a Baroque diagonal. This is a seemingly willful slash to connect two points directly, either after the fact, or within an urban design created *ab ovo* for a new quarter of the city or for an altogether new city. In this sense, the Baroque diagonal is to be distinguished from more or less accidental diagonals, which are usually the result of trying to accommodate in a regular scheme a prior stretch of road, or of the coming together of two disparate sections of urban layout.

Examples of the first condition are the Roman town of Verulamium (St. Albans) in England, where the Roman surveyors incorporated an oblique stretch of old
231 Watling Street; Kathmandu, where a high road running from Tibet to India was trapped, in the frame of the developing city, among several patches of gridded blocks; and of course Broadway in New York, which the early 19th-century grid retained from the Dutch/British period of the city. The military connection probably also belongs here. I refer to diagonals that are remnants of arrow-headed bastions between the old core and modern development; American examples are Wall Street in Salt Lake City, Water and Cumberland Streets in Charleston.

The ancient Roman use of the diagonal is commoner than one might think, and the reasons are not always clear. It tends to be a feature that comes from an early chapter in the history of the city, or a late one. In the first instance, we are dealing with a pattern of roads established prior to the imposition of a formal Roman order, of which the coordinates are a *cardo* and *decumanus* crossing at right angles. Celtic roads account for the diagonals of Lyon, for example. In the second instance, the planned Roman town has outgrown its boundaries, and the *cardo* or *decumanus* has been extended on an oblique to reach the river or the new amphitheater in a direct line, as in Fréjus, or to run between two extramural installations, as in Arles—also in southern France—where the Rue de la Redoute bent the axis of the actual *decumanus* southward to pass between the theater and the amphitheater, and reach an important gate in the latest city walls.

But the case of Nîmes is not so clear. The *cardo-decumanus* system there is contradicted by diagonals that start right at the crossing, with one going northeast to

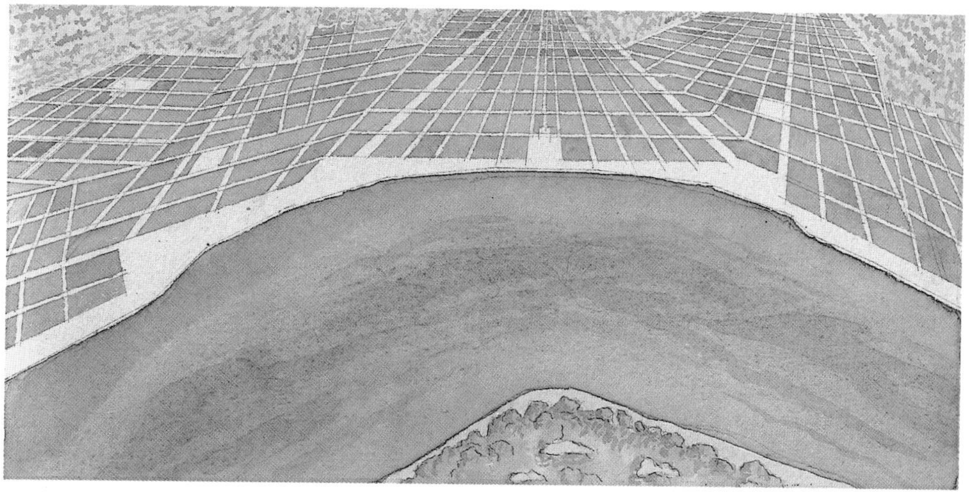

231–233 Ad hoc *diagonals: in Kathmandu* (top), *following the high road to Tibet; San Francisco* (above), *at the meeting of two discrete gridded layouts; New Orleans* (above right), *tracing the oblique canal system of the original French settlers.*

the Porte d'Uzès and the other starting at a corner of the forum (where the Maison Carrée stands) and heading due west to the Porte de Nages.

Examples of the second condition, where the "diagonal" is actually nothing more than the meeting line between two independently laid out segments of town, are not uncommon in America. San Francisco's Market Street, Denny Way in Seattle, *232*
Charleston Street in Las Vegas, and Hennepin Avenue in Minneapolis come to mind. The original settlement is often at right angles to a water landing; the later *102*
grid lays down its own competitive frame of settlement, and others would likely follow in time. The dividing line usually corresponds to a break in the topography like a valley. Since the railroads followed these breaks, that is where, on the "diagonal," we are likely to find the railroad station (e.g., Portland, Oregon; Kansas City, Missouri). Incidentally, as Grady Clay points out, these breaks will later be targets for new expressways and other urban renewal projects.[24] Even on level ground, the railroad tracks were likely to seek a direct line regardless of the National Survey grid, and the accompanying town might have all of its streets on a bias parallel to the tracks, only to revert to the coordinates of the survey in later additions (e.g., Hays, Kansas). If the town predated the coming of the railroads, the tracks might cut right through the orthogonal order, creating an industrial axis at odds with Main Street, or displacing Main Street altogether.

The case of New Orleans is unique. Its accidental Baroque, the great fanning *233*
boulevards that separate the grid of the French quarter from later developments along the meandering Mississippi, goes back to the "long lots" of the French settlers. These lots were perpendicular to the river, but not parallel to one another since the river was not straight. The oblique boundary lines of the fields were reinforced when drainage canals were dug along their paths. As the space between them was laid out with the coming of the Americans, the main streets of the individual developments ran alongside the canals, which were eventually filled in and turned into wide boulevards. In the American sector these New Orleanian boulevards converge upon a central focus like a Baroque sunburst, only "because they are radii of a half-circle whose circumference was already drawn by the Mississippi River."[25]

Such early materializations of the diagonal in the United States should not be confused with the wholehearted welcome of the Grand Manner in the early 20th century during the so-called City Beautiful movement. Then planners systematically set out to update the prosaic grids of towns across America with Baroque accents, specifically diagonal runs against the regular grain of rectangular blocks. The City

235 Beautiful grid run through by diagonals comes to be referred to in Europe as the "American grid." It shows up with the subtitle "à l'américaine" in an angry sketch
234 of Le Corbusier's from the Twenties, entitled "il faut tuer la 'rue-corridor'!" (We must kill the "corridor street"!), among the various strands of academic and organic planning he disapproves of.

Now the combination of the grid and the Baroque esthetic had been worked out as
208 a coherent, one-of-a-kind design in L'Enfant's plan for Washington, as we saw; and it was precisely the rekindling of interest in this great (and badly obscured) blueprint on the occasion of the capital's Centennial celebrations in 1902 that started the national career of the City Beautiful movement.

L'Enfant's legacy had been negligible until then. Andrew Ellicott, who had a hand in the revision of the Washington plan and was given custody of it when the Frenchman was summarily dismissed, designed Erie, Pennsylvania, in 1795 as if L'Enfant had never existed—a simple grid with no radial or diagonal streets.
216 Woodward's Detroit, which did emulate L'Enfant, had long ago reverted to a manageable regularity. The state of Wisconsin seemed taken with the Grand Manner for a while. In its 1836 plan Madison was given four radials centering on the square reserved for the State Capitol, but there "was no provision for open spaces, triangles, circles," the American Institute of Architects' 1917 review of City Beautiful projects complained, and the lakefronts were ignored altogether. Milwaukee's grid of about the same time had "a system of diagonal streets radiating into the open country. Later these highways were wiped from the map by the thoughtless extension of the checkerboard streets."[26]

The AIA report, summarizing a chorus of similar criticism over more than a decade, calls the conventional grid a "tiresome system" and "old-fashioned." It is faulted for "deep cuts and fills on irregular land," as in Harrisburg, Pennsylvania,
147 whereas City Beautiful streets "follow the lines of least resistance." Philadelphia's plan is called an "unyielding and ugly rectangular system," and Nicholas Scull is scolded for repeating it at Reading, Pennsylvania, on a *hilly* site.[27] This classic plan, which had originated with Penn, now received a strong diagonal called Fairmount Parkway linking City Hall with a new palatial art museum set in a pre-existing park.

For Daniel Burnham, the apostle of the City Beautiful, diagonals save time, and "prevent congestion by dividing and segregating traffic." Their job is to get us to the center as quickly as possible, to divert unnecessary traffic from the center, and to let those who want to cross the center without stopping do so directly. His Chicago
235 Plan of 1909 stages a tremendous concentration on the business district with a series

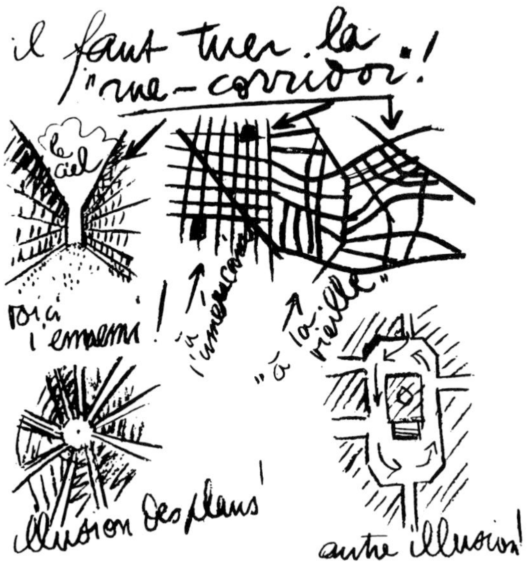

234 Le Corbusier, drawing attacking "corridor streets," from his Précisions sur un état présent de l'architecture *(1930).*

235 Detail from Daniel Burnham and Edward Bennett, Plan of Chicago *(1909). The drawing shows the center of town, with the projected City Hall at the confluence of diagonal arteries, and, in the foreground, the zone of the railway stations west of the river.*

of diagonals plunging through the famous grid toward a new civic center. But his final word is on the side of esthetic satisfaction. "There is a true glory in mere length," he writes, "in vistas longer than the eye can reach, in roads of arrow-like purpose that speed unswerving in their flight."[28]

One final "advantage" of the diagonal extolled by City Beautiful partisans was actually a disadvantage of the Grand Manner, now presented as a blessing. A diagonal cutting through a grid, or through a less regular extant pattern based on traditional building lots, will create triangular blocks hard to subdivide and occupy. In the case of Haussmann's Paris, these blocks were adjusted internally, with pairs of *Pl.23* back-to-back building lots that were regularly spaced toward the streets flanking the long sides of the triangle and became progressively shallower until they turned into one or more single-span lots toward the tip. Not concerned with details of housing, on the other hand, the City Beautiful saw in these triangular blocks opportunities for public buildings of unusual design. Left in the hands of private owners, small corner lots of this sort would be of little worth and probably be seen as a nuisance. Stretched to a good part of a block or the whole of it, the shape would inspire a noteworthy public statement.[29]

TRIVIUM AND *POLYVIUM*

In building up a plan in the Grand Manner, the main skill lies in the coordination of diagonal arteries. The simplest systematic grouping is the *trivium*.

The *trivium*, a meeting of three radial streets at, or their divergence from, a piazza, is of course affiliated with Renaissance experiments with radial schemes of urbanism; but it is less totalitarian and much more flexible. It has enormous potential to concentrate an urban area of variable size upon a crucial rallying point to which all traffic will flow, or conversely, from which all traffic will fan out evenly.

This device has no exact precedent in antiquity or the Middle Ages, except for the more or less regular Y intersections that were common in "organic" layouts, and the uneven convergence of streets at critical points like city gates or bridges. The occasional presence of a third irregular arm at a Y-intersection does not constitute a *trivium* in the Baroque sense. (An example is the place known in medieval Rome as the "Trevio," which survives in the name of the Trevi Fountain.) In the planned *trivium*, the central prong is axial, and the side ones in equal or near-equal relationship to it; and there is always a square as the source space of the three prongs.

The first application of this Baroque device was in Rome. If we discount a very imperfect specimen that took shape by 1500 on the Vatican side of the Castel S. Angelo bridge, it appeared at two spots almost simultaneously, in the 1530s. In at *237* least one case, and probably both, the *trivium* was a completion of previous street arrangements and not an idea fully conceived and executed at one time. The Banchi *trivium* opened up the congested neighborhood at the only crossing point to the Vatican territory on the right bank; the Popolo *trivium* brought order to the ragged unbuilt area in front of Piazza del Popolo, and channeled visitors from the north *Pl.21* toward all sectors of the historic city.[30]

The Banchi *trivium*, on the city side of the river, owed its middle prong to a short medieval street on axis with the Ponte S. Angelo, which became the financial center of the city in the 15th century and was accordingly renamed Via de' Banchi. The western prong, opened under Pope Paul III (1534–49) at an acute angle to Via de' Banchi, had a reasonable excuse: it joined in a short straight line the bridge with the new church of the Florentines started by the Medici Pope Leo X (1513–21). It was when Paul, quite arbitrarily and as a purely esthetic decision, matched this new street with one to the east run at an almost equivalent angle that the Banchi *trivium* took shape.

The same happened a little earlier, and on a much larger scale, at the Piazza del
237 Popolo. The central line of the Corso there corresponded to the ancient Via Lata, the
Pl.21 urban stretch of the Flaminian Way. Leo ran a straight street, the present Via di Ripetta, at an oblique angle to the Via Lata, from Piazza del Popolo to the Medici palace (later known as Palazzo Madama). He may also have started planning a corresponding eastern prong. But it was under Paul that this prong, the present Via del Babuino, then called Via Paolina Trifaria or "of the three ways," was actually built. The three streets do not meet exactly at a point. Although the angle between the Corso and the side streets is the same (23.5 degrees), Via del Babuino meets the Corso axis a little farther south than Via di Ripetta, so that the head plots are unequal in size. That was to be the challenge of the 17th century—to build two
Pl.22 domed churches on these plots that would be made to look identical by artfully manipulating the plans.

This striking urban conceit of the *trivium* found no immediate favor. At the end of the century, we find a marginal echo of Rome in the little nearby town of Bagnaia. The European discovery of the *trivium* comes, rather, in the middle of the 17th century—not out of urban experiments but through garden design. Le Nôtre deserves most of the credit, and his great scheme for Vaux-le-Vicomte, the place of honor. His way was prepared by the gardens of the château of Richelieu in Touraine, from 1627–37, designed by J. Lemercier. What the direct inspiration from
236 Italian gardens might have been proves almost impossible to ascertain. The *trivium* at the Villa Montalto on the Esquiline, the estate of the future Pope Sixtus V (1585–90) whose general plan for Rome is commonly viewed as the opening episode of Baroque urbanism, was very similar in origin to the two first urban *trivia* in Rome: the northern ray followed the line of an extant suburban street, the Strada di Suburra; the southern merely reflected this angle.[31] These rays fan out *towards* the villa from a gate in the garden walls. Le Nôtre reverses this orientation, making the main building the point of emanation.

238 At any rate the superb *patte d'oie* of Versailles linking up with the highways of Paris is surely an urban rendition of landscape design, as its magnificent pendant at the garden end of the palace affirms. There is considerable evidence to believe that Le Nôtre was responsible for both. The focal point was now the princely palace, the head plots were grandly designed (after a brief hesitation) as the royal stables, and the three avenues were lined with trees. This was probably the first Western example of the tree-lined urban street, if we discount the special case of Dutch canal streets (for which see below).[32]

It was the prestigious and magisterial example of Versailles that popularized the *trivium*, and even then convincing urban successors are few. In the 18th century, under the Bourbon kings of Spain and Naples, two residence-cities, Aranjuez and Caserta, imitated Versailles. The *trivium* emanating from the palace at Caserta was to organize the town, but the urban component of this plan was never executed. St.
240 Petersburg had the greatest princely *trivium* of the 18th century. The three radials fan out from the Admiralty Building with its focal tower. The scheme was fully formulated first in 1737–38. It took advantage of the already extant Nevsky
258 Prospekt, laid out between 1712 and 1718 to connect the Admiralty with the old Novgorod Road at the periphery, and Gorokhovaia Street which became the central prong. Kalinin (Tver) also developed an impressive *trivium* emanating from a semicircular square (now Soviet Square) and given Neoclassical head pavilions in the spirit of the salient twin churches at the Piazza del Popolo. The *trivium* in

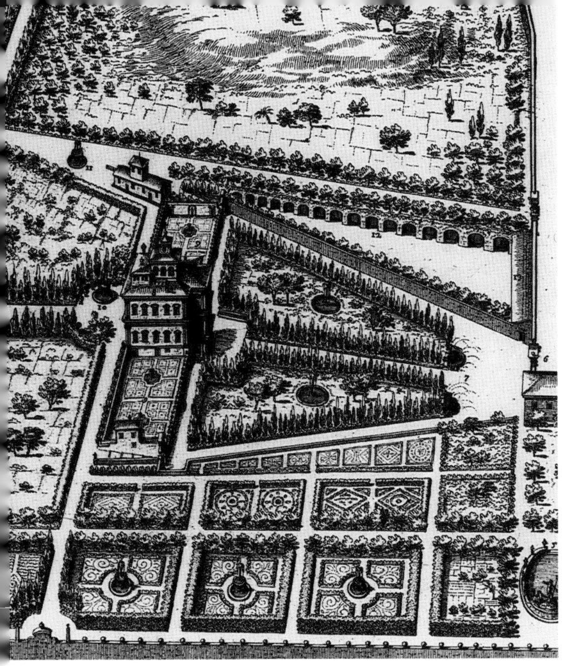

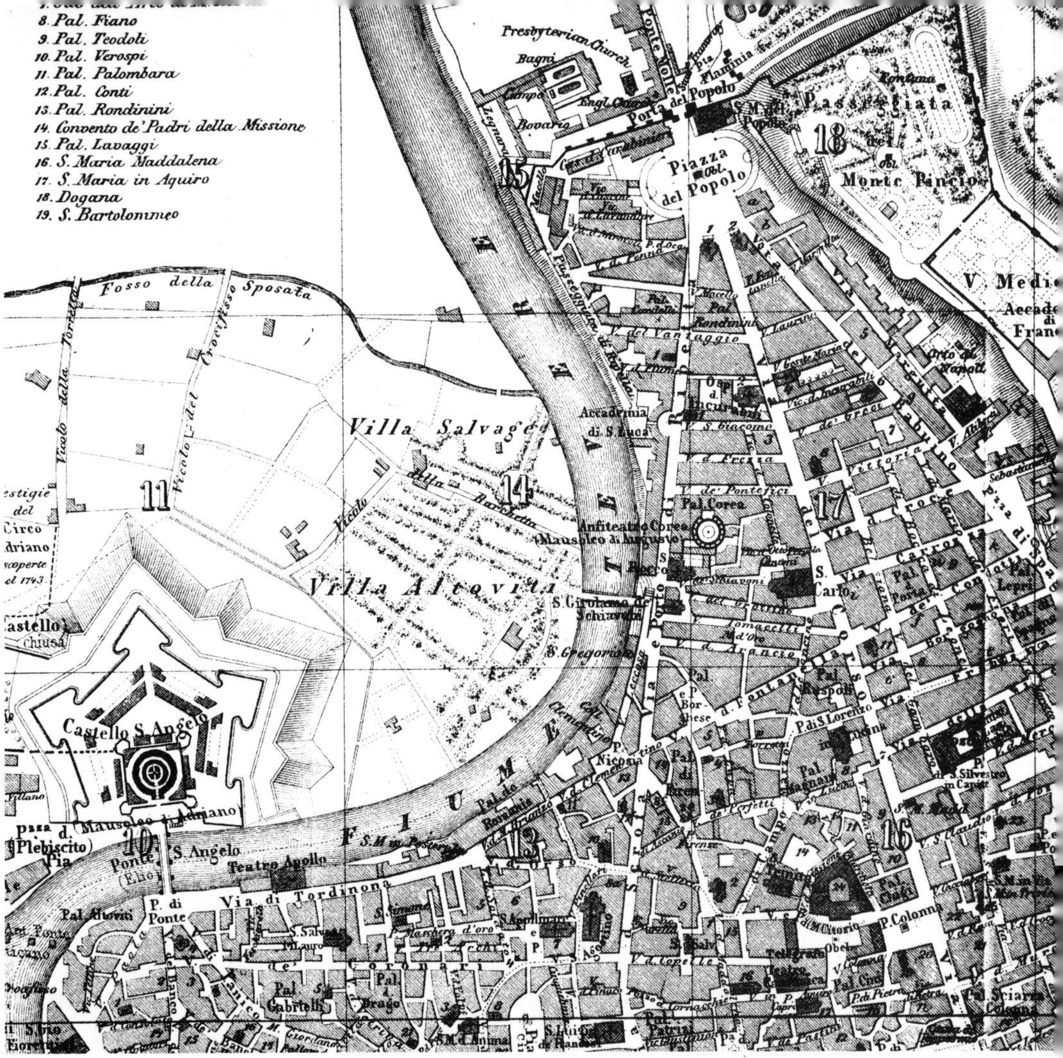

236 *Rome, Villa Montalto, garden* trivium*; engraving from G. B. Falda's* Li giardini di Roma *(1642).*

237 *Rome, Baedeker map of 1883, showing the* trivium *at Piazza del Popolo at the north entrance to the city (top, right of river), and the Banchi* trivium *across from Castel S. Angelo (bottom left).*

238 *Versailles (France), view of the palace and town.*

241, Berlin's new quarter of Friedrichstadt, which focused on a circular open space
253 known as the Rondell, had trees only in one side fork. (The *trivium* did not survive the bombing of the Second World War, though the circular plaza, drastically rebuilt as Mehring-Platz, is there after a fashion.) In the early 19th century, the plan for the new Athens, capital of the kingdom of Greece, reiterated with great effect for a modern city the palace-*trivium* combination of Versailles.

A generation or two later, past the mid-century, the symbolism in even such faint-hearted imitations of absolute power was thoroughly anachronistic. The appetite of modern traffic resisted formal elegancies, and the *trivium* made way for more practical, stellated patterns. It survived chiefly in two areas. The first was in the replanning that followed the demolition of city walls, where the configuration of bastions and the points of focus constituted by the old city gates suggested three-
242 pronged systems. A good example is Joseph Stübben's design of 1888 for Cologne's semicircular suburban extension over its demolished ramparts, with a series of small *trivia* marking the spots where the gates had been. The same idea was at work earlier in the century in the Nouvelle Athènes section of Louis-Philippe's Paris, along the boulevard that traces the line of the dismantled wall of the Farmers-General.

A second opportunity was the railroad terminal, the new city gate. The *trivium* in classic or approximate form fronts the station at places like Strasbourg, Grenoble, Sélestat, and Remiremont in France, and would have at Amsterdam South according
Pl.19 to H. P. Berlage's 1915 plan had the station been built. Since a lateral approach road along the façade was a natural provision in the planning of the station area, the three prongs might not meet at a point converging on the station, but rather the side prongs might be moved out to the edges of a kind of street-plaza that underscored the stretch of the façade (e.g. Le Mans).

The fanning out of radials in groups larger than three can proceed from orthogonal, polygonal, or circular cores. Four diagonal streets may emanate from the corners of a square or rectangular public space, more or less regularly. Perfect examples are rare: Madison, Wisconsin, has already been cited. The proliferation in stages of Haussmann's design for the Paris of the Second Empire produced flexible schemes of diagonals reaching out to targets at unequal distances. Examples would include the Place du Château-d'Eau (now Place de la Republique) and Place de l'Opéra.

The ideal of the circular arrangement is the full *rond-point* like the Place de
Pl.23 l'Etoile in Paris, with its sunburst of twelve streets. By contrast, earlier attempts like

239 Paris, Place de France, a project of the time of Henri IV (1589–1610). The area in question was just inside the old city wall between Porte St.-Antoine and Porte du Temple. The only executed elements of the scheme were the present Rue Charlot and Rue de Turenne, which converge at the Boulevard du Temple.

240 St. Petersburg (Russia), map of 1834 (after a drawing by W. B. Clarke), detail showing the Admiralty Building and the three avenues emanating radially from it. Nevsky Prospekt is the northernmost prong.

241 below *Berlin, the* trivium *of the* Rondell, *in a painting by an anonymous artist, 1735. The view is looking north over Friedrichstadt, a gridded new quarter added to the medieval city in 1688 and extended in 1721. The middle prong is Friedrichstrasse, which meets Unter den Linden at the extreme north (cf. Ills. 252, 253). The bent left prong was subsequently straightened at the expense of a curved hook at the Rondell. The circular* platz *was actually much larger than it appears here.*

242 below right *Cologne (Germany), master plan for a suburban ring development along the former walls, by Joseph Stübben, 1888. The trident intersections mark the sites of the former city gates.*

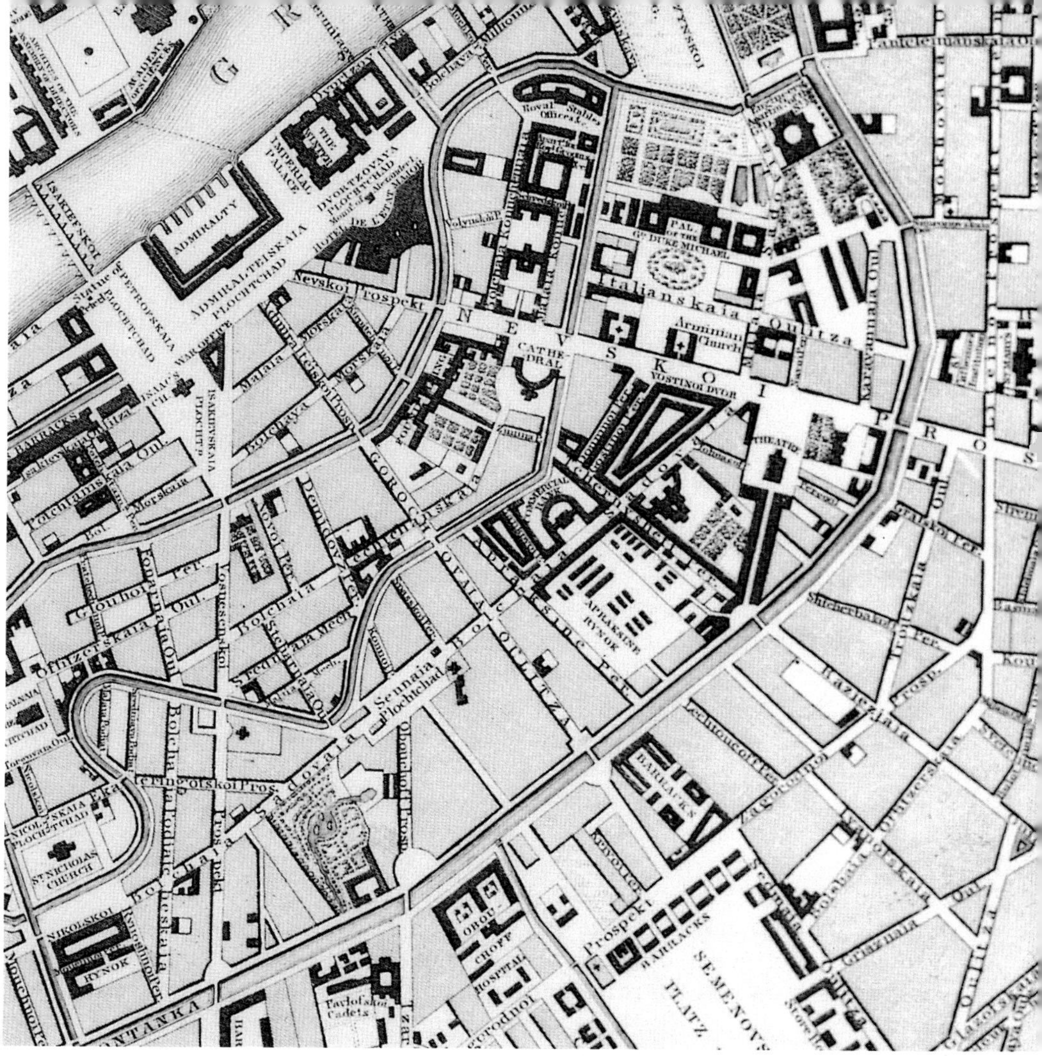

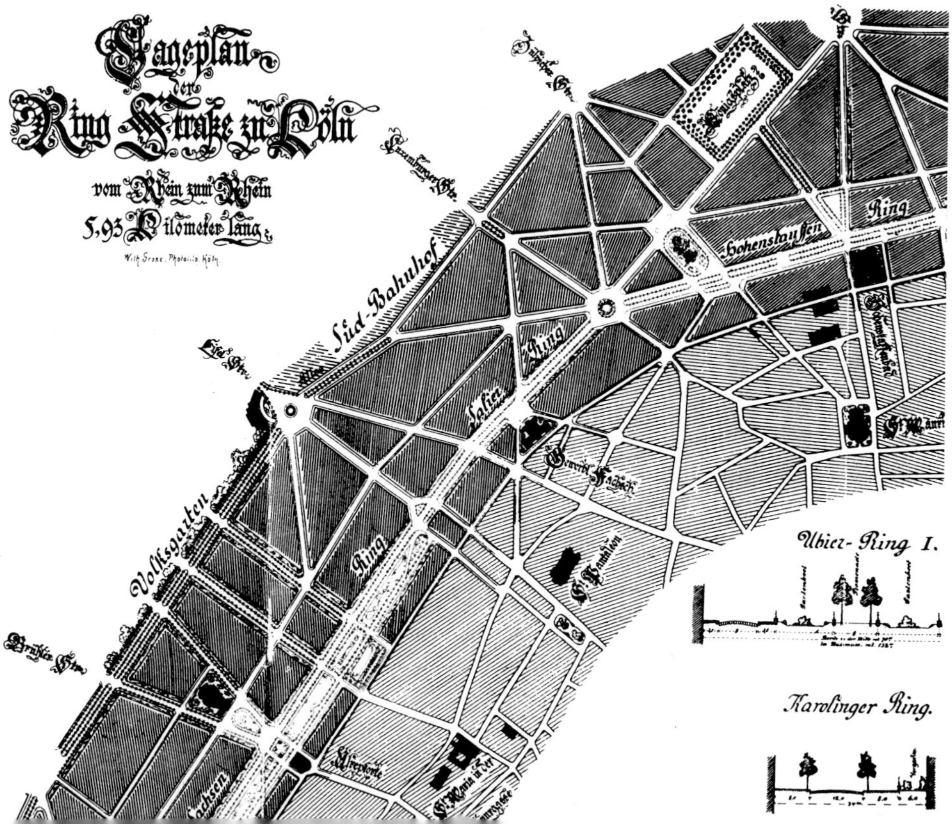

the early 17th-century Place des Victoires, also in Paris, seem botched. The *rond-*
225 *point* originates in landscape design, where it refers to a large circular clearing in the
woods. Its initial transfer was probably extra-urban. The gardens of the château of
Chambord were probably the first to feature these circular clearings, where court
ladies gathered to socialize and follow ongoing boar or stag hunts in the forest cut
through by radiating *allées*. The English version of the urban *rond-point* is the so-
called "spider web," in which main hubs are connected with straight feeder streets
212 drawn at right angles to the radials. This is a feature of the Wren and Evelyn plans
176 for post-Fire London, and will reappear in Edwin Lutyens's plan for New Delhi. The
inspiration may have come from ideal town plans like those in D. Speckle's
159 *Architectura von Festungen* of 1608, or even Palmanova itself.

The half-circle is also a cross-over from gardens. One of the definitions of *rond-*
point in garden terminology was the half-circle facing the main entrance to an estate.
The urban form has at its inception the famous Parisian project for the Place de
239 France, planned under Henri IV. This was intended as a new city-gate square in
the vicinity of the Temple: avenues would radiate from it between seven public buildings bordering the open space. Symbolically it would be the gate to the whole of France: the avenues were to be named after seven major provinces, the ring streets that connected them after others, and the extensions of the radials beyond the ring streets after others still. Another magnificent project was that by Victor Louis at Bordeaux from 1785: a generous semicircular *place* on the waterfront opened up toward the city with thirteen radial avenues representing the thirteen newly independent United States of America with which Bordeaux's merchants traded heavily. At the Place de l'Odéon in Paris of 1779–82 a modest version of these schemes was at last fully realized.

THE GRAND MANNER

The Grand Manner is not the currency of little towns. It is neither practical nor modest. Perceived as an expansive pattern of sweeping vistas, its relation to topography and prior urban arrangements is arbitrary, its effects often grandiloquent. Typically, behind designs in the Grand Manner stands a powerful, centrist State whose resources and undiluted authority make possible the extravagant urban vision of ramrod-straight avenues, vast uniformly bordered squares, and a suitable accompaniment of monumental public buildings. This is, in fact, a public urbanism. It speaks of ceremony, processional intentions, a regimented public life. The street holds the promise of pomp: it traverses the city with single-minded purpose and sports accessories like triumphal arches, obelisks and free-standing fountains. All this architectural drama subsumes the untidiness of our common routines. Shielded by the spacious envelopes, most of us continue to manage our plain existence, ready to gather into attendant crowds when the high business of the Grand Manner city needs its popular complement.

Pl.20 Palmyra (Syria), looking from the tetrapylon down the grand colonnade to the monumental arch—embellishments made to this Roman provincial city in the late 2nd and early 3rd centuries AD. *Both tetrapylon and arch serve as hinges where the angle of the colonnade street changes.*

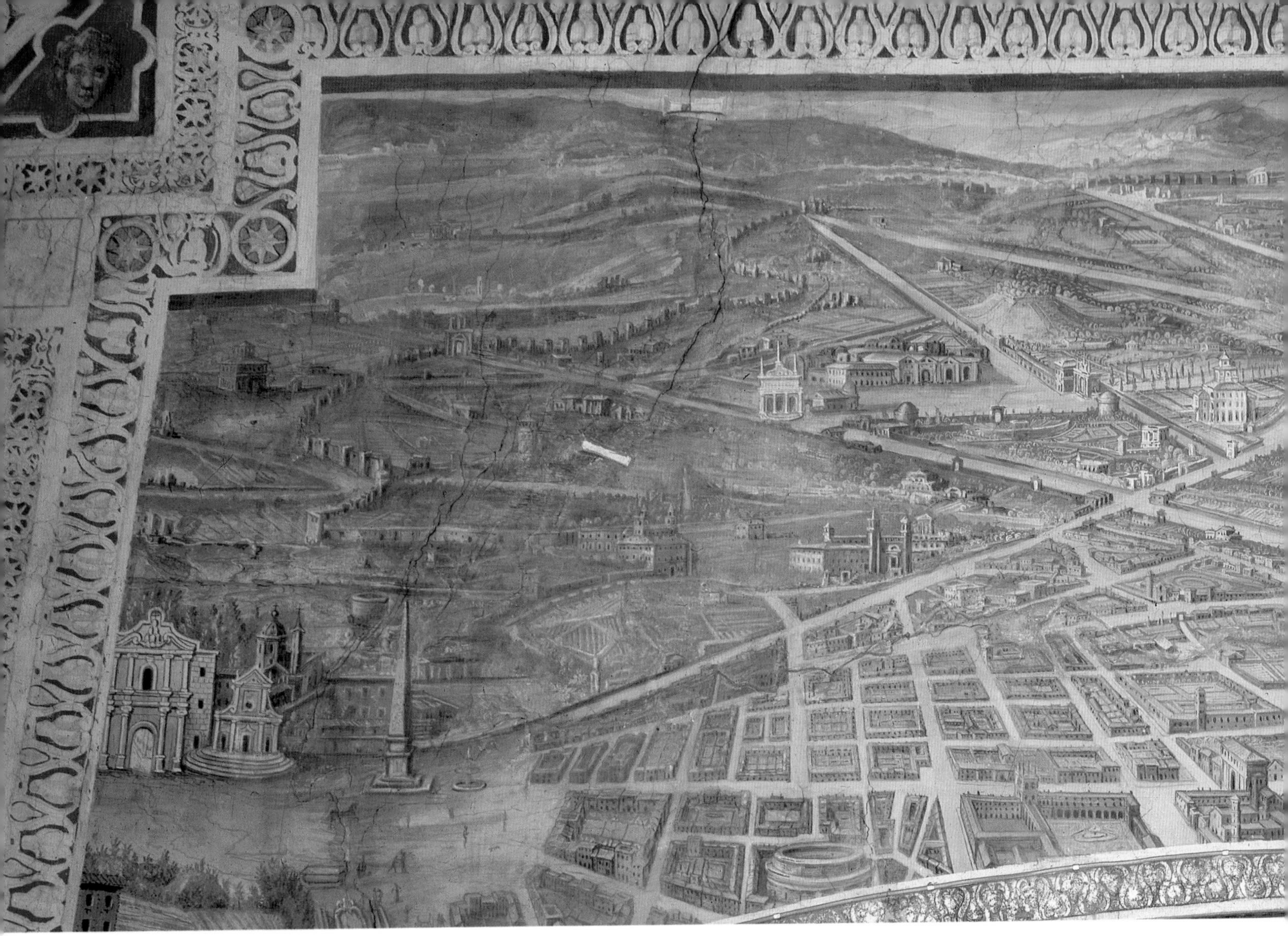

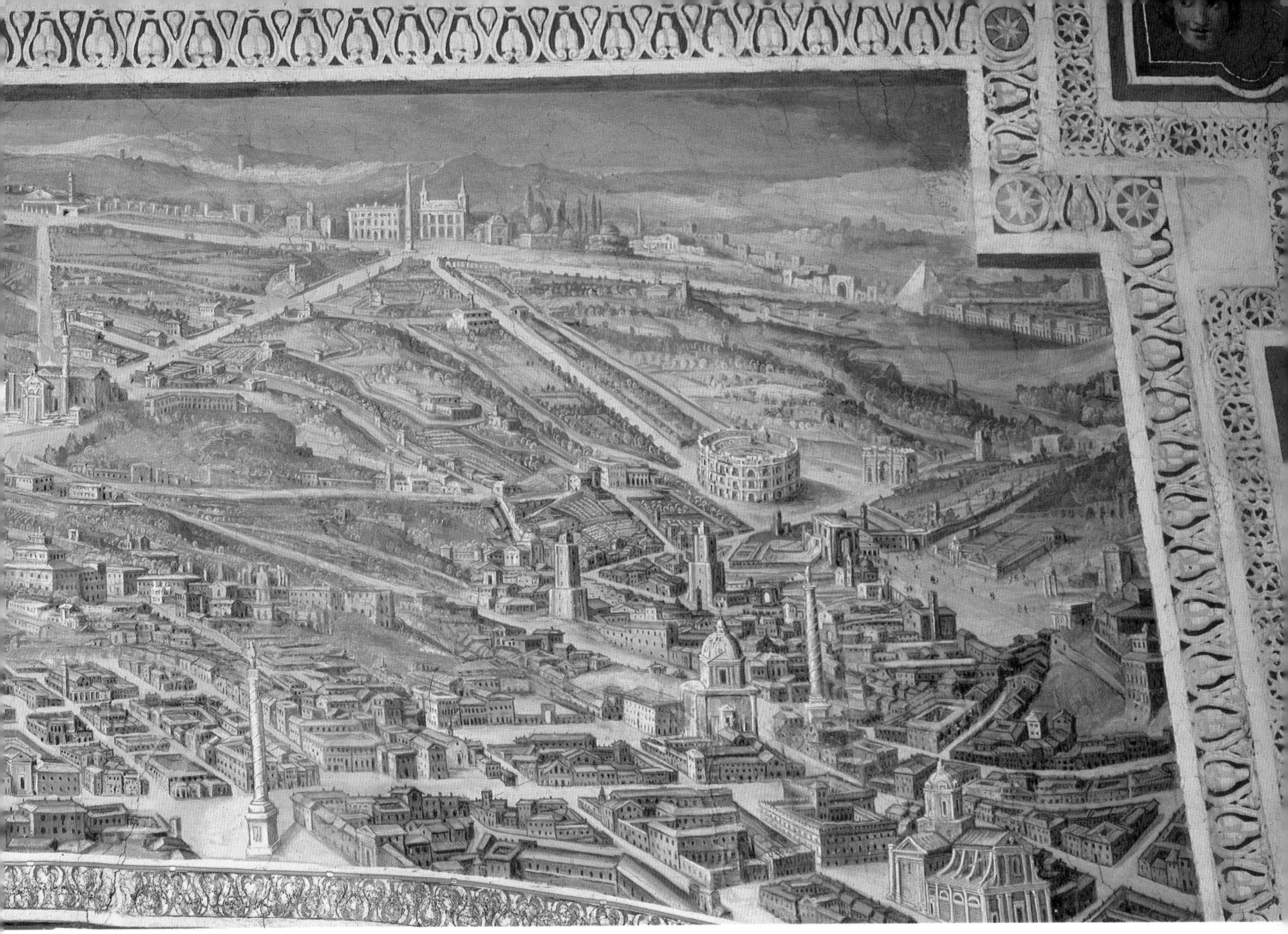

The making of Baroque townscape: Rome

Pl.21 above *The replanning of Rome in the 1530s, and chiefly in 1585–90 by Pope Sixtus V and his architect, Domenico Fontana, introduced the most enduring themes of the Baroque Grand Manner—notably the* trivium, *emphatic straight and diagonal streets, and a variety of urban markers and monuments. A contemporary fresco in the Vatican Library displays Sixtus and Fontana's great plan.*

We are looking east, with the Piazza del Popolo at the far left and the Capitol at the far right, linked by the straight Corso. The Piazza del Popolo stands at the head of the trivium *created in the 1530s. Sixtus marked it with an obelisk, and projected a fourth street to the east, that would have slashed past the Trinità dei Monti to S. Maria Maggiore and on to the Lateran, both also punctuated by obelisks (a scheme only partly realized). Halfway between the Trinità and S. Maria Maggiore is the "bellissima croce" where this Strada Felice crossed the Strada Pia, leading out to the Porta Pia in the northeastern walls. In the center foreground is the column of Marcus Aurelius; to the right, Trajan's Column.*

Pl.22 far left *The twin Baroque churches of S. Maria di Montesanto and S. Maria dei Miracoli, built in the 1660s–70s to give architectural shape to the Piazza del* Popolo trivium *(far left in the fresco,* above) *and mask its slight irregularity.*

The grand axis

Pl.23 left *Paris, looking southeast. The course of the Champs-Elysées is interrupted by a burst of radial avenues sharing the Arc de Triomphe as a terminal vista.*

Pl.24 above *Canberra (Australia): a view from Mount Ainslie down the axis linking the War Memorial to the new Parliament Building.*

Spaces, markers and monuments

Pl.25 The Grand Manner deals in lavish space. Lyon's Place Bellecour is one of the largest squares not only in France but in Europe, and was particularly vast in proportion to the historic city. From a drill ground in the 16th century it became a public square in the 17th, with rows of trees and a pall-mall field. As a place royale *under Louis XIV, it was ennobled by an equestrian statue of the king—a favorite urban focal marker—and palatial façades at its two narrower ends. Both had a political message of absolutism; and both were destroyed at the Revolution. In an equally political reply, Napoleon I had the façades rebuilt, and Charles X replaced the statue.*

From the hillside beyond, the square is overlooked by the late 19th-century basilica of Notre-Dame de Fourvière and the "Tour Métallique" (1893), inspired by the Eiffel Tower.

Pl.26 The fountain as urban focus: the Piazza Nettuno in Bologna (Italy) was created to display Giambologna's Neptune Fountain of 1563.

Pl.27 above right *The skyscraper as axial vista marker: the Transamerica Building in San Francisco (by Pereira Associates, 1973) fixes the view down Columbus Avenue, which cuts diagonally across the city.*

Pl.28 right *The triumphal arch: the All India War Memorial Arch in New Delhi's grand axis, King's Way (now Rajpath), by Sir Edwin Lutyens (1931), commemorates Indian Army dead; for Lord Chelmsford, a former viceroy, it was a monument to "the ideal and fact of British rule over India." Beyond is an empty canopy that formerly held a statue of George V.*

CLUB DE LA PRESSE

BOULEVARDS AND AVENUES

In modern parlance these two street types are considered interchangeable, but their origins and early history in the Baroque period are in fact quite distinct. What they have in common is that they were both extra-urban, fringe elements that found themselves incorporated within an extending city fabric, and thereby provided urban models for the future.

The boulevard started as a boundary between city and country. Its structure rests on the defensive wall, which by the Baroque period was usually an earthen rampart *243*
rather than a stone curtain. The practice of planting trees on ramparts goes back to the late 16th century. Speckle recommends the practice on the grounds that landscaped ramparts would conceal the precise edge of town from the approaching enemy, especially in flat areas with scant vegetation. For military engineers, the roots of big trees were a means to strengthen the embankments against concentrated cannon fire during an attempted breach. When visibility became a problem, the trees would be cut down. But the citizens saw the chance of a pleasant shady promenade with fine views of the countryside from on high. It was this notion that prevailed wherever bastioned walls lost their urgency as means of defense.

In 1670, with the destruction of the medieval walls of Paris and the filling of the old moats, these sites were transformed into broad elevated promenades, planted with double rows of trees and accessible to carriages and pedestrians. They were crossed by only a few streets at the old city gates, which were in turn replaced by grand triumphal arches. These tree-lined ramparts eventually became a system of connected public promenades, "a recreational zone at the edge of the city."[33] But they were not intended as transportation arteries. First they were called *cours* or *remparts*, but soon the name that stuck was *boulevards*, after a former bastion, the Grand Boulevart, north of Porte St.-Antoine. By the late 18th century, the west end boulevards of Paris were lined with luxury stores, cafés and theaters.

This fashion of changing fortifications to promenades was not widespread in Europe until Napoleon. Before his time city walls were decommissioned only in France. Where the walls came down, ambitious provincial intendants in the later 18th century, and the planners of Napoleon in the first decade of the 19th projected distended systems of boulevards and connecting public spaces as magnificent frames for the city edge. Bordeaux replaced its ramparts with *cours* under the intendant Aubert de Tourny and extended its crown of squares all along the riverfront. Toulouse was earlier. Of the full ring of vast *allées* that were to replace the old walls, *244*
the Promenade de l'Esplanade and the oval Grand-Rond with its six radiating arteries were completed in 1752–54—a small fragment of the projected ensemble—and this without the uniform houses that were intended to border the public spaces. In the Netherlands, a school of landscape designers specializing in the greening of ramparts was active throughout the 19th century, represented best by three generations of the Zocher family—Johann David Zocher (1763–1817), Jan David Zocher, Jr. (1791–1870), and the latter's son, Louis Paul Zocher.

The origin of the avenue is largely rural. Avenues, François Loyer, a recent student of 19th-century Paris, writes, were roads in the country "lined with tall trees to distinguish them from the surrounding landscape of leafy forests, low hedges, and fields of crops."[34] They were abstract and straight, to contrast with the undulating rural landscape, and they were approach axes to important features in that landscape—an aristocrat's estate, a farm, or a village. In the 16th century a version of this rural avenue became ubiquitous in France with the practice of planting trees along the principal post roads. By the late 17th century avenues led right up to city

Pl.29 Kalinin Prospekt in Moscow restates the monumental urbanism of Socialist Realism in a Modernist idiom; M. V. Posokhin, designer-in-chief, 1962–67.

Pl.30 Post-Modern Grand Manner: Montpellier (France), view from the Place du Nombre d'Or in the new residential quarter of Antigone, designed by Ricardo Bofill and the Taller de Arquitectura in 1978–80. "Each construction is a monument," Bofill proclaims, "each public space a theater."

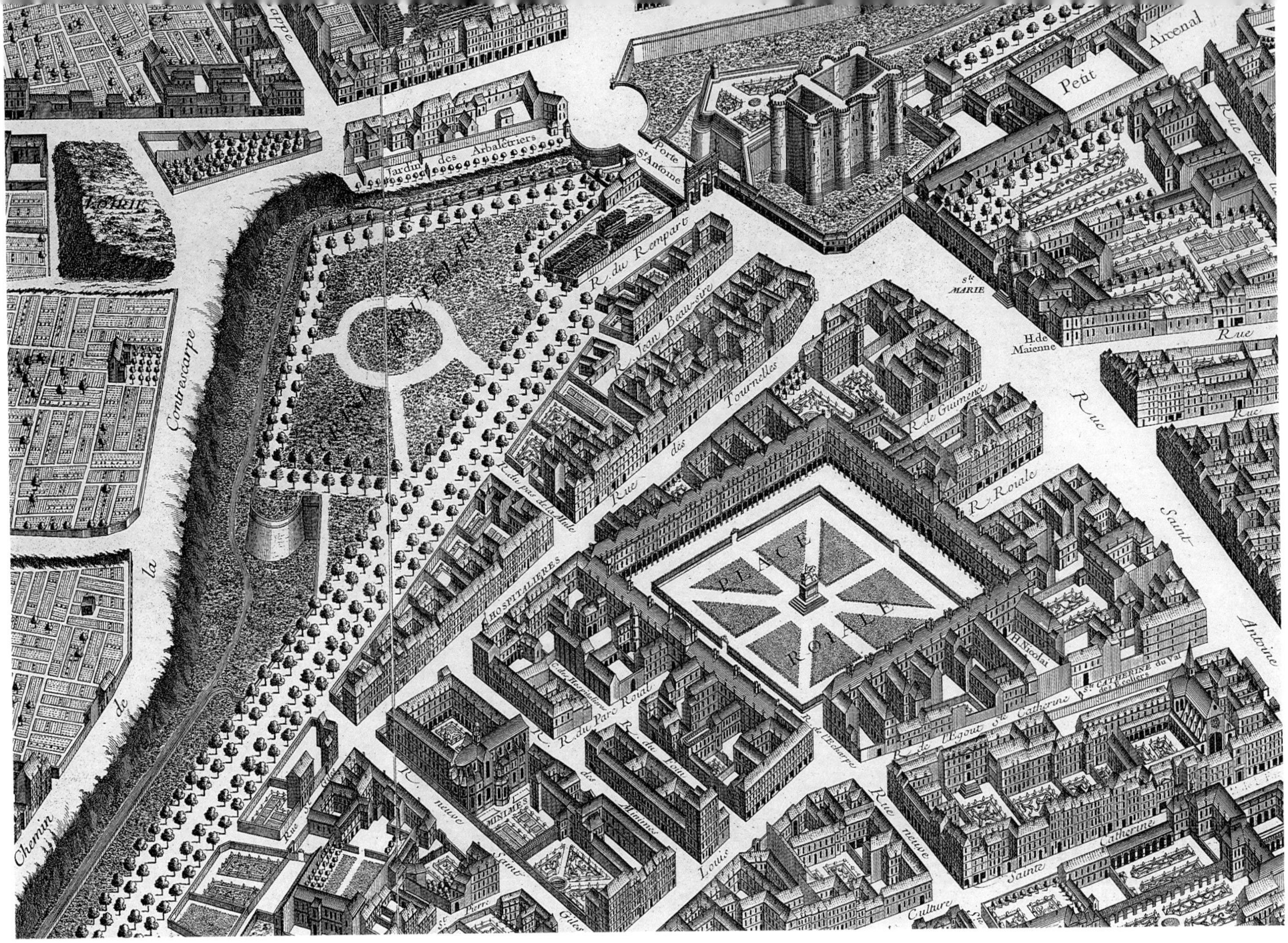

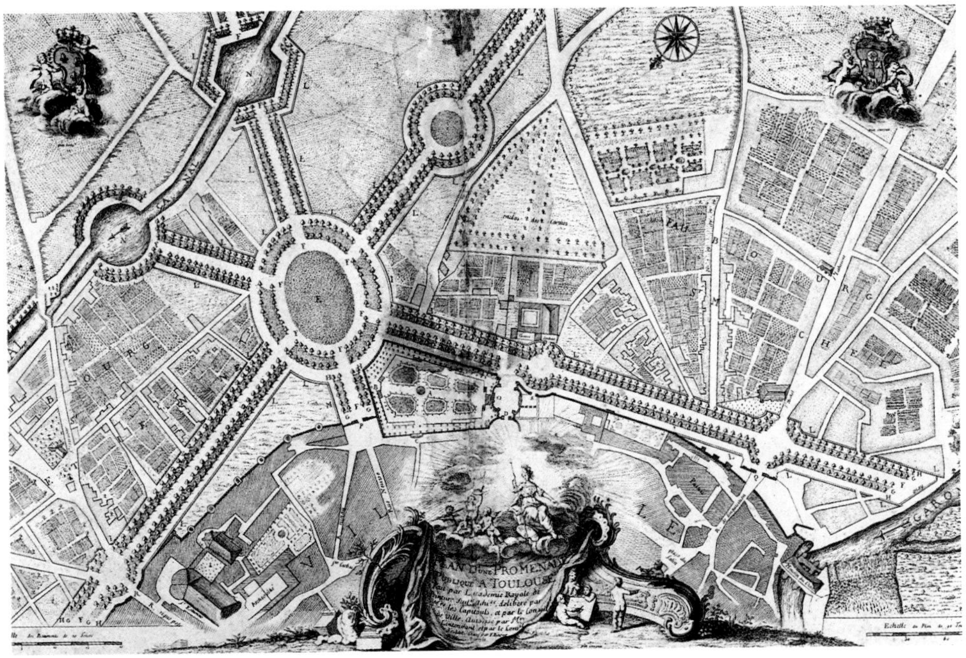

243 *Paris, detail of the Turgot Plan (1734–39) showing the landscaping of the ramparts at the Porte St.-Antoine, by the Bastille. The bastion is the Grand Boulevart. Place Royale (now des Vosges), the first of the planned royal squares (1605–12), is at bottom center, just within the tree-lined extension of the Rue du Rempart.*

244 *Toulouse (France), project for the Promenade de l'Esplanade and the Grand-Rond, 1752.*

gates, as well as large institutions like hospitals at the city edge. In Paris, the new Hôtel des Invalides on the southwestern fringe had three avenues converging upon its main southern front—a proper *trivium* in the mode of Versailles—and an esplanade on the opposite side leading down to the river.[35] A tree-lined avenue between Scheveningen and The Hague was installed in 1667 through the dunes, intended as a patrician promenade.

An equivalent of the rural avenue in garden design was the *allée*, a pathway lined with trees. The *allée* started in Renaissance Italy as the frame for the spatial organization of a new formal style of landscape garden. In France, the *allée* became an independent element in the garden plan, used for promenading and games, and it was sometimes extended beyond the enclosing wall of the garden. A famous example in Paris was the Avenue des Tuileries from the 1670s which Le Nôtre used as an extension of the central *allée* of the Tuileries gardens. This was the direct predecessor of the Avenue des Champs-Elysées in the modern city. 225

Two additional novelties belong in this story—the *cours* and the mall. Both have their origin in late 16th-century Italy, where they were the settings of new recreational pastimes. Both figured at the city edge, in proximity to the walls or in their residual spaces.

245 Paris, Cours la Reine, laid out in 1616; engraving by Aveline. It ran along the Seine to the west of the Tuileries gardens, just outside the city walls. Today it is part of the riverside road that passes the Grand and Petit Palais.

The *cours* was intended as an exclusive run for pleasure carriages. Its importance for the present discussion is that it transformed the garden *allée* into a place for vehicles. The origin of the idea may have been the Corso outside Florence, along the Arno. Marie de Médicis, the queen of Henri IV, introduced the ritual of coach rides to Paris in 1616, where a walled quadruple *allée*, the Cours la Reine, was laid out 245
for the purpose beside the Seine below the Tuileries. It had a circle in the middle and a stately arch at the entry. "Here it is," Evelyn wrote in his *Diary*, "that the Gallants, & the Ladys of the Court take the ayre & divert themselves, as with us in Hide-Parke, the middle Circle being Capable to Containe an hundred coaches to turne commodiously, & the larger of the Plantations for 5 or 6 coaches a breast." Others followed: in Paris, the Cours de Vincennes; in Madrid, the Prado; in Rome, the Forum whose ruin-filled central space was levelled and tree-lined in 1656.

The mall was initially installed for the game of pall-mall. It consisted of a flat strip of packed surface some 400 yards (365 m.) long, planted with grass, which served as the bowling green, and lanes of traffic on either side. Since the hard ball could be dangerous, the mall was closed in on either side by high fences. The game was of French origin, being played in the south of France as early as the 13th century, but it became a favorite of high society in the 17th century. The first recorded malls were in Italy, and then in Paris, adjacent to the city walls, in 1597 and 1599. Charles I introduced the game to England and set it up at Pall Mall. Charles II moved it to the Mall in St. James's Park, a broad avenue with four lines of trees, while Pall Mall 246
itself became a public road soon bordered with fine houses.

The avenues planted for pall mall became places of promenade, and since they were usually on or near the fortifications, also of military parades. Promenades were also laid out for their own sake, the earliest in England being at the spa of Tunbridge Wells, from 1638. In early Boston, several tree-lined walks on Boston Common were called malls, and there is record of other malls in Newburyport, Massachusetts, and Brunswick, Maine.[36]

One other place of public promenade was offered by some of the new formal squares that proliferated in Europe during the 18th century. An early and rather unlikely example is Queen Square in Bristol, laid out behind the river quays starting in 1699. It was a residential square in the English manner, but was cut into equal quadrants by straight rows of trees: three rows edged the square, and a double-row cross axis formed the quadrants.

Even these urban locations, however, did not bring about the transformation of the *allée* into a true urban avenue. For that one needed the orderly assembly of buildings, traffic, and rows of trees, and the incorporation of this design as part of the street system of a city interior. The key locations for this development were Amsterdam and Versailles.

247 The tree-lined canal street was a Dutch invention of the early 17th century, and was given its classic form in the 1607 expansion plan of Amsterdam. The three new girdle canals were lined with burgher houses, and between the houses and the canals, rows of elms were planted. If this created a pleasant waterside promenade, it was also a traffic artery and a working quay. But this particular arrangement remained an isolated regional form.

The more consequential model was the tree-lined avenue as it appeared in the
238 main *trivium* of Versailles. By the mid-18th century, the tree-lined avenue had become standard for French urban design in expansion projects like those at
244 Toulouse and Lyon. When Napoleon's armies swept across Europe, the avenue came with them as a familiar stamp of French imperium. His local governors laid them out, and built waterside promenades, "in Brussels, Düsseldorf, Koblenz, Lucca, Rome, and Burgos between 1809 and 1814, and began the boulevards of Turin, which were later planted."[37]

240 The layout of St. Petersburg combined the French and Dutch fashions, in line with Peter the Great's foreign sympathies. The great *trivium* focused on the Admiralty Building was of course a Versailles transplant, but main canal streets cut across the avenues. The Venetian man of letters Count Francesco Algarotti, during his visit in the summer of 1739, asserted that this homage to Dutch planning was mere affectation, without the practical logic of the original source. "It was solely in memory of Holland," he wrote, "that he planted rows of trees along the streets and bisected them with canals, which certainly do not serve the same purpose here as do those of Amsterdam and Utrecht."[38]

By the second half of the 19th century, the distinction between "avenue" and "boulevard" in Europe had largely evaporated. With the planted stretches of the old walls, the original boulevards, now within the limits of the expanding cities, look-alikes were spawned that were independent of the line of urban defenses. As early as the 1830s, the introduction of new design features, popularized in Great Britain, both to the interior avenue and to the original boulevards created a level of uniformity. These features included underground storm drains and sewers, and, visible to the eye, macadam paving, house numbering, mail boxes, and most important of all, sidewalks. To accommodate these changes the Grands Boulevards in Paris were regraded, shaving away as much as six feet (2 m.) of earth and clearing away the remains of old ramparts and counterscarps. Haussmann had this precedent to fall back on when he launched his epic campaign to modernize the capital some twenty years later. His new boulevards, beginning with the Boulevard
259, de Sébastopol, brought a once exclusively suburban scale and form into the old
225 center of Paris, and were used to subdivide it.

248 The urban boulevard was divided into three distinct strips. The sidewalks were for shoppers and shopping; the roadway was for rapid traffic; and the rows of trees provided the break between these two functions. "Moreover," Loyer writes, "the boulevards created the large-scale network needed to give the city as a whole a clearly defined structure. The boulevard was a line of communication, and also a boundary line between areas of town."[39] The houses did not count in the overall

246 opposite *London, Pall Mall and the Mall in St. James's Park; detail of an early 18th-century engraving by Johannes Kip. The Mall, now London's principal route for ceremonial processions, originated as a pall-mall playing field. It was laid out in 1660 by the great French landscape architect Le Nôtre as a part of Charles II's plan for St James's Park. Although the game fell out of favor within a century, the Mall retained its popularity as a fashionable promenade for courtiers, fortune seekers, and "priestesses of Venus." Charles I's earlier pall-mall field, transformed into an elegant residential street, runs parallel to the left.*

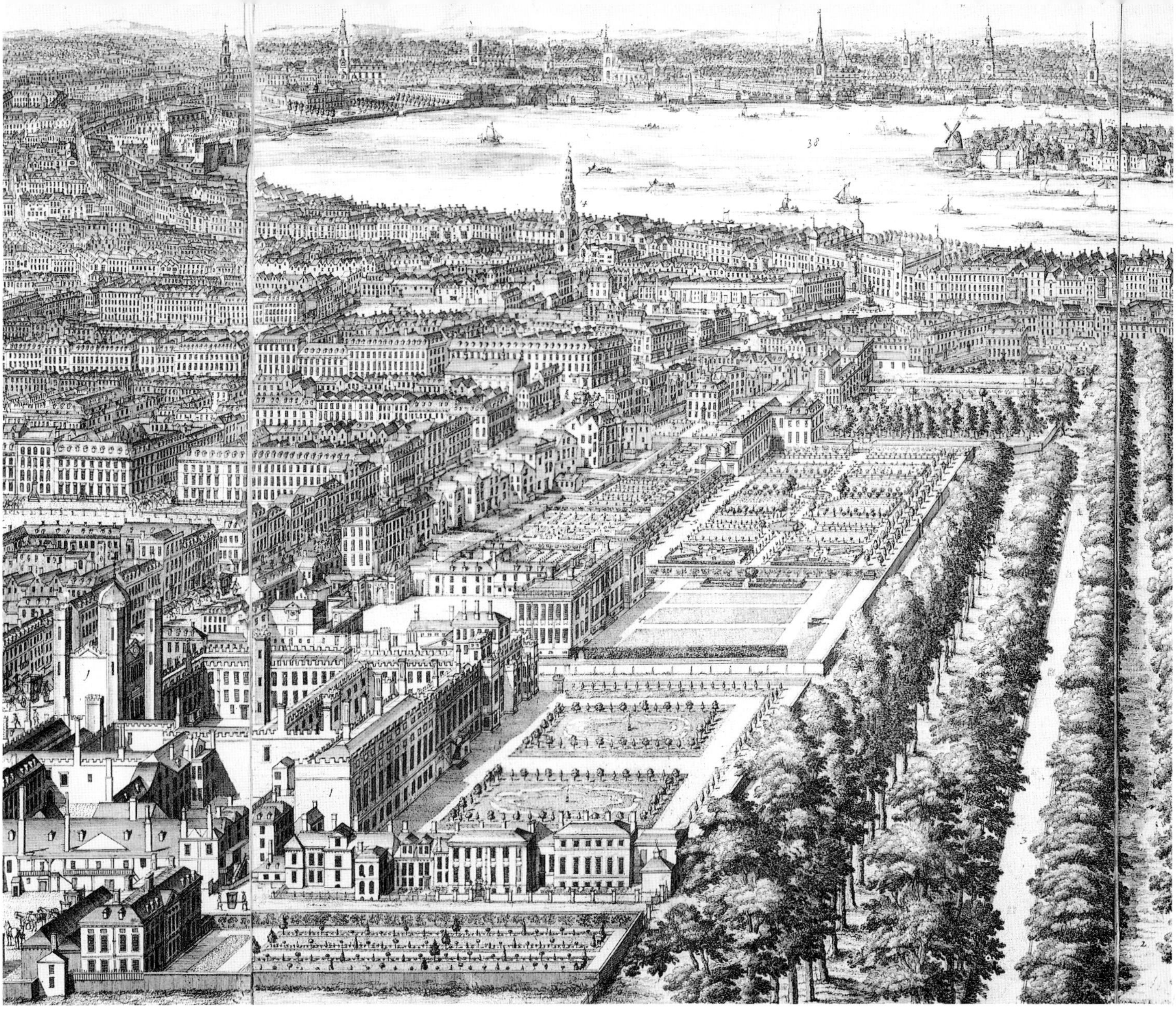

247 right *Leiden (The Netherlands), view from the Borstel bridge near the Hoogstraat, engraving by N. van de Meer, 1764. The tree-lined canal streets of Holland, unlike princely expressions of the tree-lined vista elsewhere in Europe, were built by collective city administrations as urban tributaries of a commercial port system.*

impression, which was one of fluid movement, beyond setting the outer limit of the boulevard space.

248 This space was too wide to be read as the closed volume of a traditional street, despite the commercial activity and social life it was able to shelter. The shopping zones, hidden from the roadway by the tree screens, acted independently, as if each sidewalk were its own street. Many at the time found the scale of the wide open prospects, and the insistent similarity, alienating. These boulevards disrupted the integrity and social structure of the old close-knit working-class *quartiers*, as they were intended to. But within a generation the popularity of the boulevards was assured.

The only serious attempt to modify this immensely successful format of the Haussmannian boulevard came early in this century. This was the *boulevard à*
249 *redans* of Eugène Hénard, the planning head of the city, which indented the street front at regular intervals alternating wedge-shaped building blocks in sharp points, in a manner reminiscent of Vauban's bastion systems, with trees. His rationale was that this new freedom would bring relief to the rigidity of flat continuous street walls and the unwavering rows of trees, and that it would reduce the number of interior courts and would enhance the economic value of the property by increasing direct street frontage. A variant type of *alignement brisé* serrated the street wall into shallow zigzags. Neither of these schemes caught on, but they may well have had some bearing on later Modernist massing. The jagged plan of the housing estate on Frankfurt's Burchfeldstrasse, of the 1920s, is probably acknowledging Hénard's *alignement brisé*.

To the English and the Americans, trees were a feature of residential streets, not of the town center. At the turn of the century London had almost no tree-lined streets except for the Thames Embankment. In the United States, "avenue" and "boulevard" had their own connotations. "Avenues" were primary traffic streets, and therefore not likely to encourage elegant tenancy. "Boulevards" were the green
250 connectors of parks in the periphery, and were made popular by Frederick Law Olmsted in his park systems even before the City Beautiful movement. Broad and straight, with landscaped medians and fine bordering houses in generous landscaped lots behind dense rows of trees, boulevards were designed as idyllic stretches for pedestrians and slow coaches. Once safely out in the suburbs, they became "parkways," that moved in gentle curves along natural contours, looking out on broad expanses of landscape. The boulevard/parkway was a new type of residential

248 above left *Paris, junction of the Boulevard Voltaire and Boulevard Richard-Lenoir, 19th-century postcard. The monumental tree-lined boulevard matured into its fully developed form late in Haussmann's administration. Only with the building code of 1859's standardization of design elements (and generous provisions for their enforcement by city inspectors) could the extraordinarily coherent "urban vernacular" of Paris's boulevards be realized.*

249 above *Eugène Hénard, proposal for a variation of the classic boulevard: the* boulevard à redans, *where the building line is serrated to allow for an alternating arrangement of building blocks and tree clusters.*

250 Chicago (Illinois), Grand Boulevard, a view from 1892: the American idea of a "boulevard," not only tree-lined but with a planted median strip.

neighborhood for a genteel class that, Olmsted said, "is influenced by associations and natural tastes that unquestionably deserve to be fostered and encouraged." Commercial traffic, when allowed, was restricted to roadways on the far sides. It was only later that the car would usurp the boulevards/parkways for fast, unencumbered travel, and change their character into general traffic arteries.

UNIFORMITY AND THE CONTINUOUS FRONTAGE

In celebrating the straight line, symbol of order and speed, the Grand Manner downplays the individual character of the buildings that make up the street wall in favor of visual continuities. In new development, the streets are subjected to a uniform design, which may in fact run no deeper than the street wall itself. Otherwise, unifying elements are applied after the fact to conceal the irregularities of pre-existing streets.

Hellenistic and Roman practice provides clear examples of both kinds. In the old Greek cities, Hellenistic planners brought a semblance of uniform order through the judicious use of architectural curtains. The Hellenistic reworking of the agora at Athens preserves several such renegotiated effects: on the west side, for example, a continuous colonnade brought together a new archives building and the adjacent oddly grouped administrative complex.

The most deliberate urban enterprise of this kind, starting in the 1st century BC, was the colonnaded avenue that ran through the whole length of a town. The 256 elevations were not necessarily consistent, but even so they were quite ordered compared to the inturned, uncommunicative house lines of residential streets in Mesopotamian towns, say, or the customary jumble of market streets. A common aspect of this avenue was that the roadway was sunk below the bordering features, and continuous lateral steps made it easy to socialize and gave a powerful visual directionality to the street.

The often improvisational arcades that cadence the ground floor of many medieval streets are inspired less by an esthetic appreciation of the uniform street wall than they are by the desire for shelter from the discomforts of the weather and the convenience of street-oriented shops. As late as the *Laws of the Indies* which governed city-making in New Spain, arcades were prescribed for the plaza and the four principal streets that set out from it, because "they are of considerable convenience to the merchants who generally gather there" (Article 115).

The creation of continuous street walls that will enhance the perspective drive of the street channel begins in earnest during the 16th century. Building codes like the one for Rome promulgated in the bull of Pope Gregory XIII (1571–85) called *Quae publice utilia* (On Matters of Public Utility) laid down that proprietors of empty lots giving onto new streets must put up high walls along the front. The Roman code also sought to eliminate the narrow passages between houses which older legislation, based on a concept of proprietorship where a building lot was to be isolated on all four sides, had created. These corridors, often less than two feet (0.6 m.) wide, could now be utilized by the adjoining proprietors.

Standardization and uniformity were prized aspects of new towns or town extensions during the Baroque period. Urban planning in 18th-century Europe had a close correspondence to the philosophy of the period. Regularly shaped open spaces, uniform frontages, etc. were the physical counterparts of the century's preference for regulation and rationality in behavior. The codification of streets and house types in St. Petersburg, for example, went along with Peter the Great's orders for the shaving of beards and the adoption of standard "German," i.e., Western, dress. The street in a traditional Russian town was considered a restraint to the natural spread of the house, especially the courtyard or *dvor* which was the real focus of urban life. The urban order of St. Petersburg made daily life more public and disciplined, and according to no less a judge than Catherine the Great, made "the inhabitants . . . more docile and polite, less superstitious."[40]

The first uniformly designed ensembles had to do with rowhouses built as a group by single clients. In Rome speculative row housing, called *case in serie*, becomes familiar in the Renaissance. But there are even earlier medieval cases, such as the Borgo Ognissanti in Florence laid out in 1278, or the Goodramgate Terrace (also known as Our Lady's Row) in York from the 14th century. The rebuilding of the Petit Pont in Paris joining the Ile de la Cité with the Left Bank, traditionally assigned to Fra Giocondo around 1502–10, gave Paris its earliest planned urban unit, fully a century ahead of the first royal *places*. There were 34 identical arcaded houses on each side of the bridge, "built uniformly of brick with stone corners and . . . decorated with the statues of saints and the city coat of arms." But even the original bridge had 60 uniform houses built upon it in 1421.[41]

251 Ferrara (Italy), Via Mortara: uniform façades in the so-called Herculean Addition, a new gridded quarter laid out about 1490 under Ercole d'Este (1471–1505) to the designs of Biagio Rossetti.

John Evelyn insists on this sort of uniformity for the squares and streets of his own London plan. He cautions about courts, yards and gardens for houses "because of the fractions they will make," i.e., breaks in the street frontage of rowhouses; these yards and gardens should "therefore rarely [be] towards any principal street."[42] Uniformity was, of course, articulated. The royal *places* in Paris which Evelyn so admired tempered the curtain façades unified by continuous cornices and ground-story arcades, either by individuating the high slate roofs of the houses (as in the
243 Place des Vosges), or where the hipped roof ran uninterrupted around the square (Place Vendôme), by supplying the cut-off corners and centers of the long sides with pediments that broke the steady march of the dormers.

A particularly effective Baroque device was the exceedingly long building façade of uniform design, like the Manica Lunga, the service wing of the Palazzo del Quirinale stretching along the Strada Pia (now Via XX Settembre). Institutional buildings where such protracted length and sameness would be defensible were poorhouses, hospitals, and occupational housing. At random we might instance the Ospedale S. Michele in Rome's Trastevere quarter, and two 18th-century examples from Naples—the Albergo dei Poveri and the Quartiere dei Granili.

252, Among European cities, two of the most regimented were Dresden and Berlin.
253 Dresden, the capital of the electorate of Saxony, turned the process of issuing

252 *Berlin, Friedrichstrasse, rowhouses under construction; painting attributed to Dismar Dägen, 1732.*

253 *Berlin, detail of a map of 1737. North is at the bottom (cf. Ill. 151). The fortified medieval city has been extended by two planned suburbs—Dorotheenstadt immediately to the south of the River Spree, laid out in 1674, and the much larger triangular development of Friedrichstadt further south culminating in the circular plaza of the Rondell (see Ill. 241). The long central street is Friedrichstrasse* (above). *Unter den Linden ran between the two suburbs, from the palace grounds in the medieval city to the royal park, the Tiergarten (right center). The city wall was razed on the side of the new suburbs by 1760.*

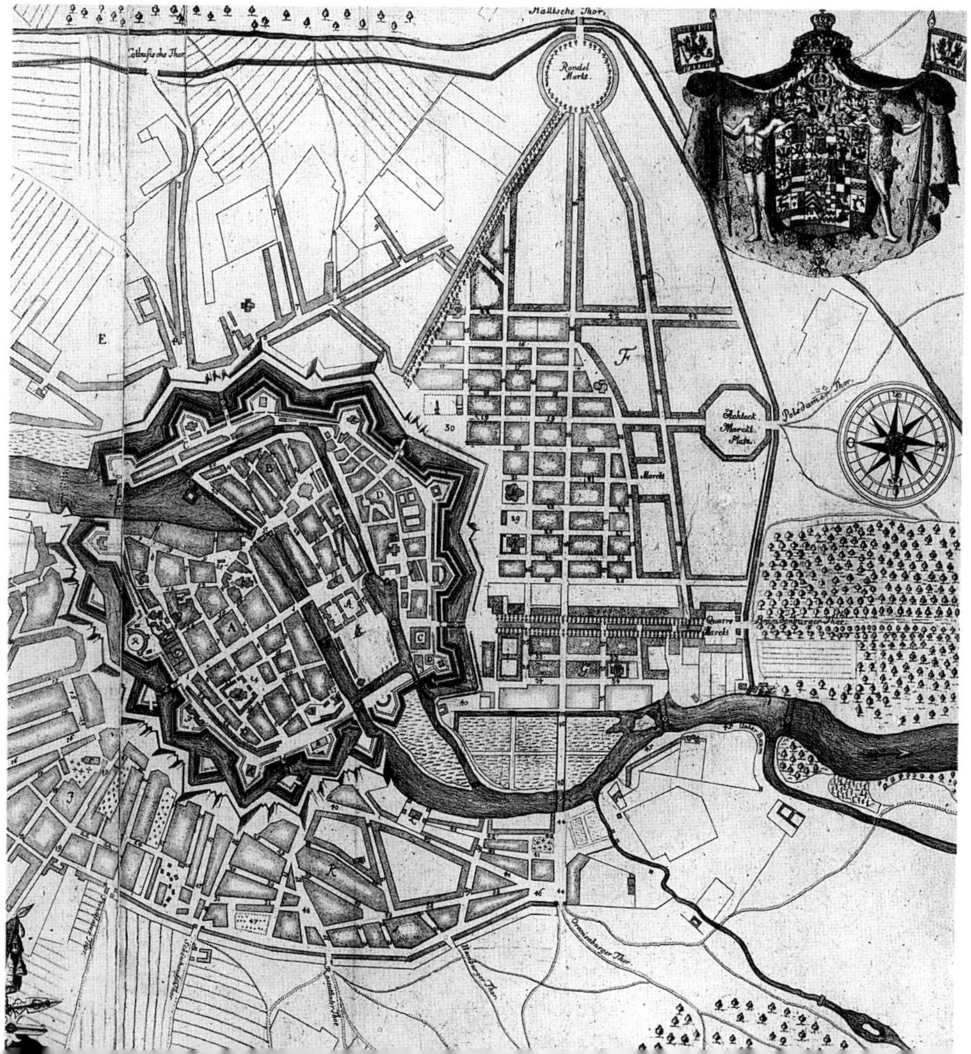

building permits for middle-class houses into a thorough review of each proposed design. The applicant was obliged to show not only the plans of his own house, but also "the outlines of neighboring houses and the layout of the streets."[43] Esthetic 252 coherence was even more Prussian in the new additions to Berlin during the late 17th century (with a final extension in 1721). The streets of Dorotheenstadt and Friedrichstadt were painted a uniform, very light gray; everything was prescribed, every house was carefully planned and numbered.[44]

Outside Europe, we have a carefully documented case study by Roberta Marx Delson for Portugal's new towns in Brazil.[45] In contrast to the 16th-century *Laws of the Indies* for New Spain, which prescribed the layout of towns but left their execution to the settlers, Portugal stipulated uniform façades from 1716 onwards throughout the 18th century. In the orders of 1747 for the town of Aracaty, to be built on the site of an older fishing hamlet, it is set down that when an old house has to be rebuilt, "it should be rebuilt in the form that [would give it] the same profile and appearance as the new houses." For the creation of Rio Negro, the *carta regia* of 1755 determines that the houses are to be "constructed in the same way on the exterior, while inside, each [resident] could do as he liked." And Governor Luis Antonio de Souza, in a communication of 1766, wrote to a judge that in the port community of Santos all future buildings were to follow prescribed norms, for

> one of the things to which the most cultivated nations are giving their attention at the present time is the symmetry and harmony of the buildings of new cities and towns. This is not only of practical benefit, but also gives pleasure, in that such good order expresses the lawfulness and culture of the inhabitants.

The effects of such regulatory vigilance can still be seen here and there in Brazil. Delson points out that in Mariana today you can still see that "the two-story colonial houses (*sobrados*) adjacent to each other resemble one enormous building, rather than separate houses."

An interesting twist in the case for standardization concerned the attitude of the colonial administration toward native Indians. As Governor José Xavier Machado Monteiro reasoned, in the new towns for Indians if all inhabitants were given identical amenities, including standardized houses with the same number of windows and doors, and standard-sized garden plots, "then all causes for envy and resulting dissension would be eliminated."[46] The unmentioned dividend was that standardization would also destroy the social structure resident in the old settlement patterns.

This use of rational planning to eradicate traditional living arrangements, and with them loyalties that may be at odds with the policies of the state, has modern correspondences. In Fascist plans for new native towns in Ethiopia, for example, the ancient grouping of native huts was regimented into strict rows. The housing policies of socialist states had similar underpinnings. A last, fortunately suspended, chapter was the master plan of the late dictator of Rumania, Ceaucescu, to demolish villages and replace them with uniform housing slabs of concrete.

The advent of the elevator-reliant tall building toward the end of the 19th century presented designers of the Grand Manner with worries. If the tall building were allowed to express itself as a sculptural, midspace object, it could not very easily be the constituent unit of an unbroken street wall. If it were forced to contiguous, street-defining conformity, cliffs of ten stories or more would tower over dark sunless canyons of public space. But the dawn of the skyscraper city was not imminent, not in Europe at least, and anticipatory designs did not find the collaboration of the tall building and the practices of the Grand Manner impossible.

254 Otto Wagner, proposal for the twenty-second district of Vienna, from his Die Grossstadt *(1911).*

Otto Wagner's 1911 *Grossstadt* project for the future metropolis (in his case Vienna) is, in fact, a modern reaffirmation of the Grand Manner. If Haussmann could bring a multi-story, mixed use uniformity to the boulevards he carved into medieval and later Paris, Wagner would apply the same uniformity to an entire new city. The apartment blocks would be taller and more massive than Haussmann's, the street channel would be wider, and the public domain would differ from the residential only in the size of its open spaces, the furnishings of fountains and monuments, and the lavish use of architectural ornament. 254

Burnham too, like Wagner, saw nothing incompatible between tall building blocks and the formal planning conventions of the Grand Manner. But he practiced in a country which, like England, had long been wedded to the ideal of the single-family house. The tall building was to be consigned to the city center, which would be devoted primarily to business. There now the Americans went higher than anyone else. In cities like Chicago and New York, they forced their great invention, the skyscraper, to produce the traditional urban effects of directional street corridors and enclosed public spaces. 235

It was against what seemed to them an artificial and near-sighted restraint of the skyscraper form that Modernists like Le Corbusier would begin to inveigh in the Twenties. Skyscrapers were marvelous, but not as servants of traditional street-scapes. The skyscraper "is a wonderful instrument of concentration: to be placed in the midst of vast open spaces," Le Corbusier wrote. In that pronouncement and others like it, the Modernists were preparing the demise of the historical city, and with it the international language of the Grand Manner.

But their triumph would have to wait until after the Second World War. In the intervening decades the Grand Manner was to write a spectacular new chapter. Most Western states were loath to replace the prescriptions of an urban design that so forcefully imaged power, authority, social order, and nationalist pride. Fascist Italy and Nazi Germany come foremost to mind. We think of the Haussmannizing
230 of Rome under Mussolini, and of the master plan for Berlin that was the brainchild
263 of the Führer himself aided by his young architect Albert Speer. But the same urban vision, without the grandiloquent rhetoric, touched many other cities across the world, from Reims and Madrid to Ankara, Meshhed and Baku.

How did planning authorities ensure the execution of uniform streets and squares? The surest way was to do the actual building themselves. Totalitarian states where the housing industry is centralized have no other alternative. A less costly method for the State, and the Baroque centuries availed themselves of it, was to build only the outer sheaths, the continuous façades, and leave the construction of the houses to the individuals who owned the plots. Louis XIV's Place Vendôme in Paris is a celebrated case. As period views show, the frame was finished first, in 1701, and only then did the sale of the building lots begin. In the end there was no connection between the subdivisions on the façades surrounding the *place* and the arrangement of courtyards and rooms behind them. Again, the Commission for the Building of St. Petersburg set up in the 1760s proposed that "the government erect façades on the squares and allow the houses behind them to be built as the owners planned."[47]

In Turin, a laboratory of the Baroque esthetic during its decades of expansion from the late 16th century to the early 18th, the rulers of the house of Savoy tried strict supervision.[48] Having issued design guidelines for the Città Nuova addition to the south of the Roman grid, drawn by the court engineer Carlo di Castellamonte in 1621, Charles Emanuel set up a committee of pre-eminent state officials accountable directly to him to make sure that all construction was in compliance. In addition to respecting these blueprints, the land owners were obliged to use only those building materials produced in the area of the Città Nuova. Twenty years later the Regent
255 Maria Cristina made personal grants of land around the new Piazza S. Carlo to high officials, bankers and aristocrats who were more susceptible to court pressure in building their residences according to the uniform design of Castellamonte. In the old city, the Via Nuova leading from the castle southward to the Roman walls called for a modern uniform casing of the medieval blocks. Finally, in the remaking of the cathedral square, owners ready to conform to the official design were given columns of white marble for their section of the continuous porticoes bordering the public space.

The habits established in these projects of the 17th century continued to mold a unified appearance for Turin and its new quarters for a long time. Even the most exuberant of Baroque architects, Guarino Guarini for example, did not extend the spatial intricacies of their architectural interiors onto the street façades. These were by and large restrained, almost self-effacing, willing to blend in with the continuous flow of the street channels. Only in Rome and its field of influence—notably Sicily—are Baroque buildings often not content with being definers of urban space. The street space becomes positive, something with shape and dynamism. Abutting

255 Turin (Italy), Piazza Reale, now Piazza S. Carlo, from a print in a collection of Turin images published in Amsterdam in 1682. The piazza was designed by Carlo di Castellamonte, 1621 ff., as the focus of a new gridded extension to the city. The Via Nuova (now Via Roma) connected it with Piazza Castello to the north, of 1584, and ran southward between the two churches of S. Carlo and S. Cristina shown at the far end of this view.

buildings are integrated with the pattern of movement defined by the street. Only there, in the work of architects like Bernini and Borromini, are the building fronts seen as expressive masses, stepping out into, and interacting with, the street space. The street, as Paolo Portoghesi puts it, "is animated by multiple episodes that challenge its quality of an inert corridor compressed between parallel planes."[49]

But then neither are the Baroque streets of Turin inert corridors. The power inherent in uniform street fronts is to create a sweeping perspective view and to direct it toward a terminal landmark. The vista is a prime device in urban design bound by the Baroque esthetic. So is the sense of spatial sweep, the corollary of speed.

VARIETY IN UNITY

The dangers of uniformity, the boredom of walking through urban spaces subject to the constant repetition of the same design, began to be voiced at the time of Laugier, in the mid-18th century. The Abbé spoke of "excessive uniformity, this greatest of all faults." Returning to the comparison between town and garden, he enjoined the planner to look at the work of Le Nôtre, where the formal and informal, the regular and the irregular, symmetry and variety are neighbors. So too the planning architect should vary details to such an extent that, walking through a town, each quarter will seem new and different, resulting in "a kind of irregularity and chaos which suits great towns so well."[50]

Variety was to be sought at several levels. A simple grid of streets was unimaginative. It was easy to lose your way with every quarter subjected to the same figure. Within the space of the streets, the façades of houses should not be left to the pleasure of private owners: public authority should determine the height limit in accordance with the width of each street, and should vary the type of façade from block to block. Laugier thought that the wealth of the Classical decorative system would be equal to the task.

Finally, there was the question of squares. Here Laugier was in good company. His contemporary the Abbé Ponz in Spain exhorted planners to set out a variety of neighborhood squares,

> the diversity of whose form will impart to the city as a whole a new beauty: some rectangular, others circular or elliptical, others still of three, six or eight angles, they will provoke enchantment and surprise in the eyes of the inhabitants themselves, and will arouse much admiration among strangers.[51]

And towns in the 18th century delivered on this score. For example, when in the
253 1730s Friedrich Wilhelm I of Prussia approved a series of squares inside the gates of the new customs wall surrounding Friedrichstadt, the planned extension of Berlin, they came in orthogonal, circular and octagonal shapes, with no pressing or self-evident grounds of practicality. The designers of new towns in Andalusia heeded their countryman Ponz's admonition not to emulate Holland, where "once you have seen one city, you might say you have seen them all." And the city-planners of Catherine the Great, busily urbanizing the Black Sea territories conquered from the Ottomans, devised squares as if they were illustrating a textbook on geometry.

The little-known work of William Hastie in Russia from about 1800 to 1820 is relevant here.[52] Formal public spaces of great geometric diversity are Hastie's most notable Baroque trait; otherwise, he advocated the grid. His plan of 1813 for Moscow envisaged a semicircular chain of squares along a ring road around the Kremlin and Kitai Gorod, at the junctures with the radial streets that converged on the city center. At Zemlianoi Gorod, he planned seven new squares which, along with the four existing ones, would follow the old rampart where it was met by the radial highways. These semicircular, round and polygonal spaces were projected on privately owned land, and ignored the city's prior fabric. For the city of Ekaterinoslav fifteen squares were projected; the high point of the plan was a semicircle with five streets converging upon it, to highlight Potemkin's palace.

The contest between variety and unity continued to occupy urban designers in the modern stages of the Grand Manner. The Paris of Haussmann relied on a uniform repertory of street furnishings and paving to subdue the façade variations permissible within the restrictions of the building code. Granite curbs, gray asphalt sidewalks, cobblestone roadways (at least until the fall of the Second Empire), and identical rows of plane trees or chestnuts established an overall monotony, which was accentuated by standardized street lamps, metal tree grates, pillar-shaped billboards, kiosks, and cast-iron drainpipes. The street walls themselves were basically monochrome.

When the reaction set in, it was as much against this overwhelming grayness as it was against the repetitiveness of façade design. In 1869 Charles Garnier's precocious outcry protested against "big straight streets that, although beautiful, are as cold and stiff as a dowager." He dreamed of the day when "a man will be able to build his house as he pleases, without worrying about whether or not it fits with his neighbor's. Cornices will shine with the colors of eternity; gold friezes will sparkle on façades."[53] By the turn of the century a new building code condoned, indeed incited, surface novelty and sculptural and picturesque effects.

Pl.19 Berlage's advocacy of uniform street fronts in Amsterdam around the time of the First World War had a more contemporary basis. Straight streets and housing

256 Timgad (Algeria), the colonnaded main east-west street and the Arch of Trajan, 2nd century AD.

blocks of strict architectural unity were prerequisites of the ideal socialist city form he saw as the blueprint of the future. Individual houses, even the apartment buildings of which city blocks were made in modern cities, were pointless artifacts of the past. Their fine articulations frittered away the street edge and ignored the collective nature of the new society. The solution had to be to group residences into single, block-filling buildings, deployed on a city-wide scale. The blocks on either side of a street were to be designed in concert; beyond the intersection, the design could change, as long as it remained consistent within its own block. The benefit of this orthodoxy was not just esthetic. By eliminating their outward architectural expression, class distinctions themselves would be eliminated.[54]

THE VISTA

The primary purpose of a vista is the framing of a distant view, so that it is seen through a composed foreground and is fixed at the opposite end by some worthy marker. Often one has one or the other of these effects, but not both. Since the foreground brackets and the terminal object play the main role in setting up a vista, the street channel in between need not hold to rigidly uniform elevations, provided it is straight and has enough visual direction to create a strong sense of perspective.

The formal vista was not unknown in Classical antiquity. The Romans were masters of it, but there is Hellenistic precedent as well. A good example is the redoing of the agora complex at Priene in the 2nd century BC where the arched
eastern gate framed a vista of stoa colonnades. The arch spanning a roadway is the 214
commonest ancient Roman vista device. The same feature often framed the vista at 256

257 Rome, Strada Pia, designed by Michelangelo for Pope Pius IV (1559–65); painting in the Lateran Palace. The terminal feature is Michelangelo's gate set against an ancient fortified gate just north of the original Porta Nomentana. In the foreground, the statues of the Dioscuri (Castor and Pollux) as horse-tamers are shown in a clearing at the summit of the Quirinal Hill.

257 both ends. (The Strada Pia in Rome terminating at the façade which Michelangelo set up in front of the old Porta Pia is in the antique tradition of ending the perspective of major urban streets at an arched gateway.) The Romans also used *nymphaea* and other such hinge buildings to provide a climax at the end of an approach and incidentally to conceal an awkward bend in the street line. Two examples: at Palmyra, a small theater was used to tie a new street in to the main axis; at Leptis, as the city was expanded along the main axis, which topography forced to bend, the wedge space between the old grid and the extension was filled by two market buildings. Also typical are four-sided markers for major crosspoints, roofed or unroofed, that offered no bar to one's path. An example of the latter is the tetrapylon
Pl.20 in Palmyra, in the center of a round plaza marking an intersection; the plaza was surrounded by stores and offices.

Pl.21 The example of Rome as re-planned by Sixtus V in the late 16th century refines the esthetic of the urban vista in a number of ways. The most effective, perhaps, is the use of the obelisk as a space marker. These thin, vertical accents fix the terminal point of a straight street without blocking what is behind. At the same time we have also the actual or proposed use of other historic remnants—the columns of Trajan and Marcus Aurelius; matching statues framing the street passage, rather than fixing the spatial extension of the roadway (the Horse-Tamers at the Quirinal, for example, actually projected by Michelangelo for his Strada Pia); ancient monuments like the Colosseum. 257

We should underline one further characteristic of Sistine Rome that enters the permanent legacy of the Baroque esthetic. It has to do with the cadence created along a single undeviating axis through the composition of bifocal segments. The main axis through the eastern hills, as it is rendered in the famous fresco in the Vatican Library, is cadenced by the Lateran obelisk at the southeastern end, the obelisk of S. Maria Maggiore on the Esquiline, the hilltop church of the Trinità dei Monti, and the Piazza del Popolo obelisk. In the same way, the Champs-Elysées and its extension that forms the great *voie triomphale* of Paris was later punctuated by the Horse-Tamers of Marly at the Tuileries end, the Arc de Triomphe, and the statue called *La Défense de Paris* set up in 1883 on the Montagne de Chante-Coq across the Pont de Neuilly, to provide the western focus of this matchless monumental axis. Pl.21 259, 260

Whatever the device, the vista is terminated in one of three ways that remain constant in later phases of the Grand Manner: it is *closed* as by a curtain (Michelangelo's Porta Pia, the Victor Emanuel Monument at the end of Via del Corso, also in Rome); it is *framed* by means of flanking or spanning features that allow for throughviews beyond (the Quirinal Horse-Tamers, the Arc de Triomphe); or it is *fixed* by means of some tall, unconcealing marker with a slender silhouette (e.g., the obelisks of Rome). The experience of any of these markers will depend on a range of factors, such as their size, the proportions of the avenue itself, and our position along its path.

A vista does not need to be defined by built walls, as long as the prospect is physically enclosed in some manner. Nevsky Prospekt in St. Petersburg, or Bolshaya Perspektiva (literally "Great Vista") as it was originally called, was an arrow-straight approach to the city from the east; having crossed the city edge at the Fontanka River, it ran through an unbuilt area with the Admiralty Building's tall thin spire as its beacon. Paved in stone and lined with rows of trees, it was an urban avenue without buildings, which started going up only after 1730. 240 258

258 St. Petersburg, Nevsky Prospekt crossing the Fontanka River, mid-18th-century drawing by M. I. Makhaev. The Anichkov Palace is on the left and the Admiralty in the distance (cf. Ill. 240).

The use of unattached midspace buildings in setting up vistas is a relatively modern option. It is encouraged by the Neoclassical penchant for public buildings set in their own pool of space, and becomes a central issue of urbanism with the later 19th-century debate on "disencumbering," that is, the clearing of attached structures from the frame of historic monuments and their presentation in the middle of an open space as if on a platter. Now of course nothing prevents a part of an attached building, the spire of a church for example, from becoming the vista marker of an avenue, but that is not quite the same thing as having the whole freestanding building act in the same capacity. Evelyn was precocious in this respect. He wanted the parish churches in his London plan built in the centers of "*spacious*
212 *areas, piazzas* &c. so as to be conspicuous to several streets, crossing upon them, as some of the Roman obelisks are; and others at the abutments and extremities of them."[55]

In this century, the skyscraper, when used within the urban conventions of the Grand Manner rather than catering exclusively to the skyline, can function effectively in the making of vistas. It has height on its side and roof-tops that can be molded into intentionally arresting crowns. As a spatial terminus for an urban vista, its potential was dramatized in a project by Eliel Saarinen of about 1920, where he anchored a high-speed thoroughfare through Grant Park in Chicago with a tall hotel building, like an oversized obelisk scaled to our modern prospects.[56] In practice, and much less dramatically, the same effect is produced by the RCA Building at Rockefeller Center in New York, at the end of the pedestrian street created off Fifth
Pl.27 Avenue, or more recently by the Transamerica Building in San Francisco as seen at the end of Columbus Avenue. As framing devices for a perspective, tall buildings have done service from Villeurbanne next to Lyon in the early Thirties to East
224 Berlin's Stalinallee (now Karl-Marx-Allee) in the Fifties.

MARKERS AND MONUMENTS

The Grand Manner has employed freestanding monuments for two purposes—to accent a vista, and to fix the space of a formal square. When the squares and the avenues leading into and out of them are correlated, a single monument can fulfill both purposes.

The repertory of monumental accents is quite limited, and most originate in Classical antiquity. Triumphal arches, commemorative columns, and equestrian statues were all familiar to Roman practice. They reappeared and prospered from the 15th century onward. We shall look at them in greater detail below.

In the case of public fountains, ancient Rome and the Baroque kept their own counsel. Antique fountains, whether of a plain basin or tub type or with an elevated architectural backdrop, held to the side of the streets. The freestanding midspace fountain with rich sculptural decoration is a signature of European Baroque. Evelyn praises them in his plan for London, these public fountains in the middle of piazzas which are "not as formerly immured with blind and melancholy walls."

The beginnings of the transformation of fountains into ornamented public monuments were in the later Middle Ages, especially in Italy. Distinguished examples are the Fontana Maggiore in Perugia by Nicola and Giovanni Pisano, and the Fonte Gaia by Jacopo della Quercia in Siena's Campo. In the 16th and 17th centuries, the scale expanded along with that of the public spaces, and hydraulic improvements added vigor and drama to the play of water. Squares were sometimes especially created to display a particularly splendid fountain. In Bologna, for
Pl.26 instance, Giambologna's Fountain of Neptune came first, in 1563, and the Piazza

Nettuno was shaped to contain it, including the demolition of extant property "per la veduta della Fontana" (so the fountain may be seen).[57]

With steps and perches for people to sit on, water to enjoy, and sculpture to admire, the fountains had all the makings of lively gathering places. The sculptural decor favored Classical mythology, and an elevated content of political and dynastic allegory often tempered the innocence of these popular monuments. The fountain of the Four Rivers in the Piazza Navona in Rome spoke of the rule of the Pamphili Pope Innocent X (1644–55) and of the Church Triumphant. The program might be distributed over two or more fountains. In the Maximilianstrasse of Augsburg, three fountains were built to a unified plan between 1589 and 1606: one honored Augustus, the city's founder; the middle one Mercury, the god of trade; and the northernmost, Hercules.[58]

The obelisk is a special case; it had no specifically urban destiny in its original Egyptian setting, nor in the use made of those transported by the emperors to Rome. It was Sixtus V who had the inspiration, perhaps on his architect Domenico Fontana's advice, to set up surviving ones in public places, beginning at the Piazza of *Pl.21* St. Peter's. The popularity of these formidable monoliths was due in good measure to their exotic origin and the feat of erecting them. One of the last to go up was the obelisk at the Place de la Concorde in Paris, a present from the Viceroy of Egypt, Mohammed Ali, to King Louis-Philippe in 1831. Always alert to conjuring parallels between ancient Rome and his regime, Mussolini transported stelae from Ethiopia, called them obelisks, and raised one of them on the axis of the so-called Via dei Trionfi (now Via di S. Gregorio) in Rome, at the opposite end from the Arch of Constantine.

Triumphal arches

The great surviving specimens in Rome which inspired modern phases of the Grand Manner—the arches of Titus, Septimius Severus, and Constantine—had a long pedigree and a large family throughout the Empire. The beginnings go back to the Republic, in the early 2nd century BC; according to Pliny, the purpose of the arches was "to raise the men whose statues stood upon them above all other mortals." These first arches were rather simple affairs with a single opening. That of Fabius Maximus spanned the Via Sacra at the entrance to the Roman Forum. With Augustus, monumental versions articulated by columns and architraves and elaborated with sculptural ornament made their appearance. They were erected both within cities and on the high roads of the Empire, on the occasion of an emperor's triumphal passage or, in the provinces, in honor of an imperial visit. The fancier among them had three openings, and most were topped by a triumphal chariot or quadriga. The attic of the Arch of Titus in Rome may have contained the eponymous emperor's ashes, but that was unusual.

Triumphal arches began to replace the simpler arched city gates in the Augustan era, the late 1st century BC and early 1st century AD. They also formed the entrance *256* to enclosed spaces like forums. An impressive triumphal arch formed the entrance to the Forum of Trajan in Rome, and an equestrian statue in honor of the Emperor stood in the middle of the open space; behind the basilica, in the court between two library buildings, rose a column 100 feet (30 m.) high decorated with a narrative frieze of his Dacian wars and surmounted by his statue. Here in one imperial complex, then, we encounter the full array of monumental effects available to the ancient Roman designer.

If we distinguish the triumphal arch among many other types of urban arches, both attached and freestanding, that punctuated Roman city form and the highways

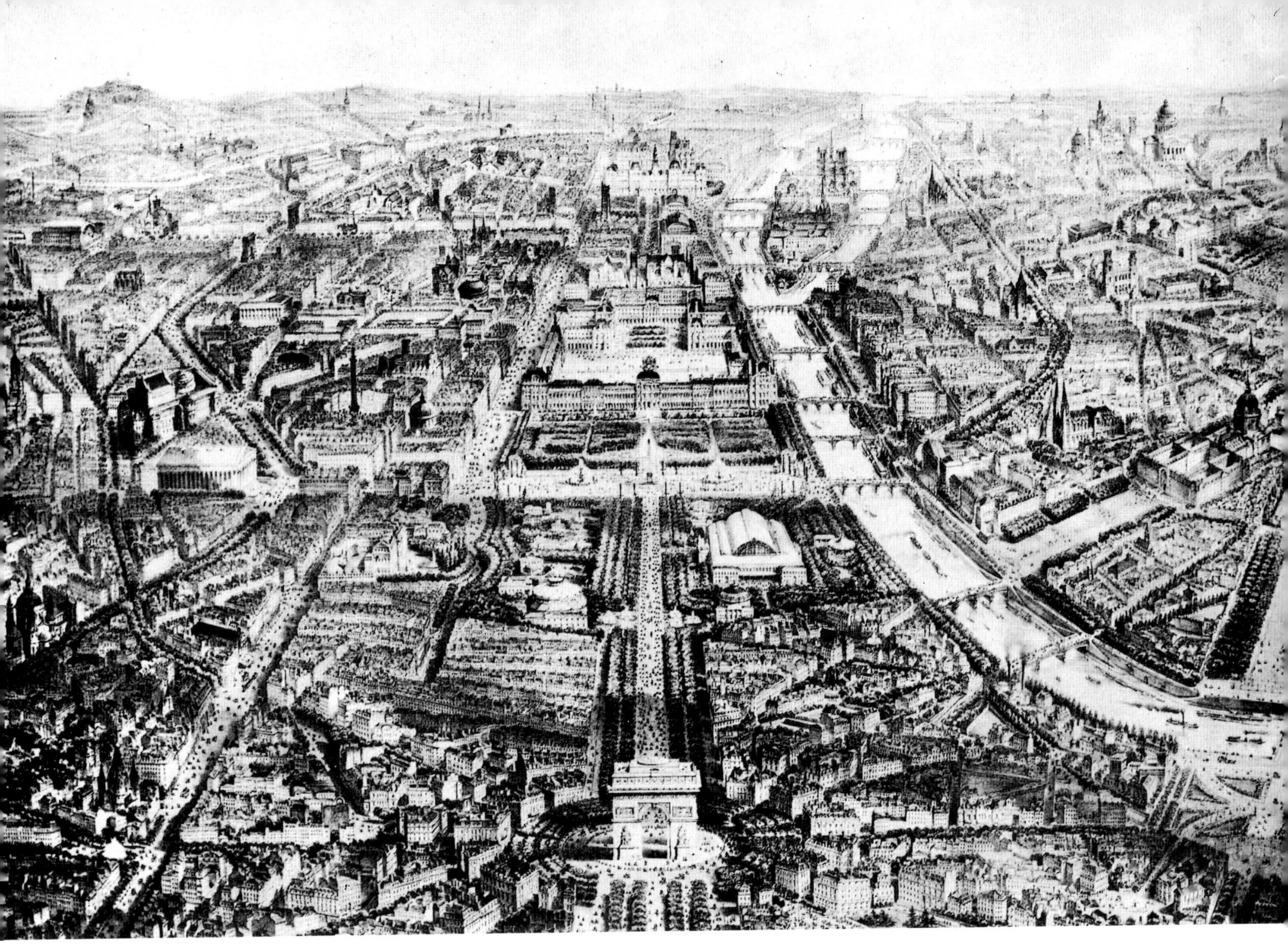

beyond it, it is because that was what carried the primary appeal in the Baroque period.[59] The 17th century resurrected the type both for its architectural form and for its political connotations. To enter a city through a triumphal arch was to celebrate the myth of a transcendent regime. It is certainly not fortuitous that the first systematic application of the triumphal arch for a city's gates was in Colbert's
259 plan for Paris for the 1670s, of which a few were executed. Laugier a century later had that example in mind when he deplored the mundane toll stations of the customs barrier, and called for magnificent triumphal arches to mark all major entrances to a well-ordered town. By the end of the century, Berlin's Branden-
262 burg Gate leading into Unter den Linden combined Roman motifs like the quadriga with a chaste Greek source—the entrance to the Acropolis of Athens called the Propylaea.

Some city gates gained historical legitimacy for their triumphal form by commemorating an actual victory. But the most celebrated monument of this kind is freestanding, and set on an eminence on an official approach road to the city. The
Pl.23 Arc de Triomphe in Paris was a key image in Napoleon Bonaparte's revival of Roman imperial iconography. At the opposite end of the Champs-Elysées another

259 Paris, a mid-19th-century bird's-eye view looking southeast toward the Arc de Triomphe, the Tuileries Palace, the Louvre, and the historic center (cf. Pl. 23). The city is still marked on the left by the curve of its walls (transformed into tree-lined boulevards), but slashed across by Haussmann's new streets. Note especially the straight Boulevard de Sébastopol, running north (left) on a line with Notre-Dame; its cutting, Haussmann wrote, "meant the disembowelling of the old Paris . . . by a wide central street piercing through and through this almost impossible maze" (see Ill. 225). Near the left-hand end of this boulevard two of Colbert's late 17th-century triumphal arches can be seen.

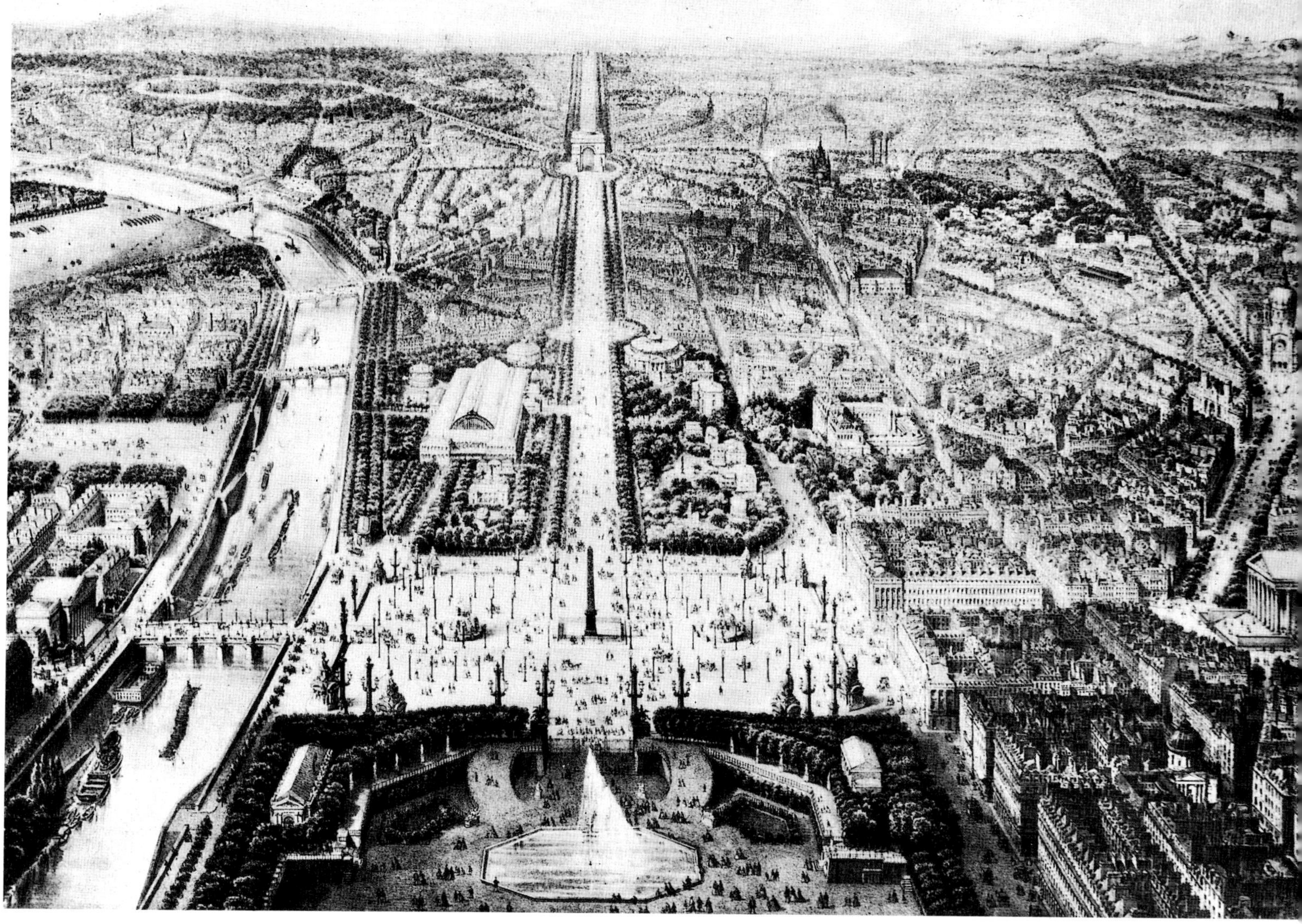

260 The pair to the view opposite, *looking northwest from above the Tuileries Gardens across the Place de la Concorde toward the Arc de Triomphe: the Champs-Elysées races toward an open horizon at La Défense, today the site of "La Grande Arche" (Ill. 311).*

triumphal arch, in memory of the Napoleonic victories over the Austrians in 1805, dignified the main entrance to the court of the Tuileries.

The triumphant message of imperialism, or at least of victory, is sounded as clearly in more recent uses of this motif, like the triple-arched Gateway of India in Bombay, or the All India War Memorial Arch in New Delhi, completed in 1931 as the terminal feature of King's Way and meant to celebrate the "ideal and fact of British rule over India."[60] With Mussolini's boast of reviving the ancient Roman Empire, the arches set up by his regime in North African cities like Tripoli and Somalia made the symbolism literal. *Pl.28*

Commemorative columns

The survival of two Classical commemorative columns in Rome itself, that of Trajan in his Forum and the Column of Marcus Aurelius on the Via Lata, kept this urban example of imperial triumph in the public eye until the revivalist swell of the Renaissance. Pope Sixtus V depaganized the two columns by replacing the imperial statues at their summit with statues of SS. Peter and Paul. This Christian takeover inspired similar imagery. With a Virgin Mary at the top, the column became a *Pl.21* favorite marker of squares in Catholic Germany, especially in Austria. One of the best examples is the Mariensäule in Munich. The instigation might be a doctrinal celebration (the Column of the Immaculate Conception in Rome, 1854) or a votive column of thankgiving for divine intercession in the stilling of a disaster (the Pestsäule in Vienna, 1679). Columns were also erected in honor of rulers, for example, the Column of King Sigismund III in Warsaw of 1644 undertaken by Ladislaus IV to commemorate his father.

The theme of military victory is the most enduring. The crowning figure is the victorious general, as in the column of the Place Vendôme in Paris (1806–10) topped by Napoleon I in the costume of a Roman emperor, and in the Nelson Columns in
261 London and Dublin; or the figure of Victory, as in the Siegessäule in Berlin (1873).

Alternatively, the victory column may celebrate dominion or national sovereignty. The Monument of National Independence (1910), topped by a winged Victory, stands at the head of the Paseo de la Reforma in Mexico City. The Jaipur Column in the forecourt of the Viceroy's House in New Delhi is surmounted by a glass star, the star of India, sprouting from a bronze lotus blossom; it was a gift from the Maharaja of Jaipur, to commemorate the creation of the new capital, the plan of which was carved on the pedestal. Sketches by Lutyens show that he had Trajan's Column in mind.

Statues

In the traditions of the Grand Manner, the chief use of public statuary has been along ceremonial streets and within squares. A pre-Classical convention had rows of statues set on the ground flanking a ceremonial way (e.g., the Avenue of the Sphinxes at Thebes). The Roman parallel put statues of patrons on consoles along a colonnaded avenue they had donated funds for.

At the Place du Petit Sablon in Brussels stand 19th-century statues of Counts Horn and Egmont, 16th-century champions of the Low Countries against Spanish rule; a cast-iron railing that circumscribes the square is interrupted by forty-eight bronze
261 statuettes representing the city guilds. The Siegesallee in Berlin and Monument Avenue (1890 ff.) in Richmond, Virginia, are both axial settings for heroic statues. The former was flanked by lifesize portraits of margraves, electors and kings of the Prussian ruling houses; it ran south from the Königsplatz, where the just mentioned Siegessäule stood on axis between monuments to Bismarck and Von Moltke. (The ensemble was moved in 1938 to a site in the Tiergarten in line with Unter den Linden,
263 to make way for the Nazi "grand axis," of which more below.) At Richmond, statues to Confederate heroes stood on a median strip down the length of the avenue, with the equestrian figure of Robert E. Lee on the major cross axis.

The equestrian statue was a rather late idea in Roman Imperial history. The famous bronze figure of Marcus Aurelius later set up on the Campidoglio originally stood in the grounds of the Emperor's family property on the Lateran. A few equestrian statues on public display were celebrated, e.g., Trajan's in his Forum in Rome, and Justinian's in the Forum of Augustus in Constantinople. This is the precedent revived in the French royal *places* in the Baroque period: the king's statue in a formally designed square—e.g., Louis XIV in the Place des Victoires, a proposed Louis XV for what became the Place de la Concorde. (The occasional equestrian statues set up in city markets during the Middle Ages, like Otto I's in Magdeburg ca. 1240, fall outside the limits of the Grand Manner; so do the Colleoni and Gattamelata monuments.) The statues almost always show the king on horseback and lifted high enough on a pedestal to stand out against the uniform walls of the square. In the case of one of the earliest of these royal squares, Henri IV's triangular Place Dauphine on the Ile de la Cité (begun in 1607), the figure of the King

261 Berlin, view up the Siegesallee to the Siegessäule, erected in 1873 to commemorate recent wars against Denmark, Austria and France; photograph of ca. 1903.

was placed on axis outside, at the tip of the triangle on the adjacent bridge. Another equestrian statue on a bridge is King George I on Essex Bridge in Dublin.

This standard repertory has been hard to get out of. Socialist iconography, beyond the obvious images of Lenin, Marx, Stalin, the hammer and sickle, and the star of Communism, included a popular postwar theme, the monument to the Soviet army, which became a fixture of formal squares, especially in the Sixties. There were three main variants: the Soviet soldier on a pedestal; the traditional column or obelisk; and the tank or artillery weapon taken from the battlefield and mounted on a stone base.[61]

THE CEREMONIAL AXIS

"Proportioned to the greatness which . . . the Capital of a powerful Empire ought to manifest."

These words of Pierre L'Enfant about the future Washington, cited at the beginning of this chapter, have been the principal subtext throughout the discussion of the Grand Manner. We have found ample proof that the Grand Manner is an urbanism of dominion. It is about empires and their capital outlets. It is about the staging of power.

The *staging* of power. All cities are, of course, repositories of power in varying degrees and patterns. Cities designed in the Grand Manner employ conventions that make power physically manifest. They do so in the structure of the urban space and the full panoply of fittings that give it substance. Theirs is an idealized urbanism, a dissembling order that subsumes reality. There is much in an urban product of the Grand Manner that is real, which is to say much that is uncomformable. It must be concealed. The staging of power is a matter of managing appearances. The managers have a choice audience in mind, an impression they wish to create for it, and a visual language that can bespeak, in proper measure, regimentation, pomp, and delight.

The nexus of this web of illusion is the ceremonial axis. It is the *voie triomphale*, the "royal way," the *magistrale*.[62] It is the predicate for the focal point of power, the sovereign's palace or its modern substitute. The royal way of pre-Classical antiquity, like the main processional avenue at the Babylon of Nebuchednezzar II that ran behind the principal public buildings lined along the river front, and
culminated in the sumptuously tiled Ishtar Gate, sets the tone. The colonnaded
256 avenue of the Roman provincial metropolis supplies a visual model for an urban
Pl.20 prospect that wants to be significantly entered, and traversed in ceremony.

A model, for clearly any street has this potential: we can turn an everyday environment into something celebratory with temporary props and ornaments, banners, rows of guards. The processional route of Christian Rome for a thousand years, the Via Papalis stretching for 3 miles (5 km.) from the Lateran to the Vatican, was in its daily existence a patchwork of streets of different width and indifferent rectitude, flanked by a scraggly line of buildings, stumps of ruins, open fields and vineyards. Here we are concerned, rather, with a permanent setting for the exhibition of power, with attempts to orchestrate the formality of ceremonial occasion.

177, The path is straight and wide, the rituals intentional: the program is political
229 legitimization and the management of history. The design may be cumulative or all of a piece; it is bound to shift, along with the structure of meanings it plays host to, and even be overhauled tempestuously. Once past the Middle Ages, the straight line of the "royal way" was drawn from the lord's country estate to the city palace where he sat in state. The apposite city gate was treated as a monument. Processions and military parades marched down the length of this straight path, which in its urban stretch doubled as a fashionable commercial street patronized by the court, as well as a residential district for nobility and the wealthy bourgeois. With the waning of absolutism, institutions of the liberal state would weight the iconography toward a bourgeois culture, and 20th-century regimes would make of the "royal way" what use their dogma allowed them to, or would rationalize retaining what is there.

222 Unter den Linden, the "royal way" of Berlin, illustrates this progress. Initially an outreach of the imperial palace or Schloss (formerly the castle) through open country, it was laid out as a parade ground and a processional way in 1647 by the Great Elector, Friedrich Wilhelm, and it became a symbol of the rise of the Prussian State. In this role, Unter den Linden was the Baroque extension of the medieval triumphal route of the electors, the later Königstrasse, leading from the Königstor, past the Berlin Rathaus (city hall), to the Lange Brücke, and then across the Spree to
the square in front of the Schloss. The buildings that were erected along this axis
262 from 1650 on had military significance: an arsenal, a triumphal gate (Brandenburg) through the center opening of which only the emperor could pass, a Catholic church (St. Hedwig's) where the troops in the garrison attended obligatory services.

In stages throughout the 19th century, and in response to changes in the political climate, the martial character of the avenue was softened with the appearance of cultural buildings—museums, an Academy of Fine Arts, a State Library, and Humboldt University (which started life in the 18th century as a palace for Frederick the Great's brother Prince Heinrich). Even in the royal pleasure grounds into which the avenue debouched at the end towards old Berlin, Schinkel's Altes Museum stood in the company of the Schloss and the Cathedral.

Hitler found the grandeur of Unter den Linden insufficient and its history
263 compromised. He planned his own royal way further west, crossing it at right

262 Berlin, the Brandenburg Gate, by K. G. Langhans, 1789–94, looking from Unter den Linden toward the Tiergarten in the 1930s. Since 1938 the Siegessäule has focussed this vista in the distance.

angles. Then with the division of the city after the War, the Brandenburg Gate was blocked; an impressive memorial to the Soviet army went up just outside it, attempting to colonize, as it were, the Western extension of the avenue, while within, East Block embassies and government ministries, no-nonsense slabs in a modern style, muscled in among the restored shells of the historic monuments. The Western part became something of a dead end until the proud Prussian standard of victory, the Siegessäule, was quickly deritualized, and the axis was linked beyond the Column to the highways of modern Berlin. And now, as this is written, with the Wall dismantled and the two Germanys reunified, Unter den Linden stands poised for yet another amendment.

To follow the Hitler-Speer partnership on the great north-south axis of the "thousand-year Reich" is to become party to a retrospective, wishful dream in the Grand Manner. Rhetoric and design invoke the roll-call of honor. The Führer, according to Speer, thinks of Washington, Karlsruhe and Canberra. He calls Paris "the most beautiful city in the world." He considers Haussmann the greatest city planner in history. He sketches from memory the building of Vienna's Ringstrasse. But all he can think to do by way of emulating these masterpieces of the Grand Manner in his capital is to go them one bigger. The great axis of Berlin is to be wider than the Champs-Elysées, and two and a half times as long; the domed hall, the *Stadtkrone*, that would terminate it to the north is to be taller than the United States Capitol; the triumphal arch at the other end would stand 450 feet (140 m.) high and have all 1,800,000 names of German soldiers who died in the Great War carved upon it. It is well the dream was shattered before it could be installed. The models and 263 drawings of this enormity are surely more flattering, and easier to admire, than the embodied great axis could ever be.

Stalin's socialist *magistrale* did get built. The revival of this very specter of European absolutism as the parade ground of the proletariat took some explaining. The 1935 Moscow Plan, where the idea first emerged, conformed to the revivalist philosophy then prevailing in all Soviet arts, namely, that a true socialist culture would absorb and redeem the greatest artistic achievements of all epochs of history. (All epochs of the Grand Manner, we might be permitted to say, for Stalinist historicism was certainly selective, and overwhelmingly championed Classical loftiness and discipline.) Seen in this light, the *magistrale*'s absolutist ancestry presented no contradictions for designers advocating its use as an organizing element in Soviet socialist cities. On the contrary, the solidly framed street corridor with its orderly progression of symmetrical building ensembles, representational ornament, and unifying cadences of cornice and window lines suggested the transfer of centralized power which, in the 18th century, could mold the city into an image of supreme order, to the People as represented by the socialist state.

The neo-Baroque urban esthetic was based on the architectural ensemble applied
295 to the entire city. Streets would be designed as a continuous uniform composition, and "even the widest streets and boulevards of advanced capitalist cities would be surpassed."[63] Paradigmatically, the new *magistrale* in Moscow would be a thoroughgoing transformation of Ulitsa Tverskaya—which was the last stretch of the Czarist royal way from the Winter Palace in St. Petersburg to the Kremlin and also Moscow's premier shopping street—into Ulitsa Gorkovo (Gorky Street), the "celebratory highway of the capital" of world socialism. This narrow and uneven
264 thoroughfare was broadened to 200 feet (60 m.) for its ultimate 500-yard (450 m.) descent toward Red Square. A new curtain of street frontages defined the channel—apartment houses with shops on the ground floor, but decorated with sculpture celebrating the collectivization of agriculture. Against this backdrop, mass pageants choreographed to celebrate Communist life could be staged. But the new *magistrale* also localized the institutions of privilege that were the sole domain of the *nomenclatura*, that army of managers charged with coordinating the formidable machinery of a centrally planned economy. They worked in the commissariats, dined in the restaurants, and stayed in the hotels that were the institutional accents of the new *magistrale*. Leningrad's *magistrale* (Stalin Prospekt, now Moskovsky Prospekt), designed in the late 1930s, encased the last urban segment of the land route that leads to Moscow. It shielded something else: the factories and the city dump of this edge area which was being rehabilitated as a new downtown away from the classic core of old St. Petersburg.

The apogee of postwar Soviet expansion brought the socialist *magistrale* to Eastern Europe. As "urban slipcover" it was used to good effect to mask the landscape of rubble and stray remnants in these firebombed cities. Berlin's
224 Stalinallee (later Karl-Marx-Allee) from the early 1950s is exemplary. Its tall neo-Classical building fronts provided a processional route of imperial splendor: behind them hid the patched up ruin of a war-ravaged city. Other realized examples of the socialist *magistrale*, mostly fragments, include Rostock's Langestrasse, Dresden's Ernst-Thälmann-Strasse, and Warsaw's Ulica Marszalkowska.[64]

In the West, the hideous war that ended the thousand-year Reich, and now pitted the confraternity of democracies against an allegedly monolithic Communism, had bankrupted the Grand Manner as a language of urban design. There, the Modernist idiom finally had its day. History-denying and value-free, disdainful of memory and monumentality, this stripped unrhetorical style seemed appropriate for the brave

263 Berlin, model of the projected north–south axis, seen from the south; Albert Speer, designer-in-chief, 1938 ff. In the foreground is the square of the south railroad station; further north, a triumphal arch intended to carry the names of soldiers who died in the First World War. The two highrise buildings on the left are a hotel and the offices of the Army High Command.

264 Moscow, Gorky (formerly Tverskaya) Street, approaching the Kremlin; A. Mordvinov, designer-in-chief, 1937–39.

new world that had to be designed now without sentiment. There was no turning back—ever. And for most of three decades the prophecy held true. In the *grands ensembles* of France and the "urban renewal" of American city centers, in new cities like Chandigarh and Brasilia, the gospel of Le Corbusier brooked no exceptions.

After the death of Stalin, the East took up the challenge in the spirit of an ideological agon. It abruptly repealed historicism in favor of the new Western look: but it did not altogether abandon the urban armature of the Grand Manner. The *magistrale* went Modernist architecturally, while holding on to its nobly framed volumes and the perspective vista, and finding new ways to advertise the State. The first example of the Modernist *magistrale* was Moscow's Kalinin Prospekt; the last, *Pl.29*
Bucharest's Calea Victoriei. Inaugurated in 1967 as part of the fiftieth anniversary celebrations of the October Revolution, Kalinin Prospekt was an update of a project in the 1935 Plan of Moscow for a new boulevard run through the Arbat, one of the city's most historic residential districts. Now the uncompromising straight line was bulldozed through, and lined with Modernist skyscrapers and slabs. But the Socialist Realist heritage is immediately apparent in the heretical use of the Modernist repertory to define a street channel, and the didactic function of the three-story-high, propaganda-emblazoned electronic billboard that closes the vista.

POST-MODERN BAROQUE

But the tide turned once again in the West. The stone cities of multi-layered tradition began to be rediscovered in the Sixties, and the Modernist ideal rejected as destructive and vacuous. A young generation who barely remembered the War could turn to the *rond-points* and the Baroque diagonals and even the accursed ceremonial axis, reject their symbolism, and find in them something guiltless and eternal, "the poetic content and esthetic quality of space," as Rob Krier put it in his book of 1975, *Stadtraum* (Urban Space). History admitted no break. In every city what we did must be a "formal response to pre-existing spatial conditions."[65] And in many European cities of the first order these spatial conditions had been dictated by the Baroque esthetic.

Ricardo Bofill, also a contented formalist, could even turn the tables on the princely sources of the Baroque esthetic, and proclaim it the medium of the working-class environment.

> The urban design of our era will take the structure, if not the dimension, of the historical city into account. It will, however, invert the symbolic values. Everyday life will take the center of the stage, while the public edifice and facility will recede into the background.[66]

The work of the Taller de Arquitectura, under his direction, consists in fact of a
Pl.30 series of public housing projects in France which recreate the stony monumentality of the Grand Manner, specifically the neo-Classical architecture and urbanism of 18th-century France, in prefabricated concrete. The inspiration is even prosaically acknowledged in the droll name of one of these housing estates—Les Echelles du Baroque (Baroque Scales), in the 14th *arrondissement* of Paris.

But these compulsive shells from the Age of Absolutism, with their densely packaged imagery and manipulative scale, betray their source with modern, even Modernist, obliquities. The building materials and methods, first of all, are post-industrial: if this is Baroque, it stands through sleight of hand, indebted to the ruling technocrats of our own building industry. The typology of housing is also contemporary. Behind the colossal orders and the *disjecta membra* of Classical monumentality hide serial housing units in the Modernist tradition of *Siedlungen* and Corbusian *unités d'habitation*. The mass, unitary and sculptural, encases cellular ranges in the hierarchic sheaths of the Baroque. And one last paradox. The expansive spatial order of the Baroque that amplifies cities and propels them into the countryside is concentrated here—at Les Arcades du Lac (St Quentin-en-Yvelines), at Antigone (Montpellier), at the Palace of Abraxas (Marne-la-Vallée)—within the moulded shape of a single Baroque building. "The center of a city," Bofill writes, "can be imagined as a Baroque church: all you need to do is transform into dwellings the thickness of its walls and into streets and squares its internal spaces."[67] The aim, at any rate, is to exalt daily life by situating it in extraordinary settings. But since there is no public life to speak of in these transfixed environments, they can achieve little else than to embalm domesticity.

Also geared to the domestic scale, in this instance the suburban environment of
265 America, is the work of Duany & Plater-Zyberk.[68] Here, however, instead of the hallucinatory gigantism of Bofill that concentrates the public forms of European Baroque in urban fragments unconnected to an urban plan, the plans themselves are elegant recollections of the Grand Manner which, from the ground up, revert to the insubstantial airiness of American suburbia. In Seaside, a north Florida resort town,

265 Seaside (Florida), laid out by Duany & Plater-Zyberk in 1983.

the axes, the vistas terminating in identifiable landmarks, the tree-lining of avenues are all there in two dimensions, as in a Burnham fragment. This formal urban diagram is in fact the covenant of a public realm. But though the building lines are held firm, the buildings are mostly evocative suburban residences—the Anglo-American reverie of the detached house on its plot of land—and a low continuous picket fence establishes the street line at the foot of the sloping front yards. This is the Baroque esthetic as domesticated by the Garden City movement, and it is not surprising that Duany & Plater-Zyberk should profess to hold Raymond Unwin's *Town Planning in Practice* of 1909 as their bible.

So the Grand Manner, it would appear, is not a closed story. The last laugh is on the Modernists. The Kriers and Bofills in Europe, and American revivalists younger still, are determined to connect. These present *places* and triumphal ways are heading straight back, beyond the skyscraper parks and *Siedlung* slabs, to the days of Fontana and Haussmann, of Burnham, Speer and his Italian counterpart Marcello Piacentini.

5 · THE URBAN SKYLINE

INTRODUCTION

In 1979 the city of Melbourne held an international competition, whose object was to secure a distinctive landmark for itself. The overseeing committee stated that after studying great cities in the world "where the landmarks have evolved over centuries . . . it became clear to us that Melbourne needed a big idea—something unique, something remarkable, something to give us more pride in ourselves and a far more significant place in the global itinerary . . ."[1]

Two things stand out in this extraordinary initiative: the urgency to have a signature building that would fix the city's identity, and "put Melbourne on that elusive world map"; and the recognition that such visual means of recall were not randomly acquired in the past, but developed over time. The urban silhouette, what the Germans called the "city portrait" or *Stadtbild*, was the result of a cumulative process, and its reading was calculated. The landmarks that stood out in this picture were symbols of a collective life; they advertised civic priorities, and made palpable the hierarchy of public institutions.

PUBLIC AND PRIVATE SKYLINES

Our word "skyline," traditionally, meant "the line where earth and sky meet." The use of "skyline" to refer to buildings on the horizon is recent—not earlier than 1876, and common by the 1890s. Not at all accidentally, another word, "skyscraper," had come into use during the intervening decade. It was this new building type, or rather an agglomeration of its specimens, that dramatically redefined the way city-form related to its natural setting and the civic messages it conveyed.

There were tall buildings before, of course, from the Mesopotamian ziggurat to the Eiffel Tower. These were unique beacons, their height not particularly useful except in a symbolic sense. Nobody lived or worked in medieval belltowers or the dome of the United States Capitol. Skyscrapers, on the other hand, were stacked up methodically for their functional payoff, and the symbolism was a bonus.

And they were *public* beacons, those others—of religion, or government, or simply, as with the Eiffel Tower, of technological progress in the abstract. The skyscraper was the product of *private* enterprise, and so it remained by and large,

266 A classic image of the privatized skyline: in New York City, the RCA Victor (by Cross & Cross, 1930–31), Chrysler (William Van Alen, 1928–30) and Waldorf Astoria (Schultze & Weaver, 1930–31) buildings stretch their Art Deco crowns in rival claims of dominance for their owners.

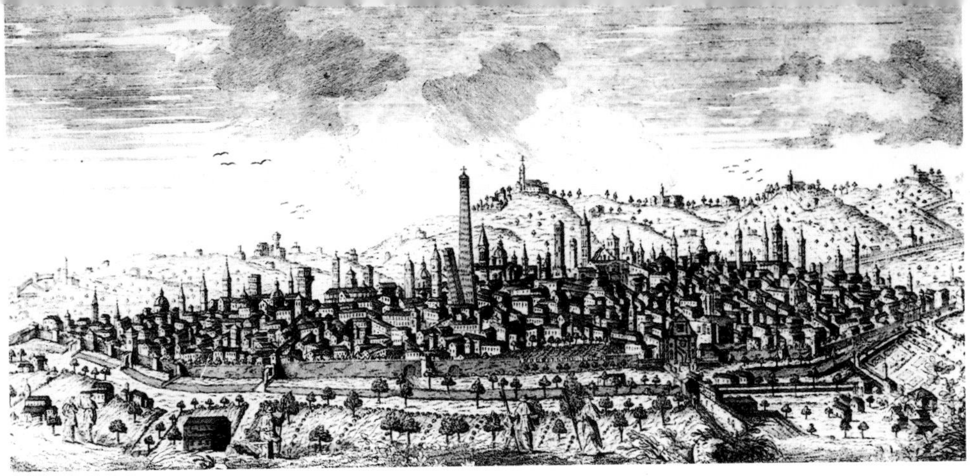

267 The skyline of Bologna, 18th-century engraving. A handful of surviving medieval family towers are shown among the many campanili. The tallest feature in the skyline is the leaning tower of the Asinelli family, from the early 12th century, which is still the city's prime landmark.

however it might have come to dominate visually the image of the city, and to stand as the very embodiment of its public realm.

The only structure comparable to the skyscraper in these respects—its utility and privacy—is the baronial tower-house of the Middle Ages. This tall urban feature
267 was characteristic of cities in central and northern Italy, in the south of France, and in central and southern Germany. There were many of them; they had defensive as
Pl.31 well as advertising intentions; and they dominated the city image, even though they represented not a collective program at all, but the most atomized self-interest—the welfare of individual clans. Alberti speaks of the time in the later Middle Ages, "about two hundred years ago, when people seemed to be seized with a kind of general infection of building high watchtowers, even in the meanest villages, insomuch that scarce a common housekeeper thought he could not be without his turret: By which means there arose a perfect grove of spires . . ." (*Ten Books on Architecture*, viii. 5). The towers were square at the base and made of brick: and they could go astoundingly high. The still-surviving Asinelli tower in Bologna, bent at a crazy angle reputedly to be safe during thunderstorms, is over 300 feet (almost 100 m.) high.

In Germany these towers tended to be bulky and squat; in northern Italy, slim and lofty. In Italy, the towers were either attached to individual family houses or central to a group of families who shared their facilities and protection. "Tower associations" in Florence brought together large numbers of people.[2] The legal basis for the construction of the towers was traced back to the ancient royal privilege to fortify—a privilege passed on to tenants upon their investiture. When the nobility moved into towns, the right to defend the family compound came with them.[3]

The communes, in their ascendancy, had mixed feelings about this privatized skyline. The danger to city interest was real. Mid-13th-century statutes in Bologna "prescribe that anyone who launches projectiles or other instruments against the palace or against the curia of the Commune would be fined and his tower demolished."[4] We have much on record to show that communal governments repeatedly and sternly regulated the height of the tower-houses, and demolished many of them in the name of communal self-assertion. In Rome Brancaleone degli Andalò, the strong-willed senator, destroyed or truncated 140 of them in the 1250s, while Florence in the same years brought down 59 towers of the discredited Guelph faction.

This attack on height is very instructive. It had two related motives. It was connected to an opening up of the city-form, the elimination of jurisdictional pockets that undermined the central authority of the commune. At the same time, since medieval city-form was meant to be visually expressive of the prevailing social and political order, it was necessary to have no towers higher than that of the town hall, so that the primacy of the public order, as against private interests, would be made palpable on the skyline.

But often commune officers were drawn from the clans, and had no wish to diminish the family structure and its proudest landmark. Even where violent civil struggles among factions and families targeted the tower-houses, cities still gloried in the bristling skyline they made. It bore witness to the power of a city that played host to so many mighty families. An example of this medieval attitude: in Perugia, in 1342, the commune prohibited the sale or destruction of towers, citing them for their "grandissima bellezza" (very great beauty).[5]

In a similar way, we ourselves, during the span of one century of tall buildings, have found glamor and vitality in the spectacle of a skyscraper-strewn downtown. The skyscraper was a monument to the growing prominence of the modern American corporation. In New York and Chicago and the other big cities of 20th-century America, the political contest was between Wall Street, banks, trusts and corporations on one side, and farmers and workers on the other. And the skyline transformed this conflict into a visual, esthetic experience, and thus neutralized it. You could hate corporations and still love the art objects that housed them. The corporate tower became the universal American symbol of the city, and desirable for itself as proof of civic pride and prosperity. As the President of the American Civic Association put it in 1926, "It is noticeable that every American city and town that aspires to metropolitan importance wants to have at least one skyscraper—one that can be illustrated on a picture postcard and sent far and wide as an evidence of modernity and a go-ahead spirit."[6]

Photography helped glamorize this urban image. The skyline of tall buildings was a great subject, and Alfred Stieglitz and his school abstracted it into stylish silhouettes and planes. The public dissemination of these icons popularized this exciting new way of picturing cities. In New York, people took the Staten Island Ferry to George Washington Bridge to see the city as the photographers saw it. Identifying the tall buildings became part of this ritual. So identifying the domes of Baroque Rome had been a tourist's ritual in an earlier era, and it was memorialized in the captioned Baedeker fold-out of the city's skyline as seen from S. Pietro in 268
Montorio on the Janiculum, with St. Peter's at one end of the panorama and S. Paolo fuori le Mura at the other.

The only other privatized skyline, in the West at any rate, besides the tower forest of urban feudalism in the Middle Ages and the corporate feudalism of the skyscraper

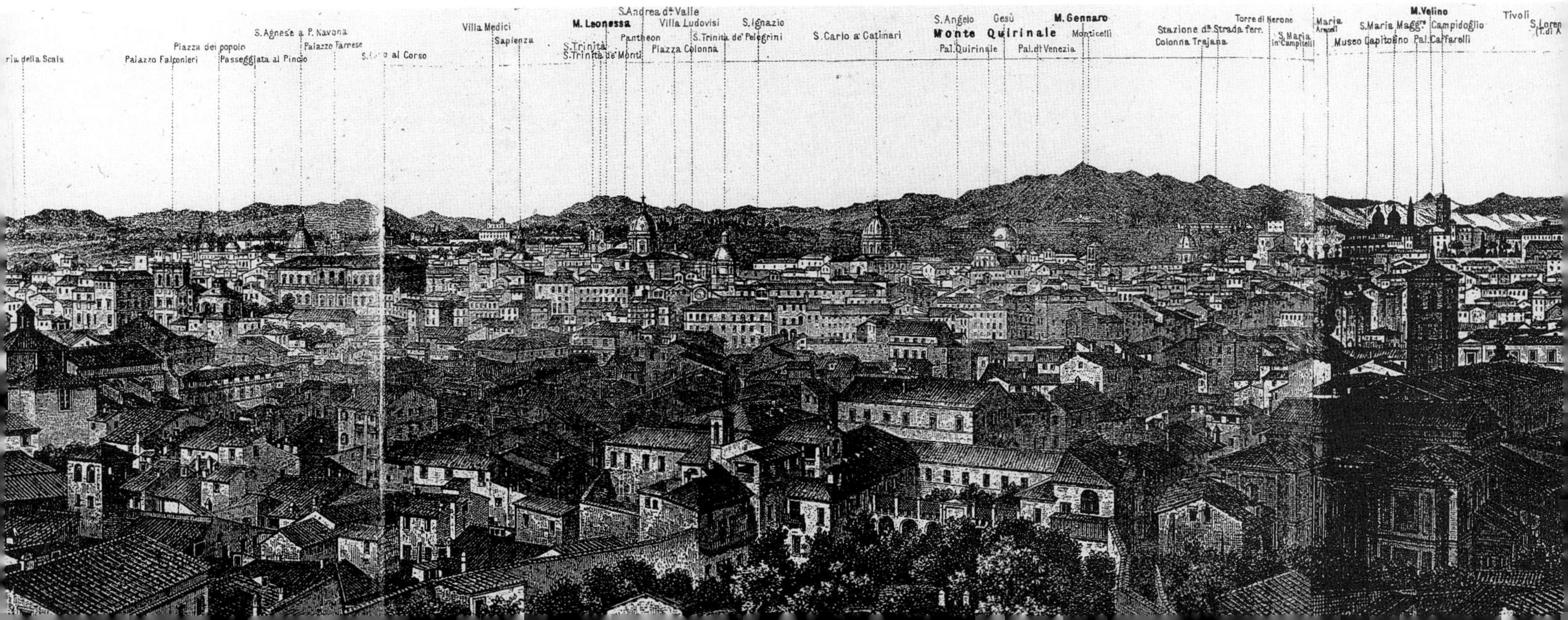

268 The skyline of Rome, center section of a foldout engraving from an 1883 Baedeker guide. The view is from S. Pietro in Montorio on the Janiculum Hill.

Pl.37 city, was the industrial landscape of smokestacks and furnace cones and water towers. Here again, the reaction was polar. You could take pride in this bristling, smoking array of industry, the harsh signature of employment and prosperity. Or you could deplore the crass overshadowing of the traditional symbols of the urban collective, the skyline of faith and governance, by symbols of driving greed—Blake's "dark satanic mills."

In like manner, Henry James was to lament, upon his return to America in 1904 after a twenty-five-year absence, that the new New York skyline of office towers had robbed the spire of Trinity Church of the distinction of being the tallest tower in the
303 city, which it had enjoyed until 1875, and left it "so cruelly overtopped and so barely distinguishable . . . in its abject helpless humility."[7]

What upset James was an uncaring attitude evident in New York toward a hierarchical cityscape, and therefore a bankrupted commitment to the traditional order of the social structure. So A. W. N. Pugin a half-century before him would
270 juxtapose the new skyline of the industrial city in England, a grim, stark silhouette of factories and tenements and workhouses, with the spire-pricked piety of the
269 medieval cityscape, to make his point about the erosion of traditional values in the modern world.

Indeed, the point to be iterated is that until the advent of the Industrial Revolution, the urban skyline celebrated institutional landmarks, buildings of communal importance having to do with religion and political power. The source of wealth, of economic power, was itself sometimes institutionalized in representational buildings like cloth halls, with their stately towers proudly rising within the storied shape of the urban center. With the arrival of industry, a confusion of skyline priorities begins. If a town grew around a factory or mill, the new skyline acquired an inherent logic at least. The shock came in the older towns subjected to industrial invasion. In America, Pittsburgh may be a good example—the smokestacks lined against the fiery red night sky, the curving rivers with their steel-girdered bridges, the blazing furnaces: an appropriate symbol for a city that became the hearth of the nation by 1880, but a startling contrast to the city that was.

Since the Industrial Revolution, the notion that private structures should not be allowed to overwhelm the collective symbols of the city has been regularly voiced. "The final contention remains," as Thomas Sharp put it in 1963 in his defense of the historic skyline of Cambridge, "that a minority of private interests should not be allowed to dominate the town architecturally any more than it should socially."[8] And the opposite point of view would have it that traditional cities were indeed set aside by modern practices, and that our cities are no longer cathedral cities but commercial or industrial centers which deserve their own skyline.

269, 270 Images from A. W. N. Pugin's Contrasts *(1836) in praise of the landscape of the Gothic city as against the crassness of the modern industrial city.*

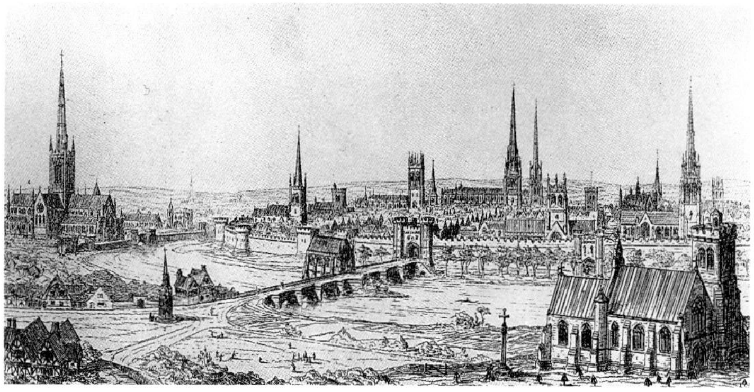

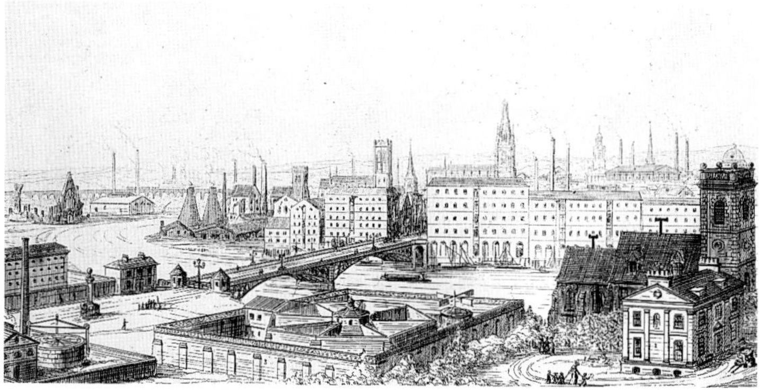

271 The Three Marys at the Open Sepulcher, *attributed to Hubert or Jan van Eyck, before 1420; detail showing the skyline of Jerusalem. The octagonal Dome of the Rock, although inflated in scale, is accurately represented. The rest of the city is a fantasy of Western and Oriental architecture transposed against a rolling northern European landscape.*

THE SKYLINE PORTRAYED

The central issue of these debates is that the shape of the skyline matters to the residents. It is the familiar, fond icon of the city-form, a vision to cherish and come home to; it is also their urban advertisement to the world, the front they present to *Pl.31* visitors, and a disseminative shorthand for a broader audience still. Royal seals with city views have had currency since at least the 12th century. Cities appeared on Renaissance coins and medals, on prints and paintings, and on their cheaper modern counterparts, postcards, T-shirts, refrigerator magnets.

Since to be conceptualized it has to be imaged, the skyline of cities, by whatever name it might be called, has always been indebted to the artist's representation of it. Until the Renaissance, city pictures were mostly ideal—conventional formulas modeled on the Heavenly Jerusalem, with little basis in reality. Although key buildings might be specifically labeled, their style is likely to be that of the time when the picture was made rather than of their own time. Even when this ideal representation was not altogether staged, but was based in some degree on visual reality, it broadcast nonetheless a formal statement of the city's self-conception—or rather the conception of the patron who commissioned the artist to make the portrait of the city.

Most commonly, this patron was the sovereign power that administered the city. It was Prince Baltasar Carlos and Philip IV of Spain, for example, who ordered Juan Bautista del Mazo to paint his *View of Saragossa* in 1646; likewise, the *Pl.6* commission for Claude-Joseph Vernet's *Ports of France* series came from the French Crown in 1753. So the city portrait highlighted those features of the cityscape important to the purposes of the sovereign power.

With the complication of defenses during the era of artillery warfare, the purpose in commissioning city views became primarily military. Princes acquired maps and

town views to study current applications of defense systems, improve their own arrangements, and plan attack strategies. Many town views from the 17th and 18th
20 centuries, for this very reason, emphasize overwhelmingly the bastioned periphery.
272 One specialty was the siege view—a meticulous record of the deployment of armed forces in the countryside surrounding the city. The ruler's interest in his own realm was as crucial, especially if he were uncertain of his grip. One of the earliest attempts at a systematic documentation was undertaken by Philip II (1556–98) of Spain, who commissioned the topographic artist Anton van der Wyngaerde to illustrate the principal cities of Spain, and Jacob van Deventer to draw up precise plans of towns in the Low Countries, a new and restive part of the King's domain.

Representing cities accurately to these ends was of prime importance, and princely patronage bolstered experiments in graphic techniques. The medium was usually a print of some sort—a woodcut or an engraving—and the diffusion was carefully controlled. The princely gift of a town plan or view was a special favor. Strict plans were less common than the perspective or bird's-eye view, which commonly took an artificially high viewpoint in order to make legible the entire urban panorama in continuous recession. In the foreground would be the part of town most formally identified with the sovereign power. In views of Rome, this is the Borgo area with the Vatican Palace and St. Peter's.

An older tradition of visualizing the city was to compose a panoramic profile of the side that mattered most for formal, representational purposes. (The Germans call this a *Schauseite*.) It is this convention that was resorted to when, in narrative painting of the 14th and 15th centuries, representations of a particular city were used as the backdrop for a specific event that took place there. So a view of Cologne appears behind *The Arrival of St. Ursula* by the Veronica Master (1411–14), and a
Pl.5 view of Naples forms the setting for the return to the home port of the victorious Aragonese fleet in 1464. The profile city view had great currency in the Netherlands in the 17th century. Often the city is seen from across a body of water, as in Rembrandt's etched view of Amsterdam of about 1643 and the famous *View of Delft* by Vermeer of about 1660.[9]

Sometimes the initiative for a city picture might come from a loyal subject. The
273 huge woodcut profile view of Cologne rendered by Anton Woensam of Worms in 1531 was sponsored by the local publisher Peter Quentel on the occasion of the election at Cologne of Ferdinand of Austria as King of the Romans, and it is dedicated to him along with the Emperor, the Archbishop of Cologne, and other dignitaries of the Empire and the city. But the commission might be more personal.

272 *The siege of Valenciennes, from F. Strada,* Primera decada de la guerra de Flandes *(1681).*

273 Cologne, woodcut view by Anton Woensam of Worms, 1531.

The famous picture of the Ile de la Cité in Paris by the Limbourg Brothers in the *Très riches heures* of the Duc de Berry has a careful view of the royal palace with the Sainte-Chapelle, which was the view from the Duke's house, the Hôtel de Nesle (on the Left Bank, where the Institut de France now stands).[10] Similarly, Canaletto has a
marvellous view of London and the Thames, commissioned by the second Duke of *Pl.35*
Richmond, grandson of Charles II, painted from Richmond House, the terrace of which is featured in the foreground.

Individual cities also commissioned portraits of themselves, often rendered by native artists, as a matter of civic pride. In print form, these were inserted into books sponsored by the cities in their own honor. An example is Saenredam's view of Haarlem for Ampzing's *Description and Praise of the Town of Haarlem* (1628).

Another important patron was the tourist. Travel books with capsule illustrations of cities have a venerable tradition. Surviving guides for the pilgrimages to Rome and Jerusalem have plans highlighted with elevations of important monuments. The first famous *printed* travel book is *Peregrinationes in Terram Sanctam* of 1486, recording the pilgrimage to the Holy Land of Bernhard von Breydenbach, Dean of Mainz. The pictures of cities were done by Erhard Reuwich of Utrecht, and were widely copied, for example by Anton Koberger in his *Weltchronik* of 1493. The cities included are Venice, Parenzo, Corfu, Candia, Rhodes and Jerusalem.

The next great attempt was a hundred years later, and set out to show what the
cities of the world looked like. This is the monumental *Civitates Orbis Terrarum* by *159*
Georg Braun, a German priest, and Franz Hogenberg of Antwerp, who did the engravings. The drawings for the engravings were done by Georg Hoefnagel, also from Antwerp. Five volumes were published between 1572 and 1598, with a sixth volume in 1617. Hoefnagel is one of the first to put closeups of famous buildings
at the edges of the map, as insets.[11] *293*

El Greco has a gloss on this in a remarkable painting of Toledo still in that city. *274*
The Hospital de Tavera is shown as a separate inset, and the explanation for this is given in a map of the city in the right foreground. "It has been necessary to put the hospital of Don Juan Tavera [outside the view], because it not only happened to conceal the Visagra gate, but thrust up its dome in such a manner that it overtopped the town . . ."[12]

By the time of El Greco's *Toledo*, accurate, realistic portraits of cities, depicted for their own sake, were at least half a century old. Until the mid-16th century, there was almost always an official, representational intention behind every city picture.

Captions clarified this message, allegorical figures added emblematic flourishes. A
273 long poem on Woensam's Cologne, for example, extolls the merits of the city—its fine buildings and busy markets, its relics and wise administration. By contrast a large woodcut view of Cairo from 1549 has the simple title, "An Accurate Representation of the Great City of Cairo"; and ten years later Anton van der Wyngaerde inscribes his view of Genoa with this sentiment: "Of all pleasures offered by the delightful and ingenious [art of] painting, none do I esteem more highly than the depiction of places."[13]

We should probably distinguish these full-scale portraits from the souvenir *capriccio*, a composed assemblage of urban landmarks without respect for their actual place in the cityscape or their interrelationships. An early imposing specimen
275 is the 16th-century painting boldly emblazoned with the words "SEPTEM ADMIRATIONES CIVITATIS BRUGENSIS" (the seven wonders of Bruges), where the monuments are shown without any interstitial fabric. To the extent that the artist in question planned to turn a quick profit, these views became formulaic, and by the 18th century were a common purchase of travellers, in pricy painted form or budget print, as mementoes of their visits.

Once an artist had developed a successful formula for a city picture, it was widely copied. The bird's-eye view of London by van der Wyngaerde of the 1540s was drawn from Southwark, from a point below London Bridge. A few years later an anonymous woodcut did another version from Southwark, but just above London Bridge. It showed old St. Paul's with the steeple that was destroyed in the fire of 1561.

274 *El Greco,* View of Toledo, *ca. 1610–14. The city plan is held up by a boy (possibly El Greco's son).*

275 The Seven Wonders of Bruges, *attributed to P. Claessens the Elder, second half of the 16th century. The "wonders" include the spire and porch of Notre-Dame (left), the Hotel des Sept Tours (rear center), the headquarters of the Hanseatic League (rear right), and the market hall crowned by the great civic belfry (right).*

Today 110 different versions of this view exist, all the way up to the Fire of London in 1666.

The Renaissance is the starting point for the great skyline imagery of early modern Europe, beginning with the *catena* ("chain", because of its linked frame) view of Florence from about 1480. On its heels comes Jacopo de' Barbari's view of
Venice (1500). Other celebrated 16th-century names are Jörg Seld for his views of 73
Augsburg (1521) and Lübeck (1552), Woensam for the 1531 view of Cologne we 273
referred to, and Conrad Merian who depicted a number of Austrian cities as well as Strasbourg, Frankfurt, Ulm and Paris. Merian had a distinctive style that showed the *top* side of the bastioned curtain, not the foreground as was usual.[14]

In general, the technique emphasized main buildings in silhouette against a blank sky. This is actually a fairly enduring notion, perhaps the inevitable graphic device to conceptualize "skyline." Ordinary houses were drawn with some care, especially in profile views, as if to emphasize that there can be no monuments without the standard residential structure that gives them their scale and dignity. In all these 16th-century samples, the perspective is not unified; the emerging naturalism of the Renaissance is still wedded to the medieval concept of an ideal city. It seems, furthermore, in Woensam's Cologne, that celestial and terrestrial space do not follow the same perspective convention. In most cases, the churches were shown larger than life to underline their importance. Streets and squares were not emphasized. By contrast, in the 17th century, public spaces were exaggerated, and general urban decay was contrasted to the grand princely palaces. In the mid-18th century, Vernet's *Ports* created a heroic genre of cityscape painting that rivaled history painting. His example was imitated across Europe from St. Petersburg to Naples.

276 Amiens (France), the town and its cathedral; early 20th-century photograph.

SKYLINE FEATURES

There are two ways, not mutually exclusive, to fix a skyline. You can do it through
277 extraordinary landscape features (the Acropolis and Lycabettos in Athens, Sugar
Loaf at Rio, Table Mountain at Cape Town). Or you can do it through pre-eminent
276 buildings (the Eiffel Tower, the cathedral or church of a medieval town like Vézelay
278 or Salisbury, the castle as at Edinburgh, where the natural rock greatly heightens the
effect).

Topography is important. The primary distinction is between flat land, like the site of most Dutch towns, and towns on a hill. Both are easy to mark. The windmill and the tower hover on the low Dutch horizon because there is no competition from nature. A church or fort on the hilltop is an equally simple advantage.

But urban landscapes are rarely that direct; and urban intentions are rarely clearcut and unchanging.

To address the landscape first: cities with a complicated topography might try to emblematize nature, as with the so-called Seven Hills of Rome, a conceit transposed along with other distinctive attributes to its eastern pendant, Constantinople. Taken seriously, the conceit could have provided a great opportunity to have a ranked or reverberating skyline. By crowning several of the summits of Constantinople with
Pl.34 the same shape, the domed mosque, the Ottomans indeed succeeded to a degree in
reshaping the profile of the former Byzantine capital more sharply than their predecessors; furthermore, the number of minarets allotted each mosque, from a single one to the grand total of six for the mosque of Sultan Ahmed I (1609–17), was an effective device to suggest a hierarchy. Rome, ancient or modern, and Byzantine Constantinople have no visual purity of this sort.

On the second point, the intended reading of the skyline, cities with a long history might tellingly juxtapose the symbols of competing powers, or of changes in their structure, within the urban profile. There are classic skyline confrontations of cathedral and town hall (Siena, Florence), of princely castles and civic centers, of rival monastic orders, and even of parish churches, as in the stately balance of St. Lorenz and St. Sebaldus across the Pegnitz, representing the two independent districts that united to create Nuremberg.[15]

But often the nature of the skyline is not determined by one or more distinctive building shapes, as much as it is by the repetitive use of one architectural feature: minarets, domes, spires, industrial chimneys, and the like.

277 Athens, with the Acropolis hill crowned by the Parthenon, photographed ca. 1870.

278 Edinburgh (Scotland), the city seen from the south.

279, 280 Skyline features, East and West. The left-hand panorama shows the large variety of Islamic minarets, from the 9th century to the present; the right-hand panorama presents a selection of church towers from about 1000 to the 19th century.

The categories of these markers through history would constitute a fairly limited list, but the local treatment of each one makes for a rich spectrum of skyscapes. The
279 dominant types of minarets in the Muslim world, for example, include the telescoped, squared towers of North Africa, massive as in Kairawan, laced and tiled as the Kutubiya of Marrakesh; the strongly tapered brick cylinders of Iran, with upper balconies on shelves of stalactite ornament; and the grey pencil-thin Ottoman minarets ending in steeply pointed roofs.

Many of these markers were crested with symbols appropriate to their meaning, or simply eye-catching toppings. St. Michael resided at the pinnacle of both churchly and civic towers; at the Old Town Hall of Bruges, he is shown expelling Satan. The point of the Admiralty steeple at St. Petersburg carried a weather-vane in the form of a sailing ship, while the dome of Bulfinch's Massachusetts State House in Boston carried a gilded pine cone. Such modestly scaled ornaments were lost in the distant view, but retained their iconographic validity nonetheless. Some were designed
305 to be visible from afar: William Penn's statue on the dome of the Philadelphia City Hall was diligently protected until recently from being obscured by the developing skyline (see p. 334).

SACRED HEIGHTS

Until the coming of the secular state, which means until relatively recently, the dominant accent of the skyline was the architecture of sacred buildings. These were often situated on eminences, natural or artificial, their architectural mass was piled up high, and their visual prominence was enhanced by sky-aspiring props.

The native religions of Southeast and East Asia developed early on a variety of such skyline accents. Hindu temples themselves were built as great ornamented mounds, but they were often overshadowed by tall multi-story portal towers (*gopuras*). There are surviving examples of these towers in India from the 7th to the 16th centuries, the most impressive among them in Madurai, Vijayanagara, and the district of Kerala. Their elaborately ornamented tapering form is capped by a characteristic barrel-vaulted roof crown.

Buddhist stupas, dome-shaped grave mounds, were surmounted by an ornamental capping structure ending in an umbrella shape. In places like Bangkok, the overall shape is a bell or a symbolic stepped mountain, crowned by tall spires.

The Chinese pagoda, in an otherwise uniformly low urban mass, often dominated the urban skyline. This is true of the White Pagoda at Fuzhou, the many-times rebuilt Great Pagoda at Suzhou, and outside of China, the gilt Shwe Dagon Pagoda in Rangoon which, in a 14th-century renovation, had reached a height of 295 feet (90 m.).

280 The classic dominants of church architecture are belltowers and domes. Going beyond domes and spires, particular segments of the building mass may also announce the church on the skyline. The "choir-façades" of Cologne, as in S. Maria im Capitol, are a case in point—the heritage of the tall and imposing "westwork" in

Carolingian church design. The apse itself is sometimes the skyline feature, in cases where the land falls beneath the church. Several Italian examples come to mind: Massa Marittima; S. Barnaba in Scarperia; Rossellino's cathedral at Pienza; and most memorably, Cefalù, where the tall, regal east end of apse and transept dwarfs the cursory nave with its stubby west towers.

The belltower as a detached structure to one side of the church is an Italian specialty, going back to the 9th century. North of the Alps, the multi-towered composition was the chief aspiration of medieval church builders since the age of Charlemagne. The main elements for this sky-aspiring mass—stair towers, belfries and spires—had appeared at St. Riquier (Centula) as early as 800, and they were elaborated with tenacity in the main abbeys and cathedrals despite frequent structural failings. The classic twin-towered façade that characterizes the main *276*
elevation of most Gothic cathedrals derives from the great Norman churches of William the Conqueror and his wife in centers like Caen and Jumièges. Less common was the single western tower over an entrance porch, as in St.-Benoît-sur-Loire and the Romanesque predecessor of Chartres Cathedral, and later Ulm and Freiburg-im-Breisgau.

In an ideal exterior design, towers would bracket the west façade, mark the end bays of one or two transepts, flank the choir, and rise over the crossing where nave and transepts overlapped in an architectural enactment of the symbol of the cross. The original Gothic design for Chartres Cathedral called for the full panoply of nine towers. Reims Cathedral projected a seven-towered pile, in emulation of the battlemented City of Heaven, each tower rising above a system of slender buttresses where angels stood guard. A rare achievement like the cathedral at Tournai in *281*
Belgium, mostly from the 12th century, gives some feeling for such magnificent reverberating verticality. But as a rule this ideal superstructure remained unat-

281 Tournai (Belgium), the cathedral and its surroundings.

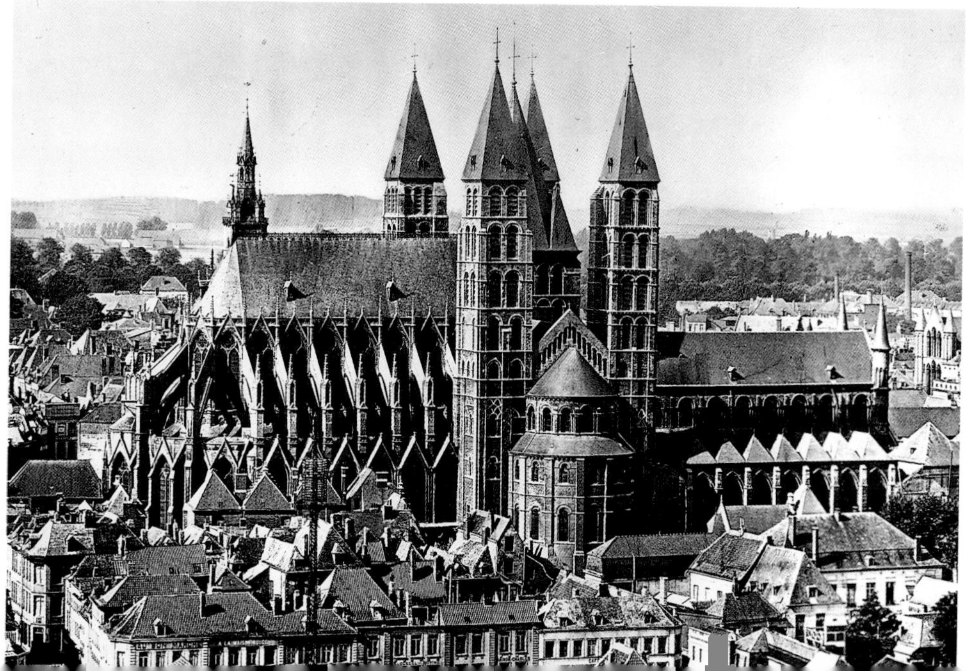

tainable, sometimes wholly unrealized, often incomplete. Time and again what was proudly, perhaps hubristically, lifted was ravaged by lightning or collapsed of its own weight. A chronicler, writing around 1200 of the collapse of the transept tower at Beverley Minster, blames the architects for sacrificing solidity to appearance.[16] At Beauvais, where the overweening dimensions of the mid-13th-century cathedral had brought on catastrophic results, a 497-foot (151.5 m.) tall tower, three stories of stone and one of wood, was built between 1558 and 1569, only to collapse spectacularly four years later.

Pl.33 Brunelleschi's dome for Florence Cathedral inaugurates, in history books, the career of the Renaissance style—and also a renowned series of magisterial domes that focused for all time the skyline of their cities. The generative archetypes were Michelangelo's dome for St. Peter's in Rome, Palladio's for his churches in Venice, *Pl.35* and Wren's for St. Paul's in London, "stand[ing] out of the welter so bravely," as E. M. Forster writes of it in *Howard's End*, "as if preaching the gospel of form." These domes exploited the possibilities of a double shell—the inner scaled to the space of the church crossing, the outer to the urban skyline.

But the dome antedates the *duomo* of Florence in the religious architecture of the West, as the cathedrals of Pisa and Siena and the domed churches of Aquitaine confirm. In the Orthodox East, in Byzantium and its sphere of influence, the dome has a colorful and long history. The low spherical forms of the early centuries are *Pl.34* represented by the grand survivor, Justinian's Hagia Sophia in Istanbul from the 6th century, whose shallow dome, substantially original, is still in place. In the later stages of Byzantine architecture, scalloped, saucer, or onion domes on tall perforated drums, grouped for the canonical Middle Byzantine scheme (a Greek-cross plan with nine bays and five domes), marked the churches of Greece and Sicily, Russia and Serbia. These domes, brightly colored in the Russian case, still announce historic cities like Kiev, Vladimir, Gračanica, Thessaloniki, Mistra and Palermo. The onion dome had also a separate and late career in Western Europe, beginning in the 16th century. First raised in the Netherlands and in Prague, the onion-shaped spire became a characteristic skyline feature in southern Germany, Czechoslovakia, Austria and the Dolomite region of Italy, for both religious and secular buildings. This spire has been interpreted as an effort to modify Gothic linear forms in accordance with the domical conventions imported from the South.[17]

Indeed, as the post-medieval urban esthetic, favoring low massing and horizontal continuities, suppressed much of the picturesque silhouette of the church form,

282 Rostov (Russia), skyline of the town with its onion-domed churches; the kremlin is on the left.

283 *Rome, spire of S. Ivo della Sapienza, by Francesco Borromini, ca. 1650.*

patrons and architects sought to recast the Gothic skyline through permissible attenuations of Classical form. Italy found ways to dematerialize the dome. Borromini's S. Ivo della Sapienza in Rome, begun in 1642, replaced the usual cupola above the drum with a spiral that twists around for several loops and culminates in a wire sculpture. Guarino Guarini's diaphanous domes in Turin went after similar effects. 283

But the most memorable revocation of a Gothic profile on a citywide scale was the crowd of Wren steeples that rose over London in the wake of the Great Fire of 1666.[18] The Fire destroyed 87 churches, but some parishes were amalgamated and only 51 were rebuilt, on the designs of Wren, who was assisted by Robert Hooke. Most of the churches were finished by 1685; the steeples dragged on for 15–20 years after that. Wren himself talks of the importance of "handsome spires, or Lanterns, rising in good Proportion above the neighbouring Houses"; and in *Parentalia* his intention is said to have been to rebuild "all the Parish Churches in such a Manner as to be seen at the End of a Vista of Houses, and dispersed in such distances from each other, as to appear neither too thick, nor thin in Prospect."[19]

The steeples were telescoped into several stories, marrying Gothic proportions and Classical detail. A handful were actually Gothic. The better-known high steeples were built of white Portland stone; more modest ones used lead. St. Margaret Pattens had a timber spire in the Gothic manner. The whole could be quite tall. The steeple of St. Mary-le-Bow is 225 feet (68.5 m.) high. The placement was always studied for maximum visibility. St. Edmund's, set in a narrow street, had its tower placed opposite a small cross street to save it from obscurity. In a number of churches the tower was moved to the edge of the building lot, and projected beyond the church mass, so it could make the best visual impact from a distance.

In their time the Wren steeples made a great impression. Canaletto who visited
Pl.35 London in 1746 painted several views of the river, all showing a forest of steeples, needle-thin against the great mass of St. Paul's, and these in turn rising from a forest of straight tallboys that held up the newly fashionable chimneypots.

Post-Fire London houses were about three stories high and of red brick. In the 1860s height limits were raised in the City, and many of Wren's steeples were obscured by Victorian and Edwardian office blocks. The original height of surrounding buildings had doubled by the early 20th century. This changing urban scale was a universal phenomenon after the 1850s. It put pressure on conventional skyline features to seek new heights.

Domes now grew taller through the progressive extension of the drum, a trend
Pl.4 which had already started in the 18th century in churches like St. Charles's in Vienna and Soufflot's Ste.-Geneviève (the Panthéon) in Paris, and was pushed to exotic extremes in multi-story drums like Alessandro Antonelli's for S. Gaudenzio in Novara (1841–88). As architects gained confidence in the use of metal reinforcement, the dome could go taller without structural worries. Monumental examples of reinforced domes are St. Isaac's (1817–57) in Leningrad, entirely framed in iron, and, in the secular realm, and United States Capitol (1851–65) by Thomas U. Walter.

Church towers also wrote a new chapter. In Russia between the 1830s and 1860s, Neoclassical horizontality and regularity which owed so much to Peter the Great's St. Petersburg and the building policies of Catherine the Great clashed with the return of medieval forms. At the time of the Byzantine-inspired multidome church, northern Russia had nurtured a vernacular tradition of wooden verticality. The so-called "tower churches" of Muscovy were built as a single tower of interlocking logs capped by an elongated octagonal cone. In the 17th century Patriarch Nikon banned the practice in the name of Orthodoxy, but under Peter and his successors the people's love for lofty sacred architecture was indulged again with the now stone towers displaying freshly imported Baroque flourishes (e.g., Moscow's Church of the Archangel Gabriel from 1701–7, known as the "Meshnikov Tower"). The 19th-century movement was seen, rather, as a return to the authentic traditions of Old Russia. New belltowers appeared along streets leading to the town center; in Moscow these belfries were brought right up to the street line, highlighting old monasteries and churches.

Similar traditionalist sentiment propped up the Gothic Revival in the West. This reaffirmation of "Christian" styles had at least two further motives. One was resurgent nationalism. The completion of Cologne Cathedral in Germany, begun in 1841 in celebration of the collapse of Napoleon's empire, is a case in point.

The other motive is the countering of the threat of the Industrial Revolution—fighting the massiveness of factories and the godlessness of the industrial work force. In England, Pugin's crusade for a revival of 13th-century Gothic, and the exertions of *The Ecclesiologist* to lay down the rules for a dogmatic church design, have been well scrutinized in the scholarly literature. A striking image of the new Christian

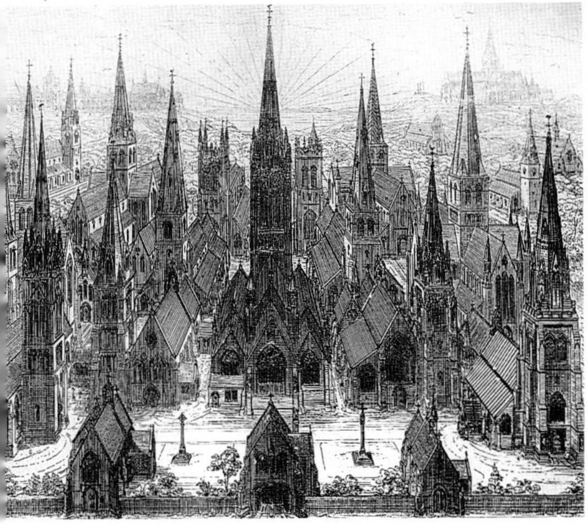

284 A. W. N. Pugin, "The Present Revival of Christian Architecture," frontispiece of his Apology for the Revival of Christian Architecture *(1843).*

"skyscraper city" is the frontispiece of Pugin's *Apology*, entitled "The Present Revival of Christian Architecture." In Kenneth Clark's words, "It represents twenty-two churches and chapels, chosen from his work, ranged like a Gothic New Jerusalem before the rising sun."[20] *284*

The name of W. F. Hook, Vicar of Leeds, is less well known. In the late 1830s he planned slum missions, grand pageant-like services to impress the poor. New churches built for them were to have transepts and a large choir higher than the nave, in defiance of the rule that parish churches ought not to look like cathedrals. Hook said that in these slum churches, "the choral system must be allied to the cathedral system [and] planted among gigantic mills and crowded alleys." A. J. B. Beresford-Hope, in his book *The English Cathedral of the Nineteenth Century* (1861), explained the need for these oversized churches by citing the scale and vitality of new urban buildings like railroad stations and "great central hotels." *Pl.38* "Can then the influence of this same spirit—," he wrote, "this increased appreciation of vastness—this greater aptitude for living and moving in a crowd—not make itself felt in man's religious transactions?"[21] The towers of these churches were to be set out as independent units, with clearly defined bases and caps.

An early urban minster is St. Mary Magdalene, Munster Square, London, begun in 1849. It combines the tower, asymmetrically placed at the southwest corner, with a small entrance courtyard, an early example of the tower-porch which will at times straddle the sidewalk (e.g., St. James the Less, Westminster, London). All Saints, Margaret Street, again in London, designed by William Butterfield, also began in 1849. Beresford-Hope takes some credit for the way the church was able to "domineer by its elevation over the haughty and Protestantized shopocracy."[22] The tower had the tallest spire in London at the time, variously reported to be 222 or 227 feet (67.7/69.2 m.). From that point on and for a decade or two, the High Victorian Gothic church tower, enhanced by structural polychromy in brick and stone and frequently diapered, became an assertive accent of urban vistas. G. E. Street was the great specialist of elaborate church towers, some planted away from home, on the streets of Rome and Mürren, Switzerland. In a famous essay of 1850 in *The Ecclesiologist*, "On the Proper Characteristics of a Town Church," Street wrote: "Height is of immense importance, and is to be obtained at all costs."

In France the neo-Gothic churches often had a single tower attached axially to the west façade, e.g., St.-Lubin at Rambouillet (1865–69), or Notre-Dame-de-la-Croix in Paris (1863–80); and in a more classical vein, St.-Pierre de Montrouge in Paris. The style of the striped Byzantinizing cathedral of Marseilles (1852–93) by Léon Vaudoyer, and its emulation by his student Henri-Jacques Espérandieu in Notre-Dame-de-la-Garde (1853–64), which dominated the hill on one side of the port, had no lasting influence. But the hilltop location, and that of later 19th-century churches like Notre-Dame-de-Fourvière in Lyon and the Sacré-Coeur in Paris, sought to *Pl.25* compensate for the irreparably secularized, elephantine modern cityscape.

LANDMARKS OF THE SECULAR CITY

Some of the features reviewed above have both a religious and a secular destiny. Within the same cultural sphere, the pagoda accents Buddhist temples as well as gates of city walls. The dome, of course, is ubiquitous and cross-cultural. It marks government buildings, baths, and tombs as readily as it does churches; and it is used in Baroque Rome, Safavid Isfahan, and medieval Novgorod with comparable distinction. The appeal to the skyline is evident in most of them, since the exterior profile of the dome has no correspondence to the space shaped within. In some instances, Bulfinch's State House in Boston for example, there is no sign at all inside the building of the dome's existence.

The belfry is also a good case. We associate it chiefly with the church and the ringing of bells for religious services. But there are secular belfries as well, associated with government. The skyline of Flemish towns was often highlighted by a belfry that was a separate building in the marketplace. It served both as rallying point for
275 the townsfolk and as civic landmark in the flat countryside. At Bruges it measured 330 feet (100 m.) in height; at Ghent 300 feet (91 m.); at Dunkirk, 295 feet (90 m.); at Ypres, 230 feet (70 m.). The belfry also occurs occasionally in northern France; in places like Soissons and St.-Quentin, it takes the form of a tower attached to a castle. Most frequently the belfry is a fixture of important public buildings in medieval communes—a sign of their sovereignty and civic pride. Such towers appear with special frequency in central Italy and Northern Europe. In addition to town halls, they accent markets (as at Bruges), and monuments to powerful guilds like cloth halls (as at Ypres).

In these cityscapes, a visual contrast is often set up between church and state through the prominent civic tower and the belfry of the cathedral. Height is of course the most obvious element of this contest, but other design discriminations can be as effective. In Tuscany different building materials, which read as contrasts of color, make a skyline statement with unmistakable clarity. At Siena, the brick tower of the city hall lifts its attenuated shaft from the floor of the Campo to respond to the white mass of the cathedral and its campanile on the hilltop of Città. Florence, prior to the splendid concentration of its skyline by Brunelleschi's dome, pitted the dark brooding towers of government—those of the Palazzo Vecchio and the Bargello (Palazzo del Podestà)—against the radiant marble-encrusted form of
Pl.33 "Giotto's Campanile" for S. Maria del Fiore. The civic towers, in addition, were often massively built and opaque, and their flat-topped summit articulated with the *ballatoio*, a machicolated cornice borrowed from military architecture. The adoption of this secular form by Giotto's successors for the campanile in the later 14th century, rejecting his original spired scheme based on North European models, was probably intended to signify that the cathedral was in the care of the commune—in effect a civic monument.[23]

THE URBAN SKYLINE

Skylines are urban signatures. They are the shorthand of urban identity, and the chance for urban flourish. Cities of all descriptions and periods raise aloft distinctive landmarks, to celebrate faith and power and special achievement. These landmarks focus city forms and highlight city portraits. The presentation itself is contrived. It is chiefly meant for an external audience. The artist composes the urban skyline with the pilgrim, the official visitor, the common tourist in mind. This image changes slowly and deliberately. Contrasts like that of Canaletto's London and the city today were a long time in the making. Radical transformations—the thrust of factory smokestacks or corporate towers—signify cultural upheavals. When the towered railway terminal and its hotel lifts up its silhouette in emulation of the urban cathedral, we know that the old values are reduced or overtopped. When the city center ends up as an aggregate of tall office buildings, we recognize that the city image has succumbed to the advertising urges of private enterprise. The skyline, in the end, is a negotiated symbol. What stands out as the city's official silhouette was given license to do so.

Pl.31 right *The patron saint of San Gimignano (Italy) holds an image of the city crowned by feudal towers, in a late 14th-century altarpiece by Taddeo di Bartolo.*

Pl.32 above *A tourist's view of the New York City skyline, from the Staten Island ferry, 1975.*

Hierarchies and rivalries

Pl.33 above *Florence (Italy), a painting of ca. 1500 based on the* catena *woodcut view. At the heart of the city is the cathedral; surrounding it, a ring of walls, and then its hinterland. The radiantly white S. Maria del Fiore, crowned by Brunelleschi's dome and flanked by Giotto's Campanile, is set against the dark, lesser-towered buildings of the secular government—the Bargello and Palazzo Vecchio, to the right.*

Pl.34 right *Istanbul (Turkey) seen from the Suleymaniye Mosque, 1844. The bulky dome in the distance is that of the 6th-century Byzantine church of Hagia Sophia. The Ottomans Islamicized it by adding four minarets, and built echoes of it across the city's skyline. The Blue Mosque of Sultan Ahmed, far right, is unique in having six minarets. This large view was painted by the Austrian artist Hubert Sattler and exhibited throughout Europe in his "cosmorama."*

From towers of God to towers of man

Pl.35 London in 1746, painted by Canaletto from the house of his patron, the second Duke of Richmond (near the present New Scotland Yard). St. Paul's Cathedral rules the skyline, attended by a host of stone and leaden spires—almost all designed by Wren as well. Only two secular features appear (both at the far right): the tall columnar Monument to the Great Fire of 1666, and a dark conical bottle oven on the industrial south bank.

Pl.36 London in 1990, looking back toward the City from Greenwich. Now the only sacred marker is the dome of St. Paul's, scarcely visible at the far left between two rectangular slab blocks. The tallest skyscraper near it is the National Westminster Bank building. In Greenwich, the view of the Queen's House and Hospital is closed by the controversial new business district under construction across the river, dominated by Cesar Pelli's Canary Wharf tower, the tallest building in England to date.

The 19th-century skyline

Pl.37 Sheffield (England) in the 1850s: a world center for the production of steel cutlery and tools, and, since the coming of the railroad, of large castings such as armor plating for ships. William Ibbitt's image records the unprecedented transformation of townscape by mechanized industry, as factory chimneys became the belfries and minarets of the new age.

Pl.38 right A 19th-century answer to the London at the Midland Grand, now St. Pancras, by George Gilbert Scott, 1868–70. The lower tower on the right is that of King's Cross Station. To the left are the spire of St. Pancras Church (ca. 1820) and the slightly later dome of University College. Painting by John O'Connor, 1881 (detail).

NEWS
BILL POSTERS
80 HIGH S^T
ISLINGTON
DAILY NEWS

The belfry and steeple of the church was the only idiom of architectural grandeur known to Colonial America; so that is what topped Independence Hall in Philadelphia in 1750, a tall steepled tower that dominated the land for miles away. In a reverse borrowing, the gilded spire of the cathedral of SS. Peter and Paul in St. Petersburg from the 1730s was intentionally reminiscent of the one on Copenhagen's Exchange built a century earlier.

In the Victorian era, public buildings of all sorts—city halls, law courts, railway stations—hoisted towers. "How many are there," Leopold Eidlitz wrote in 1881, *Pl.38*
"who are willing to forego a tower simply because it is not needed either physically or aesthetically, . . . if by an ingenious argument it may be justified."[24] The debate of how far to extend the Gothic Revival beyond strictly religious architecture was quite heated in England. Schools and charitable buildings required no special pleading. Government buildings, commercial architecture, and the new traveling landscape of hotels and railroad terminals proved more contentious. In Germany, towered Gothic city halls from the late Middle Ages could justify the neo-Gothic Rathaus in Franz Joseph's Vienna, and none other than G. G. Scott, already famous for the *Pl.4*
elaborate tower of the Protestant church of St. Nicholas in Hamburg from 1844–45, could defend his project for the Hamburg Rathaus ten years later on the grounds that "The very idea of a town hall or a civic hall is Gothic. The town councils which they symbolize are essentially teutonic, in terms of both origin and character, and must be regarded as one of the most worthy German institutions and one that deserves to be commemorated."[25] Lacking this specific historic precedent, the ambitious Victorian town halls of industrial England, like of that of Leeds by Cuthbert Brodrick from the 1850s, gave their towers an impressive civic classicism, although the Gothicists had their day in places like Manchester. But the Houses of Parliament with its two great Gothic towers had established national skyline symbols that were echoed throughout the century. The clock tower with Big Ben combined ornamental features from Flemish belfries, like that of the Cloth Hall at Ypres, with the sheerness of Italian campanili, while the 337-foot (103 m.) high Victoria Tower in its foursquare mass recalled both late Perpendicular crossing towers and the tradition of castles and country estates.

Railroad terminals were an unprecedented, exclusively modern institution, but as the new gates of cities they took to imposing clock towers from the very start. The Italian campanile had a short vogue, and there were exotic specimens, like the twin towers and truncated entrance pagoda of Union Station in New Haven by Henry Austin (1848–49), intended to convey the excitement of distant places. But medievalizing towers were quite popular from mid-century onward, and the unease of religious associations was never completely stilled. Boston's Park Square Station, a contemporary source found, "resembles more nearly a church edifice . . . and aiding still more to mislead the spectator as to the nature of the edifice is a well-proportioned tower 125 feet [38 m.] high."[26]

Exclusively secular skyline features before the Industrial Revolution must begin with the city walls. To an approaching traveler on the high roads, this was the first *286*
and mightiest visual impression of Carcassonne or Marrakesh. The walls were themselves etched against the sky with vertical accents like towers, turreted gates, pagodas and the like.

This is the medieval tradition of cityscape; good examples are in the Guidoriccio da Fogliano painting by Simone Martini at the Palazzo Pubblico of Siena, where the *285*
condottiere is shown riding between two strongholds, Sassoforte and Montemassi. Since the issue is subjection, the city image is appropriately martial. When Siena portrays itself, on the other hand, in the *Allegory of Good Government* by

Pl.39 Hong Kong at night, an urban vision unimaginable in earlier centuries. The star players—at the moment—in this international show are the Hongkong and Shanghai Bank on the left (Foster Associates, completed 1986) and the even more recent and taller Bank of China building (I. M. Pei).

285 *Simone Martini,* Guidoriccio da Fogliano, *1328, fresco in the Palazzo Pubblico, Siena (Italy). The two towns between which Guidoriccio is shown riding are said to represent Sassoforte and Montemassi, both conquered in 1328, but the decision to add the rider to a conventional landscape of cities may have been an afterthought.*

Ambrogio Lorenzetti, it is satisfied with showing the agglomerate of its civil structures, especially its houses. In between these two contexts, there is the purely descriptive townscape of the picture in the Pinacoteca at Siena called *A City by the Sea*, also perhaps by Lorenzetti, which includes in the skyline the constituent elements of an Italian town—the *rocca* or castle, churches, civil buildings, and the encompassing walls.

In traditional curtain walls, when the rendition is sufficiently realistic, the city highpoints (church steeples, etc.) appear above the line of the walls like masts of ships. With bastioned walls of the 16th century and later, the main monuments are more visible from outside because of the low-lying walls, but the distance created by these sprawling modern fortifications between the approaching visitor and the urban skyline is a new problem.

A number of miscellaneous vertical accents in the pre-industrial city have a functional excuse. Lighthouses, fire watchtowers and the like have to be tall in order to be visible. But it is the Industrial Revolution that creates and makes banal the technological landmarks of a working skyline. The tall generic brick smokestack
Pl.37 becomes the belfry and minaret of the new age. More specialized shapes are invented for the tasks at hand, and are installed as the empowering symbols of towns. Bristol adds to its profile the bottle-shaped kilns of its pottery- and glass-making industry. The grain elevator towers at the end of Main Street in the small Midwestern towns of Iowa and Kansas or looms by the river or the railroad tracks. In Oklahoma and Texas oil rigs proclaim the wealth and pride of their communities.

113 Water towers are a 19th-century phenomenon. In flat country, the pressure needed to force water into the upper stories of buildings could be attained only through storing water at sufficient heights. In American railroad towns from about 1840 onward, the water tower that tanked up the steam locomotives became the principal skyline object, along with grain elevators. The construction was stone or brick; then, at the turn of the century, the spherical containers began to be made of sheet metal.

Water towers notable for their architectural treatment include the Beyazit Tower
309 in Istanbul, the old Water Tower in Chicago, and in Germany the Mannheim Water Tower in the park of the Rose Garden, and the tower at Worms built, like the cathedral, of red sandstone, and made to conform stylistically to the famous

Romanesque monuments of the city. At Mönchengladbach, the water tower was built as a self-conscious architectural monument on the principal summit of the city, with the streets running toward it on axis.

In recent decades, water towers have been made of steel or concrete. The elevated water tanks of concrete, pioneered by Sweden and Finland, are flattened conical shells; they are bunched together dramatically in water-hungry countries like Saudi Arabia—modern age surrogates of the great hypostyle halls of Luxor and Karnak.[27]

As the 20th-century change ran its course from a manufacturing to a service and communication age, transmission towers in thin scaffolds of steel took positions of unchallenged prominence. Beginning with Stuttgart's in 1954–55 a number of transmission towers were built of concrete instead of steel, with round or hexagonal
shafts. Examples are in Berlin, Frankfurt, London, Johannesburg, Wuhan (China), 287
and Moscow. Kyoto's sits on top of a ten-story hotel, and that of Riyadh (Saudi Arabia) has a shaft of marble and a head of glass in the shape of a cut diamond in which stars shine at night. Toronto's CN Tower is currently the tallest in the world (1,748 feet or 533 m.), but these distinctions are short-lived.[28]

To get us to know and love them, telecommunication towers had viewing platforms and restaurants at the top. And towers were also set up specifically as sky restaurants, like the Space Needle in Seattle for the 1962 World's Fair, the freestanding restaurant tower of the Reunion Hotel in Dallas, Texas (1976), and the

286 Avila (Spain), general view showing the still extant medieval walls.

287 *Berlin, Marienkirche* and Fernsehturm *(television tower). The late 18th-century neo-Gothic spire of the 15th-century Marienkirche is overwhelmed by its 20th-century neighbor, built by the former East German government. At 1,197 feet (365 m.), the television tower was at the time of its completion in 1969 second in stature only to Moscow's. It boasts a spherical "Tele-Café" suspended more than 50 stories above the city.*

Sunsphere Tower for the 1982 World's Fair in Knoxville, Tennessee. These are novelty landmarks of the sort we have embraced since the Eiffel Tower. Free of the associations of industry and unburdened by the tensions of a collective past, these oddities work well to unify the city-form, especially when the skyline is not in itself memorable: they are also testimony to the impoverishment of traditional symbols of urbanized culture.

DESIGNING THE SKYLINE

If the overriding theme of this chapter is to determine the extent to which the urban silhouette is premeditated and purposely revised, we have already said enough to establish the fact that, the modern capitalist experience notwithstanding, laissez-faire skylines are not the norm. But we need to specify and elaborate further.

We should reflect, as a beginning, that an expressive skyline has not always been a manifest need. In some cultures or periods of urban history, cities maintained uneventful, flat profiles.

China is one. In the Chinese city, houses, business structures, temples, government buildings were all essentially one-story buildings, or one- and two-story parts forming single units. All of them enclosed open ground. Materials and style were more or less uniform. Since these cities had no autonomy, there was clearly no effort at the skyline level to emphasize communal government with civic monuments and city halls. The pagodas of some temples did stand out, as did some pagoda-shaped towers of the city walls, the drum tower at the central intersection, and the bell tower. The skyline, then, was determined by and large by the ring of walls and, in the case of imperial cities, the modest rise of the imperial palace which occupied a higher platform than the rest of the public buildings.

Ancient Rome is another interesting case. Roman cities, in the later stages of their history, acquired something of a skyline through the bulk of buildings like baths and amphitheaters at the city edge. Otherwise, the domes were shallow, the obelisks were on spines of circuses, which meant on low ground, so nothing terribly high stood out. The exception would be the lighthouses of ports, and the occasional "skyscraper" of rental flats like the one near the Pantheon referred to by Tertullian (*Adv. Val.* 7).

A second consideration has to do with multicultural cities, for example Jerusalem, where more than one dominant culture is forced to exist, or Istanbul, where one culture has been overcome and replaced by another without being wiped out completely. In the case of Istanbul, the appropriation of the Byzantine skyline by *Pl.34*
means of minarets added to the domed churches is well known. In Jerusalem, the premier landmark of the now subject culture, the Dome of the Rock, still controls the skyline of the old city, although the Jewish periphery of public buildings and 289
housing has certainly redefined the relationship of settlement to landscape. In Ireland, at Armagh, when the emancipated Catholics came to build their cathedral in the 19th century they placed it on a height overlooking the town where the

288 Edo (Tokyo), in an 1865 photograph by Felice Beato (cf. Ill. 179). The daimyo *compound is in the foreground. The Japanese city, like its Chinese contemporaries, shows a horizontal roofscape of one- and two-story wooden structures, with few or no vertical skyline accents.*

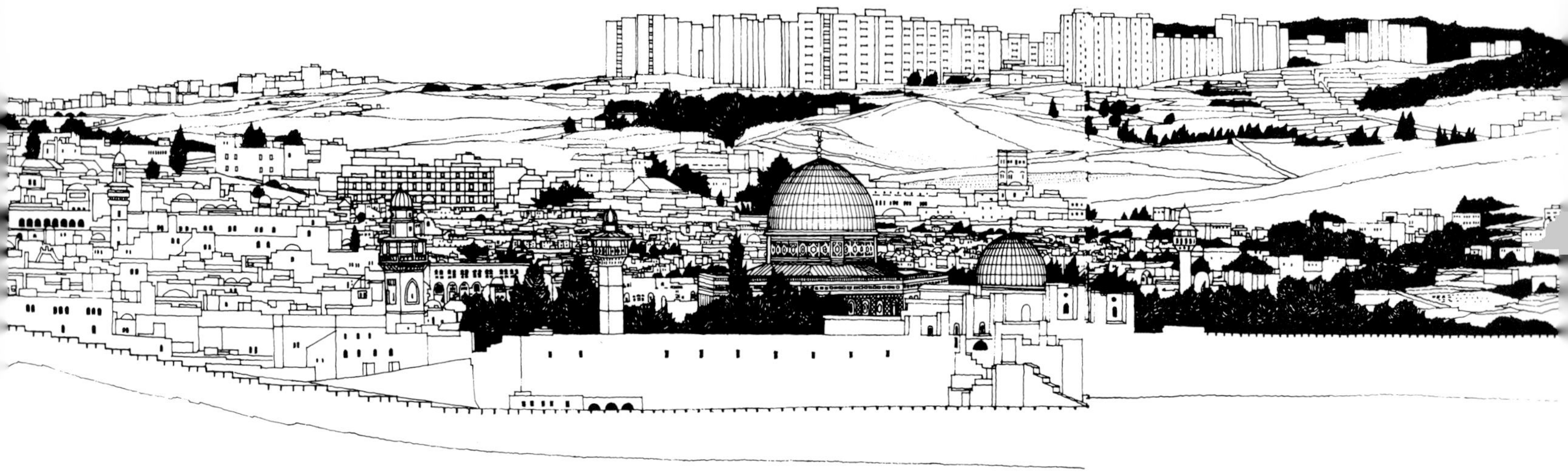

medieval—hence Church of Ireland—cathedral crowned an ancient hill, and gave the new cathedral tall steeples to be sure to outdo the Protestants.

Conquerors, aware of the importance of the skyline, at times imposed restrictions regarding it on the subject people. The Ottomans, for example, did not allow their Christian subjects in countries like Bulgaria to have domes, towers or belfries on their churches and prescribed that their churches and houses had to be lower than those of the Muslims.[29] And after independence came to Bulgaria, the main public buildings like the school and the church, the belfry and the clocktower, were often situated on high sites, deliberately overtopping the hitherto dominant mosque.

289 *Jerusalem, a drawing by Arthur Kutcher published in his* The New Jerusalem *(1973). The historic skyline in the foreground tries to hold its own against modern development, like the housing estate on French Hill.*

SOME PRINCIPLES

A number of design criteria can be isolated which determine the physical validity of the skyline: among them, *height*, *shape*, and *approach*. The first two refer to the landmark features of the skyline, the third to the skyline as a whole. This is a good point to remind ourselves that what the Germans call the *Stadtbild* is much more than landmarks. The term refers to the entirety of the urban profile as it relates to its site, which is sometimes primarily the massing of the outer houses and the layering of the rooftops. This is notably the case with Italian hill towns.

Height

Height is a relative matter—relative to a landmark's surroundings. There is pride in being the tallest building in Europe, or east of the Rockies, or in the world. But the actual impression the building will make depends on what is around it.

So we have ideal competitions and local ones. The Gothic cathedrals of the Ile-de-France were keen to surpass each other in nave height, and the number and height of
276 towers. But each one dominated the appearance of its own city unchallenged. Catherine the Great, in her eponymous new city of Ekaterinoslav which she founded in 1787, projected a magnificent cathedral "an *arshin* [ca. 28 inches/0.7 m.] higher than St. Peter's in Rome."[30] But the inhabitants would not have experienced this overscaling: to them, the cathedral would have been just a very tall church.

The skyscraper contest is, again, both generic and place-specific. Every year we hear of one somewhere in the world that supersedes all others in height. But the actual fight for the skyline happens locally, as the IDS Building crushes Foshay's obelisk in downtown Minneapolis, or the Sears Tower overwhelms the competition in Chicago, the very cradle of skyscraping.

Height limits are a recurrent theme in city-making. Augustan Rome had them, so did Elizabethan London. Though these limits had to do with structural safety and the dread of fires, their impact on the city silhouette is obvious.

In shaping the skyline, cities exempted certain kinds of buildings from prevailing height limits. The London Act of 1888, for example, which set a limit of 80 feet (24.5 m.) or the width of the street in question, exempted church steeples. In Stockholm building height was regulated to privilege church steeples until after the Second World War. Nowadays most height restrictions exempt impermanent attachments to buildings, and so television aerials get off easily.

Los Angeles in 1926 exempted by popular vote its new City Hall from the *290*
prevailing 150-foot (46 m.) building height limit, so it could climb up to almost three times that height—equivalent to 32 stories—and fix the then unremarkable skyline. Two other buildings were also exempted: the Hall of Justice and the United States Post Office. Both of them were built substantially lower than City Hall, and so did not challenge its pre-eminence. The 150-foot limit, first set in 1911, remained in effect, primarily because of earthquake fears, until 1956 when it was lifted by an amendment to the city charter. As a consequence, skyscraper construction bypassed Los Angeles which alone among major American cities has nothing to show of the national crop of several generations of highrises. An observer in 1941 noted that the central business district resembled that of a small town. "The metropolitan aspect is lacking because of the absence of skyscrapers," he concluded.[31]

Restrictions on highrises existed probably as early as the 1880s in Chicago. That city, which had settled for a maximum height limit of 130 feet (39.6 m.) at the turn of the century (to Boston's 125 feet/38.4 m.), had doubled it by 1920. New York's zoning ordinance of 1916 legalized the concept of the setback. The maximum height was defined as a multiple of the street width. There were five height districts, from the "one-time" district where the maximum height was equal to the street width, to the "two-and-a-half times" district where the height was equal to the street width multiplied by 2.5. Above this height, the building had to be set back according to a variable ratio. In the "two-and-a-half times" district, the setback had to be a foot for each 5 feet of height above the limit. Otherwise, there was no absolute height restriction, a strict adherence to which yields monotonous skylines like Honolulu's, "as uniform as teeth in a comb extending several miles along the oceanfront."[32]

In the United States a limited authority is granted the Federal Aviation Administration to question the height limit of buildings which might affect the navigable airspace over cities—which usually means the path of runways around metropolitan airports. Technically any building which intends to go higher than 200 feet (61 m.) is required to submit notice to the FAA, but the ultimate determination of matters of height and zoning resides with local government.

290 Los Angeles (California), City Hall, 1926. The building has been overtopped since 1956, when the height limit in effect since 1911 was lifted, by a forest of office highrises.

How do we measure ahead of time what a new building will do to the skyline? There are "home remedies." To this day, it is not uncommon in residential neighborhoods to put up a pole indicating the height of a projected building. That does not do for skyscrapers, of course, but here too there are home remedies. In England the height of the tall building was set for a long while by the 100-foot (30 m.) length of the fireman's ladder. And when Cambridge University proposed in 1962 to build three high towers on the New Museums site, "a number of balloons were sent up to the heights to which it was proposed to build, so that some probable effects of the building could be judged."[33] The specter was scary enough to induce the planning authority to reject the towers.

More sophisticated devices are the photomontage, where doctored pictures show the new buildings in place and juxtaposed to familiar extant landmarks. This form

of presentation could be more or less elaborate. In the case of the Millbank Tower in London, an extensive series of photographs were taken "from numerous points within a mile radius of the site and an accurately calculated montage superimposed on each."[34] Today even these methods seem archaic. Computers and simulation techniques prepare data of various sorts on which decisions affecting huge fortunes and the future of cities are based. When first set up in 1969, the Environmental
291 Simulation Laboratory at the University of California at Berkeley was primarily concerned with the immediate environmental impact of a projected tall building, but it also made possible the accurate visualization of skyline changes. If we condone enormities today it is not for lack of quantifiable knowledge.

291 Environmental Simulation Laboratory, University of California at Berkeley.

But the power and greed of major developers, and our tolerance of vertical reach, have yet to subside appreciably. The pre-Second World War crop of skyscrapers now look modest at a time when the fifty-story highrise is a commonplace. Loath to interfere with the plans of international corporations and risk losing them to other cities, local governments are nevertheless making a feeble effort to protect natural and monumental views. Some of these are gentlemen's agreements, but not everybody is a gentleman. It is clear that if cities are serious about keeping central symbols of government unobscured, they will have to legislate controls.

Several American cities have taken the lead. Madison, Wisconsin, in legislation passed in 1977, decreed that

> No portion of any building or structure located within one mile of the center of the State Capitol Building shall exceed the elevation of the base of the columns of said Capitol Building . . . This prohibition shall not apply to any flagpoles, communications towers, church spires, elevator penthouses, and chimneys exceeding such elevation, when approved as conditional uses.

Similar legislation in Little Rock, Arkansas, the following year stated that, "Since the symbolic importance of the Capitol Building is greatly dependent on the visual prominence of the Capitol dome as a unique form on the city skyline, no new development should extend above the base of the dome."[35]

The one American exception, as always, is the federal city of Washington, D.C. It is the nation's horizontal city, thanks to an unrepealed Act of 1910 which set the maximum building height at 130 feet (39.6 m.), similar to that of Boston and Chicago at the time. There is no mention in the Act of the skyline or the Capitol or any other monument. The alleged correspondence with the height of the Capitol dome is wide off the mark, since that is 315 feet (96 m.). But the Act has served the city well. Attempts by the real estate and building industry lobbies to revise the figure upward have been effectively counterbalanced by the preservation movement, which fought to declare all of the L'Enfant plan off limits to highrise development and push beyond until the surrounding rim of hills.

Shape

The general mass and shape of buildings is a good device to distinguish different competing programs within one historical frame—castle versus town hall—or else the supercession of one regime or historical era by another—Brunelleschi's
Pl.33 cathedral dome in the medieval context of Florence. In strident shifts of power, incoming regimes will try to invent some skyline feature to set themselves apart from the rest of history. The Fascists proposed (unsuccessfully) the "Torre Littoria" as a device for appropriating the skyline of Italian cities.

In Moscow, the Palace of the Soviets was intended to transfix the urban skyline upon one landmark. Iofan's 1933 design featured a squat three-tiered tower, with a

60-foot (18 m.) high figure of "the Emancipated Proletarian" capping its façade. A new design the following year stretched the palace vertically, and crowned it with a 295
260-foot (79 m.) high statue of Lenin in what would become the canonical pose—one arm cradling a sheaf of papers, the other extended toward his audience and the future. This revised monument became the focal point for the 1935 "Stalin" Plan of Moscow. Construction began in 1937, but the palace became a victim of the war.

In the Twenties, the young Weimar republic also sought to distinguish itself from the overthrown *ancien régime* in Berlin by promoting for the heart of the city the dashing new building type of the office tower, which was touted as the symbol of "big city democracy." Several competitions were held to give the city a highrise profile. "The people pant under their daily burden," Martin Wagner wrote in 1922, "but the architects—dream! They build high towers. The idea of highrises and towers has seized them. As they formerly planned and built the Bismarck towers, so now company and office buildings rise towerlike into the sky, albeit a sky of paper."[36] The proposals were freely inventive, abstract forms consciously removed from the historicist skyscrapers of America. The most striking project was Mies van der Rohe's glass skyscraper, prophetic of the reflective highrise surfaces of 292
the period after the Second World War.

But the Weimar years passed without installing beacons of this originality. The company buildings that were built were by and large stocky piles almost never over ten stories high, located not where city designers had planned with an eye to redefining the skyline of Berlin, but at the site of company headquarters or of priorly owned land parcels. By the time of the Nazi takeover in 1933, the design of highrises emphasized the horizontal floor lines. The new regime disdained the skyscraper as un-German, and used it inconspicuously. On the great axis planned by Hitler and Speer, the two projected tall buildings were for mundane destinations—a hotel and 263
the office component of the Army High Command—and set back from the main building walls of the avenue.

After the War, West Germany welcomed the tall building although it resolved to keep it out of the old historic centers. The debate within the German Democratic Republic was more complicated. According to the reconstruction law of 1950, "political, cultural and administrative facilities were to be located in city centers . . . and the silhouette was to be characterized by major monumental buildings."[37] A skyscraper of some sort was important to have in this ensemble, in order to distinguish the skyline of regional administrative centers. Local preferences were sometimes at odds with these broad policies. In Dresden, for example, city officials favored the historic preservation of the bombed city, which would mean the restitution of the *old* skyline, and resisted the desires of the Communist Party and especially the central government for a dominant modern tower that would have disrupted the historic atmosphere.[38]

292 Ludwig Mies van der Rohe, entry for the 1922 Friedrichstrasse station competition, Berlin. Mies's proposal would have added a revolutionary glass and steel skyscraper to the traditional center of Berlin. The project, ignored by the competition's jurors, is said to have been inspired by the sight of American steel-framed highrises under construction.

At any rate, plans to place a single tower for the Party's centralized apparatus in Berlin, Dresden, Magdeburg and Stalinstadt, and in other satellite capitals like Sofia and Bucharest, were never realized. But the concept of a unique skyline-crowning tower block survived the fall of Stalin and of Socialist Realism. Under subsequent regimes a Modernist idiom was embraced, and the iconography of bureaucratic power shifted to one of scientific and technological prowess. The signature towers were now designed as industrial and technical research headquarters. Two were built in East Germany, on university campuses. In Jena the skyscraper was circular, symbolic of the lens and so the local optical industry; in Leipzig, a publishing center, it was triangular to symbolize the open book. Meantime, the parallel use of towers as housing units was accorded a homey symbolism. Of his highrise residential blocks

224 on East Berlin's Stalinallee (Karl-Marx-Allee), the rehabilitated Modernist Hermann Henselmann wrote: "The tower is for our people—as for scarcely any other—an expression of steadfastness, endurance, and strength. The people use the concept of the tower in their language to express the same ideas."[39]

While on the subject of shapes, I should also bring up bulk. There is obviously a major difference between a television aerial or a space needle and the coolers of a nuclear plant. The dominance of one or the other on the skyline is clearly not a function of height or height alone. In his book *Skylines*, Wayne Attoe reminds us that in England at Durham in 1944 the debate around a proposed power plant three-quarters of a mile (1 km.) north of the cathedral was not over height but over bulk. It was the enormous bulk of the power plant that would detract from the famous cathedral, the opposition claimed, even though the plant was considerably lower and a fair distance away. (The company abandoned plans to build, and the Durham skyline is now protected by law.) In the same vein, the City Architect of Oxford, in his recommended guidelines for the design review of new buildings in 1962, emphasized the "extreme fragility" of the skyline, "the spikeyness of its silhouette. The introduction into it of any bulky elements would unavoidably destroy this essential characteristic."[40]

Approach

This issue concerns the direct experience of skyline features by the visitor to the city. The traditional city was small and was experienced more directly because it was
286 seen without suburban sprawl. In fact, the walls were usually the first element of the skyline to be encountered. Today, the cities are large and uncircumscribed, and all sorts of skyline features begin to appear in the urban fringe before we are allowed to read the symbolic relationships of the city center even were they to be preserved by law. In the case of Washington, D.C., for example, the highrise rim that surrounds the horizontal city of L'Enfant has to be ignored until we glimpse the Monument and the Capitol dome. Today there is also a need to announce cities to freeway drivers speeding toward them at some odd angle and extravagant level. Aerial views of cities have also become so commonplace that canonizing those particular images from the
Pl.23 sky proved unavoidable. Cameron's *Above* series is today's equivalent of Feininger's or Stieglitz's skyline images.

Traditionally, there were three kinds of urban skyline views that mattered—
Pls.5,6 those you had from approach roads by land; waterfront views along a river or the seacoast; and the views to be had from high vantage points within the city limits and
268 in the environs, places like the Pincio and the Janiculum in Rome, Brunate in Como, and Montmartre in Paris. The earliest views of Paris are, in fact, from Montmartre (1415 ff.).[41] Besides natural viewing platforms, the city looked down upon itself from the summits of tall buildings. Climbing belfries and domes has been a popular sport for hundreds of years. The modern case involves, of course, the highrise. The rooftop observatory of the RCA Building at Rockefeller Center in New York City "was the nation's most extensive; the building's length gave nearly half a million yearly visitors ample room to stroll."[42] At San Francisco's Empire Hotel, the "Sky Room" restaurant with its 360-degree view (from about 1938) provided the model for the later revolving restaurants which will find their ultimate perch, as we saw, on telecommunications towers and towers specifically designed for dining to a view.

Pl.32 Views from the water are often panoramic and progressively revelatory. The urban skyline is the fixed element of an ambience in motion: water and sky make a flattering frame for the meanest city-form. The distant silhouette becomes richer and more varied as the vessel draws near. An effective skyline is therefore one which

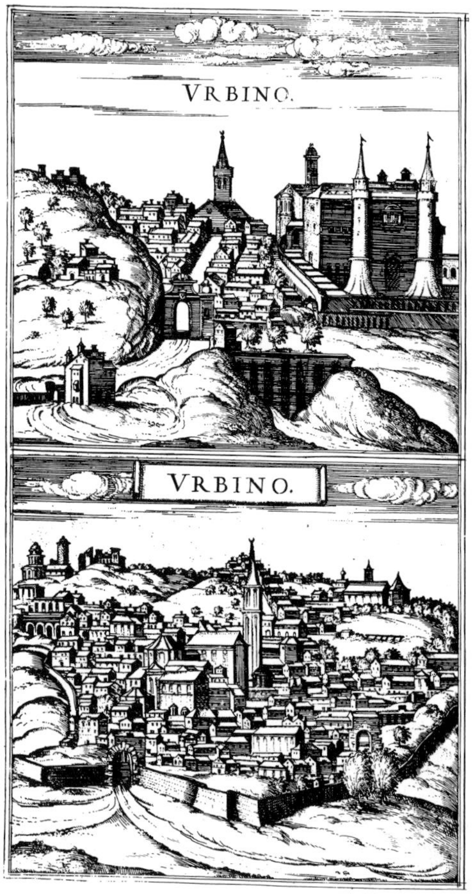

293 *Urbino (Italy), two views from* Civitates Orbis Terrarum *(1587), from the south (top) and east (above). By the mid-16th century the standard image of the city had shifted from the east-facing vista, with its emphasis on the town and its cathedral, to the south view dominated by the ducal palace and its towered frontispiece.*

has features scaled to a succession of viewpoints. A tall lighthouse like the famous Pharos of Alexandria, or an oversized statue like the Colossus of Rhodes or New York's Statue of Liberty, make fair signposts for the cityscape that is to open up behind them. A crowning feature of a building—a dome or a spire—may play a similar anchoring role. Landbound cities wanting to announce themselves to seafaring visitors must rely on height. The gleaming white outline of the Parthenon on the high outcrop of the Acropolis announced Athens to the boats entering the port of Piraeus. The spear tip of Athena Promachos, a great bronze statue of the goddess at the entrance to the Acropolis, was visible from further out at sea. *Pl.5*

Land routes focus the city more intently. To the extent that a city cared about this introductory image, it would manipulate the direction of the road and compose the scene with some picturesque or ideological aim in mind. The practice of directing approach routes toward skyline features is persistent. As Braunfels says, "Napoleon was not the first to direct cross-country roads toward church spires. The majority of roads in the Middle Ages were also built in such a way as to lead directly to the spires of the cathedral or city church."[43]

Urbino is a celebrated case of the composed city. Recent scholarship has drawn *293*
attention to the reorientation of its skyline during the 15th century to suit the policies of its lord, Federigo da Montefeltro. The key event was the addition to his new palace of a triumphal arch frontispiece, to be seen first as one came up to the city from the south on the high road from Rome, following the ancient path of the Via Flaminia. Henceforth the city skyline begins to be rendered from that side, as opposed to rarer views showing it from the east. I have summarized elsewhere the significance of this shift—the special relation of Federigo to Pope Sixtus IV, who raised his title from count to duke and installed him as Standard-Bearer of the Church and Knight of St. Peter.[44] The palace corresponded to this newfound dignity, and its orientation outward in the direction of Rome acknowledged the client-patron bond with the Roman Pontiff. The eastern view of the skyline, on the other hand, highlighted the religious buildings, with the palace registering only as a mere cipher at the extreme upper left.

These singleminded arrangements are only possible in towns of the size of Urbino. When the city-form is more widespread and complicated, skyline management must, at some point, address the distribution of landmarks in relation to approaches. John Evelyn recognizes this fact when he writes, in the report accompanying his post-Fire plan for London, that his new parish churches are to be *212*
"so placed and interspersed, as may have some reference to the adornment of the profile of the city upon all its avenues, and therefore at studied intervals . . ."[45]

The resident conflict is between the age-old tradition of a dense monumental core and the outward spread of the open city. The metropolitan central business district, or "CBD," of 20th-century America demonstrates this conflict for the modern period. The notion that the skyscraper skyline ought to be dispersed citywide, rather than compulsively crowded into a few blocks of the center, can be traced back to the late Twenties. It was then that several schemes of this sort were proposed for New York. E. Maxwell Fry, who worked on the 1929 New York Regional Plan, was the author of one of them. Raymond Hood was another. Hood proposed to put skyscrapers at major subway stations across the extant city. In Hugh Ferriss's *The Metropolis of Tomorrow* (1929) the skyscrapers are also widely spaced, though the *294*
matrix is still the grid of Manhattan. Ferriss makes it clear that "while they [the tall buildings] are not all precisely equidistant, and their relation does not suggest an absolutely rectangular checkerboard scheme, yet it is obvious that they have been located according to some citywide plan." But the major economic adjustments

294 "Imaginary Metropolis," a charcoal drawing by Hugh Ferriss from his Metropolis of Tomorrow *(1929), envisions 1,000-foot (305 m.) high skyscrapers distributed evenly over an urban background of 6-story buildings. This was Ferriss's answer to the tightly clustered highrise business district that had developed in New York and Chicago. The base of each of his skyscrapers covers 6–8 city blocks.*

called for and the changes in zoning practices were not forthcoming, so these projects remained on the boards. Even now voluntary negotiating techniques are largely ineffectual in the orderly dispersal of tall buildings. These include the transfer of the right to use a property's potential for development to another property, which is usually a way to save a historic building; and the encouragement of dispersal by rewarding developers who are willing to build in an area away from the CBD with tax reductions, tax credits, or delayed payments.

Moscow also picked up on this strategy of the citywide composition of a modern skyline with a public determination of where the tall buildings will go. There, the scheme could be, and was, realized. Having abandoned, after the Second World War, the plans for a centralized skyline fixed upon the Palace of the Soviets with its
295 colossal Lenin atop, a new proposal was advanced in 1947 for a "system of highrise landmark buildings." The intention was to re-establish the legibility of the skyline as a means of orientation, a legibility formerly characteristic of Moscow but lost in the indiscriminate spread of uniform six- to eight-story housing estates during the Thirties. This "necklace of vertical benchmarks" was strung along Moscow's outer ring boulevard, the Sadovoye Koltso, with a single more distant highrise—that of the University—serving as the terminus of the new urban axis which extended in a series of broad boulevards from Dzerzhinsky Square just northwest of the Kremlin toward the Lenin Hills.

295 *An artist's conception of the reconstruction of Moscow, ca. 1950. The view looks southwest over the center of the city, with the Kremlin in the foreground. The unrealized Palace of the Soviets is to the right of the river; the 36-story skyscraper of Moscow University, completed in 1953, at the top left. The other three skyscrapers are, from left to right, the Ministry of Foreign Affairs (27 stories, built 1951), the Hotel Ukraina (29 stories, 1956), and the Pl. Vosstaniya apartment tower (18 stories, 1954).*

296 above right *Warsaw's Palace of Culture, 1952–55. The diagrams compare it to some of the city's historic landmarks (a) in absolute size, and (b) in relative scale, as seen from an approach to the city along the eastern bank of the Vistula.*

Eight city-edge highrises were planned for strategic points—nine if we include the comparatively stubby tower of the Hotel Peking (1946–50). All but one were built. Had the Palace of the Soviets been realized in Moscow, the resulting skyline would have repeated, on a grandiose scale, the historic silhouette of the Kremlin: an ensemble of smaller towers arrayed along the palace walls, encircling the 265-foot (80 m.) high Ivan the Great Belltower which was once the tallest structure in Russia and was visible at a distance of 15 miles (25 km.).

The completed skyscrapers serve to celebrate entry into the city. Six occur at the intersection of radial highways with the ring road, and three of those are in close proximity to railway stations. Beyond this visual rationale, the buildings do not feel obliged to adopt a single function. Three (counting the Peking) are hotels, two are ministries, two are apartment blocks, and one is a university. Pleased with the spacing and form of these tall buildings, and anxious to set them apart from the skyscrapers of the U.S.S.R.'s ideological adversary, Soviet authorities, through the *Soviet Encyclopedia* of 1954, were therefore able to denounce the American skyscraper (*Neboskreb*, literally "cloud-scraper") as a symbol of capitalist greed whose disorderly cluster destroys community values and urban quality.[46]

The standard form of the freestanding Soviet skyscraper features a rectangular body with recessed stages toward the top, culminating in some sort of thin spire. "Wedding cake" is the inevitable nickname, and the Germans speak of "the confec-

tionery style." In the early Fifties the type spread to Eastern Europe. Warsaw's
296 Palace of Culture and Science, "a gift of the Soviet Union," is the most renowned specimen. It stands 768 feet (234 m.) high, its upper reaches decorated with motifs borrowed from medieval Polish secular architecture (like the town hall at Gdansk), and was intended to focus Warsaw's new city center a mile (1.6 km.) south of the historic old town.

The placement is not accidental. The planners of post-war Warsaw were anxious to demonstrate that the inevitable new skyline features would work with the extant fabric rather than against it. The debate over recomposing the skyline of the devastated city was lively and had a sense of urgency. In the words of one of the protagonists:

> The almost complete destruction of the city quarters in the immediate neighborhood of the river made it possible to revert, in the master plan, to the former principles of composition . . . The problem of the architectural forms of the individual parts of the city, and in particular of the distribution of those accentuating height, will be so solved as to take into acount both the traditional system and the creative shaping of the all-over silhouettes of the city as viewed from various points.[47]

The main point seemed to be this: though the new skyscraper(s) would be several times the height of the tallest buildings in the reconstructed old city, the approaches to them would be controlled in such a way that the historic public monuments, seen first, might act as foreground figures to the distant silhouette of the tall buildings. Presumably by the time you were close to the tall buildings, the old city was behind you and so free of domination.

COLOR AND LIGHT

> The aspect of Moscow, on approaching it, is extraordinary [Baron von Haxthausen wrote in 1856], and I know no city in Europe which can be compared with it: the finest view is from the heights called Sparrow Hills. Those countless golden and green cupolas and towers (every church has at least three, most of them five, some even thirteen, and there are about four hundred churches) rising from a sea of red housetops, the Kremlin in the midst upon a hill, towering like a crown over all . . .[48]

The Baron had reason to be impressed. That kind of multicolored skyline is rare not only in Europe but in the world at large. Yet color has always been a standard means to highlight the urban silhouette. Brunelleschi's famous dome of Florence Cathedral stands out as much through the contrast of brick panels and ribs and lantern of white Carrara marble as it does through its noble shape. In Asia, *gopuras* and pagodas were brilliantly colored. Much of this original color has faded or disappeared; some is being brought back. The *gopuras* at Madurai were restored at mid-century to the original bright colors mentioned in inscriptions, following the results of a referendum.

On the other hand, the calculated exterior chromatism of Art Deco skyscrapers in New York is not now very legible. Highrises like the Master Building of 1928–29 on Riverside Drive, probably inspired by German Expressionism, used shaded brick starting with deep purple at the base and graduating to light grey at the top. This was an optical device said to make a building look taller and to give the illusion of sunlight even on an overcast day.[49]

Gilding was a common device to highlight landmark buildings. Ancient Rome used gold tiles to roof Trajan's Basilica Ulpia and the Pantheon. The Shwe Dagon Pagoda in Rangoon is sheathed with more than eight thousand gold plates, and its peak is decorated with diamonds, rubies and sapphires. Gold leaf was applied to the dome of Boston's State House in 1874, almost a century after it went up; that decision served the building well, helping it to remain a landmark long after the stature of the dome was pre-empted on the skyline.

Cities also have their own overall hue. Paris is grey; San Francisco is white. It is not unknown to have policies aimed at maintaining this distinctive hue. In Jerusalem, for example, all modern buildings of the periphery must, by law, be faced with Jerusalem stone, naturally pastel in color; at daybreak, and again at sunset, the stone gives the city a golden glow.

The invention of electricity, and its extensive urban application about one hundred years ago, made possible a night-time skyline unknown in history. And the *Pl.39* later development of neon lights worked up to the gaudy tracery of Las Vegas. The early possibilities of this technology of light must have seemed a marvel. We have eyewitness accounts of the impression the World's Columbian Exposition of 1893 made upon visitors when the lights came on at night and the White City stood aglow on the lake at Jackson Park on the South Side of Chicago. Thirty-five years later the giant sign with the letters "PSFS" in scarlet neon on the roof of the Philadelphia Savings Fund Society Building was a milestone of another kind.

In 1937 luminous red stars were mounted on five of the Kremlin towers. As redesigned after the war, the ruby-glass stars framed in gilded stainless steel were shaped and scaled individually to match the architectural character of their respective towers. They shine around the clock and rotate slowly with the breezes. That sort of skyline magic could not have been imagined by Ivan the Terrible or Peter the Great.

THE MODERN SKYLINE

The context for the modern skyline can be sketched simply enough. The reality is this. On the one hand, a general increase in the scale of ordinary buildings overpowered the traditional public symbols of the skyline. Haussmann's Paris turned the apartment house into a monument and created a whole townscape of *Pl.23* public proportions, so that the ability of the genuine monument to stand out was severely tested. At the same time an intermediate scale of monumentality was devised, given dramatic roofs, and allowed to dominate a corner of the city. The railway stations in Paris are an example; so is the remade Louvre. But by the same token, a hierarchy among symbolic monuments had to prevail. The new Hôtel de Ville had to be larger, more monumental, than the town hall of a mere *arrondissement* or a parish church, which in turn had to be more assertive than a hospital or a secondary school.

On the other hand, this pervasive new monumentality also ennobled private businesses and other prosaic institutions—banks, department stores and the like—so that the traditional distinction of civic and religious buildings by their size and prominence in the cityscape could no longer be maintained.

How could one distinguish governmental and religious institutions in the general elephantiasis of city form; and if their supercession was accepted and explained

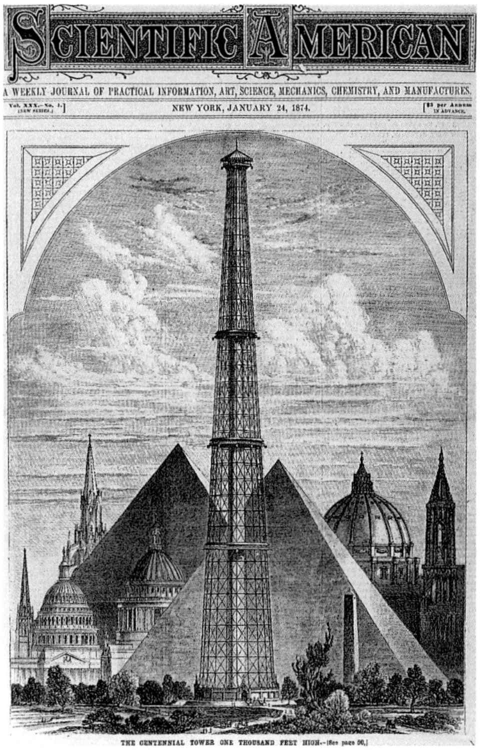

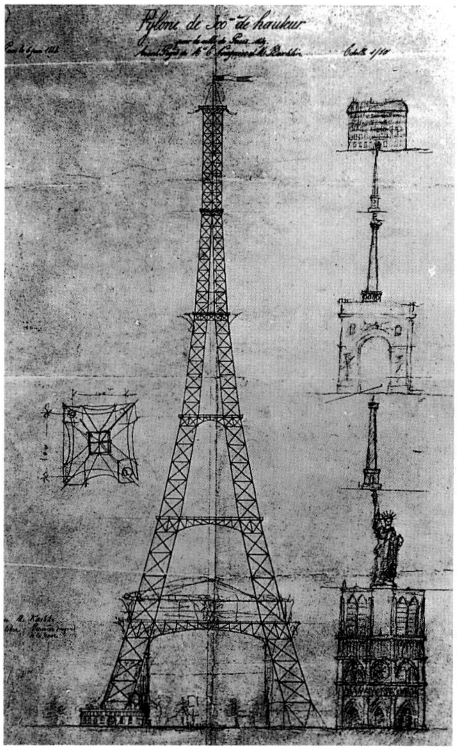

away, what new monuments to the modern age could one conceive that would have some of the value-laden publicness and social significance of churches and city halls?

For a while, cities tried to compete according to the standards set by the new urban scale. The Sacré-Coeur church in Paris not only has a 272-foot (83 m.) dome, higher than the towers of Notre-Dame, but it also sits on a hill 340 feet (104 m.)
300 above the level of the Seine. Daniel Burnham's projected new City Hall in his Chicago Plan of 1909 looms above the skyscrapers with a towering dome several times their height. One strategy was to abandon the city proper as too cluttered visually for any meaningful civic imprint and to rely on some extra-urban landmark instead. The Sacré-Coeur qualifies, but more to the point is the great Christ of Rio or, more recently, the statue of the Motherland atop the Ukrainian Museum of the History of the Great Patriotic War (1941–45) on a hillside at the edge of Kiev. But the contest could not be joined in earnest, and the competitive swagger of the private world of business enslaved the skyline.

The one notable 19th-century initiative to redress the balance has to do with the persistent vision of creating a prodigy of modern inspiration—one that would serve as advertisement for, and monument to, the spectacular advances in engineering ushered in by the new metal technology. The great metal bridges, especially those which perfected suspension systems, were already supplying memorable landmarks in this spirit of technological progress, but their form was not dominant on the urban skyline.

The first impulse was to build monumental towers in commemoration of important cultural or political events. The pioneering project was by the British engineer Richard Trevithick for a 1,000-foot (305 m.) columnar tower of gilded cast iron to honor the Reform Act of 1832. Most other comparable ideas which followed were connected with international expositions. For example, a "Centen-
297 nial Tower," also 1,000 feet high, was proposed for the Philadelphia Centennial

297 above left *Project for the Centennial Tower, by Clark, Reeves and Company, intended for the Philadelphia Centennial Exposition of 1876; from* Scientific American, *January 1874.*

298 above centre *Original design for the Eiffel Tower in Paris, 1884. The idea came from Maurice Koechlin and Emile Nouguière, two engineers in Eiffel's office. They show their tower—which was erected, in a slightly modified form, for the Paris Exposition of 1889—as equivalent in height to seven other structures stacked on top of one another, among these Notre-Dame in Paris, the Statue of Liberty, and the Arc de Triomphe.*

299 above *Turin (Italy), the Mole Antonelliana, 1863–88, so named after its architect Alessandro Antonelli. It was originally intended as the city's synagogue.*

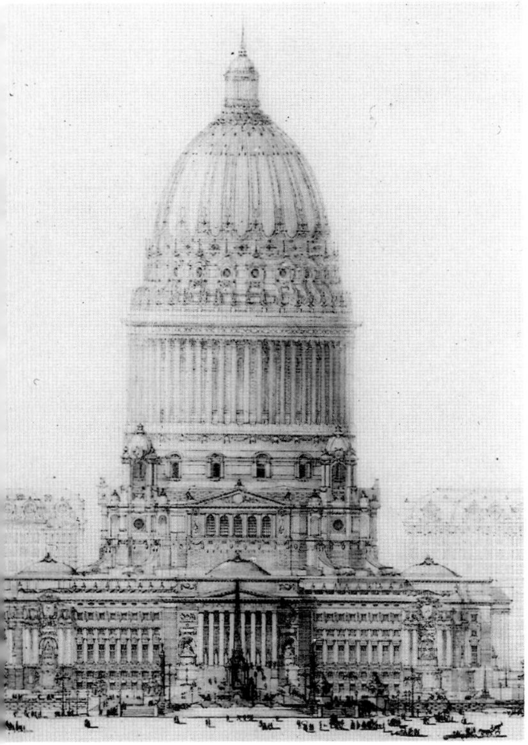

300 Chicago (Illinois), proposed new City Hall, from Burnham and Bennett's Plan of Chicago *(1909). To keep its prominence among modern skyscrapers, the City Hall is given a colossal dome, as high as a 36-story building, modeled after that of St. Peter's in Rome.*

Exposition of 1876. It is shown, in a magazine of the time, *Scientific American*, against a background of Egyptian pyramids, cathedral spires and famous domes, which are of course dwarfed by the proposed tower. This round figure of 1,000 feet, and the metal technology needed to attain it, set up an international challenge: the tower would be proof of the supremacy of the country which could produce it. "Not only shall we commemorate our birthday by the loftiest structure ever built by man," the magazine in question editorialized, "but by an edifice designed by American engineers, reared by American mechanics, and constructed of material purely the produce of American soil."[50]

The winner of course was France with the Eiffel Tower, 984 feet (300 m.) tall. One *298*
reason for its success was that its cost was met by a State subsidy, but the Tower had paid for itself within a year through phenomenal ticket sales. The British were incensed. William Morris, who saw it in 1889, called it "a hellish piece of ugliness." Hoping for a home triumph, the financier Sir Edward Watkin sponsored a competition in October of that year for a London tower that would be taller than Eiffel's. The competition produced a wild crop of submissions, mostly iron and steel specimens but also some of stone and concrete, and Eiffel haunted them all. The winning design was almost a replica of the Paris monument, and construction began in 1892 on a site in Wembley Park. The project was abandoned two years later for lack of funds. The same fate met the proposed tower for the World's Columbian Exposition of 1893 in Chicago, another Eiffel clone; and its successor of 1900 intended for the same fairgrounds, the 1,500-foot (ca. 460 m.) "Beacon of Progress" which its French architect Constant Desiré Despradelle said would "typify the apotheosis of American civilization," also came to naught.

The great, and unlikely, rival of Eiffel proved to be a synagogue at Turin—or so it *299*
started, until the city took over the colossal structure from its Jewish community disgruntled with the megalomania of the architect that turned their initial commission into a personal monument. The architect was Alessandro Antonelli, and construction stretched from 1863 to 1888. The total height of building, square dome and spire finally reached 167.5 meters (550 ft.), or about half the height of the Eiffel Tower; but it was all done in traditional masonry construction, and made up of superimposed columnar stories. This "Mole Antonelliana" as it is known is, in fact, the tallest masonry building in the world. So whereas the Eiffel Tower represents a century of technological progress, the Mole is a unique structure raised in an area of Europe that had remained a paleoindustrial backwater.[51]

FORGING THE *STADTKRONE*

The Germans gave much thought to the *Stadtkrone*, the crown of the modern city. In the 19th century the idea may have been a Walhalla, a heroes' monument. Now in the 20th century the search was for a structure that would be a symbol of communal life—a focal building that would make people noble, brotherly and good. Johannes Baader, a principal representative of Dada, had already designed a "World Temple" in 1906, and in 1907 the Munich architect Theodor Fischer had written of a building that would be "a house, not for single families to live in but for everyone . . . not for worship according to this or that cult but for devotion and inner experience." Indeed, in December 1917 a People's Building Association was founded; and in 1920 a competition was held for a "People's Building and House of Worship" with an entry by Hans Scharoun which would aim "to direct oneself and the hopeful mass of people to elevation and the crown."[52]

The question, then, was not to refortify traditional religion as the Sacré-Coeur and the finishing of Cologne Cathedral were attempting to do. Those were nationalist gestures, and their spiritual appeal was for a blissful afterlife. The concept of the *Zukunftkathedrale*, the cathedral of the future, was primarily socialist in aim. It was to be a monument for the happiness of the masses in this world, center of a communitarian utopia beyond regional or national parochialisms. If the metaphor was the Gothic cathedral, it was because that was believed to have been a structure brought forth by the collaboration of the whole of society—a total work of art which focused the labor of the citizens at large, and called upon all the crafts to serve the stability and embellishment of its form.

During the First World War, Bruno Taut and a following of other Expressionists promoted with passion this visionary agenda of a new physical environment consonant with a world free of conflict. Taut's preoccupations were with new materials, especially the potential of an all-glass architecture (here he was influenced by the writings of Paul Scheerbart, the Expressionist poet and novelist), and the restoration of a city center to the chaotic modern metropolis. His book of 1919
301 called *Die Stadtkrone* argued that the most damaging consequence of the modern
302 metropolis or *Grossstadt* was "the loss of the center," the cultural core with its
cumulative symbolic content around which the old city had grown. This center had been choked off and overcome by rental barracks, factories, and shops, while rapid transit had allowed the city-form to stretch out without definition or end. Taut contrasted this spreading miasma, with its overflow of a purposeless mob, to the traditional city with its organic collectivity, where houses and civic buildings formed a single construct culminating in the temple or the cathedral.[53]

So he conceived of a new urban utopia, cut of one cloth and anchored by a single crowning building, the *Stadtkrone*, that was to be the architectural symbol of the synthesis of the social and sacred needs of the community. This building was to be the modern equivalent of "the cathedral over the old city, the pagoda over the huts of the Indians, the enormous rectangular temple district of the Chinese city, and the acropolis over the simple dwellings of the ancient city." It alone would prevent "the obliteration of that borderline between big and small, sacred and profane, from which our time suffers."[54]

And Martin Wagner, in a similar mode, spoke of the *Stadtkrone* as the "we-symbol" (*Wir-Sinnbild*) of the new city:

> only *one* building shall rise above the level, earth-bound city houses and as a *city-crown* dominate the whole city-form, and the we-symbol of the new city, the People's- and Festival-House of its citizens, with its ceremonial plaza and its pair of churches, shall produce a city forum of the highest artistic form.[55]

In another visionary book of the same year, *Alpine Architektur*, Taut cascaded great cathedrals of crystal from the highest mountain chain of Europe—his answer to the raging war and its stupefying destructiveness. The old cities were now totally abandoned, and the efforts to refocus them with a *Stadtkrone* rescinded, in favor of a pristine environment of new alternatives, a world of glass and color. The *Stadtkronen* of these spacious Alpine cities were to be giant crystal dome structures crowning the mountain peaks, "dedicated to music and contemplation . . . and surrounded by tier upon tier of ancillary glass buildings."[56]

The irony is ready-made. These socialist utopias cannot ever be realized without a centralized power structure of some sort that can will them, finance them and execute them. It is not surprising that Nazi theorists would pick up on these phantasmagorical visions, and give them the practicality of *Realpolitik*. The hoped-

301, 302 Bruno Taut, Die Stadtkrone, *silhouette* (top) *and bird's-eye view, 1916.*

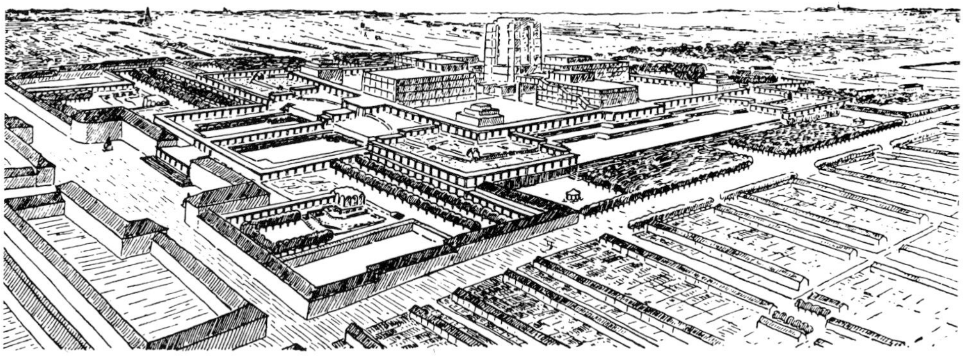

for socialist collectivity would be regimented by the Party and equated with the State: the great domed *Stadtkrone* of Hitler's new Berlin would be, not a 263
supranational People's House, but the stage where tens of thousands of recharged citizens would enter into a solemn, mystic union with the Supreme Leader of the German Nation.

Actually, a chief aim of the Nazi propagandists in flirting with Tautian ideas was to endow with spiritual character new factory towns like the Volkswagen works at Wolfsburg and the Hermann-Goering steel works, now the town of Salzgitter, both founded in 1938. A *Stadtkrone* was planned for Wolfsburg on a nearby natural hill, with a 750-meter (820 yd) long stair-street connecting it with the city; the building of this street was put in hand in 1941, but nothing came of the *Stadtkrone*, which was reminiscent of Leo von Klenze's Walhalla. The plan for Salzgitter was especially dependent on Bruno Taut's utopian ideal, including the city crown. There were two alternative proposals, one with a monumental structure in the center of town, and another with a *Stadtkrone* on an artificial hill opposite the town. Goering pre-empted the hilltop for a flak tower, and left a garden suburb at the foot of the hill. Flak towers in fact became the grim *Stadtkronen* of the early Forties. Vienna raised six of them in its periphery, paired in a precise citywide triangle. It was the end of the road for the pure crystalline sky-house of the Tautian brotherhood of man.

SKYSCRAPER CITY

To utopian Expressionists and Nazi purists alike, the American skyscraper was an unacceptable urban symbol. It was a monument to self-interest and the aggressive competitiveness of capitalism; its symbolism of laissez faire was therefore wholly inappropriate either for a cooperative socialist future or for selfless loyalty to a monolithic State.

For these very reasons, the skyscraper cluster was the perfect American *Stadtkrone*. It was a little more than one hundred years ago, in the 1870s and 1880s,
that the first skyscrapers began to go up in Chicago and New York—elevator 303
buildings of exceptional height, laboriously built in traditional masonry construction, and then, from about 1890 on, as fireproofed steel frames on which the exterior sheath could be hung like a curtain. They were exciting, unconventional urban structures, and they had many enthusiasts, their architects and clients chief among

them. Chicago's John Wellborn Root saw these first skyscrapers, in their mass and proportion, as conveying "in some large elemental sense an idea of the great, stable, conserving forces of modern civilization." The vision seemed to presage the birth of yet another legendary cosmopolis, like Babylon of antiquity with its Tower of Babel, and so a new age. Where Babylon had but one tower, here there was a whole brood of them, cheek by jowl in an artificially created field of congestion in the midst of abundant space. The skyscrapers' field of vision spread out for miles, and indeed they seemed to want to be viewed from some far away vantage point, like vast paintings in a museum we have to move away from in order to see properly.

This skyline described a premeditated human order, one indebted solely to technology and the profit-seeking designs of man. It was a great shift from the traditional view of the city, enveloped by sky and earth, at once nurtured and held in check by this primordial frame. The frame was even there in views of the industrial
Pl.37 city, the first urban silhouette of modern times not to be determined by steeples and domes. But whereas those chimneys and furnace cones and water towers could be explained away as the unavoidable hardware of industrial processes, there was a willfulness about the new landscape of highrises, an element of choice and boast, that sounded a premonitory note.

On a purely esthetic level, the architectural critic Montgomery Schuyler found the new urban prospect chaotic: "New York has no skyline at all," he wrote in the *Architectural Record* of January–March 1899. "It is all interruptions, of various heights and shapes and sizes . . . scattered or huddled towers which have nothing to do with each other or with what is below." Schuyler allowed a crude symbolic power, a picturesque sort of beauty, to this privatized skyline. He wrote that "it is in the aggregation [of the tall buildings] that the immense impressiveness lies. It is not an architectural vision, but it does, most tremendously, 'look like business'." And so he helped to articulate a growing unease about a city sundered, a raw upstaging attempt of private power to appropriate civic pride.

To distinguish the public monuments of government and culture from this vertically disposed skyline of business, their architectural character had to be

304 New York City, New York Public Library, by Carrere and Hastings, 1897–1911; one of the first of a generation of public buildings influenced by the formal classicism of the World's Columbian Exposition of 1893, Chicago's "White City." These chalky horizontal buildings scaled to the pedestrian were meant to represent the public realm against the private skyline of commercial highrises.

303 opposite *New York City, comparative skylines in 1873 and 1898, detail of a drawing by August Will. The spire of Trinity Church, the overtopping of which so distressed Henry James, can be glimpsed right of center. (The "North River" is the Hudson.)*

different. Civic beauty came to be rendered, therefore, in Classical envelopes of marble with continuous level lines of base platforms and cornices that defined urban space and monumentalized pedestrian perspectives. We were meant to pit the visual babble of Lower Manhattan skyscrapers against the public, street-enhancing monumentality of the New York Public Library, of Pennsylvania Station and Grand *304*
Central Station, of Columbia University and the Metropolitan Museum of Art.[57]

But it was not enough. Spread out through the city, the public monuments were easily overshadowed by the voraciously mushrooming landscape of commerce. As Charles Mulford Robinson, the City Beautiful advocate, put it in 1903, the presence of the civic realm would be compromised if public buildings "were scattered about the town and lost in a wilderness of commercial structures." The answer was to group them in harmonious Beaux-Arts ensembles around grand plazas adorned with public statues and fountains, thus defending them against commercial interests that "put in jeopardy the beauty and dignity of public structures through the possibility of mingling inharmonious architecture . . . or of destroying scale by the erection of a 'skyscraper', or any colossal building, that would dwarf the public structures."[58]

The skyscraper was a paradoxical building. It was at once highly materialistic *and* redolent of poetry, hardnosed in terms of urban economics *and* arbitrary. To the first clients of Chicago skyscrapers, it was a vehicle to maximize profits on their plot of land—a no-frills, sound business proposition. But at the same time the tall building began to behave in ways that were not in keeping with this insistence on a commonsensical business proposition. Ornament appeared to grace the frame almost immediately. The shape began to respond to impulses that were clearly not dictated by sound, practical exigencies. And a competitive craze over height for its own sake seized the makers of the tall buildings, a competition which is best exemplified in New York's Newspaper Row, also called Printing House Square, next to City Hall, where the *New York Times*, the *Tribune*, the *Sun*, and Pulitzer's *World* fought it out in a totally irrational way in the 1870s and 1880s.

A similar exhibition enveloped the new Philadelphia City Hall, an enormous pile *305*
that started going up in 1871. In the late Eighties, at that same juncture of Broad and Chestnut Streets, the Girard Trust built an eight-story building, and then the beer

305 Philadelphia (Pennsylvania), City Hall, capped by a statue of William Penn, seen among neighboring highrises, ca. 1908.

baron John F. Betz instructed his architect to go higher. Girard responded with an additional six stories, and Betz matched the height and surpassed it. Caught in this private contest, the City Hall lifted its tower to the unobstructed sky and set Penn's statue on top like an archangel of old, defender of heights and dominant symbol of the city of man.

A second paradox had to do with the forced density of the skyscrapers in a fairly restricted area of the city center. The intensification of the American central business district had started before the serious advent of the skyscrapers. Since the middle of the 19th century, the urban core in most cities had slowly been deprived of its residential component as those who could moved out to the suburbs. The towers joined an increasingly specialized center-city, which emptied of its working crowds at the end of the day. The highrise building came to be identified with this CBD as the monumental accent of the occupational landscape of urban America.

The density of the CBD enhanced the competitive challenge of the skyscraper. To make your statement in the company of others, to take your position in a tight
266 display of image buildings—that is what gave the whole exercise its energy, and the American city its cumulative symbol of capitalist power.

A third paradox had to do with the architectural nature of the skyscraper. Ideally it was a midspace thing, meant to be admired from all sides and to command a large visual territory. But practically it had to function within the relatively fine-grained checkerboard of the American city and the block structure that came with it. The more tall buildings were crammed into the CBD, the more each one was deprived of this breathing space and of the impact its distinctive shape might make. The more tall buildings respected the logic of the grid and the street channels it created, the more they would be forced to function as space-defining, rather than midspace, masses.

As an image-making tower in its own right, the skyscraper will ultimately give us Dallas or Vancouver—a collection of tall objects concerned with the visual effect they are creating among others who posture in like manner, keen on holding a distinctive place in the skyline as it will appear on photographs and T-shirts, or from the revolving restaurant of the space needle. As a standard urban unit, the skyscraper will be intent on marking the pre-established prospects of the urban form, or re-creating such familiar prospects. This means that a certain regularity and sameness will be sought for the tall buildings, and the attention will be for the near- and middle-range effects, experienced from within the city-form, rather than the distant skyline specter.

For the starkest effect, the freestanding tower should rise alone in the center of the city-form, and define it as the Gothic cathedrals did the towns of the Ile-de-France or the dome of St. Paul's defined London until recently. But what modern institution might deserve such distinction?

The State had little use for the skyscraper, unwilling to transpose to its mastlike form the symbolic eminence of the state house or the city hall. Even in this post-skyscraper world, government relied by and large on traditional domed imagery to make its point. There were only a few notable exceptions in the Teens and Twenties,
306 among them Bertram Goodhue's Nebraska State House at Lincoln, and the Los
290 Angeles City Hall by John C. Austin which was heavily influenced by Goodhue.

Religion comes to mind next. In the strongly felt loss of the churches' long-enjoyed primacy, a loss given voice to by Henry James, the skyscraper could atone for its enormity, as it were, by being forced to celebrate God. The attempt was made. Under the slogan "Restore the Cross to the Skyline," or "Churches Aloft," several cities set out to create skyscraper churches, which predictably amounted to

306 Lincoln (Nebraska), State Capitol, by Bertram Grosvenor Goodhue, winner of the 1919 competition. He followed this success with a second civic tower, the Los Angeles County Public Library of 1924.

307 right *Chicago (Illinois), Chicago Temple by Holabird and Roche, 1924, the first of the "revenue churches." The conventional 19-story office tower is topped by an elaborate Gothic "sky chapel" accessible by express elevator. The sanctuary relief shows Christ approvingly contemplating Chicago's business district from the heights of a nearby rooftop.*

308 far right *New York, Woolworth Building, by Cass Gilbert, 1911–13. Frank Woolworth, a chain store millionaire from Utica, New York, proclaimed that his office tower would be "like a giant signboard to advertise around the world." In the distance is the tower of the Singer Building, by Ernest Flagg, 1908.*

marrying church and office tower. The Chicago Temple by Holabird and Roche *307*
(1924), for the First Methodist Church, did just that. And there were sky churches in Miami, Pittsburgh, Minneapolis, and the Broadway Temple in New York City.

But beyond the improbability of converting the skyscraper form as generally built into a credible house of God, what was problematic about a highrise church was that in America, unlike Europe's cathedral cities, the concept of a singleminded religious focus, which had existed in Colonial Spanish cities and the New England townships with their meeting house, was abandoned. The young nation disallowed centralized religion, and made God at home in multisectarian neighborhoods. To restore the Cross to the skyline, cities would have had to endure the same spectacle as Newspaper Row, as Methodists, Catholics, Episcopalians, and all the others challenged the height of rival towers in order to claim the sky.

A cathedral of learning? It was tried once, and is still there, in Pittsburgh, an irregularly tapering mass of 535 feet (163 m.), in a dress of textured limestone on a massive steel frame cased in concrete (1926–27). It was meant, as its program put it, "to express the meaning of a University as a great high building," and its ground floor is taken up by a vast hall in the guise of a Gothic cathedral, ringed by eighteen classrooms each designed in a different national style to celebrate Pittsburgh's multinational heritage.

But the true message of the skyscraper in America was the celebration of one man's enterprise. In the end, the most suitable iconography for the American *Stadtkrone* was American business. Wilbur Foshay, the kitchen-utensils magnate from Minneapolis, put all his fortune into an obelisk building, his name indelibly engraved on all four sides of it, *the* tower in the city at the time—even if the building of it ruined him and he ended up in jail. Horace Greeley's *Tribune* Tower in New York started the great skyscraping competition of Newspaper Row.

The attempts to ennoble these monuments to commercial success with borrowed symbolism are nonetheless expressive of the inflationary value Americans came to attach to private enterprise at the expense of the public realm by the end of the 19th century; they are expressive of a general willingness to find communal pride in the atomized monumentality of office buildings. If the skyscraper could not be appropriated by public institutions, if it could not become the standard clothing for those enduring mechanisms of community—government and faith and education—then the business of individual men would be elevated to the rank of a new secular
308 religion. So the Woolworth Building in New York (1913) was officially christened "the Cathedral of Commerce" by an eminent divine, Dr. S. Parkes Cadman, who wrote in 1916:

> When seen at nightfall bathed in electric light or in the lucid air of summer morning, piercing space like a battlement of the paradise of God, which St. John beheld, it inspires feelings even for tears. The writer looked upon it and at once cried out "the Cathedral of Commerce"—the chosen habitation of that spirit in man which, through means of change and barter, binds alien people into unity and peace.[59]

The architect himself, Cass Gilbert, in a pamphlet called *The Master Builders*, lauded the Woolworth for ushering in, as it were, a social peace, since it brought together capital and labor, employer and employed, landlord and tenants.

But it is the fate of these private celebrations to be challenged and superseded in short order, as it is the fate of private success to be ephemeral. The tower to one man's enterprise cannot focus the city, because other enterprising men will not allow it. And when we get a constantly growing and shifting crop of towers, we will have to look for that one among them extraordinary enough—the highest, the freakiest,
Pl.27 the most resplendent—to become, for a time, *the* landmark—the Transamerica in San Francisco, LTV in Dallas, IDS in Minneapolis, and, at the time of writing, One Liberty Place in Philadelphia. Perhaps Frank Lloyd Wright had a point. Perhaps the only way to stop this spectacle of urban grandstanding is to make the entire city into a tower and plant it deep in the middle of Noplace.

Or to deglamorize the skyscraper, and turn it into an undemonstrative urban unit, intent on making orderly cities with high street walls, rather than punctuating the city-form with exclamation marks. A name to reckon with here is Daniel Burnham, the man whose firm had an active role in the development of the skyscraper form and then went on to propose appropriate urban uses for it. It was his Plan of Chicago of 1909 that took Schuyler's "aggregation," the picturesque collection of specimens, and disciplined it into a unified urban vision. Burnham had nothing against the tall building; what he objected to was its anarchic variety. So in the Plan, as Thomas van Leeuwen put it, "the chaotic primeval city with its irregular skyline is razed as if by a gigantic lawnmower."[60]

The period of the first generation of skyscrapers reflected the boisterous individualism of the post-Civil War boom—the era of robber barons, land grabs, and unruly urbanization. As we have seen, Burnham was the evangelist of the City Beautiful movement at the opening of the new century, one of the many ways in which America sought to bring some consolidation and order into its life. The making of cities should represent this desire for order.

248 The latest and grandest such remaking was Haussmann's Paris. It was the unity of street frontages that was stressed there, not the eccentricity of individual buildings.

309 Chicago (Illinois), commercial towers at Michigan Avenue Bridge: on the left, the Wrigley Building of 1919–21 by Graham, Anderson, Probst and White; on the right, the Chicago Tribune Tower of 1925 by Howells and Hood. Hailed as the city's new gateway, these buildings and those on the other end of the ornate bridge, and the adjoining plazas, were considered proof of the civic excellence that can result from the cooperation of the private and public spheres. In the distance is the neo-medieval Water Tower, of 1869.

BANK
FLAKES

Haussmann's boulevards were lined with five- or six-story apartment blocks holding to the same cornice line. In America it was possible to build higher. The trick was to line streets and squares with these tall buildings, while reproducing the smooth continuities and the uniform order of the French capital. In this way Burnham hoped to heal Schuyler's schism between the private monumentality of business, with its stress on the vertical and the unique, and the civic monumentality of continuous, uniform frontages. He saw the skyscraper as a constituent element of a new kind of urbanism, at once traditional and modern.

The Chicago Plan left its mark on the city, even though it was far from being realized as a whole. Stuart Cohen has recently analyzed North Michigan Avenue at
309 the Bridge as just such a Burnhamesque fragment. Four skyscrapers designed independently of one another—the Wrigley Building (1919–21), the North Michigan Avenue Building (1922–23), the *Tribune* Tower (1925), and the London Guarantee Building (1927–28)—nevertheless choose to work together to define a very specific urban space. The city and its configurations, in other words, are more important than the single buildings that are made to stand within them.[61] Outside
224 the United States, the fragments of Socialist Realism in places like East Berlin and Leipzig are late, and extremely competent, replays of that Burnhamesque combination of tall buildings and Beaux-Arts ensemble planning.

But is it true, as I have suggested, that the American skyscraper faced a choice between expressing its individuality on the urban skyline as an architectural advertisement for its client, and generalizing its form for the sake of enclosing urban volumes? The truth is that for several decades skyscrapers knew how to do both. The common formula in New York until the First World War was to top a conventional block holding to the street line with a tower element, often set to one
308 side, away from the main façade, as in the Singer Building by Ernest Flagg (1908) or the Woolworth Building.

Two things consolidated these practices. The New York Ordinance of 1916 with its setback requirements provided a legal challenge that nudged the designer's imagination into marrying the skyscraper's fancy to be a proud and soaring thing with its responsibility to street-level prospects. And the rejection of the early highrise formulas of the Chicago School—those abstracted plaid frames capped by level cornices—for historicist dress justified a riot of revivalist crowns, be they
266 mansarded, domed, spired or pyramidal. The Art Deco style contributed its own imaginative summitry. But throughout, the relationship to the street was carefully calculated. On the ground, the skyscrapers respected the street or plaza on which they were being built by using a fairly planar ten stories or so of their façade to create the abutting frame that these urban spatial units needed. Beyond that point, uninhibitedly designed terminal blocks—stepped up, faceted and pinnacled—related to the macroscale, to the distant view, that is, to image-projecting skyline considerations.

TOWERS OF GLASS

The demise of these civilities lay, unforeseen, in the impassioned prophecies of young European radicals on the architectural fringe, who could see no possible compromise between the skyscraper form and traditional urban space-making. The Futurists were first. Their concepts inchoate, their images of a new urban environment fragmentary, theirs was nonetheless the first theoretical utterance of the multilevel, apocalyptic skyscraper city worshipping motion and machine. "We must invent and rebuild ex novo our modern city . . . and the modern building like a gigantic machine . . . as big as need dictates, not merely as zoning rules permit, must rise from the brink of a tumultuous abyss."[62]

The drawings of Antonio Sant'Elia and Mario Chiattone, devoid of people, gave few clues on how the rendered fragments would connect to make workable urban systems. Ten years later, Le Corbusier's urban vision was unambiguous. This vision *310*
would not allow for the enclosure of space in the traditional manner of the city. Le Corbusier had no quarrel with the arrival of the skyscraper city as installed on the grid of Manhattan. He approved of the concentration and single-mindedness of a highrise business district. But the skyscraper was not the definer of public spaces. In his *City of Tomorrow* (1924) he shows us a business core consisting of twenty-four skyscrapers, all of them alike. They are standing, not in the thick of an old city, but in vast open parks. They are experienced from fast-speed motorways. And they are made of glass. He writes:

> Here we have, not the meager shaft of sunlight which so faintly illumines the dismal streets of New York, but an immensity of space. . . . Here is the CITY with its crowds living in peace and pure air, where noise is smothered under the foliage of green trees. . . . There is sky everywhere . . . Their outlines softened by distance, the skyscrapers raise immense geometrical façades all of glass.

This vivid Modernist interpretation of the skyscraper city lived on, unrealized but palpably imaginable thanks to Le Corbusier's drawings and words, until the end of the Second World War. Then Americans went out for it—and so did Europe. The invention in the Fifties of thick float glass by British glass companies fulfilled Modernist predictions of a transparent architecture, and advances in skyscraper engineering removed height restrictions on technical grounds.

In the United States, the home of the skyscraper, glass towers began to rise in plazas of their own, the plazas linked into private interiorized office parks; and slabs were mounted on tall podia, a formula popularized by Lever House in New York (1951–52). The historicist sheaths were denounced and dropped—and along with them, the expressive crowns that had livened the skyline. Reticulate or vertically striated, and always flat-topped, the new generation of metal-and-glass cages—towers and slabs alike—sat in their own pools of space unmindful of pre-extant avenue or square. The urban renewal policies of the Fifties and Sixties made room for them. We tore down the old city and built the new in an impoverished celebration of the Modernist "city in the park"—without the park.

When the Seventies sought to make amends for these immense squared off stacks of rental floors, these "decapitated" skyscrapers, with a sort of expressionist Modernism, and went for oval or shiplike shapes and cantilevered or raked tops, nothing was gained for the clarity of urban structure. We were caught in the one-of-each syndrome, which made for a more lively skyline but did little for the groundline. And the Post-Modern historicism of the Eighties went no deeper than mere cladding. Only a few gestures were made to address traditional urban typologies. Philip Johnson, in the most noteworthy example, deftly related the lobby of the AT & T Building (1978) to the channel of Madison Avenue. For all the notoriety of the broken pediment at the top, it was this deference to the street channel that linked the AT & T back to those versatile urban landmarks of the Thirties—the Empire State, the RCA, the McGraw-Hill—that could fit in and stand out at the same time.

The European case was traumatic. Here there had been none of the intervening American stages of easing the skyscraper into the city fabric. Also, the European cities were much older, so the sudden postwar contrast was more of a shock. And then, the visual impact of the tall building on an American grid is quite different from the unpredictable impact within more complicated city patterns like Paris's or London's.

First there were single episodes, like freak accidents in the storied urban landscapes of Europe. Around 1960, of a sudden, there was Portland House in London, at 334 feet (102 m.) dominating not only its built surroundings but St. James's Park, Green Park, and the private gardens of Buckingham Palace. A full 600 feet (183 m.) tall, the National Westminster Bank headquarters (1981) completely
Pl.36 outsized St. Paul's. The glass-walled Montparnasse tower in Paris, begun in 1969, at 56 stories (690 feet/210 m.) the tallest building in Europe at the time, shocked the fabric of Haussmann's city. And then it became old hat as the Porte Maillot got a
311 hotel tower and the Corbusian skyscraper business district went up at La Défense. The 1967 Paris master plan echoed his language when it predicted that the aspect of the great city would change drastically in the future. "One would no longer go about between parallel walls, in these corridors, the streets, but in spaces alternating with buildings and greenery."[63]

Alarmed, Denmark and Holland rushed to endow local authorities with the power to prevent the erection of tall buildings. Amsterdam made only one exception initially, along the waterfront, where W.M. Dudok designed the harbor building next to the Central Station. In West Germany, meantime, cities whose historic skylines were being threatened developed urban image plans. These cities included Ulm, Esslingen, Stuttgart, Lübeck, Cologne, Frankfurt, and Freiburg. After an urban image analysis, design criteria were laid out for architects of new buildings, either as suggestions or legal guidelines enacted in local by-laws.

But it was too late. The housing slabs, that other component of the Modernist city, took over everywhere. They became the new cliché of the city edge, from

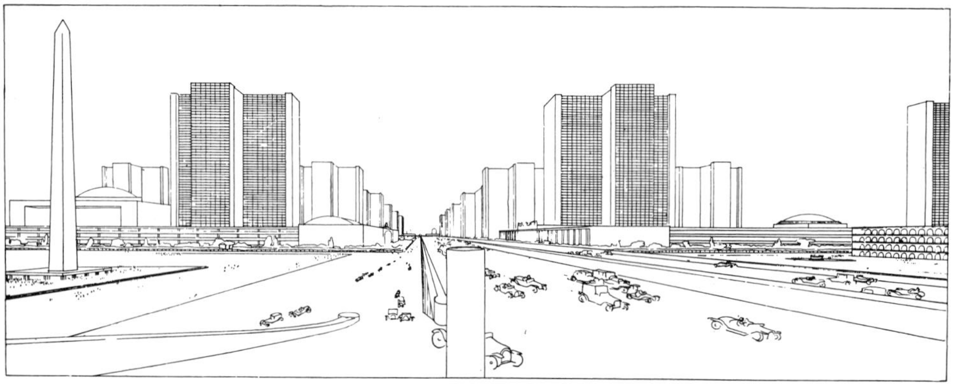

310 left *Le Corbusier's "City for Three Million People," a project of 1922; here the city center as seen from its main thoroughfare.*

311 *Paris, La Défense district seen from Avenue Charles De Gaulle—a modern fulfillment of the Corbusian prophecy. The vista is closed by "La Grande Arche," an office building by J. O. von Spreckelsen, 1988.*

312 Frankfurt (Germany), the modern skyline against the lines of the historic city.

Moscow and Bratislava to Rotterdam and Stevenage. Combined with towers in the *grands ensembles* of France, they concretized a history-free urban order. The German "success" was also qualified. In most of the major cities, it is the historic center—the *Altstadt*—only that escaped. Right next to it the skyscrapers often make their stand. In Frankfurt the hitherto essentially low-rise Westend has 312 acquired a Manhattan-type skyline which dominates the Altstadt itself. In Munich, on the other hand, the highrise buildings are well to the east of the Altstadt, and the government offices in Bonn are grouped in compounds on fringe locations and along Adenauerallee between the old established centers of Bonn and Bad Godesberg.[64]

"AND THEY LEFT OFF TO BUILD THE CITY" (*Genesis* 11)

Since the mid-Sixties a new mood has been gaining strength—both in Europe and in the United States. Its managers go beyond the debate of how best to make skyscrapers fit in our towns. They question the wisdom of having them at all. The policies of urban renewal, which freely sacrificed old building stock for most of a furious decade, are now openly discredited. In London people react with distaste at the erections in the vicinity of St. Paul's, at the scale and image of the Barbican. Meantime, the promised millennium of the Modernists seems to celebrate an impoverishment of culture. The arbitrary rambling of highrises in Modernist estates like Gropiusstadt in Berlin (1962ff.), the withdrawn, almost clinically circumscribed daily life of "the city in the park," hardly make up for the urban legacy we were asked to sacrifice. Hence the appeal for a pre-skyscraper, indeed pre-industrial, urban form by the likes of Leon Krier. Now extended high patronage, Krier is ready to carry us back to the urban organisms of a Europe before the Fall and the innocence of village life.

But this is an extreme position. The skyscraper city as it has existed for one hundred years *is* tradition by now. The issue is how to curb it, and give it an appropriate place in the scheme of things. The alternatives are to discourage it altogether by opting as a community for a no-growth policy; or to regulate the proliferation, siting, and appearance of the skyscraper.

Building high is no longer a technical challenge—the question rather has become, "Should we?" Doubts are being expressed more and more openly about the equation of tall buildings with urban progress—both in economic terms and in terms of the quality of life. Recent advances in measuring the impact of the skyscraper city on the citizens' well-being point out much to be worried about.[65] "Environmental impact" reports, required in the United States for all new significant building projects since 1969, could be extremely impressionistic. Drawings and models almost never dealt with the real world of the pedestrian functioning at the foot of these behemoths.

The main point, not addressed by such reports, was, in any case, that there are cumulative effects of the skyscraper city that cannot be calculated on a building-by-building basis. The issue of destroying famous views and altering the structure of topography is deeply felt in cities like San Francisco. The San Francisco Urban Design Plan of 1971 dealt with *height* and *bulk*, as had the New York Ordinance of 1916, with some concession to topography. But what about the concatenated pattern of spaces and volumes that gives blocks their identity? people wanted to know. What about the issue of human-scaled amenities at the base of the tall building, to redress the alienation and adverse effects of its great height? What about problems of shape? the effects on the microclimate, the additional shadows, the making of cold and windy streets? What about the symbolic issues of dominance? An activist campaign to take matters away from wheeling-dealing politicians and developers led to the passage in September 1985 of a new plan for the city center. The plan put a ban on the replacement of many landmarks, including older generations of highrises; shifted new office towers away from the overcrowded financial district; and added a ceiling to the actual amount of building that could take place in any one year—the so-called "growth cap."

And the debate has spread nationwide. Seattle has just passed restrictions similar to those of San Francisco. In Philadelphia, when a developer's project for Liberty Place was allowed to overturn the long-respected height limit of Penn's statue on City Hall, Philadelphians who cared were split between those who professed a loss they could not specifically quantify, and those who cried "Good riddance!" to an archaic and sentimental urban affectation. Some prominent outsiders, Paul Goldberger of the *New York Times* chief among them, thought that the offending structure by Helmut Jahn was a skyscraper of such distinction that it had *ipso facto* a perfect right to define for the future the skyline of Philadelphia.[66] The ultimate gauge for what should be permissible in our own cities, Goldberger seems to be saying, is the quality of architecture as judged by architectural critics. It is on these esthetic grounds that he is willing to consign the determination of the Philadelphia skyline, and the rearrangement of the traditional priorities of the city, to a developer and his architect. "[The building] transcends the old order, and establishes a new one, at a level of quality good enough to justify throwing away the old."

The judgment of quality is, alas, notoriously arbitrary. As Geoffrey Scott, author of the famous essay of 1914 on *The Architecture of Humanism*, put it during a comparably pluralist interval:

313 The delicate onion domes of Moscow's mid-17th-century church of St. Simon the Stylite provide a striking contrast to the 24-story apartment blocks of the Kalinin Prospekt.

We subsist on a number of architectural habits, on scraps of tradition, on caprices and prejudices, and above all on this mass of more or less specious axioms, of half-truths, unrelated, uncriticised and often contradictory, by means of which there is no building so bad that it cannot with a little ingenuity be justified, or so good that it cannot plausibly be condemned.[67]

The value of symbols is of a different order. Symbols are carriers of meaning. Urban symbols are presumably carriers of some collective meaning of those who live and work there. Who should be allowed to design a city's skyline? Who should have the privilege to represent us on the horizon? These are the fundamental questions.

Throughout history, as we have repeatedly observed in this book, urban form has been firmly legislated. The much-admired medieval Siena had a premeditated form, down to the shape of the windows and the enforced use of brick. The design prescriptions that controlled Haussmann's Paris extended to the smallest details: pilasters on façades could not be more than 40 centimeters (about 16 in.) in depth, balconies required official permission and even so could not project more than 80 centimeters (31.5 in.), corbelling was strictly prohibited, and so on.

In the last half-century cities have effectively turned over their skylines to powerful developers, corporations, and their architects. But the interests of the community are not synonymous with the interests of developers and corporations. They put up the tall buildings; the community is asked to look after them. As early as 1926, the President of the American Civic Association underscored this fatal flaw in the skyscraper mystique. "There is a very close relation," he wrote, "between the privilege to owners of erecting high buildings, and the burden thrown upon the community of taking care of the consequences."[68]

The importance of the civic dimension of the skyline has yet to be fully grasped in the culture of the skyscraper city. It is still true today as it was at the beginning that, to quote Thomas Adams, the chief author of the 1931 Regional Plan for New York, "In the American city the disposal of the lots to individuals with liberty to make the best of them for their private purposes was the governing factor in development, rather than architectural control in the interests of the community."[69]

This is the import of San Francisco's new plan, and others like it. They remind us that the skyscraper city, like all other negotiated settings of our past, cannot be praised or excoriated as an esthetic container alone. It is in that juggling act between private interests and the public good, supervised by the citizenry, that something more precious may reside. The esthetic vision of how our cities will look will always be supplied by professional designers, of course. But it is perfectly appropriate, indeed imperative, for the citizens to control the limits of that vision. While private interests are entitled to seek their advantage in the urban fabric, and city authorities and their experts are paid to find wholescale planning solutions to the problems of unfettered growth, it is the citizens as a collective voice who must ultimately decide the shape of their city. Like the communes of Tuscany which took charge of their city-form in the later Middle Ages and shaped it to reflect their governance, their political and social priorities, so it is given to us to do the same.

If we still believe that cities are the most complicated artifact we have created, if we believe further that they are cumulative, generational artifacts that harbor our values as a community and provide us with the setting where we can learn to live together, then it is our collective responsibility to guide their design.

NOTES

INTRODUCTION (pp. 9–41)

1. L. Mumford, *The City in History* (New York/London 1961), 423.
2. See Kostof, "Urbanism and Polity: Medieval Siena in Context," *International Laboratory for Architecture and Urban Design Yearbook*, 1982, 66–73.
3. See Kostof, *Do Buildings Lie? Hegel's Wheel and Other Fables*, The John William Lawrence Memorial Lectures, 9 (New Orleans 1980).
4. O. Grabar, *The Formation of Islamic Art* (New Haven/London 1973), 69.
5. K. Lynch, *A Theory of Good City Form* (Cambridge, Mass./London 1981), 73–98.
6. M. P. Conzen, "Morphology of Nineteenth-Century Cities," in R. P. Schaedel et al., eds., *Urbanization in the Americas from the Beginnings to the Present* (The Hague 1980), 119.
7. H. Carter, *The Study of Urban Geography* (1972; 3rd ed., London 1981), 335.
8. ibid., 333.
9. See especially "The Use of Town Plans in the Study of Urban History," in H. J. Dyos, ed., *The Study of Urban History* (London 1968), 113–30; see also Kostof, "Cities and Turfs," *Design Book Review* 10, Fall 1986, 35–39.
10. See below, Ch.2, n.50.
11. See F. Braudel, *The Structures of Everyday Life* (London 1981/New York 1985), 515–20
12. See J. E. Vance, Jr., "Land Assignment in the Precapitalist, Capitalist, and Postcapitalist City," *Economic Geography* 47, 1971, 101–20.
13. F. E. Ian Hamilton in R. A. French and Hamilton, eds., *The Socialist City* (Chichester 1979), 200.
14. *Archaeology*, Nov.–Dec. 1987, 38–45.
15. See A. Wright in G. W. Skinner, ed., *The City in Late Imperial China* (Palo Alto, Calif., 1977), 33.
16. See K. Polanyi et al., *Trade and Market in the Early Empires* (Glencoe, Ill., 1957).
17. See, e.g., P. Wheatley in R. W. Steel and R. Lawton, eds., *Liverpool Essays in Geography* (London 1967), 315–45.
18. G. Sjoberg, *The Preindustrial City* (New York/London 1960), 67–68. For a major critique of Sjoberg's thesis, see P. Wheatley in *Pacific Viewpoint* 4.2, Sept. 1963, 163–88.
19. *The Muqaddimah*, transl. F. Rosenthal, vol. 2 (New York 1958), 235.
20. Wheatley (n.17 above), 318.
21. M. Aston and J. Bond, *The Landscape of Towns* (London 1976), 21.
22. *American Journal of Sociology* 44, 1938, 8.
23. L. Mumford, *The Culture of Cities* (New York/London 1938), 3.
24. Braudel (n.11 above), 481–82.
25. See Kostof, "Junctions of Town and Country," in J.-P. Bourdier and N. AlSayyad, eds., *Dwellings, Settlements and Tradition*: (Lanham/London 1989), 107–33.
26. Lynch (n.5 above), 36.
27. *American Behavioral Scientist* 22.1, 1978, 134.

1. "ORGANIC" PATTERNS (pp. 43–93)

1. F. Castagnoli, *Orthogonal Town-Planning in Antiquity* (Cambridge, Mass./London 1971), 124.
2. R. M. Delson, *New Towns for Colonial Brazil* (diss., Syracuse Univ., N.Y., 1979), 90.
3. "The Urban Street Pattern as a Culture Indicator: Pennsylvania, 1682–1815," *Annals of the Association of American Geographers* 60.3, Sept. 1970, 428–46.
4. W. Braunfels, *Urban Design in Western Europe*, transl. K. J. Northcott (Chicago/London 1988), 6.
5. H. Gaube, *Iranian Cities* (New York 1979), 57.
6. M. W. Barley, ed., *European Towns* (London 1977), 193–96.
7. Quoted by H. Blumenfeld in *Town Planning Review*, April 1953, 44.
8. See Sherry Olson, "Urban Metabolism and Morphogenesis," *Urban Geography* 3.2, 1982, 87–109.
9. Lynch (Intro. n.5 above), 95.
10. For the Weiss argument, see his "Organic Form, Scientific and Aesthetic Aspects," *Daedalus* 89.1, Winter 1960, 176–90.
11. *Perspecta* 6, 1960, 53.
12. G. L. Burke, *The Making of Dutch Towns* (London 1956), 33. The following discussion of Dutch urban typologies is based on this book, and on A. M. Lambert, *The Making of the Dutch Landscape* (London 1971).
13. See D. Ward, "The Pre-Urban Cadaster and the Urban Pattern of Leeds," *Annals of the Association of American Geographers* 52.2, June 1962, 150–66.
14. Quoted by A. King in R. Ross and G. J. Telkamp, eds., *Colonial Cities* (Dordrecht/Lancaster 1985), 26.
15. "The Morphogenesis of Iranian Cities," *Annals of the Association of American Geographers* 69.2, June 1979, 208–24.
16. See R. J. McIntosh, "Early Urban Clusters: Arbitrating Social Ambiguity," to be published in *Journal of Field Archaeology*.
17. Thucydides II.8.
18. See Wheatley (Intro. n.17 above), 335.
19. See C. Winters, "Traditional Urbanism in the North Central Sudan," *Annals of the Association of American Geographers* 67.4, Dec. 1977, 517.
20. The following paragraphs are based on B. S. Hakim, *Arabic-Islamic Cities, Building and Planning Principles* (London 1986).
21. ibid., 95.
22. See R. Fonseca, "The Walled City of Old Delhi," *Landscape* 18.3, Fall 1969, 12–25.
23. R. Arnheim, *The Dynamics of Architectural Form* (Berkeley/London 1977), 164.
24. See P. Andrews et al., "Squatters and the Evolution of a Lifestyle," *Architectural Design*, 1973, no. 1, 16–25.
25. See E. Griffin and L. Ford, "A Model of Latin American City Structure," *Geographical Review* 70.4, Oct. 1980, 397–422.
26. See H. Dietz, "Urban Squatter Settlements in Peru," *Journal of Inter-American Studies* 11, 1969, 353–70.
27. W. M. Bowsky, *A Medieval Italian Commune* (Berkeley/London 1981), 295.
28. J. W. Reps, *Town Planning in Frontier America* (Princeton 1969), 80.
29. ibid., 167.
30. Cited in M. Aston and J. Bond, *The Landscape of Towns* (London 1976), 186. See also D. Tomkinson, "The Landscape City," *Journal of the Town Planning Institute*, May 1959.
31. A. Fein, *Landscape into Cityscape* (New York 1967), 329.
32. Cited by Peter Marcuse in *Planning Perspectives* 2, 1987, 302.
33. *Architectural Review* 163, June 1978, 361–62.
34. All quotations in R. Plunz, *A History of Housing in New York City* (New York 1990), 117–18.
35. J. Nolen, *New Towns for Old* (Boston 1927), 93.
36. For the Greenbelt Towns, see J. L. Arnold, *The New Deal in the Suburbs* (Columbus, Ohio, 1971).
37. See C. Tunnard and B. Pushkarev, *Man-Made America* (New Haven 1963), 90ff.
38. G. R. Collins and C. C. Collins, *Camillo Sitte and the Birth of Modern City Planning* (1965; repr. New York 1986), 120–21.
39. P. Lavedan, *Histoire de l'urbanisme, Renaissance et temps modernes* (Paris 1959), 126.
40. In a letter of 1921, quoted by Jean Dethier in L. Carl Brown, ed., *From Madina to Metropolis* (Princeton 1973), 203.
41. Quoted in J. Tyrwhitt, ed., *Patrick Geddes in India* (London 1947), 17.
42. Werner Knapp, cited by C. F. Otto in *Journal of the Society of Architectural Historians* 24.1, March 1965, 72.
43. See R. Smelser, "How Modern were the Nazis? DAF Social Planning and the Modernization Question," *German Studies Review* 13.2, May 1990, 291–92.
44. The piece was called "Construction des villes," a direct translation of the word *Städte-Bau* in Sitte's title. It was begun in 1910, and in the first outline sent to his teacher L'Eplattenier, Le Corbusier (then Charles Jeanneret) says that he intends to "cite plans and views in the manner of Camillo Sitte"—a promise he kept. He based the La Chaux-de-Fonds suburb on Hellerau outside Dresden, which he knew well. See H. Allen Brooks, "Jeanneret and Sitte: Le Corbusier's Earliest Ideas on Urban Design," in H. Searing, ed., *In Search of Modern Architecture* (New York/London 1982), 278–97.
45. D. I. Scargill, *Urban France* (New York/London 1983), 128.

2. THE GRID (pp. 95–157)

1. *The City of Tomorrow*, transl. F. Etchells (enlarged 1929 ed., repr. London 1987), 5–6.
2. Cited by S. E. Rasmussen in D. Walker, *The Architecture and Planning of Milton Keynes* (London 1982), 7.
3. This description is based on R. S. Johnston, "The

Ancient City of Suzhou," *Town Planning Review* 54.2, April 1983, 194–222.

4. See J. Puig i Cadafalch, "Idees teòriques sobre urbanisme en el segle XIV: un fragment d'Eiximenis," in *Homenatge a Antoni Rubio i Lluch* (Barcelona 1936), 1–9.

5. For these details, see G. P. R. Métraux, *Western Greek Land Use and City-Planning in the Archaic Period* (New York 1978).

6. E. A. Gutkind, *Urban Development in Western Europe, Great Britain, and the Netherlands* (New York 1971), 35.

7. J. W. Reps summarized by M. P. Conzen, in T. R. Slater, ed., *The Built Form of Western Cities* (Leicester 1990), 146.

8. Braunfels (Ch.1 n.4 above), 174–75.

9. This discussion of the Mormons mostly depends on Reps (Ch.1 n.28 above), 410–25.

10. See H. Lilius, *The Finnish Wooden Town* (Rungsted Kyst 1985), 155.

11. *American Notes* (London 1850 ed.), 67.

12. Buls, *Esthétique des villes* (Brussels 1893), 8–9.

13. Sitte ed. Collins (Ch.1 n.38 above), 126.

14. See P. Groth, "Streetgrids as Frameworks for Urban Variety," *Harvard Architecture Review* 2, Spring 1981, 68–75.

15. J. E. Vance, Jr., *This Scene of Man* (New York 1977), 44–45.

16. See P. J. Parr, "Settlement Patterns and Urban Planning in the Ancient Levant," in P. J. Ucko et al., eds., *Man, Settlement and Urbanism* (London 1972).

17. *Politics* II.5 and VII.10.

18. F. Grew and B. Hoblet, eds., *Roman Urban Topography* (CBA Research Report, 59, 1985), ix–x.

19. See G. Downey, *Ancient Antioch* (Princeton 1963), 33–34.

20. *Histories* VI.31, transl. F. Hultsch and E. S. Shuckburgh (Bloomington, Ind., 1962), 484.

21. Drinkwater in *Roman Urban Topography* (n.18 above), 52–53.

22. The information for this paragraph comes from Burke (Ch.1 n.12 above), 53–63.

23. See: Isidore, *Etymologia* IX.4; Hrabanus, *De Universo* XVI.4; Vincent of Beauvais, *Speculum doctrinale* VII.4.

24. *De regimine principum* II.1. For full text, see G. B. Phelan's transl., *On the Governance of Rulers* (Toronto 1935).

25. This argument is developed by S. Lang, "Sull' origine della disposizione a scacchiera nelle città medioevali," *Palladio* 5, 1955, 97–108.

26. M. Girouard, *Cities and People* (New Haven/London 1985), 222.

27. J. W. Konvitz, *Cities and the Sea* (Baltimore/London 1978), 18.

28. I owe this reference to the kindness of J. P. Protzen at Berkeley, whose monograph on Ollantaytambo is now in press.

29. P. Marcuse, "The Grid as City Plan: New York City and Laissez-faire Planning in the Nineteenth Century," *Planning Perspectives* 2, 1987, 287–310, esp. 290–96. For what follows, see also Reps (Ch.1 n.28 above), 193–203.

30. Mumford (Intro. n.1 above), 422.

31. On the grid in the United States, see generally M. Conzen (Intro. n.6 above). Also J. C. Hudson, *Plains County Towns* (Minneapolis 1985).

32. Also worth mentioning in this context are the "Sunday towns" (*villas do Domingo*) of Brazil, created because of the need for social intercourse on the part of the sparse and scattered population of the remote hinterland. Most of these towns started with a private gift of land to the Church made with the donor's understanding that it would be used to found a town. There were also towns of lay origin, often carrying the name of the founder (e.g., Paulopolis, Orlandia). In either case, the city form was a simple grid with the church and the plaza at the core, a hotel which was usually the first building to go up, and a jail. See P. Deffontaines, "The Origin and Growth of the Brazilian Network of Towns," *Geographical Review* 28, July 1938, 390ff.

33. See the chapter on "The City Edge" in the companion volume to the present work, *The City Assembled*.

34. J. F. Drinkwater in *Roman Urban Topography* (n.18 above), 53.

35. *Built Form* (n.7 above), 193.

36. D. Friedman, *Florentine New Towns* (New York/London 1988), 51.

37. The term used for this division, *per strigas*, was actually coined by a modern scholar, F. Castagnoli (see Ch.1 n.1 above). *Striga* in Latin means "a long line of grass or corn cut down, a swath," by extension a "plough furrow." In Roman parlance the system of *strigae* and *scamnae* referred to an old method of land division adopted especially in public arable land in the provinces, where strips were arranged lengthwise (*strigae*) and breadthwise (*scamnae*) in relation to the surveyor's orientation. See O. A. W. Dilke in *Geographical Journal*, Dec. 1961, 424n.

38. See Dilke, "Ground survey and measurement in Roman towns," in *Roman Urban Topography* (n.18 above), pt. II, 6–13.

39. See F. Boucher, "Medieval Design Methods, 800–1560," *Gesta* 11.2, 1972, 43, fig. 15; and amendments by Friedman (above, n.36), 132–33.

40. See n.36 above.

41. For what follows, see P. G. Hamberg, "Vitruvius, Fra Giocondo and the City Plan of Naples," *Acta archaeologica* 36, 1965, 105–25.

42. The very nomenclature of *platea* and *angiportus* (Latin for *stenopos*), first used by Vitruvius (I.vi.1) and also in a passage of Caesar's *De bello civile* (I.27), must refer to the Greek grid (see p.127 above), and not the Roman where there is no such distinction of street widths. So even though the blocks in Fra Giocondo's woodcut are square, i.e., Roman rather than Greek, the differentiation of street widths and the use of the words *platea* and *angiportus* imply that he was thinking of a Greek system.

43. The surveyor's transit, for one thing, was now able to fix a topographical feature relative to two or more points by simple triangulation. Alberti's transit had a circular dial divided into 48 degrees. Leonardo's transit consisted of "a circular, dial-like surface with its circumference divided into eight parts corresponding to the eight winds, each further subdivided into eight degrees. At the center of this disk was a magnetic compass." (J. A. Pinto in *Journal of the Society of Architectural Historians* 35, March 1976, 40.) At the beginning of the survey, magnetic north was lined up with the north wind (*tramontana*). The magnetic meridian thus provided a constant reference for observations taken from a number of different points. Also pivoted at the center was a movable sight vane. Alberti had described a process similar to that used by Leonardo at Imola in his *Descriptio urbis Romae*, dating from ca. 1450. Johannes Praetorius's much touted "invention" of the modern surveyor's transit about 1600 was probably nothing more than the standardization of instruments already in use throughout the 16th century.

44. Scamozzi was among the first to reverse the customary graphic differentiation between blocks and streets by shading the streets and squares rather than the blocks.

45. J. W. Hall, *Japan from Prehistory to Modern Times* (New York 1970), 54.

46. The township was divided and distributed according to merit, the size of each allotment reflecting either the relative amount each settler contributed to the initial expense of the enterprise, or the extent of his personal property. There was a class hierarchy of proprietors, first settlers, and latecomers.

47. See C. Tunnard, *The City of Man* (2nd ed., New York 1970), 118–19; Reps (Ch.1 n.28 above), 235–38.

48. S. Hurtt, "The American Continental Grid: Form and Meaning," *Threshold* 2, Autumn 1983, 32–40.

49. Burke (Ch.1 n.12 above), 55–57.

50. K. W. Forster, "From 'Rocca' to 'Civitas': Urban Planning at Sabbioneta," *L'arte*, March 1969, 5–40. This Gonzaga emblem was expressed architecturally in the maze gardens of the Palazzo del Tè in Mantua, the private estate of the Gonzaga, and in the famous ceiling of the Sala del Labirinto in the Ducal Palace there.

51. C. Platt, *The English Medieval Town* (London/New York 1976), 32–33.

52. See E. T. Price, "The Central Courthouse Square in the American County Seat," *Geographical Review*, Jan. 1968, 29–60.

53. See S. Tobriner, *The Genesis of Noto* (London 1982); and his "Angelo Italia and the Post-Earthquake Reconstruction of Avola in 1693," in *Le arti in Sicilia nel Settecento, Studi in Memoria di Maria Accascina* (Palermo 1985), 73–86.

54. See principally P. Boudon, *La Ville de Richelieu* (Paris 1972).

55. M. Beresford, *New Towns of the Middle Ages* (London/New York 1967), 147.

56. A. Ruegg, ed., *Materialien zur Studie Bern* (privately produced for the 4th-year course of D. Schnebli and P. Hofer at the Eidg. Technische Hochschule, Zurich, 1974–75).

57. See S. Muthesius, *The English Terraced House* (New Haven/London 1982), 107.

58. C. Bauer, *Modern Housing* (Boston 1934), 59. For New York generally, see now R. Plunz, *A History of Housing in New York City* (New York 1990).

59. Cerdà, an engineer in the central Government's department of roads and bridges, elaborated on his urban thinking in a book entitled *Teoria general de la urbanización*, published in Madrid in 1867; it was followed by a second volume on the Barcelona plan. A third volume was left unfinished. The recent focus on his work started with an exhibition mounted in Barcelona in 1976 on the occasion of the one-hundredth anniversary of his death, for which a catalogue was published. Two architectural journals in the city also dedicated entire issues to Cerdà: *Cuadernos de arquitectura y urbanismo*, nos. 100–101, 1974; and *Construcción de la ciudad*, Jan. 1977. See also "Barcelona: Planning and Change 1854–1977," *Town Planning Review* 50, 1979, 185–203.

60. See R. D. McKenzie, *Metropolitan Community* (New York 1933).

61. J. Dahir, *The Neighborhood Unit Plan* (Russell Sage Foundation, New York 1947), 22.

62. ibid., 38.

63. See A. B. Yeomans, ed., *City Residential Land Development* (Chicago 1916), 105.

64. See his *Rehousing Urban America* (New York 1935).

65. Groth (n.14 above), 75, paraphrasing J. P. Hallihan in *Annals of the American Academy of Political and Social Science* 133, Sept. 1927, 66.

66. See Hilbersheimer's *The Nature of Cities* (Chicago 1955).

67. Cited by V. M. Lampugnani in *Domus* 685, July–Aug. 1987, 27.

68. See n.2 above.

3. THE CITY AS DIAGRAM (pp. 159–207)

1. Soleri's books include: *Arcology: The City in the Image of Man* (Cambridge, Mass./London 1969) and *The Bridge between Matter and Spirit is Matter*

Becoming Spirit (Garden City, N.Y., 1973). For an early assessment of his work, see Kostof, "Soleri's Arcology: A New Design for the City?" *Art in America* 59.2, March–April 1971, 90–95.

2. Workshopper statements in J. Shipsky, "Diary of an Arcosanti Experience," *American Institute of Architects Journal* 71.5, May 1982, 30, 35.

3. Cited in *Arts and Architecture* 2.4, 1983, 60; and *Art in America* 67.3, May–June 1979, 67.

4. See chiefly L. Di Sopra, *Palmanova* (Milan 1983).

5. J. S. Buckingham, *The Eastern and Western States of America*, I (London 1842), 351; quoted in Carter (Intro. n.7 above), 151–52.

6. This esoteric literature is surveyed in S. Lang's "The Ideal City from Plato to Howard," *Architectural Review* 112, Aug. 1952, 91–101, along with the work of theorists like Filarete, Alberti and Ledoux. She reaches the curious conclusion that her survey proves the historical absence of an art of building towns, and asserts the indifference of the past to town planning as a visual art. Her editors agree, and close with the perverse aside that "there do exist, nevertheless, many examples of actual townscape, for which we have to thank accident or the intuition of their creators"!

7. See J. E. Olson, *O'Donnell, Andersonville of the Pacific* (privately published, 1985), 55.

8. See A. H. Leighton, *The Governing of Men* (Princeton 1945).

9. U. Bauche et al., eds., *Arbeit und Vernichtung* (Hamburg 1986).

10. The classic account is W. Horn and E. Born, *The Plan of St. Gall* (Berkeley/London 1979).

11. D. Hayden, *Seven American Utopias* (Cambridge, Mass./London 1976), 77 and *passim.*

12. This and following quotations from A. Holroyd, *Saltaire and its Founder* (Saltaire 1871).

13. Quoted in L. Benevolo, *The Origins of Modern Town Planning*, transl. J. Landry (London 1967), 112–16.

14. See T. P. Verma et al., eds., *Varanasi through the Ages* (Benares 1986), esp. 303–11. For a modern urban geography of the city, see R. L. Singh, *Banaras* (Benares 1955).

15. At Madurai, the central temple to Shiva, the temple of Minakshi Sundaresvarar, goes back to the 12th century. For the symbolism of the city's plan, see S. Lewandowski, "The Hindu Temple in South India," in A. D. King, ed., *Buildings and Society* (London 1980), 123–50, esp. 131–34.

16. See, e.g., T. G. McGee, *The Southeast Asian City* (London 1967), 29–41.

17. Braunfels (Ch.1 n.4 above), 174. See also G. Eimer, *Die Stadtplanung im schwedischen Ostseereich* (Stockholm 1961), 100–104.

18. The classic discussion remains P. Wheatley, *The Pivot of the Four Quarters* (Edinburgh 1971/Chicago 1972).

19. See N. S. Steinhardt in *Journal of the Society of Architectural Historians* 45.4, Dec. 1986, 349.

20. See P. Wheatley and T. See, *From Court to Capital* (London/Chicago 1978), 113–31.

21. Quoted by A. Wright (Intro. n.15 above), 46. The most current studies of Chinese imperial cities are by Nancy S. Steinhardt; see her recent book, *Chinese Imperial City Planning* (Honolulu 1990). On Chang'an under the Han dynasty, see Wang Zhongshu, *Han Civilization* (New Haven/London 1982).

22. The quotations in this and the following paragraphs come from R. G. Irving, *Indian Summer: Lutyens, Baker and Imperial Delhi* (New Haven/London 1981), 73, 76.

23. See A. D. King, *Colonial Urban Development: Culture, Social Power and Environment* (London 1976), 244–46.

24. See J. W. Hall in *Far Eastern Quarterly* 15.1, Nov. 1955, 37–56.

25. See G. Michell, "Jaipur: Form and Origins," in N. Gütschow and T. Sieverts, eds., *Stadt und Ritual* (Darmstadt 1977), 78–81.

26. This is based on J. R. Stilgoe, *Common Landscape of America, 1580 to 1845* (New Haven/London 1982), 43ff.

27. Friedman (Ch.2 n.36 above), 201–03.

28. See H. Baron, *The Crisis of the Early Italian Renaissance*, (rev. ed., Princeton 1966), 200–201.

29. While they are detailed, they are sometimes unclear. The best interpretation is by J. Lassner, in his *Topography of Baghdad in the Early Middle Ages* (Detroit 1970).

30. Lines 1004–9; cited in Lang (n.6 above), 96, n.43.

31. Lang (n.6 above), 95–96.

32. Braunfels (Ch.1 n.4 above), 149–50.

33. Lynch (Intro. n.5 above), 373.

34. ibid., 374–75.

35. S. Moholy-Nagy, *Matrix of Man* (London 1968), 76.

36. R. E. Lapp, *Must We Hide?* (Cambridge, Mass., 1949), 161–65.

37. See E. Battisti, "San Leucio presso Caserta," *Controspazio*, Dec. 1974, 50–71. The revolution of 1799 interrupted the project.

38. M. Foucault, *Discipline and Punish*, transl. A. Sheridan (New York/London 1977), 200, and 195–209 in general.

39. See P. V. Turner, *Campus, An American Planning Tradition* (New York 1984), 191ff.

40. Singh (n.14 above), 49–51.

41. See J. Pratt, "La Réunion, the Fourierist Last Hurrah," *Arts & Architecture*, 2.4, Summer 1984, 30–33.

42. S. Moholy-Nagy (n.35 above), 75–78, for a general review. The best account of Pemberton and his influence on Howard is in J. Rockey, "From Vision to Reality," *Town Planning Review* 54.1, Jan. 1983, 83–105.

43. Hayden (n.11 above), 288–317. For another copy of Howard's diagram, Prozorovska, see above, p.78.

44. H. C. Andersen and E. Hébrard, *Creation of a World Center of Communication* (1912), published a year later in Paris in English and in French (as *Création d'un centre mondial de communication*). See also H. Barnes, "Messrs. Andersen and Hébrard's Scheme," *Architectural Review* 46, Dec. 1919, 137–42.

45. M. Maruyama, "Designing A Space Community," *The Futurist*, Oct. 1976, 273.

4. THE GRAND MANNER (pp. 209–77)

1. The story of the founding and development of Washington is best told in J. W. Reps, *Monumental Washington* (Princeton 1967). See also an official history by the National Capital Planning Commission and F. Gutheim, *Worthy of the Nation* (Washington, D.C., 1977).

2. M. Coppa, *Storia dell'urbanistica. Le età ellenistiche* (Rome 1981), *passim.*

3. W. L. MacDonald, *The Architecture of the Roman Empire, II. An Urban Appraisal* (New Haven/London 1986).

4. J. Evelyn, *London Revived*, ed. E. S. de Beer, (Oxford 1938), 30.

5. ibid., 34.

6. In *A Character of England*, 1659, the supposed comments of a French observer; see Evelyn (n.4 above), 5.

7. J. A. F. Orbaan, *Sixtine Rome* (New York 1911), 72–73.

8. Recently the claim has been made that the first capital of Annapolis, St. Mary's City founded in 1634, had acquired a Baroque overlay in a carefully laid-out plan of the 1660s. The state house sat on a promontory near St. Mary's River, on the highest point of land in the town. The church was at the opposite end of town, and, like the state house, was 1,400 feet (427 m.) from the center of the town square. When the main buildings are connected by lines, the town plan yields two triangular wings touching at the town square. The planner may have been Jerome White, Surveyor General of the Maryland colony in the 1660s, who had lived for a time in Italy. See John Hartsock, "Vanished Colonial Town Yields Baroque Surprise," *New York Times*, 6 Feb. 1989.

9. See R. Krautheimer, *The Rome of Alexander VII, 1655–1667* (Princeton/Guildford 1985), 3–7 and *passim.* For the discussion in the following paragraph, see an earlier Krautheimer study, "The Tragic and Comic Scene of the Renaissance," *Gazette des Beaux-Arts*, 6th ser., vol. 33, 1948, 327–46.

10. Onians, *Bearers of Meaning* (Princeton/Cambridge 1988), 287ff., esp. 295.

11. Evelyn (n.4 above), 23.

12. M. Carlson, *Places of Performance* (Ithaca, N.Y./London 1989), 22.

13. The playwright Victorien Sardou, cited in T. J. Clark, *The Painting of Modern Life* (Princeton/London 1984), 42.

14. K. Junghanns in *Deutsche Architektur* 4, 1955, 34.

15. Cited in *Design Book Review* 17, Winter 1989, 60.

16. W. Herrmann, *Laugier and 18th Century French Theory* (London 1962), 136.

17. Quoted by A. Vidler in S. Anderson, ed., *On Streets* (Cambridge, Mass./London 1978), 38.

18. P. Herlihy, *Odessa: A History, 1794–1914* (Cambridge, Mass., 1986), 140.

19. Braudel (Intro. n.11 above), 498.

20. In a letter from Michele Ferno to the humanist Mario Maffei. I owe this reference to the kindness of Dr. Richard Ingersoll.

21. See Kostof, *Third Rome, 1870–1950: Traffic and Glory* (Berkeley 1973), 18, 60–63.

22. For a list, see W. Lotz in *Studi offerti a Giovanni Incisa della Rocchetta* (Miscellanea Società Romana di Storia Patria, 23; Rome, 1973), 247ff.

23. *Coach and Sedan* (repr. of 1636 ed., London 1925). See also R. Straus, *Carriages and Coaches, Their History and Their Evolution* (London 1912).

24. G. Clay, *Close-up: How to Read the American City* (Chicago/London 1973, 1980), 42–48.

25. P. Lewis, *New Orleans, The Making of an Urban Landscape* (Cambridge, Mass., 1976), 42.

26. American Institute of Architects, Committee on Town Planning, *City Planning Progress in the United States*, ed. G. B. Ford, (1917), 93, 97.

27. ibid., 71–72, 151.

28. D. H. Burnham and E. H. Bennett, *Plan of Chicago* (Chicago 1909, repr. New York 1970), 89–90.

29. See C. M. Robinson, *Modern Civic Art* (New York 1903), 224–25.

30. See especially Allan Ceen, "The Quartiere de' Banchi: Urban Planning in Rome in the First Half of the Cinquecento" (diss., Univ. of Pennsylvania, 1977), 66–88.

31. See M. Quast, "Villa Montalto: Genesi del sistema assiale," *Atti del XXIII Congresso di Storia dell'Architettura*, vol. 1 (Rome 1989), 212–13.

32. Prior examples in Holland during the 1580s—at Willemstad and Klundert—where the trees of a square extended a little way into converging avenues did not catch on. For this and other details that follow, see Henry W. Lawrence, "Origins of the Tree-lined Boulevard," *Geographical Review* 78.4, Oct. 1988, 355–74.

33. Lawrence (n.32 above), 365.

34. F. Loyer, *Paris Nineteenth Century, Architecture and Urbanism*, transl. C. L. Clark (New York 1988), 313.

35. For what follows, I am principally relying on

Lawrence (n.32 above).

36. See R. J. Favretti, "The Ornamentation of New England Towns: 1750–1850," *Journal of Garden History* 2.4, 1982, 325–42.

37. Lawrence (n.32 above), 374.

38. Cited in J. Cracraft, *The Petrine Revolution in Russian Architecture* (Chicago/London 1988), 229.

39. Loyer (n.34 above), 113, 116.

40. J. Garrard, ed., *The Eighteenth Century in Russia* (Oxford 1973), 322ff.

41. J. Babelon in P. Francastel, ed., *L'Urbanisme de Paris et l'Europe* (Paris 1969), 48.

42. Evelyn (n.4 above), 50.

43. Braunfels (Ch.1 n.4 above), 223.

44. ibid., 217.

45. See ch.1 n.2 above.

46. For citations, ibid., 44, 90, 128 and 67. (I have made minor editorial revisions.)

47. H. Blumenfeld in *Journal of the Society of Architectural Historians* 4, 1944, 31.

48. The major publication for Turin is A. Cavallari-Murat et al., *Forma urbana e architettura nella Torino barocca* (Turin 1968).

49. P. Portoghesi, *Roma barocca* (Cambridge, Mass. 1970), 13.

50. Cited in Herrmann (n.16 above), 138.

51. Cited by A. B. Correa in *Forum et Plaza Mayor dans le monde hispanique* (Madrid/Paris 1978), 94.

52. See A. J. Schmidt, "William Hastie, Scottish Planner of Russian Cities," *Proceedings of the American Philosophical Society* 114.3, June 1970, 226–43.

53. Cited by Loyer (n.34 above), 360–61.

54. See, among others, V. van Rossem in S. Polano, ed., *Berlage: Opera completa* (Milan 1987).

55. Evelyn (n.4 above), 39.

56. See *The American Architect* 124, Dec. 1923, 486–514, esp. 504.

57. N. Miller, *Renaissance Bologna* (New York 1989), 53.

58. See H. Friedel, *Die Bronzebildmonumente in Augsburg* (Augsburg 1974); and Braunfels (Ch.1 n.4 above), 123–24.

59. For a full discussion of Roman arches, see MacDonald (n.3 above), 75–99.

60. Lord Chelmsford, cited in Irving (Ch.3 n.22 above), 259.

61. A. Aman, "Symbols and Rituals in the People's Democracies During the Cold War," in C. Arvidsson and L. E. Blomqvist, eds., *Symbols of Power: The Esthetics of Political Legitimation in the Soviet Union and Eastern Europe* (Stockholm 1987), 48.

62. The term *magistrale* means main or arterial road in the Slavic languages. It entered the vocabulary of East German architects and planners with the Soviet occupation, and is routinely used in the Fifties and Sixties to refer to the principal city-center avenue.

63. L. Perchik, *The Reconstruction of Moscow* (Moscow 1936), 67.

64. See G. Castillo, "Cities of the Stalinist Empire," in N. AlSayyad, ed., *Forms of Dominance: On the Architecture and Urbanism of the Colonial Experience* (in press).

65. R. Krier, *Urban Space* (New York/London 1979), 19, 89.

66. On Bofill, see T. Schuman, "Utopia Spurned," *Journal of Architectural Education* 40.1, Fall 1986, 20–29.

67. Cited in *Domus*, Jan. 1986, 4–5.

68. See J. Abrams in *Lotus International* 50.2, 1986, 6–26.

5. THE URBAN SKYLINE (pp. 279–335)

1. Quoted in W. Attoe, *Skylines* (Chichester 1981), 2.

2. J. Heers, *Family Clans in the Middle Ages*, transl. B. Herbert (Amsterdam/Oxford 1977), 194.

3. Friedman (Ch.2 n.36 above), 215.

4. Miller (Ch.4 n.57 above), 30.

5. Heers (n.2 above), 188.

6. Frederic A. Delano in *The American City Magazine*, Jan. 1926, 1.

7. Quoted in T. A. P. van Leeuwen, *The Skyward Trend of Thought* (Cambridge, Mass., 1988), 7.

8. T. Sharp in *Town Planning Review*, Jan. 1963, 274.

9. For much of this discussion, I rely on J. Schulz's excellent essay, "Jacopo de' Barbari's View of Venice," *Art Bulletin* 60, Sept. 1978, 425–74; see also S. Alpers, *The Art of Describing* (Chicago 1983), 152–59.

10. This image is illustrated in J. G. Links, *Townscape Painting and Drawing* (London/New York 1972), fig. 18.

11. Among 17th-century collections of city views, also note Eric Dahlberg's *Suecia antiqua et hodierna*, published during the 1670s.

12. Links (n.10 above), 120.

13. Schulz (n.9 above), 472.

14. Braunfels (Ch.1 n.4 above), 114ff.; and his essay, "Anton Wonsams Kölnprospekt von 1531 in der Geschichte des Sehens," *Wallraf-Richartz Jahrbuch* 22, 1960, 115–36.

15. See Braunfels (Ch.1 n.4 above), 129–30.

16. O. von Simson, *The Gothic Cathedral* (New York 1964), 10.

17. See H. Schindler in *Journal of the Society of Architectural Historians* 40.2, May 1981, 138–42.

18. See A. Keen, *Sir Christopher Wren* (London 1923), 31ff.; M. Whinney, *Wren* (London/New York 1971), 66ff.

19. Quoted in G. Beard, *Our English Vitruvius* (Edinburgh 1982), 21.

20. K. Clark, *The Gothic Revival* (London 1949; repr. New York 1962), 135.

21. Quoted in G. L. Hersey, *High Victorian Gothic* (Baltimore/London 1972), 94–95.

22. ibid., 105.

23. See M. Trachtenberg, *The Campanile of Florence Cathedral* (New York 1971), esp. 174–79. A similar contrast was commonly made in 19th-century France between the civic belltower (*beffroi*), symbol of civic liberty, and the church belltower (*clocher*).

24. Quoted in C. L. V. Meeks, *The Railroad Station* (New Haven 1956/London 1957), 95.

25. See G. Germann, *Gothic Revival in Europe and Britain* (London 1972/Cambridge, Mass., 1973), 159.

26. Meeks (n.24 above), 102.

27. For water towers, see E. Heinle and F. Leonhardt, *Towers, A Historical Survey* (London/New York 1989), 262–75.

28. ibid., 222–57.

29. E. A. Gutkind, *Urban Development in Eastern Europe, Bulgaria, Romania, and the USSR* (New York 1972), 43.

30. Schmidt (Ch.4 n.52 above), 237.

31. C. M. Zierer in G. W. Robbins and L. D. Tilton, eds., *Los Angeles* (Los Angeles 1941), 44.

32. J. Pastier in *Design Quarterly* 140, 1988, 14.

33. Sharp (n.8 above), 275.

34. D. Marriott quoted in Attoe (n.1 above), 9.

35. For both instances, see Attoe (n.1 above), 86.

36. See K. H. Hüter, *Architektur in Berlin 1900–1933* (Dresden 1987), 298ff.

37. J. M. Diefendorf in *Urban Studies* 26, 1989, 139.

38. See generally F. Bergmann in *Deutsche Architektur* 5, 1956, 552–57; and for Dresden in particular, J. Paul in J. M. Diefendorf, ed., *Rebuilding Europe's Bombed Cities* (Basingstoke 1990), 170–89.

39. See C. Borngräber, "Residential Buildings in Stalinallee," *Architectural Design* 52.11–12, 1982, 37.

40. Attoe (n.1 above), 32–34, 89.

41. Links (n.10 above), figs. 21–22, 27.

42. Pastier (n.32 above), 11 and fig. 20.

43. Braunfels (Ch.1 n.4 above), 39.

44. Kostof, *A History of Architecture* (New York/Oxford 1985), 421–24.

45. Evelyn (Ch.4 n.4 above), 38.

46. See A. Ling in *Town Planning Review* 34, April 1963, 7–18; and J. Gottmann in *Geographical Review* 56, April 1966, 190–212.

47. *Town Planning Review*, Oct. 1957, 215–16.

48. Quoted in Gutkind (n.29 above), 362.

49. C. Robinson and R. H. Bletter, *Skyscraper Style* (New York 1975), 23.

50. Quoted by R. Jay in *Journal of the Society of Architectural Historians* 46, June 1987, 146.

51. See F. Rosso, *Catalogo critico dell' Archivio Alessandro Antonelli* (Museo Civico di Torino, Turin 1975); and C. L. V. Meeks, *Italian Architecture 1750–1914* (New Haven 1966), 193–202.

52. Quoted in D. Kautt, "Stadtkrone oder städtebauliche Dominante," *Die alte Stadt* 2, 1984, 140.

53. A clear analysis of these arguments will be found in G. Ricci, *La Cattedrale del Futuro, Bruno Taut 1914–1921* (Rome 1982). See also D. Sharp, *Modern Architecture and Expressionism* (London/New York 1966), 85–96.

54. B. Taut, *Die Stadtkrone* (Jena 1919), 51.

55. Quoted in R. Rainer, *Städtebauliche Prosa* (Tübingen 1948), 144.

56. Sharp (n.8 above), 91.

57. See T. Bender and W. R. Taylor, "Culture and Architecture: Some Aesthetic Tensions in the Shaping of Modern New York City," in W. Sharpe and L. Wallock, eds., *Visions of the Modern City* (Baltimore/London 1987), 189–219.

58. *Modern Civic Art or the City Made Beautiful* (New York 1903), cited by D. M. Bluestone in *Journal of the Society of Architectural Historians*, Sept. 1988, 256.

59. Quoted in van Leeuwen (n.7 above), 60.

60. ibid., 30.

61. See S. Cohen, "The Tall Building Urbanistically Reconsidered," *Threshold* 2, Autumn 1983, 6–13.

62. From the catalogue of *Città Nuova*, May 1914, text attributed to Sant' Elia, as quoted in R. Banham, *Theory and Design in the First Machine Age* (London 1960), 129.

63. Quoted by N. Evenson in H. Allen Brooks, ed., *Le Corbusier* (Princeton 1987), 244.

64. J. G. Hajdu in *Town Planning Review* 50, 1979, 274.

65. See, for example, D. Conway, ed., *Human Response to Tall Buildings* (Stroudsburg, Pa., 1977).

66. *New York Times*, 15 Nov. 1987. Goldberger claims that the Jahn building transformed "what had been the flattest of any American city to one of the richest." Another influential critic, Martin Filler (in *House and Garden*, March 1988), considers the building offensive: "it is not only an egotistical usurpation but also a visual assault, marring the face of the city for decades to come."

67. G. Scott, *The Architecture of Humanism* (London 1914; repr. Garden City, N.Y., 1956), 8.

68. Delano (n.6 above), 8.

69. Quoted in van Leeuwen (n.7 above), 79.

BIBLIOGRAPHY

The following is a very limited selection from the extensive literature consulted in the writing of the text; further specific sources will be found in the chapter notes.

INTRODUCTION

General surveys of urban history to which reference is made in the notes to this and other chapters are K. Lynch, *A Theory of Good City Form* (Cambridge, Mass./London 1981); W. Braunfels, *Urban Design in Western Europe* (Chicago 1988); E. A. Gutkind, *Urban Development in Western Europe, Great Britain, and the Netherlands* (New York 1971) and *Urban Development in Eastern Europe, Bulgaria, Romania, and the U.S.S.R.* (New York 1972); P. Lavedan, *Histoire de l'urbanisme, Renaissance et temps modernes* (Paris 1959); M. Girouard, *Cities and People* (New Haven/London 1985); H. Carter, *The Study of Urban Geography* (3rd ed., London 1981); J. E. Vance, Jr., *This Scene of Man* (New York 1977); L. Mumford, *The City in History* (New York/London 1961) and *The Culture of Cities* (New York/London 1938); and L. Benevolo, *Storia della città* (Bari 1976). Several others should also be mentioned: J. Stübben, *Der Städtebau*, first published in 1890 and in print through the Twenties, influential both as history and planning manual; F. R. Hiorns, *Town-building in History* (London 1956); E. Egli, *Geschichte des Städtebaues*, I, *Die alte Welt*, II, *Das Mittelalter* (Ansbach 1959, 1962); and A. E. J. Morris, *History of Urban Form* (London 1972). In addition, M. Morini's *Atlante di storia dell'urbanistica* (Milan 1963), newly reissued, remains an invaluable pictorial source book. The multivolume *Storia dell'urbanistica* published by Laterza of Bari through the Seventies and Eighties aims to be exhaustive; the most relevant volumes are V. F. Pardo, *Storia dell'urbanistica dal Trecento al Quattrocento* (1982); E. Guidoni and A. Marino, *Il Cinquecento* (1982) and *Il Seicento* (1979); P. Sica, *Il Settecento* (1979), *L'Ottocento* (1977), and *Il Novecento* (1978, 1985).

Period surveys include: (a) Antiquity—P. Lampl, *Cities and Planning in the Ancient Near East* (New York/London 1968); M. Hammond, *The City in the Ancient World* (Cambridge, Mass. 1972); J. B. Ward-Perkins, *Cities of Ancient Greece and Italy* (New York/London 1974); and a series of articles in *Town Planning Review* on Egypt (vol. 20, 1949, 32–51), Mesopotamia (vol. 21, 1950, 98–115), the prehistoric Aegean (vol. 23, 1953, 261–79); Greek cities (vol. 22, 1951, 102–21); Hellenistic cities (vol. 22, 1951, 177–205), and Etruscan and early Roman cities (vol. 26, 1955, 126–54).
(b) The Middle Ages—W. Braunfels, *Mittelalterliche Stadtbaukunst in der Toskana* (Berlin 1953); E. Herzog, *Die ottonische Stadt* (Berlin 1964); E. Ennen, *The Medieval Town* (Amsterdam 1979); T. Hall, *Mittelalterliche Stadtgrundrisse* (Stockholm 1980).
(c) The modern period—L. Benevolo, *The Origins of Modern Town Planning* (London 1967); R. Ross and G. J. Telkamp, eds., *Colonial Cities* (Dordrecht/Lancaster 1985); also A. Sutcliffe, *Towards the Planned City* (Oxford 1981) which deals with Germany, Britain, France and the United States during the period 1780–1914; and G. Broadbent, *Emerging Concepts in Urban Space Design* (London 1990).

A number of regional studies are best listed here.

For Africa, see W. Bascom, "Urbanization among the Yoruba," *American Journal of Sociology* 60.5, 1955, 446–54; A. L. Mabogunje, *Urbanization in Nigeria* (New York 1968). For the Middle East, I. Lapidus, ed., *Middle Eastern Cities* (Berkeley 1969); L. Carl Brown, ed., *From Madina to Metropolis* (Princeton 1973), with useful essays by P. English on Herat, J. Abu-Lughod on Cairo, and J. Dethier on French Morocco; G. H. Blake and R. I. Lawless, *The Changing Middle Eastern City* (New York/London 1980); A. Raymond, *The Great Arab Cities in the 16th–18th Centuries* (New York/London 1984).

For China, the most current studies are those of N. S. Steinhardt, in *Journal of the Society of Architectural Historians* 45.4, Dec. 1986, and her book *Chinese Imperial City Planning* (Honolulu 1990). For earlier studies, see G. Rozman, *Urban Networks in Ch'ing China and Tokugawa Japan* (Princeton 1973); G. W. Skinner, ed., *The City in Late Imperial China* (Palo Alto 1977), particularly A. Wright on the cosmology of the Chinese city, Sen-Dou Chang on walled capitals, and F. W. Mote on 14th-century Nanjing; and A. Schinz, *Cities in China* (Berlin 1989). For Japan, besides Rozman (see China above), see J. W. Hall, "The Castle Town and Japan's Modern Urbanization," *The Far Eastern Quarterly* 15.1, Nov. 1955, 37–56. For India, see P. P. Karan, "The Pattern of Indian Towns," *Journal of the American Institute of Planners* 23, 1957, 70–75; and G. Breese, "Urban Development Problems in India," *Annals of the Association of American Geographers* 53.3, Sept. 1963, 253ff. See also T. G. McGee, *The Southeast Asian City* (New York 1967).

For Central Europe, there exists a monumental urban history edited by W. Rausch, each volume organized as a collection of essays by various authors, beginning with the 12th–13th centuries: *Beiträge zur Geschichte der Städte Mitteleuropas* (Linz 1963–84).

For Eastern Europe and the Soviet Union, besides Gutkind (see general surveys above), see M. F. Hamm, ed., *The City in Russian History* (Lexington 1976), with essays by F. W. Skinner on Odessa, B. M. Frolic on the Sixties Moscow city plan and S. F. Starr on 20th-century planning; R. A. French and F. E. Ian Hamilton, *The Socialist City* (Chichester 1979).

For South America, see H. Wilhelmy and A. Borsdorf, *Die Städte Südamerikas* (Berlin/Stuttgart 1984), vol. 3 of an excellent series called *Urbanisierung der Erde* edited by W. Tietze.

1. "ORGANIC" PATTERNS

On the Islamic city form, see B. S. Hakim, *Arabic-Islamic Cities, Building and Planning Principles* (London 1986), and also S. Al Hathloul, *Tradition, Continuity and Change in the Physical Environment: The Arab Muslim City* (Ann Arbor 1981); but a critique of their tradionalist stance is provided by N. AlSayyad, "Building the Arab Muslim City" (diss., Univ. of California, Berkeley 1988).

On Alberti's sympathies for medieval cities, see W. A. Eden, "Studies in Urban Theory: The *De re aedificatoria* of Leon Battista Alberti," *Town Planning Review* 19–20, 1943, 10–28; and M. Saura, "Architecture and The Law in Early Renaissance Urban Life: Leon Battista Alberti's *De re aedificatoria*" (diss., Univ. of California, Berkeley 1987).

On the planned picturesque, see W. L. Creese, *The Search for Environment* (New Haven/London 1966); A. M. Edwards, *The Design of Suburbia* (London 1981). The Olmsted bibliography is too extensive even to sample; the places to begin are A. Fein, *Frederick Law Olmsted and the American Environmental Tradition* (New York 1969), And L. W. Roper, *FLO: A Biography of Frederick Law Olmsted* (Baltimore/London 1973). On the American picturesque tradition, see R. G. Wilson, "Idealism and the Origin of the First American Suburb: Llewellyn Park, New Jersey," *American Art Journal*, Oct. 1979, 79–90; K. T. Jackson, *Crabgrass Frontier* (New York/Oxford 1985), 73–102; D. Schuyler, *The New Urban Landscape* (Baltimore/London 1986); and *Architectural Design* 51. 10–11, 1981, a special issue on the Anglo-American suburb edited by R. A. M. Stern. See also R. S. Childs, "The First War Emergency Government Towns for Shipyard Workers," *Journal of the American Institute of Architects* 6, 1918, 237–51.

On Garden Cities, see D. MacFadyen, *Sir Ebenezer Howard and the Town Planning Movement* (1933; Manchester 1970); P. Batchelor, "The Origin of the Garden City Concept of Urban Form," *Journal of the Society of Architectural Historians* 28, 1969, 184–200; A. Schollmeier, *Gartenstädte in Deutschland* (Münster 1988); and the June 1978 issue of *The Architectural Review* devoted to the subject. Raymond Unwin's *Town Planning in Practice*, first published in 1909, is an essential primer, and there is a good recent biography of him by F. Jackson, *Sir Raymond Unwin: Architect, Planner and Visionary* (London 1985). For the United States, see C. S. Stein, *Toward New Towns for America* (Chicago/Liverpool 1951, 3rd ed. 1966).

On Camillo Sitte, see G. R. Collins and C. C. Collins, *Camillo Sitte and the Birth of Modern City Planning* (1965; repr. New York 1986). On Patrick Geddes: J. Tyrwhitt, ed., *Patrick Geddes in India* (London 1947), and also H. Meller, *Patrick Geddes* (London 1990). For the Frankfurt housing estates by E. May, see among others *Ernst May und das Neue Frankfurt 1925–1930* (Berlin 1986), and D. W. Dreysse, *May—Siedlungen* (Frankfurt 1987). For the essential biographical data on Reichow, see W. Durth, *Deutsche Architekten* (3rd ed., Brunswick/Wiesbaden 1988); also W. Durth, "Verschwiegene Geschichte: Probleme der Kontinuität in der Stadtplanung, 1940–1960," *Die alte Stadt* 14.1, 1987, 28–50. In addition to his magnum opus, *Organische Stadtbaukunst, organische Baukunst, organische Kultur* (Brunswick 1948), Reichow also wrote *Die autogerechte Stadt* (Ravensburg 1959), commissioned by the West German Ministry of Housing.

On Team X: P. Eisenman, "From Golden Lane to Robin Hood Gardens," *Oppositions* 1, Sept. 1973, 27–56; G. Candilis et al., "Recent Thoughts in Town Planning and Urban Design," in D. Lewis, ed., *The Pedestrian in the City* (Princeton 1966), 183–96.

2. THE GRID

For Classical antiquity, see F. Castagnoli, *Orthogonal Town Planning in Antiquity* (Cambridge, Mass./London 1971); G. P. R. Métraux, *Western Greek Land Use and City-Planning in the Archaic Period* (New York 1978); and M. Coppa, *Storia dell'urbanistica. Le età ellenistiche* (Rome 1981); also F. Grew and B. Hobley, *Roman Urban Topography in Britain and the Western Empire* (London 1985), esp. P. Crummy on the plan of Colchester; G. Tibiletti, "La struttura topografica antica di Pavia," *Atti del convegno di studio sul centro storico di Pavia* (Pavia 1968), 41–58.

On the *Laws of the Indies* and New Spain in general: G. Kubler, "Mexican Urbanism in the Sixteenth Century," *Art Bulletin* 24, 1942, 160–71, and his *Mexican Architecture of the Sixteenth Century*, I (New Haven 1948), 68–102; D. P. Crouch et al., *Spanish City Planning in North America* (Cambridge, Mass., 1982).

On medieval new towns in Europe: M. Beresford, *New Towns of the Middle Ages* (London/New York 1967), still the classic account for France, England, and Wales; A. Lauret et al., *Bastides* (Toulouse/Milan 1988); and D. Friedman, *Florentine New Towns* (New York/London 1988).

On the American grid, see M. P. Conzen, "Morphology of Nineteenth-Century Cities," in R. P. Schaedel et al., *Urbanization in the Americas from the Beginnings to the Present* (The Hague 1980); and works cited in Ch.2 nn.14, 29, 31, 48. On the National Survey, see H. B. Johnson, *Order upon the Land* (New York 1976); and Kostof, *America by Design* (New York/Oxford 1987), 292–304. On Savannah: S. Anderson, "The Plan of Savannah and Changes of Occupancy During Its Early Years," *Harvard Architecture Review* 2, Spring 1981, 60–67.

A full Cerdà bibliography is given in Ch.2 n.59. On Hobrecht's plan of Berlin, see J. F. Geist, *Das Berliner Mietshaus 1740–1862* (Munich 1980).

3. THE CITY AS DIAGRAM

For a broad view of ideal cities, including conceptions of painters, poets and writers, see I. Todd and M. Wheeler, *Utopia* (London 1978); and from a strict art historical perspective, S. Lang, "The Ideal City from Plato to Howard," *Architectural Review* 112, Aug. 1952, 91–101, H. Rosenau's *Ideal Cities* (London 1974, 1983), and W. Braunfels, *Urban Design in Western Europe* (Chicago/London 1988), Ch.5. N. Johnston's *Cities in the Round* (Seattle/London 1983) is a useful pictorial collection.

On the round city of Baghdad, see Lassner (Ch.3 n.29), and also G. Le Strange, *Baghdad during the Abbasid Caliphate* (1900; New York 1972).

For Filarete's text, see the edition of J. R. Spencer, *Filarete's Treatise on Architecture* (New Haven 1965). For the bastioned city, see L. Di Sopra, *Palmanova* (Milan 1983); and also H. de La Croix, "Military Architecture and the Radial City Plan in the 16th Century," *Art Bulletin* 42.4, 1960, 263–90, and his *Military Considerations in City Planning* (New York 1972). On Vauban, see R. Bornèque, *La France de Vauban* (Paris 1984), and the regional account *Vauban et ses successeurs en Franche-Comté* (Besançon 1981).

On socialist utopias of the 19th century, see L. Benevolo, *The Origins of Modern Town Planning* (London 1967); and D. Hayden, *Seven American Utopias* (Cambridge, Mass./London 1976); also R. Lifchez, "Inspired Planning: Mormon and Fourierist Communities in the 19th Century," *Landscape* 20.3, Spring 1976, 29–35. On Ledoux's Chaux: A. Braham, *The Architecture of the French Enlightenment* (London/Berkeley and Los Angeles 1980), 180–84, and the bibliography cited in his n.181.

On "world capitals," in addition to Andersen and Hébrard's scheme (Ch.3 n.44), see G. Gresleri and D. Matteoni, *La città mondiale* (Venice 1982), esp. 21–45. On Soleri, see Ch.3 n.1. On space cities, see T. A. Heppenheimer, *Colonies in Space* (Harrisburg, Pa., 1977); and F. M. Branley, *Space Colony* (New York 1982).

4. THE GRAND MANNER

On Washington, D.C., see Ch.4 n.1. On Detroit, J. Reps, "Planning in the Wilderness: Detroit, 1805–1830," *Town Planning Review* 25, 1954–55, 240–50. On Turin, see: A. Cavallari-Murat et al., *Forma urbana e architettura nella Torino barocca* (Turin 1968); and also M. Pollak, "Turin 1564–1680: Urban Design, Military Culture and the Creation of an Absolutist Capital" (diss., Univ. of Chicago 1989). On St. Petersburg, J. Cracraft, *The Petrine Revolution in Russian Architecture* (Chicago 1988); and also I. A. Egorov, *The Architectural Planning of St. Petersburg* (Athens, Ohio, 1969). On Berlin, J. P. Kleihues, ed., *750 Jahre Architektur und Städtebau in Berlin* (Berlin 1987), an exemplary exhibition catalogue which carries us to the present; on Hitler's Berlin, L. O. Larsson, *Albert Speer, Le plan de Berlin 1937–1943* (Brussels 1983, publ. in German 1978), and S. Helmer, *Hitler's Berlin: The Speer Plans for Reshaping the Central City* (Ann Arbor 1985). See also C. Keim, *Städtebau in der Krise des Absolutismus* (Marburg 1990), for Kassel, Darmstadt and Wiesbaden.

The best account of the Grand Manner in Roman antiquity is W. L. MacDonald, *The Architecture of the Roman Empire, II. An Urban Appraisal* (New Haven/London 1986); see also A. Pelletier, *L'urbanisme romain sous l'Empire* (Paris 1982). Baroque planning usually concentrates on a number of exemplary documents. Of these, the Rome plan of Sixtus V is best discussed in S. Giedion, *Space, Time and Architecture* (4th ed., Cambridge, Mass., 1963), 75ff., and L. Spezzaferro, "La Roma di Sisto V," in *Storia dell'arte italiana*, 5.3 (Turin 1983), 363–405; see also J. A. F. Orbaan, *Sixtine Rome* (New York 1911). On Le Nôtre, see among others B. Jeannel, *Le Nôtre* (Paris 1985).

For coaches, see Ch.4 n.23, and now also P. Waddy, *Seventeenth-Century Roman Palaces* (New York 1990), 61–66.

Haussmann's planning of Paris is steadily being reevaluated; see F. Loyer, *Paris Nineteenth Century, Architecture and Urbanism* (New York 1988), and also D. H. Pinkney, *Napoleon III and the Rebuilding of Paris* (Princeton 1958); T. J. Clark, *The Painting of Modern Life* (Princeton/London 1984), 23–78; and D. Harvey, *Consciousness and the Urban Experience* (Baltimore/Oxford 1985), 63–220. On Hénard, see P. M. Wolf, *Eugène Hénard and the Beginning of Urbanism in Paris* (1968).

On the City Beautiful movement in the United States, see the contemporary publications cited in Ch.4 nn.26, 28, 29 and also W. H. Wilson, "The Ideology, Aesthetics and Politics of the City Beautiful Movement," in A. Sutcliffe, ed., *The Rise of Modern Urban Planning* (London 1980), 165–98; R. E. Foglesohn, *Planning the Capitalist City* (Princeton/Guildford 1986); and M. Manieri-Elia in G. Ciucci et al., *La città americana* (Bari 1973), 3–146.

On the Socialist *magistrale*, see a series of articles in *Deutsche Architektur* by W. Weigel (on that of Frankfurt a.d. Oder, 5.10, 1956, 471–72), G. Funk (on Dresden's, 3.6, 1954, 240–47), and H. Bächler (on Dresden's, 9.4, 1960, 196–98).

On Ricardo Bofill, T. Schuman, "Utopia spurned," *Journal of Architectural Education*, 40.1, Fall 1986, 20–29; *Domus*, Jan. 1986, 1–7; and *Architecture, Mouvement, Continuité*, Oct. 1983, 28–36 and Oct. 1984, 32–43.

5. THE URBAN SKYLINE

There are no general surveys of the subject, except W. Attoe, *Skylines* (Chichester 1981).

On city images and their artists, in addition to works cited in Ch.5 nn.9, 10, and 14, see also P. Lavedan, *Représentation des villes dans l'art du Moyen Age* (Paris 1954); and J. Pahl, *Die Stadt im Aufbruch der perspektivischen Welt* (Frankfurt/Berlin 1963).

The skyscraper literature is immense; for sources dealing with skyline aspects, see Ch.5 nn.7, 32, 46, 57, 58 and 61; also W. Taylor, "New York et l'origine du *Skyline*: la cité moderne comme forme et symbole," *Urbi* 3, 1980, 3–21; M. Tafuri in G. Ciucci et al., *La città americana* (Bari 1973), 417–550; and Kostof, "The Skyscraper City," *Design Quarterly* 140, 1988, 32–47. For the debate in East Germany, see F. Bergmann, "Zentrales Haus als Turmhochhaus oder Turm mit hohem Haus," *Deutsche Architektur* 6.12, 1956, 552–57.

On the New York zoning ordinance of 1916, see S. Toll, *Zoned America* (New York 1969); H. Kantor, *Modern Urban Planning in New York* (diss., New York Univ, 1971), and C. Willis, "Zoning and Zeitgeist; the Skyscraper City in the 1920s," *Journal of the Society of Architectural Historians* 45, 1986, 47–59.

On Bruno Taut, see Ch.5 nn.53 and 54; and also K. Junghanns, *Bruno Taut 1880–1938* (2nd ed., Berlin 1983), 34–52.

ACKNOWLEDGMENTS FOR ILLUSTRATIONS

Sources of photographs and locations of images illustrated, in addition to those mentioned in the captions, are as follows:

ACL 275, 281 – Nezar AlSayyad 74 – Alinari 219 – in Amsterdam: Gemeentelijke Archiefdienst Pl.19; Rijksmuseum 73; Stedelijk Museum 136 – Maryland State Archives, Annapolis, Marion E. Warren Photographic Collection (MSA SC 1890–02–348) 217 – Arcaid/Ian Lambot Pl.39 – Instituto Municipal de Historia, Barcelona 152 – University of California at Berkeley (courtesy The Bancroft Library) 105, (courtesy Environmental Simulation Laboratory) 291 – in Berlin: Berlin Museum/Landesarchiv Berlin 253; Landesbildstelle 261; Märkisches Museum 241; Staatliche Museen zu Berlin 211 – Klaus G. Beyer 282 – Biblioteca dell'Archiginnasio, Bologna 267 – Lansdowne Library, Bournemouth 80 – City of Bradford Metropolitan Council 169 – Werner Braun 156 – Béguinage, Bruges (photo ACL) 275 – Cameron & Company Pl.23 – National Museum of Wales, Cardiff (reconstruction by Alan Sorrell) 164 – Greg Castillo 44, 92, 99, 121, 224, 264, 287, 311, 313, Pls. 27–30 – Thomas Jefferson Papers, Special Collections Dept., Manuscripts Division, University of Virginia Library, Charlottesville 198 – in Chicago: Chicago Historical Society 250; Oriental Institute, University of Chicago (F.N. AE 676) 162 – Museum der Stadt Köln, Cologne (photo Rheinisches Bildarchiv) 273 – Ohio State University Libraries, Columbus 132 – Compagnia Generale Ripreseaeree, Parma, Italy Pl.17 – Baker Library, Dartmouth College 77 – Ray Delvert 112, 124, Pl.16 – courtesy of the Burton Historical Collection of the Detroit Public Library 216 – Kupferstichkabinett, Dresden (photo Deutsche Fotothek Dresden) 218 – in Florence: Archivio di Stato 60; Biblioteca Mediceo Laurenziana 61 – Fotocielo 76 – Stadtarchiv, Frankfurt 98 – copyright Georg Gerster, John Hillelson Agency Pl.9 – By courtesy of the Goodwood Trustees Pl.35 – courtesy the Museum of Finnish Architecture, Helsinki 189, 190 – Historic Urban Plans Ithaca (N.Y.) 119 – Martin Hürlimann 262 – Illinois Department of Corrections 197 – Richard Ingersoll Pl.22 – Bildstelle der Stadt Karlsruhe 186 – H.D. Keilor 278 – Kentuckiana Historical Services 148 – Bundesarchiv, Koblenz 263 – KLM Luchtfotografie 68 – Collection Spiro Kostof 7, 229 – Mirko Krizanovic 312 – Landslides, Copyright Alex S. Maclean 88, 207 – courtesy Emily Lane 113, 237, 268, Pls. 12, 24–26, 32 – First Garden City Heritage Museum, Letchworth 82, 226 – Nebraska State Historical Society, Lincoln 306 – in London: Australian Overseas Information Service 192; British Architectural Library 235, 254, 300; the Trustees of the British Library 103, 151; the Trustees of the British Museum 136, 239; Courtauld Institute of Art (Conway Library) 236, (Witt Library) 258; Fine Art Society Pl.34; Guildhall Library 212; India Office Library 177; courtesy Italian State Tourist Office (E.N.I.T.) 227; Museum of London Pl.38; Victoria and Albert Museum 179 – in Los Angeles: California Historical Society/Ticor Title Insurance, Los Angeles. Dept. of Special Collections, University of Southern California 290; Security Pacific Photographic Collection/Los Angeles Public Library 8 – Museo del Prado, Madrid (photo Mas) Pl.6 – Mas Pl.6 – Georgina Masson 283 – Collection Carroll L.V. Meeks 299 – Middlesbrough Borough Council and Cleveland County Council 149 – Milton Keynes Development Corporation 155 – From the American Geographical Society Collection, University of Wisconsin-Milwaukee Library 116 – Montreal, Collection Centre Canadien d'Architecture/Canadian Centre for Architecture 288 – Michael Moran 265 – Museo S. Martino, Naples (photo Scala) Pl.5 – NASA Pl.8 – in New York: Museum of the City of New York (The J. Clarence Davis Collection) 303, (photo Irving Underhill, The Underhill Collection) 308; courtesy, Mies van der Rohe Archive, The Museum of Modern Art 292; courtesy The New-York Historical Society 118, Pl.15; New York Public Library (Manuscripts and Archives Division) 304, (I.N. Phelps Stokes Collection) 104; courtesy of the Rockefeller Archive Center 84 – Curators of the Bodleian Library, Oxford Pl.7 – in Paris: Bibliothèque Nationale 90, 199, 225, 243, 245, 248, 249; Caisse Nationale des Monuments Historiques et des Sites/SPADEM 238; Institut Géographique National 146 – Atwater Kent Museum, Philadelphia 147 – Daniel Philippe 45 – courtesy David R. Phillips (Chicago Architectural Photography Co.) 307, 309 – Auroville Planning Group, Pondicherry 206 – Staatliche Schlösser und Gärten Potsdam-Sanssouci 222, 252 – Private Collection 259, 260 – Private Collection, London Pl.33 – J.P. Protzen Pl.10 – Pubbli Aerfoto Pl.3 – The Radburn Association, Fairlawn (N.J.) 85, 86 – Cervin Robinson 266 – in Rome: Fototeca Unione 110, 111, 131, 230, 256; Musei Vaticani, Archivio Fotografico 257, Pl.21 – in Rotterdam: Museum Boymans–van Beuningen 271; Stichting Atlas Van Stolk 24 – Musei Civici, San Gimignano (photo Scala) Pl.31 – Ediciones Garcia Garrabella, Saragossa 286 – Scala 285, Pls. 5, 11, 31 – E. Schmidt, courtesy Mary Helen Schmidt Foundation 182 – Werner Schumann Pl.14 – Sheffield City Museums Pl.37 – in Siena: Museo dell'Opera del Duomo 75; Palazzo Pubblico 285 – courtesy Dr Soleri, The Cosanti Foundation 157, 158 (photo Ivan Pintar) – Spectrum Colour Library Pl.20 – courtesy Ian Sutton 276 – photo Swissair Pl.18 – courtesy Michael Tapscott 277 – Brian Brace Taylor Pl.13 – Richard Tobias 4–6, 9–12, 14–19, 27–43, 46–49, 52–59, 62–67, 70–72, 78, 108, 109, 123, 125–129, 134, 138, 140–144, 160, 165, 166, 168, 170, 171, 174–176, 180, 181, 194, 195, 213–215, 231–233, 279, 280 – Museo y Casa del Greco, Toledo 274 – Musée Paul Dupuy, Toulouse 244 – U.S. Department of Commerce, Coast and Geodetic Survey 102 – Varig Brazilian Airlines 178 – Historisches Museum der Stadt Wien, Vienna 223, Pl.4 – Loke Wan-Tho 172 – courtesy Derek Walker Associates (photo John Donat) 154 – Library of Congress, Washington, D.C. 21, 51, 137, 208, 209, 305 – Henry Wilson Pl.1 – Andrew Wilton Pl.36 – Windsor Castle, Royal Library. Reproduced by gracious permission of Her Majesty the Queen 130 – Sam Winklebleck 23, 202, 296 – Mainfränkisches Museum, Würzburg 13 – ETH-Bibliothek, Zurich 298

An Atlas of Old New Haven (New Haven 1924) 117 – Walter Bigges, *A Summarie [and True Discourse] of Sir Francis Drakes Indian Voyages* (London 1586) 115 – J.S. Buckingham, *National Evils and Practical Remedies* (London 1849) 201 – Georges Candilis, *Toulouse Le Mirail* (Stuttgart 1975) 100 – Le Corbusier, *Oeuvre Complète 1910–1929* (Zurich 1964) 310; *Oeuvre Complète 1946–1952* (Zurich 1961) 153; *Précisions sur un état présent de l'architecture* (Paris 1930) 234 – O. Dapper, *Historische Beschryving der Stadt Amsterdam* (Amsterdam 1663) 136 – R.W. DeForest and L. Veiller, *The Tenement House Problem* (New York 1903) 150 – Gottfried Feder, *Die neue Stadt* (Berlin 1939) 96 – E. Goldzamt, *Architektura: zespolow srodmiejskichi i problemy dziedzictwa* (Warsaw 1956) 295 – Werner Hegemann, *City Planning, housing* (New York 1936) 98 – Eugène Hénard, *Etudes sur les transformations de Paris* (Paris 1903–9) 191, 249 – Jan Jansson, *Theatrum exhibens illustriore principesque Germaniae superioris civitates* (Amsterdam 1657) 20 – Johannes Kip, *Nouveau Théâtre de la Grande-Bretagne* (London 1720–40) 246 – Robert Owen, *Report to the Committee for the Relief of the Manufacturing Poor* (1817) 200 – Georges Perrot and Charles Chipiez, *Histoire de l'art dans l'antiquité* (Paris 1884) 163 – Sebastiano Serlio, *Architettura* (Venice 1551) 220, 221 – Simon Stevin, *Materiae Politicae Burgerlicke Stoffen* (Leyden 1649) 114 – after Kakichi Suzuki, *Early Buddhist Architecture in Japan* (Tokyo/New York 1980) 139 – Bruno Taut, *Die Stadtkrone* (Jena 1919) 301, 302 – *Theatrum Statum Regiae Celsitudinis Sabaudiae Ducis* (Amsterdam 1682) 255 – *Town Planning Review* (October 1910) 93 – J.B. Ward-Perkins, *Cities of Ancient Greece and Italy: Planning in Classical Antiquity* (New York/London 1974) 106, 107 – Frederick de Widt, *Collection of Remarkable Towns, Cittys and Forts in the Seaven United Provinces* (Amsterdam 1670(?)) 133.

INDEX

Figures in *italic* type refer to illustrations—page numbers for black-and-white images, plate numbers ("*Pl.1*") for color.

A

B

C

D

E

F

G

H

I

J

K

L

M

N

O

P

Q

R

S

Y

Z